THE
unofficial GUIDE®
ᵀᴼWalt Disney World® with Kids

2020

COME CHECK US OUT!

Supplement your valuable guidebook with tips, news, and deals by visiting our websites:

theunofficialguides.com

touringplans.com

Also, while there, sign up for The Unofficial Guide newsletter for even more travel tips and special offers.

Join the conversation on social media:

 @theUGSeries    theUnofficialGuides

 theUGSeries    theUGSeries

 TheUnofficialGuideSeries

Other Unofficial Guides

The Disneyland Story: The Unofficial Guide to the Evolution of Walt Disney's Dream

Universal vs. Disney: The Unofficial Guide to American Theme Parks' Greatest Rivalry

The Unofficial Guide to Disney Cruise Line

The Unofficial Guide to Disneyland

The Unofficial Guide to Las Vegas

The Unofficial Guide to Mall of America

The Unofficial Guide to Universal Orlando

The Unofficial Guide to Walt Disney World

The Unofficial Guide to Washington, D.C.

THE *unofficial* GUIDE®

TO Walt Disney World® with Kids

2020

BOB SEHLINGER *and* LILIANE J. OPSOMER
with LEN TESTA

(Walt Disney World® is officially known as Walt Disney World® Resort.)

AdventureKEEN

Published by:
AdventureKEEN
2204 First Ave. S, Ste. 102
Birmingham, AL 35233

Cover design by Scott McGrew

Text design by Vertigo Design with modifications by Annie Long

For information on our other products and services or to obtain technical support, please contact us from within the United States at 888-604-4537 or by fax at 205-326-1012.

AdventureKEEN also publishes its books in a variety of electronic formats. Some content that appears in print may not be available in electronic formats.

ISBN 978-1-62809-100-7 (pbk.); ISBN 978-1-62809-101-4 (ebook)

Distributed by Publishers Group West

Manufactured in the United States of America

5 4 3 2 1

CONTENTS

LIST *of* MAPS

ACKNOWLEDGMENTS

THANKS TO OUR TEAM OF YOUNG PUNDITS—Felicity Pipe, Isabelle Sanders, Lucy Bravo, Sabrina Martins, A. J. Kwiatkowski, and Brendan Reilly—for their unique wisdom and fun-loving attitude (gotta have attitude, right?). Also thanks to Hannah Testa, Katie Sutton, Eve Zibart, Idan Menin, Ian Geiger, Shelton Siegel, Isaac and Ethan Leifert, Julia Aronberg, Erin Haffreingue, Ricky Vosburgh-Tyson, Rachel and Isaac Bloom, and Alex and Kieran Duncan.

The cartoons were drawn by Tami Knight, possibly the nuttiest artist in Canada, and Chris Eliopoulos, a talented illustrator–Disney fanatic based in New Jersey. Disney historian Jim Hill provided insightful and funny glimpses of the World behind the scenes. Thank you to Darcie Vance for her help with fact-checking.

For research and contributions concerning family dynamics and child behavior, thanks to psychologists Karen Turnbow, Susan Corbin, Gayle Janzen, and Joan Burns. Kudos also to Unofficial Guide Research Director Len Testa and his team for the data collection and programming behind the touring plans in this guide.

To the Ortiz-Valle gang: we love your annual reports from the parks and look forward to hearing about your next adventures.

Thanks also to Amber Kaye Henderson for her editorial and production work on this book. Steve Jones and Cassandra Poertner created the maps, Potomac Indexing prepared the index, and Annie Long did the layout. Also, thank you to Scott McGrew for patiently helping us find the best cover.

—*Bob Sehlinger, Liliane Opsomer,*
and Len Testa

INTRODUCTION

WHY "UNOFFICIAL"?

DECLARATION OF INDEPENDENCE

THE AUTHORS AND RESEARCHERS OF THIS GUIDE specifically and categorically declare that they are and always have been totally independent of the Walt Disney Company, Inc.; of Disneyland, Inc.; of Walt Disney World, Inc.; and of any and all other members of the Disney corporate family not listed.

The authors believe in the wondrous variety, joy, and excitement of the Walt Disney World attractions. At the same time, we recognize that Walt Disney World is a business. In this guide, we represent and serve you, the consumer. If a restaurant serves bad food, a gift item is overpriced, or a certain ride isn't worth the wait, we can say so, and in the process we hope to make your visit more fun, efficient, and economical.

YOUR UNOFFICIAL TOOLBOX

WHEN IT COMES TO WALT DISNEY WORLD, a couple with kids needs different advice than a party of seniors going to the Epcot International Flower & Garden Festival. Likewise, adults touring without children and honeymooners all require their own special guidance.

To meet the varying needs of our readers, we've created *The Unofficial Guide to Walt Disney World,* or what we call the Big Book. At 800 pages, it contains all the information that anyone traveling to Walt Disney World needs to have a super vacation. It's our cornerstone.

As thorough as we try to make the main guide, though, there just isn't sufficient space for all the tips and resources that may be useful to certain readers. Therefore, we've developed additional guides that provide information tailored to specific visitors. Though some advice from the Big Book, such as arriving early at the theme parks, is echoed in these guides, most of the information is unique.

Here's what's in the toolbox:

The guide you're reading now presents detailed planning and touring tips for a family vacation, along with special touring plans for families that you won't find in any other book. *The Unofficial Guide to Walt Disney World with Kids* is the only Unofficial Guide created with the guidance of a panel of kids, all of varying ages and backgrounds.

The Unofficial Guide to Universal Orlando, by Seth Kubersky with Bob Sehlinger and Len Testa, is a comprehensive guide to Universal Orlando. At 408 pages, it's the perfect tool for understanding and enjoying Universal's ever-expanding complex, consisting of theme parks, a water park, eight resort hotels by summer 2020, nightclubs, and restaurants. The guide includes field-tested touring plans that will save you hours of standing in line.

THE MUSIC OF LIFE

THOUGH IT'S COMMON in our culture to see life as a journey from cradle to grave, Alan Watts, a noted late-20th-century philosopher, saw it differently. He viewed life not as a journey but as a dance. In a journey, he said, you are trying to get somewhere and are consequently always looking ahead, anticipating the way stations and thinking about the end. Though the journey metaphor is popular, particularly in the West, it is generally characterized by a driven, goal-oriented mentality: a way of living and being that often inhibits those who subscribe to the journey metaphor from savoring each moment of life.

When you dance, by contrast, you hear the music and move in harmony with the rhythm. Like life, a dance has a beginning and an end. But unlike a journey, your objective is not to get to the end but to enjoy the dance while the music plays. You are totally in the moment and care nothing about where on the floor you stop when the dance is done.

As you begin to contemplate your Walt Disney World vacation, you may not have much patience for a philosophical discussion about journeys and dancing. But you see, it is relevant. If you are like most travel guide readers, you are apt to plan and organize and to anticipate and control, and you like things to go smoothly. And truth be told, this leads us to suspect that you are a person who looks ahead and is outcome-oriented. You may even feel a bit of pressure concerning your vacation. Vacations, after all, are special events and expensive ones as well. So you work hard to make the most of your vacation.

We also believe that work, planning, and organization are important, and at Walt Disney World they are essential. But if they become your focus, you won't be able to hear the music and enjoy the dance. Though a lot of dancing these days resembles highly individualized seizures, there was a time when each dance involved specific steps, which you committed to memory. At first you were tentative and awkward, but the steps became second nature and you didn't think about them anymore.

Metaphorically, this is what we want for you and your children or grandchildren as you embark on your Walt Disney World vacation.

We want you to learn the steps ahead of time, so that when you're on your vacation and the music plays, you will be able to hear it, and you and your children will dance with grace and ease.

YOUR PERSONAL TRAINERS

WE'RE HERE TO WHIP YOU INTO SHAPE by helping you plan and enjoy your Walt Disney World vacation. Together we'll make sure that it really *is* a vacation, as opposed to, say, an ordeal or an expensive way to experience heatstroke. Our objective, simply put, is to ensure that you and your children have fun.

Because this book is specifically for adults traveling with children, we'll concentrate on your special needs and challenges. We'll share our most useful tips, as well as the travel secrets of more than 500,000 families interviewed.

So who *are* we? There's a bunch of us, actually. Your primary personal trainers are Liliane and Bob. Helping out big time are Felicity, Isabelle, Lucy, Sabrina, A. J., and Brendan.

Felicity is 8 years old and lives in Swindon, South West England. Also known as Tink, she fancies all things Disney and enjoys singing, drawing, and making new friends. Tink adores meeting all the princesses, and like Princess Ariel, she loves playing in the water. She always looks forward to her next Florida vacation.

Felicity

Our observer on the ground is 12-year-old Isabelle. She began visiting the parks when she was just 6 months old and has been an annual pass holder since the age of 3. She enjoys reading, especially the Harry Potter books, and plays soccer and the saxophone. She has been on more than 20 cruises and is a frequent contributor to the Disney Cruise Line blog podcast.

Isabelle

Her favorite ride is Rock 'n' Roller Coaster Starring Aerosmith, and her favorite restaurant is Chef Art Smith's Homecomin'. Isabelle lives in Orlando and dislikes busy, crowded days at the parks.

Twelve-year-old Lucy spends her time swimming, reading, and crafting, but most of all she loves to travel. She dotes on all animals, but her favorites are dogs. Lucy even has her own YouTube channel, where she shares all her hobbies. She lives in Rogers, Arkansas, though she wishes it were Orlando. She visits her pal Mickey several times a year.

Lucy

Sabrina is 7 years old and loves all things Disney. She's very active and plays softball, hockey, and basketball. Her favorite rides are Journey into Imagination with Figment and Space Mountain. She goes to Les Halles Boulangerie–Patisserie in Epcot every chance she gets.

Sabrina

A. J., a 12-year-old black belt from Fanwood, New Jersey, participates in basketball and soccer, plays video games, and writes. His hamster, Nacho, also gets lots of playtime and attention. Together with his family, he visits Walt Disney World regularly, and when it's time to start planning, A. J. is hands-on. He is thrilled to share his tips with our readers.

A. J.

Nine-year-old Brendan resides in Trophy Club, Texas. Some of his hobbies include acting, strumming the ukulele, golfing, playing Fortnite, and watching Disney shows, such as *Coop & Cami Ask the World.* Slinky Dog Dash is his new favorite ride, and Evil Mr. Pork Chop is his favorite Disney character. He is very big on pin trading. Brendan visits Walt Disney World a few times each year.

Brendan

Faithful readers will note that, except for Felicity, this is a brand-new crew. After contributing for years to this guide, our former contributors have set out on new adventures. We thank them for their witty contributions and wish them magical trails. They will forever be part of our Unofficial family.

LILIANE

Liliane, a native of Belgium, moved to Birmingham, Alabama, in 2014 after having spent 25 years in New York City. She's funny and very charming in the best European tradition, and she puts more energy into being a mom than you would think possible without performance-enhancing drugs. Optimistic and happy, she loves the sweet and sentimental side of Walt Disney World. You might find her whooping it up at the *Hoop-Dee-Doo Musical Revue,* but you'll never see her riding a roller coaster with Bob.

Speak of the devil, Bob isn't a curmudgeon exactly, but he likes to unearth Disney's secrets and show readers how to beat the system. His idea of a warm fuzzy might be the Rock 'n' Roller Coaster, but he'll help you save lots of money, find the best hotels and restaurants, and return home less than terminally exhausted. These caricatures pretty much sum up the essence of Bob and Liliane.

BOB

If you're thinking that the cartoons paint a somewhat conflicted picture of your personal trainers, well, you're right. Admittedly, Bob and Liliane have been known to disagree on a thing or two. Together, however, they make a good team. You can count on them to give you both sides of every story. Let's put it this way: Liliane will encourage you to bask in the universal-brotherhood theme of It's a Small World. Bob will show up later to help you get the darned song out of your head.

Len is our research dude. His really complicated scientific wizardry will help you save a bundle of time—would you believe 4 hours in a single day?—by staying out of those pesky lines.

Oops, almost forgot: There's another team member you need to meet. Called a Wuffo, she's our very own character. She'll warn you when rides are too scary, too dark, too wet, or too rough, and she'll tell you which rides to avoid if you have motion sickness. You'll bump into her throughout the book doing, well, what characters do.

ABOUT *This* GUIDE

DISNEY WORLD HAS BEEN OUR BEAT for more than three decades, and we know it inside out. During those years, we've observed many thousands of parents and grandparents trying—some successfully, others less so—to have a good time at Walt Disney World. Some of these, owing to unfortunate dynamics within the family, were handicapped right from the start. Others were simply overwhelmed by the size and complexity of Walt Disney World; still others fell victim to a lack of foresight, planning, and organization.

Disney World is a better destination for some families than for others. Likewise, some families are more compatible on vacation than others. The likelihood of experiencing a truly wonderful Disney World vacation transcends the theme parks and attractions offered. In fact, the theme parks and attractions are the only constants in the equation. The variables that will define the experience and determine its success are intrinsic to your family: things like attitude, sense of humor, cohesiveness, stamina, flexibility, and conflict resolution.

The simple truth is that Disney World can test you as a family. It will overwhelm you with choices and force you to make decisions about how to spend your time and money. It will challenge you physically as you cover miles on foot and wait in lines touring the theme parks. You will have to respond to surprises (both good and bad) and deal with hyperstimulation.

This guide will forewarn and forearm you. It will help you decide whether a Disney World vacation is a good idea for you and your family at this particular time. It will help you sort out and address the attitudes and family dynamics that can affect your experience. Most important, it will provide the confidence that comes with good planning and realistic expectations.

LETTERS AND COMMENTS FROM READERS

MANY WHO USE *The Unofficial Guide to Walt Disney World with Kids* write us to comment or share their own touring strategies. We appreciate all such input, both positive and critical, and encourage our readers to continue writing. Their comments and observations are frequently incorporated into revised editions of the guide and have contributed immeasurably to its improvement.

BOB In this book, you'll read experienced Disney World visitors' opinions of the parks that you can apply to your own travel circumstances.

Privacy Policy

If you write us or complete our reader survey, rest assured that we won't release your name and address to any mailing-list companies, direct mail advertisers, or other third parties. Unless you instruct us otherwise, we'll assume that you don't object to being quoted in the guide.

How to Contact the Authors

Bob, Liliane, and Len
The Unofficial Guide to Walt Disney World with Kids
2204 First Ave. S, Ste. 102
Birmingham, AL 35233
info@theunofficialguides.com
Facebook: TheUnofficialGuideToWaltDisneyWorldWithKids
Twitter: @TheUGSeries

When emailing us, please tell us where you're from. If you snail mail us, put your address on both your letter and envelope; the two sometimes get separated. It's also a good idea to include your phone number. Because we're travel writers, we're often out of the office for long periods of time, so forgive us if our response is slow. Unofficial Guide email isn't forwarded to us when we're traveling, but we'll respond as soon as possible after we return.

Online Reader Survey

Express your opinions about your Walt Disney World visit at touring plans.com/walt-disney-world/survey. This online questionnaire lets every member of your party, regardless of age, tell us what he or she thinks about attractions, hotels, restaurants, and more.

If you'd rather print out and mail us the survey, send it to the address above. In any case, let us know what you think!

A **QUICK TOUR** *of a* **BIG WORLD**

WALT DISNEY WORLD COMPRISES more than 40 square miles, an area twice as large as Manhattan. Situated strategically in this vast expanse are the **Magic Kingdom, Epcot, Disney's Animal Kingdom,** and **Disney's Hollywood Studios** theme parks; 2 swimming theme parks; a sports complex; 4 golf courses; 42 hotels and a campground; more than 200 restaurants; 4 interconnected lakes; a shopping and entertainment complex; 6 convention venues; a nature preserve; and a transportation system consisting of four-lane highways, elevated monorails, a network of canals, and a gondola system.

In 2017 Disney introduced a Lyft-like service that connects the theme parks and the resorts. Guests can request private point-to-point transportation inside Walt Disney World (WDW) in Minnie Vans driven by cast members.

THE MAJOR THEME PARKS

The Magic Kingdom

When people think of Walt Disney World, most think of the Magic Kingdom, opened in 1971. It consists of adventures, rides, and shows featuring Disney cartoon characters, as well as Cinderella Castle. It's only one element of Disney World, but it remains the heart.

The Magic Kingdom is divided into six "lands," with five arranged around a central hub. First you come to **Main Street, U.S.A.,** which connects the Magic Kingdom entrance with the hub. Clockwise around the hub are **Adventureland, Frontierland, Liberty Square, Fantasyland,** and **Tomorrowland.** The Magic Kingdom has more rides, shows, and entertainment than any other WDW theme park. A comprehensive tour takes 2 days; a tour of the highlights can be done in 1 full day.

Four hotels (**Contemporary Resort** and **Bay Lake Tower, Polynesian Village & Villas,** and **Grand Floridian Resort & Villas**) are connected to the Magic Kingdom by monorail and boat. Two other hotels— **Shades of Green** (operated by the US Department of Defense), as well as **Wilderness Lodge** and its adjacent time-share permutations, **Boulder Ridge Villas** and **Copper Creek Villas & Cabins**—are nearby but aren't served by the monorail. Also nearby and served by boat and bus is **Fort Wilderness Resort & Campground.** The next addition to the Magic Kingdom resorts will be **Reflections–A Disney Lakeside Lodge.** The Disney Vacation Club property is being built on the shore of Bay Lake, adjacent to Fort Wilderness, on the site of the former River Country water park. We expect the resort to open in 2022.

Epcot

Opened in October 1982, Epcot is twice as big as the Magic Kingdom and comparable in scope. It has two major areas: **Future World** consists of pavilions concerning human creativity and technological advancement; **World Showcase,** arranged around a 40-acre lagoon, presents the architectural, social, and cultural heritages of almost a dozen nations, each country represented by replicas of famous landmarks and settings familiar to world travelers.

The Epcot resort hotels—the **BoardWalk Inn & Villas, Dolphin, Swan,** and **Yacht & Beach Club Resorts and Beach Club Villas**—are within a 5- to 15-minute walk of the International Gateway, the World Showcase entrance to the theme park. **The Cove** is set to open in 2021. The hotels are also linked to Epcot and Disney's Hollywood Studios by canal and walkway. Epcot is connected to the Magic Kingdom and its hotels by monorail. The **Caribbean Beach Resort** and **Disney's Riviera Resort** are also Epcot resorts. Free bus service is provided from Caribbean Beach and the Riviera to all theme parks, the two water parks, and Disney Springs. The new Skyliner gondola system connects Epcot with Disney's Hollywood Studios, as well as the Art of Animation, Pop Century, Caribbean Beach, and Riviera Resorts.

Disney's Animal Kingdom

About five times the size of the Magic Kingdom, Disney's Animal Kingdom combines zoological exhibits with rides, shows, and live entertainment. The park is arranged in a hub-and-spoke configuration somewhat like the Magic Kingdom. A lush tropical rain forest serves as Main

continued on page 12

South Orlando

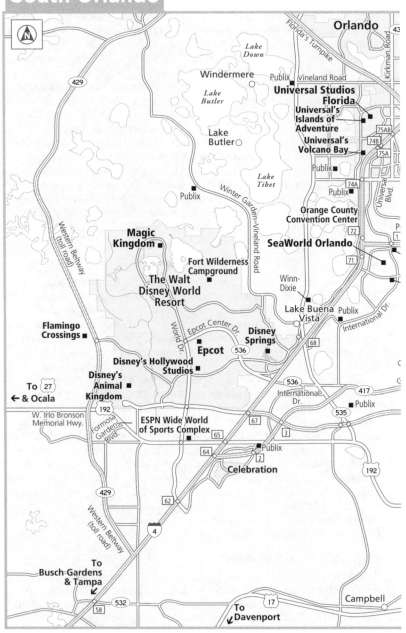

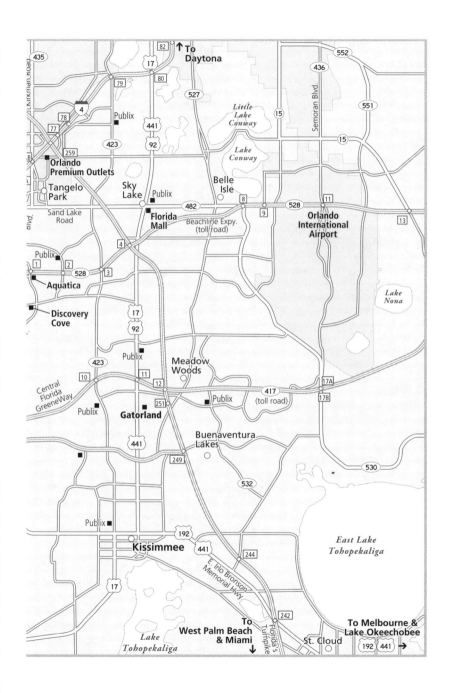

Walt Disney World

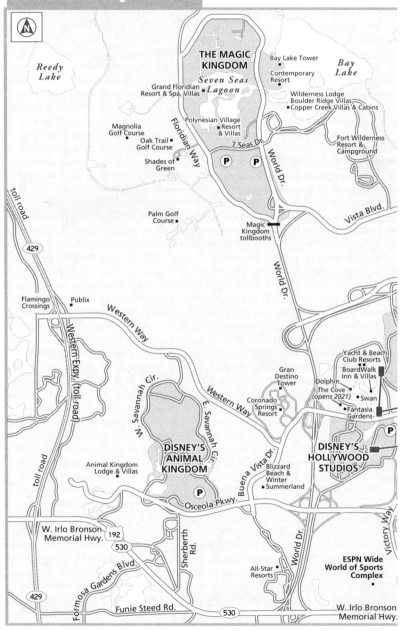

N

Reedy Lake

THE MAGIC KINGDOM

Seven Seas Lagoon

Bay Lake Tower
Contemporary Resort

Bay Lake

Grand Floridian Resort & Spa, Villas

Wilderness Lodge
Boulder Ridge Villas
Copper Creek Villas & Cabins

Magnolia Golf Course

Oak Trail Golf Course

Polynesian Village Resort & Villas

Fort Wilderness Resort & Campground

Floridian Way

7 Seas Dr.

World Dr.

Shades of Green

P   P

Vista Blvd.

Palm Golf Course

Magic Kingdom tollbooths

Magic Kingdom tollbooths

World Dr.

toll road

429

Flamingo Crossings

Publix

Western Way

Western Expy. (toll road)

Yacht & Beach Club Resorts

BoardWalk Inn & Villas

Gran Destino Tower

Dolphin
The Cove (opens 2021)

Swan

W. Savannah Cir.

Western Way

Coronado Springs Resort

Fantasia Gardens

E. Savannah Cir.

P

DISNEY'S ANIMAL KINGDOM

DISNEY'S HOLLYWOOD STUDIOS

Animal Kingdom Lodge & Villas

Blizzard Beach & Winter Summerland

Buena Vista Dr.

P

toll road

Osceola Pkwy.

W. Irlo Bronson Memorial Hwy.

192

530

Sherberth Rd.

World Dr.

Victory Way

Formosa Gardens Blvd.

All-Star Resorts

ESPN Wide World of Sports Complex

429

Funie Steed Rd.

530

W. Irlo Bronson Memorial Hwy.

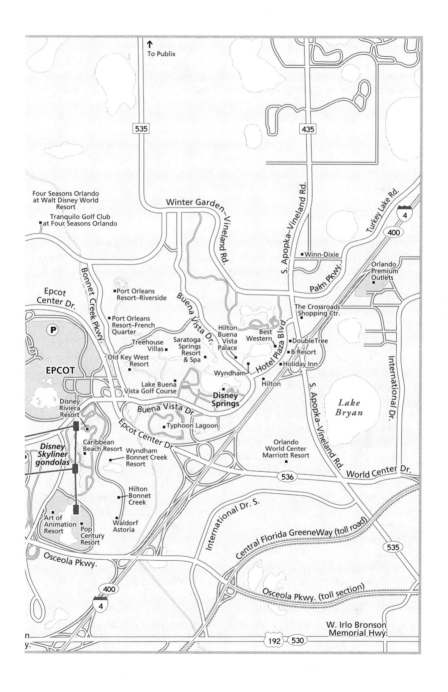

continued from page 7

Street, funneling visitors to **Discovery Island,** the park's hub. Dominated by the park's central icon, the 14-story-tall, hand-carved **Tree of Life,** Discovery Island offers services, shopping, and dining. From there, guests can access the themed areas: **Pandora, Africa, Rafiki's Planet Watch, Asia,** and **DinoLand U.S.A.** Discovery Island, Africa, Rafiki's Planet Watch, and DinoLand U.S.A. opened in 1998, followed by Asia in 1999. Africa, the largest themed area at 100 acres, features free-roaming herds in a re-creation of the Serengeti Plain.

Finally, on May 27, 2017, **Pandora: The World of Avatar,** a 12-acre extension, opened to much fanfare. Based on James Cameron's *Avatar* film, Pandora includes two headliner rides, plus one restaurant. The big draw, however, is Pandora's scenery—including "floating mountains" and glow-in-the-dark plants—which Disney has replicated here. See page 337 for more details.

Disney's Animal Kingdom has its own parking lot and is connected to other Walt Disney World destinations by the Disney bus system. The **All-Star Resorts, Animal Kingdom Lodge & Villas, Art of Animation Resort, Coronado Springs Resort** and **Gran Destino Tower,** and **Pop Century Resort** are all nearby.

Disney's Hollywood Studios

Opened in 1989 as Disney-MGM Studios in an area a little larger than the Magic Kingdom, Disney's Hollywood Studios (DHS) consists of two areas. One, occupying about 50% of the Studios, is a theme park focused on movies, music, and TV. Park highlights include a re-creation of **Hollywood and Sunset Boulevards** from Hollywood's Golden Age, several rides and musical shows, and a movie stunt show. **Mickey & Minnie's Runaway Railway,** replacing The Great Movie Ride inside the replica of the Grauman's Chinese Theatre, opens in the spring of 2020. The other half of DHS is two immersive lands based on popular Disney film franchises. The 11-acre **Toy Story Land,** with two highly themed but relatively simple rides for small children, opened June 30, 2018. The 14-acre **Star Wars: Galaxy's Edge**—with two cutting-edge, large rides for older children, teens, and adults—opened in August 2019. See page 354 for details.

DHS is connected to other Walt Disney World areas by highway, canal, and gondola but not by monorail. Guests can park in the Studios' pay parking lot or commute by bus. Guests at most Epcot resort hotels can reach the Studios by boat, on foot, or by gondola. The new Skyliner gondola system connects DHS with Epcot, as well as the Art of Animation, Pop Century, Caribbean Beach, and Riviera Resorts.

THE WATER PARKS

DISNEY WORLD HAS TWO MAJOR water parks: **Typhoon Lagoon** and **Blizzard Beach.** Opened in 1989, Typhoon Lagoon is distinguished by a wave pool capable of making 6-foot waves. Blizzard Beach opened in 1995 and features more slides. Both parks are beautifully landscaped and pay great attention to atmosphere and aesthetics. Typhoon Lagoon and Blizzard Beach have their own adjacent parking lots and can be reached by Disney bus.

OTHER WALT DISNEY WORLD VENUES

Disney Springs

Themed to evoke a Florida waterfront town, Disney Springs encompasses the **Marketplace** on the east, **West Side** on the west, **The Landing** on the waterfront, and **Town Center** in the middle, all featuring shops and restaurants and a Florida–meets–Spanish Colonial architectural theme.

Three multistory parking garages (Orange, Lime, and Grapefruit) serve the area. The Lemon and Mango surface parking lots are preferred parking lots and come with a fee of $10. Parking spaces for guests with disabilities are available in all lots and garages; a valid disability parking permit is required.

Disney Springs is accessed via Disney transportation from Disney resorts. Bus service from the four Disney theme parks to Disney Springs operates daily from 4 p.m. to 11 p.m., or 2 hours after theme parks close, whichever is earlier. There is no transportation from Disney Springs to the theme parks.

Disney's BoardWalk

Near Epcot, the BoardWalk is an idealized replication of an East Coast 1930s waterfront resort. Open all day, the BoardWalk features upscale restaurants, shops and galleries, a brewpub, and an ESPN sports bar. In the evening, a nightclub with dueling pianos and a DJ dance club join the lineup; both are for guests age 21 and up only. There's no admission fee for the BoardWalk, but the piano bar levies a cover charge at night. This area is anchored by the **BoardWalk Inn & Villas,** along with its adjacent convention center. The BoardWalk is within walking distance of the Epcot resorts, Epcot's International Gateway, and Disney's Hollywood Studios. Boat transportation is available to and from Epcot and Disney's Hollywood Studios, the Skyliner gondolas connect the BoardWalk to the Studios and the hotels on its route, and buses serve other Disney World locations.

ESPN Wide World of Sports Complex

The 220-acre Wide World of Sports is a state-of-the-art competition and training facility consisting of a 9,500-seat ballpark; an 8,000-seat arena; a field house; and venues for baseball, softball, tennis, track and field, volleyball, and dozens of other sports. The complex also hosts a mind-boggling calendar of professional and amateur competitions. Walt Disney World guests not participating in events may pay admission to watch any of the scheduled competitions.

Disney Cruise Line: The Mouse at Sea

In 1998 the Walt Disney Company launched (literally) its own cruise line with the 2,400-passenger *Disney Magic.* Its sister ship, the *Disney Wonder,* first sailed in 1999. In 2011 and 2012, respectively, the **Disney Dream** and the **Disney Fantasy** joined the fleet. Most cruises depart from Port Canaveral, Florida (about a 90-minute drive from Walt Disney World), or Miami on 3-, 4-, or 7-night itineraries, though New York, California, and Texas also serve as departure points for sailings to California, Alaska, Hawaii, Canada, Mexico, the Mediterranean, the Panama Canal, and Europe. Caribbean and Bahamian cruises include a day at **Castaway Cay,** Disney's private island. Cruises can be packaged with a stay at Disney World. Some of the sailings are themed, such as the popular Halloween on the High Seas cruise, the Very Merry Time Christmas cruise, the Star Wars Day at Sea, and the Marvel Day at Sea cruises. Disney will add three more ships to its fleet in 2021, 2022, and 2023 respectively. The new ships will be two decks taller than the *Disney Dream* and the *Disney Fantasy* and will have 1,250 staterooms each. In 2019 Disney Cruise Line (DCL) purchased the Lighthouse Point property on the island of Eleuthera. Development of Lighthouse Point will start in the near future and should be operational sometime between 2021 and 2023. Lighthouse Point won't only be for DCL guests; free access will also be available to local residents, as 190 acres of the 700-acre property will be turned into a national park. The new port is expected to receive three to five ship visits per week.

LILIANE Board the ship as early as possible. Check on your dining rotation, and reserve Palo or Remy, spa treatments, and kids' programs. Relax and get ready for the departure party.

Disney cruises are perfect for families and for kids of all ages. Though the cruises are family-oriented, extensive children's programs and elaborate childcare facilities allow grown-ups plenty of opportunities to relax and do adult stuff. The ships are modern ocean liners with classic steamship lines. Cabins are among the most spacious in the cruise industry, and the staff is very attentive and accommodating. From the waitstaff at breakfast, lunch, and dinner to the cabin stewards, yours truly has not experienced any better.

Cabin design reveals Disney's finely tuned sense of the needs of families and offers a cruise-industry first: a split bathroom with a bathtub and shower combo and sink in one room, and toilet, sink, and vanity in another. This configuration, found in all but standard inside cabins, allows any family member to use the bathroom without monopolizing it. Decor includes unusual features such as bureaus designed to look like steamer trunks. Cabins also have a phone, TV, hair dryer, and a cooling box. In some cabins, pull-down Murphy beds or drop-down bunk beds allow for additional daytime floor space. Storage is generous, with deep drawers and large closets.

SABRINA Bring lots of magnets to decorate the door of your cabin, and put your room key on a lanyard around your neck, so you don't lose it.

A big party with appearances by Mickey and Minnie marks departures, when the ship's horn toots "When You Wish Upon a Star." Halfway through your voyage, Disney throws a deck party, where Mickey saves all passengers from Captain Hook and his evil plans.

Dining is a true pleasure. Each night, passengers move to a different family restaurant—each with its own unique theme and menu—and take their table companions and waitstaff with them. In addition to the family restaurants, the ships have a range of cafés offering pizza, burgers, sandwiches, and ice cream bars. Room service is available 24-7.

LILIANE Disney strictly enforces a minimum age limit (18) for dining at Palo and Remy, and a jacket (tie optional) is a must.

For a night out without kids, Palo, which offers tables with a view, is a must. Reservations are also a must, and a surcharge of $40 per person is added for this service to your onboard bill. The food is excellent, the ambience sophisticated.

In addition to Palo, the *Dream* and the *Fantasy* crank it up a notch with Remy. Chefs Scott Hunnel of Victoria & Albert's and Arnaud

SABRINA Don't eat too much ice cream just because it's free. You may end up feeling sick.

Lallement from L'Assiette Champenoise—a Michelin three-star restaurant outside Reims, France—created the French-inspired menu, served in an Art Nouveau–style dining room. This upscale dining experience on the high seas costs $125 per person. If you think this is a little over the top, we completely agree. Whatever happened to the no-frills, great-food philosophy we learned from Remy in *Ratatouille*?

The Disney ships offer 15,000-plus square feet of playrooms and other kids' facilities. Programs include interactive activities, play areas supervised by trained counselors, and a children's drop-off service in the evening. Passengers can register their children for the nursery, and group babysitting is available for select hours every day. The cost is $9 per hour for one child and $8 an hour for each additional child in the same family. **Oceaneer Clubs** on the *Dream* and *Fantasy* feature Andy's Room, a *Toy Story*–themed area for small children; Pixie

LILIANE Check out our *Unofficial Guide to Disney Cruise Line* for in-depth information on DCL, including our advice on cruising with kids and teens.

ISABELLE The Oceaneer Club and Oceaneer Lab have interactive activities and lots of arts and crafts. If you leave the crafts you make behind, there is a chance they will be tossed. Bring a small bag with you to save your masterpieces!

Hollow, a Tinker Bell–themed dress-up and play area; and a *Star Wars*–themed play area. On the *Dream* the *Star Wars* area is a life-size *Millennium Falcon*, and on the *Fantasy* it's a Command Post holotable, where children can train with X-wing pilots. The showpiece of the *Fantasy*'s Oceaneer Club is the Marvel Super Hero Academy. On the *Magic* the four play areas are Andy's Room, Pixie Hollow, Marvel's Avengers Academy, and the Mickey Mouse Club. The club aboard the *Wonder* offers a Frozen Adventures play area with visits from Anna and Elsa; Club Disney Junior, featuring storytelling and visits from Disney Junior characters such as Doc McStuffins; Andy's Room; and the Marvel Super Hero Academy. Most programs are perfect for kids ages 3–7, though children up to age 12 can participate.

Oceaneer Lab offers high-tech play. Kids wear ID bracelets, and parents receive pagers. There are also special clubs for tweens (**Edge**) and teens (**Vibe**). Participation at Oceaneer Club and Oceaneer Lab are free of charge.

Big with kids of all ages are the pools and the nightly entertainment on board, which show Disney at its best. The **Walt Disney Theatre** stages several musical productions each cruise, and the **Buena Vista Theatre,** with its full-screen cinema, shows first-run and digital 3-D movies as well as classic Disney films. Movies are also played poolside on a state-of-the-art 24-by-14-foot LED screen affixed to the forward funnel in the ships' family-pool areas.

The *Dream* and the *Fantasy* feature the first-ever onboard water coaster. At 765 feet long and the height of four decks, **AquaDuck** is a major attraction for kids and grown-ups alike (the *Magic's* counterpart, similar though not identical, is **AquaDunk**). Following an initial drop, guests glide through a translucent tube in a loop that extends 12 feet over the side of the vessel, allowing them to look down on the ocean 150 feet below. The ride lasts about 90 seconds and comes with climbs and drops, twists and turns. If you can keep your eyes open while riding, the AquaDuck will provide you with a spectacular view of the ship.

Senses Spa & Salon is a great place to relax, not just for adults but also for teens, who get their own separate area called **Chill Spa.** The treatments are pricey, and there's a surcharge ($16/day) for the use of the Rainforest Room, the spa's suite of saunas, steam rooms, and aromatic showers. The fitness center's showers and lockers are free.

Keys, the piano bar on the *Magic,* and **Cadillac Lounge,** on the *Wonder,* are the most relaxing and beautiful lounges on the seven seas. Make a before- or after-dinner drink there part of your routine.

Shore excursions depend on the itinerary, but all Caribbean and Bahamian cruises make at least one call at **Castaway Cay,** Disney's 1,000-acre private island. The natural environment and miles of white-sand beaches have been nicely preserved. The best way to enjoy the island is to disembark first thing in the morning and secure a prime spot at the beach, complete with hammock and shade. **Castaway Family Beach** is served by a tram running every 5 minutes (or it's a 0.25-mile walk). **Cookie's BBQ** and **Cookie's Too** serve an array of food that is included in the price of your cruise. Programs for kids on Castaway Cay give parents a chance to enjoy **Serenity Bay,** the adults-only beach.

ISABELLE On Castaway Cay get two cookies from Cookie's BBQ or Cookie's Too tand put ice cream in between to make your own ice cream sandwich.

Another great family experience is a wedding or vow renewal, offered both at sea and on Castaway Cay. **Disney's Fairy Tale Wedding** packages on Castaway Cay start at $4,000 for a party of 16 guests plus the couple; the charge for additional guests is $20 per person age 3 years and older. Each package includes the ceremony, a wedding coordinator, and the officiant. Also included are live music during and after the wedding, a bouquet for the bride and a boutonniere for the groom, and a reception aboard the ship. The couple is also treated to dinner at Palo and a $100 onboard stateroom credit. A photographer, a surprise visit by Disney characters, and much more can be booked for an additional cost. For more information, check out disneyweddings.com/cruise.

Disney Cruise Line is thriving. Sailings enjoy high occupancy these days, and a number of new itineraries have been added. Friends of Disney's *Frozen* can experience the country that inspired the icy kingdom of Arendelle on a Norwegian fjord cruise of 7 or 11 nights.

Cruises are a terrific value in travel. Deals abound. Check websites such as cruisecritic.com, cruisemates.com, vacationstogo.com, and lastminutetravel.com for the latest discounts. Search engine kayak .com is another great resource for uncovering cruise bargains. If you prefer to buy directly from Disney, here's how to get in touch:

Disney Cruise Line
☎ 800-951-6499 or 800-951-3532
disneycruise.com

DCL offers a free planning e-brochure and online video that tells you all you need to know about Disney cruises and then some. Visit disneycruise.disney.go.com/cruise-planning-tools.

Finally, to get the most out of your cruise, we recommend *The Unofficial Guide to Disney Cruise Line,* by Erin Foster with Len Testa and Ritchey Halphen, which presents advice for first-time cruisers; money-saving tips for booking your cruise; and detailed profiles for restaurants, shows, and nightclubs, along with deck plans and thorough coverage of the ports visited by DCL.

DISNEY-SPEAK POCKET TRANSLATOR

THOUGH IT MAY COME AS A SURPRISE to many, Walt Disney World has its own somewhat peculiar language. Here are some terms you're likely to bump into.

DISNEY-SPEAK	ENGLISH DEFINITION
ADVENTURE	Ride
ATTRACTION	Ride or theater show
ATTRACTION HOST	Ride operator
BACKSTAGE	Behind the scenes, out of view of customers
CAST MEMBER	Employee
CHARACTER	Disney character impersonated by an employee
COSTUME	Work attire or uniform
DARK RIDE	Indoor ride
DAY GUEST	Any customer not staying at a Disney resort
FACE CHARACTER	A character who does not wear a head-covering costume (Snow White, Cinderella, Jasmine, and the like)

continued on page 18

DISNEY-SPEAK POCKET TRANSLATOR

(continued)

DISNEY-SPEAK	ENGLISH DEFINITION
FASTPASS+	Timed reservation system for rides and other attractions
GENERAL PUBLIC	Same as day guest
GREETER	Employee positioned at an attraction entrance
GUEST	Customer
HIDDEN MICKEYS	Frontal silhouette of Mickey's head worked subtly into the design of buildings, railings, vehicles, golf greens, attractions, and just about anything else
OFF-SITE	A hotel located outside Walt Disney World's boundaries
ON-SITE	A hotel located inside Walt Disney World's boundaries and served by Disney's transportation network
ONSTAGE	In full view of customers
PRESHOW	Entertainment at an attraction prior to the feature presentation
RESORT GUEST	A customer staying at a Disney resort
SECURITY HOST	Security guard
SOFT OPENING	Opening a park or attraction before its stated opening date
TRANSITIONAL EXPERIENCE	An element of the queuing area and/or preshow that provides a story line or information essential to understanding the attraction

PART ONE

BASIC CONSIDERATIONS

IS WALT DISNEY WORLD *for* EVERYONE?

ALMOST ALL VISITORS ENJOY WALT DISNEY WORLD on some level and find things to see and do that they like. In fact, for many, the theme park attractions are just the tip of the iceberg. The more salient question, then—this is a family vacation, after all—is whether the members of your family basically like the same things. If you do, fine. If not, how will you handle the differing agendas?

A mother from Toronto described her husband's aversion to Disney's (in his terms) "phony, plastic, and idealized version of life." As they toured the parks, he was a real cynic and managed to diminish the experience for the rest of the family. As it happened, however, Dad's pejorative point of view didn't extend to the Disney golf courses. So Mom packed him up and sent him golfing while the family enjoyed the parks.

If you have someone in your family who doesn't like theme parks or, for whatever reason, doesn't care for Disney's brand of entertainment, it helps to get that attitude out in the open. Our recommendation is to deal with the person up front. Glossing over or ignoring the contrary opinion and hoping that "Tom will like it once he gets there" is naive and unrealistic. Either leave Tom at home or help him discover and plan activities that he will enjoy, resigning yourself in the process to the fact that the family won't be together at all times.

KNOW THYSELF, AND NOTHING TO EXCESS

THIS GOOD ADVICE WAS MADE AVAILABLE to ancient Greeks courtesy of the oracle of Apollo at Delphi. First, concerning the "know thyself" part, we want you to do some serious thinking about what you want in a vacation. We also want you to entertain the notion that having fun on your vacation may be very different from doing and seeing as much as possible. Because Walt Disney World is expensive, many families confuse "seeing everything" in order to "get our money's worth" with having a great time. Sometimes the two are compatible, but more often they are not. So if sleeping in late, sunbathing by the pool, or taking a nap ranks high on your vacation hit parade, you need to accord them due emphasis on your Disney visit, even if it means you see less of the theme parks.

LILIANE You can enjoy a perfectly wonderful time in the World if you're realistic, organized, and prepared.

Which brings us to the "nothing to excess" part. At Walt Disney World, especially if you are touring with children, less is definitely more. Trust us—you cannot go full tilt dawn to dark in the theme parks day after day. First you'll get tired, then you'll get cranky, and then you'll adopt a production mentality ("We have three more rides, and then we can go back to the hotel"). Finally, you'll hit the wall because you just can't maintain the pace.

Plan on seeing Walt Disney World in bite-size chunks with plenty of sleeping, swimming, napping, and relaxing in between. Ask yourself over and over in both the planning stage and while you are at Walt Disney World: what will contribute the greatest contentedness, satisfaction, and harmony? Trust your instincts. If stopping for ice cream or returning to the hotel for a dip feels like more fun than seeing another attraction, do it—even if it means wasting the remaining hours of an expensive admissions pass.

BOB Get a grip on your needs and preferences before you leave home, and develop an itinerary that incorporates all the things that make you happiest.

The **AGE THING**

THERE IS A LOT OF SERIOUS REFLECTION among parents and grandparents in regard to how old a child should be before embarking on a trip to Walt Disney World. The answer, not always obvious, stems from the personalities and maturity of the children, as well as the personalities and parenting style of the adults.

WALT DISNEY WORLD FOR INFANTS AND TODDLERS

WE BELIEVE THAT traveling with infants and toddlers is a great idea. Developmentally, travel is a stimulating learning experience for even the youngest of children. Infants, of course, will not know Mickey Mouse from a draft horse but will respond to sun and shade, music, bright colors, and the extra attention they receive from you. From first steps to full mobility, toddlers respond to the excitement and spectacle of Disney World, though of course in a much different way than you do. Your toddler will prefer splashing in fountains and clambering over curbs and benches to experiencing most attractions, but no matter: he or she will still have a great time.

BOB Sehlinger's Law postulates that the number of adults required to take care of an active toddler is equal to the number of adults present, plus one.

Somewhere between 4 and 6 years old, your child will experience the first vacation that he or she will remember as an adult. Though more likely to remember the coziness of the hotel room than the theme parks, the child will be able to experience and comprehend many attractions and will be a much fuller participant in your vacation. Even so, his or her favorite activity is likely to be swimming in the hotel pool.

As concerns infants and toddlers, there are good reasons and bad reasons for vacationing at Walt Disney World. A good reason for taking your little one to Disney World is that you want to go and there's no one available to care for your child during your absence. Philosophically, we are very much against putting your life (including your vacation) on hold until your children are older.

LILIANE Traveling with infants and toddlers sharpens parenting skills and makes the entire family more mobile and flexible, resulting in a richer, fuller life for all.

Especially if you have children of varying ages (or plan to, for that matter), it's better to take the show on the road than to wait until the youngest child reaches the perceived ideal age. If your family includes a toddler or infant, you will find everything from private facilities for breastfeeding to changing tables in both men's and women's restrooms to facilitate baby's care. Your whole family will be able to tour together with fewer hassles than on a picnic outing at home.

An illogical reason, however, for taking an infant or toddler to Disney World is that you think it's the perfect vacation destination for babies. It's not, so think again if you are contemplating Disney World primarily for your child's enjoyment. For starters, attractions are geared more toward older children and adults. Even designer play areas such as Tom Sawyer Island in the Magic Kingdom are developed with older children in mind.

That said, let us stress that, for the well prepared, taking a toddler to Disney World can be a totally glorious experience. There's truly nothing like watching your child respond to the color, the sound, the festivity, and, most of all, the characters. You'll return home with scrapbooks of photos that you will treasure forever. Your little one won't remember much, but never mind. Your memories will be unforgettable.

LILIANE Baby supplies, including disposable diapers, formula, and baby food, are for sale, and there are rockers and special chairs for nursing mothers.

If you elect to take your infant or toddler to Disney World, rest assured that their needs have been anticipated. The major theme parks have centralized facilities for infant and toddler care. Everything necessary for changing diapers, preparing formula, and warming bottles and food is available. Dads in charge of little ones are welcome at the centers and can use most services offered. In addition, men's rooms in the major theme parks have changing tables.

Infants and toddlers are allowed to experience any attraction that doesn't have minimum height or age restrictions. A Minneapolis mom suggests using a baby sling:

The baby sling was great when standing in lines—much better than a stroller, which you have to park before getting in line (and navigate through crowds). My baby was still nursing when we went to Disney World. The only really great place I found to nurse in the Magic Kingdom was a hidden bench in the shade in Adventureland between the snack stand (next to the Enchanted Tiki Room*) and the small shops. It is impractical to go to the baby station every time, so a nursing mom should be comfortable about nursing in very public situations.*

Two points in our reader's comment warrant elaboration. First, the rental strollers at all of the major theme parks are designed for toddlers and children up to 3 and 4 years old but are definitely not for infants. If you bring pillows and padding, the rental strollers can be made to work. You can bring your own stroller, but unless it's collapsible, you will not be able to take it on Disney trams, buses, or boats.

LILIANE In addition to providing an alternative to carrying your child, a stroller serves as a handy cart for diaper bags, water bottles, and other items you deem necessary.

Even if you opt for a stroller (your own or a rental), we nevertheless recommend that you also bring a baby sling or baby/child backpack. Simply put, there will be many times in the theme parks when you will have to park the stroller and carry your child.

The second point that needs addressing is our reader's perception that there are not many good places in the theme parks for breastfeeding unless you are accustomed to nursing in public. Many nursing moms recommend breastfeeding during a dark Disney theater presentation. This works, however, only if the presentation is long enough for the baby to finish nursing. *The Hall of Presidents* at the Magic Kingdom and *The American Adventure* at Epcot will afford you about 23 and 29 minutes, respectively.

Many Disney shows run back-to-back with only 1 or 2 minutes in between to change the audience. If you want to breastfeed and require more time than the length of the show, tell the cast member on entering that you want to breastfeed and ask if you can remain in the theater and watch a second showing while your baby finishes. Also keep in mind that many shows may have special effects or loud soundtracks that may make children even as old as 7 uncomfortable.

If you can adjust to nursing in more public places with your breast and the baby's head covered with a shawl or some such, nursing will not be a problem at all. Even on the most crowded days, you can always find a back corner of a restaurant or a comparatively secluded park bench or garden spot to nurse. Finally, the Baby Care Centers, with their private nursing rooms, are centrally located in all of the parks except the Studios.

A mom from Georgia wrote to us, and we totally agree with her:

Many women have no problem nursing uncovered, and they have the right to do so in public without being criticized. Even women who want to cover up may have a baby who won't cooperate and flings off the cover; plus, it's not necessary to sit through all of The Hall of Presidents *to feed your child. Babies will eat almost anywhere, and mothers shouldn't feel pressured to sneak off when a baby is hungry.*

WALT DISNEY WORLD FOR 4-, 5-, AND 6-YEAR-OLDS

CHILDREN AGES 4–6 VARY immensely in their capacity to comprehend and enjoy Walt Disney World. With this age group, the go-no-go decision is a judgment call. If your child is sturdy, easygoing, and fairly adventuresome, and demonstrates a high degree of independence, the trip will probably work. On the other hand, if your child tires easily, is temperamental, or is a bit timid or reticent in embracing new experiences, you're much better off waiting a few years. Whereas the travel and sensory-overload problems of infants and toddlers can be addressed and (usually) remedied on the go, discontented 4- to 6-year-olds have the ability to stop a family dead in its tracks, as this mother of three from Cape May, New Jersey, attests:

> *My 5-year-old was scared pretty badly on a dark ride our first day at Disney World. For the rest of the trip, we had to reassure her before each and every ride before she would go.*

If you have a tiring, clinging, and/or difficult 4- to 6-year-old who, for whatever circumstances, will be part of your group, you can sidestep or diminish potential problems with a bit of pretrip preparation. Even if your preschooler is plucky and game, the same prep measures (described later in this section) will enhance his or her experience and make life easier for the rest of the family.

Parents who understand that a visit with 4- to 6-year-old children is going to be more about the cumulative experience than it is about seeing it all will have a blast, as well as wonderful memories of their children's amazement.

THE IDEAL AGE

THOUGH OUR READERS REPORT both successful trips and disasters with children of all ages, the consensus is that the ideal children's ages for family compatibility and togetherness at Walt Disney World are 8–12 years. This age group is old enough, tall enough, and sufficiently stalwart to experience, understand, and appreciate practically all Disney attractions. Moreover, they are developed to the extent that they can get around the parks on their own steam without being carried or collapsing. Best of all, they're still young enough to enjoy being with Mom and Dad. From our experience, ages 10–12 are better than 8 and 9, though what you gain in maturity is at the cost of that irrepressible, wide-eyed wonder so prevalent in the 8- and 9-year-olds.

WALT DISNEY WORLD FOR TEENS

TEENS LOVE WALT DISNEY WORLD, and for parents of teens, the World is a nearly perfect, albeit expensive, vacation choice. Though your teens might not be as wide-eyed and impressionable as their younger sibs, they are at an age where they can sample, understand, and enjoy practically everything Disney World has to offer.

For parents, Walt Disney World is a vacation destination where you can permit your teens an extraordinary amount of freedom. The entertainment is wholesome; the venues are safe; and the entire complex of hotels, theme parks, restaurants, and shopping centers is accessible via the Disney World transportation system. The transportation system allows you, for example, to enjoy a romantic dinner and an early bedtime while your teens take in the late-night fireworks at the theme parks. After the fireworks, a Disney bus, boat, or monorail will deposit them safely back at the hotel.

Because most adolescents relish freedom, you may have difficulty keeping your teens with the rest of the family. Thus, if one of your objectives is to spend time with your teenage children during your Disney World vacation, you will need to establish some clear-cut guidelines regarding togetherness and separateness before you leave home. Make your teens part of the discussion and try to meet them halfway in crafting a decision everyone can live with. For your teens, touring on their own at Walt Disney World is tantamount to being independent in a large city. It's intoxicating, to say the least, and can be an excellent learning experience, if not a rite of passage. In any event, we're not suggesting that you just turn them loose. Rather, we are just attempting to sensitize you to the fact that, for your teens, there are some transcendent issues involved.

Most teens crave the company of other teens. If you have a solitary teen in your family, do not be surprised if he or she wants to invite a friend on your vacation. If you are invested in sharing intimate, quality time with your solitary teen, the presence of a friend will make this difficult, if not impossible. However, if you turn down the request to bring a friend, be prepared to go the extra mile to be a companion to your teen at Disney World. Expressed differently, if you're a teen, it's not much fun to ride Space Mountain by yourself.

One specific issue that absolutely should be addressed before you leave home is what assistance (if any) you expect from your teen in regard to helping with younger children in the family. Once again, try to carve out a win-win compromise. Consider the case of the mother from Indiana who had a teenage daughter from an earlier marriage and two children under age 10 from a second marriage. After a couple of vacations where she thrust the unwilling teen into the position of being a surrogate parent to her half-sisters, the teen declined henceforth to participate in family vacations.

Many parents have written *The Unofficial Guide* asking if there are unsafe places at Walt Disney World or places where teens simply should not be allowed to go. Though the answer depends more on your family values and the relative maturity of your teens than on Disney World, the basic answer is no. Though it's true that teens (or adults, for that matter) who are looking for trouble can find it anywhere, there is absolutely nothing at Disney World that could be construed as a precipitant or a catalyst.

As a final aside, if you allow your teens some independence and they are getting around on the Walt Disney World transportation system, expect some schedule slippage. If your teen happens to just miss the bus, he or she might have to wait 15–45 minutes (more often 15–20 minutes) for the next one. If punctuality is essential, advise your independent teens to arrive at a transportation station an hour before they are expected somewhere to allow sufficient time for the commute.

About **INVITING** *Your* **CHILDREN'S FRIENDS**

IF YOUR CHILDREN WANT TO INVITE FRIENDS on your Walt Disney World vacation, give your decision careful thought. There is more involved here than might be apparent. First, consider the logistics of numbers. Is there room in the car? Will you have to leave something at home that you had planned on taking to make room in the trunk for the friend's luggage? Will additional hotel rooms or a larger condo be required? Will the increased number of people in your group make it hard to get a table at a restaurant?

If you determine that you can logistically accommodate one or more friends, the next step is to consider how the inclusion of the friend will affect your group's dynamics. Generally speaking, the presence of a friend will make it harder to really connect with your own children. So if one of your vacation goals is an intimate bonding experience with your children, the addition of friends will probably frustrate your attempts to realize that objective.

If family relationship building is not necessarily a primary objective of your vacation, it's quite possible that the inclusion of a friend will make life easier for you. This is especially true in the case of only children, who may otherwise depend exclusively on you to keep them happy and occupied. Having a friend along can take the pressure off and give you some much-needed breathing room.

If you decide to allow a friend to accompany you, limit the selection to children you know really well and whose parents you also know. Your Disney World vacation is not the time to include "my friend Eddie from school" whom you've never met. Your children's friends who have spent time in your home will have a sense of your parenting style, and you will have a sense of their personality, behavior, and compatibility with your family. Assess the prospective child's potential to fit in well on a long trip. Is he or she polite, personable, fun to be with, and reasonably mature? Does he or she relate well to you and to the other members of your family?

Because a Disney World vacation is not, for most of us, a spur-of-the-moment thing, you should have adequate time to evaluate potential candidate friends. A trip to the mall, including a meal in a sit-down restaurant, will tell you volumes about the friend. Likewise, inviting the friend to share dinner with the family and then spend the night will provide a lot of relevant information. Ideally this type of evaluation should take place early on in the normal course of family events, before you discuss the possibility of a friend joining you on your vacation. This will allow you to size things up without your child (or the friend) realizing that an evaluation is taking place.

By seizing the initiative, you can guide the outcome. Ann, a Springfield, Ohio, mom, for example, anticipated that her 12-year-old son would ask to take a friend on their vacation. As she pondered the various friends her son might propose, she came up with four names. One, an otherwise sweet child, had a medical condition that Ann felt unqualified to monitor or treat. A second friend was overly aggressive with younger children and was often socially inappropriate for his age. Two other friends, Chuck and Marty, with whom she'd had a generally positive experience, were good candidates for the trip. After orchestrating some opportunities to spend time with each of the boys, she made her decision and asked her son, "Would you like to take Marty with us to Disney World?" Her son was delighted, and Ann had diplomatically preempted having to turn down friends her son might have proposed.

We recommend that you do the inviting instead of your child and that you extend the invitation to the parent (to avoid disappointment, you might want to sound out the friend's parent before broaching the issue with your child). Observing this recommendation will allow you to query the friend's parents concerning food preferences, any medical conditions, how discipline is administered in the friend's family, and how the friend's parents feel about the way you administer discipline.

Before you extend the invitation, give some serious thought to who pays for what. Make a specific proposal for financing the trip a part of your invitation. For example: "There's room for Marty in the hotel room, and transportation's no problem because we're driving. So we'll just need you to pick up Marty's meals, theme park admissions, and spending money."

A FEW WORDS *for* SINGLE PARENTS

BECAUSE SINGLE PARENTS GENERALLY are also working parents, planning a special getaway with your children can be the best way to spend some quality time together. But remember, the vacation is not just for your child—it's for you too. You might invite a grandparent or a favorite aunt or uncle along; the other adult provides nice company for you, and your child will benefit from the time with family members. You might likewise consider inviting an adult friend.

Though bringing along an adult friend or family member is the best option, the reality is that many single parents don't have friends, grandparents, or favorite aunts or uncles who can make the trip. And while spending time with your child is wonderful, it is very difficult to match the energy level of your child if you are the sole focus of his or her world.

One alternative: Try to meet other single parents at Walt Disney World. It may seem odd, but most of them are in the same boat as you; besides, all you have to do is ask. Another option, albeit expensive, is to take along a trustworthy babysitter (18 or up) to travel with you.

The easiest way to meet other single parents at the World is to hang out at the hotel pool. Make your way there on the day you arrive, after traveling by car or plane and without enough time to blow a full admission ticket at a theme park. In any event, a couple of hours spent poolside is a relaxing way to start your vacation.

If you visit Walt Disney World with another single parent, get adjoining rooms; take turns watching all the kids; and, on at least one night, get a sitter and enjoy an evening out.

Throughout this book we mention the importance of good planning and touring. For a single parent, this is an absolute must. In addition, make sure that you set aside some downtime back at the hotel every day.

Finally, don't try to spend every moment with your children on vacation. Instead, plan some activities for your children with other children. Disney programs for children, for example, are worth considering. Then take advantage of your free time to do what you want to do: Read a book, have a massage, take a long walk, or enjoy a catnap.

While pricey, one of the best ways for single parents to relax is to add a 3- or 4-night cruise to their Disney stay. Onboard activities will keep your child occupied and give you time to relax.

"He Who Hesitates Is Launched!"
TIPS *and* WARNINGS *for* GRANDPARENTS

SENIORS OFTEN GET INTO PREDICAMENTS caused by touring with grandchildren. Run ragged and pressured to endure a blistering pace, many seniors just concentrate on surviving Walt Disney World rather than enjoying it. The theme parks have as much to offer older visitors as they do children, and seniors must either set the pace or dispatch the young folks to tour on their own.

An older reader from Alabaster, Alabama, writes:

Being a senior is not for wusses. At Disney World particularly, it requires courage and pluck. Things that used to be easy take a lot of effort, and sometimes your brain has to wait for your body to catch up. Half the time, your grandchildren treat you like a crumbling ruin and then turn around and trick you into getting on a roller coaster in the dark. Seniors have to be alert and not trust anyone—not their children or even the Disney people, and especially not their grandchildren. When your grandchildren want you to go on a ride, don't follow along blindly like a lamb to the slaughter. Make sure you know what the ride is all about. Stand your ground and do not waffle. He who hesitates is launched!

If you don't get to see much of your grandchildren, you might think that Walt Disney World is the perfect place for a little bonding and togetherness. Wrong! Disney World can potentially send children into system overload and can precipitate behaviors that pose a challenge even to adoring parents, never mind grandparents. You don't take your grandchildren straight to Disney World for the same reason you don't buy your 16-year-old son a Ferrari: handling it safely and well requires some experience.

Begin by spending time with your grandchildren in an environment that you can control. Have them over one at a time for dinner and to spend the night. Check out how they respond to your oversight and discipline. Determine that you can set limits and that they will accept those limits. When you reach this stage, you can contemplate some outings to the zoo, the movies, the mall, or the state fair. Gauge how demanding your grandchildren are when you are out of the house. Eat a meal or two in a full-service restaurant to get a sense of their social skills and their ability to behave appropriately. Don't expect perfection, and be prepared to modify your own behavior a little too. As a senior friend of mine told her husband, "You can't see Walt Disney World sitting on your butt."

If you have a good relationship with your grandchildren and have had a positive one-on-one experience taking care of them, you might consider a trip to Disney World. If you do, we have two recommendations. First, visit Disney World without them to get an idea of what you're getting into. A scouting trip will also provide you with an opportunity to enjoy some of the attractions that won't be on the itinerary when you return with the grandkids. Second, if you are considering a trip of a week's duration, you might think about buying a Disney package that combines 4 days at Disney World with a 3-day cruise. In addition to being a memorable experience for your grandchildren, the cruise provides plenty of structure for children of almost every age, thus allowing you to be with them but also to have some time off. Call Disney Cruise Line at ☎ 800-951-3532 or visit disneycruise.com.

Tips for Grandparents

1. It's best to take one grandchild at a time, two at the most. Cousins can be better than siblings because they don't fight as much. To preclude sibling jealousy, try connecting the trip to a child's milestone, such as finishing the sixth grade.

2. Let your grandchildren help plan the vacation, and keep the first one short. Be flexible and don't overplan. Take a break in the afternoon.

3. Discuss mealtimes and bedtime. Fortunately, many grandparents are on an early dinner schedule, which works nicely with younger children. Plan your evening meal early to avoid long waits. And make Advance Reservations if you're dining in a popular spot, even if it's early. Take some crayons and paper to keep younger kids occupied.

4. Gear plans to your grandchildren's age levels, because if they're not happy, you won't be happy. Take a day off between visits to the parks.

5. Create an itinerary that offers some supervised activities for children in case you need a rest.

6. If you're traveling by car, this is the one time we highly recommend earbuds. Kids' musical tastes are vastly different from most grandparents'. It's simply more enjoyable when everyone can listen to his or her own preferred style of music, at least for some portion of the trip.

7. Take along a night-light.

8. Carry a notarized statement from parents for permission for medical care in case of an emergency. Also be sure you have insurance information and copies of any prescriptions for medicines the kids may take. Ditto for eyeglass prescriptions.

9. Tell your grandchildren about any medical problems you may have, so they can be prepared if there's an emergency.

10. Many attractions and hotels offer discounts for seniors, so check ahead of time for bargains.

ORDER *and* DISCIPLINE *on the* ROAD

OK, OK, WIPE THAT SMIRK OFF YOUR FACE. Order and discipline on the road may seem like an oxymoron to you, but you won't be hooting when your 5-year-old launches a screaming stem-winder in the middle of Fantasyland. Your willingness to give this subject serious consideration before you leave home may well be the most important element of your pretrip preparation.

Discipline and maintaining order are more difficult when traveling because everyone is, as a Boston mom put it, "in and out" (in strange surroundings and out of the normal routine). For children, it's hard to contain the excitement and anticipation that pop to the surface in the form of fidgety hyperactivity, nervous energy, and, sometimes, acting out. Confinement in a car, plane, or hotel room only exacerbates the situation, and kids are often louder than normal, more aggressive with siblings, and much more inclined to push the envelope of parental patience and control. Once in the theme parks, it doesn't get much better. There's more elbow room, but there's also overstimulation, crowds, heat, and miles of walking. All this coupled with marginal or inadequate rest can lead to meltdown in the most harmonious of families.

The following discussion was developed by leading child psychologist Dr. Karen Turnbow, who has contributed to The Unofficial Guides for years and who has spent many days at Walt Disney World conducting research and observing families.

Sound parenting and standards of discipline practiced at home, applied consistently, will suffice to handle most situations on vacation. Still, it's instructive to study the hand you are dealt when traveling. For starters, aside from being jazzed and ablaze with adrenaline, your kids may believe that rules followed at home are somehow suspended when traveling. Parents reinforce this misguided intuition by being inordinately lenient in the interest of maintaining peace in the family. While some of your home protocols (cleaning your plate, going to bed at a set time, and such) might be relaxed to good effect on vacation, differing from your normal approach to discipline can precipitate major misunderstanding.

Children, not unexpectedly, are likely to believe that a vacation (especially a vacation to Walt Disney World) is expressly for them. This reinforces their focus on their own needs and largely erases any consideration of yours. Such a mind-set dramatically increases their sense of hurt and disappointment when you correct them or deny them something they want. An incident that would hardly elicit a pouty lip at home could well escalate to tears or defiance when traveling.

LILIANE Discuss your vacation needs with your children and explore their wants and expectations well before you depart on your trip.

The stakes are high for everyone on a vacation—for you because of the cost in time and dollars but also because your vacation represents a rare opportunity for rejuvenation and renewal. The stakes are high for your children too. Children tend to romanticize travel, building anticipation to an almost unbearable level. Discussing the trip in advance can ground expectations to a certain extent, but a child's imagination will, in the end, trump reality every time. The good news is that you can take advantage of your children's emotional state to preestablish rules and conditions for their conduct while on vacation. Because your children want what's being offered *sooooo* badly, they will be unusually accepting and conscientious regarding whatever rules are agreed upon.

According to Dr. Turnbow, successful response to (or avoidance of) behavioral problems on the road begins with a clear-cut disciplinary policy at home. Both at home and on vacation, the approach should be the same and should be based on the following key concepts:

1. LET EXPECTATIONS BE KNOWN. Discuss what you expect from your children, but don't try to cover every imaginable situation. Cover expectations in regard to compliance with parental directives, treatment of siblings, resolution of disputes, schedule (including wake-up and bedtimes), courtesy and manners, staying together, and who pays for what.

2. EXPLAIN THE CONSEQUENCES OF NONCOMPLIANCE. Detail very clearly and firmly the consequences of unmet expectations. This should be very straightforward and unambiguous. If you do X (or don't do X), this is what will happen.

3. WARN YOUR KIDS. You're dealing with excited, expectant children, not machines, so it's important to issue a warning before meting out discipline. It's critical to understand that we're talking about one unequivocal warning rather than multiple warnings or nagging. These undermine your credibility and make your expectations appear relative or less than serious. Multiple warnings or nagging also effectively pass control of the situation from you to your child (who may continue to act out as an attention-getting strategy).

4. FOLLOW THROUGH. If you say that you are going to do something, do it. Period. Children must understand that you are absolutely serious and committed.

5. BE CONSISTENT. Inconsistency makes discipline a random event in the eyes of your children. Random discipline encourages random behavior, which translates to a nearly total loss of parental control. Long-term, both at home and on the road, your response to a given situation or transgression must be perfectly predictable. Structure and repetition, essential for a child to learn, cannot be achieved in the absence of consistency.

ACTIVE LISTENING AND A FEELING VOCABULARY

THOUGH THE PREVIOUS FIVE are the biggies, several other corollary concepts and techniques are worthy of consideration.

First, understand that whining, tantrums, defiance, sibling friction, and even holding the group up are ways in which children communicate with parents. Frequently, the object or precipitant of a situation has little or no relation to the unacceptable behavior. On the surface, a fit may appear to be about the ice cream you refused to buy little Robby, but there's almost always something deeper, a subtext that is closer to the truth (this is the reason why ill behavior often persists after you give in to a child's demands). As often as not, the real cause is a need for attention. This need is so powerful in some children that they will subject themselves to certain punishment and parental displeasure to garner the attention they crave.

To get at the root cause of the behavior in question requires both active listening and empowering your child with a "feeling vocabulary." Active listening is a concept that's been around for a long time. It involves being alert not only to what a child says but also to the context in which it is said, to the language used and possible subtext, to the child's emotional state and body language, and even to what's not said. Sounds complicated, but it's basically being attentive to the larger picture and, more to the point, being aware that there is a larger picture.

Helping your child to develop a feeling vocabulary consists of teaching your child to use words to describe what's going on. The idea is to teach the child to articulate what's really troubling him, to be able to identify and express emotions and mood states in language.

It all begins with convincing your child that you're willing to listen attentively and take what he's saying seriously. Listening to your child, you help him transcend the topical by reframing the conversation to address the underlying emotional state(s). That his brother hit him may have precipitated the mood, but the act is topical and of secondary importance. What you want is for your child to be able to communicate how that makes him feel and to get in touch with those emotions. When you reduce an incident (hitting) to the emotions triggered (anger, hurt, rejection, and so on), you have the foundation for helping him to develop constructive coping strategies. A child who can tell his mother why he is distressed is a child who has discovered a coping strategy far more effective (not to mention easier for all concerned) than a tantrum.

Until you get the active listening and feeling vocabulary going, be careful not to become part of the problem. There's a whole laundry list of adult responses to bad behavior that only make things worse. Hitting, swatting, yelling, name-calling, insulting, belittling, using sarcasm, pleading, nagging, and inducing guilt ("We've spent thousands of dollars to bring you to Disney World and now you're spoiling the trip for everyone!") figure prominently on the list.

DEALING WITH UNWANTED BEHAVIORS

RESPONDING TO A CHILD appropriately in a disciplinary situation requires thought and preparation. Following are key things to keep in mind and techniques to try when your world blows up while waiting in line for Dumbo.

1. BE THE ADULT. It's well understood that children can push their parents' buttons faster and more lethally than just about anyone or anything else. They've got your number, know precisely how to elicit a response, and are not reluctant to go for the jugular. Fortunately (or unfortunately), you're the adult, and to deal with a situation effectively, you must act like one. If your kids get you ranting and caterwauling, you effectively abdicate your adult status. Worse, you suggest by way of example that being out of control is an acceptable expression of hurt or anger. No matter what happens, repeat the mantra, "I am the adult in this relationship."

2. FREEZE THE ACTION. Being the adult and maintaining control almost always translates to freezing the action. Instead of a knee-jerk response, freeze the action by disengaging. Wherever you are or whatever the family is doing, stop in place and concentrate on one thing and one thing only: getting all involved to calm down. Practically speaking, this usually means initiating a time-out. It's essential that you take this action immediately. Grabbing your child by the arm or collar and dragging him toward the car or hotel room only escalates the turmoil by prolonging the confrontation and by adding a coercive physical dimension to an already volatile emotional event. If, for the sake of people around you (as when a toddler throws a tantrum in church), it's essential to retreat to a more private place, choose the first place available. Firmly sit the child down and refrain from talking to him until you've both cooled off. This might take a little time, but the investment is worthwhile.

3. ISOLATE THE CHILD. You'll be able to deal with the situation more effectively and expeditiously if the child is isolated with one parent. Dispatch the uninvolved members of your party for a break or have them go on with the activity or itinerary without you (if possible) and arrange to rendezvous later at an agreed time and place. In addition to letting the others get on with their day, isolating the offending child with one parent relieves him of the pressure of being the group's focus of attention and object of anger. Equally important, isolation frees you from the scrutiny and expectations of the others in regard to how to handle the situation.

4. REVIEW THE SITUATION WITH THE CHILD. If, as discussed previously, you've made your expectations clear, stated the consequences of failing those expectations, and administered a warning, review the situation with the child and follow through with the discipline warranted. If, as often occurs, things are not so black-and-white, encourage the child to communicate his feelings. Try to uncover what occasioned the acting out. Lecturing and accusatory language don't work well here, nor do threats. Dr. Turnbow suggests that a better approach (after the child is calm) is to ask, "What can we do to make this a better day for you?"

5. FREQUENT TANTRUMS OR ACTING OUT. The preceding four points relate to dealing with an incident as opposed to a chronic condition. If a child frequently acts out or throws tantrums, you'll need to employ a somewhat different strategy.

LILIANE Tantrums are about getting attention. Giving your child attention when things are on an even keel often preempts acting out.

Tantrums are cyclical events evolved from learned behavior. A child learns that he can get your undivided attention by acting out. When you respond, whether by scolding, admonishing, threatening, or negotiating, your response further draws you into the cycle and prolongs the behavior. When you accede to the child's demands, you reinforce the effectiveness of the tantrum and raise the cost of capitulation next time around. When a child thus succeeds in monopolizing your attention, he effectively becomes the person in charge.

To break this cycle, you must disengage from the child. The object is to demonstrate that the cause-and-effect relationship (that is, tantrum elicits parental attention) is no longer operative. This can be accomplished by refusing to interact with the child as long as the untoward behavior continues. Tell the child that you're unwilling to discuss his problem until he calms down. You can ignore the behavior, remove yourself from the child's presence (or vice versa), or isolate the child with a time-out. The important thing is to disengage quickly and decisively with no discussion or negotiation.

Most children don't pick the family vacation as the time to start throwing tantrums. The behavior will be evident before you leave home, and home is the best place to deal with it. Be forewarned, however, that bad habits die hard, and a child accustomed to getting attention by throwing tantrums will not simply give up after a single instance of disengagement. More likely, the child will at first escalate the intensity and length of his tantrums. By your consistent refusal over several weeks (or even months) to respond to his behavior, however, he will finally adjust to the new paradigm.

Children are cunning as well as observant. Many understand that a tantrum in public is embarrassing to you and that you're more likely to cave in than you would at home. Once again, consistency is the key, along with a bit of anticipation. When traveling, it's not necessary to retreat to the privacy of a hotel room to isolate your child. You can carve out space for time-out almost anywhere: on a theme park bench, in your car, in a restroom, even on a sidewalk. You can often spot the warning signs of an impending tantrum and head it off by talking to the child before he reaches an explosive emotional pitch.

6. SALVAGE OPERATIONS. Children are full of surprises, and sometimes the surprises are not good. If your sweet child manages to make a mistake of mammoth proportions, what do you do? This happened to an Ohio couple, resulting in the offending kid pretty much being grounded for life. Fortunately there were no injuries or lives lost, but the parents had to determine what to do for the remainder of the vacation. For starters, they split the group. One parent escorted the offending child back to the hotel, where he was effectively confined to his guest room for the duration. That evening, the parents arranged for in-room sitters for the rest of the stay. Expensive? You bet, but better than watching your whole vacation go down the tubes.

A family at the Magic Kingdom had a similar experience, though the offense was of a more modest order of magnitude. Because it was their last day of vacation, they elected to place the child in time-out, in the theme park, for the rest of the day. One parent monitored the culprit while the other parent and the siblings enjoyed the attractions. At agreed times, the parents would switch places. Once again, not ideal, but preferable to stopping the vacation.

PART TWO

GETTING *Your* ACT TOGETHER

Visiting Walt Disney World is a bit like childbirth—you never really believe what people tell you, but once you've been through it yourself, you know exactly what they were saying!

—Hilary Wolfe, a mother and *Unofficial Guide* reader from Swansea, Wales, United Kingdom

GATHERING INFORMATION

IN ADDITION TO USING THIS GUIDE, we recommend that you visit our sister website, touringplans.com. The companion blog has breaking news for Walt Disney World, Universal Orlando, Disney Cruise Line, and Disneyland.

Touringplans.com complements and augments the information in our books, and it provides real-time personal services that are impossible to build into a book. The book is your comprehensive reference source; touringplans.com is your personal concierge. Sign up for free here: touringplans.com/walt-disney-world/join/basic.

With that free access, you'll be able to create custom touring plans, follow them in the parks, and get updates to them if conditions change while you're there. You'll also find up-to-the-minute information on rides, restaurants, crowds, park hours and operations, and more.

A few parts of the site require a small subscription fee to access: a detailed, day-by-day crowd calendar, for example, or a service that sends your hotel-room request directly to Disney. That subscription covers the costs of the extra people, technology, and external companies that it takes to provide them, beyond what's needed for the books.

Here's a brief rundown of some of the things you'll find on the site:

CUSTOM TOURING PLANS *Our best and most efficient touring plans are those provided in this guide.* For families with unique circumstances, we provide custom touring plans online. You can also customize the plans in this book by simply skipping any attractions that don't interest you.

DETAILED 365-DAY CROWD CALENDAR FOR EACH THEME PARK
Subscribers can see which parks will be the least crowded every day of
their trip, using a 1-to-10 scale.

HOTEL ROOM VIEWS AND ONLINE FAX SERVICE We have photos of the
views from every hotel room in Walt Disney World—more than 30,000
images—and we'll give you the exact wording to use with Disney to
request a specific room. For subscribers, we'll even automatically fax
your room request to Disney right before you arrive. Disney will try to
accommodate your request, but its ability to do so depends on a number
of variables that we can't control. The majority of the faxed requests we
send on behalf of readers are honored in full or partially, but sometimes
Disney just can't make it work.

TICKET DISCOUNTS A customizable search helps you find the cheapest
tickets for your specific needs. The average family can save $20–$80 by
purchasing admission from one of our recommended ticket wholesalers.

FASTPASS+ INFORMATION We show every FastPass+ reservation available at every attraction in the parks on a single page of our site.

ANSWERS TO YOUR TRIP-PLANNING QUESTIONS Our online community includes tens of thousands of Disney experts and fans willing to help
with your vacation plans. Ask questions and offer your own helpful tips.

LINES APP Our in-park app, Lines, is available on the Apple App Store
and Google Play. It has lots of interesting, free features, designed to
accompany you in the parks. It provides ride and park information that
Disney doesn't, including:

- **Posted and actual wait times at attractions** Lines is the only Disney-
  parks app that displays both posted wait times and the actual times you'll
  wait in line. The wait time you see posted outside of a ride is often much longer than the real wait time, often because Disney is trying to do crowd control. With Lines, you can make better decisions about what to see.

- **"Ride now or wait" recommendations** Lines shows you whether ride wait
  times are likely to get longer or shorter. If you find a long line at a particular
  attraction, Lines tells you the best time to come back.

- **Real-time touring plan updates while you're in a park** Lines automatically updates your custom touring plan to reflect actual crowd conditions
  at a given moment. You can also restart your plan and add or change attractions, breaks, meals, and more.

- **In-park chat feature with our Lines community** Have a quick question
  while you're in the parks? Ask our community of thousands of Liners and
  get a response within seconds.

The Unofficial Guide and touringplans.com, along with the Lines
app, were created to work together to provide the most comprehensive planning and touring support possible. This mom from St. Louis
shares her experience using all the tools in our toolbox:

*I read the book cover to cover and then referred back to it. After
reading the book, I had a good idea of what hotels I was interested
in and had must-do and must-eat places somewhat picked out. I then
switched to the website to personalize our touring plans and use as*

an easy reference when needed. The book and the website together made our trip INCREDIBLE. My husband even complimented me on our touring plans—they worked perfectly and were supereasy to use and manipulate.

The Unofficial Guides' website, theunofficialguides.com, features free content, and we invite you to follow us on Facebook (facebook .com/TheUnofficialGuideToWaltDisneyWorldWithKids), Instagram (@theUGSeries), YouTube (@theunofficialguideseries), and Twitter (@LilianeOpsomer) for tips and updates.

Next, we recommend that you obtain the following:

1. **WALT DISNEY WORLD RESORT VACATION-PLANNING VIDEOS** Disney has online videos advertising the complex's offerings. To view them, fill out a short survey at disneyplanning.com. You can also access videos about Disneyland, Disney Cruise Line, and other Disney destinations from the same website.

2. **VISIT ORLANDO VACATION PLANNING KIT** If you're considering lodging outside Disney World or if you think you might patronize out-of-the-World attractions and restaurants, check out visitorlando.com, which includes discounts for hotels, restaurants, ground transportation, shopping, dinner theaters, and theme parks and attractions. For more information call ☎ 800-643-9492 or 407-363-5872, 8 a.m.–8 p.m. Eastern time.

3. **KISSIMMEE VISITOR'S INFO** If you intend to lodge outside of Disney World, visit experiencekissimmee.com, which has information on hotels, rental houses, time-shares, and condominiums, as well as a directory of attractions, restaurants, special events, and other useful info. You can also call the Kissimmee Convention and Visitors Bureau at ☎ 407-569-4800.

4. **"GUIDEBOOK FOR GUESTS WITH DISABILITIES"** Available at Guest Relations within the parks, at resort front desks, and at wheelchair-rental areas (listed in each theme park chapter). More-limited information is located at disneyworld.disney.go.com/guest-services/guests-with-disabilities.

IMPORTANT WALT DISNEY WORLD TELEPHONE NUMBERS

WHEN YOU CALL the main information number, you'll be offered a menu of options for recorded information on operating hours, recreation areas, shopping, entertainment, tickets, reservations, and driving directions. See the table on page 38 for a list of phone numbers.

DISNEY ONLINE: OFFICIAL AND OTHERWISE

THE WALT DISNEY COMPANY features a set of high-tech enhancements in its theme parks and hotels. Known as **MyMagic+,** the technology includes **FastPass+** and rubber wristbands (**MagicBands**) with embedded computer chips that function as admission tickets and hotel keys.

FastPass+ requires that you make reservations months in advance to ride Disney's attractions, if you want any chance of avoiding long waits in line. Other features, such as MagicBands, require you to enter detailed information about your traveling party, and restaurant reservations require you to know the exact time you want to eat, and where, six months before you arrive.

• Important WDW Telephone Numbers •

General Information ☎ 407-824-4321 or 407-824-2222

General Information for the Hearing-Impaired (TTY) ☎ 407-827-5141

General Information for Guests with Disabilities ☎ 407-939-7807

Accommodations/Reservations ☎ 407-W-DISNEY (934-7639) • UK 0800 028 0778

Advent Health Centra Care • Kissimmee ☎ 407-390-1888
• Lake Buena Vista ☎ 407-934-2273 • Universal-Dr. Phillips ☎ 407-291-8975

Blizzard Beach Information ☎ 407-560-3400

Dining Advance Reservations ☎ 407-WDW-DINE (939-3463)

ESPN Wide World of Sports Complex ☎ 407-939-4263 or 407-939-1500

Golf Reservations and Information ☎ 407-WDW-GOLF (939-4653)

Guided-Tour Information ☎ 407-WDW-TOUR (939-8687)

Lost and Found • **Today:** Visit Guest Relations in the park
• **Yesterday or before** (*all Disney parks*) ☎ 407-824-4245
• **Yesterday or before** (*Disney Springs*) ☎ 407-828-3150

Outdoor Recreation Reservations and Information ☎ 407-WDW-PLAY (939-7529)

Resort Dining and Information ☎ 407-WDW-DINE (939-3463)

Security ☎ 407-560-7959 (*routine*) or 407-560-1990 (*urgent*)

Tennis Lessons ☎ 321-228-1146

Ticket Inquiries ☎ 407-939-7679

Typhoon Lagoon Information ☎ 407-560-4120

Walt Disney Travel Company ☎ 407-939-6244

Weather Information ☎ 407-827-4545

Wrecker Service ☎ 407-824-0976 (*or call Security after hours; see above*)

Disney's website (disneyworld.com) and mobile app are the "glue" that binds all of this together. Because you have to plan so much before you leave home, we're covering the basics of Disney's website and app in this section. Full coverage of MagicBands starts on page 64; details on the FastPass+ system start on page 238. You should read the FastPass+ section before making any reservations.

My Disney Experience at DisneyWorld.com

In this area of the Disney website, you can make hotel, dining, and some recreation reservations; buy admission; and get park hours, attraction information, and much more. The most important of the site's features support My Disney Experience (MDE). See page 239 for step-by-step instructions.

My Disney Experience Mobile App

In addition to its website, Disney offers a companion app on iTunes and Google Play (search for "My Disney Experience"). My Disney Experience is optimized for the latest phones and tablets, so some features may not be available on all devices. The app includes park hours, attraction operating hours and descriptions, wait times for buses, restaurant hours with descriptions and menus, the ability to make FastPass+ and dining reservations, GPS-based directions, the locations of park photographers, and more. The app also offers mobile ordering at select quick-service restaurants and can even be used to open your Disney resort room.

Our Recommended Websites

Searching online for Disney information is like navigating an immense maze for a very small piece of cheese: There's a lot of information available, but you may find a lot of dead-ends before getting what you want. Our picks follow.

BEST Q&A SITE Walt Disney World has a **Mom's Panel,** chosen from among 10,000-plus applicants. The panelists have a website, disney worldmoms.com, where they offer tips and discuss how to plan a Disney World vacation. Several moms have specialized experience in areas such as Disney Cruise Line; some speak Spanish too.

BEST GENERAL UNOFFICIAL WALT DISNEY WORLD WEBSITE We highly recommend Deb Wills's **allears.net** to friends who want to make a trip to Disney World. Updated several times a week, the site includes breaking news, tons of photos, Disney restaurant menus, resort and ticket information, tips for guests with special needs, and more. We also check **wdwmagic.com** for news and happenings around Walt Disney World.

BEST MONEY-SAVING SITE MouseSavers (mousesavers.com) keeps an updated list of discounts for use at Disney resorts. Discounts are separated into categories such as "For the general public" and "For residents of certain states." Anyone who calls or books online can use a current discount. Savings can be considerable—up to 40% in some cases. MouseSavers also has discounts for rental cars and non-Disney hotels in the area.

BEST WALT DISNEY WORLD PREVIEW SITE If you want to see what a particular attraction is like, **touringplans.com** offers free videos or photos of every attraction. Videos of indoor ("dark") rides are sometimes inferior to those of outdoor rides due to poor lighting, but even the videos and photos of indoor rides generally provide a good sense of what the attraction is about. **YouTube** is also an excellent place to find videos of Disney and other Central Florida attractions.

SOCIAL MEDIA Facebook, Twitter, and **Instagram** are popular places for Disney fans to gather online and share comments, tips, and photos. Following fellow Disneyphiles as they share their in-park experiences can make you feel like you're there, even as you're stuck in a cubicle at work. You can also join more than 9,000 fans for news and insights on our very own Facebook page: **facebook.com/TheUnofficialGuideToWalt DisneyWorldWithKids.**

BEST THEME PARK-INSIDER SITE Jimhillmedia.com has insider accounts of the politics, frantic project management, and pipe dreams that somehow combine to create the attractions that Disney and Universal build.

BEST DISNEY DISCUSSION BOARDS There are tons of these; among the most active are **disboards.com, forums.wdwmagic.com, forum.touring**

plans.com, and, for Brits, **thedibb.co.uk** (*DIBB* stands for "Disney Information Bulletin Board").

BEST SITES FOR TRAFFIC, ROADWORK, CONSTRUCTION, AND SAFETY INFORMATION Visit **cfxway.com** for the latest information on roadwork in the Orlando and Orange County areas. The site also contains detailed maps, directions, and toll-rate information for the most popular tourist destinations. A seven-year construction project to improve I-4 was launched in 2015. Information on the northern section between Kirkman Road (near Universal) and downtown Orlando can be found at **i4ultimate.com.** Construction updates on the southern section from Kirkman Road to US 27 in Polk County are available at **i4beyond.com.** Check **tinyurl.com/childsafetyFL** to learn about state child-restraint requirements. Finally, we like **Google Maps** for driving directions.

Liliane's Favorite Podcasts

If you just can't make it through the year without the Mouse, don't despair. Sounds, images, and news from the World are available in abundance online. Here are some of my favorites.

BE OUR GUEST A fun, high-energy, Disney-related podcast. Visit **beourguestpodcast.podbean.com** for more info.

THE DISNEY DISH Join theme park historian Jim Hill and Touring Plans' Len Testa at **podbean.com/podcast-detail/k2jbz-349ea** for insightful and fun shows filled with theme park news, rumors, and history.

DISNEY DREAM GIRLS Recorded in the UK, this all-female podcast promotes Disney girl power. Visit **disneydreamgirlspodcast.blogspot.co.uk.**

THE DISNEY MOVIE REVIEW A great podcast for movie fans. The podcast, found at **thedisneymoviereview.com/category/disney-movies,** covers live-action and animated feature-length films from Walt Disney Studios, including films from Pixar and Marvel.

THE DIS UNPLUGGED PODCAST Tune into this weekly roundtable discussion, which covers all aspects of planning a Walt Disney World vacation: **disunplugged.com/category/orlando-podcast-episodes.**

GEEKIN' ON WDW All Disney geeks will enjoy this passionate and enthusiastic podcast at **geekinonwdw.com/category/podcast,** hosted by a father–daughter team.

ORLANDO TOURISM REPORT A weekly show covering Central Florida hospitality news: **orlandotourismreport.com/category/podcast.** It's also live on Friday, 10 a.m.–noon, on 91.5 FM WPRK (Winter Park) radio.

RADIO HARAMBE and the accompanying website, **jamboeveryone.com,** are a celebration of Disney's Animal Kingdom. Listen to Dave and Safari Mike as they keep you updated on all that is happening at the park. Visit **radioharambe.podbean.com.**

THE PARKSCOPE UNPROFESSIONAL PODCAST Sit back and listen to four dudes talk about their love of theme parks: **parkscope.net/p/podcast_5.html.**

SOUNDS OF DISNEY Join Jeff Davis, also known as The Sorcerer, as he delights his audience with music, news, and Disney songs from the parks. In addition to the podcast, Davis's website, **srsounds.com,** provides music, videos, pictures, and a message board.

THE UNOFFICIAL UNIVERSAL ORLANDO PODCAST This biweekly podcast highlights news, interviews, and discussions about the Universal Orlando Resort. Visit **uuopodcast.com.**

ALLOCATING TIME

YOU SHOULD ALLOCATE 6 days for a whirlwind tour (7–10 days if you're old-fashioned and insist on some relaxation during your vacation). If you don't have 6-plus days, then you need to be prepared to make some hard choices.

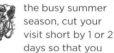 **BOB** If you must visit during the busy summer season, cut your visit short by 1 or 2 days so that you will have the weekend or a couple of vacation days remaining to recuperate when you get home.

A seemingly obvious point lost on many families is that Walt Disney World is not going anywhere. There's no danger that it will be packed up and shipped to Iceland anytime soon. This means that you can come back if you don't see everything this year. Disney has planned it this way, of course, but that doesn't matter. It's infinitely more sane to resign yourself to the reality that seeing everything during one visit is impossible. We recommend, therefore, that you approach Walt Disney World the same way you would an eight-course French dinner: leisurely, with plenty of time between courses.

WHEN TO GO TO WALT DISNEY WORLD

LET'S CUT TO THE ESSENCE: Disney World between mid-June and mid-August is rough. You can count on large summer crowds as well as Florida's trademark heat and humidity. Avoid these dates if you can. Ditto for Memorial Day and Labor Day weekends. Other holiday periods (such as Easter, spring break, Halloween, Thanksgiving, Christmas, and so on) are very crowded, but the heat is not as bad.

BOB Though crowds have grown in September and October as a result of promotions aimed at families without school-age children and the international market, these months continue to be good for touring.

The least-busy time *historically* is from Labor Day in September through the beginning of October—but see our caveat below. Next slowest are the weeks in mid-January after the Martin Luther King Jr. holiday weekend up to Presidents' Day in February (except when the Walt Disney World Marathon runs after MLK Day). The weeks after Thanksgiving and before Christmas are less crowded than average, as is mid-April–mid-May, after spring break and before Memorial Day.

Late February, March, and early April are dicey. Crowds ebb and flow according to spring break schedules and the timing of Mardi Gras and Presidents' Day weekend. Besides being asphalt-melting hot, July brings throngs of South American tourists on their winter holiday.

The basic rule of thumb is that Disney World is more crowded when school is out and less crowded when kids are in school. However, Disney has become adept at loading slow periods of the year with special events, conventions, food festivals, and the like. Discounts on rooms and dining during slower periods also figure in.

In short: The World can be packed at any time, and you need to dig a little deeper than merely the time of year to pinpoint the least crowded dates. For a calendar of scheduled Disney events, see touringplans.com /walt-disney-world/events#. Huge conventions at the Orange County Convention Center also contribute to the problem (see page 44).

Other factors affecting crowding and long lines include a combination of closed rides and the number of employees Disney decides to use in the parks. As a result, we've added more data about ride closures to our Crowd Calendar forecasts. Last but certainly not least, Disney, in an effort to save money, reduces ride capacity and schedules fewer cast members to work the rides during slower periods of the year, resulting in longer wait times even when the parks are not crowded.

So, parents, what to do? If your children are of preschool age, definitely go during a cooler, less-crowded time. If you have school-age children, look first for an anomaly in your school-year schedule: in other words, a time when your kids will be out of school when most schools elsewhere are in session. Anomalies are most often found at the beginning or end of the school year (for example, school starts late or lets out early), at Christmas, or at spring break. In the event that no such anomalies exist, and providing that your kids are good students, our recommendation is to ask permission to take your children out of school either just before or after the Thanksgiving holiday. Teachers

ANNUAL ATTENDANCE PATTERNS AT THE MAGIC KINGDOM

Visitors Per Day (*thousands*)

Christmas   New Year's

Thanksgiving

Easter

Labor Day   Presidents' Day   Memorial Day

College Spring Break

120 — 100 — 80 — 60 — 40 — 0

Sept Oct Nov Dec Jan Feb Mar Apr May Jun Jul Aug

can assign lessons that can be made up at home over the Thanksgiving holiday, either before or after your Disney World vacation.

If none of these options are workable for your family, consider visiting Disney World the week immediately before school starts (excluding Labor Day weekend) or the week immediately after school lets out (excluding Memorial Day weekend). This strategy should remove you from the really big mob scenes by about a week or more.

The time that works best for families with kids is the week before school ends. Because grades must be finalized earlier, there is often little going on at school during that week. Check far in advance with your child's teacher to determine if any special exams or projects will occur in that last week. If no major assignments are on the child's schedule, then go for it.

Incidentally, taking your kids out of school for more than a few days is problematic. We have received well-considered letters from parents and teachers who don't think taking kids out of school is such a hot idea. A Fairfax, Virginia, dad put it thus:

My wife and I do not encourage families to take their children out of school. My wife is an eighth-grade science teacher. She has parents pull their children, some honor roll students, out of school for vacations, only to discover when they return that the students are unable to comprehend the material. Several students have been so thoroughly lost in their assignments that they ask if they can be excused from the tests. Parental suspicions about the quality of their children's education should be raised when children go to school for 6 hours a day yet supposedly can complete this same instruction with less than an hour of homework each night.

A Martinez, California, teacher offers this compelling analogy:

There are a precious 180 days for us as teachers to instruct our students, and there are 185 days during the year for Disney World. I have seen countless students struggle to catch up the rest of the year due to a week of vacation during critical instructional periods. It's like walking out of a movie after watching the first 5 minutes, and then returning for the last 5 minutes and trying to figure out what happened.

But a schoolteacher from Penn Yan, New York, expresses a different opinion:

As a teacher and a parent, I disagree with the comments from teachers saying that it's horrible for a parent to take a child out for a vacation. If a parent takes the time to let us know that a child is going to be out, we help them get ready for upcoming homework the best we can. If the child is a good student, why shouldn't they go have a wonderful experience with their family? I also don't understand when teachers say they can't get something together for the time the student will be out. We all have to plan ahead, and we know what we are teaching days, if not weeks, in advance. Take 20 minutes out of your day and set something up. Learn to be flexible!

If possible, ask your child's teacher for a list of topics they'll be covering while you're away. Have your child study these on the plane or in the car, during midday breaks, and at night before bed.

BE UNCONVENTIONAL The Orange County Convention Center in Orlando hosts some of the largest conventions and trade shows in the world. Hotel rooms anywhere near Walt Disney World are hard to find when there's a big convention—rooms less than $75 or more than $200 a night (that is, budget and upscale) go quickly. Check the convention schedule for the next seven months at calendar.occc.net/calendar; click on any meeting during your Disney dates to view the expected attendance. (Don't worry about conventions with fewer than 10,000 attendees unless you want to book a hotel in the International Drive area.)

DON'T FORGET AUGUST Kids go back to school pretty early in Florida (and in a lot of other places too). This makes mid- to late August a good time to visit Disney World for families who can't vacation during the off-season. A New Jersey mother of two school-age children spells it out:

> The end of August is the PERFECT time to go. There were virtually no wait times, 20 minutes at the most.

JUNE AND THE EARLY BIRD It's not an easy turnaround, but heading for Walt Disney World in late May or early June as soon as school is out will net big rewards. Late May through about June 12 is still considered shoulder season, so the crowds will not have spiked to summer levels. Also the weather is usually cooler than in late August. An exception to the above is Memorial Day weekend, though the week following the holiday is one of the best of the whole summer crowd-wise.

High-Low, High-Low, It's Off to Disney We Go

We strongly recommend going to Disney World in the fall, winter, or spring because of the milder weather, generally smaller crowds, and deeper discounts. However, these benefits come with some trade-offs. The parks often close early during the off-season, either because of low crowds or special events, and even when crowds are small, it's difficult to see big parks such as the Magic Kingdom between 9 a.m. and 7 p.m. Early closing also usually means no evening parades or fireworks. And because these are slow times, some rides and attractions may be closed. Finally, Central Florida temperatures fluctuate wildly during late fall, winter, and early spring; daytime highs in the 40s and 50s aren't uncommon.

On the other hand, Disney generally has the best lodging offers during these times of the year, including free dining plans. If you plan to stay on-property, this could represent some serious savings.

We realize that off-season touring isn't possible for many families. We want to make it clear, therefore, that you can have a wonderful experience regardless of when you go. Our advice, irrespective of season, is to arrive early at the parks and avoid the crowds by using one of our touring plans. If attendance is light, kick back and forget the touring plans.

• Walt Disney World Climate •

	JAN	FEB	MAR	APR	MAY	JUN	JUL	AUG	SEP	OCT	NOV	DEC
AVERAGE DAILY HIGH												
	71°F	73°F	78°F	83°F	89°F	91°F	92°F	92°F	90°F	84°F	78°F	72°F
AVERAGE DAILY HEAT INDEX (TEMPERATURE + HUMIDITY)												
	76°F	75°F	80°F	88°F	104°F	109°F	116°F	117°F	110°F	92°F	80°F	74°F
AVERAGE DAILY TEMPERATURE												
	60°F	61°F	67°F	71°F	77°F	81°F	82°F	83°F	81°F	75°F	68°F	62°F
AVERAGE DAILY HUMIDITY												
	62%	73%	71%	70%	71%	70%	74%	76%	76%	75%	74%	73%
AVERAGE RAINFALL PER MONTH												
	2.9″	2.7″	4.0″	2.3″	3.1″	8.3″	7.0″	7.7″	5.1″	2.5″	2.1″	2.9″
NUMBER OF DAYS OF RAIN PER MONTH												
	6	6	7	5	8	14	16	16	13	8	5	6

Holidays and Special Events at Walt Disney World

YOU CAN'T BEAT THE HOLIDAYS for live entertainment, special events, parades, fireworks, and elaborate decorations at the theme parks and resort hotels. Unfortunately, you also can't beat holiday periods for crowds. A mom from Ogden, Utah, puts it this way:

> We know the lines will be outrageous, but the special shows, parades, and decorations more than make up for it. For first-timers who want to see the rides, Christmas is not ideal, but for us it's the most colorful and exciting time to go.

Here's a look at the larger special events and major holidays at Walt Disney World.

JANUARY Held January 8–12, 2020, the **Walt Disney World Marathon** pulls in 60,000 runners and their families—enough people to affect crowd conditions and pedestrian traffic throughout Disney World. Information on all Disney running events can be found at rundisney.com.

SABRINA There are lots of marathons every year, and you can sign up for cool races and get different medals.

Each year the China Pavilion in Epcot has a **Chinese New Year** celebration (usually late January or early February), typically with Chinese acrobats and special activities for kids.

Epcot International Festival of the Arts, a celebration of art, food, and entertainment, takes place daily mid-January–mid-February, with Disney on Broadway performances held Friday–Monday.

FEBRUARY **Black History Month** is celebrated throughout Walt Disney World with displays, artisans, storytellers, and entertainers.

Presidents' Day is February 17, 2020, and **Mardi Gras** is February 25, 2020, bringing increases in attendance starting the weekend before. The **Princess Half-Marathon** (February 20–23, 2020) schedule includes a health expo, kids' races, a family 5K, a 10K, and the big race. The event draws more than 30,000 runners, enough to increase park attendance and affect vehicular and pedestrian traffic.

MARCH Epcot International Flower & Garden Festival runs annually March–May. The 30 million blooms from some 1,200 species will make your eyes pop, and best of all, the event doesn't seem to affect crowd levels at Epcot. Food and beverage kiosks at the festival make it more like fall's International Food & Wine Festival (see page 47), only with flowers. Check out Liliane's 2019 review at tinyurl.com/2019epcotflower for lots of pictures and tips for visiting the festival with kids. The Spike's Pollen Nation Exploration game (map and stickers are $6.99 plus tax) is a great way to occupy children during the festival. Spike the honeybee has pollinated the different festival gardens, and the task is to find Spike and apply corresponding stickers on the map. Once done, kids can claim a prize—a set of three embroidered sew-on patches. Different sets are available.

In Disney Springs, the **Mighty St. Patrick's Day Festival,** a weeklong celebration culminating on St. Patrick's Day (March 17), pays tribute to Irish music, dance, and food. Check out tinyurl.com/disneystpattys day for Liliane's 2014 review.

Most of March and early April are peak spring break season.

APRIL The Magic Kingdom showcases Mickey, Minnie, and the gang, all dressed in their Sunday best, in the **Easter Parade** (Easter is April 12, 2020), which takes place prior to the Festival of Fantasy Parade that makes its way down Main Street, U.S.A. The merriment includes Mr. and Mrs. Easter Bunny, Daisy Duck, Thumper and Ms. Bunny, Rabbit from Winnie the Pooh, White Rabbit, Clara Cluck, and the Azalea Trail Maids from Mobile, Alabama. About 10 days prior to Easter, guests can meet the Easter Bunny in the Town Square courtyard. Ask at the front desk about activities (such as egg hunts) at your hotel and other Disney resorts.

At Epcot kids will love the **Egg-stravaganza** game (map and stickers are $6.99 plus tax) offered early April through Easter. Be on the lookout for a dozen hidden Disney character–themed eggs. The eggs are 1.5 feet tall! Upon completion of the game, kids can choose one Disney character–themed egg as a prize.

Star Wars Half Marathon—Rival Run (April 16–19, 2020) includes Stormtroopers along the course, plus plenty of appearances by other *Star Wars* characters. Due to the popularity of *Star Wars*, expect the parks to be crowded when visiting Darth Vader's turf.

A fan-organized event, **Dapper Day,** when guests visit the parks wearing period costumes from the 1920s to 1950s, occurs in April and November (November 16–17, 2019). Visit dapperday.com for more information.

JULY Independence Day at Disney World basically means crowds and more crowds. All parks are in a festive and patriotic mood, and the fireworks are incredible. A very special place to visit is *The Hall of Presidents* at the Magic Kingdom. We recommend watching the evening fireworks from the Polynesian Village Resort instead of from the parks.

Most parks will reach full capacity by 10 a.m., and no advance reservations will get you into a park once it has closed. So pick your park and be prepared to stay there all day.

AUGUST Since 1991, lesbian, gay, bisexual, transgender, and queer (LGBTQ) people from around the world have been converging on and around the World for **Gay Days,** a week of events centered on the theme parks. Gay Days attracts more than 160,000 LGBTQ visitors and their families and friends. Universal Studios also participates. For additional information, visit gaydays.com.

SEPTEMBER A fan-organized event, **Spooky Day** (spookydayintheparks .com), held in September, involves wearing "wicked" costumes, plus VIP events and special shopping opportunities.

Those who say Christmas is the most wonderful time of year have never been to the **Epcot International Food & Wine Festival.** Held in World Showcase, August 29–November 23, 2019, the celebration represents 25 nations and cuisines, including demonstrations, wine seminars, and tastings. Though many activities are included in Epcot admission, some workshops and tastings are by reservation only and cost more than $100. Call ☎ 407-WDW-DINE (939-3463) starting around the beginning of August for more information. We think the culinary demos and the wine-and-beverage seminars (about $15–$20 each) are the best values at the festival. Because most of the food kiosks are set up around World Showcase, it can be difficult to walk through the crowds at some of the popular spots. Wait times at Epcot's attractions, however, are affected only slightly.

Mickey's Not-So-Scary Halloween Party runs 7 p.m.–midnight at the Magic Kingdom. In 2019 the party is held 36 times, with the first one starting as early as August 16! The event includes trick-or-treating in costume, parades, live music, storytelling, and a fireworks show. Every year there is a villain show, and the latest show, the *Hocus Pocus Villain Spelltacular,* is absolutely spectacular! Held several times throughout the evening in front of Cinderella Castle, the show, like special Halloween fireworks, is very popular. We suggest attending the last show to avoid losing too much time claiming an unobstructed spot right in front of the stage. Aimed primarily at younger children, the party is happy and upbeat rather than spooky and frightening.

We recommend arriving at least an hour before the beginning of the party. Disney usually allows party guests to enter the Magic Kingdom as early as 4 p.m. Upon entering the park, you will be issued a wristband identifying you as a party guest. Also, get the special map for the event, with details and hours of all the happenings. Go straight to the rides that are on your must-do list, and after that, just enjoy the party. If trick-or-treating is a priority, do that first thing after you arrive or toward the end of the night, when crowds thin out and there are no long lines in front of the trick-or-treating stations.

An absolute must-ride is The Haunted Mansion, which is spooky but only in the sweetest way. Look for the ghost in the garden of the mansion when you're queuing up; his hilarious tales and interaction with the guests will make you forget that you're standing in line. Characters are out in force all over the park, and the **Boo-to-You Parade** is pretty amazing. Our two favorite parts of the parade are the Headless Horseman riding at full speed through the park and The Haunted Mansion's groundskeeper, with his dim lantern in one hand and his bloodhound, followed by a large group of ghosts and gravediggers.

In addition, the Mad Tea Party has spooky lighting, pirates invade and interact with sailors at Pirates of the Caribbean, and Space Mountain has a new soundtrack and special effects. The *Storybook Circus Disney Junior Jam,* a dance party, features some favorite Disney Junior characters, including Doc McStuffins. The party has become very popular, and you won't be able to see or do it all. Pick your favorite events, and enjoy the night.

Advance tickets for the 2019 event cost $84.14–$143.78 for adults, $78.81–$138.45 for kids (including tax); same-day tickets, if still available, typically cost about $6 more. Discounts are available for annual pass holders and Disney Vacation Club members. The least-crowded events are typically in September and on Tuesdays; tickets for the late-October dates usually sell out by mid-October at the latest. Here is Liliane's 2018 review of Mickey's Not So Scary Halloween party: theunofficialguides.com/2018/09/10/halloween-party-2.

Cruella de Vil hosts **Cruella's Halloween Hide-a-Way Dining Experience** at Tony's Town Square, 9:30 p.m.–12:30 a.m., each night of the party. For $99 (plus tax) guests can enjoy hors d'oeuvres and desserts, as well as beer and wine for those age 21 and over. The event includes access to a reserved viewing area for Mickey's Boo-to-You Halloween Parade at 11:15 p.m. And yes, the hostess mingles with her guests.

Most Disney resorts have some complimentary activities on Halloween, ranging from Halloween movies under the stars to trick-or-treating, costume parades, and contests. Check at the reception desk for a detailed schedule of events happening during your stay.

Teens and young adults looking for a non-Disney Halloween happening should check out the party at **Universal CityWalk.** And if you'd rather have a monster with a chain saw running after you, consider attending Universal theme parks' **Halloween Horror Nights.** (*Note:* No costumes are allowed at the parks on these special nights.) For more information, visit halloweenhorrornights.com.

NOVEMBER The **Wine and Dine Half-Marathon** weekend (October 31–November 3, 2019) includes a 5K and 10K race in addition to the half-marathon. The half-marathon is no longer a nighttime race, and the postrace party is a separately ticketed event. The number of runners and their "cheer squads"—combined with the guests who descend on Epcot for the food festival alone—blow up the crowd levels like an agitated puffer fish. Vehicular and pedestrian traffic is disturbed by the running courses throughout Disney property.

There are no special Thanksgiving events or decorations in the parks, so if you're looking for the equivalent of the Macy's Thanksgiving Parade, you're out of luck, though many of the Christmas decorations are normally in place the day after Thanksgiving. But the kids are out of school, and this is the busiest travel weekend of the year. Your best bet for the least-crowded park will be Epcot.

Remember to make your dining arrangements long before your visit, especially if you want a traditional Thanksgiving meal. While there is plenty of food at the World, note that not all restaurants offer turkey with all the trimmings. Some that do include **Liberty Tree Tavern** at the Magic Kingdom; **50's Prime Time Café** at Disney's Hollywood Studios; **Cítricos** at the Grand Floridian; and **Garden Grill Restaurant** at Epcot. For information and reservations, call ☎ 407-WDW-DINE (939-3463). Disney changes its food offerings faster than lightning, so to avoid disappointment, call the restaurant and ask about its Thanksgiving menu prior to making reservations.

The annual **Disney Parks Magical Christmas Day Parade,** televised on December 25, is taped mid- to late November or the first week of December. The parade is filmed at Disneyland, but the musical performances are taped in all four parks at Walt Disney World. The filming of the musical segments ties up pedestrian traffic on these days.

DECEMBER If you're visiting during Christmas week, don't expect to see all the attractions in a single day of touring at any park. All parks, especially the Magic Kingdom, will be filled to capacity, and Disney will stop admitting visitors as early as 10 a.m. (Not to mention that women will have to wait up to 20 minutes to use the restrooms in the Magic Kingdom.) As you might have guessed by now, your only way in is getting there early. Be at the gates with admission passes in hand at least

LILIANE Did I mention that it's going to be packed? This is not a good time for first-time visitors, but fun can be had by all at the parks, even at peak times. (I actually stayed at Disney World on Christmas Eve and Christmas Day and loved it.)

1 hour before scheduled opening time. Most of all, bring along a humongous dose of patience and humor. The daily tree-lighting ceremonies and the parades are wonderful. Again, most parks will reach full capacity by 10 a.m., and no advance reservations will get you into the park once it's closed. So *pick your park* and be prepared to stay there all day.

Also, be sure to make dinner reservations long before your visit, especially if you're spending Christmas Eve and Christmas Day at the parks. Christmas festivities at Disney World usually run November 24–December 30. From the Monday following Thanksgiving weekend until December 20 or so, you can enjoy the decorations and holiday events without the crowds. This between-holidays period is one of our favorite times of year at Disney World.

The **Magic Kingdom** is home to a stunning display of holiday decorations, a **tree-lighting ceremony** on Main Street, and **Mickey's Once Upon a Christmastime Parade** on select days. Check the *Times Guide* for times. The Magic Kingdom is also the scene of **Mickey's**

Very Merry Christmas Party, staged 7 p.m.–midnight (after regular hours) on 23 evenings in November and December. Advance tickets for the 2019 event cost $105.44–$148.04 for adults, $100.11–$142.71 for kids (including tax); same-day tickets, if available, typically cost $6 more. Tickets for busier dates usually sell out a week in advance. Included in the cost is the use of all attractions during party hours, holiday-themed stage shows featuring Disney characters, cookies and hot chocolate, performances of Mickey's Once Upon a Christmastime Parade, carolers, "a magical snowfall" on Main Street, and fireworks. The least crowded dates are usually the weeks before Thanksgiving week and the week after. Tuesday (and the rare Wednesday) parties are the slowest too. See tinyurl.com /mickeysverymerryxmas for more details. We don't recommend the party for first-time visitors. For more on the Christmas celebrations at the Magic Kingdom, check out Liliane's review at theunofficial guides.com/2018/11/12/christmas-2.

With about twice the land of the Magic Kingdom, **Epcot** is a good option on Christmas Day, but this doesn't mean it's a ghost town, just somewhat less crowded than the Magic Kingdom. Again, if your heart is set on touring a park on Christmas Day, you'll have to get up early.

Epcot's **International Festival of the Holidays** takes place November 29–December 30, 2019. Don't miss the park's **Candlelight Processional**, featuring a celebrity narrator accompanied by a huge live choir and a full orchestra. The show takes place daily at the America Gardens Theatre and is included with regular Epcot admission. Special lunch and dinner packages are available for an additional charge and include preferred seating for the processional (call ☎ 407-WDW-DINE [939-3463] for reservations). If you don't want to spring for one of the packages, we recommend lining up at least 1 hour prior to the show of your choice. Guests with preferred seating should arrive at the reserved-seating entrance 30 minutes before the beginning of the show. Seats within this section are available on a first-come, first-serve basis and are opened to general admission 15 minutes before the beginning of the show. Check the *Times Guide* for performance hours and information on the day's narrator.

Holiday Kitchens features booths scattered around the World Showcase, offering festive holiday-themed tasting portions of food and drink.

The new nightly fireworks show *Epcot Forever* is a great way to end the night; the show replaces *IllumiNations: Reflections of Earth.* For the 2020 holiday season, a brand-new nighttime spectacular will debut.

Kids will want to join **Chip & Dale's Christmas Tree Spree Scavenger Hunt** (map and stickers are $6.99 plus tax) and search for the two chipmunks and their ornaments.

At theunofficialguides.com/2018/11/08/epcot-2, check out Liliane's review of the holidays at Epcot. At the **United Kingdom Pavilion,** Father Christmas tells of his country's holiday customs. **France** is the home of Père Noël. In **Japan,** the *Daruma* seller talks about how Japanese celebrate the New Year. (*Daruma* dolls are symbols of the New Year and are said to bring good luck.) In **Italy,** meet La Befana, the good witch who brings gifts to children on Epiphany. (For more information on La Befana, check out en.wikipedia.org/wiki/befana.)

Visit **China** and enjoy the Chinese Lion Dancers, a typical part of any Chinese New Year celebration; make sure to watch the show. In **Norway,** meet the Christmas elf Julenisse, who represents simplicity and peace (to learn more, visit mylittlenorway.com/2008/12/norwegian-elf). In **Mexico,** Fiesta de Navidad includes dancers and the Mariachi Cobre band.

At the **United States Pavilion,** Santa and Mrs. Claus meet with guests, and the Voices of Liberty, clad in Dickens-period costumes, bring joy with their Christmas carols. The professional and moving performance is a most appropriate show for the season.

Disney's Animal Kingdom has festive holiday decorations, a gigantic Christmas tree, and holiday entertainment throughout the park. Also, *Up! A Great Bird Adventure* incorporates Diwali, the Hindu festival of lights.

At **Disney's Hollywood Studios,** the park is also dressed for the season. The *Sunset Seasons Greetings* sound-and-light show projected on The Twilight Zone Tower of Terror comes complete with snow falling on Sunset Boulevard and runs several times per hour. The *Jingle Bell, Jingle BAM!* nighttime show is projected on the Grauman's Chinese Theatre, and Santa takes up residence at the Once Upon a Time shop for meet and greets. Echo Lake gets a holiday overhaul, and even Gertie, the giant dinosaur, is outfitted with a Santa hat! Here is Liliane's report from the 2018 festivities: theunofficialguides.com/2018/11/22/disneys-hollywood-studios.

Minnie's Holiday Dine at Hollywood & Vine is another nice way to celebrate the season at Hollywood Studios. Minnie, joined by Mickey, Donald, Daisy, and Santa Goofy, meets with guests as they dine on holiday-themed menu items. Minnie's Seasonal Dining event costs $52 per adult and $31 per child, plus tax and gratuity, and includes table activities and souvenir party gifts. The dinner is offered early November through the first week of January.

You thought we were done? No way. There's much more to see outside the parks.

The **holiday decorations** at the Walt Disney World resorts are attractions in their own right. Generally speaking, each resort incorporates its theme into its holiday finery. At **Port Orleans Resort,** for example, expect Mardi Gras colors in the trees, while the **Yacht Club** has trees adorned with miniature sailboats. Also make sure to visit the **Grand Floridian,** where the mother of all Christmas trees—five stories tall!—dominates the lobby, flanked by

LILIANE A word of advice for families with small children: reassure the kids that Santa knows where the family is on Christmas Day. You don't want your little ones to suddenly worry that Santa won't find them on Christmas because they're not at home. Consider shipping a small tree and holiday decorations to your hotel. Kids can decorate the window of your hotel room with their drawings.

a gingerbread dollhouse and a miniature railroad. Don't miss the free daily classes in decorating gingerbread houses; guests get a free recipe brochure and a taste of freshly made gingerbread. At the **Beach Club,** poinsettias and a gingerbread carousel are the big draw. For a more natural approach, visit the **Wilderness Lodge** and **Animal Kingdom Lodge.** Check out Liliane's 2017 write-up about Christmas decorations at the resorts—again, with lots of pictures—at theunofficial guides.com/2017/12/22/resort-hopping.

If you're staying at a Disney resort over Christmas, check with the concierge to see what holiday events might be going on. Happenings can range from carolers, brass bands, and country singers to Christmas-cookie decorating, visits with Santa, and readings of *The Night Before Christmas.*

During December, Disney offers 25-minute **"sleigh" rides** through the woods from the Fort Wilderness Campground. (The horse-drawn vehicle is wheeled but made to look like a red sleigh, complete with sleigh bells!) Rides depart from Crockett's Tavern at Fort Wilderness. The cost is $84 per sleigh. (Each sleigh can accommodate up to four adults or two adults plus up to three children age 9 and under.) You can book up to 180 days in advance by calling ☎ 407-WDW-PLAY (939-7529).

In addition to a nightly tree-lighting ceremony, lots of live entertainment occurs at **Disney Springs** for the holidays. Check out Liliane's report from her 2017 visit at theunofficialguides.com/2017/11/30 /disney-springs-2. The atmosphere is festive, and shops and restaurants have special window dressings. If you're looking for the perfect Christmas card, this is the place to get it. Santa appears in his chalet at the Christmas Tree Trail, and you can take pictures with your own camera or use Disney's Memory Maker service. For a less classical picture, Santa Goofy appears in the chalet December 25–January 3. Ask at Guest Relations for the daily schedule.

Ring in the New Year with Mickey and friends. If you're in the mood for a night of partying and live entertainment, there's no better place than **Disney Springs** or **Universal CityWalk.** Both offer a choice of parties and midnight fireworks. The Magic Kingdom shows fireworks on both December 30 and 31 for those who either wish to see fireworks in multiple parks or who don't wish to be caught in the largest crowds of the year on New Year's Eve.

Though all parks, with the exception of Animal Kingdom, have spectacular fireworks at midnight, here are a few different options for the last night of the year:

- If culinary delights are your thing and money is no object, this would be a good night for dinner at Victoria & Albert's. The restaurant, inside Disney's Grand Floridian Resort, features modern American cuisine with exquisite ingredients sourced from around the world. A 10-course dinner, eclectic wines, and live harp music are all part of the experience!

- Forget the rides—the lines will be looong. Relax at your hotel pool and go out for a great dinner that night. If you have little children, get a babysitter. The trick is to arrive a day before New Year's, settle in, go to a water park, and start the touring after January 2, when crowds thin out.

- At Epcot, welcome the New Year several times. Have a drink before 6 p.m. (midnight in Germany) at the Biergarten in Germany. Then go to the Rose & Crown Pub in the United Kingdom and repeat the celebration at 7 p.m., as guests and staff alike will be welcoming the New Year in the United Kingdom. Best of all, you get to start all over again a few hours later when the clock finally strikes midnight at Epcot.

Selecting the Day of the Week for Your Visit

We receive thousands of emails and letters from readers each year asking which park is the best bet on a particular day. To make things easier for you (and us!), we provide at touringplans.com a calendar covering the next year (click "Crowd Calendar" on the home page). For each date, we offer a crowd-level index based on a scale of 1–10, with 1 being least crowded and 10 being most crowded. The calendar also lists the best and worst park(s) to visit in terms of crowd conditions on any given day.

Extra Magic Hours

This program is a perk for families staying at a Walt Disney World resort, including the Swan, Dolphin, and Shades of Green (plus Disney Springs Resort Area hotels, the Four Seasons, the Hilton Bonnet Creek, and the Waldorf Astoria Orlando through at least the end of 2020). On selected days of the week, Disney resort guests are able to enter a Disney theme park 1 hour earlier or stay in a selected theme park about 2 hours later than the official park-operating hours. Theme park visitors not staying at a Disney resort may stay in the park for Extra Magic Hour (EMH) evenings, but they can't experience any attractions. In other words, they can shop and eat.

 BOB You'll need to have a Park Hopper option on your theme park admission to take advantage of Extra Magic Hours at more than one park on the same day.

If you're not eligible for EMHs, avoid the park with morning EMHs. As a backup strategy, plan to stay until the park closes and get in line for popular attractions (such as those in Toy Story Land or Galaxy's Edge at Disney's Hollywood Studios) in the hour before closing. If you get in an attraction line before closing time, you'll get to ride even if the park has already closed.

WHAT'S REQUIRED? A valid admission ticket or MagicBand is required to enter the park, and you must show your Disney resort ID or have your MagicBand scanned when entering. For evening EMHs, you may be asked to show your Disney resort ID or MagicBand to experience rides or attractions.

WHEN ARE EMHs OFFERED? You can check the Crowd Calendar at touringplans.com for the dates of your visit, check the parks calendar at disneyworld.com, or call Walt Disney World Information at ☎ 407-824-4321 or 407-939-6244.

In addition to the hours listed in the table on the next page, it's common for Epcot to have evening EMHs on Wednesday or Thursday in September and October and for Animal Kingdom to have its two morning EMHs on any day except Tuesday and Thursday later in the year. The opening of Galaxy's Edge has altered the EMH schedule of Disney's Hollywood Studios and other parks. The Studios will have "Extra" morning Extra Magic Hours running 6–9 a.m., every day August 29–November 2, 2019. The Magic Kingdom and Animal Kingdom will run morning EMHs beginning at 7 a.m. during that time, to handle overflow guests. We expect similar schedules to be offered during other busy periods, such as Christmas and Easter.

Typhoon Lagoon and Blizzard Beach rarely offer EMHs. If they do, it's usually during the summer.

SAMPLE EXTRA MAGIC HOURS SCHEDULE *(frequently varies)*						
MORNING						
MON	**TUES**	**WED**	**THUR**	**FRI**	**SAT**	**SUN**
Animal Kingdom	—	—	Epcot	Magic Kingdom	Animal Kingdom	DHS
EVENING						
MON	**TUES**	**WED**	**THUR**	**FRI**	**SAT**	**SUN**
—	Epcot	Magic Kingdom	—	—	—	—

MORNING EXTRA MAGIC HOURS (or Early Entry) These are offered at all four theme parks throughout the year, and rarely (during summer) at Blizzard Beach and Typhoon Lagoon water parks. Several days of the week, Disney resort guests are invited to enter a designated theme park 1 hour before the general public. During this hour, guests can enjoy selected attractions opened early just for them.

During holidays and other busy times, the Magic Kingdom opens to regular guests at 8 a.m. Morning EMHs begin at 7 a.m., so you'll need to be at the Magic Kingdom entrance at around 6:30 a.m. You won't be alone, but relatively few people are willing to get up that early for a theme park, and your first hour in the parks will be (please pardon us) magical.

Morning EMHs strongly affect attendance at all the parks, especially during busier times of year. Crowds at the parks are usually larger than average, as a Winston-Salem, North Carolina, mom discovered:

Disney's Hollywood Studios was a MADHOUSE. Do NOT go on Extra Magic Hour days. After spending about 3 hours to ride three rides, I just wanted to trample the people stampeding to the exit.

In general, every park has longer ride wait times on days with morning EMHs than on days without. Wait times at Animal Kingdom are the most affected; you'll barely notice the difference at the Magic Kingdom.

If you're staying at a Disney resort, remember these three things about Extra Magic Hours:

1. The Magic Kingdom has more attractions open for morning EMHs than any other park. We think the Magic Kingdom's morning session, coupled with a good touring plan, is the most worthwhile of any EMHs at any park.

2. Morning EMHs are useful at Disney's Animal Kingdom because it's the most time-effective strategy for seeing the mega-attractions in Pandora. Morning EMHs should also be effective for the new Star Wars: Galaxy's Edge rides at Disney's Hollywood Studios.

3. If you don't think you'll be at the park with morning EMHs 30 minutes before it opens, visit another park instead.

This note from a North Bend, Washington, dad emphasizes the importance of arriving at the beginning of the early-entry period.

We only used early entry once—to Disney's Hollywood Studios. We got there 20 minutes after early entry opened, and the wait for Tower of Terror was 1.5 hours long without FastPass+. We skipped it.

During holiday periods and summer, when Disney hotels are full, getting in early makes a tremendous difference in crowds at the designated park. The program funnels so many people into the EMH park that it fills by about 10 a.m. and is practically gridlocked by noon. A mother of three from Lee's Summit, Missouri, writes:

We went to the Magic Kingdom on an early-entry day. We were there at 7:30 a.m. and were able to walk onto all the rides in Fantasyland with no wait. At 8:45 a.m. we positioned ourselves at the Adventureland rope and ran toward Splash Mountain when the rope dropped. We were able to ride Splash Mountain with no wait and then Big Thunder with about a 15-minute wait. We then went straight to the Jungle Cruise and the wait was already 30 minutes, so we skipped it. The park became incredibly crowded as the day progressed, and we were all exhausted from getting up so early. We left the park around noon. After that, I resolved to avoid early-entry days and instead be at a non–early-entry park about a half hour before official opening time.

An alternative strategy for Disney resort guests is to take advantage of morning EMHs, but only until the designated park gets crowded. At that time, if you have Park Hopper tickets, move to another park. A Dillsburg, Pennsylvania, mom has another tip:

Schedule your FastPasses for the park you're visiting second.

This works particularly well at the Animal Kingdom for the Pandora rides, and at Magic Kingdom for families with young children who love the attractions in Fantasyland. However, it will take you about an hour to commute to the second park of the day. If, for example, you depart the Magic Kingdom for Disney's Hollywood Studios at 11 a.m., you'll find the Studios pretty crowded when you arrive at about noon, as this Texas mom found:

We made the mistake of doing a morning at the Magic Kingdom and an afternoon at the Studios. Worst idea ever. By the time we got to the Studios, all the [FastPass+ reservations] were gone for Toy Story Mania!, the Tower of Terror, and Rock 'n' Roller Coaster. And all three rides had at least 90-minute waits.

Keeping these and other considerations in mind, here are some tips:

1. Use the morning-EMH/park-hopping strategy during the less busy times of year when the parks close early. You'll get a jump on the general public and add an hour to what, in the off-season, is an already short touring day.

2. Use the morning-EMH/park-hopping strategy to complete touring a second park that you've already visited on a previous day, or specifically to see live entertainment in the second park.

On any day except its EMH days, hopping to Epcot is usually good. Epcot is equipped to handle large crowds better than any other Disney park, minimizing the effects of a midday arrival. Also, World Showcase has a large selection of interesting dining options, making it a good choice for evening touring.

Don't hop to the park with morning EMHs. The idea is to avoid crowds, not join them. Finally, limit your hopping to two parks per day. Hopping to a third park in one day would result in more time spent commuting than saved by avoiding crowds.

EVENING EXTRA MAGIC HOURS These let Disney resort guests enjoy a different theme park on specified nights for about 2 hours after it closes to the general public. Guests pay no additional charge to participate but must scan their MagicBands at each attraction they wish to experience. You can also show up at the turnstiles at any point after evening EMHs have started. Note that if you've been in another park that day, you'll need the Park Hopper feature on your admission ticket to enter. As of mid-2019, evening EMHs are offered at the Magic Kingdom and Epcot. We expect evening EMHs to return to the Studios with the opening of Galaxy's Edge.

Evening sessions are usually more crowded at the Magic Kingdom than at Epcot. Those evening EMH crowds can be just as large as those throughout the day. During summer, when the Magic Kingdom's evening EMH session runs until midnight (or later), lines at headliner attractions can still be long at midnight. A mom from Fairhaven, Massachusetts, doesn't mince words:

> Steer clear of a park that is open late. There are only a few attractions open, and tons of people trying to get on them.

EARLY MORNING MAGIC AND DISNEY AFTER HOURS These are offered on select days and in select months. During Early Morning Magic at the **Magic Kingdom,** guests receive a breakfast buffet at Cosmic Ray's Starlight Café and unlimited access to seven Fantasyland attractions starting 75 minutes before regular park hours. Early Morning Magic at Toy Story Land inside **Disney's Hollywood Studios** lets guests experience Alien Swirling Saucers, Slinky Dog Dash, and Toy Story Mania! with little wait. Buzz, Woody, and Jessie are also on hand for photo ops. A breakfast buffet is served at a select quick-service dining location outside of Toy Story Land. Both Early Morning Magic experiences are $84 per adult and $73 per child. Regular park admission is not included in the cost, making this a very pricey event. Consider this upcharge only if you have very small children and limited time at the Magic Kingdom.

Disney After Hours are available at the Magic Kingdom, Disney's Hollywood Studios, and the Animal Kingdom. When the parks close to daytime visitors, guests can enjoy select attractions for 3 hours. Unlimited ice cream novelties, popcorn, and bottled beverages—available at carts stationed throughout the parks—are included in the cost of admission. A ticket purchased in advance costs $113 per adult or child, and $137 per adult or child on the day of the event. Event hours are 9 p.m.–midnight at the Animal Kingdom and Disney's Hollywood Studios, 10 p.m.–1 a.m. at the Magic Kingdom. Guests can enter all parks at 7 p.m.

Disney Villains After Hours, only at the Magic Kingdom during select months, offers guests unique, wicked experiences for 3 hours after the park closes to daytime guests. See page 298 for details.

WHICH EXTRA MAGIC HOURS SHOULD YOU USE?

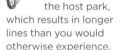

BOB Extra Magic Hours draw more Disney resort guests to the host park, which results in longer lines than you would otherwise experience.

Not many families have the stamina to take advantage of morning and evening EMHs on consecutive days. If you have to choose between morning or evening EMH sessions, consider first whether your family functions better getting up early or staying up late. Also, consider the time at which the parks close to day guests. Evening EMHs are most useful when the crowds are low and the parks close relatively early to the general public, so your family doesn't have to stay up past midnight to take advantage of the perk.

PLANNING *Your* WALT DISNEY WORLD VACATION BUDGET

HOW MUCH YOU SPEND DEPENDS on how long and when you stay at Walt Disney World. But even if you stop by only for an afternoon, be prepared to drop a bundle. Later we'll show you how to save money on lodging. This section will give you some sense of what you can expect to pay for admissions and food. And we'll help you decide which admission option will best meet your needs.

HOW MUCH DOES IT COST PER DAY?

A TYPICAL DAY WOULD COST about $937.20, excluding lodging and transportation, for a family of four—Mom, Dad, 12-year-old Abner, and 8-year-old Agnes—driving their own car and staying outside the World. They plan to stay a week in the off-season, so they buy 5-Day Base Tickets with the Park Hopper option.

A Birmingham, Alabama, mom of two begs to differ with our budget recommendation for souvenirs in the table on the next page:

Sorry, but Uncle Bob is totally out of touch when he says, "You won't have to buy souvenirs every day." In my experience, you'll head home with several sets of character ears; enough dress-up costumes to outfit the neighborhood; and countless pins, toys, and knickknacks.

HOW MUCH DOES A DAY COST?	
Breakfast for four at Denny's with tax and tip	$56.23
Epcot parking fee *(free for pass holders and resort guests)*	$25.00
Four 1-day admissions on 5-Day Tickets with Park Hopper **DAD:** *Adult 5-Day with tax is $522 divided by 5 days = $104.40* **MOM:** *Adult 5-Day with tax is $522 divided by 5 days = $104.40* **ABNER:** *Adult 5-Day with tax is $522 divided by 5 days = $104.40* **AGNES:** *Child 5-Day with tax is $503 divided by 5 days = $100.60*	$413.80
Morning break *(soda or coffee)*	$17.57
Fast-food lunch *(sandwich or burger, fries, soda)*, no tip	$69.35
Afternoon break *(soda and popcorn)*	$39.58
Dinner at Italy *(3 appetizers, 4 entrées, 3 desserts)*, with tax and tip	$251.77
Souvenirs (Mickey T-shirts for Abner and Agnes) with tax*	$63.90
1-day total (without lodging or transportation)	**$937.20**

Cheer up—you won't have to buy souvenirs every day.

The *Unofficial* No-Frills Guide to Walt Disney World

With even a bare-bones visit to the World now out of reach of many families, being frugal is becoming ever more necessary. These tips can help:

1. Buy your admission online from one of the sellers on page 62. Get tickets only for the number of days you plan to visit, and skip all add-on options.

2. Book a hotel outside of Walt Disney World. Hotels on US 192 (Irlo Bronson Memorial Highway) are usually the least expensive. Also, consider renting a vacation home (see discussion starting on page 134) if you have four or more people in your group.

3. Eat breakfast in your hotel room from a cooler; take lunch, snacks, and drinks from your cooler to the park; and eat dinner outside the World using discount coupons.

4. Avoid parking fees by using your hotel's shuttle service or by taking Disney transportation from Saratoga Springs. Park your car in the Disney Springs Lime parking lot and walk to Saratoga Springs to do so. Another option is to park at the Disney Springs Strawberry parking lot and take the Lynx #50 bus from the West Side Transfer Center. It runs every 30 minutes to the Ticket and Transportation Center at the Magic Kingdom. From there you can take a free Disney monorail to Epcot or a free bus to the Animal Kingdom or Disney's Hollywood Studios. Only use these options if you're budgeting to the penny, as they require a lot of walking and take lots of time out of your touring day. Do *not* park overnight at Disney Springs to avoid the resort parking fees; your car will be towed.

5. Buy discounted Disney merchandise from one of Orlando's two **Disney's Character Warehouse** outlets (4951 International Dr., ☎ 407-354-3255; 8200 Vineland Ave., ☎ 407-477-0222; premiumoutlets.com/orlando).

WALT DISNEY WORLD ADMISSION OPTIONS

DISNEY OFFERS MORE THAN 7,000 theme park ticket options, ranging from the humble 1-Day Base Ticket, good for a single day's entry into one Disney theme park, to the blinged-out Premium Annual Pass, good for 365 days of admission into every Disney theme or water park, plus Disney's Oak Trail Golf Course and other attractions. See the table on pages 60–61 for the most common admission types.

Date-Based Pricing and Other Surcharges

Disney introduced date-based pricing for all theme park tickets in late 2018. The price of the ticket changes based on the days of the year you're traveling.

Tickets are now generally most expensive when children are out of school: Christmas and other holidays, spring break, and summer vacation. Less-expensive tickets are generally available during non-holiday periods when children are in school and during months subject to inclement weather: January and February, for example, and peak hurricane season in September.

To avoid additional surcharges when buying tickets, you must tell Disney the first date on which you plan to visit a theme park or water park. Your ticket price will be based on that starting date, the number of days you plan to visit the theme parks or water parks, and whether you plan to visit more than one theme park per day. See "Flexible Dates" below for more details.

If you need to move your vacation dates from more-expensive to less-expensive days, Disney will not refund the difference in ticket prices—but they will charge you the incremental cost if you need to move from less-expensive to more-expensive days.

Disney has a rolling calendar of the next 8–11 months in advance, showing each day's seasonal classification.

When Tickets Expire

Disney has also shortened the amount of time you have to use your tickets. Whereas previously all tickets expired 14 days from the date of first use, ticket expiration is now based on how many days you're visiting the theme parks and water parks, as shown in the table on pages 60–61 (see the row labeled "Use Within").

Example: If you purchase a basic 4-Day Base Ticket and specify that you'll start using it on June 1, 2020, you must complete your four theme park visits by midnight on June 7, 2020. *Tickets expire even if you don't use them.*

TICKET ADD-ONS

NAVIGATING THE TICKET ADD-ONS is like ordering dinner à la carte at an upscale restaurant: many choices, mostly expensive, virtually all of which require some thought. Three add-on options are offered with the Base Ticket, each at an additional cost:

FLEXIBLE DATES This add-on allows you to visit Disney's theme parks on any day you choose without having to specify the exact date on

WDW THEME PARK ADMISSION OPTIONS

	1-DAY	2-DAY	3-DAY	4-DAY	5-DAY
USE WITHIN:	1 DAY	4 DAYS	5 DAYS	7 DAYS	8 DAYS
BASE TICKET AGES 3-9					
ALL PARKS: $111-$164	$216-$319	$316-$461	$412-$578	$418-$586
—	($108-$160/day)	($105-$154/day)	($103-$144/day)	($84-$117/day)
BASE TICKET AGE 10+					
ALL PARKS: $116-$137	$226-$330	$331-$476	$426-$597	$437-$605
—	($113-$165/day)	($110-$159/day)	($107-$149/day)	($87-$121/day)

Base Ticket admits guest to one theme park each day of use. Tickets must be used within the number of days shown in the "Use Within" row above.

PARK HOPPER *(add-on)*

	1-DAY	2-DAY	3-DAY	4-DAY	5-DAY
AGES 3-9: $175-$228	$290-$394	$391-$536	$497-$663	$503-$671
AGE 10+: $180-$233	$301-$404	$3406-$551	$511-$682	$522-$690

Park Hopper option entitles guest to visit more than one theme park on each day of use.

PARK HOPPER PLUS *(add-on)*

	1-DAY	2-DAY	3-DAY	4-DAY	5-DAY
AGES 3-9: $196-$249	$312-$415	$412-$557	$518-$684	$524-$692
AGE 10+: $202-$223	$322-$426	$427-$572	$533-$703	$543-$712
1 visit	2 visits	3 visits	4 visits	5 visits

Park Hopper Plus option entitles guest to a specified number of visits (2-10) to a choice of entertainment and recreation venues in addition to the Park Hopper option above. PHP tickets expire 1 day later than the "Use Within" days above.

which your vacation will start. This option costs anywhere from $0 to $177 per ticket, depending on how many days you're visiting the theme parks. Flexible Dates makes sense if you want to buy tickets now for a trip at some uncertain date in the future.

PARK HOPPER This add-on lets you visit more than one theme park per day. The cost is about $64–$85 (including tax) on top of the price of any ticket. The longer your stay, the more affordable it is: as an add-on to a 7-Day Base Ticket, for example, the flat fee works out to $12 per day for park-hopping privileges. If you want to visit the Magic Kingdom in the morning and eat dinner at Epcot, request this feature.

PARK HOPPER PLUS On top of the Park Hopper feature described above, the Park Hopper Plus (PHP) option gives you admission to Blizzard Beach or Typhoon Lagoon water park, Oak Trail Golf Course, Fantasia Gardens or Winter Summerland minigolf, or the ESPN Wide World of Sports Complex. The PHP option costs $85–$107 more than a Base Ticket—about $26 per ticket more than the Park Hopper option by itself, including tax.

You can't change how many Park Hopper/PHP admissions you buy with either option; it's fixed, and unused days are not refundable. You can, however, skip Park Hopper/PHP entirely and buy an individual admission to any of the venues above—that's frequently the

	6-DAY	7-DAY	8-DAY	9-DAY	10-DAY
	9 DAYS	10 DAYS	12 DAYS	13 DAYS	14 DAYS
BASE TICKET AGES 3-9					
	$425-$592	$432-$597	$448-$608	$461-$616	$472-$621
	($71-$99/day)	($62-$85/day)	($56-$76/day)	($51-$68/day)	($44-$62/day)
BASE TICKET AGE 10+					
	$445-$611	$453-$617	$469-$629	$482-$637	$493-$643
	($74-$102/day)	($65-$88/day)	($59-$79/day)	($54-$71/day)	($49-$64/day)

NOTE: ALL ADMISSION AND ADD-ON PRICES INCLUDE 6.5% SALES TAX.

Park choices are Magic Kingdom, Epcot, Disney's Hollywood Studios, or Disney's Animal Kingdom.

PARK HOPPER *(add-on)*

6-DAY	7-DAY	8-DAY	9-DAY	10-DAY
$511-$677	$518-$5682	$533-$693	$546-$701	$557-$707
$530-$697	$538-$702	$554-$714	$567-$723	$579-$728

Park choices are any combination of Magic Kingdom, Epcot, Disney's Hollywood Studios, or Disney's Animal Kingdom on each day of use.

PARK HOPPER PLUS *(add-on)*

6-DAY	7-DAY	8-DAY	9-DAY	10-DAY
$532-$698	$539-$703	$555-$715	$567-$723	$578-$728
$552-$718	$559-$724	$575-$736	$589-$744	$600-$750
6 visits	7 visits	8 visits	9 visits	10 visits

Choices are Disney's Blizzard Beach water park, Disney's Typhoon Lagoon water park, Oak Trail Golf Course, ESPN Wide World of Sports Complex, or Fantasia Gardens or Winter Summerland minigolf.

best deal if you're not park-hopping and want to visit only one of the aforementioned venues.

If you buy a ticket but then decide later that you want to add the Park Hopper/PHP option, you can do so. Note, though, that Disney doesn't prorate the cost: if you add Park Hopper/PHP on the last day of your trip, you'll pay the same price as if you'd bought it before you left home.

ANNUAL PASSES

AN ANNUAL PASS PROVIDES unlimited use of the major theme parks for one year. Two versions are available: The **Disney Platinum Pass** ($1,191.74 including tax, age 3 and up) includes free use of Disney's Memory Maker digital-photo service in addition to park access. The **Disney Platinum Plus Pass** ($1,298.24 including tax, age 3 and up) also provides unlimited use of the minor parks, ESPN Wide World of Sports, and Oak Trail Golf Course. Holders of both types of annual passes also get perks, including free parking; hotel, dining, and merchandise discounts; and seasonal offers such as a dedicated entrance line at the theme parks. These passes are not valid for special events, such

LILIANE I keep my annual passes in the same place as my passport, insurance papers, and other travel documents. And I always keep a copy of my receipt documenting the purchase.

as admission to Mickey's Very Merry Christmas Party. Finally, the **Water Parks Annual Pass** costs $148.04 for age 3 and up, tax included.

Florida Resident Passes

Disney offers several special admission options to Florida residents and members of the Disney Vacation Club time-share program. The **Gold Pass** ($744.44 including tax, age 3 and up) offers unlimited admission and park-hopping privileges to the four major theme parks, free parking, and the discounts mentioned in the previous paragraph. The Gold Pass has blackout dates, including mid-December–January 2, and the two weeks around Easter. The **Silver Pass** ($552.74 including tax, age 3 and up) offers the same park benefits as the Gold Pass, with additional blackout dates from the first week of June through the second week of August. The **Theme Park Select Pass** is $467.54 for age 3 and up, tax included. Set blackout dates for the pass include Magic Kingdom on Saturday, Epcot on Friday, and Epcot on Saturdays and Sundays during the International Food & Wine Festival; other blackout dates for the pass vary by park. The **Weekday Select Pass** ($371.69 including tax, age 3 and up) is good for visits Monday–Friday (Silver Pass blackout dates apply), and the **Epcot After 4 Annual Pass** ($329.09 including tax, age 3 and up) is good for admission to Epcot after 4 p.m.

WHERE TO PURCHASE TICKETS

YOU CAN BUY YOUR ADMISSION on arrival at Walt Disney World (with a $21 per-ticket surcharge for 3-day tickets and up) or buy them in advance to avoid that fee. Tickets are available at Disney World resorts and theme parks; they're also available at Disney Stores and at disney world.com for the same prices listed in the table on pages 60–61.

If you're trying to keep costs to an absolute minimum, consider using an online ticket wholesaler, such as **Official Ticket Center** (OTC), **Parksavers,** or **Boardwalk Ticketing,** especially for trips with 3 or more days in the parks. All tickets sold are brand new, and the savings can easily be more than $100 for a family of four. All vendors provide you with electronic tickets, just like Disney, so you'll be able to make FastPass+ reservations immediately through the My Disney Experience website.

OTC and Parksavers offer discount tickets for almost all Central Florida attractions, including Disney, Universal, and SeaWorld. Discounts for the major theme parks range from about 6% to 12%; tickets for other attractions are more deeply discounted. OTC (3148 Vineland Road, Kissimmee; daily, 8 a.m.–6 p.m. Eastern; ☎ 407-396-9020 or 877-406-4836; officialticketcenter.com) offers delivery by USPS certified mail for free; you may also pick up tickets at its office for free. For $10, it will deliver via Priority Mail or to area hotels. The savings with Parksavers (☎ 877-226-3380; parksavers.com) can be substantial—almost $120 off Disney's price for four 3-Day Park Hoppers, and about $50 better than other ticket vendors. Boardwalk (boardwalk ticketing.com) operates only online. Boardwalk and Parksavers will both send actual tickets to you through the mail (free shipping), or you can pick them up at the park entrances (also free). You may also link the admissions to MagicBands.

Finally, tickets are available at some non-Disney hotels and shopping centers, and through independent ticket brokers. Because Disney admissions are only marginally discounted in the Walt Disney World–Orlando area, the chief reason for you to buy from an independent broker is convenience. Offers of free or heavily discounted tickets abound, but the catch is that they generally require you to attend a time-share sales presentation.

LILIANE Also steer clear of passes offered on eBay, Craigslist, and the like.

Where Not to Buy Passes

In addition to the many authorized sellers of theme park admissions, a number of unauthorized sellers exist. They buy unused days on legitimately purchased passes, and then resell them as if they were newly issued. They insist that you specify exactly which dates you plan to use the ticket. They know, of course, how many days are left on the pass and when it expires. If you tell them you plan to use it tomorrow and the next 2 days, they'll sell you a ticket that has 3 days remaining and expires in 3 days. Naturally, because they don't tell you this, you assume the usual 5-day expiration period. In the case of your tickets, however, the original purchaser triggered the 5-day expiration period. If you decide to skip a day instead of using the pass on the next 3 consecutive days, you'll discover, to your chagrin, that it has expired.

FOR ADDITIONAL INFORMATION ON ADMISSION

IF YOU HAVE A QUESTION OR CONCERN regarding admissions that can be addressed only through a person-to-person conversation, contact **Disney Ticket Inquiries** at ☎ 407-566-4985 or ticket.inquiries @disneyworld.com. If you call, be aware that you may spend a considerable time on hold; if you email, be aware that it can take up to 3 days to get a response. In contrast, the ticket section of the Disney World website—disneyworld.disney.go.com/tickets—is surprisingly straightforward in showing how ticket prices breaks down.

THIS IS A JOB FOR . . . A COMPUTER!

DISNEY'S DATE-BASED PRICING SCHEME is the most complicated system it has ever used for ticket purchases—so complicated, in fact, that we wrote a computer program to analyze all the options and to look for loopholes in the new pricing rules. Visit touringplans.com and try our **Park Ticket Calculator** (tinyurl.com/ug-ticketcalculator). It aggregates ticket prices from Disney and a number of online ticket vendors. Answer a few questions relating to the size of your party and the parks you intend to visit, and the calculator will identify your four cheapest ticket options. It will also show you how much you'll save versus buying at the gate.

The program will also make recommendations for considerations other than price. For example, annual passes might cost more, but Disney often offers substantial resort discounts and other deals to annual pass holders. These resort discounts, especially during the off-season, can more than offset the price of the pass.

ANTICIPATING DISNEY TICKET PRICE INCREASES

DISNEY USUALLY RAISES PRICES ONCE A YEAR: hikes were announced in January 2019; September 2018; in February 2014–2018; in June 2011–2013; and August 2006–2010. However, we would not be surprised to see a second increase in fall 2019. We certainly expect another price increase in early 2020. If you're putting together a budget, assume an increase of around 10% per year to be safe.

TICKETS, BIOMETRICS, WRISTBANDS, AND RFID

WE'VE USED THE WORD *ticket* to describe that thing you carry around as proof of your admission to the park. In fact, Disney admission media come in two forms—neither of which is a ticket.

If you're staying at a Disney resort, your admission medium is a rubber wristband about the size and shape of a small wristwatch. Called a **MagicBand**, it contains a tiny radio frequency identifier (RFID) chip, on which is stored a link to the record of your admission purchase in Disney's computers. Your MagicBand also functions as your hotel-room key, and it can (optionally) work as a credit card for most food and merchandise purchases.

If you don't want a MagicBand, you're staying off-property, or you bought your admission from a third-party vendor, you get a flexible, credit card–size piece of plastic-coated paper, which we'll call a **park card.** If you printed your ticket at home, a cast member will scan it the first time you enter a park and exchange it for a park card for further use. We recommend that you safeguard both! For a fee you can upgrade these cards to a MagicBand. The inner workings of RFID are discussed in detail starting on the next page.

In addition to using RFID chips, Disney's computer systems store the dimensions of one finger (not a fingerprint) from your right hand, a reference to which is also stored on your MagicBand or laminated card. Recording this biometric information requires a quick and painless measurement, taken the first time you use the ticket. When you use it again, you'll be asked to scan the same finger to validate your identity. If the scans don't match—say, you use a different finger—you may be asked to present photo identification. Disney will ask for biometric finger scans for children ages 3–9; younger kids may have a parent or other adult provide their scans, or Disney may ask to photograph the child for admission verification purposes.

If you're buying admission for your entire family and you're worried that you won't be able to keep everyone's tickets straight, Disney's computer system should have every family member's data linked to every ticket, allowing anyone in your group to enter with anyone else's ticket. We've confirmed this by having a platoon of Unofficial Guide researchers (including men, women, and children) swap MagicBands with each other; all were admitted.

RFID: It's All in the Wrist

MagicBands—rubber wristbands—are a sort of wearable theme park ticket. Small and reusable across trips, a **MagicBand** is imprinted with your first name, an ID number, and some legalese, along with a Mickey logo. A tiny radio-frequency-identification (RFID) chip embedded in the wristband links to your ticket and travel information.

Disney hotel guests get a MagicBand by default but may request a plastic **park card** instead. If you're staying off-site or you bought your admission through a third party, you can upgrade to a MagicBand for a fee; otherwise you get a park card. Like the MagicBand, the card uses RFID.

Each member of your family gets his or her own MagicBand, each with a unique serial number. Along with the wristband, each family member will be asked to select a four-digit personal-identification number (PIN) for purchases—more on that below. The wristbands are removable, resizable, and waterproof, and they have ventilation holes for cooling. Several colors are available: red, blue, green, pink, purple, orange, yellow, and gray (the default). You can choose your colors and personalize your bands when you book your resort stay at the Disney World website. Further customization is available for a price.

BOB At magicyourband.com you can create stickers of almost any color or design for your MagicBand.

Some guests, particularly those with hand or wrist mobility issues, find using the MagicBand physically challenging. The center portion of the band (essentially a puck the size of a quarter) is removable. The puck can be placed inside special accessories such as a key chain, a watch slider, or a necklace, making it easier to use. Etsy is a great source for all kinds of puck holders.

RFID for Payment, Hotel-Room Access, and Photos

Disney's hotel-room doors have RFID readers, allowing you to check in and enter your room simply by tapping your wristband or park card against the reader. In fact, you can now start the check-in process 60 days before arrival. From the app, you can make room requests, add credit card information, authorize charges, submit an estimated arrival time, and request a message to alert you when your room is ready. This does not replace front desk cast members, and guests can still talk face-to-face with cast members at the front desk. To finalize your check-in, all you have to do is unlock your room door with your MagicBand.

RFID readers are installed at virtually every Disney cash register on property, allowing you to pay for food, drinks, and souvenirs by tapping your MagicBand/park card against the reader, a technology known as contactless payment. You'll be asked to verify your identity by entering your PIN on a small keypad to complete your purchase.

If you're using Disney's **Memory Maker** service (disneyworld.disney
.go.com/memory-maker), your MagicBand/park card serves as the link
between your photos and your family. Each photographer carries a
small RFID reader, against which you tap your MagicBand when having your photo taken. The Memory Maker system will link your photos
to you, and you'll be able to view them on the Disney World website.

Disney's onboard ride-photo computers incorporate RFID technology too. As you begin down the big drop near the finale of Splash
Mountain, for example, RFID sensors read the serial number on your
MagicBand and pass it to Splash Mountain's cameras. When those cameras snap your family plunging into the briar patch, they attach your
MagicBand's serial number to the photo, allowing you to see your ride
photos together after you've returned home. Because ride sensors may
not pick up the signal from an RFID card sitting in a wallet or purse,
we're fairly sure that onboard ride photos require MagicBands.

The Future of RFID

Other innovative uses of RFID technology are in the works. The last scene
of It's a Small World now says "goodbye" to your family by name. In a
more advanced scenario we've heard coming, you'll provide Disney with
some information about your child before your visit, such as his or her
favorite color and pet's name. Later, when your child visits Cinderella, an
RFID reader next to Cinderella will recognize your child's wristband and
display the previously gathered information on a hidden prompter for
Cinderella to work into conversation. And because Disney's computer
systems will know from your MagicBand which rides you've been on and
where you've eaten, Cinderella may mention those details too.

But as impressive as all this sounds, many people are understand-
ably concerned about multinational corporations tracking their movements. As noted earlier, guests who prefer not to wear MagicBands
can instead obtain park cards, which are somewhat more difficult to
track (inexpensive RFID-blocking wallets are available online). Disney claims that guests who opt out of MagicBands don't get the full
range of ride experiences, though, so there's a trade-off to be made.

RFID and MagicBands are hot topics with our readers. Here are a
few typical comments. First from a Buckley, Michigan, mom:

> *MagicBands and MyMagic+: AMAZING! We had everything we
> needed right in our wristbands! If we didn't want to take anything
> with us when we left the room, we didn't have to. The MagicBands
> acted as our room key, charge card, park passes, FastPasses, and din-
> ing plan vouchers.*

This from a newlywed couple:

> *I cannot say enough about how awesome the MagicBands are! Not
> having to root around for a room key after a long day of touring was
> bliss. The fact that they could be worn in the water made going to
> the pool or water park a snap. Also, they were linked to our credit*

card, so we didn't have to bring cash everywhere. Plus, they survived Summit Plummet!

Finally, a mom from Plano, Texas, chipped in with this:

Loved the MagicBands! They make it so convenient to spend lots of money. And you can use them at the Disney store in the airport too.

BABYSITTING

CHILDCARE CENTERS Childcare isn't available inside the theme parks, and in early 2018 Disney closed all of its childcare centers. The only childcare center still available is **Camp Dolphin** at the Dolphin and Swan. Camp Dolphin is a fun-filled club exclusively for kids ages 4–12. Hours are 5 p.m.–midnight. Reservations are required, and the price is $12 per child, per hour. A kid's meal from Picabu can be included for an additional $10. Receive up to 2 hours of complimentary time at Camp Dolphin by getting a treatment at Mandara Spa (treatment of $75 and up) or by dining at Shula's Steak House, Todd English's blue-zoo, or Il Mulino New York Trattoria. Simply present your receipt as proof of purchase when you pick up your child.

IN-ROOM BABYSITTING Two companies provide in-room sitting in Walt Disney World and surrounding areas: **Kid's Nite Out** and **Extra Hands.** Both provide sitters older than age 18 who are screened, reference-checked, police-checked, and trained in CPR. In addition to caring for your kids in your room, the sitters will, if you direct, take your children to the theme parks or other venues. (For in-park care,

• Babysitting Services •	
KID'S NITE OUT	**EXTRA HANDS**
☎ 407-828-0920 or 800-696-8105 kidsniteout.com	vacationsitterfl.com
HOTELS SERVED All WDW and Orlando-area hotels	**HOTELS SERVED** All WDW and Orlando-area hotels
MINIMUM CHARGES 4 hours	**MINIMUM CHARGES** 5 hours
BASE HOURLY RATES • 1 child, $18 • 2 children, $21 • 3 children, $24 • 4 children, $26	**BASE HOURLY RATES** • 1 child, $15 • 2 children, $16.50 • 3 children, $18 • 4 children and up, $19.50
EXTRA CHARGES Transportation fee, $10; before 8 a.m. or after 9 p.m., +$2 per hour; additional fee for holidays	**EXTRA CHARGES** Transportation fee, $10; before 8 a.m. or after 9 p.m., +$3 per hour; holidays, +$5 per hour; in parks, +$3 per hour; resort parking (if applicable)
CANCELLATION DEADLINE 24 hours before service (48 hours for holidays)	**CANCELLATION DEADLINE** 72 hours before service
FORM OF PAYMENT AE, D, MC, V; tips in cash	**FORM OF PAYMENT** D, MC, V
THINGS SITTERS WON'T DO Transport children in private vehicle, take children swimming, give baths	**THINGS SITTERS WON'T DO** Take children swimming, give baths

Kid's Nite Out charges the full cost of a ticket, while Extra Hands charges an extra $3 per hour.) A bilingual sitter may be available but is not guaranteed. (See the table on the previous page for details.)

SPECIAL PROGRAMS *for* CHILDREN

LILIANE Be aware that Disney is tinkering with prices and availability of packages now more than ever. Check ahead of time before promising your kids any activity.

SEVERAL CHILDREN'S PROGRAMS are available at Disney World parks and resorts. Many of Disney's Deluxe and Disney Vacation Club resorts offer a continuous slate of free children's activities from early morning through the evening, from storytelling and cookie decorating to hands-on activities themed to the resort.

BEHIND THE SEEDS AT EPCOT This 1-hour walking tour of The Land greenhouses and labs at Epcot has plenty of interaction for the kids, such as playing guessing games and feeding fish at the fish farm. The greenhouses are home to more than 60 crops from around the world. Did you know that the food grown in The Land is used at restaurants throughout Epcot? The price is $25 per adult and $20 per child (ages 3–9). Call ☎ 407-WDW-TOUR (939-8687) for additional information and reservations.

CAPTAIN HOOK'S PIRATE CREW This kids' program is offered nightly at Disney's Beach Club, transporting kids ages 4–12 to an environment full of excitement and adventure with Captain Hook himself in attendance! Activities include a treasure hunt, a sailing excursion on Crescent Lake, and dinner. Check-in begins at 4:30 p.m., and programing runs 5–8 p.m. for a fee of $55 plus tax. Children must be fully toilet trained, and parents must be physically present to check children in and out of the program. To book this tour call ☎ 407-WDW-PLAY (939-7529).

CARING FOR GIANTS This family-friendly, 1-hour backstage experience at the Animal Kingdom gives guests the opportunity to meet dedicated animal care experts, who provide for the care and wellness of the elephant herd. African cultural representatives share stories of Disney's conservation efforts. The tour is offered throughout the day 9:30 a.m.–4 p.m. Pricing for all ages is $30 and does not include park admission. Children must be at least 4 years old to attend; children age 17 or under must be accompanied by an adult. To book this adventure, call ☎ 407-WDW-PLAY (939-7529).

DINE WITH AN ANIMAL SPECIALIST We highly recommend this experience at Sanaa, one of the restaurants at Animal Kingdom Lodge. Not only will you and your family be treated to a fabulous African-inspired lunch, but you'll also get to spend time with a caretaker who shares fun facts about his or her work with the animals. After lunch, guests are taken outside and behind the gates to meet an endangered animal.

Limited to 12 participants, the lunch is offered Wednesdays and Saturdays at 11 a.m. The price—$60 for adults and $35 for kids ages 3–9 (it's best suited for age 8 and up)—includes tax and tip. At the end of the meal, guests are invited to make a voluntary $5 donation to the Disney Conservation Fund. It's educational, fun, and a great value. Check out Liliane's review at tinyurl.com/lunchwithanimalspecialist.

DISNEY'S FAMILY MAGIC TOUR This is an approximately 2-hour guided tour of the Magic Kingdom for the entire family. Even children in strollers (no younger than age 3) are welcome. The tour combines information about the Magic Kingdom with a guided scavenger hunt with riddles. There's usually a marginal plot such as saving Wendy from Captain Hook, in which case the character at the end of the tour is Wendy. The tour departs Monday, Tuesday, Friday, and Saturday at 10 a.m. The cost is about $39 per person plus tax, and a valid Magic Kingdom admission. Maximum group size is 20 persons. Reservations can be made up to 180 days in advance by calling ☎ 407-WDW-TOUR (939-8687).

DISNEY'S PERFECTLY PRINCESS TEA It certainly takes a princely sum to cover the tab on this Grand Floridian shindig, hosted by Rose Petal, an enchanted storytelling rose. Your little princess gets to sip tea with Princess Aurora. Girls receive an 18-inch My Disney Girl Princess Aurora doll dressed in a gown plus accessories. Other loot includes a tiara, silver bracelet, fresh rose, sticker page, "Best Friend" certificate for the doll, and a cinch bag. Princes who attend the tea party will receive a sword and shield, a souvenir pin, a Disney plush, and a "Best Friend" certificate. A luncheon is served as well. The cost is about $334 with tax and gratuity for one adult and one child ages 3–9; add an additional guest age 10 and up for $99 or an additional child for $235 (adults-only bookings not available). *Note:* **This event is not covered by the Disney Dining Plan.** Your credit card will be charged beforehand, and you can book up to 180 days in advance. The tea party is held on select days, 10:30 a.m.–noon. Call ☎ 407-939-6983 for reservations and information. Check in 15 minutes prior to reservation time.

An Illinois mom ponied up for two of the programs:

The Perfectly Princess Tea was nice but a bit too long with all the singing and stories. Not easy for a 4-year-old to sit that long. I would not do it again. The Wonderland Tea Party was a much better cost, and I thought my daughter would love decorating a cupcake. She was so freaked out by the Mad Hatter that the nice workers there called and asked me to come get her. They said many kids are scared of him, so I'm not sure why they don't have Alice and another character. I was pleased that they gave me a full refund (she was in there maybe 10 minutes).

DISNEY'S THE MAGIC BEHIND OUR STEAM TRAINS Kids must be age 10 or older for this 3-hour tour, presented Sunday–Thursday. At the 7:30 a.m. start time, join the crew of the Walt Disney World Railroad as they prepare their steam locomotives for the day. Cost is about $54 per person plus tax, and a valid Magic Kingdom admission. Call ☎ 407-WDW-TOUR (939-8687) for information and reservations.

FORT WILDERNESS ARCHERY EXPERIENCE Loyal fans of Princess Merida, this is your activity! Guests 7 years of age and up can learn how to hold and fire a compound bow in this 90-minute archery program. With class sizes limited to 10 guests, this is a wonderful experience held at the campsites at Fort Wilderness Resort. The fee for the program is $47.93, including tax. The archery experience is available Tuesday–Saturday, 2:45–4:15 p.m. For reservations call ☎ 407-WDW-PLAY (939-7529).

STAR WARS GUIDED TOUR This 7-hour *Star Wars*–themed guided tour takes place at Disney's Hollywood Studios. Highlights include a screening of *Star Wars: Path of the Jedi*; a reserved viewing area for *Star Wars: A Galaxy Far, Far Away* and *Star Wars: A Galactic Spectacular* nighttime fireworks show; and a *Star Wars*–inspired dinner at Backlot Express. Children ages 4–12 receive guaranteed enrollment and participation in *Jedi Training: Trials of the Temple*. Guest also have VIP access to Star Tours—The Adventures Continue and *Star Wars* characters. The tour costs $99, including tax, for all ages and requires valid park admission. If you don't mind the astronomical price tag, call ☎ 407-WDW-PLAY (939-7529).

UP CLOSE WITH RHINOS This 60-minute tour is offered daily at 11 a.m. at the Animal Kingdom. The tour discusses the behavior and biology of the park's white rhinos, as well as the challenges that threaten the animal in the wild. Participants must be 4 years of age or older; guests under the age of 18 must be accompanied by a paying adult. No cameras, video equipment, or cell phones may be used while on this backstage tour. The price for all ages is $40 plus tax. To book this tour call ☎ 407-WDW-PLAY (939-7529).

WILD AFRICA TREK This backstage tour of the Animal Kingdom is not made for the faint of heart, but you, and especially your kids, will get a real sense of adventure. On this 3-hour walking and driving tour, you will visit Harambe Wildlife Reserve and the savanna for up close encounters with giraffes, rhinos, tigers, and lions. At some point in the tour, secured to an overhead track with a safety harness, you will walk a wobbly bridge and get incredible views of hippos and crocodiles. Halfway through the tour guests will indulge in gourmet eats in an outdoor setting on the savanna. Morning tours enjoy air-dried beef and prosciutto, smoked salmon roulade, several cheeses, yogurt, and fresh fruit. Afternoon tours are served chicken curry salad, hummus with mini pitas, marinated tandoori shrimp, smoked salmon roulade, air-dried beef and prosciutto, and fresh fruit. Your encounters with the animals will be captured by a professional

LILIANE Love, love, love this tour. I wish I could go on it every time I visit and capture tigers and lions and more with my camera.

photographer, and at the end of the tour, guests receive a photo code to access and download the images. You can bring your own camera or smartphone too, but only if you have a strap that can be attached to the provided vest or if you can hang the camera securely around your neck.

Wear comfortable clothes and sneakers, and bring a strap for your glasses or sunglasses. Participants also receive a complimentary souvenir, which currently is a water bottle that clips to your vest. For anything you cannot attach to your vest, Disney provides lockers. The guides are incredibly knowledgeable, and a wireless headset allows you to hear the guide at all times. The price is $201.29 per person and jumps up to $265.19 during peak seasons such as December and Easter. Participants must be 8 years of age or older, at least 48 inches tall, and 45–300 pounds with the harness gear on. The trek is available multiple times daily. Call ☎ 407-WDW-TOUR (939-8687) for reservations.

WONDERLAND TEA PARTY This event is held Monday–Friday, 2–3 p.m., at 1900 Park Fare restaurant at the Grand Floridian. The price tag is $52.19, including tax (ages 4–12). The program consists of decorating and eating cupcakes and having "tea" with characters from *Alice in Wonderland*. Small children might get scared meeting the White Rabbit or Mad Hatter. Reservations can be made by calling ☎ 407-WDW-DINE (939-3463) 180 days in advance.

BIRTHDAYS AND SPECIAL OCCASIONS

GUESTS WHO ARE CELEBRATING A BIRTHDAY or visiting Walt Disney World for the first time can pick up a button corresponding to the celebration at Guest Relations when entering any of the parks. Often upon check-in, clerks at the Disney resorts will ask if any member of your party is celebrating a special event. It's especially fun for birthday kids, as cast members will congratulate your child throughout the day in the hotel, on the bus, in the park, and at restaurants throughout the World. A Lombard, Illinois, mom put the word out and was glad she did:

> My daughter turned 5 while we were there, and I asked about special things that could be done. Our hotel asked me who her favorite character was and did the rest. We came back to our room on her birthday and there were balloons, a card, and an autographed Cinderella 5-by-7-inch photo! When we entered the Magic Kingdom, we received an It's My Birthday Today pin (FREE!), and at the restaurant she got a huge cupcake with whipped cream, sprinkles, and a candle. IT PAYS TO ASK!!

Another great and reasonably priced treat is to have your child's hair cut at the **Harmony Barber Shop** on Main Street, U.S.A. at the Magic Kingdom. Rest assured that your kid will walk away with a good haircut, and you may even be treated to a song by the Dapper Dans, Disney's famous barbershop quartet. The best time to go is during a parade. You get a good view, and the staff sings along with the parade music. It's a great photo op. An Ohio mom celebrated her child's first haircut at the barber shop:

> *The barbershop makes a big deal with baby's first haircut—pixie dust, photos, a certificate, and "free" mouse ears hat!*

An adult haircut is $19, children's is $18, and the special My First Haircut package is $25. There is a $10 no-show fee. For reservations call ☎ 407-WDW-PLAY (939-7529).

Lest you think the Harmony Barber Shop is strictly a boys' domain, a fashion- and dollar-conscious Kalamazoo, Michigan, mom writes that it's a great option for little girls who want to get gussied up:

> *You don't need reservations. They put my daughter's hair into a teased bun and used brightly colored paints and colorful confetti to match the princess dress she had on.*

"No, no, really, it's OK. It's just not what I was expecting."

PART THREE

WHERE *to* STAY

WHEN TRAVELING WITH CHILDREN, your hotel is your home away from home, your safe harbor, and your sanctuary. Staying in a hotel is in itself a great adventure for children. They take in every detail and delight in such things as having a pool at their disposal and obtaining ice from a noisy machine. Of course, it's critical that your children feel safe and secure, but it adds immeasurably to the success of the vacation if they really like the hotel.

BOB In our opinion, if you're traveling with a child age 12 or younger, one of your top priorities should be to book a hotel within easy striking distance of the parks.

In truth, because of their youth and limited experience, children are far less particular about hotels than adults, but kids' memories are like little steel traps, so once you establish a lodging standard, that's pretty much what they'll expect every time. A couple from Gary, Indiana, stayed at the pricey Yacht Club Resort at Walt Disney World because they heard that it offered a knockout swimming area (which it does). When they returned 2 years later and stayed at one of Disney's All-Star Resorts for about a third of the price, their 10-year-old carped all week. If you're on a budget, it's better to begin with modest accommodations and move up to better digs on subsequent trips as finances permit.

"YOU CAN'T ROLLER-SKATE IN A BUFFALO HERD"

THIS WAS A SONG TITLE FROM THE 1960S. If we wrote that song today, we'd call it "You Can't Have Fun at Disney World if You're Drop-Dead Tired." Believe us, Disney World is an easy place to be penny-wise and pound-foolish. Many families who cut lodging expenses by booking a budget hotel end up so far away from Disney World that it's a major hassle to return to the hotel in the middle of the day for swimming and a nap. By trying to spend the whole day at the theme parks, however, they wear themselves out quickly, and the dream vacation suddenly disintegrates into short tempers and exhaustion. And don't confuse this advice with a sales pitch for Disney hotels. You will find dozens of hotels outside Disney World that are as close or closer to certain Disney parks than some of the resorts inside the World. Our main point—our only point, really—is that you should be able to return to your hotel easily when the need arises.

LODGING CONSIDERATIONS

COST

AT WALT DISNEY WORLD, standard hotel-room rates range from about $125 to more than $1,800 per night during the holidays. Outside, rooms are as low as $80 a night. Clearly, if you are willing to sacrifice some luxury and don't mind a 10- to 25-minute commute, you can really cut your lodging costs by staying outside Walt Disney World. Hotels in the World tend to be the most expensive, but they also offer some of the highest quality, as well as a number of perks not enjoyed by guests who stay outside the World. The cost shown in the WDW Resorts At a Glance table on pages 104–106 is rounded to the nearest $50.

Animal Kingdom Villas, Bay Lake Tower, Beach Club Villas, Board-Walk Villas, Boulder Ridge Villas, Copper Creek Villas & Cabins, Old Key West, Polynesian Villas, Riviera Resort, Saratoga Springs Resort, and **The Villas at Grand Floridian Resort** offer condo-type accommodations with one-, two-, and (at Animal Kingdom Villas, Bay Lake Tower, BoardWalk Villas, Copper Creek Villas & Cabins, Grand Floridian Villas, Old Key West, Riviera Resort, and Saratoga Springs) three-bedroom units with kitchens, living rooms, DVD players, and washers and dryers. Studios have a kitchenette (with microwave, mini-fridge, and sink) but no washer or dryer. Prices range from $405–$773 per night for a studio suite at Animal Kingdom Villas to more than $4,295 per night for a two-bedroom bungalow at the Polynesian. Fully equipped cabins (minus a washer and dryer) at **Fort Wilderness Resort & Campground** cost $402–$597 per night. Family Suites at the All-Star Music and Art of Animation Resorts have kitchenettes, separate bedrooms, and two bathrooms. A few suites without kitchens are available at the more expensive Disney resorts.

The nightly surcharge for each extra adult in a room (more than two) is $15 at Value resorts, $25 at Moderate resorts, and $35 at Deluxe resorts, plus tax. Disney Deluxe Villas (DDV) do not levy a surcharge.

Also at Disney World are the seven hotels of the **Disney Springs Resort Area (DSRA).** Accommodations range from fairly luxurious to motel-like. While the DSRA is technically part of Disney World, staying there is like visiting a colony rather than the motherland. For more information on DSRA properties, see page 107.

LOCATION AND TRANSPORTATION OPTIONS

ONCE YOU'VE DETERMINED YOUR BUDGET, think about what you want to do at Walt Disney World. Will you go to all four theme

COSTS PER NIGHT OF DISNEY HOTEL ROOMS, 2019 *(rack rate)*	
Rates are for standard rooms except as noted.	
ALL-STAR RESORTS	$112–$217
ALL-STAR MUSIC RESORT FAMILY SUITES	$277–$497
ANIMAL KINGDOM LODGE	$389–$622
ANIMAL KINGDOM VILLAS *(studio, Jambo/Kidani)*	$379–$773
ART OF ANIMATION FAMILY SUITES	$366–$631
ART OF ANIMATION RESORT	$153–$271
BAY LAKE TOWER AT CONTEMPORARY RESORT *(studio)*	$557–$861
BEACH CLUB RESORT	$456–$749
BEACH CLUB VILLAS *(studio)*	$511–$800
BOARDWALK INN	$498–$786
BOARDWALK VILLAS *(studio)*	$511–$800
BOULDER RIDGE VILLAS *(studio)*	$478–$693
CARIBBEAN BEACH RESORT	$194–$322
CONTEMPORARY RESORT *(Garden Wing)*	$465–$728
COPPER CREEK VILLAS & CASCADE CABINS *(studio)*	$497–$723
CORONADO SPRINGS RESORT	$208–$331
DOLPHIN *(Sheraton)*	$325–$431
FORT WILDERNESS RESORT & CAMPGROUND *(cabins)*	$377–$655
GRAN DESTINO TOWER	$320–$390
GRAND FLORIDIAN RESORT & SPA	$664–$957
GRAND FLORIDIAN VILLAS *(studio)*	$665–$988
OLD KEY WEST RESORT *(studio)*	$395–$590
POLYNESIAN VILLAGE RESORT	$552–$861
POLYNESIAN VILLAS & BUNGALOWS *(studio)*	$592–$915
POP CENTURY RESORT	$130–$245
PORT ORLEANS RESORT *(French Quarter & Riverside)*	$232–$350
RIVIERA RESORT *(studio; opens late 2019)*	$392–$632
SARATOGA SPRINGS RESORT & SPA *(studio)*	$395–$590
SWAN *(Westin)*	$325–$431
TREEHOUSE VILLAS	$958–$1,601
WILDERNESS LODGE	$378–$669
YACHT CLUB RESORT	$456–$749

parks, or will you concentrate on one or two? If you'll be driving a car, the location of your Disney hotel isn't especially important unless you plan to spend most of your time at the Magic Kingdom. (Disney transportation is always more efficient than your car in this case because it deposits you right at the theme park entrance.)

Most convenient to the Magic Kingdom are the three resorts linked by monorail: the **Grand Floridian** and its **Villas,** the **Contemporary** and **Bay Lake Tower,** and the **Polynesian Village.**

Wilderness Lodge, Boulder Ridge Villas, and **Copper Creek Villas & Cabins,** along with **Fort Wilderness Resort & Campground,** are linked to the Magic Kingdom by boat and to everywhere else in the World by bus. **Shades of Green** only has bus service.

The most centrally located resorts in Walt Disney World are the Epcot hotels—**BoardWalk Inn & Villas, Yacht & Beach Club Resorts, Beach Club Villas, Riviera Resort, Swan,** and **Dolphin**—and **Coronado Springs** (including the new **Gran Destino Tower**), near the Animal Kingdom. The Epcot hotels are within easy walking distance of Disney's Hollywood Studios (DHS) and Epcot's International Gateway. Except at Coronado Springs, boat service is also available at these resorts, with vessels connecting to DHS.

LILIANE Just for the record, the Epcot resorts within walking distance of the International Gateway are a long, long walk from Future World, the section of Epcot where families tend to spend most of their time.

Caribbean Beach, Riviera, Pop Century, and **Art of Animation Resorts** are just south and east of Epcot and DHS. They are connected to Epcot and DHS by the Skyliner gondola and to everything else by bus. Along Bonnet Creek, **Old Key West** and **Port Orleans Resorts** also offer quick access to those parks. **Saratoga Springs** is connected to Disney Springs via a pedestrian bridge; boat and bus service are available.

Though not centrally located, the **All-Star Resorts** and **Animal Kingdom Lodge & Villas** have good bus service to all Disney World destinations and are closest to Animal Kingdom.

BOB If you plan to use Disney transportation to visit all four major parks and the water parks, book a centrally located resort that has good transportation connections, such as the Epcot resorts: the **Polynesian Village, Caribbean Beach, Art of Animation, Pop Century, Coronado Springs, Port Orleans,** or **Riviera Resorts.**

Wilderness Lodge and **Fort Wilderness** have the most inconvenient transportation service of the Disney hotels. Also, buses run less frequently to and from Old Key West than they do at other Disney resorts. Spotty bus service is also a drawback shared by **Saratoga Springs** and **Treehouse Villas.**

Disney Skyliner, a new aerial tramway gondola system, connects the **Art of Animation, Pop Century,** and **Caribbean Beach Resorts,** as well as other locations, with DHS and the International Gateway entrance at Epcot. Disney has also started a point-to-point transportation system called **Minnie Van** service. Similar to Lyft, the Minnie Mouse–themed midsize SUVs will transport guests, on demand, throughout Walt Disney World. The SUVs accommodate up to eight passengers.

Open the Lyft app from anywhere within Walt Disney World Resort to access the Minnie Van service, driven by Disney cast members, to request a ride. Prices vary based on distance traveled. The service is available 6:30 a.m.–12:30 a.m. for transportation on Disney property only, which includes the four main theme parks, all Disney-owned resorts, Disney's two water parks, and Disney Springs. In addition to the fact that the Minnie Van service is restricted to transportation within Disney property only, it's more expensive than Uber.

A Minnie Van airport shuttle is available 7 a.m.–11:59 p.m. for a flat rate of $150, gratuity not included. The pick-up location at the airport is by the baggage claim escalators. Please note that the Minnie Van airport shuttle is not available for the Swan and Dolphin, the Four Seasons, Disney Springs Resort Area hotels, Walt Disney World Gateway hotels, and Walt Disney World Good Neighbor hotels.

To reserve an accessible vehicle that accommodates a wheelchair or electronic convenience vehicle, call ☎ 407-828-3500. Vans accommodate up to six guests and six medium-size suitcases, and they can be equipped with up to three complimentary car seats.

Last but not least, you can book a Minnie Van transfer between a Walt Disney World resort and Port Canaveral. The transfer from the port to a Disney resort at the end of your cruise is also available. The transfer is a flat fee of $240, one way, gratuity not included, and must be booked by calling the Disney Cruise Line embarkation services at ☎ 800-395-9374.

COMMUTING TO AND FROM THE THEME PARKS

FOR VISITORS LODGING INSIDE WALT DISNEY WORLD With three important exceptions, the fastest way to commute from your hotel to the theme parks and back is in your own car. And though many guests use the Disney transportation system and appreciate not having to drive, based on timed comparisons, it's almost always less time-consuming to drive. The exceptions are these: (1) commuting to the Magic Kingdom from the hotels on the monorail (Grand Floridian, Polynesian Village, and Contemporary Resort and Bay Lake Tower); (2) commuting to the Magic Kingdom from any Disney hotel by bus or boat; and (3) commuting to Epcot on the monorail from the Polynesian Village Resort via the Transportation and Ticket Center (TTC).

If you stay at the Polynesian, you can catch a direct monorail to the Magic Kingdom, and by walking 100 yards or so to the TTC, you can catch a direct monorail to Epcot. At the nexus of the monorail system, the Polynesian is certainly the most convenient resort. From either the Magic Kingdom or Epcot, you can return to your hotel quickly and easily whenever you want.

Second to the Polynesian in terms of convenience are the Grand Floridian and Contemporary, also on the Magic Kingdom monorail, but they cost as much as or more than the Polynesian. Less expensive Disney hotels transport you to the Magic Kingdom by bus or boat. For reasons described below, this is more efficient than driving a car.

DRIVING TIME TO THE THEME PARKS FOR VISITORS LODGING OUTSIDE WALT DISNEY WORLD For vacationers staying outside Walt Disney World, we've calculated the approximate commuting time to the major theme parks' parking lots from several off-World lodging areas. Add a few minutes to our times to pay your parking fee and to park. Once parked at the TTC (Magic Kingdom parking lot), it takes an average of 20–30 more minutes to reach the Magic Kingdom. At Epcot and Animal Kingdom, the lot-to-gate transit time is 10–15 minutes; at Disney's Hollywood Studios (DHS), it's 8–12 minutes. If you haven't purchased your theme park admission in advance, tack on another 10–20 minutes.

DRIVING TIME TO THE THEME PARKS				
MINUTES TO: FROM:	MAGIC KINGDOM PARKING LOT	EPCOT PARKING LOT	DISNEY'S ANIMAL KINGDOM PARKING LOT	DISNEY'S HOLLYWOOD STUDIOS PARKING LOT
Downtown Orlando	35	31	37	33
North International Drive and Universal Orlando	24	21	26	22
Central International Drive and Sand Lake Road	26	23	27	24
South International Drive and SeaWorld	18	15	20	16
FL 535	12	9	13	10
US 192, west of I-4	10–15	7–12	5–10	5–10
US 192, east of I-4	10–18	7–15	5–12	5–13

Our WDW Resorts At a Glance table on pages 104–106 shows the commuting time, not including getting to and from the parking lot to the turnstiles, to the Disney theme parks from each hotel listed. Those commuting times represent an average of several test runs. Your actual time may be shorter or longer depending on many variables.

SHUTTLE SERVICE FROM HOTELS OUTSIDE WALT DISNEY WORLD Many hotels in the Walt Disney World area provide shuttle service to the theme parks. They represent a fairly carefree alternative for getting to and from the parks, letting you off near the entrance (except at the Magic Kingdom) and saving you the cost of parking. The rub is that they might not get you there as early as you desire (a critical point if you are using our touring plans) or be available at the time you wish to return to your lodging. Also, be forewarned that most shuttle services do not add vehicles at park opening or closing times. In the morning, your biggest problem is that you might not get a seat. At closing time, however, and sometimes following a hard rain, you can expect a lot of competition for standing space on the bus. If there is no room, you might have to wait 30 minutes to an hour for the next shuttle.

CONVENIENCE, CONVENIENTLY DEFINED Conceptually, it's easy to grasp that a hotel that is closer is more convenient than one that is far away. But nothing is that simple at Walt Disney World, so we'd better tell you exactly what you're in for. If you stay at a Walt Disney World resort and use the Disney transportation system, you'll have a 5- to 10-minute walk to the bus stop, monorail station, or dock (whichever applies). Once there, buses, trains, or boats generally run about every

15–25 minutes, so you might have to wait a short time for your transportation to arrive. Once you're on board, most conveyances make additional stops en route to your destination, and many take a less-than-direct route. Upon arrival, however, they deposit you fairly close to the entrance of the theme park. Returning to your hotel is the same process in reverse and takes about the same amount of time.

Regardless of whether you stay in Walt Disney World, if you use your own car, here's how your commute shakes out: After a 1- to 5-minute walk from your room to your car, you drive to the theme park, stopping to pay a parking fee or showing your MagicBand for free parking (if you're a Disney resort guest). Disney cast members then direct you to a parking space. If you arrive early, your space may be close enough to the park entrance (Magic Kingdom excepted) to walk. If you park farther afield, a Disney tram will come along every 5 minutes to collect you and transport you to the entrance.

At the Magic Kingdom, the entrance to the park is separated from the parking lot by the TTC and the Seven Seas Lagoon. After parking at the Magic Kingdom lot, you take a tram to the TTC and then board a ferry or monorail (your choice) for the trip across the lagoon to the park. This process is fairly time-consuming and is to be avoided if possible. The only way to avoid it, however, is to stay at a Disney resort and commute directly to the Magic Kingdom entrance via Disney bus, boat, or monorail. Happily, all the other theme parks are situated adjacent to their parking lots.

Because families with children tend to spend more time on average at the Magic Kingdom than at the other parks, and because it's so important to return to your hotel for rest, the business of getting around the lagoon can be a major consideration when choosing a place to stay; the extra hassle of crossing the lagoon (to get back to your car) makes coming and going much more difficult. The half hour it takes to commute to your hotel via car from the Animal Kingdom, DHS, or Epcot takes an hour or longer from the Magic Kingdom. If you stay at a Disney hotel and use the Disney transportation system, you may have to wait 5–25 minutes for your bus, boat, or monorail, but it will take you directly from the Magic Kingdom entrance to your hotel, bypassing the lagoon and the TTC.

DINING

DINING FIGURES INTO THE LODGING DISCUSSION only if you don't plan to have a car at your disposal. If you plan on using the Disney transportation system (for Disney hotel guests) or the courtesy shuttle of your non-Disney hotel, you will either have to dine at the theme parks or near your hotel. If your hotel offers a lot of choices or if other restaurants are within walking distance, then there's no problem. If your hotel is somewhat isolated and offers limited selections, you'll feel like Bob did on a canoe trip once when he ate northern pike at every meal for a week because that's all he could catch.

At Disney World, though it's relatively quick and efficient to commute from your Disney hotel or campground to the theme parks, it's a long, arduous process requiring transfers to travel from hotel to hotel. Disney hotels that are somewhat isolated and that offer limited dining choices include Old Key West, Caribbean Beach, All-Star, Pop Century, Art of Animation, Animal Kingdom Lodge, Coronado Springs, and Wilderness Lodge Resorts, as well as the Fort Wilderness Campground.

LILIANE If you share a room with your children, you all should hit the sack at the same time. Establish a single compromise bedtime, probably a little early for you and a bit later than the children's usual weekend bedtime. Observe any nightly rituals you practice at home, such as reading a book before lights-out.

If you want a condo-type accommodation so that you have more flexibility for meal preparation than eating out of a cooler, the best deals in Disney World are the prefab log cabins at Fort Wilderness Resort & Campground. Other Disney lodgings with kitchens are available at all of the villas, plus Bay Lake Tower, Old Key West, and Saratoga Springs, but all are much more expensive than the cabins at the campground. Outside Disney World, an ever-increasing number of condos are available, and some are very good deals. See our discussion of lodging outside Disney World starting on page 112.

THE SIZE OF YOUR GROUP

LARGER FAMILIES AND GROUPS may be interested in how many people can stay in a Disney resort room, but only Lilliputians would be comfortable in a room filled to capacity. Groups requiring two or more rooms should consider condo, suite, or villa accommodations, either in or out of Disney World. If there are more than six in your party, you will need either two hotel rooms, a suite (see Wilderness Lodge), a villa, or a condo.

STAYING IN OR OUT OF THE WORLD: WEIGHING THE PROS AND CONS

1. COST If cost is your primary consideration, you'll lodge much less expensively outside Walt Disney World.

2. EASE OF ACCESS Even if you stay in Disney World, you're dependent on some mode of transportation. It may be less stressful to use the Disney transportation system, but with the exception of commuting to the Magic Kingdom, the fastest, most efficient, and most flexible way to get around is usually a car. If you're at Epcot, for example, and want to take the kids back to the Contemporary Resort for a nap, forget the monorail. You'll get back much faster by car.

A reader from Raynham, Massachusetts, who stayed at the Caribbean Beach Resort, writes:

Even though the resort is on the Disney bus line, I recommend renting a car if it fits one's budget. The buses don't go directly to many destinations, and often you have to switch buses. Getting a bus back to the hotel after a hard day can mean a long wait in line.

HOTEL | MAXIMUM OCCUPANCY PER ROOM

All-Star Resorts | Standard room: 4 people plus child under age 3 in crib; Family Suite: 6 people plus child in crib

Animal Kingdom Lodge | 4 people plus child under age 3 in crib

Animal Kingdom Villas: Jambo House | Studio: 4 people; 1 bedroom: 4 or 5 people; 2 bedroom: 8 or 9 people; Grand Villa: 12 people; all plus child in crib

Animal Kingdom Villas: Kidani Village | Studio: 4 people; 1 bedroom: 5 people; 2 bedroom: 9 people; Grand Villa: 12 people; all plus child in crib

Art of Animation | Little Mermaid buildings: 4 people; Cars, Finding Nemo, and Lion King buildings: 6 people; all plus child in crib

Bay Lake Tower at the Contemporary Resort | Studio: 4 people; 1 bedroom: 5 people; 2 bedroom: 9 people; Grand Villa: 12 people; all plus child in crib

Beach Club Resort | 5 people plus child under age 3 in crib

Beach Club Villas | Studio and 1 bedroom: 4 people; 2 bedroom: 8 people; Grand Villa: 12 people; all plus child in crib

BoardWalk Inn | 5 people plus child under age 3 in crib

BoardWalk Villas | Studio and 1 bedroom: 4 people; 2 bedroom: 9 people; Grand Villa: 12 people; all plus child in crib

Boulder Ridge Villas and Copper Creek Villas & Cabins at Wilderness Lodge Boulder Ridge studio: 5 people; Copper Creek studio: 4 people; 1 bedroom: 4 people; 2 bedroom: 8 people; Copper Creek 3 bedroom: 12 people; all plus child in crib

Caribbean Beach Resort | 4 people plus child under age 3 in crib; 5 people in rooms with Murphy bed

Contemporary Resort | 5 people plus child under age 3 in crib

Coronado Springs Resort | 4 people plus child under age 3 in crib

Dolphin *(Sheraton)* | 5 people

Fort Wilderness Cabins | 6 people plus child under age 3 in crib

Gran Destino Tower at Coronado Springs Resort | Standard and executive rooms: 4 people; 1 bedroom: 5 people; Presidential suites: 8 people; all plus a child in crib

Grand Floridian Resort | 5 people plus child under age 3 in crib

Old Key West Resort | Studio: 4 people; 1 bedroom: 5 people; 2 bedroom: 9 people; Grand Villa: 12 people; all plus child in crib

Polynesian Village Resort | 5 people plus child under age 3 in crib

Polynesian Villas & Bungalows | Studio: 5 people plus child in crib; 2 bedroom bungalow: 8 people plus child in crib

Pop Century Resort | 4 people plus child under age 3 in crib

Port Orleans–French Quarter | 4 people plus child under age 3 in crib

Port Orleans–Riverside | 4 people plus child under age 3 in crib or trundle bed; 5 people in rooms with Murphy bed

Riviera Resort | Tower Studio: 2 people; Deluxe Studio and 1 bedroom: 5 people; 2 bedroom: 9 people; Grand Villa: 12 people; all plus a child in crib

Saratoga Springs Resort | Studio and 1 bedroom: 4 people; 2 bedroom: 8 people; Grand Villa: 12 people; all plus child in crib

Swan *(Westin)* | 4 people

Treehouse Villas at Saratoga Springs Resort | 9 people plus child in crib

The Villas at Grand Floridian Resort | Studio and 1 bedroom: 5 people; 2 bedroom: 9 or 10 people; Grand Villa: 12 people; all plus child in crib

Wilderness Lodge | Standard room: 4 people plus child under age 3 in crib; Deluxe room with sleeper sofa: 6 people

Yacht Club Resort | 5 people plus child under age 3 in crib

Readers complain about problems with the Disney transportation system more than most topics. These comments from a Columbus, Ohio, reader are typical:

It sometimes felt like we were visiting Mass Transit World instead of Walt Disney World. More and more [of our] energy was devoted to planning and getting from point A to point B than in the past. I've never rented a car on property, but after this trip I will consider it.

Though it's only for the use and benefit of Disney guests, the Disney transportation system is nonetheless public, and users must expect inconveniences: conveyances that arrive and depart on their schedule, not yours; the occasional need to transfer; multiple stops; time lost loading and unloading passengers; and, generally, the challenge of understanding and using a large, complex transportation network.

Traffic on I-4 is the largest potential problem with staying at an off-site hotel, especially if you're coming or going during rush hours. Thus, the closer your off-site hotel is to Disney property, the less risk there is of being stuck in I-4 traffic.

3. YOUNG CHILDREN Though the hassle of commuting to most non-Disney hotels is only slightly (if at all) greater than that of commuting to Disney hotels, a definite peace of mind results from staying in the World. Regardless of where you stay, make sure you get your young children back to the hotel for a nap each day.

4. SPLITTING UP If your party will likely split up to tour (as frequently happens in families with children of widely varying ages), staying in Walt Disney World offers more transportation options, and therefore more independence.

5. SLOPPIN' THE HOGS If you have a large crew that chows down like pigs at the trough, you may do better staying outside the World, where food is far less expensive. Also, many off-site hotels' prices include some sort of complimentary breakfast.

6. VISITING OTHER ORLANDO-AREA ATTRACTIONS If you plan to visit SeaWorld, Kennedy Space Center, the Universal theme parks, or other area attractions, it may be more convenient to stay outside the World. Remember the number one rule, though: stay close enough to return to your hotel for rest in the middle of the day.

WALT DISNEY WORLD LODGING

BENEFITS OF STAYING IN WALT DISNEY WORLD

IN ADDITION TO PROXIMITY—especially easy access to the Magic Kingdom—Walt Disney World resort hotel and campground guests are accorded other privileges and amenities unavailable to those staying outside the World. Though some of these perks are only advertising gimmicks, others are potentially quite valuable. Here are the benefits and what they mean:

1. EARLY ACCESS TO RIDE AND RESTAURANT RESERVATIONS Disney hotel and campground guests—along with guests staying at the Swan and Dolphin resorts, the Disney Springs Resort Area (DSRA) hotels, the Hilton Bonnet Creek, the Waldorf Astoria, the Four Seasons, and Shades of Green—can make FastPass+ ride reservations 60 days before they arrive, 30 days earlier than the general public. However, only guests staying at a **Disney-owned and -operated resort** can make dining reservations up to 180 days before their visit for the entire length of their stay, up to 10 days.

2. EXTRA MAGIC HOURS AT THE THEME PARKS Guests of all Disney resorts, the Swan and Dolphin, the DSRA hotels, the Hilton Bonnet Creek, the Waldorf Astoria, the Four Seasons, and Shades of Green enjoy this perk, discussed in detail starting on page 53.

3. THEME All of the Disney hotels are themed, in pointed contrast to non-Disney hotels, which are, well, mostly just hotels. Each Disney hotel is designed to make you feel that you're in a special place or period of history. See the table on page 84 that lists the hotels and their themes.

Themed rooms are a huge attraction for children, firing their imaginations and really making the hotel an adventure and a memorable place. Some resorts carry off their themes better than others, and some themes are more exciting. **Wilderness Lodge,** for example, is extraordinary. The lobby opens eight stories to a timbered ceiling supported by giant columns of bundled logs. One look eases you into the Northwest wilderness theme. The isolated lodge is heaven for kids.

Animal Kingdom Lodge & Villas replicate the grand safari lodges of Kenya and Tanzania and overlook their own African-inspired game preserve. By far the most exotic of the Disney resorts, they're made for families with children.

Another kids' favorite is **Treehouse Villas at Saratoga Springs Resort.** Designed in the adventurous image of their 1970s predecessors, the tree houses are nestled in the woods alongside the Lake Buena Vista Golf Course.

The **Polynesian Village Resort & Villas** convey the feeling of the Pacific islands. It's great for families. Kids don't know Polynesia from amnesia, but they like those cool "lodge" buildings and all the torches at night. Many waterfront rooms on upper floors offer perfect views of Cinderella Castle and the Magic Kingdom fireworks across the Seven Seas Lagoon.

Grandeur, nostalgia, and privilege are central to the **Grand Floridian Resort & Villas,** the **Yacht & Beach Club Resorts,** the **Beach Club Villas, Saratoga Springs Resort,** and **BoardWalk Inn & Villas.** Kids appreciate the creative swimming facilities of these resorts but are relatively neutral toward their shared Eastern-seaboard theme.

Port Orleans Resorts lack the mystery and sultriness of New Orleans's French Quarter, but it's hard to replicate the Big Easy in a sanitized Disney version. The Riverside section of Port Orleans, however, hits the

WALT DISNEY WORLD RESORT HOTEL THEMES	
**HOTEL	THEME**	
ALL-STAR RESORTS	Sports, movies, and music
ANIMAL KINGDOM LODGE & VILLAS	East African game-preserve lodge
ART OF ANIMATION RESORT	Disney's animated films
BAY LAKE TOWER AT THE CONTEMPORARY	Ultramodern high-rise
BEACH CLUB RESORT & VILLAS	New England beach club of the 1870s
BOARDWALK INN	East Coast boardwalk hotel of the early 1900s
BOARDWALK VILLAS	East Coast beach cottages of the early 1900s
CARIBBEAN BEACH RESORT	Caribbean islands
CONTEMPORARY RESORT	The future as envisioned by past and present generations
CORONADO SPRINGS RESORT	Northern Mexico and the American Southwest
DOLPHIN *(Sheraton)*	Modern Florida resort
GRAN DESTINO TOWER	Spanish architecture
GRAND FLORIDIAN RESORT & VILLAS	Turn-of-the-20th-century luxury hotel
OLD KEY WEST RESORT	Florida Keys
POLYNESIAN VILLAGE RESORT & VILLAS	Hawaii and South Seas islands
POP CENTURY	Popular-culture icons from various decades of the 20th century
PORT ORLEANS–FRENCH QUARTER	Turn-of-the-19th-century New Orleans
PORT ORLEANS–RIVERSIDE	Antebellum Louisiana plantation and bayou
RIVIERA RESORT	Inspired by the grand hotels of Europe with Mediterranean-themed pools and European-style cuisine
SARATOGA SPRINGS RESORT	1880s Victorian lakeside resort
SWAN *(Westin)*	Modern Florida resort
TREEHOUSE VILLAS	Rustic vacation homes with modern amenities
WILDERNESS LODGE, BOULDER RIDGE VILLAS, AND COPPER CREEK VILLAS & CABINS	Grand national park lodge of the early 1900s
YACHT CLUB RESORT	New England seashore hotel of the 1880s

LILIANE Coronado Springs and the Port Orleans Resorts are among my favorites.

mark with its antebellum Mississippi River theme, as does **Old Key West Resort** with its Florida Keys theme. Children like each of these resorts, even though the themes are a bit removed from their frame of reference. The **Caribbean Beach Resort**'s theme is much more effective at night, thanks to creative lighting. By day, the resort looks like a Miami condo development. Its pirate-themed suites are a big hit with little buccaneers, and the playground and swimming pool fit in nicely with the pirate theme.

Riviera Resort, the 15th Disney Vacation Club property, will open December 2019. Built on several acres of land that were previously part of the Caribbean Beach Resort, the resort is designed to capture the magic of Europe. Lush landscaping, beautiful gardens, and fountains enhance the hotel's waterfront setting. The pools and the S'il Vous Play interactive water play area are sure to impress kids.

Coronado Springs Resort offers several styles of Mexican and Southwestern American architecture. Though the lake setting is lovely and the resort is attractive, the theme (with the exception of the main swimming area) isn't especially stimulating for kids. But like the Caribbean, it's beautiful at night.

The **All-Star Resorts** comprise almost 35 three-story, T-shaped hotels with almost 6,000 guest rooms. There are 15 themed areas: 5 celebrate sports (surfing, basketball, tennis, football, and baseball), 5 recall Hollywood movies, and 5 have musical motifs. The resort's design—with entrances shaped like giant Dalmatians, Coke cups, footballs, and the like—is pretty adolescent, sacrificing grace and beauty for energy and novelty. Guest rooms are small, with decor reminiscent of a teenage boy's bedroom. **Pop Century Resort** is pretty much a clone of All-Star Resorts, only here the giant icons symbolize decades of the 20th century (Big Wheels, 45-rpm records, silhouettes of people doing period dances, and such), and period memorabilia decorates the rooms. Across the lake from Pop Century is **Art of Animation Resort,** with icons and decor based on *Cars, Finding Nemo, The Lion King,* and *The Little Mermaid.*

Pretense aside, the **Contemporary, Bay Lake Tower, Swan,** and **Dolphin** are essentially themeless but architecturally interesting. The Contemporary is a 15-story, A-frame building with monorails running through the middle. Views from guest rooms in the Contemporary are among the best at Walt Disney World. Bay Lake Tower at the Contemporary Resort is a sleek, curvilinear high-rise offering bird's-eye views of Bay Lake. The Swan and Dolphin hotels are massive yet whimsical.

4. GREAT SWIMMING AREAS Disney World resorts offer some of the most imaginative swimming facilities that you are likely to find anywhere. Exotically themed; beautifully landscaped; and equipped with slides, fountains, and smaller pools for toddlers, Disney resort swimming complexes are a quantum leap removed from the typical rectangular hotel pool. The **Grand Floridian** and the **Polynesian** also offer a sand beach on Seven Seas Lagoon. Others, such as the **Caribbean Beach** and **Port Orleans Resorts,** have elaborately themed playgrounds near their swimming areas.

BOB Alligators can be found in almost all bodies of water in Florida, including those at Disney World. Though alligator-related deaths are rare, people can be attacked near the water's edge. Alligators are most active in the late afternoon and at dark. Give them a wide berth (they can run faster than you) and do NOT feed them.

5. DISNEY'S MAGICAL EXPRESS If you arrive in Orlando by air, Disney will collect your checked baggage and send it directly to your Disney World resort, allowing you to bypass baggage claim. Baggage service is available daily, 5 a.m.–10 p.m.; free bus service to your hotel is available 24 hours a day. If your flight arrives in Orlando close to or after 10 p.m., you must collect your own bags and bring them with you on the bus.

When it's time to go home, you can check your baggage and receive your boarding pass at the front desk of your Disney resort.

DISNEY WORLD RESORT POOLS: *Rated and Ranked for Kids*	
RANK/HOTEL	POOL RATING
1. Yacht & Beach Club Resorts and Beach Club Villas *(shared complex)*	★★★★★
2. Grand Floridian Resort & Villas	★★★★½
3. Animal Kingdom Villas *(Kidani Village)*	★★★★½
4. Wilderness Lodge and Boulder Ridge & Copper Creek Villas	★★★★½
5. Port Orleans Resorts	★★★★½
6. Saratoga Springs and Treehouse Villas	★★★★
7. Animal Kingdom Lodge & Villas *(Jambo House)*	★★★★
8. Caribbean Beach Resort	★★★★
9. Coronado Springs Resort and Gran Destino Tower	★★★★
10. Art of Animation Resort	★★★★
11. Riviera Resort	★★★★
12. All-Star Resorts	★★★★
13. Polynesian Village, Villas, & Bungalows	★★★★
14. BoardWalk Inn & Villas	★★★★
15. Bay Lake Tower	★★★★
16. Contemporary Resort	★★★½
17. Swan	★★★½
18. Dolphin	★★★½
19. Old Key West Resort	★★★
20. Fort Wilderness Resort & Campground	★★★
21. Pop Century Resort	★★★
22. Shades of Green	★★★

This service is available to all guests at Disney-owned resorts—but not the Swan, Dolphin, Shades of Green, or Disney Springs resorts—even those who don't use the Magical Express service (folks who have rental cars, for example). Resort check-in counters are open 4 a.m.– noon, and you must check in no later than 4 hours before your flight. Participating airlines are **Alaska, American, Delta** (US domestic flights only), **JetBlue, Southwest,** and **United.** All of the preceding airlines have restrictions on the number of bags, checking procedures, and related items; consult your carrier before leaving home for specifics.

A word about baggage fees: Cast members know that there is no fee for two checked bags on Southwest; for all other airlines, bring proof of prepaid or waived baggage fees when you drop your bags off at the Magical Express service.

Magical Express will pick you up at your resort approximately 3 hours before your scheduled domestic flight, 4 hours prior to an international

LILIANE Just in case your luggage is delayed or your room isn't ready, always pack a change of clothes and bathing suits for all family members in your carry-on luggage. Also keep your MagicBand in your carry-on; you'll be asked for it before boarding Disney's Magical Express.

flight. If your flight departs from Orlando before 8 a.m., Magical Express may pick you up before the Magical Express desk at your resort is open. In this case, you cannot use the resort check-in for your bags or to get your boarding pass. You'll need to handle your own luggage and get your boarding pass at the airport.

Travel agents report few complaints about Magical Express, though it's not without its faults. Luggage is transported by truck to Disney World instead of accompanying you on the bus. Readers have complained of luggage delivered to their hotel rooms hours late, sometimes in the middle of the night. If you want, you can collect your own luggage at baggage claim and bring it with you on the bus; if your room isn't ready when you arrive, the hotel will store your luggage and provide a number you can call to check the status of your room. Some buses go directly to your resort, while others make multiple stops at other resorts. Regarding the return trip to the airport, some readers report barely getting to the airport in time for their flight, while others have been made to depart from their hotel very early.

BOB If you're flying to Orlando and staying on-property, Disney's free transportation network—coupled with ride-hailing services like Lyft and Uber—means you won't need to rent a car.

6. PRIORITY THEME PARK ADMISSIONS On days of unusually heavy attendance, Disney may restrict admission into the theme parks, in which case guests staying at Disney resorts get priority.

7. CHILDREN SHARING A ROOM WITH THEIR PARENTS There's no extra charge per night for children younger than age 18 sharing a room with their parents. Many hotels outside Disney World also offer this perk.

8. FREE PARKING AT THE PARKS Disney resort guests with cars do not pay parking fees at the theme parks; however, Disney charges for overnight parking at its hotels.

WALT DISNEY WORLD HOTELS:
Strengths and Weaknesses for Families

IN THIS SECTION, we've grouped the Disney resorts by location. Closest to the Magic Kingdom are the **Contemporary Resort** and **Bay Lake Tower, Grand Floridian Resort & Villas,** and **Polynesian Village Resort, Villas, & Bungalows,** all on the monorail; **Fort Wilderness Resort & Campground** and the **Wilderness Lodge, Boulder Ridge Villas,** and **Copper Creek Villas & Cabins,** which are connected to the Magic Kingdom by boat; and the US military resort, **Shades of Green,** served by bus. If you are contemplating a stay at a resort on the Magic Kingdom monorail, determine the status of monorail operations before reserving. During much of 2018 and 2019, the monorails (including the Epcot monorail) cut hours of service and frequently were not operating at all. This applies especially to the Grand Floridian and the Polynesian. Service problems have less impact on the Contemporary and Bay Lake Tower because they're within easy walking distance of the Magic Kingdom.

Close to Epcot are the **BoardWalk Inn & Villas, Caribbean Beach, Riviera,** the non-Disney-owned **Swan** and **Dolphin,** the **Yacht & Beach Club Resorts,** and the **Beach Club Villas.** These are also the closest hotels to Disney's Hollywood Studios (DHS).

The **All-Star, Art of Animation, Coronado Springs,** and **Pop Century Resorts** are near both DHS and Animal Kingdom. Closest to the Animal Kingdom is **Animal Kingdom Lodge & Villas.**

Closer to Disney Springs and Bonnet Creek are **Old Key West, Port Orleans,** and **Saratoga Springs Resorts.** Also nearby are the seven independent hotels of the **Disney Springs Resort Area (DSRA).**

Guests at some resorts can now use a smartphone as a room key. You must first opt in and activate the feature on check-in day via the My Disney Experience app. Then you can tap the "Unlock Door" button and simply hold the phone against the door lock. The program started at Wilderness Lodge and will be rolled out at other resorts in stages. Liliane thinks now is a good time to buy an extra charger for your smartphone. Bob wonders when the very expensive, annoying, and wasteful MagicBand system will be discontinued.

MAID SERVICE At some resorts, Disney will offer you $10 per day in gift cards to forgo regular housekeeping service, part of a new program called **Service Your Way.** If you accept the offer, you can still call anytime to have housekeeping remove trash and bring fresh towels, free of charge.

PARKING FEES Guests staying at a Value resort pay $15 per night, those staying at a Moderate resort are charged $20 nightly, and guests at Deluxe resorts are asked to fork over a hefty $25 per night. Shades of Green charges $9 a night. Valet parking at Deluxe resorts is $33. Disney Vacation Club (DVC) members are not charged, regardless of whether they used vacation points or another form of payment for their stay. Complimentary parking is available for guests with disabilities, guests traveling as part of a group or convention, and guests staying at campsites at Fort Wilderness. Guests who wish to dine, shop, enjoy activities, or visit a resort for the day are not charged parking fees.

SECURITY After the Las Vegas and Pulse nightclub shootings, Disney implemented mandatory daily hotel room inspections. These usually happen during each room's normal housekeeping visit. If your room inspection hasn't been completed, call the front desk and have it done before you nap or shower.

MAGIC KINGDOM RESORTS

Disney's Contemporary Resort & Bay Lake Tower

THE CONTEMPORARY RESORT has a sleek, ultramodern look, with an A-frame design that allows the monorail to pass through. And it has lots

STRENGTHS	• Excellent dining options on-site and via monorail
• On the Magic Kingdom monorail	**WEAKNESSES**
• Easy walk to the Magic Kingdom	• Monorail aside, the theme leaves children cold
• Iconic architecture; the only hotel that the monorail goes *through*	• Magic Kingdom–view rooms mostly look out at parking lots and are overpriced
• Large, very attractive guest rooms with nice views of Bay Lake	• Very small studios in Bay Lake Tower sleep no more than 2 people comfortably
• Excellent children's pool	
• Convenient parking	
• Marina	• Bus transportation to DHS, Animal Kingdom, water parks, and Disney Springs shared with other resorts
• Recreational options, including super games arcade	

to offer the active family: six lighted tennis courts, three swimming pools, a health club, volleyball courts, a beach, and a marina that rents boats of various sizes—you must be at least 18 years old, which helps limit the traffic a little. Guest rooms are quite stunning and, in our opinion, the nicest to be found at Walt Disney World. There's no compelling theme, but then show us a child who isn't wowed by monorails tearing though the inside of a hotel.

Bay Lake Tower is a high-rise DVC property situated on Bay Lake between the Contemporary Resort and the Magic Kingdom. Like other DVC developments, it offers studios and one-, two-, and three-bedroom suites. Features include a fireworks-viewing deck, a rooftop lounge (for DVC owners only), a lakeside pool, and a sky bridge linking the tower to the Contemporary Resort's monorail station. Bay Lake Tower has its own check-in desk, as well as its own private pool and pool bar, plus a small fire pit on the beach.

Disney's Fort Wilderness Resort & Campground

STRENGTHS	• Convenient self-parking
• Informality	**WEAKNESSES**
• Children's play areas	• Isolated location
• Best recreational options at WDW	• Complicated bus service
• Special day and evening programs	• Confusing campground layout
• Campsite amenities	• Lack of privacy
• Plentiful showers and toilets	• Very limited on-site dining options
• *Hoop-Dee-Doo Musical Revue* dinner show	• Extreme distance to store and restaurant facilities from many campsites
• Off-site dining options via boat at the Magic Kingdom	• Crowding at beaches and pools
	• Small baths in cabins

IF CAMPING IS ONE OF YOUR HOBBIES, you can rough it in beautiful territory at Fort Wilderness for as little as $75 per campsite. Either set up a tent and use the restrooms, showers, and laundry down the lane, or borrow your parents' RV. With the accessibility of two markets on-site, most visitors here choose to do their own cooking; if you do so, this becomes the absolute rock-bottom-priced Disney World vacation. Prices for a campsite range from $75 for a no-frills tent or pop-up campsite in the off-season to $194 for a full hook-up, premium site during peak season. Cabins ($357–$557) sleep up to six guests. Both options offer free boat and bus service. Complimentary parking for one vehicle is included in the nightly rate.

BOB All loops have a comfort station with showers, toilets, phones, an ice machine, and a coin laundry.

Fort Wilderness is ideal for nature lovers. For the less active, golf carts are for rent. Also available are pools; a marina; a beach; and outdoor activities such as basketball, volleyball, canoeing, biking, and even tennis and horseback riding. If you really get into the mood, you can sit around the evening campfire and watch a movie with the other happy campers. The campsites allow you to have pets (not running loose, of course).

Here's what you *can't* do: drive anywhere *within* the campground (of course, you can drive to enter or exit the campground), not even from your campsite back to the trading post. You must take the bus, rent a bike or golf cart, or walk. Bus or boat transportation to the theme parks can be laborious.

Obviously, Fort Wilderness draws a lot of families (did we mention the wagon rides?) and, in hot weather, a lot of bugs and thunderstorms. If you want things a little more comfortable, ask for a full-service hookup and get water, electricity, an outdoor grill, sanitary disposal, and even a cable-TV connection. If you want super privacy and even more amenities, rent one of the prefab log cabins, which get you a full bathroom, a full kitchen, a living room, a patio and grill, housekeeping services, air-conditioning, and, yes, cable TV.

Disney is constructing a new 900-room hotel called **Reflections–A Disney Lakeside Resort** in the northwest section of Fort Wilderness, just west of the Tri-Circle-D Ranch and on the land of the former River Country water park. Until it opens in 2022, daytime construction activity may be heard in nearby campsite loops.

Disney's Grand Floridian Resort & Spa, Grand Floridian Villas

STRENGTHS	WEAKNESSES
• Boat and monorail transportation to the Magic Kingdom	• Very expensive resort
• Large rooms with daybeds	• Children don't get the theme
• Character meals	• Dining more adult-oriented than at other resorts
• Fantastic *Alice in Wonderland*–themed splash area for kids	• Self-parking across the street
• Diverse recreational options	• Bus transportation to DHS, Animal Kingdom, water parks, and Disney Springs shared with other resorts
• Good restaurant selection via monorail	• Noise from Magic Kingdom and boat horns and whistles
• Brand-new Bibbidi Bobbidi Boutique	

THE GRAND FLORIDIAN HAS A LOT TO OFFER: a white-sand beach, a spa and fitness center, tennis courts, elaborate theatrical dining (from high tea to personal butler service), and so on. But the tone strikes some people as rather hoity-toity, the music in the lobby can be disconcertingly loud, the rooms are not as expansive or good-looking as the public spaces, and the complex is frequently crowded with sightseers. Also, because a wedding chapel is on the grounds, there are frequently receptions, photo sessions, and bridezilla fits—which, depending on your outlook, add charm or are inconveniences. The Villas at the Grand Floridian, a DVC property situated between the main building and the Polynesian Village Resort, along Seven Seas Lagoon, has 200 rooms in studio, one-, two-, and three-bedroom configurations, along with a 0.25-acre kids' pool.

Disney's Polynesian Village Resort, Villas, & Bungalows

STRENGTHS	• Excellent swimming complex and recreational options
• Most family-friendly dining on the monorail loop	**WEAKNESSES**
• Fun South Seas theme that kids love	• Bungalows obstruct the view of some buildings
• Boat and monorail transportation to the Magic Kingdom; walking distance to Epcot monorail	• Noise from boat horns and whistles
	• Inadequate self-parking
• Rooms among the nicest at WDW	• Bus transportation to DHS, Animal Kingdom, water parks, and Disney Springs shared with other resorts
• Character meals	
• Beach and marina	

THE POLYNESIAN IS ARRAYED along the Seven Seas Lagoon facing the Magic Kingdom. It's a huge complex, but the hotel buildings, laid out like a South Seas–island village around a ceremonial house, are of a decidedly human scale compared with the hulking Grand Floridian and Contemporary Resorts. From the tiki torches at night to the bleached-sand beach, kids love the Polynesian.

The villas and bungalows are part of DVC. The bungalows, built on stilts on the Seven Seas Lagoon, offer spectacular views of the Magic Kingdom fireworks and the Electrical Water Pageant on the Seven Seas Lagoon but obstruct the view for some buildings that previously had it. The noise level at the bungalows is terrible. Every time a ferry leaves the dock, which is about every 12 minutes from about an hour before the parks open until an hour after they close, the ferry sounds a warning horn. It's so loud and frequent that we don't recommend staying there if you want to relax during the day, get a baby to nap, or have a good night's sleep. The resort's location at WDW's transportation nexus makes it the most convenient resort for those without a car.

Shades of Green

THIS DELUXE RESORT IS OWNED and operated by the US Armed Forces and is open only to US military personnel (including members of the National Guard and reserves, retired military, employees of the US Public Health Service and the Department of Defense, and their families, as well as foreign military personnel attached to US units and some civilian

SHADES OF GREEN

STRENGTHS	
• Large guest rooms	• Video arcade and game room with pool tables
• Discount tickets for military personnel	**WEAKNESSES**
• Views of golf course from guest rooms	• No interesting theme
• Convenient self-parking	• Limited on-site dining
• Swimming complex, fitness center	• Limited bus service
• On-site car rental in the mornings (Alamo and National)	• No free parking at the theme parks

contractors). Shades of Green consists of one three-story building nestled among three golf courses that are open to all Disney guests. Tastefully nondescript, Shades of Green is at the same time pure peace and quiet. There's no beach or lake, but there are two pools. If you qualify to stay here, don't even think about staying anywhere else. Shades of Green has its own website, shadesofgreen.org.

Disney's Wilderness Lodge, Boulder Ridge Villas, and Copper Creek Villas & Cascade Cabins

STRENGTHS	WEAKNESSES
• Along with Animal Kingdom Lodge, it's the least expensive Deluxe resort	• Transportation to Magic Kingdom is by bus or boat only
• Magnificently rendered theme that children can't get enough of	• Bus transportation to the Magic Kingdom sometimes shared with Fort Wilderness
• Good on-site dining	• Smallest rooms and baths of Disney's Deluxe resorts
• Great views from guest rooms	
• Close to recreational options at Fort Wilderness	• Noise from main building's lobby can be heard inside nearby rooms
• Elaborate swimming complex	• Rooms in main lodge sleep only 4 people (plus child in crib)
• Convenient self-parking	
• Character meal	

THIS DELUXE RESORT IS INSPIRED by national park lodges of the early 20th century. The Wilderness Lodge complex, which includes the DVC properties Boulder Ridge Villas and Copper Creek Villas & Cascade Cabins, ranks with Animal Kingdom Lodge & Villas as one of the most impressively themed and meticulously detailed Disney resorts. It's also the hands-down favorite of children. You won't have any trouble convincing the kids to abandon the theme parks for rest and a swim if you stay at Wilderness Lodge.

On the shore of Bay Lake, the lodge consists of an eight-story central building flanked by two seven-story guest wings and a wing of studio and one- and two-bedroom condominiums. The hotel features exposed timber columns, log cabin–style facades, and dormer windows. The grounds are landscaped with evergreen pines and pampas grass. The lobby boasts an 82-foot-tall stone fireplace and two 55-foot

Pacific Northwest totem poles. Timber pillars, giant tepee chandeliers, and stone- and wood-inlaid floors accentuate the lobby's rustic luxury. Though the resort isn't on vast acreage, it does have a beach, a children's water-play area, and a delightful pool modeled on a mountain stream, complete with waterfall and geyser.

Kids will enjoy the new Story Book Dining at Artist Point, where a forestlike environment inspired by *Snow White and the Seven Dwarfs* awaits. Snow White, a few of her forest-dwelling friends, and the Evil Queen are your hosts.

While prohibitively expensive, the luxurious two-bedroom, two-bathroom lakefront Cascade Cabins are absolutely breathtaking. They come with a fully equipped kitchen, a washer and dryer, a fireplace, and a screened-in wraparound porch with a built-in hot tub. The peaceful, quiet setting is perfect after a busy day in the parks.

EPCOT RESORTS
Disney's BoardWalk Inn & Villas

STRENGTHS	• 3-minute walk to BoardWalk midway and dining options
• Lively seaside and amusement-pier theme	**WEAKNESSES**
• Within walking distance of Epcot's International Gateway and DHS	• Limited quick-service dining options suitable for kids; no character meals
• Boat and Skyliner service to Epcot and DHS	• Limited children's activities
• Modest but well-themed swimming complex	• No transportation to Epcot main entrance
• Health and fitness center	• Bus service to the Magic Kingdom, Animal Kingdom, water parks, and Disney Springs shared with other Epcot resorts
• Views from waterside guest rooms	

ON CRESCENT LAKE, the BoardWalk Inn is a Deluxe resort. The complex is a detailed replica of an early 20th-century Atlantic coast boardwalk. Facades of hotels, diners, and shops create an inviting and exciting waterfront skyline. In reality, behind the facades, the BoardWalk Inn & Villas are a single integrated structure. Restaurants and shops occupy the boardwalk level, while accommodations rise up to six stories above. The inn and villas share one pool with an old-fashioned amusement park theme and have two quiet pools.

Disney's Caribbean Beach Resort

THE CARIBBEAN BEACH RESORT OCCUPIES 200 acres surrounding the 45-acre Barefoot Bay. This midpriced resort, modeled after resorts in the Caribbean, consists of the registration area (Custom House) and five two-story "villages," each with its own pool, laundry room, and beach. The Caribbean motif is maintained with blue-metal roofs, widow's walks, and wooden-railed porches. The atmosphere is cheerful, with buildings painted blue, lime green, and sherbet orange. Rooms in the Trinidad South village are themed to *Finding Nemo* and *Pirates of the Caribbean*.

DISNEY'S CARIBBEAN BEACH RESORT

STRENGTHS	• Skyliner service to Epcot and DHS
• Colorful Caribbean theme	
• Children's play areas	**WEAKNESSES**
• Rooms with *Pirates of the Caribbean* and *Finding Nemo* themes	• Lackluster on-site dining
	• No character meals
• Lakefront setting	• Check-in far from rest of resort
• Large food court	• Multiple bus stops
• One of two Moderate resorts that can sleep five (with a Murphy bed)	• Dining gets low marks from readers
	• Some "villages" a good distance from restaurants and shops
• Five pools and children's activities	

In addition to the five village pools, the resort's main pool is themed as an old Spanish fort, complete with slides and water cannons.

Old Port Royale is home to check-in, shops, and Center Town Market, a counter-service food court. Sebastian's Bistro, the casual table-service restaurant, blends Latin and Caribbean flavors and offers waterfront seating. The resort has plenty of free children's activities, and a pirate adventure (for a fee) is offered daily, weather permitting. The 2-hour, kids-only treasure hunt sets sail from Old Port Royale. On Thursday evenings the Unsolved Mysteries of Barefoot Bay cruise and scavenger hunt is offered for buccaneers ages 10–16. Call ☎ 407-WDW-PLAY (939-7529) for pricing and reservations. The new gondola system connects the resort to DHS and Epcot.

Disney's Riviera Resort *(opens December 2019)*

STRENGTHS	WEAKNESSES
• Character breakfast	• Theme meaningless to children
• Pool with interactive water play area for children	• Except for character breakfast, dining more adult-oriented than at other resorts
• Skyliner service to Epcot and DHS	

DISNEY'S NEWEST, DELUXE French Riviera–themed DVC is located next to the Caribbean Beach Resort. In addition to deluxe studios and one-, two-, and three-bedroom villas, the resort offers tower studios designed for two guests.

The Riviera's restaurants include the quick-service Primo Piatto with grab-and-go options; Le Petit Café, a lobby coffee bar that turns into a wine bar in the evening; and the Bar Riva pool bar serving European- and Mediterranean-style fare. The rooftop Topolino's Terrace is a Signature restaurant, with great views of the nightly fireworks at Epcot and Disney's Hollywood Studios and a prix fixe character breakfast. Did you know that in Italy Mickey Mouse is called Topolino?

The main pool includes S'il Vous Play, an interactive water play area for children. For a more relaxing experience, guests retreat to the Beau Soleil quiet pool.

The Skyliner gondola system connects the resort to Epcot and Hollywood Studios, and the rest of Disney World is accessed via bus.

Walt Disney World Swan & Walt Disney World Dolphin

STRENGTHS	WEAKNESSES
• Best-priced location on Crescent Lake	• Tiny bathrooms at the Swan
• Extremely nice guest rooms	• Spotty front desk service and housekeeping at the Swan
• Good on-site and nearby dining	
• Very nice swimming complex	• Primarily adult convention and business clientele
• Only hotel with on-site childcare	
• Children's programs, character meals	• Distant guest self-parking; daily resort fee
• Only hotels within walking distance of minigolf (Fantasia Gardens)	• No Disney's Magical Express or Disney Dining Plan
• On-site car rental (National and Alamo)	• Bus service to the Magic Kingdom, Animal Kingdom, water parks, and Disney Springs shared with other Epcot resorts
• Participates in Extra Magic Hours program and FastPass+ reservations 60 days out	
• Within walking distance of Epcot's International Gateway and DHS	• Construction noise in west-facing rooms at the Swan through early 2021

THE SWAN AND DOLPHIN HOTELS are not Disney-owned properties, though guests have most of the perks that Disney resort guests have. While Disney handles their reservations, they're owned by Sheraton (Dolphin) and Westin (Swan) and can be booked directly through their parent companies too. Both are served by Disney transportation to the theme parks and are within walking distance to Disney's Hollywood Studios. The Swan and Dolphin also participate in Extra Magic Hours and FastPass+, but neither offers Disney's Magical Express bus service nor participates in the Disney Dining Plan. Besides those, the same amenities found at Disney Deluxe resorts are found at the Dolphin. Both resorts have a $30-per-night resort fee, as well as a nightly parking fee (as do Disney hotels). (Disney theme park parking is still free.)

The Swan and Dolphin are patronized by business types and adult travelers rather than families, and their theme is more surrealistic than whimsical. That said, a quick glance at the Swan and Dolphin's strengths will verify that they have as much or more to offer families than the Disney resorts. Multiple pools, a sandy beach, swan boats, the Grotto Pool's waterfall, and a waterslide are sure to wow kids.

A new 14-story hotel called The Cove is being constructed across the street from the Swan and Dolphin, adjacent to Disney's Fantasia Gardens miniature golf course. When The Cove opens in 2021, it will have 198 standard rooms, 151 high-tech suites aimed at business travelers, a restaurant, a pool, and meeting space.

Disney's Yacht & Beach Club Resorts and Beach Club Villas

SITUATED ON CRESCENT LAKE across from Disney's BoardWalk, the Yacht & Beach Club Resorts are connected and share a boardwalk,

DISNEY'S YACHT & BEACH CLUB RESORTS AND BEACH CLUB VILLAS

STRENGTHS	• Best pool complex of any WDW resort
• Fun nautical New England theme	• Convenient self-parking
• Attractive guest rooms	• View from waterside guest rooms
• Children's programs, character meals	**WEAKNESSES**
• Boat and Skyliner service to Epcot and DHS	• Bus service to the Magic Kingdom, Animal Kingdom, water parks, and Disney Springs shared with other Epcot resorts
• Within walking distance of Epcot's International Gateway	• No convenient counter-service food
• Close to many BoardWalk and Epcot dining options	• Views and balcony size are hit-or-miss

marina, and swimming complex. The Yacht Club Resort has a breezy Nantucket and Cape Cod atmosphere with its own lighthouse, lots of polished wood, and burnished brass. Its sibling resort, the Beach Club, shares most of the facilities but is a little sportier and more casual in atmosphere. The DVC Villas at the Beach Club are available for rent, have their own small pool, and may offer more privacy. The resorts offer a shared mini–water park, Stormalong Bay, with a white-sand beach and marina, as well as an unusual number of facilities for sports, such as tennis and volleyball, plus fitness rooms and more. Many of the guest rooms have balconies, though a relatively small percentage look across the lake toward the BoardWalk. Pirates ages 4–12 can embark on the Albatross Treasure Cruise sailing around Crescent Lake and Epcot's Showcase Lagoon. The 2-hour, kids-only treasure hunt departs from the Bayside Marina on Monday, Wednesday, and Friday. Call ☎ 407-WDW-PLAY (939-7529) for pricing and reservations.

ANIMAL KINGDOM RESORTS
Disney's All-Star Resorts: Movies, Music, & Sports

STRENGTHS	WEAKNESSES
• Least expensive of the Disney resorts	• Older rooms feel small and in need of update
• Very kid-friendly theme	
• Lots of pools	• No full-service dining; food courts often overwhelmed at mealtimes
• Food courts and in-room pizza delivery	• No character meals
• Family Suites at All-Star Music are less expensive than those at Art of Animation	• All three resorts share buses during slower times of year; bus stops often crowded
• Convenient parking	• Limited recreation options

DISNEY'S VERSION OF A BUDGET RESORT features three distinct themes executed in the same hyperbolic style. Spread over a vast expanse, the resorts comprise 30 three-story motel-style guest room buildings. Each resort has its own lobby, food court, and registration area. All-Star Sports features huge sports equipment: bright football helmets, tennis rackets, and baseball bats, all taller than the buildings they adorn. Similarly, All-Star Music features 40-foot guitars, maracas, and saxophones, while All-Star Movies showcases giant popcorn boxes and icons from Disney films. Lobbies of all are loud (in both decibels and brightness) and cartoonish, with checkerboard walls and photographs of famous athletes, musicians, or film stars, and they also have a dedicated area for kids to watch Disney shows and movies while parents are checking in.

At 260 square feet, guest rooms are very small—so small, in fact, that a family of four attempting to stay in one room might redefine *family values* by week's end. The All-Stars are the noisiest Disney resorts, though guest rooms are well soundproofed and quiet. Each resort has two main pools, all featuring replicas of Disney characters.

All-Star Music has 192 Family Suites in the Jazz and Calypso Buildings. Suites measure roughly 520 square feet, slightly larger than the cabins at Fort Wilderness but slightly smaller than Art of Animation's Family Suites. Each suite, formed from the combination of two formerly separate rooms, includes a kitchenette with mini-fridge, microwave, and coffee maker. Sleeping accommodations include a queen bed in the bedroom, plus a pullout sleeper sofa, a chair bed, and an ottoman bed. A hefty door separates the two rooms.

All-Star Resorts, starting with the All-Star Movies' rooms, are being refurbished, and we love the new look. The work is yet to be completed. If you wish to get a refurbished room, make a request for the Toy Story or Fantasia rooms (no guarantees). Disney hasn't announced how long it will take to complete the renovations and when the other All-Stars will be done. We expect the last resort refurbishments to be completed in 2021.

We receive a lot of letters commenting on the All-Star Resorts. From a Massachusetts family of four:

> I would never recommend the All-Star for a family. It was like dormitory living. Our room was about 1 mile from the bus stop, and the room was tiny—you needed to step into the bathroom, shut the door, and then step around the toilet that blocked half the tub.

But a Baltimore family had a positive experience:

> Yes, the rooms are small, but the overall magic there is amazing. The lobby played Disney movies, which is perfect if you get up early and the buses aren't running yet. Customer service was impeccable.

Disney's Animal Kingdom Lodge & Villas

TAILOR-MADE FOR FAMILIES, Animal Kingdom Lodge is a snazzy take on safari chic, with balcony views of wildlife that alone may be worth the tab. Its distance from the other parks may be a drawback for those planning to explore all of Disney World, but on the other hand, if you have a car, it's the closest resort to the affordable family restaurants lining US 192 (Irlo Bronson Memorial Highway).

DISNEY'S ANIMAL KINGDOM LODGE & VILLAS

STRENGTHS	WEAKNESSES
• Exotic theme	• On-site nature programs and storytelling
• Most rooms have private balconies	**WEAKNESSES**
• View of savanna and animals from guest rooms	• Remote location
• Creatively themed swimming areas	• Rooms are dark and outdated, in need of refurbishment
• Excellent on-site dining, including a buffet	• Savanna views can be hit-or-miss
	• Limited counter-service dining
	• Erratic bus service
• Proximity to non-Disney restaurants on US 192	• Jambo House villas are smaller than those at Kidani Village

The lodge fuses African tribal architecture with the rugged style of grand East African national park lodges. Five-story thatched-roofed wings fan out from a vast central rotunda that houses the lobby and features a huge mud fireplace. Public areas and many rooms offer panoramic views of a private 21-acre wildlife preserve punctuated with streams and elevated kopje (rock outcrops) and populated with some 200 free-roaming hoofed animals and birds. Most of the lodge's guest rooms boast hand-carved furnishings and richly colored upholstery. Almost all rooms have full balconies.

Studio and one-, two-, and three-bedroom villa accommodations are available at Jambo House (the main building) and adjacent Kidani Village, a DVC property. Having stayed at Kidani Village, we think it's a quieter, more relaxed experience. The lobby and rooms have a more personal feel than Jambo House's, and Kidani's distance from Jambo House makes it feel remote. The bus stops are a fair distance from the main building too, and it's easy to head in the wrong direction when you're coming back from the parks at night.

Except for the three-bedroom units, most rooms at Kidani are larger than their counterparts at Jambo House, anywhere from 50 square feet for a studio to more than 200 square feet for a two-bedroom unit. Kidani's villas also have one more bathroom for one-, two-, and three-bedroom units.

Besides theming, Jambo House's strength is its upscale dining options: readers place all three sit-down restaurants at Animal Kingdom Lodge among Walt Disney World's top 10. Other amenities include a village marketplace, outdoor movies nightly, and a nightly campfire hosted by African cast members.

A Starlight Safari tour is offered to guests age 8 and up. The tour costs $79 (tax included) and leaves nightly (weather permitting) at 8:30 p.m. and 10 p.m. Cast members meet participants at Sanaa, and, equipped with night-vision goggles, they board a safari truck for their 1-hour trip through the savanna. Guests staying on other WDW properties and even non-Disney properties can book this tour.

Disney's Art of Animation Resort

STRENGTHS	• Skyliner service to Epcot and DHS
• Exceptional theming	**WEAKNESSES**
• Family Suites are well designed	• Most expensive Value resort
• Best pool of the Value resorts	• No full-service dining or character
• Food court	meals
• Some buildings offer interior hallways	• Rooms not as nice as new rooms at
• One bus stop	Pop Century and All-Star Movies

ART OF ANIMATION RESORT DRAWS its inspiration from four Disney animated films: *The Lion King* and *The Little Mermaid,* as well as Disney-Pixar's *Finding Nemo* and *Cars.*

The Value resort, located across Hour Glass Lake from Pop Century, has 864 rooms and 1,120 Family Suites. The latter have two separate bathrooms, a master bedroom, three separate sleeping areas within the living space, and a kitchenette. The resort consists of four-story buildings and a series of themed swimming pools, including a large feature pool at the *Finding Nemo* courtyard. A water-play area, as well as a 68,800-square-foot commercial building with shopping and dining space, completes the picture. As at Pop Century, large, colorful icons stand in the middle of each group of buildings; here, though, they represent film characters rather than pop-culture touchstones.

Three of the four sets of themed buildings have pools; the *Lion King* complex has a playground instead. Like the other Value resorts, Art of Animation has a central building—here called Animation Hall—for check-in and bus transportation; it also holds the food court, Landscape of Flavors; a gift shop; and a video arcade.

Reader reports on Art of Animation have mostly been positive. A mom from Blountville, Tennessee, says:

> The Art of Animation Resort was the highlight of our trip! Our daughter loves The Little Mermaid, *and the rooms, while small and basic, were adorable. The courtyards, the pools, the main lobby areas, etc.— Disney is fantastic at attention to detail. Our daughter loved pointing out* Lion King, Finding Nemo, *and* Little Mermaid *characters.*

Disney's Coronado Springs Resort & Gran Destino Tower

TO SAVE A LITTLE MONEY without giving up services, consider Coronado Springs Resort, a rich, Old Mexico–style complex with courtyards, fountains, stucco and terra-cotta buildings, a few Mayan ruins here and there, several swimming pools, a mini–water park, a white-sand beach, a fitness center, a walking path circling a 14-acre lake, and a nightclub. Rix Sports Bar and Grill serves both lunch and dinner, while the Maya Grill serves Mexican fare at dinner. The former Pepper Market food court has been renamed El Mercado de Coronado and is open for breakfast, lunch, and dinner. Because Coronado Springs is also a convention hotel, expect a high percentage of guests to be business travelers.

DISNEY'S CORONADO SPRINGS RESORT & GRAN DESTINO TOWER

STRENGTHS	WEAKNESSES
• Nice renovated guest rooms; beautiful guest rooms at Gran Destino Tower	• Conventioneers may be off-putting to vacationing families
• Food court	• No character meals
• Mayan-themed swimming area with waterslides	• Multiple bus stops
• Setting is beautiful at night	• Extreme distance of many guest rooms from dining and services
• Rooftop dining at Gran Destino Tower	• Theme at Gran Destino Tower meaningless to children
• Plenty of on-site dining at Gran Destino Tower	• Dining more adult-oriented at Gran Destino Tower than at other resorts

The resort has particularly good access to Animal Kingdom and Blizzard Beach. The rooms were refurbished in 2017 and 2018.

LILIANE I enjoy dining at the brand-new Toledo rooftop restaurant at the Gran Destino Tower while watching the nighttime fireworks.

In July 2019 the 15-story Gran Destino Tower opened. The tower is now the main lobby for the entire resort. Toledo offers tapas, steak, and seafood in a rooftop setting overlooking Lago Dorado and the fireworks from nearby parks.

The decor of Gran Destino Tower is inspired by Spanish architecture. The new tower has 545 rooms, including standard rooms and executive, one-bedroom, and presidential suites.

Nestled in the middle of the lake is Three Bridges Bar & Grill. The eatery is connected to the resorts by three walkways across the lake.

Disney's Pop Century Resort

STRENGTHS	WEAKNESSES
• Large swimming pools	• Theming holds more appeal for adults than for kids and teens
• Food court and in-room pizza delivery	
• Convenient self-parking	• Small rooms are the same size as All-Stars' but slightly more expensive
• Fast check-in	
• Stylish new room design	• No full-service dining or character meals
• One bus stop	
• Skyliner service to Epcot and DHS	• Limited recreation options

ON VICTORY WAY near the ESPN Wide World of Sports Complex is Pop Century Resort, an economy resort and a near-clone of the All-Star Resorts (that is, four-story, motel-style buildings around a central pool, food court, and registration area). Decorative touches make the difference. Where the All-Stars display larger-than-life icons from sports, music, and movies, Pop Century draws its icons from decades of the 20th century. Look for such oddities as building-size Big Wheels and Hula-Hoops, punctuated by silhouettes of people dancing the decade's fad dance.

The public areas are marginally more sophisticated than the ones at the All-Star Resorts, with 20th-century period furniture and decor

rolled up in a saccharine, those-were-the-days theme. The food court, bar, playground, pools, and so on emulate the All-Star model in size and location, but a Pop Century departure from the All-Star precedent has merchandise retailers thrown in with the fast-food concessions in a combination dining-and-shopping area. (The Hippy Dippy pool will be closed for refurbishment beginning in 2020.) The resort is connected to Epcot and DHS by the Skyliner gondola and to the rest of Walt Disney World by bus, but because of the limited dining options, we recommend having a car.

After a major refurbishment in 2018, we think Pop Century has the best rooms of any Disney Value resort. The carpet has been replaced with a modern hardwood-floor look, and space-saving storage areas, including built-in shelving, are everywhere. The second bed in the room is a fold-down option, as at the Art of Animation. When the bed isn't in use, it disappears into the wall, freeing up floor space (and turning into a desk). The bathroom overhaul is stylish and efficient, with lots more shelf space, plenty of storage, and a modern shower. A lake separating Pop Century from the Art of Animation Resort offers water views not available at the All-Star Resorts.

A reader from Dublin, Georgia, likes Pop Century for several reasons:

> *(1) It's far superior to the All-Star Resorts. (2) There's a lake and a view of fireworks. (3) The courtyards have Twister games and neat pools for children. (4) The memorabilia is interesting to us of a certain age. (5) I love the gift shop, food court, and bar combo. The [dinner entrées are among] the best bargains and the best food anywhere. (6) Bus transportation is better than anywhere else, including Grand Floridian! (7) The layout is more convenient to the food court. (8) The noise from neighbors is not worse than anywhere else. (9) Where else do the cast members do the shag to oldies?*

BONNET CREEK/DISNEY SPRINGS AREA RESORTS
Disney's Old Key West Resort

STRENGTHS	WEAKNESSES
	• Boat service to Disney Springs
• Largest villas of the DVC/DDV resorts, with full kitchens	**WEAKNESSES**
	• Theme meaningless to children
• Quiet, lushly landscaped setting	• Large, confusing layout
• Convenient self-parking	• Multiple bus stops
• Small, more private swimming pools in each accommodations cluster	• Mediocre on-site dining, no character meals
• Nice family pool with waterslide and free sauna for parents inside lighthouse	• No easily accessible off-site dining
• Recreation options	• Extreme distance of many guest rooms from dining and services

THIS WAS THE FIRST DVC PROPERTY. Though the resort is a time-share property, units not being used by owners are rented on a nightly basis.

Old Key West is a large aggregation of two- to three-story buildings modeled after Caribbean-style residences and guesthouses of the Florida Keys. Arranged subdivision-style around a golf course and along Bonnet Creek, the buildings are in small neighborhood-like clusters and feature pastel facades, white trim, and shuttered windows. The registration area—along with a full-service restaurant, modest fitness center, marina, and sundries shop—is in Conch Flats Community Hall. Each cluster of accommodations has a quiet pool; a larger pool is at the community hall. A waterslide in the shape of a giant sandcastle is the primary kid pleaser at the main pool.

Each villa has a private balcony with views of the golf course, the landscape, or a waterway; the waterway views are among the best of any Walt Disney World resort. The resort completed its latest refurbishment in the summer of 2019.

Disney's Port Orleans Resorts–French Quarter and Riverside

STRENGTHS	• Varied recreational offerings
• Aquatic play area and creative pool	• Boat service to Disney Springs
• Riverside is one of two Moderate resorts that can sleep 5 (with a Murphy bed at Alligator Bayou)	**WEAKNESSES**
	• No full-service dining at French Quarter; no character meals
• Disney princess–themed rooms at Magnolia Bend (Riverside)	• Extreme distance of many guest rooms from dining and services
• Food courts	
• Convenient self-parking	• French Quarter and Riverside may share bus service during slower times of year
• Children's play areas	

THE PORT ORLEANS RESORTS are good-looking, lower-cost hotel alternatives with fairly easy access to Disney Springs, and they're pretty popular among families too.

The 1,008-room French Quarter section is a sanitized Disney version of the New Orleans French Quarter. Consisting of seven three-story buildings next to the Sassagoula River, the resort suggests what New Orleans would look like if its buildings were painted every year and its garbage collectors never went on strike. Wrought iron filigree, shuttered windows, and old-fashioned iron lampposts festoon prim pink-and-blue guest buildings. In keeping with the Crescent City theme, French Quarter is landscaped with magnolia trees and overgrown vines. The centrally located Mint, containing the registration area and food court, is a reproduction of a turn-of-the-19th-century building where Mississippi Delta farmers sold their harvests; the registration desk features a vibrant Mardi Gras mural and old-fashioned bank-teller windows. The Doubloon Lagoon swimming complex surrounds a colorful fiberglass creation depicting Neptune riding a sea serpent. We think French Quarter has the most attractive and tasteful rooms of any of the Disney Moderate resorts. If your visit falls on Mardi Gras, be sure to watch the annual cast member parade and enjoy free activities at the courtyard party at French Quarter.

Port Orleans Resort–Riverside draws on the lifestyle and architecture of Mississippi River communities in antebellum Louisiana. Spread along the Sassagoula River, which encircles Ol' Man Island (the section's main swimming area), Riverside is subdivided into two more themed areas: the "mansion" area, featuring plantation-style architecture, and the "bayou" area, with tin-roofed imitation-rustic wooden buildings. Mansions are three stories tall, while bayou guesthouses are a story shorter. A set of 512 rooms is themed to Disney's *The Princess and the Frog*. Rooms in Alligator Bayou started a refurbishment program in late 2018 that continues into 2019. Riverside's food court houses a working cotton press powered by a 35-foot waterwheel. The table-service Boatwright's Dining Hall is located inside the main Sassagoula Steamboat Company building, between the River Roost Lounge and the Riverside Mill food court. The restaurant is open for dinner only and serves Southern fare. The main reader gripes about Riverside are its food options and its bus service.

Disney's Saratoga Springs Resort & Spa and Treehouse Villas

STRENGTHS	• No character meals
• Lushly landscaped setting	• Rooms in need of refurbishment
• Very nice spa and fitness center	• Theme and atmosphere not very kid-friendly
• Convenient self-parking	
• Closest resort to Disney Springs and Typhoon Lagoon	• Limited number of units makes the Treehouses among the most difficult accommodations to book at WDW
• Nice themed swimming complex	
• Hiking, jogging, and water recreation	• Bus service takes some time to get out of the (huge) resort; internal bus service slow and inconvenient
WEAKNESSES	
• Limited dining options	

THE MAIN POOL IS THIS RESORT'S FOCAL POINT. Called High Rock Spring, it tumbles over boulders into a clear, free-form heated pool. The area offers a waterslide that winds among the rocks, two hot tubs, and an interactive water-play area for children. Saratoga Springs is the largest DVC resort, with a path and a pedestrian bridge connecting it to the Disney Springs shopping area (across the lake). There is boat and bus service at the facility, though the boats don't run if lightning threatens. The resort's decor plays on the history and retro-Victorian style of the upstate New York racing resort, with traditional horse-country prints and drawings, stable-boy uniforms for the bellhops, and so on. The spa has a fitness center attached.

Favorites of kids are the Treehouse Villas, nestled in a pinewood bordering the golf course. With the living and sleeping areas about 10 feet off the ground, you really do feel like you're in a tree house. There are only 60 three-bedroom units, so if you want to reserve one, book well in advance. Bus travelers connect via Saratoga Springs, a major hassle.

continued on page 107

WDW RESORTS AT A GLANCE

All-Star Movies Resort ★★★½
1901 W. Buena Vista Dr.
Lake Buena Vista, FL 32830
☎ 407-939-7000
tinyurl.com/allstarmovies

| ROOM RATING | 80 |
| COST | $150+ |

Commuting times to parks (in minutes):
MAGIC KINGDOM	6:15
EPCOT	5:45
ANIMAL KINGDOM	4:15
DHS	5:15

All-Star Music Resort ★★★
1801 W. Buena Vista Dr.
Lake Buena Vista, FL 32830
☎ 407-939-6000
tinyurl.com/allstarmusicresort

| ROOM RATING | 73 |
| COST | $150+ |

Commuting times to parks (in minutes):
MAGIC KINGDOM	6:15
EPCOT	5:45
ANIMAL KINGDOM	4:15
DHS	5:15

All-Star Sports Resort ★★★
1701 W. Buena Vista Dr.
Lake Buena Vista, FL 32830
☎ 407-939-5000
tinyurl.com/allstarsports

| ROOM RATING | 73 |
| COST | $150+ |

Commuting times to parks (in minutes):
MAGIC KINGDOM	6:15
EPCOT	5:45
ANIMAL KINGDOM	4:15
DHS	5:15

Art of Animation Resort
★★★½
1850 Animation Way
Lake Buena Vista, FL 32830
☎ 407-938-7000
tinyurl.com/artofanimationresort

| ROOM RATING | 80 |
| COST | $200+ |

Commuting times to parks (in minutes):
MAGIC KINGDOM	12:00
EPCOT	10:00
ANIMAL KINGDOM	12:00
DHS	3:00

**Bay Lake Tower at
Contemporary Resort**
★★★★½
4600 N. World Dr.
Lake Buena Vista, FL 32830
☎ 407-824-1000
tinyurl.com/baylaketower

| ROOM RATING | 95 |
| COST | $650 |

Commuting times to parks (in minutes):
MAGIC KINGDOM	on monorail
EPCOT	11:00
ANIMAL KINGDOM	17:15
DHS	14:15

Beach Club Resort ★★★★
1800 Epcot Resorts Blvd.
Lake Buena Vista, FL 32830
☎ 407-934-8000
tinyurl.com/disneybeachclub

| ROOM RATING | 89 |
| COST | $550+ |

Commuting times to parks (in minutes):
MAGIC KINGDOM	7:15
EPCOT	5:15
ANIMAL KINGDOM	6:45
DHS	4:00

**Boulder Ridge Villas at
Wilderness Lodge** ★★★★
901 Timberline Dr.
Lake Buena Vista, FL 32830
☎ 407-824-3200
tinyurl.com/wlvillas

| ROOM RATING | 84 |
| COST | $550 |

Commuting times to parks (in minutes):
MAGIC KINGDOM	by ferry
EPCOT	10:00
ANIMAL KINGDOM	15:15
DHS	13:30

Caribbean Beach Resort
★★★½
1114 Cayman Way
Lake Buena Vista, FL 32830
☎ 407-934-3400
tinyurl.com/caribbeanbeachresort

| ROOM RATING | 80 |
| COST | $250+ |

Commuting times to parks (in minutes):
MAGIC KINGDOM	8:00
EPCOT	6:00
ANIMAL KINGDOM	7:15
DHS	4:15

Contemporary Resort
★★★★½
4600 N. World Dr.
Lake Buena Vista, FL 32830
☎ 407-824-1000
tinyurl.com/contemporarywdw

| ROOM RATING | 91 |
| COST | $550+ |

Commuting times to parks (in minutes):
MAGIC KINGDOM	on monorail
EPCOT	11:00
ANIMAL KINGDOM	17:15
DHS	14:15

Fort Wilderness Resort (cabins)
★★★★½
4510 N. Fort Wilderness Trail
Lake Buena Vista, FL 32830
☎ 407-824-2900
tinyurl.com/ftwilderness

| ROOM RATING | 90 |
| COST | $500− |

Commuting times to parks (in minutes):
MAGIC KINGDOM	13:15
EPCOT	8:30
ANIMAL KINGDOM	20:00
DHS	14:00

**Gran Destino Tower at
Coronado Springs Resort**
★★★★½
1000 W. Buena Vista Dr.
Orlando, FL 32830
☎ 407-939-1000
tinyurl.com/coronadosprings

| ROOM RATING | 92 |
| COST | $350+ |

Commuting times to parks (in minutes):
MAGIC KINGDOM	5:30
EPCOT	4:00
ANIMAL KINGDOM	4:45
DHS	4:45

Grand Floridian Resort & Spa
★★★★½
4401 Floridian Way
Lake Buena Vista, FL 32830
☎ 407-824-3000
tinyurl.com/grandflresort

| ROOM RATING | 93 |
| COST | $750− |

Commuting times to parks (in minutes):
MAGIC KINGDOM	on monorail
EPCOT	4:45
ANIMAL KINGDOM	11:45
DHS	6:45

Animal Kingdom Lodge
★ ★ ★ ★
2901 Osceola Pkwy.
Lake Buena Vista, FL 32830
☎ 407-938-3000
tinyurl.com/aklodge

| ROOM RATING | 86 |
| COST | $450+ |

Commuting times to parks (*in minutes*):
MAGIC KINGDOM	8:15
EPCOT	6:15
ANIMAL KINGDOM	2:15
DHS	6:00

Animal Kingdom Villas (Jambo House) ★ ★ ★ ★
2901 Osceola Pkwy.
Lake Buena Vista, FL 32830
☎ 407-938-3000
tinyurl.com/akjambo

| ROOM RATING | 86 |
| COST | $450 |

Commuting times to parks (*in minutes*):
MAGIC KINGDOM	8:15
EPCOT	6:15
ANIMAL KINGDOM	2:15
DHS	6:00

Animal Kingdom Villas (Kidani Village) ★ ★ ★ ★ ½
3701 Osceola Pkwy.
Lake Buena Vista, FL 32830
☎ 407-938-7400
tinyurl.com/akkidani

| ROOM RATING | 90 |
| COST | $550– |

Commuting times to parks (*in minutes*):
MAGIC KINGDOM	8:15
EPCOT	6:15
ANIMAL KINGDOM	2:15
DHS	6:00

Beach Club Villas ★ ★ ★ ★
1800 Epcot Resorts Blvd.
Lake Buena Vista, FL 32830
☎ 407-934-8000
tinyurl.com/beachclubvillas

| ROOM RATING | 86 |
| COST | $600– |

Commuting times to parks (*in minutes*):
MAGIC KINGDOM	7:15
EPCOT	5:15
ANIMAL KINGDOM	6:45
DHS	4:00

BoardWalk Inn ★ ★ ★ ★
2101 N. Epcot Resorts Blvd.
Lake Buena Vista, FL 32830
☎ 407-939-6200
tinyurl.com/boardwalkinn

| ROOM RATING | 89 |
| COST | $550+ |

Commuting times to parks (*in minutes*):
MAGIC KINGDOM	7:15
EPCOT	-5:30
ANIMAL KINGDOM	7:00
DHS	3:00

BoardWalk Villas ★ ★ ★ ★
2101 N. Epcot Resorts Blvd.
Lake Buena Vista, FL 32830
☎ 407-939-6200
tinyurl.com/boardwalkvillas

| ROOM RATING | 89 |
| COST | $450+ |

Commuting times to parks (*in minutes*):
MAGIC KINGDOM	7:15
EPCOT	5:30
ANIMAL KINGDOM	7:00
DHS	3:00

Copper Creek Villas & Cabins at Wilderness Lodge ★ ★ ★ ★ ½
901 Timberline Dr.
Lake Buena Vista, FL 32830
☎ 407-824-3200
tinyurl.com/wdwcoppercreek

| ROOM RATING | 90 |
| COST | $550+ |

Commuting times to parks (*in minutes*):
MAGIC KINGDOM	by ferry
EPCOT	10:00
ANIMAL KINGDOM	15:15
DHS	13:30

Coronado Springs Resort
★ ★ ★ ★
1000 W. Buena Vista Dr.
Orlando, FL 32830
☎ 407-939-1000
tinyurl.com/coronadosprings

| ROOM RATING | 88 |
| COST | $250+ |

Commuting times to parks (*in minutes*):
MAGIC KINGDOM	5:30
EPCOT	4:00
ANIMAL KINGDOM	4:45
DHS	4:45

Dolphin ★ ★ ★ ★
1500 Epcot Resorts Blvd.
Lake Buena Vista, FL 32830
☎ 407-934-4000
swandolphin.com

| ROOM RATING | 87 |
| COST | $300 |

Commuting times to parks (*in minutes*):
MAGIC KINGDOM	6:45
EPCOT	5:00
ANIMAL KINGDOM	6:15
DHS	4:00

Old Key West Resort
★ ★ ★ ★ ½
1510 N. Cove Road
Lake Buena Vista, FL 32830
☎ 407-827-7700
tinyurl.com/oldkeywest

| ROOM RATING | 91 |
| COST | $450+ |

Commuting times to parks (*in minutes*):
MAGIC KINGDOM	10:45
EPCOT	6:00
ANIMAL KINGDOM	14:30
DHS	10:30

Polynesian Village Resort
★ ★ ★ ★
1600 Seven Seas Dr.
Lake Buena Vista, FL 32830
☎ 407-824-2000
tinyurl.com/wdwpolyvillage

| ROOM RATING | 87 |
| COST | $650– |

Commuting times to parks (*in minutes*):
MAGIC KINGDOM	on monorail
EPCOT	8:00
ANIMAL KINGDOM	16:15
DHS	12:30

Polynesian Villas & Bungalows (studios) ★ ★ ★ ★
1600 Seven Seas Dr.
Lake Buena Vista, FL 32830
☎ 407-824-2000
tinyurl.com/wdwpolyvillage

| ROOM RATING | 88 |
| COST | $650 |

Commuting times to parks (*in minutes*):
MAGIC KINGDOM	on monorail
EPCOT	8:00
ANIMAL KINGDOM	16:15
DHS	12:30

WDW RESORTS AT A GLANCE (continued)

Pop Century Resort ★★★½
1050 Century Dr.
Lake Buena Vista, FL 32830
☎ 407-938-4000
tinyurl.com/popcenturywdw

ROOM RATING	80
COST	$200-

Commuting times to parks (in minutes):

MAGIC KINGDOM	8:30
EPCOT	6:30
ANIMAL KINGDOM	6:15
DHS	5:00

Port Orleans Resort–French Quarter ★★★★
2201 Orleans Dr.
Lake Buena Vista, FL 32830
☎ 407-934-5000
tinyurl.com/portorleansfq

ROOM RATING	87
COST	$300-

Commuting times to parks (in minutes):

MAGIC KINGDOM	12:00
EPCOT	8:00
ANIMAL KINGDOM	16:15
DHS	12:30

Port Orleans Resort–Riverside ★★★★
1251 Riverside Dr.
Lake Buena Vista, FL 32830
☎ 407-934-6000
tinyurl.com/portorleansriverside

ROOM RATING	83
COST	$300-

Commuting times to parks (in minutes):

MAGIC KINGDOM	12:00
EPCOT	8:00
ANIMAL KINGDOM	16:15
DHS	12:30

Riviera Resort ★★★★½
1080 Sea Breeze Dr.
Lake Buena Vista, FL 32830
☎ 407-939-7762
tinyurl.com/disneyriviera

ROOM RATING	95
COST	$500-

Commuting times to parks (in minutes):

MAGIC KINGDOM	8:00
EPCOT	6:00
ANIMAL KINGDOM	7:15
DHS	4:15

Saratoga Springs Resort & Spa ★★★★
1960 Broadway
Lake Buena Vista, FL 32830
☎ 407-827-1100
tinyurl.com/saratogawdw

ROOM RATING	84
COST	$450+

Commuting times to parks (in minutes):

MAGIC KINGDOM	14:45
EPCOT	8:45
ANIMAL KINGDOM	18:15
DHS	14:30

Shades of Green ★★★★½
1950 W. Magnolia Palm Dr.
Lake Buena Vista, FL 32830
☎ 407-824-3400
shadesofgreen.org

ROOM RATING	91
COST	$100+

Commuting times to parks (in minutes):

MAGIC KINGDOM	3:30
EPCOT	4:45
ANIMAL KINGDOM	9:30
DHS	6:15

Swan ★★★★
1200 Epcot Resorts Blvd.
Lake Buena Vista, FL 32830
☎ 407-934-3000
swandolphin.com

ROOM RATING	89
COST	$350

Commuting times to parks (in minutes):

MAGIC KINGDOM	6:30
EPCOT	4:45
ANIMAL KINGDOM	6:15
DHS	4:00

Treehouse Villas at Saratoga Springs Resort & Spa ★★★★½
1960 Broadway
Lake Buena Vista, FL 32830
☎ 407-827-1100
tinyurl.com/saratogawdw

ROOM RATING	90
COST	$1,050+

Commuting times to parks (in minutes):

MAGIC KINGDOM	12:45
EPCOT	7:15
ANIMAL KINGDOM	16:45
DHS	12:30

The Villas at Grand Floridian Resort & Spa ★★★★½
4401 Floridian Way
Lake Buena Vista, FL 32830
☎ 407-824-3000
tinyurl.com/grandfloridianvillas

ROOM RATING	93
COST	$700+

Commuting times to parks (in minutes):

MAGIC KINGDOM	on monorail
EPCOT	4:45
ANIMAL KINGDOM	11:45
DHS	6:45

Wilderness Lodge ★★★★
901 Timberline Dr.
Lake Buena Vista, FL 32830
☎ 407-824-3200
tinyurl.com/wildernesslodge

ROOM RATING	86
COST	$450+

Commuting times to parks (in minutes):

MAGIC KINGDOM	by ferry
EPCOT	10:00
ANIMAL KINGDOM	15:15
DHS	13:30

Yacht Club Resort ★★★★½
1700 Epcot Resorts Blvd.
Lake Buena Vista, FL 32830
☎ 407-934-7000
tinyurl.com/yachtclubwdw

ROOM RATING	91
COST	$550

Commuting times to parks (in minutes):

MAGIC KINGDOM	7:15
EPCOT	5:15
ANIMAL KINGDOM	6:45
DHS	4:00

continued from page 103

INDEPENDENT HOTELS OF THE DISNEY SPRINGS RESORT AREA

THE SEVEN HOTELS of the Disney Springs Resort Area (DSRA) were created in the days when Disney had far fewer of its own resorts. The hotels—**Best Western Lake Buena Vista, B Resort, DoubleTree Guest Suites, Hilton Orlando Buena Vista Palace, Hilton Orlando Lake Buena Vista, Holiday Inn Orlando,** and **Wyndham Garden Lake Buena Vista**—are chain properties with minimal or nonexistent theming, though the Hilton Orlando Buena Vista Palace, especially, is pretty upscale.

The main advantage to staying in the DSRA is being in Disney World and near Disney Springs. Guests at the two Hiltons, Wyndham Garden, and Holiday Inn are an easy 5- to 15-minute walk from the Marketplace on the east side of Disney Springs. Guests at Best Western, B Resort, and DoubleTree are about 10 minutes farther by foot. Another bonus is that one can book these hotels with reward points instead of money. Disney transportation can be accessed at Disney Springs, though the Disney buses take a notoriously long time to leave due to the number of stops throughout the shopping and entertainment complex. Though all DSRA hotels offer shuttle buses to the theme parks, the service is provided by private contractors and is somewhat inferior to Disney transportation in frequency of service, number of buses, and hours of operation. All these hotels are easily accessible by car and are only marginally farther from the Disney parks than several of the Disney resorts (and DSRA hotels are quite close to Typhoon Lagoon).

Free parking at the theme parks isn't offered, but guests staying at a DSRA hotel can enjoy Extra Magic Hours at Walt Disney World theme parks. Guests who have booked a Walt Disney Travel Company package, including a stay at one of the hotels and theme park admission, are able to link their hotel reservation on mydisneyexperience .com, and with a linked, valid theme park ticket, these guests have a 60-day booking window for FastPass+ selections. These perks are valid through 2020.

All DSRA hotels try to appeal to families. Some have pool complexes that rival those at any Disney resort, whereas others offer a food court or all-suite rooms. A few sponsor Disney-character meals and organized children's activities; all have counters for buying Disney tickets, and most have Disney gift shops.

Take a peek at the combined website for the DSRA hotels at disney springshotels.com. The hotels we recommend in this area are profiled beginning on page 122.

HOW *to* GET DISCOUNTS *on* LODGING *at* WALT DISNEY WORLD

THERE ARE SO MANY GUEST ROOMS in and around Walt Disney World that competition is brisk, and everyone, including Disney, wheels and deals to fill them. Here are some tips for getting price breaks at Disney properties:

1. SEASONAL SAVINGS You can save 15%–35% or more per night on a Walt Disney World hotel room by scheduling your visit during the slower times of the year (see page 41).

2. ASK ABOUT SPECIALS Disney's website will display discounts available to the general public for your dates. Look for the words "special offer" near the top of the page, in the section that asks whether you're booking a room-only or package deal. You must click on the particular special to get the discount; otherwise, you may be charged the full rack rate. If you're calling Disney, ask the reservationist specifically about specials. For example, "What special rates or discounts are available at Disney hotels during the time of our visit?"

3. CHECK MOUSESAVERS The folks at **MouseSavers** (mousesavers.com) maintain an updated list of discounts for Disney resorts. The discounts are separated into categories such as "for anyone," "for residents of certain states," and "for annual pass holders." Anyone calling ☎ 407-W-DISNEY (934-7639) can use a current discount. Discounts for the general public will also appear on Disney's website (see "Ask About Specials" above); however, MouseSavers shows you targeted discounts that Disney's website may not.

MouseSavers has a great historical list of when discounts were released and what they encompassed at mousesavers.com/historical wdwdiscounts.html. You can also sign up for the MouseSavers newsletter, with discount announcements, Disney news, and exclusive offers not available to the general public.

4. INTERNET SELLERS Online travel sellers **Expedia** (expedia.com), **Hotels.com, One Travel** (onetravel.com), **Priceline** (priceline.com), and **Travelocity** (travelocity.com) offer discounted rooms at Disney hotels, but usually at a price approximating the going rate obtainable from the Walt Disney Travel Company or Walt Disney World Central Reservations. Most breaks are in the 7%–25% range. Always check these websites' prices against Disney's. Hotels.com offers a point system, where you earn one point for each night you book. Ten points will give you 1 free night at a hotel of your choice. Note that the value of the free night equals the average price you paid for 10 nights. Once you accrue 10 nights, you can put the value of your free night toward a night at any hotel you choose.

5. RENTING DISNEY VACATION CLUB POINTS The Disney Vacation Club (DVC) is Disney's time-share condominium program. DVC resorts, also known as Disney Deluxe Villa (DDV) resorts, at Disney World are **Animal Kingdom Villas, Bay Lake Tower** at the Contemporary, **Beach Club Villas, BoardWalk Villas, Boulder Ridge Villas** and **Copper Creek Villas & Cabins** at Wilderness Lodge, **Gran Destino Tower** at Coronado Springs, **Old Key West Resort, Polynesian Villas & Bungalows, Riviera Resort, Saratoga Springs Resort & Spa, Treehouse Villas** at Saratoga Springs, and **The Villas at Grand Floridian Resort. Reflections–A Disney Lakeside Lodge** opens in late 2020 or 2021. Each resort offers studios and one- and two-bedroom villas (some resorts also offer three-bedroom villas; the Polynesian only has studios and two-bedroom bungalows). Studios are equipped with kitchenettes, wet bars, and fridges; the villas come with full kitchens. Most accommodations have patios or balconies.

DVC members receive a number of points annually that they use to pay for their Disney accommodations. Sometimes members elect to "rent" (sell) their points instead of using them in a given year. Though Disney is not involved in the transaction, it allows DVC members to make these points available to the general public. The going rental rate is $12–$17 per point when you deal with members directly; third-party brokers often charge more for acting as middleman. Renting a studio for a summer week at Animal Kingdom Lodge & Villas would run you $2,368 with tax during summer if you booked through Disney. The same studio costs the DVC member 88 points for a week. If you rented those points at $15 per point, the same studio would cost you $1,380 with tax—about $1,000 less.

You have two options when renting points: go through a company that specializes in DVC points rental, or locate and deal directly with the selling DVC member. For a fixed rate of around $17 per point, **David's Vacation Club Rentals** (dvcrequest.com) will match your request for a specific resort and dates to its available supply. The per-point rate is a bit higher than if you did the legwork yourself, but David's takes requests months in advance and notifies you as soon as something becomes available; plus, it takes credit cards. We've used David's for huge New Year's Eve events and last-minute trips, and it's tops. In addition to David's, some readers have had good results with **The DVC Rental Store** (dvcrentalstore.com).

When you deal directly with the selling DVC member, you pay him or her directly, such as by certified check (few members take credit cards). The DVC member makes a reservation in your name and pays Disney the requisite number of points. Usually your reservation is documented by a confirmation sent from Disney to the owner and then passed along to you. Though the deal you cut is strictly up to you and the owner, you should always insist on receiving the afore-mentioned confirmation before making more than a 1-night deposit.

We suggest checking online at one of the various Disney discussion boards if you're not picky about where you stay and when you go and are willing to put in the effort to ask around. If you're trying to book a particular resort, especially during a busy time of year, there's something to be said for the low-hassle approach of a points broker.

6. CRACK THE (PIN) CODE Disney maintains a list of recent Disney World visitors and those who have inquired about a Disney World vacation. During slow times of the year, Disney will send these folks direct mail and emails with personalized discounts. Each offer is uniquely identified by a long string of letters and numbers, called a PIN code.

The PIN code is required to get the discount (thus, it can't be shared), and Disney will verify the street or email address to which the code was sent is yours.

To get your name in the Disney system for a PIN code, call ☎ 407-W-DISNEY and request written information. If you've been to Walt Disney World before, your name and address will of course already be on record, but you won't be as likely to receive a PIN-code offer as you would by calling and requesting to be sent information. Go to disneyworld.com and sign up to automatically be sent offers and news at your email address. You might also consider getting a **Disney Rewards Visa Card,** which entitles you to around 2 days' advance notice when a discount is released (visit disney.go.com/visa for details).

7. TRAVEL AGENTS We believe a good travel agent is the best friend a traveler can have. And though we at *The Unofficial Guide* know a thing or two about the travel industry, we always give our agent a chance to beat any deal we find. If she can't beat it, we let her book it anyway if she can get commission from it, thus nurturing the relationship.

Each year we ask our readers to rate the travel agents who helped plan their Disney trip. This year we received surveys on over 1,700 agents. None of them charge a fee for their services. The best of the best include **Sue Pisaturo** of **Small World Vacations,** who contributes to this guide (sue@smallworldvacations.com); **Darren Wittko** (darren @magicalvacationstravel.com); **Mike Rahlmann** (mike.rahlmann@the magicforless.com); **Kathy Achue** (kathy@smallworldvacations.com); **Candice Stoves** (candice@magicalvacationstravel.com); **Kristin Moore** (kristin@magicalvacationstravel.com); **Brandi Pold** (brandi@magical vacationstravel.com); **Wendy Ott** (wendy@smallworldvacations.com); **Samantha Loureiro** (samantha@magicalvacationstravel.com); **Darcy Phelps** (darcy@magicalvacationstravel.com); **Holly Biss** (holly@magical vacationstravel.com); **Jacki York** (jacki.york@meitravel.com); **Lauren Masarik** (lauren@pixievacations.com); **Lisa Cameron** (lisac@magical vacationstravel.com); and **Sue Kelly** (sue@magicalvacationstravel.com).

8. OTHER AVAILABLE DISCOUNTS If you're a member of AARP, AAA, or any travel or auto club, ask whether the group has a discounts program before shopping elsewhere. Government workers, teachers, nurses, military, and AAA and Entertainment Coupon Book members can save on their rooms at the Dolphin or Swan (when space is available, of course). Call ☎ 888-828-8850.

9. MILITARY DISCOUNTS The Shades of Green Armed Forces Recreation Center offers luxury accommodations at rates based on a service member's rank, as well as tickets to the theme parks. For rates and other information, call ☎ 888-593-2242 or visit shadesofgreen.org.

WALT DISNEY TRAVEL COMPANY PACKAGES

DISNEY'S TRAVEL-PACKAGE PROGRAM mirrors the admission-ticket program. Here's how it works: You begin with a base package room and tickets. Tickets can be customized to match the number of days you intend to tour the theme parks and range in length from 2 to 10 days. As with theme park admissions, the package program offers strong financial incentives to book a longer stay. An adult 1-Day Base Ticket for the Magic Kingdom (including tax) costs $116–$169, depending on the day of your visit, whereas if you buy a 7-Day Base Ticket, the average cost per day drops to $65–$88. You can purchase add-ons to your Base Tickets, such as hopping between theme parks or visiting water parks or the ESPN Wide World of Sports Complex.

With Disney's packages, you can avoid paying for features you don't intend to use. On a 1-week vacation, for example, you might want to spend only 5 days in the Disney parks, saving a day each for Universal Studios and SeaWorld. (That is, even if your Disney hotel stay is 7 days, you can buy admission tickets lasting anywhere from 2 to 10 days; the ticket length doesn't need to match your hotel stay length.) Likewise, if you don't normally park-hop, you can purchase multiday admissions that don't include the Park Hopper feature. Best of all, you can buy the various add-ons at any time during your vacation.

The basic components of a Disney package are as follows:

- 1 or more nights of accommodations at the Disney resort of your choice
- Base Ticket for the number of days you tour the theme parks (must be at least 2-day tickets for packages)
- Unlimited use of the Disney transportation system
- Free theme park parking
- Official Walt Disney Travel Company luggage tag (one per person)

The various **Dining Plans,** an optional but very popular component, are covered in detail beginning on page 139.

Number-Crunching

Comparing a Disney Travel Company package with purchasing the package components separately is a breeze.

1. Pick a Disney resort and decide how many nights you want to stay.
2. Next, work out a rough plan of what you want to do and see so you can determine the admission passes you'll require.
3. When you're ready, call the Disney Reservation Center (DRC) at ☎ 407-W-DISNEY (934-7639) and price a package, including tax, for your selected resort and dates. The package will include both admissions and lodging. It's also a good idea to get a quote from a Disney-savvy travel agent (see page 110).
4. To calculate the costs of buying accommodations and admission separately, call the DRC a second time. This time, price a room-only rate for the same resort and dates. Be sure to ask about the availability of any special deals. While you're still on the line, obtain the prices, including tax, for the admissions you require. If you're not sure which of the various admission options will best serve you, consult our free Ticket Calculator at touringplans.com.

5. Add the room-only rates and the admission prices. Compare this sum to the DRC quote for the package.

6. Check for deals and discounts on packages, room-only rates, and theme park admission.

Throw Me a Line!

If you buy a package from Disney, don't expect reservationists to offer suggestions or help you sort out your options. Generally, they respond only to your specific questions, ducking queries that require an opinion. A reader from North Riverside, Illinois, complains:

> *The representatives from WDW were very courteous, but they only answered the questions posed and were not eager to give advice on what might be most cost-effective. I feel a person could spend 8 hours on the phone with WDW reps and not have any more input than you get from reading the website.*

If you can't get the information you need from a Disney reservationist, get in touch with a good travel agent.

LODGING *Outside* WALT DISNEY WORLD

AT THIS POINT YOU'RE PROBABLY WONDERING how a hotel outside Walt Disney World could be as convenient as one inside. Well, Mabel, Disney World is a *muy largo* place, but like any city or state, it has borders.

Just south of Walt Disney World on US 192 are a bunch of hotels and condos—some great bargains—that are closer to Animal Kingdom and Disney's Hollywood Studios than are many hotels in Disney World. Similarly, there are hotels along Disney's east border, FL 535, that are exceptionally convenient if you plan to use your own car.

Lodging costs outside of Walt Disney World vary incredibly. If you shop around, you can find a clean motel with a pool within a few minutes of Disney World for as low as $80 a night. You can also find luxurious, expensive hotels. Because of hot competition, discounts abound.

GOOD NEIGHBOR HOTELS

SOME HOTELS PAY DISNEY a marketing fee to display a GOOD NEIGHBOR designation. Usually a ticket shop in the lobby sells full-price Disney tickets. Other than that, the designation means nothing for the consumer. It doesn't guarantee quality—some Good Neighbor hotels are very nice; others, not so much. Some are close to Disney World, while others are quite far away. Disney requires Good Neighbor hotels to provide shuttle service to Walt Disney World.

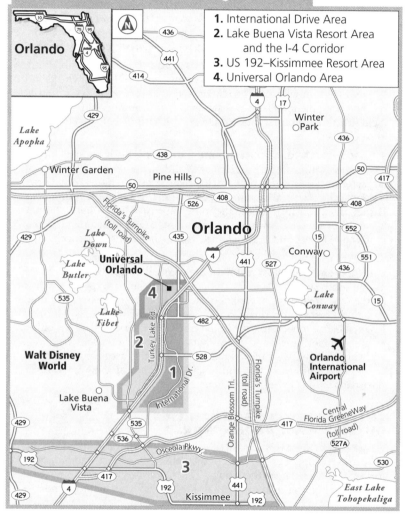

Hotel Concentrations Around Walt Disney World

1. International Drive Area
2. Lake Buena Vista Resort Area and the I-4 Corridor
3. US 192–Kissimmee Resort Area
4. Universal Orlando Area

SELECTING AND BOOKING A HOTEL OUTSIDE WALT DISNEY WORLD

THERE ARE FOUR PRIMARY out-of-the-World areas to consider:

1. INTERNATIONAL DRIVE AREA This area, about 15–25 minutes northeast of Walt Disney World, parallels I-4 on its eastern side and offers a wide selection of both hotels and restaurants. Accommodations range from about $80 to $500 per night. The chief drawbacks are terribly congested roads, countless traffic signals, and inadequate access to westbound I-4. While I-Drive's biggest bottleneck is its intersection with Sand Lake Road, the mile between Kirkman and Sand Lake Roads is almost always gridlocked. This increases the odds that you'll hit traffic going to a theme park in the morning, returning in the evening, or both.

2. LAKE BUENA VISTA AND THE I-4 CORRIDOR A number of hotels are situated along FL 535 and west of I-4 between Walt Disney World and I-4's intersection with the Florida Turnpike. These properties are easily reached from the interstate and are near a large number of restaurants, including those on International Drive. The Visit Orlando website lists most of them.

3. US 192/IRLO BRONSON MEMORIAL HIGHWAY This is the highway to Kissimmee, southeast of Walt Disney World. In addition to a number of large, full-service hotels, some small, privately owned motels often offer a good value. Several dozen properties on US 192 are closer to the Disney theme parks than are the more expensive hotels in the Disney Springs Resort Area. A variety of restaurants are located along US 192. Hotels on US 192 and in Kissimmee can be found at experiencekissimmee.com, or call ☎ 407-569-4800.

4. UNIVERSAL ORLANDO AREA In the triangular area bordered by I-4 on the southeast, Vineland Road on the north, and Turkey Lake Road on the west are Universal Orlando and the hotels most convenient to it. Running north–south through the middle of the triangle is Kirkman Road, which connects to I-4. On the east side of Kirkman are a number of independent hotels and restaurants. Universal hotels, theme parks, and CityWalk are west of Kirkman. Traffic in this area is not nearly as congested as on nearby International Drive, and there are good interstate connections in both directions.

THE BEST HOTELS FOR FAMILIES OUTSIDE WALT DISNEY WORLD

WHAT MAKES A SUPER FAMILY HOTEL? Roomy accommodations, an in-room fridge, a great pool, complimentary breakfast, and programs for kids are a few of the things *The Unofficial Guide* hotel team researched in selecting the top hotels for families from among hundreds of properties in the Disney World area. Some of our picks are expensive, others are more reasonable, and some are a bargain. Regardless of price, each of these hotels understands a family's needs.

Though most of the hotels in the next section offer some type of shuttle to the theme parks, some offer very limited service. Call the hotel before you book and ask what the shuttle schedule will be when you visit. Because families, like individuals, have different wants and needs, we haven't ranked these properties; they're listed geographically and then alphabetically.

INTERNATIONAL DRIVE & UNIVERSAL AREAS

DoubleTree by Hilton Orlando at SeaWorld ★★★★½

Rate per night $159–$179. **Pool** ★★★½. **Fridge in room** Standard in premium rooms. **Shuttle to parks** Yes (Disney: $8/person round-trip; Universal, Volcano Bay, SeaWorld, Aquatica: free). **Maximum number of occupants per room** 4. **Comments** Good option if visiting Universal, SeaWorld, or Aquatica. $19.95/night resort fee plus tax (includes 1 appetizer with purchase of entrée at Laguna, a 10% discount on spa services, and 2 bottles of water). Pets welcome (1/room, 25-pound limit, $75/stay).

10100 International Dr. Orlando
☎ 407-352-1100 or 800-327-0363
dtresortorlando.com

ON 28 LUSH, TROPICAL ACRES, the DoubleTree is adjacent to SeaWorld and Aquatica water park. The 1,094 rooms and suites—classified as resort or tower—are suitable for business travelers or families. We recommend the tower rooms for views and the resort rooms for convenience. Laguna serves steak and seafood, along with breakfast; you can also get a quick bite at The Market or the pool bar. Relax and cool off at one of the two pools (plus one just for kids), or indulge in a spa treatment. A fitness center, minigolf course, children's day camp, and game area afford even more diversions. The resort is about a 15-minute drive to Walt Disney World, a 12-minute drive to Universal, or a short walk to SeaWorld.

Hard Rock Hotel Orlando ★★★★½

Rate per night $334–$618. **Pool** ★★★★. **Fridge in room** Yes (microwave $15/day). **Shuttle to parks** Yes (Universal, Volcano Bay, SeaWorld, Discovery Cove, Aquatica). **Maximum number of occupants per room** 5 (2 queens plus rollaway)/3 (king plus rollaway); $25/night (plus tax) for rollaway. **Comments** Pets welcome ($50/night; maximum $150). $27/night self-parking.

5800 Universal Blvd. Orlando
☎ 407-503-2000 or 888-464-3617
hardrockhotelorlando.com

THE HARD ROCK HOTEL is the closest resort to Universal's theme parks. The exterior has white stucco walls, arched entryways, and rust-colored roof tiles. Inside, the lobby is a tribute to rock-and-roll style, with marble, chrome, and stage lighting.

The eight floors hold 650 rooms and 29 suites, with the rooms categorized into standard, deluxe, and club-level tiers. Standard rooms measure 375 square feet and are furnished with two queen beds, a TV, a refrigerator, a coffee maker, and an alarm clock with a 30-pin iPhone docking port.

A six-drawer dresser and separate closet with sliding doors ensure plenty of storage space. In addition, most rooms have a reading chair and a small desk with two chairs. An optional rollaway bed, available for an extra charge, allows standard rooms to sleep up to five people.

Each room's dressing area features a sink and hair dryer. The bathroom is probably large enough for most adults to get ready in the morning while another person gets ready in the dressing area. We rate the rooms at Hard Rock slightly ahead of the more expensive Portofino Bay.

LILIANE The Rock Star Suites in the Hard Rock Hotel are for tweens, teens, and anyone who ever dreamed of performing onstage. Sign me up anytime!

International Drive & Universal Hotels

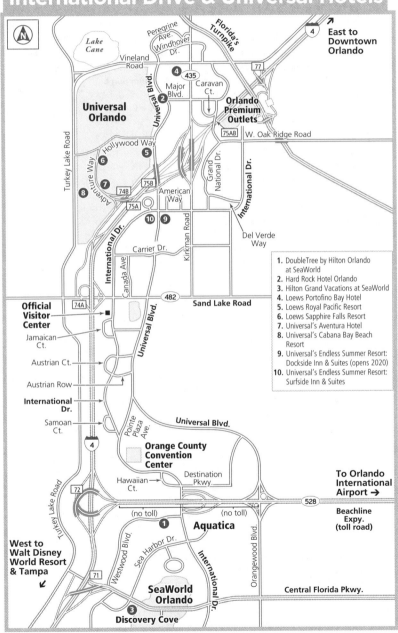

1. DoubleTree by Hilton Orlando at SeaWorld
2. Hard Rock Hotel Orlando
3. Hilton Grand Vacations at SeaWorld
4. Loews Portofino Bay Hotel
5. Loews Royal Pacific Resort
6. Loews Sapphire Falls Resort
7. Universal's Aventura Hotel
8. Universal's Cabana Bay Beach Resort
9. Universal's Endless Summer Resort: Dockside Inn & Suites (opens 2020)
10. Universal's Endless Summer Resort: Surfside Inn & Suites

In 2018 the hotel added newly redesigned Rock Star Suites, complete with an in-room stage, lights, a selection of Fender guitars, and priceless memorabilia in each room, sure to make the heart of any rock fan beat faster. Every one-of-a-kind Rock Star Suite consists of a king room that connects through a "stage door" to a room with two twin beds and roadie case–inspired furniture. You can also listen to some records on a Crosley turntable.

Situated in the middle of the resort's C-shaped main building, the 12,000-square-foot pool includes a 250-foot waterslide, a sand beach, and underwater speakers so you can hear the music while you swim. Adjacent to the pool are a fountain play area for small children, a sand-volleyball court, hot tubs, and a poolside bar. The Hard Rock also has a small, functional fitness center. Like all Universal Orlando Resort hotels, the Hard Rock has a business center and video arcade.

On-site dining includes The Kitchen—a casual full-service restaurant open for breakfast, lunch, and dinner—featuring American food such as burgers, steaks, and salads. The Palm Restaurant is an upscale steak house available for dinner only. And, of course, the Hard Rock Café is just a short distance away at Universal CityWalk.

The hotel offers Camp Lil' Rock, a children's activity center for kids ages 4–14. The camp offers arts and crafts, stories, computers, video games, movies, board games, and more, under the supervision of trained counselors. The fee is $15 per hour, per child, and $15 per meal. Reservations are required. Hours are Sunday–Thursday, 5–11:30 p.m., and Friday–Saturday, 5 p.m.–midnight.

Hilton Grand Vacations at SeaWorld ★★★★

Rate per night $235–$400. **Pool** ★★★★. **Fridge in room** Yes (full kitchen in suites). **Shuttle to parks** Yes (Universal, SeaWorld). **Maximum number of occupants per room** 2 (studio)/8 (3 bedroom). **Comments** Guests get front-of-line access to some SeaWorld rides.

6924 Grand Vacations Way
Orlando
☎ 407-239-0100
tinyurl.com/seaworldhgv

ACROSS THE STREET FROM SEAWORLD, Hilton Grand Vacations is within a 15-minute drive of both Walt Disney World and Universal Orlando. While that means spending more time in a car, you get a lot more room for your money: one-bedroom suites are 878 square feet, compared to around 520 for Disney's Value Family Suites and Fort Wilderness Cabins, and they cost less than those at Disney. Plus Grand Vacations has free parking.

Unofficial Guide readers give this Hilton an A for room quality and a solid B for room quietness. Studios have kitchenettes. Suites come equipped with a washer and dryer, kitchen with utensils, dishwasher, oven/range, microwave, coffee maker, and TVs. One-bedroom suites have a sofa bed and one bathroom; two-bedroom suites have two baths, and three-bedroom suites have three. Decor isn't the most modern, but it is bright, clean, functional, and comfortable.

Amenities include three pools with cabanas, a fitness center, a kids' playground, basketball and tennis courts, and a business center. One sit-down and one counter-service/grab-and-go restaurant serve 6:30 a.m.–11 p.m.

Loews Portofino Bay Hotel ★★★★½

5601 Universal Blvd.
Orlando
☎ 407-503-1000 or
888-464-3617
loewshotels.com
/portofino-bay-hotel

Rate per night $359–$635. **Pool** ★★★★. **Fridge in room** Yes (microwave $15/day). **Shuttle to parks** Yes (Universal, Volcano Bay, SeaWorld, Discovery Cove, Aquatica). **Maximum number of occupants per room** 5 (2 queens plus rollaway)/3 (king plus rollaway); $25/night (plus tax) for rollaway. **Comments** Pets welcome ($100/stay). $27/night self-parking.

UNIVERSAL'S TOP-OF-THE-LINE HOTEL evokes the Italian seaside city of Portofino, complete with a man-made bay past the lobby. To Universal's credit, the layout, color, and theming of the guest-room buildings are a good approximation of the architecture around the harbor in the real Portofino (Universal's version has fewer yachts, though).

Most guest rooms are 450 square feet and have either one king bed or two queen beds. Rooms come furnished with a 32-inch TV, a refrigerator, a coffee maker, and an alarm clock with a 30-pin iPhone docking port. Other amenities include a small desk with two chairs, a comfortable reading chair with lamp, a chest of drawers, and a standing closet. Guest bathrooms at Portofino Bay are the best on Universal property.

Kids love the Despicable Me Kids' Suites. The two-bedroom suites (connected via a door to the adults' room) offer privacy for Mom and Dad and a kids' room with two twin beds or a bunk bed designed to capture the excitement of Gru's Lab.

Portofino Bay has three pools, the largest of which is the Beach Pool, on the west side of the resort. Two smaller quiet pools sit at the far end of the east wing and to the west of the main lobby. The Beach Pool has a zero-entry design and a waterslide themed after a Roman aqueduct, plus a children's play area, hot tubs, and a poolside bar and grill. The Villa Pool has private cabana rentals for that Italian Riviera feeling. Rounding out the luxuries are the full-service Mandara Spa; a complete fitness center with weight machines, treadmills, and more; a business center; and a video arcade. On-site dining includes three sit-down restaurants serving Italian cuisine; a deli; and a café serving coffee and gelato.

Loews Royal Pacific Resort ★★★★

6300 Hollywood Way
Orlando
☎ 407-503-3000 or
888-464-3617
loewshotels.com
/royal-pacific-resort

Rate per night $299–$556. **Pool** ★★★★. **Fridge in room** Yes (microwave $15/day). **Shuttle to parks** Yes (Universal, Volcano Bay, SeaWorld, Discovery Cove, Aquatica). **Maximum number of occupants per room** 5 (2 queens plus rollaway)/3 (king plus rollaway); $25/night (plus tax) for rollaway. **Comments** Saturday character breakfast. Pets welcome ($100/stay). $27/night self-parking.

THE SOUTH SEAS-INSPIRED theming at Royal Pacific Resort is both relaxing and structured. Guests enter the lobby from a walkway two stories above an artificial stream that surrounds the resort. Once you're inside, the lobby's dark teakwood accents contrast nicely with the enormous amount of light coming in from the windows and three-story A-frame roof. Palms line the walkway through the lobby, and through these you see that the whole lobby surrounds an enormous outdoor fountain.

The 1,000 guest rooms are spread among three Y-shaped wings attached to the main building. Standard rooms are 335 square feet and feature one king or two queen beds, fitted with 300-thread-count sheets. Rooms have modern monochrome wall treatments and carpets, accented with boldly colored floral graphics, and include a TV, a refrigerator, a coffee maker, and an alarm clock with a 30-pin iPhone docking port. Other amenities include a small desk with two chairs, a comfortable reading chair, a chest of drawers, and a large closet. A dressing area with sink is separated from the rest of the room by a wall. Next to the dressing area is the bathroom, with a tub, shower, and toilet. Kids brave enough will want to stay in the *Jurassic World* suites.

The Royal Pacific's zero-entry pool includes a sand beach, a volleyball court, a play area for kids, a hot tub, and cabanas for rent, plus a poolside bar and grill.

Amenities include a 5,000-square-foot fitness facility, a business center, a video arcade, a full-service restaurant (open for breakfast and dinner), three bars, and a luau.

Loews Sapphire Falls Resort   ★★★★

6601 Adventure Way
Orlando
☎ 407-503-5000 or
888-464-3617
loewshotels.com
/sapphire-falls-resort

Rate per night $234–$365. **Pool** ★★★★. **Fridge in room** Yes (microwave $15/day). **Shuttle to parks** Yes (Universal, Volcano Bay, SeaWorld, Discovery Cove, Aquatica). **Maximum number of occupants per room** 5 (2 queens plus rollaway)/3 (king plus rollaway); $25/night (plus tax) for rollaway. **Comments** Pets welcome ($100/stay). $25/night self-parking.

SAPPHIRE FALLS RESORT brings a sunny Caribbean island vibe to the moderate-price market with its 1,000 rooms. Opened in summer 2016 and sandwiched between Royal Pacific and Cabana Bay, both physically and price-wise, Sapphire Falls sports all the amenities of Universal's three Deluxe hotels, including water taxi transportation to the parks, with the crucial exception of complimentary Express Passes.

Water figures heavily at Sapphire Falls, whose namesake waterfalls form the scenic centerpiece of the resort. The 16,000-square-foot zero-entry main pool features a white-sand beach, a waterslide, children's play areas, a fire pit, and cabanas for rent. A fitness room holds a sauna and hot tub. For dinner, Amatista Cookhouse offers table-service Caribbean dining, with an open kitchen and waterfront views. Drhum Club Kantine serves tapas-style small plates near the pool bar's fire pit. New Dutch Trading Co. is an island-inspired grab-and-go marketplace, and Strong Water Tavern in the lobby has rum tastings and table-side ceviche. *Caribbean Carnaval* is an interactive dinner show held every Wednesday. Prices start at $71 plus tax for adults and $36 plus tax for children ages 3–9. The price includes Caribbean-inspired fare, nonalcoholic beverages, wine, beer, punch, and gratuity.

Sapphire Falls also contains 131,000 square feet of meeting space and a business center. Covered walkways connect to a parking structure, which in turn connects to the meeting facilities at Royal Pacific, making the sister properties ideal for conventions.

The rooms range from 321 square feet in a standard queen or king to 529 square feet in the 36 Kids' Suites to 1,353 square feet in the 15 Hospitality Suites. The standard rooms have separate bath and vanity areas. The Kids' Suites include a king bed and sofa, with two twin beds in a separate bedroom that connects only to the adults' room. A sliding panel separates the vanity from the tub and toilet. All rooms have a TV, mini-fridge, and coffee maker.

Universal's Aventura Hotel ★★★★

6725 Adventure Way
Orlando
☎ 407-503-6000 or
888-464-3617
loewshotels.com/universals
-aventura-hotel

Rate per night $159–$286. **Pool** ★★★★. **Fridge in room** Yes (microwave $15/day). **Shuttle to parks** Yes (Universal, Sea-World, Discovery Cove, Aquatica). **Maximum number of occupants per room** 4 (standard)/5 (Kids' Suites). **Comment** Walking distance to Volcano Bay. $17/night self-parking.

THE ROOMS OF THIS relatively small, boutique-style modern resort are cleanly designed and are similar in size to Disney's Moderate resorts. The prices, however, are much more in line with a Value resort.

The 575-square-foot suites feature three separate sleeping areas, each with floor-to-ceiling, wall-to-wall windows. Suites in the top floors have sweeping views of Universal Orlando's theme parks and Volcano Bay. The largest room comes with a king bed, mini-fridge, TV, desk, and chairs. Separated by a three-quarter wall and a curtain is the children's sleeping area, with two twin beds and a TV. Right next to it is a separate space with a pullout sofa, a table, and a third TV mounted on the wall. Here, kids can hang out, play, and watch TV without messing up the bedrooms. The bathroom has a tub, a separate shower, toilet, and a double vanity. Several family members can get ready at the same time in this space, which is an added bonus.

The 600-room, 17-story glass tower is located across from Cabana Bay Beach Resort southwest of Sapphire Falls. Amenities include early park admission to Universal's theme parks, complimentary transportation around the resort, a pool, a hot tub, a kids' splash pad, a food hall with five different cuisines, and the rooftop bar and grill Bar 17. Aventura also has on-site car rental, a gift shop, and a fitness center. A stay at the resort does *not* include complimentary Express Passes. Aventura Hotel is a prime location for visiting Volcano Bay, and the hotel features new technology, such as an in-room tablet that allows guests to control the TV, temperature, and more.

During inclement weather, the lifeguards entertain kids on the covered bar patio with games. Here, they can also enjoy a game of table tennis, pool, or Foosball. The second floor of the hotel contains a fitness center and a virtual reality game room; the six different games (*Snowball, Longbow, Vortex, Fruit Ninja, Space Pirates,* and *Zombie Training Center*) cost $10 each to play.

Universal's Cabana Bay Beach Resort ★★★★

6550 Adventure Way
Orlando
☎ 407-503-4000 or
888-464-3617
loewshotels.com
/cabana-bay-hotel

Rate per night $159–$286 standard, $174–$376 suites. **Pool** ★★★★. **Fridge in room** Yes (microwave $15/day, free in suites). **Shuttle to parks** Yes (Universal, SeaWorld, Discovery Cove, Aquatica). **Maximum number of occupants per room** 4 (standard)/6 (suites). **Comment** Character greeting on Friday evenings. $17/night self-parking.

CABANA BAY WAS UNIVERSAL'S first on-site hotel aimed at the value and moderate markets. The theme is midcentury modern, with lots of windows, bright colors, and period-appropriate lighting and furniture.

Kids love the two large and well-themed pools (one with a lazy river), the amount of space they have to run around in, the video arcade, and the vintage cars parked outside the hotel lobby. Adults appreciate the sophisticated kitsch of the decor, the multiple lounges, the business center, and the on-site Starbucks. We think Cabana Bay is an excellent choice for price- and/or space-conscious families visiting Universal.

Each family suite has a small bedroom with two queen beds, separated from the living area and kitchenette by a sliding screen; a pullout sofa in the living area offers additional sleeping space. (Standard rooms also have two queen beds.) The bath is divided into three sections: toilet, sink area,

LILIANE Lock me up in a volcano-view tower room anytime. Did you know that Krakatau erupts once in a while? Either way, it's a sight to behold by day and night!

and shower room with additional sink. The kitchenette has a microwave, coffee maker, and mini-fridge. A bar area allows extra seating for quick meals, and a large closet has enough space to store everyone's luggage. Built-in USB charging outlets for your devices are a thoughtful touch.

Recreational options include the 10-lane Galaxy Bowl (about $15 per person with shoe rental), poolside table tennis and billiards, and a large Jack LaLanne fitness center. Outdoor movies are shown nightly near the pool.

In addition to Starbucks, a food court with seating area shows 1950s TV clips. Swizzle Lounge in the lobby, two pool bars, in-room pizza delivery, and the Galaxy Bowl round out the on-site dining options. You'll find more restaurants and clubs nearby at the Royal Pacific Resort and Universal CityWalk.

Unlike the other Universal resorts, Cabana Bay offers no watercraft service to the parks—it's either take the bus or walk. A pedestrian bridge connects Cabana Bay to CityWalk and the rest of Universal Orlando, but we recommend the bus service for most people. Bus service from Cabana Bay to the parks is superior to any bus transportation from Disney hotels to Disney parks. Cabana Bay guests are eligible for early entry at Universal and Volcano Bay but do not get complimentary Universal Express Passes.

Universal added two towers that enlarged the resort by 360 more standard guest rooms and 40 suites. Half of those rooms overlook the lush, 28-acre Volcano Bay water park, with amazing views of the rides and the 200-foot-high Krakatau volcano.

Universal's Endless Summer Resort

Rate per night $104–$259. **Pool** ★★★½. **Fridge in room** Yes (microwave $15/day, free in suites). **Shuttle to parks** Yes (Universal, Volcano Bay, SeaWorld, Discovery Cove, Aquatica). **Maximum number of occupants per room** 4 (standard)/6 (suites). **Comment** $17/night self-parking.

Surfside: 7000 Universal Blvd.
Dockside: 7125 Universal Blvd.
Orlando
☎ 407-503-7000 or
888-273-1311
loewshotels.com/surfside-inn
-and-suites

UNIVERSAL'S LATEST HOTEL COMPLEX, Endless Summer Resort features two hotel towers: Surfside Inn & Suites opened in 2019, and Dockside Inn & Suites will follow suit in 2020. The 750-room Surfside Inn & Suites includes 390 two-bedroom suites, a surfboard-shaped pool, a fitness center, a Universal Studios store, and a Universal vacation-planning center. A food court with a variety of stations serves three meals a day and is complemented by a pool bar, a coffee bar in the lobby, and in-room pizza delivery.

The sun- and surf-themed rooms come in hues of blue and green and have plenty of storage area. The two-bedroom suites have a kitchenette, a dining area, and a bathroom with separate shower and double-sink areas. The Dockside Inn will have 1,300 rooms, including standard rooms and two-bedroom suites.

This is Universal Orlando's first value resort. The hotel is located at the intersection of International Drive and Universal Boulevard, in the plot that used to be Wet 'n' Wild, and has a beach theme.

Guests staying at the Endless Summer Resort receive early park admission and free transportation to the theme parks and CityWalk but do not receive complimentary Universal Express Passes.

LAKE BUENA VISTA & I-4 CORRIDOR

B Resort ★★★½

1905 Hotel Plaza Blvd.
Lake Buena Vista
☎ 407-828-2828 or
866-759-6832
bhotelsandresorts.com

Rate per night $129–$199. **Pool ★★★½. Fridge in room** Yes. **Shuttle to parks** Yes (Disney). **Maximum number of occupants per room** 4 plus child in crib. **Comments** $30/night resort fee. $22/night self-parking fee. Guests are eligible for 60-day FastPass+ and Extra Magic Hours benefits through 2020.

LOCATED WITHIN WALKING DISTANCE of shops and restaurants and situated 5 miles or less from the Disney parks, the 394-room B Resort targets couples, families, groups, and business travelers.

Decorated in cool blues, whites, and grays, guest rooms and suites afford views of downtown Orlando, area lakes, and theme parks. Along with B Resort–exclusive Blissful Beds, each room is outfitted with sleek modern furnishings and a large interactive TV. Additional touches include a mini-fridge, in-room snacks, and gaming consoles (available on request). Some rooms are also equipped with bunk beds, kitchenettes, or wet bars.

The bathroom is spacious, with plenty of storage. The glass shower is well-designed and has good water pressure. There's absolutely nothing wrong with this hotel at this price point, except for the terrible traffic you have to endure every night because of Disney Springs.

Amenities include free Wi-Fi, a spa, a beauty salon, and a fitness center. The main restaurant, American Kitchen Bar & Grill, serves comfort food made with contemporary ingredients. Hungry guests can also choose from a poolside bar and grill; The Pickup, a grab-and-go shop just off the lobby that serves quick breakfasts, snacks, picnic lunches, and ice cream; and in-room dining 6:30 a.m.–2 a.m.

Other perks: a zero-entry pool with interactive water features, a kids' area, and more than 25,000 square feet of meeting and multiuse space.

Four Seasons Resort Orlando at Walt Disney World Resort ★★★★★

10100 Dream Tree Blvd.
Golden Oak
☎ 407-313-7777
or 800-267-3046
fourseasons.com/orlando

Rate per night $650–$995. **Pool ★★★★★. Fridge in room** Yes. **Shuttle to parks** Yes (Disney). **Maximum number of occupants per room** 4 (3 adults or 2 adults and 2 children). **Comments** The best pool complex in Disney World. Character breakfast on Thursday, Saturday, and select Tuesdays. Guests are eligible for 60-day FastPass+ and Extra Magic Hours benefits through 2020.

THE PLUSH FOUR SEASONS is the best deluxe resort in the area, with comfort, amenities, and personal service that far surpass anything Disney's Deluxes offer. The Spanish Revival–inspired architecture calls to mind Florida's grand resorts of the early 20th century.

Most of the 444 guest rooms have an 80-square-foot balcony with a table and chairs. Standard guest rooms average around 500 square feet and feature either one king bed with a sleeper sofa or two double beds (a crib is available in double rooms). Amenities include two TVs (one in the mirror above the bathroom sink), a coffee maker, a mini-fridge, a work desk with two chairs, and Bluetooth speakers for your personal audio. Each nightstand has four electrical outlets and two USB ports. Bathrooms have glass-walled showers, a separate tub, marble vanities with two sinks, mosaic-tile floors, hair dryers, and lighted mirrors.

If you're looking for family activities, the Four Seasons Resort has them. Explorer Island comprises an adult pool, a family pool, a 242-foot waterslide, a children's splash zone, a playground, and a lazy river. The free Kids for All Seasons program runs daily, 9 a.m.–5 p.m. Other amenities include a full-service spa and fitness center.

Capa, a Spanish-themed rooftop restaurant, serves seafood and steaks. Ravello serves American breakfasts and upscale Italian dishes for dinner. PB&G (Pool Bar and Grill) serves sandwiches, seafood, and salads by the main pool.

The shuttle service to the parks is free and by luxury coach, but the schedule is not as frequent as the Disney buses. Guests staying at the resort are better off having a car or taking a ride-share service.

Hilton Orlando Bonnet Creek ★★★★

Rate per night $221–$251. **Pool** ★★★★½. **Fridge in room** Yes. **Shuttle to parks** Yes (Disney). **Maximum number of occupants per room** 4. **Comments** $50/night resort fee. $30/night self-parking. Guests are eligible for 60-day FastPass+ and Extra Magic Hours benefits through 2020.

14100 Bonnet Creek Resort Lane Orlando
☎ 407-597-3600
hiltonbonnetcreek.com

THIS IS ONE OF OUR FAVORITE non-Disney hotels in Lake Buena Vista, and the value for the money beats anything in Disney's Deluxe category. Located behind Disney's Caribbean Beach and Pop Century Resorts, this Hilton is much nicer than the ones in the Disney Springs Resort Area.

Standard rooms are around 414 square feet and have either one king bed or two queens. The mattresses and linens are very comfortable. Other features include a 37-inch TV, a spacious work desk, a small reading chair with floor lamp, a nightstand, and a digital clock. A coffee maker, a mini-fridge, a hair dryer, and an iron and board are all standard, along with free wired and free wireless internet. Bathrooms include tile floors, and some have glass showers. Unfortunately, the layout isn't as up-to-date as other hotels'—where many upscale hotel bathrooms have two sinks (so two people can primp at once), the Hilton's have only one.

Families will enjoy the huge zero-entry pool, complete with waterslide, as well as the 3-acre lazy river. Even better, the Hilton staff run arts-and-crafts activities poolside during the day, allowing parents to grab a quick swim and a cocktail. Pool-facing cabanas are available for rent. A nice fitness center sits on the ground floor.

The Hilton participates in the Waldorf Astoria's Kids Club next door, for children ages 5–12. A daytime program is available 10:30 a.m.–2:30 p.m., and an evening program is available Friday–Saturday, 6–10 p.m. The price is $75 for the first child, $25 for each additional child. To make reservations call ☎ 407-597-5388.

More than a dozen restaurants and lounges are between the Hilton and the Waldorf Astoria, with cuisine including steak, Italian, sushi, and tapas. A coffee bar, an American bistro, and a breakfast buffet round out the choices. Reservations are recommended for the fancy places.

Hilton Orlando Buena Vista Palace ★★★

1900 E. Buena Vista Dr.
Lake Buena Vista
☎ 407-827-2727
buenavistapalace.com

Rate per night $164–$241. **Pool** ★★★½. **Fridge in room** Yes. **Shuttle to parks** Yes (Disney). **Maximum number of occupants per room** 4. **Comments** $39/night resort fee. $22/night self-parking. Sunday character breakfast. Guests are eligible for 60-day FastPass+ and Extra Magic Hours benefits through 2020.

THIS UPSCALE, CONVENIENT HOTEL is surrounded by an artificial lake and plenty of palms. Hilton has invested substantially in renovations since 2016, but more improvements are needed to bring the property up to par with the Hilton image. The spacious pool area comprises three heated pools, the largest of which is partially covered; a hot tub and sauna; a basketball court; and a sand volleyball court. A pool concierge will fetch your favorite magazine or fruity drink, and there is a Sunday character breakfast with Disney friends. The 897 guest rooms are posh and spacious; each comes with a desk, a coffee maker, a hair dryer, satellite TV with pay-per-view movies, an iron and board, and a mini-fridge. There are also 117 suites. In-room babysitting is available. One lighted tennis court, a fitness center, an arcade, and a playground round out the recreation options. Two restaurants and a mini-market are on-site, and if you aren't wiped out after the parks, drop by the lobby lounge for a nightcap.

Hilton Orlando Lake Buena Vista ★★★★

1751 Hotel Plaza Blvd.
Lake Buena Vista
☎ 407-827-4000
hilton-wdwv.com

Rate per night $143–$226. **Pool** ★★★½. **Fridge in room** Yes. **Shuttle to parks** Yes (Disney). **Maximum number of occupants per room** 4. **Comments** $35/night resort fee. $22/night self-parking fee. Sunday character breakfast. Guests are eligible for 60-day FastPass+ and Extra Magic Hours benefits through 2020.

THOUGH THE DECOR IS DATED, the rooms are comfortable and nicer than some others in the DSRA. On-site dining includes Covington Mill Restaurant, offering a breakfast buffet and sandwiches and salads for lunch; Andiamo, an Italian bistro; and Benihana, a Japanese steak house and sushi bar. The two pools are matched with a children's spray pool and a 24-hour fitness center. A game room and 24-hour market are on-site. Babysitting is available.

Holiday Inn Resort Lake Buena Vista ★★★½

13351 FL 535
Orlando
☎ 407-239-4500
hiresortlbv.com

Rate per night $105–$140. **Pool** ★★★. **Fridge in room** Yes (microwave). **Shuttle to parks** Yes (Disney). **Maximum number of occupants per room** 4-6. **Comments** $21.95/night resort fee. Pets welcome ($50/stay).

THE BIG LURE HERE IS KIDSUITES—405-square-foot rooms, each with a separate children's area. The kids' area sleeps two to four children in one or two sets of bunk beds. The separate adult area has its own TV, safe, hair dryer, and kitchenette with fridge, microwave, sink, and coffee maker (standard guest rooms also offer these amenities). Kid-friendly perks include the tiny Kids' Movie Theater, which shows movies all day, every day; a splash pad; and an arcade with video games and air hockey. Other amenities include a fitness center for the grown-ups and a large free-form pool complete with kiddie pool and two hot tubs. Applebee's serves breakfast, lunch, and dinner; there's also a minimart. Kids age 12 and younger eat free at breakfast and dinner from a special menu when dining with a paying adult (maximum four kids per adult), and Dive-In movies are shown at the pool seasonally on Saturday nights.

Holiday Inn Resort Orlando Suites—Waterpark ★★★½

Rate per night $129–$171. **Pool** ★★★★. **Fridge in room** Yes (microwave). **Shuttle to parks** Yes (Disney [TTC], Disney Springs, Universal, Volcano Bay, SeaWorld). **Comments** $30/night resort fee plus tax. **Maximum number of occupants per room** 8.

14500 Continental Gateway, Orlando
☎ 407-387-5437
hisuitesorlando.com

AFTER A $30 MILLION RENOVATION IN 2016, the hotel once known as Nickelodeon Suites became the Holiday Inn Resort Orlando Suites—Waterpark.

The 777 suites come in one-, two-, and three-bedroom varieties, and each suite contains a mini-fridge, a microwave, a TV, and high-speed internet. The resort also boasts a water park with seven slides, a 4-D Experience, Laser Challenge, and a 3,000-square-foot arcade. Kids will love the many free activities at the main pool.

The resort is huge, and the layout of the hotel is somewhat confusing. Unless you prefer the more remote, quiet pool area, we suggest that you request a room close to the main pool and The Market Place, the shopping and dining area of the complex. The shuttles to the parks depart from The Market Place.

Hyatt Regency Grand Cypress ★★★★½

Rate per night $159–$259. **Pool** ★★★★★. **Fridge in room** Yes, plus minibar. **Shuttle to parks** Yes (Disney, Universal, Volcano Bay, SeaWorld). **Maximum number of occupants per room** 4. **Comments** $39.38/night resort fee. Pets welcome (50-pound limit; $150/up to 6 nights). $22/night self-parking.

1 Grand Cypress Blvd. Orlando
☎ 407-239-1234
grandcypress.hyatt.com

THERE ARE MYRIAD REASONS to stay at the 1,500-acre Grand Cypress, but the pool ranks as number one. The 800,000-gallon tropical paradise has waterfalls and a suspension bridge, along with a 124-foot waterslide, a splash zone, a pool bar, and kids' rock-climbing facilities.

The 767 standard guest rooms are 360 square feet and have a Florida ambience, with green and reddish hues, touches of rattan, and private balconies. Amenities include a minibar, an iron and board, a safe, a hair dryer, a ceiling fan, and cable/satellite TV with pay-per-view movies and video games. Suite and villa accommodations offer even more amenities. Camp Hyatt provides supervised programs for kids ages 3–12, and in-room babysitting is available. Two restaurants offer dining options, and three lounges provide nighttime entertainment.

Calling all mermaids! Guests can suit up for a once-in-a-lifetime experience and learn how to swim like a mermaid. The 1-hour Mermaid Academy is $25.

Marriott's Harbour Lake ★★★★

7102 Grand Horizons Blvd.
Orlando
☎ 407-465-6100
tinyurl.com/marriotthl

Rate per night $161–$433 (1 bedroom)/$269–$501 (2 bedroom). **Pool** ★★★★. **Fridge in room** Yes. **Shuttle to parks** No. **Maximum number of occupants per room** 4 (1 bedroom)/8 (2 bedroom).

THE RESORT FEATURES STUDIOS and one- and two-bedroom villas with fully equipped kitchens, separate living and dining areas, a washer and dryer, and a screened balcony.

Kids will love the Florida Falls pool complex, with its water playground and waterslide. The larger Shipwreck Landing pool area contains a pirate ship, complete with waterslides and water cannons. The on-site fitness center and Key Lime Greens, an 18-hole minigolf course, are also sure to please.

The only drawback is the very limited on-site dining. The Outpost offers grab-and-go food, while The Patio Bar and Grill serves breakfast, lunch, and dinner. Note that the grill closes during inclement weather.

Marriott Village at Lake Buena Vista ★★★

8623 Vineland Ave.
Orlando
☎ 407-938-9001
or 800-761-7829
marriottvillage.com

Rate per night $129–$269. **Pool** ★★★. **Fridge in room** Yes (microwave). **Shuttle to parks** Yes (Disney). **Maximum number of occupants per room** 4 (Courtyard and Fairfield)/5 (SpringHill). **Comments** Free hot buffet breakfast at SpringHill or Fairfield (guests' choice).

THIS GATED HOTEL COMMUNITY includes a 388-room Fairfield Inn (★★★½), a 400-suite SpringHill Suites (★★★), and a 312-room Courtyard (★★★½). If you need a bit more space, book SpringHill Suites; if you're looking for value, try the Fairfield Inn; if you need limited business amenities, reserve at the Courtyard. Amenities at all three properties include fridge, cable TV, iron and board, hair dryer, and microwave. Cribs and rollaway beds are available at no extra charge at all locations. Swimming pools at all three hotels are attractive and medium-sized, featuring children's interactive splash zones and hot tubs; in addition, each property has its own fitness center. The incredibly convenient Village Marketplace food court includes Pizza Hut, Village Grill, Village Coffee House, and a 24-hour convenience store. Bahama Breeze and Golden Corral full-service restaurants are within walking distance. Other services and amenities include a Disney planning station and ticket sales, an arcade, and a Hertz car-rental desk.

Sheraton Lake Buena Vista Resort ★★★★

12205 S. Apopka-
Vineland Road
Orlando
☎ 407-239-0444
or 800-325-3535
sheratonlakebuena
vistaresort.com

Rate per night $96–$348. **Pool** ★★★★. **Fridge in room** Yes (microwave for a fee). **Shuttle to parks** Yes (Disney). **Maximum number of occupants per room** 4–6. **Comments** $23.95/night resort fee plus tax. $19/night self-parking. Pets welcome (40-pound limit; free).

COMPRISING 400 GUEST ROOMS and 86 Family Bunk Bed Rooms, this resort has a sleek, modern feel. Amenities in each room include Sheraton Signature Beds, free Wi-Fi, a 42-inch TV, mini-fridge, coffee maker, hair dryer, safe, alarm clock, and iron and board. The Family Bunk Bed Rooms also provide bunk beds for children. The relaxing pool area features cabanas with food service (for a fee), and youngsters can enjoy the cascading waterfall and waterslide at The Falls Pool or the zero-entry Beach Pool with basketball nets and a youth wet deck. Activities include poolside movies, crafts, and poolside games.

The Top of the Palms Spa offers massages, facials, manicures, and pedicures. Also on-site are two restaurants, a business center, a fitness center, and a gift shop.

Sheraton Vistana Resort Villas ★★★★

Rate per night $146–$327. **Pool** ★★★½. **Fridge in room** Yes (full kitchen). **Shuttle to parks** Yes (Disney, for a fee). **Maximum number of occupants per room** 4 (1 bedroom)/8 (2 bedroom). **Comments** These time-share villas are also rented nightly.

8800 Vistana Centre Dr.
Orlando
☎ 407-239-3100 or
866-208-0003
tinyurl.com/vistanaresort

IF YOU WANT A SERENE RETREAT from the theme parks, this is an excellent base. The Sheraton Vistana is deceptively large, stretching across both sides of Vistana Centre Drive. The spacious villas come in one-bedroom and two-bedroom layouts. Each villa has a full kitchen (including fridge/freezer, microwave, oven/range, dishwasher, toaster, and coffee maker, with an option to prestock with groceries and laundry products), a washer and dryer, TVs in the living room and each bedroom (one with DVD player), a stereo with CD player in some villas, a separate dining area, and a private patio or balcony in most. The grounds offer seven swimming pools (three with bars), four playgrounds, two restaurants, game rooms, fitness centers, a minigolf course, and sports equipment rental (including bikes), as well as courts for basketball, volleyball, tennis, and shuffleboard. The mind-boggling array of activities for kids (and adults) ranges from crafts to games and sports tournaments. Of special note: Vistana is highly secure, with locked gates bordering all guest areas, so children can have the run of the place without parents worrying about them wandering off. The one downside: noise, both above (from being on the flight path of a helicopter tour company) and below (from International Drive).

Sheraton Vistana Villages Resort Villas ★★★★

Rate per night $265–$536. **Pool** ★★★★. **Fridge in room** Yes (full kitchen). **Shuttle to parks** No. **Maximum number of occupants per room** 6 (2 bedroom).

THIS IS ONE OF TWO Sheraton Vistana properties in Orlando that are favorites of *Unofficial Guide* readers (the other is the Vistana Resort Villas in Lake Buena Vista, profiled above). The 1,100-square-foot, two-bedroom villas are the rooms to get. While that's double the size of a Disney one-bedroom Family Suite, rack rates are much less than Disney's.

12401 International Dr.
Orlando
☎ 407-238-5000
tinyurl.com/sheraton
villages

Suites have fully equipped kitchens and a washer and dryer. All rooms have a private balcony or patio. The resort has two pools, including one zero-entry for kids; a fitness center; and a business center.

This family from Bedford, Texas, really enjoyed their stay:

I highly recommend Vistana Villages—it's the best value for the money. Plenty of space for everyone to spread out, great pools, and fantastic location. It was 10 minutes to Epcot and Hollywood Studios and 5 minutes to Disney Springs, and lots of restaurants were nearby.

The Vistana Villages are about a 15-minute drive from Walt Disney World (and you don't have to take I-4!) and 20 minutes to Universal Orlando.

Staybridge Suites Lake Buena Vista   ★★★★½

8751 Suiteside Dr.
Lake Buena Vista
☎ 407-238-0777
tinyurl.com/sblbv

Rate per night $112–$276. **Pool** ★★★. **Fridge in room** Yes (full kitchen). **Shuttle to parks** Yes (Disney, Universal). **Maximum number of occupants per room** 4 (1 bedroom)/8 (2 bedroom). **Comments** AAA Three Diamond Award; free hot breakfast and afternoon reception.

WE FOUND THIS GEM through our reader surveys, which named this Staybridge Suites the best off-site hotel near Walt Disney World in 2016. Having stayed there, we agree. The best value is the two-bedroom suite: one bedroom has a king bed; the other, two doubles (a sleeper sofa is standard in both the one- and two-bedroom suites). Each bedroom has its own full bathroom. In between the bedrooms are a living room, small dining area, and full kitchen with dishwasher, range, microwave, and refrigerator. The suite also contains plates, cups, glasses, and cutlery, plus basic pots and pans. A large-screen TV in the living room is matched by smaller TVs in each bedroom.

The Staybridge is about 0.5 mile from the Disney Springs Resort Area, just around the corner on South Apopka–Vineland Road. Nearby are two small shopping centers, both in easy walking distance of your room.

Waldorf Astoria Orlando   ★★★★½

14200 Bonnet Creek
Resort Lane, Orlando
☎ 407-597-5500
waldorfastoriaorlando.com

Rate per night $309–$781. **Pool** ★★★★. **Fridge in room** Yes. **Shuttle to parks** Yes (Disney). **Maximum number of occupants per room** 4 plus child in crib. **Comments** Good alternative to Disney Deluxe resorts; $45/night resort fee. Guests are eligible for 60-day FastPass+ and Extra Magic Hours benefits through 2020.

BEAUTIFULLY DECORATED AND WELL MANICURED, the Waldorf Astoria is more elegant than any Disney resort. Service is excellent, and the staff-to-guest ratio is far higher than at Disney properties. It's located between I-4 and Disney's Pop Century Resort, near the Hilton Orlando at the back of the Bonnet Creek Resort property.

At just under 450 square feet, standard rooms feature either two queen beds or one king. A full-size desk allows you to get work done if necessary, and rooms also have TVs, high-speed internet, and Wi-Fi. The bathrooms are spacious and gorgeous, with marble floors, glass-walled showers, separate tubs, and enough counter space for a Broadway makeup artist.

Amenities include a fitness center, a spa, a golf course, six restaurants, and two pools (including a zero-entry pool for kids). Poolside cabanas are available for rent.

Wyndham Garden Lake Buena Vista   ★★★½

1850 Hotel Plaza Blvd.
Lake Buena Vista
☎ 407-828-4444
wyndhamlakebuenavista.com

Rate per night $104–$370. **Pool** ★★★★. **Fridge in room** Yes. **Shuttle to parks** Yes (Disney). **Maximum number of occupants per room** 4. **Comment** Character breakfast Tuesday, Thursday, and Saturday. $25/night resort fee. $15/night parking. Guests are eligible for 60-day FastPass+ and Extra Magic Hours benefits through 2020.

THE MAIN REASON TO STAY at the Wyndham is the short walk to Disney Springs. The lobby is bright and airy, and check-in service is friendly. Rooms are larger than most and have full refrigerators. Pool-facing rooms in the hotel's wings have exterior hallways that overlook the pool and center courtyard; these hallways can be noisy during summer months. The elevators are unusually slow—it's probably faster to walk to the second and third floors, assuming you're up for the exercise.

US 192 AREA

Gaylord Palms Resort & Convention Center ★★★★½

Rate per night $175–$439. **Pool** ★★★★. **Fridge in room** Yes. **Shuttle to parks** Yes (Disney: free; Universal, Volcano Bay, SeaWorld: $21/person round-trip). **Maximum number of occupants per room** 4. **Comments** $30/night resort fee. $24/night parking.

6000 W. Osceola Pkwy. Kissimmee
☎ 407-586-0000
gaylordpalms.com

THIS UPSCALE RESORT has a colossal convention facility and caters to business clientele, but it's still a nice (if pricey) family resort. Hotel wings are defined by the three themed glass-roofed atria they overlook: Key West's design is reminiscent of island life in the Florida Keys; Everglades is an overgrown spectacle of shabby swamp chic, complete with piped-in cricket noise and a robotic alligator; and the immense, central St. Augustine harks back to Spanish Colonial Florida. Lagoons, streams, and waterfalls connect all three, and walkways and bridges abound. A fourth wing, Emerald Bay Tower, overlooks the Emerald Plaza shopping and dining area of the St. Augustine atrium. These rooms are the nicest and the most expensive, and they're mostly used by conventioneers. The rooms (with perks such as high-speed internet) work better as retreats for adults than for kids. However, children will enjoy wandering the themed areas and playing in the family pool (with water-squirting octopus). In-room childcare is provided by Kid's Nite Out (see page 67).

Grand Orlando Resort at Celebration ★★★★

Rate per night $109–$159. **Pool** ★★★★½. **Fridge in room** Yes. **Shuttle to parks** Yes (Disney). **Maximum number of occupants per room** 5. **Comments** $25/night resort fee. $13/night parking.

2900 Parkway Blvd. Kissimmee
☎ 407-396-7000
or 800-634-4774
grandorlandoresort celebration.com

THE POOL ALONE IS WORTH A STAY HERE, but the hotel gets high marks in all areas. The free-form pool is huge, with a waterfall and waterslide surrounded by palms and flowering plants, plus a smaller heated pool, two hot tubs, and a kiddie pool. Other outdoor amenities include two lighted tennis courts, sand volleyball, a playground, and jogging areas. Kids can also blow off steam in the game room, while adults might visit the fitness center. Rooms are elegant, featuring Italian furnishings and marble baths. They're of ample size and include a minibar (some rooms), a coffee maker, a TV, an iron and board, a hair dryer, and a safe. Dining options include Mandolin's for breakfast (buffet) and dinner and a 1950s-style diner serving burgers, sandwiches, pizza, and more. A sports lounge with a 6-by-11–foot TV offers nighttime entertainment. Guest services can help with tours, park passes, car rental, and babysitting. While the hotel doesn't offer children's programs per se, there are plenty of activities, such as pool games,

Lake Buena Vista, I-4 Corridor, and US 192 Hotels

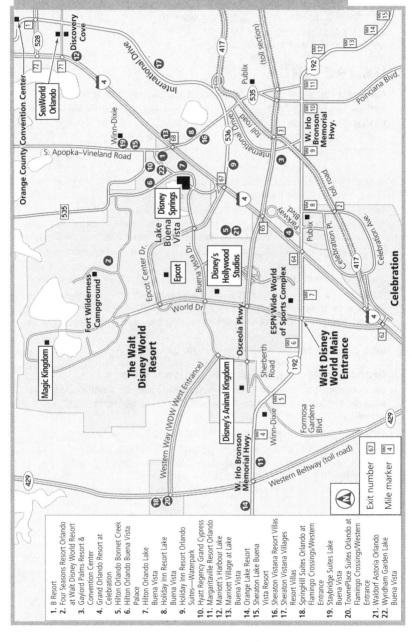

1. B Resort
2. Four Seasons Resort Orlando at Walt Disney World Resort
3. Gaylord Palms Resort & Convention Center
4. Grand Orlando Resort at Celebration
5. Hilton Orlando Bonnet Creek
6. Hilton Orlando Buena Vista Palace
7. Hilton Orlando Lake Buena Vista
8. Holiday Inn Resort Lake Buena Vista
9. Holiday Inn Resort Orlando Suites—Waterpark
10. Hyatt Regency Grand Cypress
11. Margaritaville Resort Orlando
12. Marriott's Harbour Lake
13. Marriott Village at Lake Buena Vista
14. Orange Lake Resort
15. Sheraton Lake Buena Vista Resort
16. Sheraton Vistana Resort Villas
17. Sheraton Vistana Villages Resort Villas
18. SpringHill Suites Orlando at Flamingo Crossings/Western Entrance
19. Staybridge Suites Lake Buena Vista
20. TownePlace Suites Orlando at Flamingo Crossings/Western Entrance
21. Waldorf Astoria Orlando
22. Wyndham Garden Lake Buena Vista

bingo, arts and crafts, and movies by the pool. Once the former Radisson undergoes a multimillion dollar refurbishment of its public areas and guest rooms, it will become a Delta Hotel by Marriott.

Margaritaville Resort Orlando ★★★★½

Rate per night $109–$239 (standard)/$209–$569 (1 bedroom). **Pool** ★★★★. **Fridge in room** Yes. **Shuttle to parks** Yes (Disney, Universal, SeaWorld). **Maximum number of occupants per room** 4 (standard)/6 (1 bedroom). **Comments** $30/night resort fee. $25/night parking.

8000 Fins Up Cir.
Kissimmee
☎ 407-479-0950
margaritavilleresort
orlando.com

THE MARGARITAVILLE COMPLEX, LOCATED across from Disney's Animal Kingdom, includes a hotel, vacation cottages, a dining and entertainment district, and a water park. The casual-luxe design of the 184-room resort evokes island vibes; all rooms have balconies overlooking Fins Up Beach Club and its lagoon pools. Each room includes a TV, a mini-bar, a coffee maker, and a workstation. Guest rooms range from one-bedroom to deluxe suites. Ethan Allen designed a special collection to furnish the guest rooms, restaurants, common areas, and cottages. The hotel has meeting and event spaces, a spa, and several dining options.

Child-appropriate activities, including games, arts, and crafts, are offered at the Parakeets Kids Club, while the Teen Center welcomes older kids for games, movies, and more. The clubs are free of charge. They are open daily 9 a.m.–6 p.m. and are staffed by trained counselors.

Kids will especially enjoy Island H2O Live!, the property's water park. In addition to thrill rides, a wave pool, a lazy river, and a river raft ride, the park offers sand beaches and adult-only areas. Island H20 Live! is within walking distance of the hotel. A trolley is also available for guests to commute from the resort to the water park. Daily admission to the water park is $49.99 plus tax (guests under 48″ $42.99 plus tax).

The dining and entertainment complex called Sunset Walk is opening in phases through the end of 2019. A high-tech, 12-screen dine-in movie theater opened in March 2019. Upon completion the complex will be home to a wide selection of eateries and shops. High-profile tenants will include B.B. King's World Famous BBQ, Skechers, and Lafayette's Fish House and Music Hall.

The vacation cottages are also opening in phases now through the end of 2020. Many of the planned 700 cottages have been sold and some are in varying stages of construction.

Orange Lake Resort ★★★★½

Rate per night $179–$273. **Pool** ★★★★. **Fridge in room** Yes (full kitchen). **Shuttle to parks** Yes (fee varies depending on destination). **Maximum number of occupants per room** 4 (1 bedroom)/16 (4 bedroom). **Comments** $8.95/night resort fee. If you rent directly through the resort as opposed to the sales office, you can avoid time-share sales pitches.

8505 W. Irlo Bronson
Memorial Hwy.
Kissimmee
☎ 407-239-0000 or
800-877-6522
experienceorangelake.com

YOU COULD SPEND YOUR ENTIRE VACATION never leaving this property, about 6–10 minutes from the Disney theme parks. From its seven pools and mini–water park to its golfing opportunities (36 holes of championship greens plus two 9-hole executive courses), Orange Lake offers extensive amenities and recreational opportunities. If you tire of lazing by the pool, try water-skiing, wakeboarding, tubing, fishing, or other activities on the 80-acre lake. There's also a live alligator show, exercise programs, organized competitive sports and games, arts-and-crafts sessions, and mini-golf. Activities don't end when the sun goes down. Karaoke, live music, a Hawaiian luau, and movies at the resort cinema are some of the evening options.

The 2,412 units, ranging from suites and studios to three-bedroom villas, are tastefully decorated and comfortably furnished, all with fully equipped kitchens. The resort recently refurbished its River Island rooms. In addition, the complex has two cafés, three grills, a pizzeria, and a fast-food eatery.

LILIANE These value hotels are perfect for families. Plenty of space, free Wi-Fi, and a kitchen, plus the price is right! However, the shuttle service is insufficient, and a car is a must.

Flamingo Crossings

The hotels at Flamingo Crossings, about 0.5 mile from Walt Disney World's western entrance, target both budget-minded tourists and the sports teams that participate in events at the ESPN Wide World of Sports Complex. In addition to the SpringHill and TownePlace Suites profiled below, **Holiday Inn, Hyatt House,** and **Hampton Inn** are scheduled to open in the near future. By the time all three phases of Flamingo Crossings are complete, the vast development will encompass seven hotels and 237,000 square feet of retail space, as well as nearly 1,300 apartments.

13279 Flamingo Crossings Blvd. Winter Garden ☎ 407-507-1200 tinyurl.com/fc -springhill

SpringHill Suites Orlando at Flamingo Crossings/ Western Entrance ★★★★

Rate per night $116–$192. **Pool** ★★★★ (shared). **Fridge in room** Yes. **Shuttle to parks** Yes (Disney [TTC]: $5/person). **Maximum number of occupants per room** 4 (1 bedroom)/5 (2 bedroom), plus infant in crib. **Comments** Free hot breakfast. See next profile.

13295 Flamingo Crossings Blvd. Winter Garden ☎ 407-507-1300 tinyurl.com/fc- towneplace

TownePlace Suites Orlando at Flamingo Crossings/ Western Entrance ★★★★

Rate per night $116–$267. **Pool** ★★★★ (shared). **Fridge in room** Yes. **Shuttle to parks** Yes (Disney [TTC]: $5/person). **Maximum number of occupants per room** 3 (1 bedroom)/5 (2 bedroom), plus infant in crib. **Comments** Pets welcome ($150/stay). Free hot breakfast.

WITH 250 ROOMS EACH, these adjacent hotels share parking, a huge pool complex with a pool bar, and a fitness center. The hotels include sports-practice fields and facilities—a nod to the sports groups that participate in events at the ESPN Wide World of Sports Complex. The two hotels also share a Seattle's Best coffee bar and a full-service restaurant. Amenities include complimentary Wi-Fi and a free hot breakfast.

The roomy hotel suites at SpringHill include a mini-fridge, a microwave, a sofa bed, and a coffee maker. At TownePlace, an extended-stay hotel, spacious one- and two-bedroom suites feature fully equipped kitchens.

Despite the potential for noise, the rooms are very quiet and spotless. The two-bedroom suite has a small, full kitchen, while the studio has a microwave and coffee maker. Both have only one bathroom, and we think the two-bed-room units could use a second.

Note that the Disney shuttle service is available only three times in the morning, with three return shuttles scheduled in the evening. Located as close to Walt Disney World as some on-site Disney properties, it's only about 5–7 minutes from Disney's Hollywood Studios and the Animal Kingdom. In addition, the Flamingo Crossings hotels are about a 10-minute drive to a wide variety of suburban stores on US 192, including a Publix, a Super Target, and tons of restaurants.

GETTING A GOOD DEAL ON A ROOM OUTSIDE WALT DISNEY WORLD

UNABLE TO COMPETE WITH Disney resorts for convenience or perks, out-of-World hotels lure patrons with bargain rates. The extent of the bargain depends on the season, day of the week, and local events. Here are tips and strategies for getting a good deal on a room outside Walt Disney World.

1. VISIT ORLANDO HOTEL DEALS This discount program sponsored by Visit Orlando offers discounts of up to 25% at Orlando hotels. The program also offers discounts at some area attractions, dinner theaters, museums, performing-arts venues, restaurants, shops, and more. Go to visitorlando.com and click on "Deals."

2. HOTEL SHOPPING ONLINE When we're really looking for a deal, we scour sites such as the ones below for unusually juicy deals that meet our criteria (location, quality, price, amenities).

OUR FAVORITE ONLINE HOTEL RESOURCES
mousesavers.com Best site for hotels in Disney World
hotelcoupons.com Self-explanatory
experiencekissimmee.com Primarily US 192–Kissimmee area hotels
visitorlando.com Good info; not user-friendly for booking
orlandovacation.com Great rates for condos and home rentals

If we find a hotel that fills the bill, we check it out at other websites and comparative travel search engines such as **Kayak** (kayak.com), **Hotels.com,** and **Mobissimo** (mobissimo.com) to see who has the best rate. (As an aside, Kayak sells travel products, raising the issue of whether products not sold by Kayak are equally likely to come up in a search. Mobissimo, on the other hand, only links potential buyers to provider websites.) Hotels.com is a booking engine that lets you earn points toward a future free stay. Another site is **Trivago** (trivago.com), but it requires your check-in and check-out dates to search. Your initial shopping effort should take about 15–20 minutes, faster if you can zero in quickly on a particular hotel.

BOB Always call the specific hotel, not the hotel chain's national 800 number.

Next, call the hotel or have your travel agent call. Start by asking about specials. If there are none, or if the hotel can't beat the best price you've found on the internet, share your findings and ask if the hotel can do better. Sometimes you'll be asked for proof of the rate you've discovered online—to be prepared for this, go to the site and enter the dates of your stay, and make sure the rate you've found is available. If it is, print the page or take a screenshot of this information and have it handy for your travel agent or for when you call the hotel.

3. IF YOU MAKE YOUR OWN RESERVATION Call and ask about specials before you inquire about corporate rates. Don't hesitate to bargain, but do it before you check in. If you're buying a weekend package, for example, and want to extend your stay, you can often obtain at least the corporate rate for the extra days.

CONDOMINIUMS AND VACATION HOMES

THE BEST DEALS IN LODGING in the Walt Disney World area are vacation homes and single-owner condos. In a condo, if something goes wrong, someone will be on hand to fix the problem. Vacation homes rented from a property-management company likewise will have someone to come to the rescue, though responsiveness tends to vary vastly from company to company. If you rent directly from an owner, correcting problems can often be more difficult, particularly if the owner doesn't live in the same area as the rental home.

Because condos tend to be part of large developments (frequently time-shares), amenities such as pools, playgrounds, arcades, and fitness centers often rival those found in the best hotels. In a vacation home, all the amenities are contained in the home (though in planned developments, there may be community amenities as well). Depending on the specific home, you might find a small pool, a hot tub, a two-car garage, a family room, a game room, or even a home theater. Features found in both condos and vacation homes include full kitchens, laundry rooms, TVs, and DVD players. Time-shares are clones when it comes to furniture and decor, but single-owner condos and vacation homes are furnished and decorated in a style that reflects the taste of the owner.

Location, Location, Location

The best vacation home is one that is within easy commuting distance of the theme parks. If you plan to spend some time at SeaWorld and the Universal parks, you'll want something just to the northeast of Walt Disney World (between the World and Orlando). If you plan to spend most of your time in the World, the best selection of vacation homes is along US 192 south of the park.

To get the most from a vacation home, you need to be close enough to commute in 20 minutes or less to your Walt Disney World destination. This proximity will allow for naps, quiet time, swimming, and dollar-saving meals you prepare yourself. Though traffic and road conditions are as important as the distance from a vacation home to your Disney destination, we recommend a home no farther than 5 miles away in areas northeast of Disney World and no farther than 4.5 miles away in areas south of the park.

Recommended Websites

The best websites for rental homes or condos provide the following:

- Ease of navigation
- The ability to browse without having to log in or divulge personal information
- Photos and in-depth descriptions of individual homes
- Overview maps or text descriptions that reflect how far the home or development is from Walt Disney World
- The ability to book the specific rental home of your choice on the site (some companies provide photos of a typical home instead of listing each home in their inventory)
- An easy-to-find phone number for bookings and questions

After checking out dozens upon dozens of sites, we narrowed our recommendations to the following:

Vacation Rentals by Owner (vrbo.com) is a nationwide vacation-homes listings service that puts prospective renters in direct contact with owners of rental homes. The site is straightforward and lists a large number of rental properties in Celebration, Disney's planned community situated about 8–10 minutes from the theme parks. Two similar listing services with good websites are **Flipkey** (flipkey.com), owned by TripAdvisor, and **#1 Dream Homes** (floridadreamhomes .com), which has a smaller selection of homes but a good reputation for customer service.

Visit Orlando (visitorlando.com) is the way to go when it comes to shopping for time-shares (click "Stay" on the home page) because you can bypass these developments' notoriously high-pressure sales pitches. The site also lists hotels and vacation homes.

We frequently receive letters from readers extolling the virtues of renting a condo or vacation home. This endorsement from a New Jersey family of five is typical:

> *I cannot stress enough how important it is that large families (more than two kids) rent a house for their stay! We stayed at Windsor Hills Resort. It took about 10 minutes to drive to the parks in the morning, and we had no traffic issues at all. We loved getting away from the hubbub of Disney and relaxing back at the house in "our" pool.*

HOW *to* CHILDPROOF *a* HOTEL ROOM

SMALL CHILDREN UP TO 3 YEARS OLD (and sometimes older) can wreak mayhem—if not outright disaster—in a hotel room. Chances are that you're pretty experienced when it comes to spotting potential dangers, but just in case you need a refresher course, here's what to look for.

Begin by checking for hazards that you can't fix yourself: balconies, chipping paint, cracked walls, sharp surfaces, shag carpeting, and windows that can't be secured shut. If you encounter anything that you don't like or is too much of a hassle to fix, ask for another room.

If you use a crib supplied by the hotel, make sure that the mattress is firm and covers the entire bottom of the crib. The mattress cover, if there is one, should fit tightly. Slats should be 2.5 inches (about the width of a soda can) or less apart. Make sure the drop sides work properly. Check for sharp edges and potentially toxic substances. Wipe down surfaces with disinfectant. Finally, position the crib away from drapery cords, heaters, wall sockets, and air conditioners.

A Manteno, Illinois, mom offers this suggestion:

> You can request bed rails at the Disney resorts. Our 2½-year-old was too big for the pack and play; the bed rails worked perfectly for us.

If your infant can turn over, we recommend changing him or her on a pad on the floor. Likewise, if you have a child seat of any sort, place it where it cannot be knocked over, and always strap your child in.

If your child can roll, crawl, or walk, you should bring about eight electrical outlet covers and some cord to tie cabinets shut and to bind drapery cords and the like out of reach. Check for appliances, lamps, ice buckets, and anything else that your child might pull down on him- or herself. Have the hotel remove coffee tables with sharp edges, as well as both real and artificial plants that are within your child's reach. Round up items from tables and countertops, such as courtesy toiletries and drinking glasses, and store them out of reach.

If the bathroom door can be accidentally locked, cover the locking mechanism with duct tape or a doorknob cover. Use the security chain or upper latch on the room's entrance door to ensure that your child doesn't open it without your knowledge.

Inspect the floor and remove pins, coins, and other foreign objects that your child might find. Don't forget to check under beds and furniture. *Tip:* Crawl around the room on your hands and knees to see possible hazards from your child's perspective.

If you rent a suite or a condo, you'll have more territory to childproof and will have to deal with things such as cleaning supplies, a stove, a refrigerator, cooking utensils, and low cabinet doors. Sometimes the best option is to seal off the kitchen with a safety gate. Access to a private pool should be locked at all times.

PART FOUR

DINING

DINING OPTIONS ABOUND BOTH IN AND OUT of Walt Disney World, and if you're so inclined, there are a lot of ways to save big bucks while keeping your crew nourished and happy.

◄█ DINING *in* WALT DISNEY WORLD

IF THE AVERAGE PARENTS roaming Walt Disney World were primarily concerned with pleasing their palates, the hottest dinner ticket in the parks wouldn't be the *Hoop-Dee-Doo Musical Revue*. In fact, if you want to know what Disney visitors really like, look at the numbers: every year, they consume 10 million hamburgers, 6 million hot dogs, 75 million sodas, and 150 tons of popcorn.

So for many families, food is a secondary consideration, but if you *do* care about dining out on your vacation or you'd like to experiment with different cuisines, *The Unofficial Guide to Walt Disney World* includes detailed reviews of the sit-down establishments in Disney World.

LILIANE Parents should be aware that both full- and counter-service restaurants at Disney World serve very substantial portions. You can easily split an entrée, put aside parts of dinners for lunch the next day (if you have an in-room fridge), or load up at lunch and go light on dinner.

WALT DISNEY WORLD RESTAURANT CATEGORIES

IN GENERAL, FOOD AND BEVERAGE offerings at Walt Disney World are defined by service, price, and convenience.

FULL-SERVICE RESTAURANTS Full-service restaurants are in all Disney resorts (except the Value resorts and Port Orleans French Quarter), all major theme parks, and Disney Springs. Disney operates most of the restaurants in the theme parks and its hotels, while contractors or franchisees operate the rest. Advance Reservations (see page 144) are recommended for most full-service restaurants except those in the Disney Springs Resort Area. The restaurants accept American Express, Diners

WALT DISNEY WORLD BUFFETS & FAMILY-STYLE RESTAURANTS

RESTAURANT	LOCATION	CUISINE	MEALS SERVED	CHARACTERS
AKERSHUS ROYAL BANQUET HALL	Epcot	American (B), Norwegian (L, D)	B, L, D	Yes
BIERGARTEN RESTAURANT	Epcot	German	L, D	No
BOMA—FLAVORS OF AFRICA	Animal Kingdom Lodge	American (B), African (D)	B, D	No
CAPE MAY CAFE	Beach Club Resort	American	B, Br, D	Yes (B)
CHEF MICKEY'S	Contemporary Resort	American	B, Br, D	Yes
CINDERELLA'S ROYAL TABLE	Magic Kingdom	American	B*, L, D	Yes
THE CRYSTAL PALACE	Magic Kingdom	American	B, L, D	Yes
THE DIAMOND HORSESHOE	Magic Kingdom	American	L, D*	No
FRESH MEDITERRANEAN MARKET	Dolphin Hotel	Mediterranean/ American	B, L	No
GARDEN GRILL RESTAURANT	Epcot	American	B, L, D	Yes
GARDEN GROVE	Swan Hotel	American	B, L, D	Yes (B**, D)
HOLLYWOOD & VINE	Disney's Hollywood Studios	American	B, L, D	Yes
HOOP-DEE-DOO MUSICAL REVUE	Fort Wilderness	American	D	No
LIBERTY TREE TAVERN	Magic Kingdom	American	L, D	No
1900 PARK FARE	Grand Floridian	American	B, D	Yes
'OHANA	Polynesian Village	American/Polynesian	B, D	Yes (B)
PIZZAFARI	Animal Kingdom	American	L, D*	No
SPIRIT OF ALOHA DINNER SHOW	Polynesian Village	Polynesian	D	No
TRAIL'S END RESTAURANT	Fort Wilderness	American	B, Br, D	No
TUSKER HOUSE RESTAURANT	Animal Kingdom	American (B), African (L, D)	B, L, D	Yes
THE WAVE . . . OF AMERICAN FLAVORS	Contemporary Resort	American	B, L, D	No
WHISPERING CANYON CAFE	Wilderness Lodge	American	B, L, D	No

* Serves family-style meals only at the meal(s) indicated. *Note:* The Diamond Horseshoe is open seasonally.
** Character-breakfast buffet served only on weekends.
*** Serves buffet-style meals only at the meal(s) indicated.

Club, Discover Card, Disney gift cards, Disney Dream Reward Dollars, Japan Credit Bureau, MasterCard, and Visa.

BUFFETS AND FAMILY-STYLE RESTAURANTS Many of these have Disney characters in attendance, and most have a separate children's menu with dishes such as hot dogs, burgers, chicken nuggets, pizza, macaroni and cheese, and spaghetti and meatballs. In addition to the buffets, several restaurants serve a family-style, all-you-can-eat, fixed-price meal.

Advance Reservations are required for character buffets and recommended for all other buffets and family-style restaurants. Most major credit cards are accepted.

If you want to eat a lot but don't feel like standing in yet another line, then consider one of the all-you-can-eat family-style restaurants. These feature platters of food brought to your table in courses by a server. You can eat as much as you like—even go back to a favorite appetizer after you finish the main course. The food tends to be a little better than what you'd find on a buffet line.

The table on the opposite page lists buffets and family-style restaurants (where you can belly up for bulk loading) at Walt Disney World.

FOOD COURTS Featuring a collection of counter-service eateries under one roof, food courts can be found at Disney's Moderate and Value resorts. (The closest thing to a food court at the theme parks is **Sunshine Seasons** at Epcot; see the opposite page.) Advance Reservations are not available at these restaurants.

COUNTER SERVICE Counter-service fast food is available at all theme parks, Disney Springs, and the BoardWalk. The food compares in quality with McDonald's or Taco Bell but is more expensive, though often served in larger portions.

FAST CASUAL Somewhere between hamburgers and formal dining are the establishments in this category, including three in the theme parks: **Be Our Guest** (breakfast and lunch) in the Magic Kingdom and **Sunshine Seasons** and **Les Halles Boulangerie-Patisserie** in Epcot. The menu choices are a cut above what you'd typically see at a counter-service location. At Sunshine Seasons, for example, chefs prepare grilled salmon on an open cooking surface while you watch, or you can choose from rotisserie chicken or pork, tasty noodle bowls, or large sandwiches made with artisanal breads. Entrées cost about $1–$2 more on average than traditional counter service, but the variety and food quality more than make up for the difference.

LILIANE Les Halles Boulangerie-Patisserie has amazing sandwiches, cheese platters, quiches, and the best sweets ever.

VENDOR FOOD Vendors abound at the theme parks, Disney Springs, and the BoardWalk. Offerings include popcorn, ice cream bars, churros (Mexican pastries), soft drinks, bottled water, and (in theme parks) fresh fruit. Prices include tax; many vendors are set up to accept credit cards, charges to your room at a Disney resort, and the Disney Dining Plan. Others take only cash (look for a sign near the cash register).

DISNEY DINING PLANS

DISNEY OFFERS PREPAID DINING PLANS to accompany its lodging packages (see page 111). They're available to all Disney resort guests except those staying at the Swan, the Dolphin, the hotels of the Disney

Springs Resort Area, and Shades of Green. Guests must also purchase a package from Disney (not through an online reseller), have annual passes, or be members of the Disney Vacation Club (DVC) to participate in the dining plan. Except for DVC members, a 3-night minimum stay is typically also required. The overall cost is determined by the number of nights you stay at a Disney resort hotel. All plans include tax but not gratuity.

You must purchase a Disney vacation package to be eligible for a dining plan, as a family of five from Waldron, Michigan, learned:

> We read through The Unofficial Guide and noticed that it said not to book a package during slow season. We were overwhelmed with the decisions that we had to make, so we booked the resort first, then the tickets, and then we wanted the dining plan. Well, they wouldn't add the dining plan because we had already booked everything.

In addition to food, all the plans include sweeteners, such as a free round of mini-golf, discounts on spa treatments and salon services, and deals on recreational activities such as fishing and water sports.

Disney ceaselessly tinkers with the dining plans' rules, meal definitions, and participating restaurants. Here are some recent examples:

- At sit-down restaurants, you can substitute dessert for a side salad, cup of soup, or fruit plate.
- Counter-service restaurants make no distinction between adult and child dining credits. If you have two child and two adult dining credits on your account, you may purchase four adult counter-service meals with those credits.
- You may exchange one sit-down or counter-service meal credit for three snacks, as long as you do so within the same transaction. However, using a sit-down credit for this is not a good deal.
- You can exchange a sit-down meal credit for a counter-service meal, though doing this even once negates any savings you get from using a plan in the first place.

Finally, you can use your meal credits to pay for the meals of people who are not on any dining plan. We've heard of sporadic incidents of Disney not allowing this, and we think it's due to confusion about what the dining plan rules actually say. (The rules say the meals can't be *transferred*; they say nothing about meals being *shared*.) As long as someone enrolled in the dining plan tells the server in advance that they plan to redeem the appropriate number of credits, and then orders the meals for the non-enrolled diners, everything should be within the rules. In the event a server or manager says the rules prohibit meal sharing, point out that the rules don't mention it.

DISNEY DINING PLAN This plan provides, for each member of your group (age 3 and up), for each night of your stay, one counter-service meal, one full-service meal, and two snacks at participating Disney dining locations and restaurants, including room service at some Disney resorts (type "Disney Dining Plan Locations" into your favorite search engine to find sites with the entire list). The plan also includes one refillable drink mug per person, per package, but it can be filled only at Disney resort counter-service restaurants. For guests age 10 and up, the price for 2019 is $75.49 per night; for guests ages 3–9, the price is $25.76 per night. Children younger than age 3 eat free from an adult's plate. Tax is included, but gratuity is not.

For instance, if you're staying 3 nights, you'll be credited with three counter-service meals, three full-service meals, three snacks, and one refillable mug for each member of your party. All those meals will be put into a group meal account. Meals in your account can be used by anyone in your group, on any combination of days—for example, you can skip a full-service meal one day and have two on another day.

The counter-service meal includes an entrée (sandwich, dinner salad, pizza, or the like) or a complete combo meal (such as a burger and fries), and a drink. The full-service sit-down meals include an entrée, dessert, and drink. If you're dining at a buffet, the full-service meal includes the buffet and a drink. The snacks include items normally sold from carts or stands throughout the parks and resorts: ice cream, soft drinks, fruit, and the like. When in doubt, ask a cast member what else might count. Beverage choices include unlimited soda, coffee, or tea; or one beer, glass of wine, cocktail from a predetermined list, milkshake, smoothie, or specialty hot chocolate.

Disney's top-of-the-line restaurants (dubbed **Disney Signature** restaurants in the plan)—along with Cinderella's Royal Table and Be Our Guest (dinner only), all the dinner shows, regular room service, and in-room pizza delivery—count as two full-service meals on the standard dining plan.

In addition to the preceding, the dining plan comes with several other important rules:

- Everyone staying in the same resort room must participate in the dining plan.

- Children ages 3–9 must order from the kid's menu if one is available. This rule is occasionally relaxed at Disney's counter-service restaurants, enabling older kids to order from the adult (age 10+) menu.

- A full-service meal can be breakfast, lunch, or dinner. The greatest savings occur when you use your full-service meal credits for dinner.

- The meal plan expires at midnight **on the day you check out** of the Disney resort. **Unused meals are nonrefundable.**

- Neither the Disney Dining Plan nor Disney's Free Dining can be added to a discounted room-only reservation.

QUICK-SERVICE DINING PLAN This plan includes meals, snacks, and drinks at most counter-service eateries in Walt Disney World. The cost (including tax) is $52.50 per day for guests age 10 and up, $21.75 per day for kids ages 3–9. The plan includes two counter-service meals and two snacks per day, in addition to one refillable drink mug per person, per package (eligible for refills only at counter-service locations in your Disney resort).

DISNEY DELUXE DINING PLAN This plan offers a choice of full- or counter-service meals for three meals a day at any participating restaurant. In addition to the three meals a day, the plan also includes two snacks per day and a refillable drink mug. The Deluxe Plan costs $116.25 per night for guests age 10 and older, and $40 per night for kids ages 3–9, tax included.

Things to Consider When Evaluating the Disney Dining Plan

If you prefer to always eat at counter-service restaurants, you'll be better off with the Quick-Service plan. You should also avoid the Disney Dining Plan if you have finicky eaters, you're visiting during holidays or summer, or you can't get reservations at your first- or second-choice sit-down restaurants. In addition, if you have children age 10 and older, be sure that they can eat an adult-size dinner at a sit-down restaurant every night; if not, you'd probably come out ahead just paying for everyone's meals without the plan.

If you opt for the plan, skipping one full-service meal during a visit of 5 or fewer days can mean the difference between saving and losing money. In our experience, having a scheduled sit-down meal for every day of a weeklong vacation can be mentally exhausting, especially for kids. One option might be to schedule a meal at a Disney Signature restaurant, which requires two full-service credits, and have no scheduled sit-down meal on another night in the middle of your trip, allowing everyone to decide on the spot if they're up for something formal.

As already noted, many of the most popular restaurants are fully booked as soon as their reservation windows open. If you're still interested in the dining plan, book your restaurants as soon as possible, typically 180 days before you visit. Then decide whether the plan makes economic sense. (For more on Advance Reservations, see page 144.)

If you're making reservations to eat at Disney hotels other than your own, a car allows you to easily access them. When you use the Disney transportation system, dining at the various resorts can be a logistical nightmare. Those without a car may want to weigh the immediate services of a taxi or ride-sharing, typically $9–$25 each way across Disney property, versus a 50- to 75-minute trip on Disney transportation each way.

When Disney offers Free Dining discounts (typically in September but earlier in 2019), it generally charges rack rate for the hotel. You should work out the math, but Free Dining is typically a good deal for families who have two children under age 10, are staying at a Value or Moderate resort, and book lots of character meals. Families with always-hungry teenagers may also benefit from Free Dining. Light eaters and childless couples, especially those staying at Deluxe resorts, may find it cheaper to take a room discount and pay for food separately.

Disney is known to tinker with the dining plans, so we recommend double-checking your options prior to purchasing any dining plan.

Readers who try the Disney dining plans have varying experiences. A St. Louis family of three comments:

> We got the dining plan and would never do it again. Far too expensive, far too much food, and then you have to tip on top of the expense. Much easier to buy what you want, where and when you want.

A Belmont, Massachusetts, dad likes the Quick-Service Plan:

> If you intend to eat Disney food, the counter-service meal plan is a good option. We didn't want the full plan because the restaurants seemed overpriced, and the necessity of reservations months in advance seemed crazy and a bar to flexibility.

But a reader from The Woodlands, Texas, laments that the plan has altered the focus of her vacation:

> For me, the dining plan has taken a lot of the fun out of going to Disney World. Now, dining for each day must be planned months in advance unless one is to eat just hot dogs, pizza, and other walk-up items. I want to have fun. I don't want to be locked into a tight schedule, always worrying about where we need to be when it's time to eat, and I don't want to eat when I'm not hungry just because I have a reservation somewhere.

A mom from Orland Park, Illinois, comments on the difficulty of getting Advance Reservations:

> It's impossible to get reservations anywhere good—the restaurants that are available are available for a reason. We found ourselves taking whatever was open and were unhappy with every sit-down meal we had, except lunch at Liberty Tree Tavern. I don't enjoy planning my day exclusively around eating at a certain restaurant at a certain time, but that is what you must do 6 months in advance if you want to eat at a good sit-down restaurant in Disney. That is ridiculous.

In a similar vein, a San Jose, California, reader says guests who aren't on the dining plan need to know how it affects Advance Reservations:

> When planning 90 days out for the off-season, I was told by the Disney rep to make all my Advance Reservations then because the restaurants are booked by people on the dining plan. I was told most of the sit-down restaurants don't even take walk-ins anymore. Sure enough, even though I was well over 90 days away from my vacation, a lot of my restaurant choices were unavailable. I had to rearrange my entire schedule to fit the open slots at the restaurants I didn't want to miss.

On a positive note, many readers report that Disney cast members are much more knowledgeable about the dining plan these days than in the past. A Washington, D.C.–area couple writes:

> The kinks are worked out, and everyone at the parks we talked to seemed to get it, but we still spent $40 or more at most sit-down dinners on [additional] drinks and tips.

A mum from Sutton Coldfield, England, warns that toddlers fall through the cracks:

We were traveling with two 6-year-olds and a 2-year-old. My youngest did not qualify for the dining plan, which worked well in the buffet-style restaurants where he could eat free. However, if you eat in a full-service restaurant and your 2-year-old is eating off the menu, there's no toddler option—you have to pay for a child's meal.

A Land O' Lakes, Florida, dad bumped into this problem:

We had some trouble with our dining plan being invalidated after checkout, though it was supposed to be valid until midnight of our checkout date. That was annoying because calls to the resort were needed to verify the meals left on our passes for The Crystal Palace and for some snacks later.

The dining plan left a family of five from Nashville, Tennessee, similarly dazed and confused:

What was annoying was the inconsistency. You can get a 16-ounce chocolate milk on the kids' plan, but only 8 ounces of white milk at many places. At Earl of Sandwich, you can get 16 ounces of either kind. A pint of milk would count as a snack (price $1.79), but they wouldn't count a quart of milk (price $2.39) because it wasn't a single serving. However, in Animal Kingdom, my husband bought a water-bottle holder (price $3.75) and used a snack credit.

Reader Tips for Getting the Most Out of the Plan

A mom from Radford, Virginia, shares the following:

Warn people to eat lunch early if they have dinner reservations before 7 p.m. Disney doesn't skimp on food—if you eat a late lunch, you WILL NOT be hungry for dinner.

A mom from Brick Township, New Jersey, found that the dining plan streamlined her touring:

This was great for the kids because we did a character-dining experience every day. This helped us in the parks because we didn't have to wait in line to see the characters. Instead, we got all of our autographs during our meals.

A Saskatoon, Saskatchewan, father of three says it's important to be vigilant when it comes to the outdoor food vendors:

We had a problem with a vendor who charged us meal service for each of the ice cream bars we purchased. This became evident at our final sit-down meal, when we didn't have any meal vouchers left. Check the receipts after every purchase!

ADVANCE RESERVATIONS: WHAT'S IN A NAME?

THOUGH THEY'RE CALLED ADVANCE RESERVATIONS, most dining reservations at Disney World don't guarantee you a table at a specific time, as they would at your typical hometown restaurant.

Instead of scheduling Advance Reservations for actual tables, reservations fill time slots. The number of slots available is based on the average length of time that guests occupy a table at a particular restaurant, adjusted for seasonality. When you arrive at a restaurant having made Advance Reservations, your wait to be seated will usually be less than 20 minutes during peak hours, and often less than 10 minutes. If you're a walk-in, especially during busier seasons, expect to either wait 40–75 minutes or be told that no tables are available.

BOB Disney charges a $10- to $25-per-person penalty for missing an Advance Reservation, or if you cancel on the day of the meal.

Disney's most popular restaurants can run out of reservations 6 months in advance. Also, most Disney restaurants hold no tables at all—none—for walk-in guests. That means it's important to book your dining reservations as soon as you're able (typically 180 days before your visit).

GETTING ADVANCE RESERVATIONS AT POPULAR RESTAURANTS

TWO OF THE HARDEST RESERVATIONS to get in Disney World are the 8 a.m. breakfast slots at the Magic Kingdom's **Cinderella's Royal Table** and **The Plaza Restaurant** on Main Street. Why? Cinderella's Royal Table is Disney's tiniest character restaurant, accommodating only about 130 diners at a time. The Plaza is even smaller. Starting a breakfast reservation at these places at 8 a.m.

BOB If you wonder why Disney makes everything so insanely complicated, so do we. We also wonder why people put up with it. Excellent non-Disney restaurants are listed on pages 186–187.

gets you in the park, fed, and on your way to your first ride before most people are even through the turnstiles. You'll have to put in some effort to secure an Advance Reservation at these places, especially during busier times of year.

The easiest, fastest way to get a reservation is to go to disneyworld .disney.go.com/dining starting at 5:45 a.m. Eastern, a full hour and 15 minutes before phone reservations open. To familiarize yourself with how the site works, try it out a couple of days before you actually need

ADVANCE RESERVATIONS: *The Official Line*

YOU CAN RESERVE THE FOLLOWING up to 180 days in advance:

Afternoon tea and children's programs at the Grand Floridian Resort & Spa

All Disney table-service restaurants and character-dining venues

***Fantasmic!* Dining Package** at Disney's Hollywood Studios

Hoop-Dee-Doo Musical Revue at Fort Wilderness Resort & Campground

Spirit of Aloha Dinner Show at the Polynesian Village Resort

Guests staying at Disney-owned resorts may make dining reservations for the entire length of their stay—up to 10 days—in a single booking up to 180 days before their arrival. Guests staying at the Swan, the Dolphin, Shades of Green, and the hotels of the Disney Springs Resort Area, as well as guests staying off-property, are only able to reserve one day at a time 180 days in advance.

to make reservations. You'll also save time by setting up a My Disney Experience account online (see page 239) before your 180-day booking window, making sure to enter any credit card information needed to guarantee your reservations. If you live in California and have to get up at 2:45 a.m. Pacific to make a reservation, Disney couldn't care less.

Disney's website is usually within a few seconds of the official time as determined by the US Naval Observatory or the National Institute of Standards and Technology, accessible online at time.gov. Using this site, synchronize your computer to the second the night before your 180-day window opens (if your computer hasn't done it automatically already).

Early on the morning you want to make reservations, take a few moments to type the date of your visit into a text document in MM/DD/YYYY format (for example, 11/16/2019 for November 16, 2019). Select the date, and copy it to your computer's clipboard by pressing the **Ctrl** and **C** keys simultaneously (**Command-C** on Mac) or right-clicking your mouse and selecting "Copy." This will save you from having to type in the date when the site comes online.

Next, start trying Disney's website about 3 minutes before 5:45 a.m. Under "My Disney Experience," click "Reserve Dining." You'll see a text box where you can specify the date of your visit. Click the text box and press **Ctrl-A,** then **Ctrl-V** (substitute **Command** for **Ctrl** on Mac) to paste the date; then press the tab key on your keyboard. (You can also click on the blue calendar icon to flip through a month-by-month calendar, or you can select the entire date in the text box, right-click your mouse, and select "Paste," but these are slower.) You'll also see a place to specify the location (such as "Magic Kingdom"), time of your meal, and your party size; you can fill these in ahead of time too. Then click "Search Times."

BOB For Advance Reservations, be sure you bring your confirmation number to the restaurant.

Above the "Party Size" widget is a text box with the words "Search Within Dining." Start typing your restaurant name in that text box. As soon as you start typing, the website will start guessing which restaurant you want and offer a list of suggestions. It's faster if you just type a few letters—*be our* or *cin* are enough for the site to know you mean Be Our Guest and Cinderella's Royal Table, respectively. Click on the desired restaurant in the list of suggestions. Finally, click "Search Times" or hit the Enter key on your keyboard—both submit your request.

If your date isn't yet available, a message will appear saying "There is a problem searching for reservations at this time" or something similar. If this happens, refresh the browser page and start over. If you don't see an error message, however, the results returned will tell you whether your restaurant has a table available.

Note that while you're typing, other guests are trying to make Advance Reservations too, so you want the transaction to go down as quickly as possible. Flexibility on your part counts—it's much harder to get a seating for a large group, so give some thought to breaking your group into numbers that can be accommodated at tables of four. Also make sure you have your credit card out where you can read it.

All Advance Reservations for Cinderella's Royal Table character meals, the *Fantasmic!* and *Rivers of Lights* Dining Packages, the *Hoop-Dee-Doo Musical Revue,* and the *Spirit of Aloha Dinner Show* require complete prepayment with a credit card at the time of the booking. The name on the booking can't be changed after the Advance Reservation is made. Reservations may be canceled, with the deposit refunded in full, by calling ☎ 407-WDW-DINE (939-3463) at least 48 hours before seating time.

While many readers have been successful using our strategies, some have not:

> *I got up extra early 180 days before our trip to get Thanksgiving reservations at Le Cellier for my husband's birthday. Even though I logged on to Disney's website right at 6 a.m., by the time I got done typing and clicking, the only table available was for 8:40 p.m.—too late for our children, and we would have missed the fireworks.*

On most days, a couple hundred users slam Disney's computer system within milliseconds of one another. With this volume, a 20th of a second or less can make the difference between getting a table and not getting one. As it happens, there are variables beyond your control. One is the number of computers through which your request passes before it reaches Disney's reservation system. The explanation is rather technical, but the same principle applies whether you're trying to get dining reservations online with Disney or concert seats through Ticketmaster.

If you don't have access to a computer at 5:45 a.m. on the morning you need to make reservations, Disney's phone agents begin taking calls at 6:45 a.m. Eastern. Call ☎ 407-WDW-DINE (939-3463) and follow the prompts to speak to a person. You may still get placed on hold, and you'll be an hour behind the early birds with computers. Still, you'll be well ahead of those who couldn't make it up before sunrise.

Also, if you're on the Disney Dining Plan and you want to book the *Fantasmic!* or *Rivers of Light* package, Cinderella's Royal Table, or one of the dinner shows, you may be better off reserving by phone. The online system may not recognize your table-service credits, but you can book and pay with a credit card and then call ☎ 407-WDW-DINE (939-3463) after 6:45 a.m. and have them credit the charge for the meal back to your card (a potential hassle if you get an uncooperative cast member). When you get to Walt Disney World, you'll use credits from your dining plan to "pay" for the meal. (Sometimes the online system has glitches and shows no availability; in this case, call after 6:45 a.m. to confirm whether the online system is correct.)

Reservations are also available for several WDW restaurants via OpenTable. If you're having trouble getting a dining reservation through the usual Disney channels, it may be worth checking this option. As a bonus, if you book through OpenTable, you won't be subject to the same no-show penalty fee that you're charged if you miss your reservation without canceling. However, your account will be suspended if you're a no-show for four reservations within a 12-month period. Besides just being polite, it's easy to cancel or change reservations on the website or app.

Last-Ditch Efforts

Because a fee is charged for failing to cancel an Advance Reservation in time (see page 149), you can often score a last-minute reservation: as long as the reservation-holder calls to cancel before midnight the day before, he or she won't be charged, so your best shot at picking up a canceled reservation is to repeatedly call ☎ 407-WDW-DINE (939-3463) or ping disneyworld.disney.go.com/dining as often as possible between 10 and 11 p.m.

If you *still* can't get an Advance Reservation, go to the restaurant on the day you wish to dine, and try for a table as a walk-in. Yes, we've already told you this is a long shot—that said, you *may* be able to swing it between 2:30 and 4:30 p.m., the hours when most full-service restaurants are most likely to take walk-ins, if they do at all. Your chances of success increase during less-busy times of year or on cold or rainy days during busier seasons. If you don't mind eating late, see if you can get a table during the restaurant's last hour of serving. Disney full-service restaurants in the theme parks can be very hard-nosed about walk-ins: Even if you walk up and see that the restaurant isn't busy, you may still need to visit Guest Services to make a reservation, as a Fayetteville, Georgia, reader relates:

> We walked up to Hollywood & Vine at Disney's Hollywood Studios to try for walk-in seating. It was an off time—3:30 p.m.—and we could see that the restaurant was virtually empty. But we were turned away for lack of availability. We walked to Guest Relations, obtained a reservation, walked back to the podium, and were immediately checked in.

Landing an Advance Reservation for Cinderella's Royal Table at dinner is somewhat easier than for breakfast or lunch, but the price is a whopping $65–$80 or more for adults and $45–$65 for children ages 3–9 (prices varies depending on season). If you're unable to lock up a table for breakfast or lunch, a dinner reservation will at least get your children inside the castle.

Last-Minute Dining Reservations for Last-Minute Planners

If you are planning a trip within 30 days of arrival and pixie dust couldn't get you a spot at Cinderella's Royal Table, don't despair. Try **The Crystal Palace** (Magic Kingdom), **Akershus Royal Banquet Hall** (Epcot), or **Tusker House** (Animal Kingdom) for theme park character meals. Outside the parks, try **1900 Park Fare** (Grand Floridian); **Cape May Cafe** (Beach Club); breakfast with Rapunzel, Flynn Rider, Ariel, and Prince Eric at **Trattoria al Forno** (BoardWalk); or the new Story Book Dining at **Artist Point** with Snow White (Wilderness Lodge). Check regularly online, call ☎ 407-WDW-DINE (939-3463), and, most of all, don't ever, ever give up.

THE REALITY OF GETTING LAST-MINUTE DINING RESERVATIONS

IF YOUR TRIP is more than 180 days out and you want to dine at a popular venue such as Be Our Guest Restaurant or Cinderella's Royal Table, following our advice on page 145 will get you the table you want more than 80% of the time.

The longer you wait, the more effort you'll have to put in to find a reservation. For example, if you're trying for breakfast at Cinderella's Royal Table within the next 7 days, your chance of finding any table the first time you check is less than 3%, based on our tests. But if you have the time and patience to visit Disney's website around 30 times over the next week (that's not a typo), you have a 50-50 shot at finding a last-minute cancellation.

Besides Cinderella's Royal Table and Be Our Guest, the list below shows the restaurants where capacity and demand make finding a last-minute reservation very difficult. If you're planning a trip within the next 30 days, see the section on page 148 for our recommended alternatives.

- **Chef Art Smith's Homecomin'** *(Disney Springs)* Exceptional fried chicken, desserts you'd slap your siblings to get more of, and the best cocktails in Disney Springs. Dinner reservations are hardest to get.

- **Chef Mickey's** *(Contemporary Resort)* The food isn't anything special, and neither is the venue. The draw is the Disney characters and the service, both of which are great. Lunch reservations are hardest to get.

- **Coral Reef** *(The Seas/Epcot)* One of only two sit-down restaurants in Epcot's Future World. The location and underwater views of The Seas' fish tanks make lunch reservations harder to find than at most other places.

- **The Crystal Palace** *(Magic Kingdom)* Joining Winnie the Pooh and his friends for this character buffet is difficult to do last minute, and it rarely has walk-in availability.

- **The Plaza Restaurant** *(Magic Kingdom)* The Plaza serves decent sandwiches in blessed air-conditioned comfort, but its small size makes it a difficult reservation to snag, especially at dinner.

- **Raglan Road** *(Disney Springs)* Long regarded as one of Disney Springs' best restaurants, Raglan Road is tough to book for dinner.

- **Via Napoli Ristorante e Pizzeria** *(Italy/Epcot)* The best pizza in Walt Disney World is enough reason to go. Lunch is hard to get.

No-Show Penalties

All Disney restaurants charge a no-show fee ranging from $10 to $25 per person; at **Victoria & Albert's,** it's $100 per person if you cancel 72 hours or less prior to the reservation or if you don't show up. Prepaid bookings risk losing the full amount paid. Only one person needs to dine at the restaurant for Disney to consider your reservation fulfilled, even if you have a reservation for more people. Restaurants booked on opentable.com do not have no-show penalties. Also, while Disney says it requires 24 hours' notice, you can cancel up until midnight of the day before your meal in many instances.

THEME PARK RESTAURANTS AND ADMISSION

MANY FIRST-TIME VISITORS to Disney World are surprised when making their Advance Reservations to learn that admission to a theme park is required to eat at restaurants inside of it. The lone exception is Rainforest Cafe at Animal Kingdom, which can be entered from the parking lot just outside the theme park; you must have admission, however, if you want to enter Animal Kingdom after you eat.

If you're booking a meal for a day when you weren't expecting to visit the parks, you'll need to check the restaurant's location to make sure it isn't in a theme park. Also, if you've visited a theme park earlier in the day that's different from the one in which your restaurant is located, you'll need the Park Hopper option (see page 60) to dine inside the second theme park.

DRESS

DRESS IS INFORMAL at most theme park restaurants, but Disney has a business-casual dress code for some of its resort restaurants: khakis, dress slacks, jeans, or dress shorts with a collared shirt for men and capris, skirts, dresses, jeans, or dress shorts for women. Restaurants with this dress code are **Jiko—The Cooking Place** at Animal Kingdom Lodge, the **Flying Fish** at the BoardWalk, **California Grill** at the Contemporary Resort, **Monsieur Paul** at Epcot's France Pavilion, **Cítricos** and **Narcoossee's** at the Grand Floridian Resort, **Yachtsman Steakhouse** at the Yacht Club Resort, **Il Mulino** at the Swan, and **Todd English's bluezoo** and **Shula's Steak House** at the Dolphin. **The Edison** at Disney Springs prohibits shorts and worn jeans, in addition to the rules above. **Victoria & Albert's** at the Grand Floridian is the only Disney restaurant that requires men to wear a jacket to dinner (they'll provide one if needed).

Also, be aware that smoking is banned at all restaurants and lounges on Walt Disney World property. Diners who puff must get their nicotine fix outdoors—and in the theme parks, that also means going to a designated smoking area outside the parks.

FOOD ALLERGIES AND DIETARY NEEDS

IF YOU HAVE FOOD ALLERGIES or observe a specific type of diet (such as eating kosher), make your needs known when you make your Advance Reservations. And be aware that for kosher or special dietary needs, there is a charge for canceling to cover the cost of special ordering individual meal components. Almost all Walt Disney World restaurants have dedicated allergy-friendly menus available; ask any cast member for a menu when you arrive at the restaurant. Also, many Disney sit-down restaurants have adapted their dishes so that almost anyone with a common allergy can order off the standard menu. Chefs at restaurants and quick-service locations will go out of their way to accommodate your dietary needs. Discuss your food allergies with your server on arrival at the restaurant. If you have any doubts, a chef or cast member trained in special diets will discuss your dietary needs before placing an order. For official information from Disney, email specialdiets@disney world.com or visit tinyurl.com/wdwspecialdiets.

A Phillipsburg, New Jersey, mom reports her family's experience:

My 6-year-old has many food allergies. When making my Advance Reservations, I indicated these to the clerk. When we arrived at the restaurants, the staff was already aware of my child's allergies and assigned our table a chef who double-checked the list of allergies with us. The chefs were very nice and made my son feel very special.

A Charlotte, North Carolina, mom offers this handy tip:

A website called **AllergyEats** *(allergyeats.com/disney) is a lifesaver. Put in your allergies and your park, and it shows you what you can eat.*

To request kosher or halal meals at table-service restaurants, call ☎ 407-WDW-DINE (939-3463) 24 hours in advance. All Disney menus have vegetarian options; vegans may have to talk to the chef.

A FEW CAVEATS

BEFORE YOU BEGIN EATING your way through the World, here's what you need to know:

1. Theme park restaurants rush their customers to make room for the next group of diners. Dining at high speed may appeal to a family with young, restless children, but for people wanting to relax, it's more like eating in a pressure chamber than fine dining.

2. Disney restaurants have comparatively few tables for parties of two, and servers are generally disinclined to seat two guests at larger tables. If you're a duo, you might have to wait longer—sometimes much longer—to be seated.

3. At full-service Disney restaurants, an automatic gratuity of 18% is added to your tab—even at buffets where you serve yourself.

"WAITER, THESE PRICES ARE GIVING ME HEARTBURN!"

INCREASES IN DISNEY'S TICKET COSTS are always sure to grab headlines, but most people don't notice that Disney's restaurant prices rise about as fast. For example, while the inflation-adjusted cost of a 1-day theme park ticket has increased about 73% since 2010, the average lunch entrée price at Le Cellier has gone from around $22 to just under $46—an increase of 109%. For reference, the average meal cost in a US restaurant went up 27% during the same time, according to the Federal Reserve.

You might need a stiff drink after seeing those prices, but alcohol is no bargain either. While the average bottle of wine in WDW costs three times as much as retail, some wines have much higher markups. For example, a $9 bottle of Placido pinot grigio costs $45 in Epcot and various Disney resort lounges—five times as much as the retail price. If you rent a car and eat dinner each day at non-Disney restaurants, you'll save enough to more than pay for the rental cost.

This comment from a New Orleans mom spells it out:

Disney keeps pushing prices up and up. For us, the sky is NOT the limit. We won't be back.

THE COST OF COUNTER-SERVICE FOOD	
Bagel or muffin	$2.99-$3.99
Brownie	$3.99-$7.99
Burrito	$6.99-$11.00
Cake or pie	$3.99-$8.00
Cereal with milk	$2.99-$4.99
Cheeseburger with fries	$11.99-$14.99
Chicken breast sandwich	$11.99-$14.99
Chicken nuggets with fries	$8.49-$11.49
Children's meal (various)	$5.49-$7.99
Chips	$2.99-$3.25
Cookie	$1.99-$3.99
Fried fish basket with fries	$10.99-$11.95
Fries	$2.99-$3.79
Fruit (whole)	$1.99-$3.59
Fruit cup / fruit salad	$3.79-$3.99
Hot dog	$9.49-$12.49
Ice cream / frozen novelties	$4.00-$9.95
Nachos with cheese	$3.99-$7.99
PB&J sandwich	$5.99-$6.29 (kids' meal)
Pizza (personal)	$9.99-$23.00
Popcorn	$4.25-$5.50
Pretzel	$2.95-$6.00
Salad (entrée)	$7.99-$12.99
Salad (side)	$3.29-$5.25
Smoked turkey leg	$11.75-$13.29
Soup / chili	$4.19-$7.99
Sub / deli sandwich	$9.49-$11.49
Veggie burger	$10.99
THE COST OF COUNTER-SERVICE DRINKS	
Beer	$7.25-$12.50
Bottled water	$3.00-$4.50
Coffee	$2.00-$7.99
Latte	$3.75-$6.50
Float, milkshake, or sundae	$4.49-$6.00
Fruit juice	$3.29-$4.29
Hot tea and cocoa	$1.50-$2.79
Milk	$1.99-$3.29
Soft drinks, iced tea, and lemonade	$2.59-$4.50

Each person on a Disney Dining Plan gets a free mug, refillable at any Disney resort. There is a short wait between refills: a screen on the soda fountain shows the exact amount of time until guests can fill up their mug again. If you're not on a dining plan and wish to purchase a refillable mug, the cost is $18.99 with tax for the length of your stay at Disney resorts and around $11.75 at the water parks.

MOBILE ORDERING

THE MY DISNEY EXPERIENCE APP offers this time-saving perk at many of its counter-service restaurants. Using the app, you place an order, pay for your meal online, and notify the restaurant when you've arrived for pickup. You'll be directed to a separate window or line to pick up your food, bypassing the regular line. Be sure to keep your app updated to see the latest participating restaurants.

Beyond Mobile Ordering: Tips for Saving Time and Money

Even if you confine your meals to counter-service fare, you lose a lot of time getting food in the theme parks. Not to mention that every time you buy a soda, it's going to set you back more than $3, and everything else from hot dogs to salad is

LILIANE All quick-service restaurants will give you free ice water; just ask!

comparably high. You can say, "Oh, well, we're on vacation" and pay the exorbitant prices, or you can plan ahead and save big bucks.

You could rent a condo and prepare your own meals, but you didn't travel all the way to Disney World to cook. So let's be realistic and assume that you'll eat your evening meals out—which is what most families do because, among other reasons, they're too tired to think about cooking. That leaves breakfast and lunch. Here are some ways to minimize the time and money you spend hunting and gathering:

1. Eat breakfast before you arrive. Restaurants outside the World offer some outstanding breakfast specials. Plus, some hotels have small refrigerators in guest rooms, or you can rent a fridge or bring a cooler. If you can get by on cold cereal, pastries, fruit, and juice, this will save a ton of time and money.

2. Prepare sandwiches and snacks to take to the theme parks in hip packs; carry water bottles or rely on drinking fountains. Alternatively, after a good breakfast, buy snacks from vendors instead of eating lunch.

3. All theme park restaurants are busiest between 11:30 a.m. and 2:15 p.m. for lunch and 6 and 9 p.m. for dinner. For shorter lines and faster service, don't eat during these hours, especially 12:30–1:30 p.m.

4. Many counter-service restaurants sell cold sandwiches. Buy a cold lunch minus drinks before 11:30 a.m., and carry it in small plastic bags until you're ready to eat (within an hour or so of purchase for food-safety reasons). Ditto for dinner. Buy drinks at the appropriate time from any convenient vendor.

5. Most fast-food eateries have more than one service window. Regardless of the time of day, check the lines at all windows before queuing. Sometimes a window that's staffed but out of the way will have a much shorter line or none at all. Note, however, that some windows may offer only certain items.

6. If you're short on time and the park closes early, stay until closing and eat dinner outside Disney World before returning to your hotel. If the park stays open late, eat dinner about 4 or 4:30 p.m. at the restaurant of your choice. You should sneak in just ahead of the dinner crowd.

If you opt to buy groceries, you can stock up at Publix (14928 E. Orange Lake Blvd. and 3221 Vineland Road, both in Kissimmee). There's also a Winn-Dixie on Apopka–Vineland Road, about a mile north of Crossroads Shopping Center. The Winn-Dixie at US 192 on the west side of I-4 is the closest and largest grocery for visitors staying near the Sherberth Road or World Drive entrances to Disney World. The Super Target on Rolling Oaks Boulevard is the closest to the Western Way entrance. The closest Costco, at 4696 Gardens Park Blvd., is close to Universal Orlando.

FAST FOOD IN THE THEME PARKS

BECAUSE MOST MEALS DURING a Disney World vacation are consumed on the run while touring, we'll tackle counter-service and vendor foods first. Plentiful in all theme parks are hot dogs, hamburgers, chicken sandwiches, salads, and pizza. They're augmented by special items that relate to the park's theme or the part of the park you're touring. In Epcot's Germany, for example, counter-service bratwurst and beer are sold. In Frontierland in the Magic Kingdom, vendors sell smoked turkey legs. Counter-service prices are fairly consistent from park to park.

Getting your act together at counter-service restaurants is more a matter of courtesy than necessity. Rude guests rank fifth among reader complaints. A mother from Fort Wayne, Indiana, points out that indecision can be as maddening as outright discourtesy, especially when you're hungry:

Every fast-food restaurant has menu signs the size of billboards, but do you think anybody reads them? People still don't have a clue what they want when they finally get to the counter. If by some miracle they've managed to choose between the hot dog and the hamburger, they then fiddle around another 10 minutes deciding what size Coke to order. Folks, PULEEEZ get your orders together ahead of time!

A North Carolina reader on counter-service food lines:

Many counter-service registers serve two queues each, one to the left and one to the right of each register. People are not used to this and will instinctively line up in one queue per register, typically on the right side, leaving the left vacant. We had register operators wave us up to the front several times to start a left queue instead of waiting behind others on the right.

LILIANE Look for the **DISNEY CHECK** icon on healthy menu items such as fresh fruit and low-fat milk.

Healthful Food at Walt Disney World

Health-conscious choices are available at most fast-food counters and even vendors. All the major theme parks have fruit stands.

HARD CHOICES

DINING DECISIONS WILL DEFINITELY affect your Walt Disney World experience. If you're short on time and you want to see the theme parks, avoid full service. Ditto if you're short on funds. If you do want full service, arrange Advance Reservations—again, they won't actually reserve you a table, but they can minimize your wait.

Miz ETTICKET'S LESSONS in FOOD LINE-UP MANNERS

Hmm... what SHALL I eat?

LINE ←

Lesson #36: "Know what you want to order BEFORE getting to the front of the line."

Integrating Meals into the Unofficial Guide Touring Plans

Arrive before the park of your choice opens. Tour expeditiously, using your chosen plan (taking as few breaks as possible), until about 11 or 11:30 a.m. Disney World's restaurants are busiest at 12:30 p.m. and 6:30 p.m. Once the park becomes crowded around midday, meals and other breaks won't affect the plan's efficiency. If you intend to stay in the park for evening parades, fireworks, or other events, eat dinner early enough to be finished in time for the festivities.

Character Dining

A number of restaurants, primarily those with all-you-can-eat buffets and family-style meals, offer character dining. At character meals, you pay a fixed price and dine in the presence of one to five Disney characters who circulate throughout the restaurant, hugging children (and sometimes adults), posing for photos, and signing autographs. They are served at restaurants in and out of the theme parks. See page 252 for more information.

A. J. I don't recommend getting autographs during the character dining meals unless your heart is really set on it. I found it stressful to run to the buffet, shovel food onto your plate, and run back to the table, hoping I didn't miss a character.

DISNEY DINING SUGGESTIONS

FOLLOWING ARE SUGGESTIONS for dining at each of the major theme parks. If you want to try a theme-park full-service restaurant, be aware that the restaurants continue to serve after the park's official closing time. Don't worry if you're depending on Disney transportation: buses, boats, and monorails run 1–2 hours after the parks close.

LILIANE'S TOP 10 DISNEY WORLD SNACKS

FOLLOWING IS A TOP 10 LIST of particularly decadent or unusual snacks available at WDW. We've omitted the usual funnel cakes, popcorn, and ice cream available anywhere. Also absent are the truly bizarre snacks, such as the squid treats sold at the Mitsukoshi Department Store in the Japan Pavilion at Epcot's World Showcase. These are the goodies worth scouring the parks and resorts for:

10. FROZEN CHOCOLATE-COVERED BANANA This treat is available in all parks and is Liliane's idea of a healthy snack.

9. KAKIGŌRI at the Japan Pavilion, Epcot's World Showcase A little on the sweet side but lighter than ice cream, the shaved ice at this small stand comes in unique flavors, such as honeydew melon, strawberry, and tangerine.

8. GHIRARDELLI SODA FOUNTAIN AND CHOCOLATE SHOP at Disney Springs Marketplace Everything is good, and the atmosphere has a sophisticated ice-cream-shop-plus-coffee-bar vibe. Very San Fran.

7. TURKEY LEGS Available at the Magic Kingdom and Epcot, these must come from 85-pound turkeys because they're huge, not to mention extra-juicy and flavorful. Grab some napkins and go primal on one of these bad boys, and don't worry about the stares you might attract—they're all just jealous.

6. MILKSHAKES from Beaches & Cream at the Beach Club Resort Hand-dipped, thick, and creamy. When was the last time you sported a milkshake mustache? For large crowds, or large appetites, try the Kitchen Sink: a huge sundae consisting of mountains of ice cream and toppings that is actually served in a kitchen sink.

5. CHOCOLATE-COVERED PINEAPPLE SPEARS at Big Top Treats in Fantasyland at the Magic Kingdom The only decision you will have to make is what kind of chocolate you want: milk or dark chocolate. At the nearby Karamell-Küche, the chocolate-covered spears come with caramel drizzled on top!

4. ZEBRA DOMES at Animal Kingdom Lodge Offered as a dessert on the Boma buffet, they're also available at the Mara food court, on the lower level of the resort near the pool. They consist of a layer of sponge cake topped with cream liqueur mousse, and then covered in white chocolate and drizzled with dark chocolate ganache. Fun and yum rolled into one!

3. MASTER'S CUPCAKE at Be Our Guest Restaurant in the Magic Kingdom Liliane loves Lumière's special dessert from Be Our Guest in Fantasyland so much that she gave it a try. Here is her recipe of the Master's Cupcake, topped with "grey stuff": themouseforless.com/blogworld/2015/08/grey-stuff-masters-cupcake-recipe.

2. LES HALLES BOULANGERIE–PATISSERIE at the France Pavilion, Epcot's World Showcase There are simply no words to adequately describe the pastries at this bakery. Try the frangipane or the napoleon. Oh, did we mention the flan tart, the crème brûlée, and the chocolate mousse?

But the number one snack at Walt Disney World is . . .

1. Two words: DOLE WHIP! Available in Adventureland at the Magic Kingdom, Dole Whip is a soft-serve pineapple–ice cream dream. Liliane prefers her Dole Whip with rum, available at Animal Kingdom's Tamu Tamu Refreshments.

I love Mickey ice cream bars. They're a delicious snack!

Brendan

The Magic Kingdom

Be Our Guest in Fantasyland, **Liberty Tree Tavern** in Liberty Square, **The Plaza Restaurant** on Main Street, and the **Jungle Navigation Co. Ltd. Skipper Canteen** in Adventureland are the park's best full-service restaurants. **Cinderella's Royal Table** in the castle and **The Crystal Palace** on Main Street serve decent-but-expensive character buffets. Avoid **Tony's Town Square Restaurant** on Main Street and (if it's open) **The Diamond Horseshoe** in Frontierland.

AUTHORS' FAVORITE COUNTER-SERVICE RESTAURANTS

- Be Our Guest (breakfast and lunch)　*Fantasyland*
- Columbia Harbour House　*Liberty Square*
- Pecos Bill Tall Tale Inn and Café　*Frontierland*

These three restaurants offer the most variety within the Magic Kingdom. **Be Our Guest** serves the best breakfast at the Magic Kingdom. At lunch the restaurant offers a tasty tuna salade Niçoise, a grilled ham-and-cheese sandwich, and a juicy braised-pork entrée. **Columbia Harbour House**'s offerings include lobster rolls and chicken potpie. **Pecos Bill Tall Tale Inn and Café** serves fabu-

BRENDAN There are so many details at Be Our Guest that it's hard to catch them all in one visit. And the food is good too.

lous tacos and beef nachos and has plenty of seating. Our favorite is the three soft-shell tacos with a selection of ground beef, chicken, spicy beef, or spicy breaded cauliflower (the latter topped with five-spice yogurt and pineapple salsa). Otherwise, the Magic Kingdom's fast-food eateries are undistinguished. They're also about twice as expensive as McDonald's, for about the same quality. On the positive side, portions are large, sometimes large enough for children to share.

Be Our Guest has a prix fixe dinner menu ($60 adults; $36 kids ages 3–9, plus tax). Selections are considerably more upscale and not suitable for picky eaters; escargot is one of the appetizers, and main courses include lamb chops, filet mignon, and seafood bouillabaisse, among others. Dinner requires two table-service credits on the dining plan.

Epcot

Since the beginning, dining has been an integral component of Epcot's entertainment product. World Showcase has many more restaurants than attractions, and Epcot has added bars, tapas-style eateries, and full-service restaurants faster than any park in memory.

For the most part, Epcot's restaurants have always served decent food, though the World Showcase restaurants have occasionally been timid about delivering honest representations of their host nations' cuisine. While it's true that the less adventuresome diner can find steak and potatoes on virtually every menu, the same kitchens will serve up the real thing for anyone willing to ask.

Many Epcot restaurants are overpriced, most conspicuously **Monsieur Paul** (France) and **Coral Reef Restaurant** (The Seas). Epcot restaurants that combine attractive ambience and well-prepared food with good value are **Teppan Edo** (Japan), **Via Napoli** (Italy), **Rose & Crown** (United Kingdom), **Spice Road Table** (Morocco), and **Biergarten** (Germany). Biergarten (along with **Restaurant Marrakesh** in Morocco) also features live entertainment.

A new space-themed table-service restaurant will open in late 2019. Tentatively named **Space 220,** the eatery is adjacent to Mission: Space. The France Pavilion will see the opening of a *crêperie,* featuring the cuisine of celebrity chef Jérôme Bocuse near the upcoming Remy's Ratatouille Adventure ride. No opening dates were announced as we went to print.

AUTHORS' FAVORITE COUNTER-SERVICE RESTAURANTS

- Les Halles Boulangerie–Patisserie *France*
- Sommerfest *Germany*
- Sunshine Seasons *The Land*
- Tangierine Café *Morocco*

Les Halles Boulangerie–Patisserie sells pastries, sandwiches, and quiche. The pastries are made on-site, and the sandwiches are as close to actual French street food—in taste, size, and price—as you'll get anywhere in Epcot. Another favorite is the chicken-and-lamb shawarma platter at Morocco's **Tangierine Café.** Besides juicy lamb, it comes with some of the best tabbouleh we've tasted in Florida.

In addition to these, we recommend the following ethnic counter-service specialties:

JAPAN • **Katsura Grill** for noodle dishes, teriyaki, and tempura

NORWAY • **Kringla Bakeri Og Kafe** for pastries, open-faced sandwiches, and imported beer

UNITED KINGDOM • **Rose & Crown Pub** or **Yorkshire County Fish Shop** for fish-and-chips and Harp and Bass beers; Rose & Crown also serves Guinness beer

---

FELICITY The food at Tusker House buffet is different from all other buffets. I know because I ate at all of them. I love the chicken, mashed potatoes, and gravy; I had three servings.

Disney's Animal Kingdom

We recommend that you tour early after a good breakfast, and then graze on vendor food until dinner. Then try **Yak & Yeti** for a moderately priced (for Disney), moderately paced meal, or **Tiffins** if you have a little more time and money.

Animal Kingdom offers a lot of counter-service fast food, along with **Tusker House,** a buffet-style restaurant in Africa, and **Yak & Yeti,** a table-service restaurant in Asia. You'll find plenty of traditional Disney theme park food—hot dogs, hamburgers, and the like—but even the fast food is superior to typical Disney fare. A third full-service restaurant inside the Animal Kingdom, **Tiffins** (an upscale place featuring international cuisine), is located on Discovery Island. **Rainforest Cafe** has entrances both inside and outside the theme park, meaning that you don't have to buy park admission to eat there.

AUTHORS' FAVORITE COUNTER-SERVICE RESTAURANTS

- Flame Tree Barbecue *Discovery Island*
- Harambe Market *Africa*
- Satu'li Canteen *Pandora*
- Yak & Yeti Local Food Cafes *Asia*

We like **Flame Tree Barbecue** for its waterfront dining pavilions and **Yak & Yeti Local Food Cafes** (just outside the full-service Yak & Yeti) for casual Asian dishes from egg rolls to crispy honey chicken.

Harambe Market has several smaller food windows. The park's *Avatar*-themed **Satu'li Canteen** is Pandora's answer to Chipotle's rice bowls. You pick a base of starch, grain, or lettuce; a protein; and garnishes.

Disney's Hollywood Studios

Dining at Disney's Hollywood Studios is less ethnic than at Epcot and possibly less interesting than at any other park. The Studios has five (soon to be six) restaurants where Advance Reservations are recommended: The Hollywood Brown Derby, 50's Prime Time Café, Sci-Fi Dine-In Theater Restaurant, Mama Melrose's Ristorante Italiano, and the Hollywood & Vine buffet, as well as **Roundup Rodeo BBQ** inside Toy Story Land (not open at press time). The upscale **Brown Derby** is by far the best restaurant at the Studios. For simple Italian food, including pizza, **Mama Melrose's** is fine; just don't expect anything fancy. At the **Sci-Fi Dine-In,** you eat in little cars at a simulated drive-in movie from the 1950s; you

FELICITY Mama Melrose's is a very dark restaurant and not that much fun for kids.

won't find a more entertaining restaurant in Walt Disney World. The food is somewhat better at the **50's Prime Time Café,** where you sit in Mom's time-warp kitchen and scarf down meat loaf while watching clips of vintage TV sitcoms. **Hollywood & Vine** features characters from the Disney Channel during breakfast and lunch, while Minnie and friends have seasonal-themed dinners.

AUTHORS' FAVORITE COUNTER-SERVICE RESTAURANTS

- ABC Commissary *Commissary Lane*
- Dockside Diner *Echo Lake*
- Backlot Express *Echo Lake*
- Fairfax Fare *Sunset Boulevard*
- Docking Bay 7 Food and Cargo *Star Wars: Galaxy's Edge*

Several restaurants opened with the debut of Star Wars: Galaxy's Edge. **Docking Bay 7 Food and Cargo** is the main eatery of the land. For a quick bite, visit **Ronto Roasters.** Stop at the **Milk Stand** to try the famous blue or green milk. **Oga's Cantina** is the land's main watering hole, where guests enjoy exotic beverages and small plates. At **Kat Saka's Kettle** go for some colorful kettle-cooked popcorn with sweet, spicy, and savory seasoning.

READERS' COMMENTS ABOUT WALT DISNEY WORLD DINING

EATING IS A POPULAR TOPIC AMONG *Unofficial Guide* readers. In addition to participating in our annual restaurant survey, many readers like to share their thoughts with us. The following comments are representative of those we receive.

A reader from Glendale, Illinois, had a positive experience with Disney food, writing:

> *In general, we were pleasantly surprised. I expected it to be over-priced, generally bad, and certainly unhealthy. There were a lot of options, and almost all restaurants (including counter service) had*

generally good food and some healthy options. It's not the place to expect fine cuisine—and it's certainly overpriced—but if you understand the parameters, you can eat quite well.

We've received consistent raves for Boma—Flavors of Africa:

Please stop telling everyone how wonderful Boma is. I love it so much there, and I don't want everyone to know the secret—it's already difficult to get a table!

A Laurel, Maryland, couple rave about Tiffins:

Tiffins is one of the best restaurants in all of Disney World. It's pricey, but the food is spectacular and the setting is very quiet and relaxing.

A Lombard, Illinois, mom underscores the need to make Advance Reservations:

Please stress that if you want a "normal" dining hour at a specific restaurant, call them as far in advance as possible—IT IS WORTH IT! I wanted to change one reservation about two weeks before our arrival date, and I had a choice of either 7:45 or 9 p.m. for dinner (not feasible with little ones).

A Greenwood, Indiana, family had this to say:

The food was certainly expensive, but contrary to many of the views expressed in The Unofficial Guide, *we all thought the quality was excellent. Everything we had, from chicken strips and hot dogs in the parks to dinner at the Coral Reef, tasted great and seemed very fresh.*

A family from Youngsville, Louisiana, got a leg up on other guests:

The best thing we ate were the smoked turkey legs.

A mom from Aberdeen, South Dakota, writes:

When we want great food, we'll be on a different vacation. Who wants to waste fun time with the kids at a sit-down restaurant when you know the food will be mediocre anyway?

On the topic of saving money, a Seattle woman offered this:

For those wanting to save a few bucks (or in some cases several bucks), we definitely suggest eating outside WDW for as many meals as possible. To keep down our costs, we ate a large breakfast before leaving the hotel, had a fast-food lunch in the park, a snack later to hold us over, and then ate a good dinner outside the park. Several good restaurants in the area have excellent food at reasonable prices.

COUNTER-SERVICE RESTAURANT MINI-PROFILES

TO HELP YOU FIND PALATABLE FAST FOOD that suits your taste, we provide thumbnail profiles of the theme park counter-service restaurants, listed alphabetically by park. They're rated for quality, portion size, and value. The value rating ranges A–F as follows:

A = Exceptional value, a real bargain	**D** = Somewhat overpriced
B = Good value	**F** = Significantly overpriced
C = Fair value, you get exactly what you pay for	

THE MAGIC KINGDOM

Aloha Isle

QUALITY Excellent   **VALUE** B+   **PORTION** Medium   **LOCATION** Adventureland
READER-SURVEY RESPONSES   98% 👍   **DISNEY DINING PLAN?** Yes

SELECTIONS Dole Whip floats and cups, pineapple upside-down cake, juice, and bottled water.

COMMENTS Located next door to *Walt Disney's Enchanted Tiki Room.* The pineapple Dole Whip soft-serve is a world-famous Disney treat.

Be Our Guest Restaurant

QUALITY Excellent   **VALUE** C   **PORTION** Medium   **LOCATION** Fantasyland
READER-SURVEY RESPONSES   86% 👍   **DISNEY DINING PLAN?** Yes

SELECTIONS Breakfast: cured meats and cheese with fresh marmalade, and scrambled egg whites with roasted tomatoes. Kids can feast on steel-cut oatmeal, cereals, scrambled eggs, French toast, or crepes. Lunch: French dip sandwich, braised pork with mashed potatoes, veggie quiche, quinoa salad, potato leek or onion soup. Kids' meals include grilled shrimp, carved turkey sandwich, slow-cooked pork, a tasty meat loaf, grilled cheese and turkey noodle soup, or whole-grain macaroni with marinara sauce.

COMMENTS The best counter-service restaurant in the Magic Kingdom. The assorted cured meats–and-cheese breakfast includes alpine-smoked ham, Serrano ham, *soppressata,* cheese, marmalade, fresh fruit, a baguette, and an assortment of pastries. It's Liliane's choice for a good breakfast and easily serves two. For lunch we like the croque monsieur, a grown-up version of grilled ham and cheese, with carved ham, Gruyère, and béchamel sauce and *pommes frites* on the side. For a healthier option, the generous seared-tuna salade Niçoise hits the spot. For a quick meal, Liliane recommends the French onion soup and the Master's Cupcake (also known as the Grey Stuff). However, this reader from Raleigh, North Carolina, comments:

I was very disappointed by my most recent visit. The croque monsieur, typically made with carved ham and Gruyère, used to be a staple for me. On this trip, it consisted of cold deli ham and a cheese sauce rather than actual melted cheese. A croque monsieur is, by definition, a GRILLED sandwich, and it shouldn't be legal to promise a croque monsieur and deliver the cold monstrosity I was given.

Note: Advance Reservations for breakfast and lunch are required. Breakfast is served for just 2 hours (8–10 a.m.).

Casey's Corner

QUALITY Good   **VALUE** C   **PORTION** Medium   **LOCATION** Main Street, U.S.A.
READER-SURVEY RESPONSES   85% 👍   **DISNEY DINING PLAN?** Yes

SELECTIONS Hot dogs, corn dog nuggets, fries, and brownies.

COMMENTS Best to stop at Casey's when it's extra-busy—that's the best guarantee of a fresh bun and hot fries.

Columbia Harbour House

QUALITY Good   VALUE B+   PORTION Medium   LOCATION Liberty Square
READER-SURVEY RESPONSES   91% 👍   DISNEY DINING PLAN?   Yes

SELECTIONS Grilled salmon with vegetable rice, tuna sandwich, or grilled shrimp. Other choices: lobster roll, chicken nuggets and fried fish, salad with shrimp or chicken, New England clam chowder, vegetarian chili, mac and cheese, or green beans and carrots. Seasonal cobbler or yogurt for dessert. For kids: salad with chicken, PB&J, or tuna sandwich.

COMMENTS No trans fats in the fried items, and the soups are a cut above most fast-food fare. Liliane's favorite is the lobster roll. The upstairs seating is far more quiet than downstairs.

Cosmic Ray's Starlight Cafe

QUALITY Fair-poor   VALUE C-   PORTION Large   LOCATION Tomorrowland
READER-SURVEY RESPONSES   82% 👍   DISNEY DINING PLAN?   Yes

SELECTIONS Greek salad, chicken nuggets, grilled chicken club, or Angus bacon cheeseburger; cookies and cream cheesecake or s'mores for dessert. For kids: PB&J sandwich, mac and cheese, chicken nuggets, and salad with turkey.

COMMENTS The same menu appears at all three ordering stations. Generous toppings bar.

Friar's Nook

QUALITY Good   VALUE B   PORTION Medium-large   LOCATION Fantasyland
READER-SURVEY RESPONSES   88% 👍   DISNEY DINING PLAN?   Yes

SELECTIONS Hot dogs and fried sponge snack cakes.

COMMENTS Unless you're desperate, skip it! Nearby Gaston's Tavern is a better choice.

Gaston's Tavern

QUALITY Good   VALUE C   PORTION Medium   LOCATION Fantasyland
READER-SURVEY RESPONSES   90% 👍   DISNEY DINING PLAN?   Yes

SELECTIONS Ham-and-Brie sandwich with chips, fruit and cheese platter, mixed veggies with dip, hummus and chips, chocolate croissant, warm cinnamon roll, and LeFou's Brew (frozen apple juice flavored with toasted marshmallow).

COMMENTS Clever setting, limited menu. The supersweet LeFou's Brew is basically expensive apple juice.

Golden Oak Outpost *(seasonal)*

QUALITY Good   VALUE B+   PORTION Medium-large   LOCATION Frontierland
READER-SURVEY RESPONSES   91% 👍   DISNEY DINING PLAN?   Yes

SELECTIONS Waffle fries, chicken nuggets, chili-queso fries, and chocolate chip cookies.

COMMENTS Many better quick-service options are available.

Liberty Square Market

QUALITY Good   VALUE C   PORTION Medium   LOCATION Liberty Square
READER-SURVEY RESPONSES   91% 👍   DISNEY DINING PLAN?   No

SELECTIONS Mostly fresh fruit, packaged drinks and snacks, plus fresh grilled hot dogs.

COMMENTS The best hot dogs in Disney World. There's seating nearby, but none of it is covered.

The Lunching Pad

QUALITY Fair   VALUE C   PORTION Medium   LOCATION Tomorrowland
READER-SURVEY RESPONSES   84% 👍   DISNEY DINING PLAN?   Yes

SELECTIONS Cheese-stuffed pretzel; frozen sodas; classic hot dog; sliced roast beef sandwich.

COMMENTS The frozen carbonated drinks—cola or blue raspberry—are a treat in summer's heat.

Main Street Bakery

QUALITY Good   VALUE B   PORTION Medium   LOCATION Main Street, U.S.A.
READER-SURVEY RESPONSES   93% 👍   DISNEY DINING PLAN?   Yes

SELECTIONS Coffee drinks and teas; breakfast sandwiches and pastries.

COMMENTS Disney-themed Starbucks, with the same food and drinks you'd find in any other. Very crowded at park opening and mealtimes.

Pecos Bill Tall Tale Inn and Cafe

QUALITY Good   VALUE B   PORTION Medium–large   LOCATION Frontierland
READER-SURVEY RESPONSES   86% 👍   DISNEY DINING PLAN?   Yes

SELECTIONS Pork and chicken fajita platter with rice and beans, beef nachos, Southwest salad with chicken or pork, and cheeseburger. For kids, beef nachos, mac and cheese, or PB&J with applesauce and oranges; churros or Greek yogurt for dessert.

COMMENTS These items are an improvement over the old burgers.

Pinocchio Village Haus

QUALITY Fair-poor   VALUE D   PORTION Medium   LOCATION Fantasyland
READER-SURVEY RESPONSES   81% 👍   DISNEY DINING PLAN?   Yes

SELECTIONS Flatbreads; pasta with marinara; chicken nuggets; fries; chicken Parmesan sandwiches; kids' meals of chicken nuggets, pasta with marinara or butter, turkey sandwich, or flatbreads.

COMMENTS An easy stop for families in Fantasyland, but it's usually crowded. Avoid the chicken Parmesan. Consider Columbia Harbour House only a few minutes' walk away (it's tastier too).

Tomorrowland Terrace Restaurant (seasonal)

QUALITY Fair   VALUE C-   PORTION Medium–large   LOCATION Tomorrowland
READER-SURVEY RESPONSES   82% 👍   DISNEY DINING PLAN?   Yes

SELECTIONS One-third-pound Angus bacon cheeseburger; chicken strips; Buffalo chicken salad; veggie burger; brownies or yogurt for dessert.
COMMENTS Grab an outdoor table and watch the castle lit by fireworks.

Tortuga Tavern *(seasonal)*

QUALITY Fair **VALUE** B **PORTION** Medium-large **LOCATION** Adventureland
READER-SURVEY RESPONSES 78% 👍 **DISNEY DINING PLAN?** Yes

SELECTIONS Hot dogs, turkey legs, and barbecue short ribs; chocolate chip cookie for dessert.
COMMENTS Large, shaded eating area. Rarely open.

EPCOT
L'Artisan des Glaces

QUALITY Excellent **VALUE** C **PORTION** Large **LOCATION** France
READER-SURVEY RESPONSES 96% 👍 **DISNEY DINING PLAN?** No

SELECTIONS Flavors change but can include vanilla, chocolate, mint chocolate, salted caramel, and coffee ice creams. Sorbet flavors can include strawberry, mango, lemon, and mixed berry. Over-21s can enjoy two scoops in a martini glass, topped with a shot of Grand Marnier, rum, or whipped cream–flavored vodka.
COMMENTS Hands down, the best ice cream at Disney World, freshly made on the spot. Our white chocolate–coconut had fresh shaved coconut in it. The chocolate macaron ice cream sandwich is worth every calorie.

La Cantina de San Angel

QUALITY Good **VALUE** B **PORTION** Medium-large **LOCATION** Mexico
READER-SURVEY RESPONSES 89% 👍 **DISNEY DINING PLAN?** Yes

SELECTIONS Tacos with seasoned beef, chicken, or fried fish; fried cheese empanada; grilled chicken with Mexican rice, corn, cascabel pepper sauce, and pickled onions; Mexican salad with cabbage, lettuce, black beans, and corn; guacamole and chips; churros and frozen fruit pops; margaritas. For kids, empanadas, chicken tenders, or mac and cheese.
COMMENTS The cantina is a popular spot for a quick meal, with 150 covered outdoor seats. When it's extra-busy, the back of La Hacienda's dining room is opened for air-conditioned seating.

Crêpes des Chefs de France

QUALITY Excellent **VALUE** B+ **PORTION** Medium **LOCATION** France
READER-SURVEY RESPONSES 89% 👍 **DISNEY DINING PLAN?** No

SELECTIONS Crepes filled with chocolate, strawberry preserves, ice cream, or sugar; ice cream; specialty beer (Kronenbourg 1664); espresso.
COMMENTS These crepes rate high—even with French guests.

Fife & Drum Tavern

QUALITY Fair **VALUE** C **PORTION** Large **LOCATION** United States
READER-SURVEY RESPONSES 90% 👍 **DISNEY DINING PLAN?** Yes

SELECTIONS Turkey legs, popcorn, ice cream, frozen slushes, wine, beer, alcoholic lemonade, and root beer.

COMMENTS Great place to grab a drink before a show at American Gardens Theatre. Seating is also available in and around the Regal Eagle Smokehouse, behind the Fife & Drum.

Fountain View

QUALITY Good   **VALUE** B   **PORTION** Small
READER-SURVEY RESPONSES 95% 👍   **DISNEY DINING PLAN?** Yes

SELECTIONS Coffee drinks and teas; sandwiches, salads, and pastries.

COMMENTS Disney-themed Starbucks. At press time, Disney announced it was moving Fountain View to a temporary location during Future World's upcoming renovations, so check the park map for location.

Les Halles Boulangerie–Patisserie

QUALITY Good   **VALUE** A   **PORTION** Small-medium   **LOCATION** France
READER-SURVEY RESPONSES 97% 👍   **DISNEY DINING PLAN?** Yes

SELECTIONS Tuna Niçoise salad, sandwiches (ham and cheese; turkey BLT; chicken breast; Brie, cranberry, and apple); imported-cheese plates; quiches; soups; pastries.

COMMENTS Les Halles opens at 9 a.m.—2 hours before World Showcase—so it's a wonderful spot for a quiet breakfast. Usually crowded starting at lunch and stays that way throughout the day. One of Liliane's favorite counter-service restaurants in all of Disney World.

Kabuki Café

QUALITY Fair   **VALUE** C   **PORTION** Small   **LOCATION** Japan
READER-SURVEY RESPONSES 96% 👍   **DISNEY DINING PLAN?** Yes

SELECTIONS Sushi, including California roll with cucumber, crab, and avocado, and *temari* roll with tuna, salmon, and shrimp; edamame; shaved ice flavored with fruit or milk, such as strawberry, melon, cherry, or tangerine; Japanese beer, including a frozen Kirin, slushy style; wine and sake; sodas.

COMMENTS The sushi are frequently premade and come as four bite-size pieces, small enough to be a snack without ruining your appetite for something else later in World Showcase. Share a frozen Kirin.

Katsura Grill

QUALITY Good   **VALUE** B   **PORTION** Small-medium   **LOCATION** Japan
READER-SURVEY RESPONSES 86% 👍   **DISNEY DINING PLAN?** Yes

SELECTIONS Sushi; udon noodle bowls (beef or tempura shrimp); chicken or beef teriyaki; chicken-cutlet curry; edamame; miso soup; green tea cheesecake; green tea or adzuki bean–strawberry ice cream; teriyaki chicken kid's plate; Kirin beer, sake, and plum wine.

COMMENTS Great spot to grab some sushi and sit outside.

Kringla Bakeri Og Kafe

QUALITY Good-excellent   **VALUE** B   **PORTION** Small-medium   **LOCATION** Norway
READER-SURVEY RESPONSES 96% 👍   **DISNEY DINING PLAN?** Yes

SELECTIONS Pastries and desserts; unusual sandwiches (Norwegian club with lingonberry mayo); smoked salmon and egg bagel; imported beer.

COMMENTS Try the ham-and-apple sandwich with Jarlsberg and Muenster cheeses or the rice cream (not a typo). Shaded outdoor seating.

Lotus Blossom Café

QUALITY Fair   VALUE C   PORTION Medium   LOCATION China
READER-SURVEY RESPONSES 83% 👍 DISNEY DINING PLAN? Yes

SELECTIONS Pork and vegetable egg rolls, pot stickers, sesame chicken salad, Szechuan spicy chicken, shrimp fried rice with egg roll, orange chicken, beef-noodle soup bowl, caramel-ginger or lychee ice cream, plum wine, Tsingtao beer.

COMMENTS The menu rarely changes, and the food remains mediocre.

Promenade Refreshments

QUALITY Fair   VALUE C   PORTION Large   LOCATION World Showcase Promenade
READER-SURVEY RESPONSES 96% 👍 DISNEY DINING PLAN? Yes

SELECTIONS Chili dogs, hot dogs, kettle chips, soft-serve ice cream, and beer.

COMMENTS Seating is limited to nonexistent. Be prepared to walk and chew.

Refreshment Outpost

QUALITY Good   VALUE B-   PORTION Small   LOCATION Between Germany and China
READER-SURVEY RESPONSES 91% 👍 DISNEY DINING PLAN? YES

SELECTIONS Hot dogs, soft-serve in a cone, slushes, coffee or sodas, draft Safari Amber beer, Mango Starr (mango purée and Starr African rum).

COMMENTS Home of the Frozen Brown Elephant—an adult slushy of frozen Coke and Amarula, a cream liqueur from South Africa.

Refreshment Port

QUALITY Good   VALUE B-   PORTION Medium   LOCATION Near Canada
READER-SURVEY RESPONSES 94% 👍 DISNEY DINING PLAN? Yes

SELECTIONS Poutine (fries, brisket, beef gravy, cheese curds) and ice cream.

COMMENTS Almost everyone in line is here for the ice cream. For the poutine, it helps to be Canadian. You never know what you'll find here, but chances are that it will be good.

Regal Eagle Smokehouse: Craft Drafts & Barbecue

QUALITY, VALUE, AND PORTION Too new to rate   LOCATION United States
READER-SURVEY RESPONSES Too new to rate   DISNEY DINING PLAN? Yes

SELECTIONS Craft beers and barbecue, of course! The scent emanating from the large smoker on the promenade will likely draw in guests.

COMMENTS Liberty Inn was the lowest-rated restaurant in World Showcase, but it was replaced in late 2019 by this new quick-service option.

Rose & Crown Pub

QUALITY Good   VALUE C+   PORTION Medium   LOCATION United Kingdom
READER-SURVEY RESPONSES 97% 👍 DISNEY DINING PLAN? No

SELECTIONS Fish-and-chips; Scotch egg (hard-boiled, wrapped in sausage, and deep-fried); battered bangers and chips; Guinness, Harp, and Bass beers, as well as other spirits.

COMMENTS Most of the crowd Is here to drink in an authentic British pub. Outside the pub is Yorkshire County Fish Shop (see page 167), which serves food to go. Liliane thinks there's nothing better than fish-and-chips with a cold Harp.

Sommerfest

QUALITY Fair   **VALUE** C   **PORTION** Medium   **LOCATION** Germany
READER-SURVEY RESPONSES 88% 👍   **DISNEY DINING PLAN?** Yes

SELECTIONS Bratwurst or frankfurter with sauerkraut, apple strudel, Black Forest cake, German wine and beer.

COMMENTS Grab a spot in the courtyard to indulge in a hearty sausage and a cold Pilsner. Skip the *nudelgratin* (baked macaroni with Cheddar and Swiss cheeses).

Sunshine Seasons

QUALITY Excellent   **VALUE** A   **PORTION** Medium   **LOCATION** The Land
READER-SURVEY RESPONSES 91% 👍   **DISNEY DINING PLAN?** Yes

SELECTIONS It comprises the following four areas: (1) wood-fired grills and rotisseries, with rotisserie half-chicken or slow-roasted pork loin and grilled fish with seasonal vegetables; (2) a shop with made-to-order sandwiches, with barbecue pork or rotisserie turkey breast; (3) Asian shop, with Mongolian beef, vegan korma with meatless "chicken," sweet-and-sour chicken, and stir-fried shrimp; and (4) soup-and-salad shop, with soups made daily and unusual creations such as the Power Salad (quinoa, almonds, and chicken). Breakfast includes pastries, bacon, eggs, and the like.

COMMENTS One of the best quick-service spots in Epcot.

Tangierine Café

QUALITY Good   **VALUE** B   **PORTION** Medium   **LOCATION** Morocco
READER-SURVEY RESPONSES 92% 👍   **DISNEY DINING PLAN?** Yes

SELECTIONS Chicken and lamb shawarma; hummus; tabbouleh; lentil salad; couscous salad; vegetarian hummus, tabbouleh, and couscous platter; child's burger or chicken nuggets with carrot sticks and applesauce; Moroccan wine and beer.

COMMENTS One of Epcot's top-rated restaurants but rarely busy. Grab a seat outdoors.

Yorkshire County Fish Shop

QUALITY Good   **VALUE** B+   **PORTION** Medium   **LOCATION** United Kingdom
READER-SURVEY RESPONSES 95% 👍   **DISNEY DINING PLAN?** Yes

SELECTIONS Fish-and-chips, chicken-and-mushroom pie, Victorian sponge cake, Bass Ale draft, Harp Lager.

COMMENTS There's usually a line for the crisp, hot fish-and-chips at this convenient fast-food window attached to the Rose & Crown Pub. Outdoor seating overlooks the lagoon, but we recommend claiming a bench in front of the stage where the British Revolution band performs at the United Kingdom Pavilion.

DISNEY'S ANIMAL KINGDOM

Creature Comforts

QUALITY Fair   **VALUE** C   **PORTION** Small   **LOCATION** Discovery Island near Africa
READER-SURVEY RESPONSES 97% 👍   **DISNEY DINING PLAN?** Yes

SELECTIONS Coffee drinks and teas; breakfast sandwiches and pastries.

COMMENTS Disney-themed Starbucks. The fare is largely the same you'd find at any other, plus the occasional Animal Kingdom–themed treat.

Flame Tree Barbecue

QUALITY Excellent　VALUE B-　PORTION Large　LOCATION Discovery Island
READER-SURVEY RESPONSES　92% 👍　DISNEY DINING PLAN?　Yes

SELECTIONS St. Louis–style ribs; smoked half-chicken; pulled-pork sandwich; pulled-chicken salad; ribs, chicken, and pulled pork platter; child's plate of baked chicken drumstick, hot dog, or PB&J sandwich; fries and onion rings; salted caramel apple crisp cupcake; Safari Amber beer, Bud Light, and wine.

COMMENTS Its outdoor seating offers shaded space overlooking the water. One of our favorites for lunch.

Harambe Market

QUALITY Good　VALUE B　PORTION Large　LOCATION Africa
READER-SURVEY RESPONSES　91% 👍　DISNEY DINING PLAN?　Yes

SELECTIONS Ribs, chicken, or vegetable bowl; pork sausage; beef and lamb gyro. Beer and Leopard's Eye (Snow Leopard vodka blended with kiwi-and-mango-flavored Bibo). Kids' menu includes barbecue ribs, chicken bowl, and corn dogs.

COMMENTS Plenty of shaded seating. Modeled after a typical real-life market in an African nation during the 1960s colonial era. The spice-rubbed ribs and chicken bowl are our favorites.

Kusafiri Coffee Shop and Bakery

QUALITY Good　VALUE B　PORTION Medium　LOCATION Africa
READER-SURVEY RESPONSES　94% 👍　DISNEY DINING PLAN?　Yes

SELECTIONS Danish, muffins, croissant, cookies, cake, fruit cup, yogurt, coffee, cocoa, and juice. Breakfast wrap (egg, sausage, spinach, and goat cheese) served until 10:30 a.m.; panini at lunch.

COMMENTS The only savory offering is the breakfast wrap. The colossal cinnamon roll is a favorite anytime.

Pizzafari

QUALITY Fair　VALUE C　PORTION Medium　LOCATION Discovery Island
READER-SURVEY RESPONSES　80% 👍　DISNEY DINING PLAN?　Yes

SELECTIONS Shrimp flatbread; cheese, pepperoni, or veggie personal pizzas; salad with chicken. Kids' choices: mac and cheese, cheese pizza, or PB&J. Cannoli cake for dessert. Beer available.

COMMENTS Hectic at peak mealtimes, but there's lots of seating. The pizza is unimpressive but popular. Better options are at Harambe Market. A separate dining area offers family-style dining (daily, 5–8 p.m.), where guests can enjoy two different salads and three entrées (pasta, chicken, and pizza), plus a dessert and nonalcoholic drink. It's $19.99 for adults, $11.99 for kids ages 3–9, plus tax.

Restaurantosaurus

QUALITY Fair　VALUE C　PORTION Medium-large　LOCATION DinoLand U.S.A.
READER-SURVEY RESPONSES　85% 👍　DISNEY DINING PLAN?　Yes

SELECTIONS Angus bacon cheeseburger; chicken nuggets; black bean burger; grilled chicken salad; grilled-chicken sandwich; kids' turkey wrap, chicken nuggets, cheeseburger, or PB&J. May serve breakfast during peak seasons.

COMMENTS Plenty of seating and a good burger-toppings bar.

Satu'li Canteen

QUALITY Good	VALUE A	PORTION Medium	LOCATION Pandora
READER-SURVEY RESPONSES 96%		DISNEY DINING PLAN? Yes	

SELECTIONS International-inspired cuisine. Beef, chicken, shrimp, or tofu bowls served over a base of grains or vegetables with sauce. For dessert try the blueberry cream cheese mousse served with passion fruit curd, or the chocolate cake served on a cookie layer and topped with banana cream.

COMMENTS Most meals are also available as kid's meals, with only a few non-Pandora-inspired offerings for children. The food is a welcome departure from regular park fare but doesn't work for unadventurous or picky eaters. Breakfast is offered seasonally.

Yak & Yeti Local Food Cafes

QUALITY Fair	VALUE C	PORTION Large	LOCATION Asia
READER-SURVEY RESPONSES 89%		DISNEY DINING PLAN? Yes	

SELECTIONS Honey sesame chicken with white rice, ginger chicken salad, Asian chicken wrap, teriyaki beef bowl, egg rolls, chicken fried rice. Kids' menu: chicken tenders, PB&J, or cheeseburger with fresh fruit. Breakfast bowls with scrambled eggs and sausage or sausage-and-egg muffins.

COMMENTS For filling up when you're in a hurry.

DISNEY'S HOLLYWOOD STUDIOS

ABC Commissary

QUALITY Fair	VALUE D	PORTION Medium-large	LOCATION Commissary Lane
READER-SURVEY RESPONSES 77%		DISNEY DINING PLAN? Yes	

SELECTIONS Barbecue rib platter, fish and shrimp platter, vegan burger, and Mediterranean salad. Kids will love the chicken strips, cheeseburger, or mac and cheese. For dessert try the s'more cookie or raspberry mousse. ABC Commissary has plenty of gluten-free and allergy-free menu items.

COMMENTS Continually one of the lowest-rated restaurants in Walt Disney World. Indoors, centrally located, but hard to find. Offers kosher meals.

Backlot Express

QUALITY Fair	VALUE C	PORTION Medium-large	LOCATION Echo Lake
READER-SURVEY RESPONSES 86%		DISNEY DINING PLAN? Yes	

SELECTIONS One-third-pound Angus cheeseburger, with or without barbecue pork on top; chicken tenders; Southwest chicken salad. A *Toy Story*–themed dessert (Forky's orange-hazelnut éclair) replaced the *Star Wars*–themed cupcakes.

COMMENTS BB-8's stein with unlimited refills is Liliane's favorite.

Catalina Eddie's

QUALITY Fair	VALUE B	PORTION Medium-large	LOCATION Sunset Boulevard
READER-SURVEY RESPONSES 81%		DISNEY DINING PLAN? Yes	

SELECTIONS Cheese and pepperoni pizzas, Caesar salad with or without chicken, and chocolate mousse. For kids: cheese pizza or PB&J.

COMMENTS Seldom crowded. Nothing to write home about.

Docking Bay 7 Food and Cargo

QUALITY Good–excellent	VALUE B-	PORTION Medium–large	LOCATION Galaxy's Edge
READER-SURVEY RESPONSES	Too new to rate	DISNEY DINING PLAN?	No

SELECTIONS Smoked Kaadu ribs—named after the creature Jar Jar rode in *Episode I* but actually pork—are cut vertically to give them an alien appearance, then glazed with a sticky-sweet sauce and served with down-home blueberry corn muffins. Endorian Tip-Yip (chicken) is roasted on a quinoa-curry salad or compressed into cubes, deep-fried, and served with a roasted vegetable–potato mash and herb gravy. Vegans will rejoice at not one but two meatless menu items featuring Impossible Foods, while gluten-free pescatarians can pick the chilled Yobshrimp Noodle Salad with spicy Thai dressing. For breakfast, try the Bright Suns Morning, Disney's version of eggs with cheese, potatoes, and pork sausage; the overnight oats are delicious.

COMMENTS Most items are above average in terms of quality. The *tip-yip* chicken is moist and flavorful, as are the vegetable "*kefta*" in the Felucian Garden Spread. Note that the kids' menu isn't particularly child-friendly. In keeping with the idea that you're on an alien plant, most of the food isn't in recognizable shapes or colors.

Dockside Diner

QUALITY Fair	VALUE C	PORTION Small–medium	LOCATION Echo Lake
READER-SURVEY RESPONSES	83% 👍	DISNEY DINING PLAN?	Yes

SELECTIONS Pulled-pork sandwich, chili-cheese hot dog, and loaded chili-cheese nachos; PB&J or macaroni and cheese for kids.

COMMENTS Limited seating at nearby picnic tables.

Fairfax Fare

QUALITY Fair	VALUE B	PORTION Medium–large	LOCATION Sunset Boulevard
READER-SURVEY RESPONSES	89% 👍	DISNEY DINING PLAN?	Yes

SELECTIONS Empanadas platter; pulled-pork sandwiches; chili-cheese hot dog; Fairfax Salad with barbecue pork, bacon, and corn-tomato salsa; chocolate mousse or seasonal cupcakes for dessert.

COMMENTS Go for the *mojo* pulled-pork sandwich.

PizzeRizzo *(seasonal)*

QUALITY Poor	VALUE D	PORTION Large	LOCATION Grand Avenue
READER-SURVEY RESPONSES	77% 👍	DISNEY DINING PLAN?	Yes

SELECTIONS Personal pizzas, meatball subs, and antipasto salad.

COMMENTS Unmemorable pizza. Umbrella-shaded tables outdoors.

Ronto Roasters

QUALITY Good–excellent	VALUE B+	PORTION Medium	LOCATION Galaxy's Edge
READER-SURVEY RESPONSES	Too new to rate	DISNEY DINING PLAN?	No

SELECTIONS Ronto Wrap (flatbread sandwich filled with roast pork and grilled Portuguese sausage), turkey jerky, nonalcoholic fruit punch. Breakfast options available too.

COMMENTS A disgruntled smelting droid named 8D-J8 does the cooking here, turning mysterious alien meats on a rotating spit beneath a recycled pod-racing engine. The sandwiches are dressed with spicy Szechuan Clutch Sauce, and the hand-cut jerky comes in sweet teriyaki or spicy herb flavors. Wash it down with a tart Sour Sarlacc raspberry lemonade.

Rosie's All-American Café

QUALITY Fair	VALUE C	PORTION Medium	LOCATION Sunset Boulevard
READER-SURVEY RESPONSES 83% 👍		DISNEY DINING PLAN? Yes	

SELECTIONS Cheeseburgers; fried green tomato sandwich; chicken nuggets; fries; child's turkey sandwich or chicken nuggets; strawberry shortcake, seasonal cupcakes, or chocolate mousse.

COMMENTS A quick stop on the way to Tower of Terror or Rock 'n' Roller Coaster. Plenty of shaded seating and a good fixin's bar.

Trolley Car Cafe

QUALITY Good	VALUE B	PORTION Small	LOCATION Hollywood Boulevard
READER-SURVEY RESPONSES 97% 👍		DISNEY DINING PLAN? Yes	

SELECTIONS Coffee drinks and teas; breakfast sandwiches and pastries.

COMMENTS Disney-themed Starbucks. The pink-stucco Spanish Colonial exterior calls to mind old Hollywood, while the industrial-style interior is themed to evoke a trolley-car switching station. The fare is largely the same you'd find at any other Starbucks.

Woody's Lunch Box

QUALITY Fair	VALUE B	PORTION Medium	LOCATION Toy Story Land
READER-SURVEY RESPONSES 87% 👍		DISNEY DINING PLAN? Yes	

SELECTIONS Breakfast: *Toy Story*–themed specialties, such as s'more French toast breakfast sandwich, potato barrels with brisket country gravy and scrambled eggs, fruit tarts, and soda floats. Lunch and dinner: sandwiches (barbecue brisket, smoked turkey, grilled three-cheese); tomato-basil soup; potato barrels smothered with chili, queso, and corn chips.

COMMENTS Health alert: The potato barrels and fruit tarts with icing might not be what you want for your child; healthier options are available elsewhere. Limited seating at nearby picnic tables with umbrellas. Use mobile ordering here to avoid long waits in line.

DISNEY'S FULL-SERVICE RESTAURANTS:
A QUICK ROMP AROUND THE WORLD

LILIANE Young children are the rule, not the exception, at Disney World restaurants.

DISNEY RESTAURANTS OFFER an excellent (though expensive) opportunity to introduce young children to the variety and excitement of ethnic food. No matter how formal a restaurant appears, the staff is accustomed to wiggling, impatient, and often boisterous children. **Chefs de France** at Epcot, for example, may be the nation's only French restaurant where most patrons wear shorts and T-shirts and at least two dozen young diners are attired in basic black . . . mouse ears.

Almost all Disney restaurants offer children's menus, and all have booster seats and high chairs. They understand how tough it may be for kids to sit for an extended period of time, and waiters will supply little ones with crackers and rolls and serve your dinner much faster than in comparable restaurants elsewhere. In fact, we have received lots of complaints from guests who felt rushed through their meals. At restaurants with prix fixe menus, such as 'Ohana, Disney seems to bring your food out at warp speed. Unless you have little children and welcome the quick turnaround, we say take your time and eat at your own pace.

FELICITY The San Angel Inn is really dark, making it difficult to eat. It was hard to sit through dinner knowing that the Gran Fiesta boats were nearby. I just wanted to get up and ride it over and over again.

In **Epcot,** preschoolers most enjoy Biergarten in Germany, San Angel Inn in Mexico, and Coral Reef at The Seas with Nemo & Friends Pavilion in Future World. **Biergarten** combines a rollicking and noisy atmosphere with good basic food, including pork roast and German sausages. A German oompah band entertains, and kids can often participate in Bavarian dancing. **San Angel Inn** is in the Mexican village marketplace. From the table, children can watch boats on the Gran Fiesta Tour drift beneath a smoking volcano. With a choice of chips, tacos, and other familiar items, picky children usually have no difficulty finding something to eat. (Be aware, though, that the service here is sometimes glacially slow.) **Coral Reef,** with tables beside windows looking into The Seas' aquarium, offers a colorful mealtime diversion for all ages. If your kids don't eat fish, Coral Reef also serves beef and chicken. The downside is that the food is extremely expensive. For a more affordable splurge, forget lunch or dinner and drop in during off-hours for one of the Coral Reef's decadent desserts. The San Angel Inn is likewise overpriced but not in the same league as Coral Reef. Biergarten offers reasonable value, plus good food.

LILIANE Spice Road Table is my favorite spot for watching the fireworks. Read my review here: tinyurl.com /spiceroadtable.

While certainly not cheap, **Spice Road Table** provides the added value of a great location. Situated along the edge of World Showcase Lagoon in the Morocco Pavilion, it serves Mediterranean-inspired small plates similar to Spanish tapas, and its outdoor terrace provides perfect views for fireworks at night. Kids will like sitting outside, and the small plates can be shared. The entire family will enjoy the fireworks while mom and dad have a nice glass of wine.

Be Our Guest Restaurant and **Cinderella's Royal Table,** both in Fantasyland, are the hot tickets in the **Magic Kingdom,** but reservations are often well-nigh impossible to get. For the best combination of food and entertainment, book a character meal at **The Crystal Palace.** From a strictly foodie standpoint, we think the best kids' fare is at the **Liberty Tree Tavern,** and it's easy to book too. **The Plaza** and **Tony's Town Square Restaurants** are two other options in the Magic Kingdom.

In Adventureland **Jungle Navigation Co. Ltd. Skipper Canteen** offers extensive, exciting, and very pricey choices—including *char siu* pork, lamb chops, and Kungaloosh! dessert.

FELICITY Crystal Palace is amazing. The breakfast lasagna is yummy, and the fluffy characters are super nice to cuddle.

At **Disney's Hollywood Studios,** all ages enjoy the atmosphere and entertainment at the **Sci-Fi Dine-In Theater Restaurant** and the **50's Prime Time Café.** Unfortunately, the Sci-Fi's food is close to dismal except for dessert, and the Prime Time Café's is uneven. Theme aside, children enjoy the character meals at **Hollywood & Vine,** and the pizza at **Mama Melrose's** never fails to please. **The Hollywood Brown Derby** offers fine dining in the park. **Roundup Rodeo BBQ,** a much-needed new table-service restaurant inside Toy Story Land, will be themed around a play area that Andy has set up in his backyard. No opening date has been announced, but you can be certain that it will be very popular.

A. J. The Sci-Fi Dine-In Theater is the best themed restaurant. You sit in a convertible booth, watch old sci-fi movie trailers and cartoons, and drink milkshakes. What's better than that?

FELICITY I knew you had to watch your manners and eat all your food, including the vegetables, at 50's Prime Time. This made me pretty nervous. Our server was nice and friendly, but I kept wondering if she was going to tell me off.

The four full-service restaurants at **Disney's Animal Kingdom** are **Tusker House Restaurant** (a character buffet); **Rainforest Cafe,** a great favorite of children; **Yak & Yeti Restaurant;** and **Tiffins.** Both Bob and Liliane agree that Tiffins is the best restaurant inside the theme parks.

As you've undoubtedly noticed by now, Disney World is a trend-savvy place, and every market share has its niche. But Disney World is also about stars, fantasies, and meeting characters. So if you've become accustomed to oak-fired filet of beef, the **California Grill** atop the Contemporary Resort will oblige. Great sushi can be had at **Teppan Edo** at Japan in Epcot and at **Kimonos** in the Swan. The best and biggest steaks are at **Shula's Steak House** in the Dolphin, **Le Cellier Steakhouse** at the Canada Pavilion, or **Yachtsman Steakhouse** at the Yacht Club, albeit way overpriced. At Epcot's Italy **Via Napoli,** an authentic Neapolitan pizzeria, features wood-burning ovens and imports water from a source that most resembles the water in Naples, Italy, home of some of the world's best pizza dough. The 300-seat pizzeria has both indoor and outdoor dining. In Mexico, the counter-service **La Cantina de San Angel** and the full-service **La Hacienda de San Angel** (dinner only) offer a combined 400 seats with alfresco seating for lunch and a perfect place for viewing Epcot's nightly fireworks.

Disney Springs has an amazing array of dining venues. The West Side's Exposition Park food trucks include **Fantasy Fare,** featuring shrimp and lobster macaroni and cheese, chicken and waffles with zesty maple syrup, and chicken strips with waffle fries; and **Springs' Street Tacos,** which offers steak, chicken, fish, and vegetarian bowls, as well as a taco combo. (Food truck offerings and schedules vary daily.)

The West Side has one celebrity-connected restaurant-nightclub: **House of Blues,** part of the chain of New Orleans–style music halls–restaurants once partly owned by surviving Blues Brother Dan Aykroyd. House of Blues, surprisingly enough, has done well with its Louisiana-inspired fare and gospel brunch. **The Smokehouse** is a quick-service barbecue joint operated by the House of Blues. (Bongos, a Cuban-flavored café created by Gloria Estefan and her husband, Emilio, closed in August 2019.)

The new kid on the block on West Side is **Jaleo,** a concept by world-renowned chef José Andrés, which opened in 2019. Jaleo features an extensive menu of tapas, reflecting the rich regional diversity of traditional and contemporary Spanish cuisine.

At the Landing, **Jock Lindsey's Hangar Bar,** an aviation-themed lounge located between Paradiso 37 and The Boathouse, is named after the pilot from the *Indiana Jones* films. The lounge features unique cocktails, such as Reggie's Revenge and the Fountain of Youth, both containing Florida vodkas; and Hovito Mojito and The Bitter Barkeep, both with Peruvian pisco. Other drinks worth trying are The Aviator's Flight, The Scottish Professor, and the Cool-headed Monkey with African spirits. This family-friendly, 150-seat waterfront lounge serves little plates, such as spiced meatballs on mini buns with yogurt sauce. Check out the memorabilia in the bar's indoor seating area.

Iron Chef Masaharu Morimoto brought prestige to Disney Springs when he opened the first pan-Asian restaurant there: **Morimoto Asia** highlights foods from around the continent. It's Bob's and Liliane's favorite sit-down restaurant at Disney Springs. Guests can pick from several dining lounges or the coveted spot in the show kitchen. Items on the menu include *moo shu* pork, Peking duck, lobster *chow fun,* sweet-and-sour crispy whole fish, and kung pao chicken. And kids don't need to feel left out: kid-friendly dishes such as lo mein Cantonese noodles with steamed vegetables, Japanese-style fried chicken,

---

FAVORITE EATS AT DISNEY SPRINGS

LAND | SERVICE LOCATION | FOOD SELECTIONS

MARKETPLACE   Earl of Sandwich | Sandwich paradise

Ghirardelli Soda Fountain & Chocolate Shop | Ice cream and chocolate treats

T-REX | Burgers, ribs, pasta, and kids' menu in Jurassic setting with animatronic dinosaurs | *Table service only*

WEST SIDE   Food Trucks at Exposition Park | A world of choices, including shrimp and lobster macaroni and cheese and tacos

House of Blues | Cajun food and kids' menu. For shows in the music hall next door, check out hob.com. | *Table service only*

Jaleo | Authentic Spanish cuisine, including tapas, paella, and Serrano and Ibérico ham by celebrity chef José Andrés

Pepe by José Andrés | A grab-and-go dining spot in front of Jaleo with sandwiches and sangria

Starbucks | Bistro boxes, coffee and tea, croissants, pastries, and salads

THE LANDING AND TOWN CENTER   Amorette's Patisserie | Mini cakes

Blaze Pizza, Fast-Fire'd | Best pizza ever. Lines are out the door—that should tell you enough!

Morimoto Asia | Pan-Asian food. Inside is table service only, but Morimoto Street Food, a window on the outdoor patio, serves *bao* tacos, sushi, and noodles at a reasonable price.

Raglan Road Irish Pub and Restaurant | Irish food and live music | *Table service only*

a Japanese panko–fried hamburger patty, and orange chicken served with white or brown rice are also available.

The Edison, an industrial Gothic restaurant and bar serving American food and craft cocktails, opened early 2018. Filled with themed areas (such as The Lab, The Ember Parlour, The Tesla Lounge, and Waterfront Patio) and entertainment (including palm readers, DJs, and contortionists), The Edison is a lot of fun, especially for mom and dad on a night out. The food is decent and nicely presented but overpriced. We recommend you dine elsewhere and enjoy the atmosphere and entertainment of The Edison past 9 p.m. at one of the establishment's bars.

Stay away from **Maria and Enzo's Ristorante.** The food is adequate Italian fare in a very noisy setting. **Pizza Ponte** is a quick-service eatery that's connected to Maria and Enzo's. If money isn't an issue, we recommend **Enzo's Hideaway.** The setting is a speakeasy-inspired tunnel serving Italian dishes and the largest selection of aged rums and scotches in Disney Springs.

At **The Boathouse,** an upscale seafood restaurant on the waterfront, kids enjoy watching the amphibious cars drive by. One of Liliane's favorites is **Erin McKenna's Bakery NYC,** the world's premier vegan and gluten-free bakery. **Vivoli il Gelato** serves gelato made with fresh, seasonal ingredients.

Family-friendly restaurants include **Raglan Road,** an Irish pub and restaurant featuring live Celtic music, and several outdoor food-and-beverage locations. **Paradiso 37** highlights the cuisines of the Americas (that would be North, Central, and South) served both indoors and out. **STK Orlando** is a high-end steak house with a rooftop terrace. **Chef Art Smith's Homecomin'** has become a favorite among Disney Springs visitors; it offers local farm-to-table ingredients and traditional Southern cooking. **Terralina Crafted Italian** finally opened in summer 2018 after undergoing a major refurbishment, transforming the former Portobello Country Italian Trattoria into a restaurant with dishes curated by James Beard Award–winning chef Tony Mantuano. Board a stationary "steamship" to eat at **Paddlefish;** the menu consists of seafood, sandwiches, and salads.

Town Center is also home to lots of eateries, such as **Blaze Pizza, Fast-Fire'd; D-Luxe Burger;** the table-service restaurant **Frontera Cocina** by celebrity chef Rick Bayless; and **Amorette's Patisserie. The Polite Pig,** with the same owners as The Ravenous Pig, serves wood-fired fare and beer, wine, and cocktails.

Planet Hollywood Observatory has an outdoor terrace and bar called Stargazers, which features live entertainment. The menu lacks a lot when it comes to quality and taste; however, the restaurant is a favorite among teens. In 2018 Planet Hollywood added an outdoor quick-service called **Chicken Guy,** brought to life by Robert Earl (of Planet Hollywood fame) and celebrity chef Guy Fieri, hoping to draw in the next-door movie theater crowd and those still hungry on their way to the nearby parking garage. There are so many great offerings now at Disney Springs that we recommend you skip Planet Hollywood.

For mom and dad's night out, try **Wine Bar George,** featuring recommendations by master sommelier George Miliotes. The lounge also serves small plates designed to complement the wine list. **The Basket** brings a counter-service component to Wine Bar George, serving sandwiches, cookies, and wine. **Wolfgang Puck Bar & Grill** offers the best of the chef's signature dishes.

If your kids haven't had their fill of robotic crocodiles, Abraham Lincolns, singing parrots, and the like, T-REX and Rainforest Cafe will serve up all they can handle. There are two **Rainforest Cafe** branches, one at Disney Springs Marketplace and a supertheatrical version at the entrance to Animal Kingdom, where the decor and animatronic elephants make it fit right into the scenery there. Not surprisingly in a place where the sky "rains" and the stars flicker overhead, more thought went into naming the dishes than perfecting the recipes. Also, note that the Animal Kingdom Rainforest Cafe serves breakfast.

If your kids prefer dinosaurs to pachyderms, try **T-REX,** which is located within spitting distance of the Rainforest Cafe at Disney Springs and is operated by the same folks. The food is better than Rainforest, and children go nuts about being surrounded by a life-size animatronic brontosaurus, triceratops, and such.

Film and sports stars, as well as Food Network and food-magazine stars, have been enlisted in the Disney World parade. Paul Bocuse was one of the eponymous **Chefs de France** who designed the menu for that restaurant and for **Monsieur Paul** in Epcot. Paul's son, Jérôme, will head a new *crêperie* opening at the France Pavilion by 2021. Boston star chef Todd English created **bluezoo** for the Dolphin.

LILIANE While bluezoo is a very adult dining venue, I was disappointed with the food and service. I don't recommend it.

In fact, though the official guides to Walt Disney World describe various restaurants as *delicious, delectable,* and *delightful,* the truth is that only perhaps a dozen of the nearly 100 full-service establishments are first-rate. And some of the most disappointing restaurants, in general, are the often attractive but commissary-bland ethnic kitchens.

Though a blessing in disguise to many children and picky eaters of all ages, most of the "ethnic" food at Walt Disney World is Americanized, or rather homogenized, especially at Epcot, where visitors from so many countries, as well as the United States, tend to have preconceived notions of egg rolls and enchiladas. **Teppan Edo** in the Japan Pavilion happens to be one of the better restaurants in the World, with pretty good teppanyaki (and good tempura next door)—but it specializes in a particularly Westernized form of Japanese cuisine. A new Signature Dining restaurant, **Takumi-Tei,** opened in the summer of 2019. **Nine Dragons Restaurant** in the China Pavilion serves satisfying appetizers, a respectable five-spiced fish, and crisp vegetables. The **San Angel Inn** in the Mexico Pavilion is associated with the famous Debler family of Mexico City. **Chefs de France** and **Monsieur Paul,** the brainchildren of the late master chefs Paul Bocuse, Gaston Lenôtre, and Roger Vergé, are serious dining destinations.

Liliane loves meeting the princesses at Norway's **Akershus Royal Banquet Hall,** but Bob finds the buffet stodgy, smoky, and cheese- and mayonnaise-heavy. (If smoked meats are your thing, he thinks the smoked turkey legs from the outdoor vendors are far better.)

Among the places the culinary staff actually recommends (off the record) are the classic-Continental prix-fixe **Victoria & Albert's** at the Grand Floridian, where you pay $235 a head to have every waitress introduce herself as Vicky and all the waiters as Al; the **Flying Fish; Jiko; Sanaa;** and the ultra-chic **California Grill.**

Another thing: A lot of the food at Disney World, particularly the fast food, isn't exactly healthy. (Funnel cakes? Happy Meals?) But healthy options do exist. **Sunshine Seasons** in The Land Pavilion at Epcot is a fast-casual spot where the food is freshly prepared, often when you order it, but can be carried out or taken to nearby tables. At Sunshine Seasons, there are four different fully staffed kitchens, one preparing entrée salads with chicken, almonds, and quinoa, as well as soups du jour; another stir-frying veggies and preparing Asian noodle soup; a third wood-grilling chicken, pork, and salmon; and a fourth preparing deluxe focaccia sandwiches.

Beyond that, fruit stands and juice bars are scattered around, and healthier food options include veggie sandwiches, wraps, rotisserie chicken, soft pretzels, popcorn, baked potatoes (not, frankly, prepared with the apparent care of the turkey legs but about a tenth of the calories and salt), as well as the frozen fruit bars in the ice cream freezers and frozen yogurt or smoothies at the ice cream shops. Yes, it's hard, especially with all those fudge and cookie stands practically pelting you with sugary goodness as you saunter past, but stick to your guns. Look for the fruit markets in Liberty Square in the Magic Kingdom, at The Land Pavilion in Epcot, on Sunset Boulevard in Disney's Hollywood Studios, and at the Harambe Village marketplace in Animal Kingdom.

WALT DISNEY WORLD RESTAURANTS: RATED AND RANKED

OVERALL RATING This represents the entire dining experience: style, service, ambience, and food quality. Five stars is the highest rating attainable. Four-star restaurants are above average, and three-star restaurants offer good, though not necessarily memorable, meals. Two-star restaurants serve mediocre fare, and one-star restaurants are below average. Our star ratings don't correspond to ratings awarded by AAA, Forbes, Zagat, or other restaurant reviewers.

★★★★★	Exceptional value, a real bargain
★★★★	Good value
★★★	Fair value, you get exactly what you pay for
★★	Somewhat overpriced
★	Significantly overpriced

COST RANGE The next rating tells you how much you'll spend on a full-service entrée. Appetizers, sides, soups/salads, desserts, drinks, and tips aren't included. Costs are categorized as inexpensive ($15 or less), moderate ($15–$35), or expensive ($35 and up).

QUALITY RATING The food quality is rated on a scale of one to five stars, five being the best. The criteria are taste, freshness of ingredients, preparation, presentation, and creativity of food served. Price is not a consideration.

continued on page 182

WALT DISNEY WORLD RESTAURANTS BY CUISINE

RESTAURANT	LOCATION	OVERALL RATING	COST	QUALITY RATING	VALUE RATING
AFRICAN					
BOMA—FLAVORS OF AFRICA	Animal Kingdom Lodge–Jambo	★★★★½	Exp	★★★★	★★★★
JIKO—THE COOKING PLACE	Animal Kingdom Lodge–Jambo	★★★★½	Exp	★★★★	★★★
SANAA	Animal Kingdom Villas–Kidani	★★★★	Exp	★★★★	★★★★
JUNGLE NAVIGATION CO. LTD. SKIPPER CANTEEN	Magic Kingdom	★★★½	Exp	★★★	★★★
TUSKER HOUSE RESTAURANT	Animal Kingdom	★★★	Exp	★★★	★★★
AMERICAN					
CALIFORNIA GRILL	Contemporary	★★★★★	Exp	★★★★★	★★★
BE OUR GUEST RESTAURANT	Magic Kingdom	★★★★	Exp	★★★★	★★★★
THE HOLLYWOOD BROWN DERBY	DHS	★★★★	Exp	★★★★	★★★
TIFFINS	Animal Kingdom	★★★★	Exp	★★★★	★★★
WOLFGANG PUCK BAR & GRILL	Disney Springs	★★★½	Mod	★★★★	★★★½
ARTIST POINT	Wilderness Lodge	★★★½	Exp	★★★★	★★★½
CAPE MAY CAFE	Beach Club	★★★½	Exp	★★★½	★★★★
CHEF ART SMITH'S HOMECOMIN'	Disney Springs	★★★½	Mod	★★★½	★★★½
LIBERTY TREE TAVERN	Magic Kingdom	★★★½	Mod	★★★	★★★
WHISPERING CANYON CAFE	Wilderness Lodge	★★★	Exp	★★★½	★★★★
GEYSER POINT BAR & GRILL	Wilderness Lodge	★★★	Inexp	★★★½	★★★
HOUSE OF BLUES RESTAURANT	Disney Springs	★★★	Mod	★★★½	★★★
THE CRYSTAL PALACE	Magic Kingdom	★★★	Exp	★★★½	★★★
THE EDISON	Disney Springs	★★★	Exp	★★★½	★★★
50'S PRIME TIME CAFE	DHS	★★★	Mod	★★★	★★★
ALE & COMPASS	Yacht Club	★★★	Exp	★★★	★★★
TUSKER HOUSE RESTAURANT	Animal Kingdom	★★★	Exp	★★★	★★★

WALT DISNEY WORLD RESTAURANTS BY CUISINE *(continued)*

RESTAURANT	LOCATION	OVERALL RATING	COST	QUALITY RATING	VALUE RATING
BOATWRIGHT'S DINING HALL	Port Orleans–Riverside	★★★	Exp	★★★	★★
CINDERELLA'S ROYAL TABLE	Magic Kingdom	★★★	Exp	★★★	★★
OLIVIA'S CAFE	Old Key West	★★★	Exp	★★★	★★
T-REX	Disney Springs	★★★	Mod	★★	★★
THE WAVE . . . OF AMERICAN FLAVORS	Contemporary	★★★	Exp	★★	★★
PADDLEFISH	Disney Springs	★★½	Exp	★★★½	★★½
ESPN CLUB	BoardWalk	★★½	Mod	★★★	★★★
CHEF MICKEY'S	Contemporary	★★½	Exp	★★★	★★★
HOLLYWOOD & VINE	DHS	★★½	Exp	★★★	★★★
1900 PARK FARE	Grand Floridian	★★½	Exp	★★★	★★★
GRAND FLORIDIAN CAFE	Grand Floridian	★★½	Mod	★★★	★★
BEACHES & CREAM SODA SHOP	Beach Club	★★½	Mod	★★½	★★
FRESH MEDITERRANEAN MARKET	Dolphin	★★½	Mod	★★½	★★
SPLITSVILLE	Disney Springs	★★½	Mod	★★½	★★
RAINFOREST CAFE	Animal Kingdom and Disney Springs	★★½	Mod	★★	★★
GARDEN GROVE	Swan	★★	Exp	★★★	★★
TURF CLUB BAR & GRILL	Saratoga Springs	★★	Exp	★★★	★★
SCI-FI DINE-IN THEATER RESTAURANT	DHS	★★	Mod	★★½	★★
LAS VENTANAS	Coronado Springs	★★	Mod	★★½	★★
GARDEN GRILL RESTAURANT	Epcot	★★	Exp	★★	★★★
JOCK LINDSEY'S HANGAR BAR	Disney Springs	★★	Inexp	★★	★★
BIG RIVER GRILLE & BREWING WORKS	BoardWalk	★★	Mod	★★	★★
THE FOUNTAIN	Dolphin	★★	Mod	★★	★★
THE PLAZA RESTAURANT	Magic Kingdom	★★	Mod	★★	★★
TRAIL'S END RESTAURANT	Fort Wilderness Resort	★★	Exp	★★	★★
PLANET HOLLYWOOD OBSERVATORY	Disney Springs	★½	Mod	★★	★★
DIAMOND HORSESHOE *(seasonal)*	Magic Kingdom	★	Mod	★½	★
MAYA GRILL	Coronado Springs	★	Exp	★	★
THREE BRIDGES BAR & GRILL	Coronado Springs	Too new	Mod	Too new	Too new
CITY WORKS EATERY AND POUR HOUSE *(opens 2019)*	Disney Springs	N/A	Mod	N/A	N/A

WALT DISNEY WORLD RESTAURANTS BY CUISINE (continued)

RESTAURANT	LOCATION	OVERALL RATING	COST	QUALITY RATING	VALUE RATING
ASIAN					
JUNGLE NAVIGATION CO. LTD. SKIPPER CANTEEN	Magic Kingdom	★★★½	Exp	★★★	★★★
BRITISH					
ROSE & CROWN DINING ROOM	Epcot	★★★	Mod	★★★½	★★
BUFFET					
BOMA—FLAVORS OF AFRICA	Animal Kingdom Lodge-Jambo	★★★★½	Exp	★★★★	★★★★
CAPE MAY CAFE	Beach Club	★★★½	Exp	★★★½	★★★★
THE CRYSTAL PALACE	Magic Kingdom	★★★	Exp	★★★½	★★★
TUSKER HOUSE RESTAURANT	Animal Kingdom	★★★	Exp	★★★	★★★
THE WAVE . . . OF AMERICAN FLAVORS	Contemporary	★★★	Exp	★★	★★
CHEF MICKEY'S	Contemporary	★★½	Exp	★★★	★★★
HOLLYWOOD & VINE	DHS	★★½	Exp	★★★	★★★
1900 PARK FARE	Grand Floridian	★★½	Exp	★★★	★★★
GARDEN GROVE	Swan	★★	Exp	★★★	★★
AKERSHUS ROYAL BANQUET HALL	Epcot	★★	Exp	★★	★★★★
BIERGARTEN	Epcot	★★	Exp	★★	★★★★
TRAIL'S END RESTAURANT	Fort Wilderness Resort	★★	Exp	★★	★★
DIAMOND HORSESHOE (seasonal)	Magic Kingdom	★	Mod	★½	★
CAJUN					
BOATWRIGHT'S DINING HALL	Port Orleans-Riverside	★★★	Exp	★★★	★★
CHINESE					
NINE DRAGONS RESTAURANT	Epcot	★★	Mod	★★	★★
FRENCH					
MONSIEUR PAUL	Epcot	★★★★	Exp	★★★★½	★★★
BE OUR GUEST RESTAURANT	Magic Kingdom	★★★★	Exp	★★★★	★★★★
CHEFS DE FRANCE	Epcot	★★★	Exp	★★★	★★★
GERMAN					
BIERGARTEN	Epcot	★★	Exp	★★	★★★★
GLOBAL					
PARADISO 37	Disney Springs	★★½	Exp	★★★	★★★
GOURMET					
VICTORIA & ALBERT'S	Grand Floridian	★★★★★	Exp	★★★★★	★★★★
INDIAN					
SANAA	Animal Kingdom Villas-Kidani	★★★★	Exp	★★★★	★★★★

WALT DISNEY WORLD RESTAURANTS BY CUISINE *(continued)*

RESTAURANT	LOCATION	OVERALL RATING	COST	QUALITY RATING	VALUE RATING
IRISH					
RAGLAN ROAD IRISH PUB & RESTAURANT	Disney Springs	★★★★	Mod	★★★½	★★★
ITALIAN					
TUTTO ITALIA RISTORANTE	Epcot	★★★★	Exp	★★★★	★★
VIA NAPOLI RISTORANTE E PIZZERIA	Epcot	★★★★	Exp	★★★½	★★★
MARIA & ENZO'S RISTORANTE	Disney Springs	★★★½	Exp	★★★½	★★★
TRATTORIA AL FORNO	BoardWalk	★★★½	Mod	★★★½	★★
TERRALINA CRAFTED ITALIAN	Disney Springs	★★★½	Mod	★★★	★★★
IL MULINO NEW YORK TRATTORIA	Swan	★★★	Exp	★★★	★★
MAMA MELROSE'S RISTORANTE ITALIANO	DHS	★★½	Mod	★★★	★★
TONY'S TOWN SQUARE RESTAURANT	Magic Kingdom	★★½	Exp	★★★	★★
JAPANESE					
KIMONOS	Swan	★★★★	Mod	★★★★	★★★
TEPPAN EDO	Epcot	★★★½	Exp	★★★★	★★★
MORIMOTO ASIA	Disney Springs	★★★½	Exp	★★★½	★★★★
TOKYO DINING	Epcot	★★★	Mod	★★★★	★★★
TAKUMI-TEI	Epcot	Too new	Exp	Too new	Too new
LATIN					
JUNGLE NAVIGATION CO. LTD. SKIPPER CANTEEN	Magic Kingdom	★★★½	Exp	★★★	★★★
SEBASTIAN'S BISTRO	Caribbean Beach	★★★	Exp	★★★	★★★★
MEDITERRANEAN					
CÍTRICOS	Grand Floridian	★★★½	Exp	★★★★½	★★★
FRESH MEDITERRANEAN MARKET	Dolphin	★★½	Mod	★★½	★★
TOPOLINO'S TERRACE *(opens 2019)*	Riviera	N/A	Exp	N/A	N/A
MEXICAN					
FRONTERA COCINA	Disney Springs	★★★½	Mod	★★★½	★★★
LA HACIENDA DE SAN ANGEL	Epcot	★★★	Exp	★★★½	★★½
SAN ANGEL INN RESTAURANTE	Epcot	★★★	Exp	★★★	★★
MAYA GRILL	Coronado Springs	★	Exp	★	★
MOROCCAN					
SPICE ROAD TABLE	Epcot	★★★★	Exp	★★★★	★★★
RESTAURANT MARRAKESH	Epcot	★★★	Exp	★★½	★★

WALT DISNEY WORLD RESTAURANTS BY CUISINE (continued)

RESTAURANT	LOCATION	OVERALL RATING	COST	QUALITY RATING	VALUE RATING
NORWEGIAN					
AKERSHUS ROYAL BANQUET HALL	Epcot	★★	Exp	★★	★★★★
POLYNESIAN/PAN-ASIAN					
TIFFINS	Animal Kingdom	★★★★	Exp	★★★★	★★★
MORIMOTO ASIA	Disney Springs	★★★½	Exp	★★★½	★★★★
'OHANA	Polynesian Village	★★★	Exp	★★★½	★★★
KONA CAFE	Polynesian Village	★★★	Mod	★★★	★★★★
TRADER SAM'S GROG GROTTO	Polynesian Village	★★★	Mod	★★★	★★★
YAK & YETI RESTAURANT	Animal Kingdom	★★	Exp	★★½	★★
SEAFOOD					
NARCOOSSEE'S	Grand Floridian	★★★★½	Exp	★★★½	★★
FLYING FISH	BoardWalk	★★★★	Exp	★★★★	★★★
TODD ENGLISH'S BLUEZOO	Dolphin	★★★	Exp	★★★★	★★
SEBASTIAN'S BISTRO	Caribbean Beach	★★★	Exp	★★★	★★★★
THE BOATHOUSE	Disney Springs	★★★	Exp	★★★	★★
PADDLEFISH	Disney Springs	★★½	Exp	★★★½	★★½
CORAL REEF RESTAURANT	Epcot	★★½	Exp	★★	★★
SPANISH					
JALEO	Disney Springs	★★★★	Mod	★★★★	★★★★
THREE BRIDGES BAR & GRILL	Coronado Springs	Too new	Mod	Too new	Too new
TOLEDO–TAPAS, STEAK & SEAFOOD	Coronado Springs	Too new	Exp	Too new	Too new
STEAK					
SHULA'S STEAK HOUSE	Dolphin	★★★★	Exp	★★★★	★★
STK ORLANDO	Disney Springs	★★★½	Exp	★★★★	★★½
LE CELLIER STEAKHOUSE	Epcot	★★★½	Exp	★★★½	★★★
YACHTSMAN STEAKHOUSE	Yacht Club	★★★	Exp	★★★½	★★

continued from page 178

VALUE RATING If you are looking for both quality and value, then you should check the value rating, expressed as stars.

WALT DISNEY WORLD DINNER THEATERS

SEVERAL DINNER-THEATER SHOWS play each night at Walt Disney World. When you make a reservation, you'll receive a confirmation number and be told to pick up your tickets at a Disney-hotel Guest Relations desk. Unlike Advance Reservations, your seating times for dinner shows are guaranteed. Unless you cancel your tickets at least 48 hours before your reservation time, your credit card will still be charged the full amount. Dinner-show reservations can be made 180 days in advance; call ☎ 407-939-3463.

Hoop-Dee-Doo Musical Revue   Pioneer Hall, Fort Wilderness Resort & Campground

Showtimes 4, 6:15, and 8:30 p.m. nightly. **Cost** *Category 1:* $72 adults, $43 children ages 3–9. *Category 2:* $67 adults, $39 children. *Category 3:* $64 adults, $38 children. Prices include tax and gratuity. **Discounts** Seasonal. **Type of seating** Tables of various sizes to fit the number in each party, set in an Old West–style dance hall. **Menu** All-you-can-eat barbecue ribs, fried chicken, salad, baked beans, and corn bread. **Vegetarian alternative** On request (at least 24 hours in advance). **Beverages** Unlimited beer, wine, sangria, and soft drinks. **Comments** Disney Dining Plan credits can be used for Category 2 and 3 seats but not Category 1.

HOOP-DEE-DOO IS THE LONGEST-RUNNING SHOW at Walt Disney World and a nostalgic favorite for many families. If you've ever thought *Country Bear Jamboree* would benefit from free-flowing beer and wine and barbecue, this is the show for you.

Audience participation includes sing-alongs, hand-clapping, and a finale where you may find yourself onstage. During the meal, the music continues (softly). The food itself isn't bad, and you can't complain about the portion size.

Give special consideration to transportation when planning your evening at Fort Wilderness. There is no parking at Pioneer Hall, which is only accessible by boat (Magic Kingdom and the loop between Fort Wilderness, Wilderness Lodge, and the Contemporary) and the Fort Wilderness internal bus system. After shows, buses at the Pioneer Hall stop take you to the Magic Kingdom bus depot. If driving, allow plenty of time (about an hour) to get there. The fastest option may be to take a Minnie Van (see page 76), which will drop you off as close as possible to the venue. Or do as this California dad suggests:

> Take the boat from the Magic Kingdom rather than a bus. The dock is a short walk from Pioneer Hall in Fort Wilderness, while the bus goes to the main Fort Wilderness parking lot, where you transfer to another bus to Pioneer Hall.

Boat service may be suspended during thunderstorms, so if it's raining or it looks like it's about to rain, Disney will provide bus service from the parks.

Spirit of Aloha Dinner Show   Polynesian Village Resort

Showtimes Tuesday–Saturday, 5:15 and 8:15 p.m. **Cost** *Category 1:* $78 adults, $46 children ages 3–9. *Category 2:* $74 adults, $44 children. *Category 3:* $66 adults, $39 children. Prices include tax and gratuity. **Type of seating** Long rows of tables, with some separation between individual parties. The **BOB** *The Spirit of Aloha is particularly susceptible to cancellations due to weather.* show is performed on an outdoor stage, but all seating is covered. Ceiling fans provide some air movement, but it can get warm, especially at the early show. **Menu** Tropical fruit, roasted chicken, island pork ribs, mixed vegetables, rice, and pineapple-coconut bread; grilled chicken, fish, corn dogs, and pizza for children. **Vegetarian alternative** On request. **Beverages** Beer, wine, and soft drinks.

THIS SHOW FEATURES South Seas–island native dancing followed by an all-you-can-eat "Polynesian-style" meal. The dancing is interesting and largely authentic, and the dancers are definitely PG-rated in the Disney tradition. The show has its moments and the meal is adequate, but neither is particularly special.

The show follows (tenuously) the common "girl leaves home for the big city, forgets her roots, and must rediscover them" theme. The story, however, never really makes sense as anything other than a slender thread between musical numbers. Our show lasted for more than 2 hours and 15 minutes.

The food does little more than illustrate how difficult it must be to prepare the same meal for hundreds of people simultaneously. The roasted chicken is better than the ribs, but neither is worth writing home about. We conditionally recommend *Spirit of Aloha* for special occasions, when the people celebrating get to go on stage. But go to the early show and get dessert somewhere else.

EATING *Outside*
WALT DISNEY WORLD

1. **A CAR HELPS** Access to restaurants outside of Walt Disney World can really cut the cost of your overall vacation, but you need to have wheels. If you eat only your evening meal outside the World, the savings will more than pay for a rental car.

2. **PLENTY OF CHOICES** Outside of Walt Disney World, the range of choices is quite broad and includes elegant dining options, as well as familiar chain restaurants and local family eateries.

3. **DISCOUNTS ARE EVERYWHERE** Visitor booklets containing discount coupons to dozens of out-of-the-World restaurants are available everywhere except in Disney World. The coupons are good at a broad selection of eateries, ranging from burger joints to some of the best restaurants in the area. The mother lode of booklets can be found at the **Visit Orlando Official Visitor Center** (8102 International Dr.; ☎ 407-363-5872 or 800-972-3304; visitorlando.com; open daily, 8 a.m.–8 p.m., except December 25). The center also sells slightly discounted tickets to the theme parks.

The **Kids Eat Free Card** may be a good investment if you have young children and plan to eat off Disney property frequently. It provides free kids' meals at more than 50 restaurants in the Orlando area. To see a full listing, visit kidseatfreecard.com. Each $25 card is valid for one child age 11 or younger and requires that the child be accompanied by one adult paying for a full-price entrée.

In Kissimmee, visit the **Osceola County Welcome Center and History Museum** (4155 W. Vine St.; ☎ 407-396-8644; osceolahistory.org). In addition to visitor information and restaurant coupons, the center also houses an excellent free museum tracing the colorful history of Central Florida. Also, check out couponsalacarte.com for printable coupons.

You can save money at some Disney World–area restaurants by purchasing discounted gift certificates from restaurant.com. Most certificates are for a specific amount (usually $25) at a discounted price (usually $10). The certificates do not expire and can be printed at home. You can use only one certificate per restaurant per month (meaning you could use one certificate at each restaurant during your vacation). Occasionally there are other restrictions, so be sure to read the information provided on the site carefully. Some restaurants require you to buy a certain number of entrées, for instance. Note that restaurants occasionally drop out of the program, so call the restaurant before you go to confirm it's still participating. If a restaurant is no longer a participant, you can change the certificate for another restaurant by contacting the site's customer service.

BUFFETS AND MEAL DEALS
OUTSIDE WALT DISNEY WORLD

BUFFETS, RESTAURANT SPECIALS, and discount dining abound in the area surrounding Walt Disney World, especially on US 192 (Irlo Bronson Memorial Highway) and along International Drive. The local visitor magazines, distributed free at non-Disney hotels, among other places, are packed with advertisements and discount coupons for seafood feasts, Chinese buffets, Indian buffets, and breakfast buffets, as well as specials for everything from lobster to barbecue. For a family trying to economize, some of the come-ons are mighty sweet. But are these places any good? Is the food fresh, tasty, and appealing? Are the restaurants clean and inviting? Armed with little more than a roll of Tums, the *Unofficial* research team tried all the eateries that advertise heavily in the free tourist magazines. Here's what we discovered.

CHINESE SUPER BUFFETS If you've ever prepared Chinese food, especially a stir-fry, you know that split-second timing is required to avoid overcooking. So it should come as no big surprise that Chinese dishes languishing on a buffet lose their freshness, texture, and flavor in a hurry.

In the past, we were able to find several Chinese buffets that we felt comfortable recommending; unfortunately, we would return the next year only to discover that their quality had slipped precipitously. We then searched for new buffets to replace the ones we removed from the book, and we can tell you that wasn't fun work. At the end of the day, **Ichiban Buffet** (5269 W. Irlo Bronson Memorial Hwy., ☎ 407-396-6668; 5529 International Dr., ☎ 407-930-8889; ichibanbuffet.com) and **Hokkaido Chinese & Japanese Buffet** (12173 S. Apopka–Vineland Road, ☎ 407-778-5188; 5737 W. Irlo Bronson Memorial Hwy., ☎ 407-396-0669; hokkaidobuffetorlando.com) are the best choices in their genre. Ichiban is our pick, with Japanese hibachi and sushi, plus traditional and American-style Chinese dishes, including steamed snow crab legs (for an extra charge), raw oysters, and grilled head-on shrimp. Its I-Drive location is our favorite. Hokkaido buffets are comparable, so select whichever buffet is most convenient to you. Selections dry out on buffets, so seek out a popular buffet, where dishes are replenished frequently.

INDIAN BUFFETS Indian food works better on a buffet than Chinese food; in fact, it actually improves as the flavors marry. In the Disney World area, most Indian restaurants offer a buffet at lunch only—not too convenient if you're spending your day at the theme parks. If you're out shopping or taking a day off, these Indian buffets are worth trying: **Aashirwad Indian Cuisine** (7000 S. Kirkman Road; ☎ 407-370-9830; aashirwadrestaurant.com); **Ahmed Indian Restaurant** (11301 S. Orange Blossom Trl., Ste. 104; ☎ 407-856-5970; ahmedrestaurant.com); and **Woodlands Pure Vegetarian Indian Cuisine** (6040 S. Orange Blossom Trl.; ☎ 407-854-3330; woodlandsusa.com).

CHURRASCARIAS A number of these South American–style meat emporiums have sprung up along International Drive. Our picks are **Café**

Where to Eat Outside Walt Disney World

AMERICAN

THE RAVENOUS PIG* 565 W. Fairbanks Ave., Winter Park; ☎ 407-628-2333; theravenouspig.com; moderate–expensive. New American cuisine with an award-winning menu that changes seasonally. Daily happy hour 3–6 p.m.; Sunday brunch 10:30 a.m.–3 p.m.

SLATE 8323 W. Sand Lake Road, Orlando; ☎ 407-500-7528; slateorlando.com; moderate–expensive. Grab a quick bite from the extensive menu, or try heartier fare from the copper-clad wood oven.

BARBECUE

BUBBALOU'S BODACIOUS BAR-B-QUE 5818 Conroy Road, Orlando (near Universal Orlando); ☎ 407-295-1212; kirkman.bubbalous.com; inexpensive. Tender, smoky barbecue; tomato-based Killer Sauce.

4 RIVERS SMOKEHOUSE 874 W. Osceola Pkwy., Kissimmee; ☎ 844-474-8377; 4rsmokehouse.com; inexpensive. (Closed Sunday.) Award-winning beef brisket, fried pickles, cheese grits, fried okra, and collard greens.

CUBAN/SPANISH

COLUMBIA 649 Front St., Celebration; ☎ 407-566-1505; columbiarestaurant.com; moderate. Cuban and Spanish creations such as paella and the 1905 Salad.

CUBA LIBRE 9101 International Dr. at Pointe Orlando, Orlando; ☎ 407-226-1600; cubalibrerestaurant.com; moderate. Upscale. Specializes in ceviche, tapas, and classic Cuban entrées. The 15-course tasting menu is a fabulous way to discover Cuba's cuisine.

ETHIOPIAN

NILE 7048 International Dr., Orlando; ☎ 407-354-0026; nileorlando.com; moderate. An *Unofficial Guide* favorite. Go for the meat combination platter for two (chicken *doro wat, doro alicha,* beef *alicha,* beef *tibs,* cabbage, collard greens, lentils, and split peas), or try the Taste of the Nile vegetarian platter for two.

SELAM ETHIOPIAN & ERITREAN CUISINE 5494 Central Florida Pkwy., Orlando; ☎ 407-778-3119; ethiopianrestaurantorlando.com; moderate. Excellent samosa and lamb dishes. Friendly staff.

FRENCH

URBAIN40 8000 Via Dellagio Way, Orlando; ☎ 407-872-2640; urbain40.com; moderate–expensive. Splendid interpretations of classic Lyonnaise dishes with locally inspired twists, in a 1940s New York–inspired room.

GREEK

TAVERNA OPA 9101 International Dr., Orlando; ☎ 407-351-8660; opaorlando.com; moderate. Try traditional Greek standouts like *boureki,* moussaka, and lamb *kleftiko,* plus kebabs and seafood specialties cooked on a wood fire. Live entertainment.

INDIAN

TABLA CUISINE 5847 Grand National Dr., Orlando; ☎ 407-248-9400; tablacuisine .com; moderate. It's within the Clarion Inn on I-Drive, but don't let that keep you away from one of the better Indian restaurants in the area. It also has Chinese and Thai dishes.

20 minutes or more from Walt Disney World

Mineiro (6432 International Dr.; ☎ 407-248-2932; cafemineirosteak house.com), north of Sand Lake Road, and **Boi Brazil Churrascaria** (5668 International Dr.; ☎ 407-354-0260; boibrazil.com). Both offer good value. More expensive are the Argentinean churrasco specialties at **The Knife** (12501 FL 535; ☎ 321-395-4892; thekniferestaurant

ITALIAN

ANTHONY'S COAL-FIRED PIZZA 8031 Turkey Lake Road, Orlando; ☎ 407-363-9466; acfp.com; inexpensive. Pizza, eggplant, beer and wine.

PEPERONCINO CUCINA 7988 Via Dellagio Way, Orlando; ☎ 407-440-2856; peperoncinocucina.com; moderate. Calabrian chef Barbara Alfano runs a tight and authentic kitchen, creating pastas and wood-fired pizza worthy of the name.

JAPANESE/SUSHI

J-PETAL 5135 International Dr., Ste. 7, Orlando; ☎ 407-866-0605; inexpensive. Huge variety of poke bowls. Try the savory or sweet crepes and bubble tea.

NAGOYA SUSHI 7600 Dr. Phillips Blvd., Ste. 66, in the very rear of The Marketplace at Dr. Phillips; ☎ 407-248-8558; nagoyasushi.com; moderate. A small, intimate restaurant with great sushi and an extensive menu.

LATIN

SOFRITO LATIN CAFÉ 8607 Palm Pkwy., Orlando; ☎ 407-778-4205; sofritocafe .com; inexpensive. Specializes in comfort food from Cuba, Columbia, Argentina, Chile, Puerto Rico, Peru, the Dominican Republic, Brazil, and Venezuela. Best for take-out or delivery.

MEXICAN

EL PATRON 12167 S. Apopka–Vineland Road, Orlando; ☎ 407-238-5300; elpatron orlando.com; inexpensive. Family-owned restaurant serving freshly prepared Mexican dishes. Fabulous lunch buffet. Full bar. Saturday–Sunday brunch, 11:30 a.m.–2:30 p.m., with a buffet and bottomless mimosas.

EL TENAMPA MEXICAN RESTAURANT 4565 W. Irlo Bronson Hwy., Orlando; ☎ 407-397-1981; inexpensive. Family-owned, serving an extensive menu of authentic Mexican regional fare in a small, colorful room. Try the steak dish Arrachera El Tenampa.

MOROCCAN

MERGUEZ 11951 International Dr., Orlando; ☎ 407-778-4343; merguez.restaurant; inexpensive. Bright, informal setting with alfresco option. Excellent and representative Moroccan specialties. Awesome bastilla and tagines. Couscous served only on Friday.

SEAFOOD

BONEFISH GRILL 7801 W. Irlo Bronson Memorial Hwy., Kissimmee; ☎ 321-677-0103 (or 7830 W. Sand Lake Road, Orlando; ☎ 407-355-7707); bonefishgrill.com; moderate. Casual setting. Choose your fish, then choose a sauce to accompany. Also has steaks and chicken.

CELEBRATION TOWN TAVERN 721 Front St., Celebration; ☎ 407-566-2526; thecelebrationtowntavern.com; moderate. Popular hangout for locals, with New England–style seafood. The clam chowder is a big hit.

STEAK/PRIME RIB

VITO'S CHOP HOUSE 8633 International Dr., Orlando; ☎ 407-354-2467; vitos chophouse.com; moderate. Upscale meat house with a taste of Tuscany.

THAI

THAI SILK 6803 S. Kirkman Road at International Festival Mall, Orlando; ☎ 407-226-8997; thaisilkorlando.com; moderate. Acclaimed by Orlando dining critics for its authentic Thai dishes. Delicious vegetarian options; impressive wine list.

.com); be sure to try the sweetbreads, an Argentine specialty. If you prefer chain restaurants, the pricey **Texas de Brazil** and **Fogo de Chão** also have locations in Orlando.

SEAFOOD AND LOBSTER BUFFETS These affairs don't exactly fall under the category of inexpensive dining. The main draw is all the lobster you can eat. The problem is that lobsters, like Chinese food, don't wear well on a steam table. After a few minutes on the buffet line, they make better tennis balls than dinner, so try to grab yours immediately after a fresh batch has been brought out. Two lobster buffets are on International Drive, and another is on US 192. Though all three do a reasonable job, we prefer **Boston Lobster Feast** (6071 W. Irlo Bronson Memorial Hwy., ☎ 407-396-2606; 8731 International Dr., ☎ 407-248-8606; bostonlobsterfeast.com). Both locations are distinguished by a vast variety of seafood in addition to the lobster. The I-Drive location is cavernous and noisy, which is why we prefer the Irlo Bronson location, where you can actually have a conversation over dinner. The I-Drive location has ample parking, while the Irlo Bronson restaurant does not. At about $47 for early birds (4–6 p.m.) and $52 after 6 p.m., dining is expensive at both locations.

SALAD BUFFETS The most popular of these in the Walt Disney World area is **Sweet Tomatoes** (6877 S. Kirkman Road, ☎ 407-363-1616; 12561 S. Apopka–Vineland Road, ☎ 407-938-9461; 4678 E. Colonial Dr.; ☎ 407-896-8770; sweettomatoes.com). During lunch and dinner, you can expect a line out the door, but fortunately it moves fast. The buffet features prepared salads and an extensive array of ingredients for building your own. In addition, Sweet Tomatoes offers a variety of soups, a modest pasta bar, a baked-potato bar, an assortment of fresh fruit, and ice cream sundaes. Dinner runs $12.39 for adults, and lunch is $9.99 Monday–Friday, $10.39 Saturday–Sunday. Kids ages 7–12 cost $6.39, and kids ages 3–6 are $4.39, for both lunch and dinner daily.

BREAKFAST AND ENTRÉE BUFFETS Most chain steak houses in the area, including **Ponderosa, Sizzler,** and **Golden Corral,** offer entrée buffets. Among them, they have 12 locations in the Walt Disney World area. All serve breakfast, lunch, and dinner. At lunch and dinner, you get the buffet when you buy an entrée, usually a steak; breakfast service is a straightforward buffet (that is, you don't have to buy an entrée). As for the food, it's chain-restaurant quality but decent. Prices are a bargain, and you can get in and out at lightning speed—important at breakfast when you're trying to get to the parks early. Some locations offer lunch and dinner buffets at a set price without requiring you to buy an entrée.

BOB Most chain-restaurant breakfast buffets have a number of locations in the Orlando area, but their operating hours aren't always the same. If you want to eat early or late, check online or call before you go.

Though you can argue about which chain serves the best steak, **Golden Corral** wins the buffet contest hands-down, with at least twice as many offerings as its two competitors. While buffets at Golden Corral and Ponderosa are pretty consistent from location to location, the buffet at Sizzler (7602 W. Irlo Bronson Memorial Hwy.; ☎ 407-397-0997; sizzler.com) varies a good deal from Sizzler locations out West. In addition to the steak houses, the WDW-area **Shoney's** also offers breakfast, lunch, and dinner buffets.

A New Hampshire reader notes that some off-site breakfast buffets don't open early enough:

You mention quite a few buffets for off-site dining, but it would have been nice to know their normal morning business hours. Some buffets (like Ponderosa) didn't open until 8 a.m. for breakfast. This is way too late if you're trying to get to the park at opening time.

DISNEY BUFFETS VS. OFF-SITE BUFFETS Most off-site buffets are long on selection but don't compare favorably to Disney buffets in terms of quality; likewise, the setting and ambience of Disney buffets is generally superior. An exception is **Café Osceola** (9939 Universal Blvd., Orlando; ☎ 407-996-6338; rosenshinglecreek.com/dining) at the Rosen Shingle Creek Resort. Specializing in carved meats, Café Osceola is open for breakfast, lunch, and dinner. If you're trying to save money, however, non-Disney buffets offer excellent value. At a Disney buffet, you can expect well-prepared dishes across all food categories. At an off-site buffet, though some dishes may be below par, you should find enough that's palatable to put together a more-than-acceptable meal. At any buffet, we recommend starting with small samples to sort out the winners and losers, and then going back for larger portions of your favorites.

MEAL DEALS An unbeatable deal for meat eaters is the Family Feast at **Sonny's BBQ**. For $46 per family of four, you get sliced pork and beef, plus chicken, ribs, your choice of three sides (choose from beans, slaw, fries, and others), garlic bread or corn bread, and soft drinks or tea, all served family-style. The closest Sonny's location to Walt Disney World and Universal is at 7423 S. Orange Blossom Trl. in Orlando (☎ 407-859-7197; sonnysbbq.com.)

THE GREAT ORLANDO PIZZA SCAM Plenty of reputable local pizza joints deliver to hotels in and around the theme parks; many Disney and Universal resorts offer pizza delivery as well. But for a few years now, con artists have been distributing fliers advertising delivery to hotel guests—they ask for your credit card number over the phone, but the pizza never arrives. Disregard any such fliers you find.

PART FIVE

KNOW *Before* YOU GO

The **BRUTAL TRUTH** *About* **FAMILY VACATIONS**

IT HAS BEEN SUGGESTED THAT THE PHRASE *family vacation* is a bit of an oxymoron. This is because you can never take a vacation from the responsibilities of parenting if your children are traveling with you. Though you leave your work and normal routine far behind, your children require as much attention, if not more, when traveling as they do at home.

Parenting on the road is an art. It requires imagination and organization. Think about it: you have to do all the usual stuff (feed, dress, bathe, supervise, teach, comfort, discipline, put to bed, and so on) in an atmosphere where your children are hyperstimulated, without the familiarity of place and the resources you take for granted at home. Though it's not impossible—and can even be fun—parenting on the road is not something you want to learn on the fly, particularly at Walt Disney World.

The point we want to drive home is that preparation, or the lack thereof, can make or break your Walt Disney World vacation. Believe us—you do *not* want to leave the success of your expensive Disney vacation to chance. But don't confuse chance with good luck. Chance is what happens when you fail to prepare. Good luck is when preparation meets opportunity.

Your preparation can be organized into several categories, all of which we will help you undertake. Broadly speaking, you need to prepare yourself and your children mentally, emotionally, physically, organizationally, and logistically. You also need a basic understanding of Walt Disney World and a well-considered plan for how to go about seeing it.

MENTAL *and* EMOTIONAL PREPARATION

MENTAL PREPARATION BEGINS with realistic expectations about your Disney vacation and consideration of what each adult and child in your party most wants and needs from their Walt Disney World experience. Getting in touch with this aspect of planning requires a lot of introspection and good, open family communication.

DIVISION OF LABOR

TALK ABOUT WHAT YOU and your partner need and what you expect to happen on the vacation. This discussion alone can preempt some unpleasant surprises mid-trip. If you are a two-parent family, do you have a clear understanding of how the parenting workload is to be distributed? We've seen some distinctly disruptive misunderstandings in two-parent households where one parent is (pardon the legalese) the primary caregiver. Often, the other parent expects the primary caregiver to function on vacation as she (or he) does at home. The primary caregiver, on the other hand, is ready for a break. She expects her partner to either shoulder the load equally or perhaps even assume the lion's share so she can have a *real* vacation. However you divide the responsibility, of course, is up to you. Just make sure you negotiate a clear understanding *before* you leave home.

TOGETHERNESS

ANOTHER DIMENSION TO CONSIDER is how much togetherness seems appropriate to you. For some parents, a vacation represents a rare opportunity to really connect with their children—to talk, exchange ideas, and get reacquainted. For others, a vacation affords the time to get a little distance, to enjoy a round of golf while the kids are participating in a program organized by the resort.

At Walt Disney World you can orchestrate your vacation to spend as much or as little time with your children as you desire, but more about that later. The point here is to think about both your own and your children's preferences and needs concerning your time together. A typical day at a Disney theme park provides the structure of experiencing attractions together, punctuated by periods of waiting in line, eating, and so on, which facilitate conversation and sharing. Most attractions can be enjoyed together by the whole family, regardless of age ranges. This allows for more consensus and less dissent when it comes to deciding what to see and do. For many parents and children, however, the rhythms of a Walt Disney World day seem to consist of passive entertainment experiences alternated with endless discussions of where to go and what to do next. As a mother from Winston-Salem, North Carolina, reported:

*Our family mostly talked about what to do next with very little shar-
ing or discussion about what we had seen. The conversation was
pretty task-oriented.*

Two observations: First, fighting the crowds and keeping the family moving along can easily escalate into a pressure-driven outing.
Having an advance plan or itinerary eliminates moment-to-moment
guesswork and decision making, thus creating more time for savoring and connecting. Second, external variables such as crowd size,
noise, and heat, among others, can be so distracting as to preclude any
meaningful togetherness. These negative impacts can be moderated,
as previously discussed, by your being selective concerning the time
of year, day of the week, and time of day you visit the theme parks.
The bottom line is that you can achieve the degree of connection and
togetherness you desire with a little advance planning and a realistic
awareness of the distractions you will encounter.

LIGHTEN UP

PREPARE YOURSELF MENTALLY to be a little less compulsive on
vacation about correcting small behavioral deviations and pounding
home the lessons of life. So what if Matt eats hamburgers for breakfast,
lunch, and dinner every day? You can make him eat peas and broccoli
when you get home and are in charge of meal preparation again. Roll
with the little stuff, and remember when your children act out that they
are wired to the max. At least some of that adrenaline is bound to spill
out in undesirable ways. Coming down hard will send an already frayed
little nervous system into orbit.

SOMETHING FOR EVERYONE

IF YOU TRAVEL WITH AN INFANT, toddler, or any child who
requires a lot of special attention, make sure that you have some energy

LILIANE Try to schedule some time alone with each of your children—if not each day, then at least a couple of times during the trip.

and time remaining for your other children. In
the course of your planning, invite each child to
name something special to do or see at Walt
Disney World with mom or dad alone. Work
these special activities into your trip itinerary.
Whatever else, if you commit, write it down so
you don't forget. Remember, though, that a casually expressed willingness to do this or that may be perceived as a promise by your children.

WHOSE IDEA WAS THIS, ANYWAY?

LILIANE Short forays to the parks interspersed with naps, swimming, and quiet activities such as reading to your children will go a long way toward keeping things on an even keel.

THE DISCORD THAT MANY VACATIONING
families experience arises from the kids being on
a completely different wavelength from mom and
dad. Parents and grandparents are often worse
than children when it comes to conjuring up fantasy scenarios of what a Walt Disney World vacation will be like. A Disney vacation can be many

things, but believe us when we tell you that there's a lot more to it than just riding Dumbo and seeing Mickey.

In our experience, most parents (and nearly all grandparents) expect children to enter a state of rapture at Walt Disney World, bouncing from attraction to attraction in wide-eyed wonder, appreciative beyond words of their adult benefactors. What they get, more often than not, is not even in the same ballpark. Preschoolers will, without a doubt, be wide-eyed, often with delight but also with a general sense of being overwhelmed by noise, crowds, and Disney characters as big as toolsheds. We have substantiated through thousands of interviews and surveys that the best part of a Disney vacation for a preschooler is the hotel swimming pool. With some grade-schoolers and pre-driving-age teens, you get near-manic hyperactivity coupled with periods of studied nonchalance. This last, which relates to the importance of being cool at all costs, translates into a maddening display of boredom and a "been there, done that" attitude. Older teens are frequently the exponential version of the younger teens and grade-schoolers, except without the manic behavior.

For preschoolers, keep things light and happy by limiting the time you spend in the theme parks. The most critical point is that the overstimulation of the parks must be balanced by adequate rest and more mellow activities. For grade-schoolers and early teens, moderate

LILIANE The more information your children have before arriving at Walt Disney World, the less likely they will be to act out.

the hyperactivity and false apathy by enlisting their help in planning the vacation, especially by allowing them to take a leading role in determining the itinerary for days at the theme parks. Being in charge of specific responsibilities that focus on the happiness of other family members also works well. One reader, for example, turned a 12-year-old liability into an asset by asking him to help guard against attractions that might frighten his 5-year-old sister.

Knowledge enhances anticipation and at the same time affords a level of comfort and control that helps kids understand the big picture. The more they feel in control, the less they will act out of control.

DISNEY, KIDS, AND SCARY STUFF

DISNEY ATTRACTIONS, both rides and shows, are adventures, and they focus on themes common to adventures: good and evil, life and death, beauty and the grotesque, fellowship and enmity. As you sample the attractions at Walt Disney World, you transcend the spinning and bouncing

BOB Before lining up for any attraction, check out our description of it and see our Small-Child Fright-Potential Table on pages 198–201.

of midway rides to thought-provoking and emotionally powerful entertainment. All of the endings are happy, but the adventures' impact, given Disney's gift for special effects, often intimidates and occasionally frightens young children.

There are rides with burning towns and ghouls popping out of their graves, all done with a sense of humor, provided you're old enough to understand the joke. And bones. There are bones every-where: human bones, cattle bones, dinosaur bones, even whole skel-etons. There's a stack of skulls at the headhunter's camp on the Jungle Cruise, a platoon of skeletons sailing ghost ships in Pirates of the Caribbean, and a haunting assemblage of skulls and skeletons in The Haunted Mansion. Skulls, skeletons, and bones punctuate Peter Pan's Flight and Big Thunder Mountain Railroad. And in the Animal Kingdom, an entire children's playground is made up exclusively of giant bones and skeletons.

LILIANE While there is no cer-tain way to know what will scare your kids or what will garner a big smile, many rides are so intense that they can even affect adults. I make a huge detour around The Twilight Zone Tower of Terror or Space Mountain, but I can't get enough of Slinky Dog Dash and Kali River Rapids—and I've survived the Mad Tea Party and Expedition Everest. Parents know their children best. I remem-ber braving the Tower of Terror once because I felt I.couldn't deprive my then-10-year-old just because I was a chicken. I didn't let on that this was not my cup of tea. My prayers to exit the attrac-tion were answered when he asked me shyly if we could ask a cast member to get out. The request was granted instantly by both me and the cast member.

A reader from Thibodaux, Louisiana, wrote to us about his experiences at the Magic Kingdom:

I found SO MANY of the rides to be dark and too spooky for my almost 3-year-old. She hated The Many Adventures of Winnie the Pooh and Peter Pan's Flight because they were dark. There's only so many times one can ride It's a Small World and the carousel before one starts to curse the Imagineers who created so many dark rides.

On the other hand, the special effects at Disney's Hollywood Studios seem more real and sinister than those in the other theme parks. If your child has difficulty coping with the ghouls of The Haunted Mansion, think twice about exposing him or her to Star Tours.

One reader tells of taking his preschool children on Star Tours:

*We took a 4-year-old and a 5-year-old, and they had the *^%#! scared out of them at Star Tours. We did this first thing in the morning, and it took hours of Tom Sawyer Island and It's a Small World to get back to normal.*

Preschoolers should start with Dumbo and work up to the Jungle Cruise in late morning, after being revved up and before getting hungry, thirsty, or tired. Pirates of the Caribbean is out for preschoolers. You get the idea.

LILIANE You know I scream a lot on roller coast-ers, but did you know that I don't leave my feet on the floor dur-ing *It's Tough to Be a Bug!* at the Animal Kingdom? Well, now you know I do not like bugs, and they sting too; they do, they do.

At Walt Disney World, anticipate the almost inevitable emotional overload of your young children. Be sensitive, alert, and prepared for practically anything, even behavior that is out of character for your child at home. Most young children take Disney's macabre trap-pings in stride, and others are easily comforted by an arm around the shoulder or a squeeze of the hand. Parents who know their children tend to become upset should take it slow and easy, sampling more benign adventures, gauging reactions, and discussing with the children how they felt about what they saw.

Some Tips

1. START SLOW AND WARM UP Though each major theme park offers several fairly nonintimidating attractions that you can sample to determine your child's relative sensitivity, the Magic Kingdom is probably the best testing ground. There, try Buzz Lightyear's Space Ranger Spin in Tomorrowland, Peter Pan's Flight in Fantasyland, and the Jungle Cruise in Adventureland to measure your child's reaction to unfamiliar sights and sounds. If your child takes these in stride, try Pirates of the Caribbean. Try the Mad Tea Party or The Barnstormer, both in Fantasyland, or the Astro Orbiter in Tomorrowland to observe how your child tolerates certain ride speeds and motions.

Don't assume that because an attraction is a theater presentation, it will not frighten your child. Trust us on this one. An attraction does not have to be moving to trigger unmitigated, panic-induced hysteria. Rides such as Big Thunder Mountain Railroad and Splash Mountain may look scary, but they don't have even one-fiftieth the potential for terrorizing children as do theater attractions such as *It's Tough to be a Bug!*

2. BE ATTUNED TO PEER AND PARENT PRESSURE Sometimes young children will rise above their anxiety in an effort to please parents or siblings. This doesn't necessarily indicate a mastery of fear, much less enjoyment. If children leave a ride in apparently good shape, ask if they would like to go on it again (not necessarily now, but sometime). The response usually will indicate how much they actually enjoyed the experience. There's a big difference between having a good time and just mustering the courage to get through.

3. ENCOURAGE AND EMPATHIZE Evaluating a child's capacity to handle the visual and tactile effects of Disney World requires patience, understanding, and experimentation. If a child balks at or is frightened by a ride, respond constructively. Let your children know that lots of people, adults and children, are scared by what they see and feel. Help them understand that it's OK if they get frightened and that their fear doesn't lessen your love or respect. Take pains not to compound the discomfort by making a child feel inadequate; try not to undermine self-esteem, impugn courage, or ridicule. Most of all, don't induce guilt by suggesting the child's trepidation might be ruining the family's fun. It's also sometimes necessary to restrain older siblings' taunting or teasing.

The Fright Factor

Of course, each youngster is different, but there are eight attraction elements that alone or combined can push a child's buttons:

1. NAME OF THE ATTRACTION Young children will naturally be apprehensive about something called The Haunted Mansion or The Twilight Zone Tower of Terror.

2. VISUAL IMPACT OF THE ATTRACTION FROM OUTSIDE Big Thunder Mountain Railroad and Splash Mountain look scary enough to give even adults second thoughts, and the two rides visually terrify many young children.

3. VISUAL IMPACT OF THE INDOOR QUEUING AREA Pirates of the Caribbean's caves and dungeons and The Haunted Mansion's "stretch rooms" can frighten kids even before they board the ride.

4. INTENSITY OF THE ATTRACTION Some attractions are overwhelming, inundating the senses with sights, sounds, movement, and even smell. *It's Tough to Be a Bug!* at Animal Kingdom, for example, combines loud sounds, lights, smoke, animatronic insects, and 3-D cinematography to create a total sensory experience. For some preschoolers, this is two or three senses too many.

5. VISUAL IMPACT OF THE ATTRACTION ITSELF Sights in various attractions range from falling boulders to lurking buzzards, from grazing dinosaurs to waltzing ghosts. What one child calmly absorbs may scare the bejabbers out of another.

6. DARK Many Disney World attractions operate indoors in the dark. For some children, darkness alone triggers fear. A child who is frightened on one dark ride (The Haunted Mansion, for example) may be unwilling to try other indoor rides.

7. THE RIDE ITSELF; THE PHYSICAL EXPERIENCE Some rides are wild enough to cause motion sickness, to wrench backs, and to discombobulate patrons of any age.

8. LOUD   The sound levels in some attractions and live shows are so loud that younger children flip out even though the general content of the presentation is quite benign. For toddlers and preschoolers especially, it's good to have a pair of earplugs handy.

Disney Orientation Course

We receive many tips from parents telling how they prepared their young children for the Disney experience. A common strategy is to acquaint children with the characters and stories behind the attractions by reading Disney books and watching Disney videos at home. A more direct approach is to watch videos that show the attractions. A Lexington, Kentucky, mom reports:

LILIANE   My first roller coaster experience ever was with my son. We rode The Barnstormer. I screamed his ears off. Next I took a ride with you-know-who: Bob. He tricked me into riding The Incredible Hulk Coaster at Universal's Islands of Adventure. One cannot print what I said to him. (*Editor's note:* Bob is still deaf in one ear.)

My timid 7-year-old daughter and I watched rides and shows on YouTube, and we cut out all the ones that looked too scary.

You can also view videos at disneyplanning.com. As a YouTube supplement, it gives your kids an adequate sense of what they'll see. You can also watch the **Travel Channel**'s Disney World specials streaming on Hulu or Netflix.

A MAGICAL TIME FOR MOM AND DAD

OK, LILIANE WRITING HERE. Because Bob's idea of a romantic evening is watching *Monday Night Football* on the sofa with his honey instead of sitting in his La-Z-Boy, I'm going to tackle this subject solo.

Let's face it: we all know that moms and dads deserve some special time. But the reality on the ground is that the kids come first. And when the day is over, mom and dad are way too tired to think about having a special evening alone. It's difficult enough to catch a movie or go out for a romantic dinner in our hometowns, so how realistic is a romantic parents' night out while on vacation at Walt Disney World?

The answer is: no planning, no romance! With a little magic and some advance preparation, you can make it happen. Here we offer a few suggestions.

Staying at a hotel that offers great kids' programs is a big plus. Consider signing up small children for a half-day program with lunch or dinner while you enjoy your resort. Go to the pool and read a book, and then have a meal in calm and peace. Rent a bike, a boat, or just take off outside the World. This is also a great opportunity to enjoy the thrill rides you passed up when you were busy worshipping at the altar of Dumbo.

continued on page 201

SMALL-CHILD FRIGHT-POTENTIAL TABLE

This is a quick reference to identify attractions to be wary of, and why. The table represents a generalization, and all kids are different. It relates specifically to kids ages 3–7. On average, children at the younger end of the range are more likely to be frightened than children in their 6th or 7th year.

The Magic Kingdom

- **SORCERERS OF THE MAGIC KINGDOM** Not frightening in any respect.

MAIN STREET, U.S.A.

- **TOWN SQUARE THEATER MEET AND GREETS** Not frightening in any respect.
- **WALT DISNEY WORLD RAILROAD** Not frightening in any respect.

ADVENTURELAND

- **JUNGLE CRUISE** Moderately intense, some macabre sights. A good test attraction for little ones.
- **THE MAGIC CARPETS OF ALADDIN** Much like Dumbo. A favorite of most younger kids.
- **A PIRATE'S ADVENTURE: TREASURES OF THE SEVEN SEAS** Some exhibits, such as skulls and sudden sounds, may frighten small children.
- **PIRATES OF THE CARIBBEAN** Slightly intimidating queuing area; intense boat ride with gruesome (though humorously presented) sights and a short, unexpected slide down a flume.
- **SWISS FAMILY TREEHOUSE** Kids who are afraid of heights may want to skip it.
- *WALT DISNEY'S ENCHANTED TIKI ROOM* A thunderstorm, loud volume level, and simulated explosions frighten some preschoolers.

FRONTIERLAND

- **BIG THUNDER MOUNTAIN RAILROAD** Visually intimidating from outside, with moderately intense visual effects. The roller coaster is wild enough to frighten many adults, particularly seniors. Switching-off option (see page 248).
- *COUNTRY BEAR JAMBOREE* Not frightening in any respect.
- **FRONTIERLAND SHOOTIN' ARCADE** Frightening to children scared of guns.
- **SPLASH MOUNTAIN** Visually intimidating from outside, with moderately intense visual effects. The ride culminates in a 52-foot plunge down a steep chute. Switching-off option (see page 248).
- **TOM SAWYER ISLAND AND FORT LANGHORN** Some very young children are intimidated by dark walk-through tunnels that can be easily avoided.

LIBERTY SQUARE

- *THE HALL OF PRESIDENTS* Not frightening, but boring for young ones.
- **THE HAUNTED MANSION** Name raises anxiety, as do sounds and sights of waiting area. Intense attraction with humorously presented macabre sights. The ride itself is gentle.
- *LIBERTY BELLE* RIVERBOAT Not frightening in any respect.

FANTASYLAND

- **ARIEL'S GROTTO** Not frightening in any respect.
- **THE BARNSTORMER** May frighten some preschoolers. Switching-off option (see page 248).
- **CASEY JR. SPLASH 'N' SOAK STATION** Not frightening in any respect.
- **DUMBO THE FLYING ELEPHANT** A tame midway ride; a great favorite of most young children.
- *ENCHANTED TALES WITH BELLE* Not frightening in any respect.
- **IT'S A SMALL WORLD** Not frightening in any respect.
- **MAD TEA PARTY** Midway-type ride can induce motion sickness in all ages.
- **THE MANY ADVENTURES OF WINNIE THE POOH** Frightens a few preschoolers.
- **MEET MERIDA AT FAIRYTALE GARDEN** Not frightening in any respect.
- *MICKEY'S PHILHARMAGIC* Some preschoolers may be a little scared at first, but taking the 3-D glasses off tones down the effect.
- **PETER PAN'S FLIGHT** Not frightening in any respect.
- **PETE'S SILLY SIDESHOW** Not frightening in any respect.

SMALL-CHILD FRIGHT-POTENTIAL TABLE *(continued)*

FANTASYLAND *(continued)*

- **PRINCE CHARMING REGAL CARROUSEL** Not frightening in any respect.
- **PRINCESS FAIRYTALE HALL** Not frightening in any respect.
- **SEVEN DWARFS MINE TRAIN** Marginally wild ride, dark scenes, and special effects may frighten children age 7 and under. Switching-off option (see page 248).
- **UNDER THE SEA: JOURNEY OF THE LITTLE MERMAID** Evil Ursula and dark effects frighten kids under age 7.

TOMORROWLAND

- **ASTRO ORBITER** Visually intimidating waiting area but a relatively tame ride.
- **BUZZ LIGHTYEAR'S SPACE RANGER SPIN** May frighten some preschoolers.
- *MONSTERS, INC. LAUGH FLOOR* May frighten some preschoolers.
- **SPACE MOUNTAIN** Very intense roller coaster in the dark; the Magic Kingdom's wildest ride and a scary roller coaster by any standard. Switching-off option (see page 248).
- **TOMORROWLAND SPEEDWAY** The noise of the waiting area slightly intimidates preschoolers; otherwise, not frightening. Switching-off option (see page 248).
- **TOMORROWLAND TRANSIT AUTHORITY PEOPLEMOVER** Not frightening in any respect.
- *WALT DISNEY'S CAROUSEL OF PROGRESS* Not frightening in any respect.

Epcot

FUTURE WORLD

- *AWESOME PLANET (opens early 2020)* Not frightening in any respect.
- **DISNEY & PIXAR SHORT FILM FESTIVAL** Not frightening in any respect.
- **INNOVENTIONS** Not frightening in any respect.
- **JOURNEY INTO IMAGINATION WITH FIGMENT** Loud noises and unexpected flashing lights startle younger children.
- **LIVING WITH THE LAND** Not frightening in any respect but loud.
- **MISSION: SPACE** Extremely intense space-simulation ride that has been known to frighten guests of all ages. Switching-off option (see page 248).
- **SEABASE** Not frightening in any respect.
- **THE SEAS WITH NEMO & FRIENDS** Very sweet but may frighten some toddlers.
- **SOARIN'** May frighten kids age 7 and younger, or anyone with a fear of heights. Otherwise a very mellow ride. Switching-off option (see page 248).
- **SPACESHIP EARTH** Dark, imposing presentation intimidates a few preschoolers.
- **TEST TRACK** Intense thrill ride may frighten guests of any age. Switching-off option (see page 248).
- *TURTLE TALK WITH CRUSH* Not frightening in any respect.

WORLD SHOWCASE

- **AGENT P'S WORLD SHOWCASE ADVENTURE** Not frightening in any respect.
- *THE AMERICAN ADVENTURE* Not frightening in any respect.
- *BEAUTY AND THE BEAST SING-ALONG (opens early 2020)* Not frightening in any respect.
- **FROZEN EVER AFTER** Dark. The ride ends with a plunge down a 20-foot flume, which may frighten a few preschoolers. Switching-off option (see page 248).
- **GRAN FIESTA TOUR STARRING THE THREE CABALLEROS** Not frightening in any respect.
- *EPCOT FOREVER* Fireworks may frighten small children.
- *IMPRESSIONS DE FRANCE* Not frightening in any respect.
- **MEET ANNA AND ELSA AT ROYAL SOMMERHUS** Not frightening in any respect.
- *O CANADA!* Not frightening in any respect, but audience must stand.
- *REFLECTIONS OF CHINA* Not frightening in any respect.
- **REMY'S RATATOUILLE ADVENTURE** *(opens 2020)* Dark ride; some chase scenes may frighten young children.
- **WORLD SHOWCASE PAVILIONS** Not frightening in any respect.

SMALL-CHILD FRIGHT-POTENTIAL TABLE *(continued)*
Disney's Animal Kingdom

- **THE OASIS** Not frightening in any respect.

DISCOVERY ISLAND

- **MEET FAVORITE DISNEY PALS AT ADVENTURERS OUTPOST** Not frightening in any respect.
- **THE TREE OF LIFE/*IT'S TOUGH TO BE A BUG!*** Very intense and loud, with special effects that startle viewers of all ages and potentially terrify little kids.
- **WILDERNESS EXPLORERS** Not frightening in any respect.

PANDORA: WORLD OF AVATAR

- **AVATAR FLIGHT OF PASSAGE** May frighten kids age 7 and younger. May cause motion sickness or a feeling of claustrophobia. Switching-off option (see page 248).
- **NA'VI RIVER JOURNEY** Dark boat ride but not scary.

AFRICA

- *FESTIVAL OF THE LION KING* A bit loud but otherwise not frightening.
- **GORILLA FALLS EXPLORATION TRAIL** Not frightening in any respect.
- **KILIMANJARO SAFARIS** The proximity of real animals make a few young children anxious. The nighttime version may frighten small children.
- **WILDLIFE EXPRESS TRAIN** Not frightening in any respect.

RAFIKI'S PLANET WATCH

- **THE ANIMATION EXPERIENCE** Not frightening in any respect.
- **CONSERVATION STATION/AFFECTION SECTION** Not frightening in any respect.

ASIA

- **EXPEDITION EVEREST** Can frighten guests of all ages. Switching-off option (see page 248).
- **KALI RIVER RAPIDS** Potentially frightening and certainly wet for guests of all ages. Switching-off option (see page 248).
- **MAHARAJAH JUNGLE TREK** Not frightening in any respect.
- *RIVERS OF LIGHT: WE ARE ONE* Loud with special effects. May frighten young children, but most will like it.
- *UP! A GREAT BIRD ADVENTURE* Swooping birds startle some younger children.

DINOLAND U.S.A.

- **THE BONEYARD** Not frightening in any respect.
- **DINOSAUR** High-tech thrill ride rattles riders of all ages. Switching-off option (see page 248).
- **PRIMEVAL WHIRL** A beginner roller coaster. Most children age 7 and older will take it in stride. More intense than The Barnstormer. Switching-off option (see page 248).
- **THEATER IN THE WILD/*FINDING NEMO—THE MUSICAL*** Not frightening in any respect but loud.
- **TRICERATOP SPIN** A midway-type ride that will frighten only a small percentage of younger children.

Disney's Hollywood Studios

SUNSET BOULEVARD

- *BEAUTY AND THE BEAST—LIVE ON STAGE*/**THEATER OF THE STARS** Not frightening in any respect.
- *FANTASMIC!* Loud and intense with fireworks and some scary villains, but most young children like it.
- *LIGHTNING MCQUEEN'S RACING ACADEMY* Not frightening but loud.
- **MICKEY & MINNIE'S RUNAWAY RAILWAY** *(opens spring 2020)* The darkness may frighten some preschoolers.
- **ROCK 'N' ROLLER COASTER STARRING AEROSMITH** The wildest coaster at Walt Disney World. May frighten guests of any age. Switching-off option (see page 248).
- **THE TWILIGHT ZONE TOWER OF TERROR** Visually intimidating to young children; contains intense and realistic special effects. The plummeting elevator at the ride's end frightens many adults as well as kids. Switching-off option (see page 248).

SMALL-CHILD FRIGHT-POTENTIAL TABLE *(continued)*

ECHO LAKE

- *FOR THE FIRST TIME IN FOREVER: A FROZEN SING-ALONG CELEBRATION* Not frightening in any respect.
- *INDIANA JONES EPIC STUNT SPECTACULAR!* An intense show with powerful special effects, including explosions, but young kids generally handle it well.
- *JEDI TRAINING: TRIALS OF THE TEMPLE* Some very young Padawans may get frightened when facing the *Star Wars* villains.
- **STAR TOURS—THE ADVENTURES CONTINUE** Extremely intense visually for all ages; too intense for kids under age 8. Switching-off option (see page 248).

GRAND AVENUE

- *MUPPET-VISION 3-D* Intense and loud but not frightening.

STAR WARS: GALAXY'S EDGE

- *MILLENNIUM FALCON:* SMUGGLERS RUN Intense visual effects may discombobulate droids (and guests) of all ages. Switching-off option (see page 248).
- **STAR WARS: RISE OF THE RESISTANCE** *(opens late 2019)* Intense visual effects, such as close encounters with sci-fi villains, and loud sounds may frighten small children. Switching-off option (see page 248).

TOY STORY LAND

- **ALIEN SWIRLING SAUCERS** May induce motion sickness in riders of all ages. Switching-off option (see page 248).
- **SLINKY DOG DASH** A mild first roller coaster for most kids; may frighten some preschoolers. Switching-off option (see page 248).
- **TOY STORY MANIA!** Dark ride may frighten some preschoolers.

ANIMATION COURTYARD

- *DISNEY JUNIOR DANCE PARTY!* Not frightening in any respect.
- **STAR WARS LAUNCH BAY** Small children may be scared when meeting Chewbacca because he is huge, and Kylo Ren is intimidating.
- *VOYAGE OF THE LITTLE MERMAID* Some children are creeped out by Ursula.
- *WALT DISNEY PRESENTS* Not frightening in any respect.

continued from page 197

PREPARING YOUR CHILDREN TO MEET THE CHARACTERS

FELICITY Mickey didn't speak, but meeting him made me so happy that I cried. I got to hug the greatest sorcerer in the world!

ALMOST ALL DISNEY CHARACTERS are quite large; several, like Baloo, are huge! Young children don't expect this and can be intimidated if not terrified. Discuss the characters with your children before you go. If there is a high school, college, or other sports team with a costumed mascot nearby, arrange to let your kids check it out. If not, then Santa Claus or the Easter Bunny will do.

On the first encounter, don't thrust your child at the character. Allow your little one to deal with this big thing from whatever distance feels safe to him or her. If two adults are present, one should stay near the youngster while the other approaches the character and demonstrates that it's safe and friendly. Some kids warm to the characters immediately; some never do. Most take a little time and several encounters.

There are two kinds of characters: furs, or those whose costumes include face-covering headpieces (including animal characters and such humanlike characters as Captain Hook), and face characters, those for whom no mask or headpiece is necessary. These include Tiana, Anna, Elsa, Mary Poppins, Ariel, Jasmine, Aladdin, Cinderella, Belle, Snow White, Merida, and Prince Charming, among others.

Only face characters speak. Headpiece characters don't make noises of any kind. Because cast members couldn't possibly imitate the distinctive cinema voice of the character, Disney has determined that it's more effective to keep them silent. Lack of speech notwithstanding, headpiece characters are very warm and responsive and communicate very effectively with gestures.

BOB If your child wants to collect character autographs, it's a good idea to carry a pen the width of a Magic Marker. Costumes make it exceedingly difficult for characters to wield a pen, so the bigger the writing instrument, the better. Unfortunately, a few characters, such as Buzz Lightyear, can't sign autographs at all but will gladly pose for photos.

StoryMaker uses the information stored on your MyMagic+ profile to allow certain attractions to interact with guests. The first attraction to make use of this feature was It's a Small World. Now a panel bids guests an individual goodbye at the end of the ride. StoryMaker has huge potential. Imagine Mickey Mouse or Cinderella greeting your little ones by name or wishing them a happy birthday, without being told this information by you or a cast member. The possibilities are endless.

Some character costumes are cumbersome and limit cast members' ability to see and maneuver. (Eyeholes frequently are in the mouth of the costume or even on the neck or chest.) Children who approach the character from the back or side may not be noticed, even if the child touches the character. It's possible in this situation for the character to accidentally step on the child or knock him or her down. It's best for a child to approach a character from the front, but occasionally not even this works. Duck characters (such as Donald, Daisy, and Uncle Scrooge), for example, have to peer around their bills.

It's OK for your child to touch, pat, or hug the character. Understanding the unpredictability of children, the character will keep his

feet very still, particularly refraining from moving backward or side-ways. Most characters will sign autographs or pose for pictures.

Another great way to show young children how the characters appear in the parks is to buy a *Disney SingAlong Songs* DVD. These programs show Disney characters interacting with real kids. At a min-imum, the videos will give your kids a sense of how big the charac-ters are. The best two are *Flik's Musical Adventure SingAlong Songs at Disney's Animal Kingdom* and *Campout SingAlong Songs at Walt Disney World*. *It's a Small World SingAlong Songs—Disneyland Fun* is a third offering . . . but then there's THAT SONG. No sense turning your brain to mush before even leaving home.

See "Character Analysis," page 249, for an in-depth discussion of the Disney characters.

PHYSICAL PREPARATION

YOU'LL FIND THAT SOME PHYSICAL CONDITIONING, coupled with a realistic sense of the toll that Walt Disney World takes on your body, will preclude falling apart in the middle of your vacation. As one of our readers put it, "If you pay attention to eat, heat, feet, and sleep, you'll be OK."

As you contemplate the stamina of your family, it's important to understand that somebody is going to run out of steam first, and when they do, the whole family will be affected. Sometimes a cold drink or a snack will revive the flagging member. Sometimes, however, no amount of cajoling or treats will work. In this situation it's crucial that you rec-ognize that the child, grandparent, or spouse is at the end of his or her rope. The correct decision is to get them back to the hotel. Pushing the exhausted beyond their capacity will spoil the day for them—and you. Accept that stamina and energy levels vary and be prepared to adminis-ter to members of your family who poop out. One more thing: no guilt trips. "We've driven 1,000 miles to take you to Disney World and now you're going to ruin everything!" is not an appropriate response.

PREVENT BLISTERS IN FIVE EASY STEPS

1. PREPARE You can easily cover 5–12 miles a day at the parks, and the walking at Disney World is nothing like a 5-mile hike in the woods. At Disney you will be in direct sunlight most of the time, will have to navigate through huge jos-tling crowds, will be walking on hot pavement, and will have to endure waits in line between

LILIANE Be sure to give your kids adequate recov-ery time between training walks (48 hours will usually be enough), however, or you'll make the problem worse.

bursts of walking. Though most children are active, their normal play usually doesn't condition them for the exertion of touring a Disney theme park. We recommend starting a program of family walks 6 weeks or more before your trip. A Pennsylvania mom who did just that offers the following:

We had our 6-year-old begin walking with us a bit every day one month before leaving—when we arrived [at Walt Disney World], her little legs could carry her and she had a lot of stamina.

Start with short walks around the neighborhood, on pavement, and increase the distance about 0.25 mile on each outing. Increase your distance gradually until you can do 6 miles without needing CPR. As you begin, remember that little people have little strides, and though your 6-year-old may create the appearance of running circles around you, consider that (1) he won't have the stamina to go at that pace very long, and (2) more to the point, he probably has to take two strides or so to every one of yours to keep up when you walk together.

2. PAY ATTENTION During your training program, your feet will tell you if you're wearing the right shoes. Choose well-constructed, broken-in running or hiking shoes. If you feel a "hot spot" coming on, chances are that a blister isn't far behind. The most common sites for blisters are heels, toes, and balls of feet. If you develop a hot spot in the same place every time you walk, cover it with a blister bandage or cushion before you set out.

Don't wear sandals, flip-flops, or slip-ons in the theme parks. Even if your feet don't blister, they'll get stepped on by other guests or run over by strollers.

3. SOCK IT UP Good socks are as important as good shoes. When you walk, your feet sweat like a mule in a peat bog, and the moisture only increases friction. To counteract friction, wear socks made from material such as Smartwool or CoolMax, which wicks perspiration away from your feet (Smartwool socks come in varying thicknesses). To further combat moisture, dust your feet with antifungal powder.

BOB If your children (or you, for that matter) don't consider it cool to wear socks, get over it! Bare feet, whether encased in Nikes, Weejuns, Docksides, or Birkenstocks, will turn into lumps of throbbing red meat if you tackle a Disney park without socks.

4. DON'T BE A HERO Take care of foot problems the minute you notice them. Carry a small foot-emergency kit with gauze, antibiotic ointment, disinfectant, and moleskin or blister bandages. Extra socks and foot powder are optional.

If carrying all of that sounds like too much, stop by a First Aid Center in the park as soon as you notice a hot spot on your foot.

BOB If your child is age 8 or younger, we recommend regular foot inspections, whether he or she understands the hot-spot idea or not. Even the brightest and most well-intentioned child will fail to sound off when distracted.

5. CHECK THE KIDS Young children might not say anything about blisters forming until it's too late. Stop several times a day and check their feet. Look for red spots and blisters, and ask if they have any places on their feet that hurt. If you find a blister, either treat it using the kit you're carrying, or stop by a First Aid Center.

A stroller will provide the child the option of walking or riding, and if he collapses, you won't have to carry him. Even if your child hardly uses the stroller at all, it serves as a convenient depository for water bottles and other stuff you may not feel like carrying. Strollers at Walt Disney World are covered in detail starting on page 262.

LILIANE If you have a child who will physically fit in a stroller, rent one, no matter how well conditioned your family is.

REST AND RELAXATION

PHYSICAL CONDITIONING IS IMPORTANT but is *not* a substitute for adequate rest. Even marathon runners need recovery time. If you push too hard and try to do too much, you'll either crash or, at a minimum, turn what should be fun into an ordeal. Rest means plenty of sleep at night, naps during the afternoon on most days, and planned breaks in your vacation itinerary. And don't forget that the brain needs rest and relaxation as well as the body. The stimulation inherent in touring a theme park is enough to put many children and some adults into system overload. It's imperative that you remove your family from this unremitting assault on the senses, preferably for part of each day, and do something relaxing and quiet like swimming or reading.

The theme parks are huge; don't try to see everything in 1 day. Tour in the early morning and return to your hotel around 11:30 a.m. for lunch, a swim, and a nap. Even during the off-season, when the crowds are comparatively smaller and the temperature more pleasant, the size of the major theme parks will exhaust most children under age 8 by lunchtime. Return to the park in late afternoon or early evening and continue touring. A family from Texas underlines the importance of naps and rest:

> We visited a specific park in the morning, left midafternoon for either a nap in the room or a trip to the pool, and then returned to a park in the evening. On the few occasions we skipped your advice, I was muttering to myself by dinner. I can't tell you what I was muttering . . .

When it comes to naps, this mom does not mince words:

> For parents of small kids—take the book's advice and get out of the park and take the nap, take the nap, TAKE THE NAP! Never in my life have I seen so many parents screaming at, ridiculing, or slapping their kids. (What a vacation!) Disney World is overwhelming for kids and adults. Although the rental strollers recline for sleeping, we noticed most toddlers and preschoolers didn't give up and sleep until 5 p.m., several hours after the fun had worn off, and right about the time their parents wanted them to be awake and polite in a restaurant.

A mom from Rochester, New York, was equally adamant:

> You absolutely must rest during the day. Kids went 8 a.m.–9 p.m. in the Magic Kingdom. Kids did great that day, but we were all completely worthless the next day. Definitely must pace yourself. Don't ever try to do 2 full days of park sightseeing in a row. Rest during the day. Sleep in every other day.

If you plan to return to your hotel midday and would like your room made up, let housekeeping know before you leave in the morning.

DEVELOPING *a* GOOD PLAN

ALLOW YOUR CHILDREN to participate in the planning of your time at Disney World. Guide them diplomatically through the options, establishing advance decisions about what to do each day and how the day will be structured. Begin with your trip *to* Walt Disney World, deciding what time to depart, who sits by the window, whether to stop for meals or eat in the car, and so on. For the Disney World part of your vacation, build consensus for wake-up call, bedtime, and naps in the itinerary, and establish ground rules for eating, buying refreshments, and shopping. Determine the order for visiting the different theme parks and make a list of must-see attractions. To help you with filling in the blanks of your days, and especially to prevent you from spending most of your time standing in line, we offer a number of field-tested touring plans. The plans are designed to minimize your waiting time at each park by providing step-by-step itineraries that route you counter to the flow of traffic. The plans are explained in detail starting on page 231.

BOB To keep your thinking fresh and to adequately cover all bases, develop your plan in a series of family meetings no longer than 30 minutes each. You'll discover that all members of the family will devote a lot of thought to the plan both during and between meetings. Don't try to anticipate every conceivable contingency, or you'll end up with something as detailed and unworkable as the tax code.

Generally it's better to just sketch in the broad strokes on the master plan. The detail of what to do when you actually arrive at the park can be decided the night before you go or with the help of one of our touring plans once you get there. Above all, be flexible. One important caveat, however: make sure you keep any promises or agreements that you make when planning. They may not seem important to you, but they will to your children, who will remember for a long, long time that you let them down.

The more that you can agree to and nail down in advance, the less potential you'll have for disagreement and confrontation once you arrive. Because children are more comfortable with the tangible than the conceptual, and also because they sometimes have short memories, we recommend typing up all of your decisions and agreements and providing a copy to each child. Create a fun document, not a legalistic one. You'll find that your children will review it in anticipation of all the things they will see and do, will consult it often, and will even read it to their younger siblings.

By now you're probably wondering what one of these documents looks like, so we've provided a sample on pages 208–209. Incidentally, this itinerary reflects the preferences of its creators, the Langston family, and is not meant to be offered as an example of an ideal itinerary. It does, however, incorporate many of our most basic and strongly held recommendations, such as setting limits and guidelines in advance, getting enough rest, getting to the theme parks early, touring the theme parks in shorter visits with naps and swimming in between, and saving time and money by having a cooler full of food for breakfast. As you will see, the Langstons go pretty much full tilt without much unstructured time and will probably be exhausted by the time they get home, but that's their choice. One more thing—the Langstons visited Walt Disney World in late June, when all of the theme parks stay open late.

THE GREAT WALT DISNEY WORLD EXPEDITION

CO-CAPTAINS Mary and Jack Langston

TEAM MEMBERS Lynn and Jimmy Langston

EXPEDITION FUNDING The main expedition fund will cover everything except personal purchases. Each team member will receive $50 for souvenirs and personal purchases. Anything above $50 will be paid for by team members with their own money.

EXPEDITION GEAR Each team member will wear an official expedition T-shirt and carry a hip pack.

PREDEPARTURE Jack makes Advance Reservations at Disney World restaurants. Mary, Lynn, and Jimmy make up trail mix and other snacks for the hip packs.

Notice that the Langstons' itinerary on pages 208–209 provides minimal structure and maximum flexibility. It specifies which park the family will tour each day without attempting to nail down exactly what the family will do there. No matter how detailed your itinerary is, be prepared for surprises at Walt Disney World, both good and bad. If an unforeseen event renders part of the plan useless or impractical, just roll with it. And always remember that it's your itinerary; you created it, and you can change it. Just try to make any changes the result of family discussion, and be especially careful not to scrap an element of the plan that your children perceive as something you promised them.

Routines That Travel

If you observe certain routines at home—for example, reading a book before bed or having a bath first thing in the morning—try to incorporate these familiar activities into your vacation schedule. They will provide your children with a sense of security and normalcy.

Maintaining a normal routine is especially important with toddlers, as a mother of two from Lawrenceville, Georgia, relates:

> *The first day, we tried an early start, so we woke the children (ages 2 and 4) and hurried them to get going. BAD IDEA with toddlers. This put them off schedule for naps and meals the rest of the day. It is best to let young ones stay on their regular schedule and see Disney at their own pace, and you'll have much more fun.*

LANGSTON FAMILY ITINERARY

DAY 1: FRIDAY

- **6:30 p.m.** Dinner
- **After dinner** Pack car
- **10 p.m.** Lights out

DAY 2: SATURDAY

- **7 a.m.** Wake up!
- **7:15 a.m.** Breakfast
- **8 a.m.** Depart Chicago for Hampton Inn, Chattanooga; Confirmation #DE56432; Lynn rides shotgun
- **About noon** Stop for lunch; Jimmy picks restaurant
- **7 p.m.** Dinner
- **9:30 p.m.** Lights out

DAY 3: SUNDAY

- **7 a.m.** Wake up!
- **7:30 a.m.** Depart Chattanooga for Walt Disney World, Port Orleans Resort–Riverside; confirmation #L124532; Jimmy rides shotgun
- **About noon** Stop for lunch; Lynn picks restaurant
- **5 p.m.** Check in, buy park admissions (if you haven't already), and unpack
- **6–7 p.m.** Mary and Jimmy shop for breakfast food for cooler
- **7:15 p.m.** Dinner at Boatwright's at Port Orleans–Riverside
- **After dinner** Walk along Bonnet Creek or swim a few laps in the pool
- **10 p.m.** Lights out

DAY 4: MONDAY

- **7 a.m.** Wake up! Cold breakfast from cooler in room
- **8 a.m.** Depart room to catch bus for Epcot
- **Noon** Lunch at Epcot
- **1 p.m.** Return to hotel for swimming and a nap
- **5 p.m.** Return to Epcot for touring, dinner, and fireworks
- **9:30 p.m.** Return to hotel
- **10:30 p.m.** Lights out

DAY 5: TUESDAY

- **7 a.m.** Wake up! Cold breakfast from cooler in room
- **7:30 a.m.** Depart room to drive to Disney's Hollywood Studios; tour Star Wars: Galaxy's Edge first
- **Noon** Lunch at Studios
- **2:30 p.m.** Return to hotel for swimming and a nap
- **6 p.m.** Return to Studios via car for touring. Have dinner at ABC Commissary. Consider using Mobile Ordering to save time.
- **9 p.m.** Watch *Fantasmic!*
- **10 p.m.** Return to hotel
- **11 p.m.** Lights out

We offer a sleepyhead touring plan for each park, perfect for families like this reader's.

LOGISTICAL PREPARATION

WHEN WE RECENTLY LAUNCHED into our spiel about good logistic preparation for a Walt Disney World vacation, a friend from Indianapolis said, "Wait, what's the big deal? You pack clothes, a few games

DAY 6: WEDNESDAY

- **7 a.m.** Wake up! Cold breakfast from cooler in room
- **8 a.m.** Depart room for Animal Kingdom; tour Pandora first
- **Noon** Lunch at Flame Tree Barbecue or Harambe Market
- **1 p.m.** Return to hotel for swimming and a nap
- **5 p.m.** Return to Animal Kingdom for dinner, revisit Pandora at night, and see *Rivers of Light*
- **9 p.m.** Return to hotel via bus
- **10:30 p.m.** Lights out

DAY 7: THURSDAY

- **6 a.m.** Wake up! Cold breakfast from cooler in room
- **6:45 a.m.** Depart via bus for early entry at Magic Kingdom
- **11:30 a.m.** Return to hotel for lunch, swimming, and a nap
- **4:45 p.m.** Drive to Contemporary for dinner at Chef Mickey's
- **6:15 p.m.** Walk from the Contemporary to the Magic Kingdom for more touring, fireworks, and parade
- **11 p.m.** Return to Contemporary via walkway or monorail; get car and return to hotel
- **11:45 p.m.** Lights out

DAY 8: FRIDAY

- **8 a.m.** Wake up! Cold breakfast from cooler in room
- **8:40 a.m.** Drive to Blizzard Beach water park
- **Noon** Lunch at Blizzard Beach
- **1:30 p.m.** Return to hotel for nap and packing
- **4 p.m.** Revisit favorite park, shop at Disney Springs, or do whatever we want
- **Dinner** When and where we decide
- **10 p.m.** Return to hotel
- **10:30 p.m.** Lights out

DAY 9: SATURDAY

- **7:30 a.m.** Wake up!
- **8:30 a.m.** After fast-food breakfast, depart for DoubleTree Hotel, Nashville; confirmation #SD234; Lynn rides shotgun
- **About noon** Stop for lunch; Jimmy picks restaurant
- **7 p.m.** Dinner
- **10 p.m.** Lights out

DAY 10: SUNDAY

- **7 a.m.** Wake up!
- **7:45 a.m.** Depart for home after fast-food breakfast; Jimmy rides shotgun
- **About noon** Stop for lunch; Lynn picks restaurant
- **4:30 p.m.** Home, sweet home!

for the car, then go!" So OK, we confess, that will work, but life can be sweeter and the vacation smoother (as well as less expensive) with the right gear.

CLOTHING

LET'S START WITH CLOTHES. We recommend springing for vacation uniforms. Buy for each child several sets of jeans (or shorts) and T-shirts, all matching, and all the same. For a 1-week trip, as an example, get each child three or so pairs of khaki shorts, three or so light yellow shirts, and three pairs of Smartwool or CoolMax hiking socks. What's the point? First, you don't have to play fashion designer, coordinating a week's worth of stylish combos. Each morning the kids put on their uniform. It's simple, it's time-saving, and there are no decisions to make or arguments about what to wear. Second, uniforms make your children easier to spot and keep together in the theme parks. Third, the uniforms give your family, as well as the vacation itself, some added identity. You might even go so far as to create a logo for the trip to be printed on the shirts.

LILIANE Give your teens the job of coming up with the logo for your shirts. They will love being the family designers.

When it comes to buying your uniforms, we have a few suggestions. Purchase well-made, durable shorts or jeans that will serve your children well beyond the vacation. Buy short-sleeve T-shirts in light colors for warm weather or long-sleeve, darker-colored T-shirts for cooler weather. We suggest purchasing colored shirts from a local screen printing company; they offer a wide choice of colors not generally available in retail clothing stores as well as various sizes. Plus, the shirts will cost a fraction of what a clothing retailer would charge. All-cotton shirts are a little cooler and more comfortable in hot, humid weather; polyester-cotton blends dry a bit faster if they get wet.

LABELS A great idea, especially for younger children, is to attach labels with your family name, hometown, the name of your hotel, the dates of your stay, and your cell phone number inside the shirt. For example:

**Carlton Family of Frankfort, KY; Port Orleans–Riverside
May 14–20; 502-555-2108**

Instruct your smaller children to show the label to an adult if they get separated from you. Elimination of the child's first name (which most children of talking age can articulate in any event) allows you to order labels that are all the same, that can be used by anyone in the family, and that can also be affixed to such easily lost items as hats, jackets, hip packs, ponchos, and umbrellas. If fooling with labels sounds like too much of a hassle, check out "When Kids Get Lost" (see page 259) for some alternatives.

TEMPORARY TATTOOS An easier and trendier option is a temporary tattoo with your child's name and your phone number. Unlike labels, ID bracelets, or wristbands, the tattoos cannot fall off or be lost. Temporary tattoos last about 2 weeks, won't wash or sweat off, and are not irritating to the skin. They can be purchased online from **SafetyTat** at safetytat.com, or from **Tattoos With A Purpose** at tattooswithapurpose.com. Special tattoos are available for children with food allergies or cognitive impairment such as autism.

LILIANE Equip each child with a big bandanna. Though bandannas come in handy for wiping noses, scouring ice cream from chins and mouths, and dabbing sweat from the forehead, they can also be tied around the neck to protect from sunburn.

DRESSING FOR COOLER WEATHER Central Florida experiences temperatures all over the scale November–March, so it could be a bit chilly if you visit during those months. Our suggestion is to layer: for example, a breathable, waterproof or water-resistant windbreaker over a light, long-sleeved polypropylene shirt over a long-sleeved T-shirt. As with the baffles of a sleeping bag or down coat, it's the air trapped between the layers that keeps you warm. If all the layers are thin, you won't be left with something bulky to cart around if you want to pull one or more off. Later in this section, we'll advocate wearing a hip pack. Each layer should be sufficiently compactible to fit easily in that hip pack, along with whatever else is in it.

ACCESSORIES

WE RECOMMEND PANTS with reinforced elastic waistbands for your children to eliminate the need to wear a belt (one less thing to find when you're trying to leave). If your children like belts or want to carry an item suspended from their belts, buy them military-style 1-inch-wide web belts at any Army/Navy surplus or camping-equipment store. The belts weigh less than half as much as leather, are cooler, and are washable.

SUNGLASSES The Florida sun is so bright and the glare so blinding that we recommend sunglasses for each family member. For children and adults of all ages, a good accessory item is a polypropylene eyeglass strap for glasses. The best models have a little device for adjusting the amount of slack in the strap. This allows your child to comfortably hang sunglasses from his or her neck when indoors or, alternately, to secure them fast to his or her head while experiencing a fast ride outdoors.

HIP PACKS AND WALLETS Unless you're touring with an infant or toddler, the largest thing anyone in your family should carry is a hip pack, or fanny pack. Each adult and child should have one. They should be large enough to carry at least a half-day's worth of snacks, as well as other items deemed necessary (lip balm, bandanna, antibacterial hand gel, and so on), and still have enough room left to stash a hat, poncho, or light windbreaker. We recommend buying full-size hip packs as opposed to small, child-size hip packs at outdoor retailers. The packs are light; can be made to fit any child large enough to tote a hip pack; have slip-resistant, comfortable, wide belting; and will last for years.

BOB Unless you advise the front desk to the contrary, all MagicBands (or park cards) can be used for park admission and as credit cards. They are definitely something you don't want to lose. Our advice is to void the charge privileges on your preteen children's bands or cards, and then collect them and put them together someplace safe when not in use.

Do not carry billfolds or wallets, car keys, park cards, or room keys in your hip packs because children tend to inadvertently drop their wallet in the process of rummaging around in their hip packs for snacks and other items.

You should weed through your billfold and remove to a safe place anything that you won't need on your vacation (family photos, local library card, department store credit cards, business cards, and so on). In addition to having a lighter wallet to lug around, you will decrease your exposure in the event that your wallet is lost or stolen. When we're working at Walt Disney World, we carry a small profile billfold with a driver's license, a credit card, our hotel room key, and a small amount of cash. You don't need anything else.

DAY PACKS We see a lot of folks at Disney World carrying day packs (that is, small, frameless backpacks) and/or water bottle belts that strap around the waist. Day packs might be a good choice if you plan to carry a lot of camera equipment or if you need to carry baby supplies on your person. Otherwise, try to travel as light as possible. Packs are hot, cumbersome, and not very secure, and they must be removed every time you get on a ride or sit down for a show. Hip packs, by way of contrast, can simply be rotated around the waist from your back to your abdomen if you need to sit down. Additionally, our observation has been that the contents of one day pack can usually be redistributed to two or so hip packs.

CAPS Caps protect young eyes from damaging ultraviolet rays, but the lifespan of a child's hat is usually pretty short. Simply put, kids pull caps on and off as they enter and exit attractions, restrooms, and restaurants, and . . . big surprise, they lose them.

LILIANE If your kids are little and don't mind a hairdo change, consider getting them a short haircut before you leave home. Not only will they be cooler and more comfortable, but—especially with your girls—you'll save them (and yourselves) the hassle of tangles and about 20 minutes of foo-fooing a day. Don't try this with your confident teen or pre-teen, though. Braids will do the trick for girls, and your Mick Jagger in the party will be grateful for the bandanna or sports headband, unless of course the hair is meant to keep the monsters and dinosaurs out of sight!

If your children are partial to caps, purchase a short, light cord with little alligator clips on both ends, sold at ski and camping supply stores. Hook one clip to the shirt collar and the other to the hat.

RAINGEAR Rain in Central Florida is a fact of life, though persistent rain day after day is unusual (it is the Sunshine State, after all!). Our suggestion is to check out The Weather Channel or weather forecasts online for 3 or so days before you leave home to see if there are any major storm systems heading for Central Florida. If it appears that you might see some rough weather during your visit, you're better off bringing raingear from home. If, however, nothing big is on the horizon weather-wise, you can take your chances.

At Disney World, ponchos are available in seemingly every retail shop for $12 (adults) and $10 (kids). If you insist on bringing raingear, however, any dollar store has them for exactly that: $1!

LUCY A poncho or an umbrella is a must when you visit in the summer. The weather changes quickly. A hat is also a must. I like to buy mine at the parks, but you can also bring your own. Get creative and decorate your hat.

If you do find yourself in a big storm, you'll want to have both a poncho and an umbrella. As one *Unofficial* reader put it:

Umbrellas make the rain much more bearable. When rain isn't beating down on your ponchoed head, it's easier to ignore.

Another advantage of buying ponchos before you leave home is that you can choose the color. At Disney World all the ponchos are clear, and it's quite a sight when 30,000 differently clad individuals suddenly transform themselves into what looks like an army of really big larvae. If your family is wearing blue ponchos, they'll be easier to spot.

And consider this tip from a Memphis, Tennessee, mom:

Scotchgard your shoes. The difference is unbelievable.

MISCELLANEOUS ITEMS

MEDICATION Some parents of hyperactive children on medication discontinue or decrease the child's normal dosage at the end of the school year. If you have such a child, be aware that Disney World might overly stimulate him or her. Consult your physician before altering your child's medication regimen. Also, if your child has attention deficit disorder, remember that especially loud sounds can drive him or her right up the wall. Unfortunately, some Disney theater attractions are almost unbearably loud.

SUNSCREEN Overheating and sunburn are among the most common problems of younger children at Disney World. Carry and use full-spectrum sunscreen of SPF 30 or higher. Be sure to put some on children in strollers, even if the stroller has a canopy. Some of the worst cases of sunburn we've seen were on the exposed foreheads and feet of toddlers and infants in strollers. To avoid overheating, rest regularly in the shade or in an air-conditioned restaurant or show.

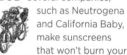

BOB Several companies, such as Neutrogena and California Baby, make sunscreens that won't burn your eyes. Look for a product *without* the active ingredient avobenzone, which is usually the culprit when it comes to stinging and burning.

WATER BOTTLES Don't count on keeping young children hydrated with soft drinks and stops at water fountains. Long lines may hamper buying refreshments, and fountains may not be handy. Furthermore, excited children may not realize or tell you they're thirsty or hot. We recommend renting a stroller for children age 6 and younger and carrying plastic bottles of water. Plastic bottles run about $3 in all major parks. You can save oodles of money by buying your own water outside the parks (Disney allows you to bring water to the parks). If you're staying in a rental home, freeze the water and use it to keep sandwiches cool. By the time you're thirsty, the water should be just right. You can also refill the water bottles at any Disney counter-service restaurant by asking for free tap water.

LILIANE About 1 week before I arrive at WDW, I ship a box to my hotel containing food, plastic cutlery, and toiletries, plus pretty much any other consumables that might come in handy during my stay. If you fly, this helps avoid baggage fees and problems with liquid restrictions for carry-on luggage.

COOLERS AND MINI-FRIDGES If you drive to Walt Disney World, bring two coolers: a small one for drinks in the car and a large one for the hotel room. If you fly and rent a car, stop and purchase a large biodegradable cooler, which can be discarded at the end of the trip. Refrigerators in all Disney resort rooms are free of charge. If you arrive at your room and there is no refrigerator, call and request one.

Coolers and mini-fridges allow you to have breakfast in your hotel room, store snacks and lunch supplies to take to the theme parks, and supplant expensive vending machines for snacks and beverages at the hotel. To keep the contents of your cooler cold, we suggest freezing a

RESPECT FOR THE SUN

Health and science writer **Avery Hurt** sheds some light on the often confusing products and methods for avoiding sunburn. Here's the basic advice from the medical experts.

• **Choose a sunscreen that is convenient for you to use.** Some prefer sprays, others lotions. The form of sunscreen doesn't matter as much as the technique of applying it.

• **Apply sunscreen a half hour before going out,** and be sure to get enough on you. For adults, 1 ounce per application is recommended—that means a full shot glass worth each time you apply. An average 7-year-old will probably take two-thirds of an ounce (20 cc). Measure 1 ounce in your hands at home, so you'll be familiar with what an ounce looks like in your palms. It's far more sunscreen than you tend to think.

• **Get a generous covering on all exposed skin.** Then reapply (another full shot glass) every 2 hours or after swimming or sweating. No matter what it says on the label, water resistance of sunscreen is limited. And none of them last all day.

• **There is very little difference in protection** between 30 or so SPF and 45 or 50 or greater. There is no need to spend more for higher SPF numbers. In fact, it's much safer to choose a lower (and typically less expensive) SPF (as long as it is at least 30) and apply it more often. However, be sure to choose a product that has broad-spectrum coverage, meaning that it filters out both UVA and UVB rays. There's no need to pay extra for special formulas made for children.

• **It's best to keep babies under 6 months old covered** and out of the sun. However, the American Academy of Pediatrics condones a small amount of sunscreen on vulnerable areas, such as the nose and chin, when you have your baby out. Be very careful to monitor your baby even if he is wearing a hat and sitting under an umbrella.

• **Use a lip balm** with an SPF of 15 and reapply often to your own lips and those of your kids.

• **Sunglasses are also a must.** Too much sun exposure can contribute to age-related macular degeneration (among other things). Not all sunglasses filter out damaging rays. Be sure to choose shades (for adults and kids) that have 99% UV protection. Large lenses and wraparound styles might not look as cool, but they offer much better protection.

• **If you do get a burn,** cool baths, aloe gels, and ibuprofen (or for adults, aspirin) usually help ease the suffering. Occasionally sunburns can be as dangerous in the short term as they are in the long term. If you or your child experience nausea, vomiting, high fever, severe pain, confusion, or fainting, seek medical care immediately.

2-gallon milk jug full of water before you head out. In a good cooler, it will take the jug 5 or more days to thaw. If you buy a biodegradable cooler in Florida, you can use bagged ice and ice from the ice machine at your hotel. Even if you have to rent a mini-fridge, you will save a bundle of cash, as well as significant time, by reducing dependence on restaurant meals and expensive snacks and drinks purchased from vendors.

Please note that Disney no longer allows guests to bring loose ice or dry ice into its theme parks and water parks. If you bring a cooler, use reusable ice packs, freeze water inside sealed bags or bottles, or request free ice from any quick-service restaurant. This change is intended to speed up security screenings at bag check locations.

FOOD-PREP KIT If you plan to make sandwiches, bring along your favorite condiments and seasonings from home. A good travel kit will include mayonnaise, ketchup, mustard, salt and pepper, and packets of sugar or artificial sweetener. Also bring some plastic knives and spoons, paper napkins, plastic cups, and a box of zip-top plastic bags. For break-fast you will need some plastic bowls for cereal. Of course, you can buy this stuff in Florida, but you probably won't consume it all, so why waste the money? If you drink bottled beer or wine, bring a bottle opener and corkscrew. If you fly, make sure the corkscrew is in your checked baggage. Liliane has donated a few to the Transportation Security Administration by leaving them in her carry-on.

ENERGY BOOSTERS Kids get cranky when they're hungry, and when that happens, your entire group has a problem. Like many parents, you might, for nutritional reasons, keep a tight rein on snacks available to your children at home. At Walt Disney World, however, maintaining energy and equanimity trumps snack discipline. For maximum zip and contentedness, give your kids snacks containing complex carbohydrates (fruits, crackers, nonfat energy bars, and the like) *before* they get hungry or show signs of exhaustion. You should avoid snacks high in fats and proteins because these foods take a long time to digest and will tend to unsettle your stomach if it's a hot day.

Bob enthusiastically recommends **Clif Shot Bloks,** chewable cubes that replace electrolytes in the body. They're light, come in several different flavors (all tasty), and don't melt even on the hottest days.

ELECTRONICS Regardless of your children's ages, always bring a night-light. Flashlights are also handy for finding stuff in a dark hotel room after the kids are asleep. If you're a big coffee drinker and if you drive, bring along a coffee maker if it's not included in your room (all Disney resort rooms have them).

Smartphones, tablets, digital music players with earbuds, and electronic games are often controversial gear for a family outing. We recommend compromise. Earbuds allow kids to create their own space even when they're with others, and that can be a safety valve. That said, try to agree before the trip on some earbud parameters, so you don't begin to feel as if they're being used to keep other family members and the trip itself at a distance.

POWERING UP Speaking of smart devices, their use has become standard in the parks. In addition to taking photos, guests also use apps to check on waiting times and score seats at restaurants. All that technology comes at a price: dead batteries. You spend all day using your phone to email photos to Great-Aunt Fern, but at the end of the day, you can't find the missing members of your party because you don't have enough power to place a call or even send a text. Having experienced the problem firsthand, Liliane has a few suggestions:

First, bring a portable phone charger and always, *always* bring the charging cable. You can purchase a portable phone charger at the theme parks for $30; the kit includes Android and iPhone cables. When it runs out of juice, simply go to one of the kiosks (available in all parks) and swap your empty battery for a charged one at no cost! Back at home, you can charge the battery via a USB cable plugged into your computer or any AC outlet. Liliane and Bob were instant fans.

You can recharge at the Baby Care Centers in the parks and at restrooms. Charging policies at restaurants vary—our experience has been that the upscale places will fuss about a request, while the counter-service places don't mind.

Here are a few good choices during lunch- or dinnertime: in the Magic Kingdom, several tables at the **Columbia Harbour House** (especially upstairs) are near electrical outlets. At **Pecos Bill Tall Tale Inn and Cafe,** a table opposite the condiments station is next to a power outlet. The tent at the back of Storybook Circus, next to **Pete's Silly Sideshow,** is set up with several charging stations and benches to rest. Another great station is in the rest area across from the *Tangled*-**themed restrooms;** outlets are located in fake tree stumps. At these stations you can charge via USB or a regular plug. Also try the shopping area at the exit to **Space Mountain.** At Disney's Hollywood Studios, don't count on the sit-down restaurants; rather, head for **Backlot Express,** which has lots of tables nestled next to power outlets. At Epcot, you'll find outlets at **Sunshine Seasons,** as well as in the single-rider line at **Soarin',** which is good for a quick 5- or 10-minute charge. Try the **Innovation Plaza** behind and to the right of Club Cool. At Animal Kingdom, try outlets at **Pizzafari** or **Tusker House.** The bar at **Tiffins** is the mother of all charging stations.

DON'T FORGET THE TENT   *Bob here:* When my daughter was preschool-age, I almost went crazy trying to get her to sleep in a shared hotel room. She was accustomed to having her own room at home and was hyperstimulated whenever she traveled. I tried makeshift curtains and room dividers and even rearranged the furniture in a few hotel rooms to create the illusion of a more private, separate space for her. It wasn't until she was around 4 years old and I took her camping that I seized on an idea that had some promise. She liked the cozy, secure, womblike feel of a backpacking tent and quieted down much more readily than she ever had in hotel rooms. So the next time the family stayed in a hotel, I pitched my backpacking tent in the corner of the room. In she went, nested for a bit, and fell asleep.

Modern tents are self-contained, with floors and an entrance that can be zipped up (or not) for privacy but cannot be locked. Affordable and sturdy, many are as simple to put up as opening an umbrella. Some tents are even specifically made to turn a bed into a fort. Kids appreciate having their own space and enjoy the adventure of being in a tent, even one set up in the corner of a hotel room. Light and compact when stored, a two-adult-size tent in its own storage bag (called a stuff sack) will take up about one-tenth or less of a standard overhead bin on a commercial airliner. Another option for infants and toddlers is to drape a sheet over a portable crib or playpen to make a tent.

"THE BOX" *Bob again:* On one memorable Disney World excursion when my kids were young, we started each morning with an involuntary scavenger hunt. Invariably, seconds before our scheduled departure to the theme park, we discovered that some combination of shoes, billfolds, sunglasses, hip packs, or other necessities were missing. For the next 15 minutes we would root through the room like pigs hunting truffles in an attempt to locate the absent items. Finally, I swung by a liquor store and mooched a big empty box. From then on, every time we returned to the room, I had the kids deposit shoes, hip packs, and other potentially wayward items in the box. After that the box was off-limits until the next morning, when I doled out the contents.

PLASTIC GARBAGE BAGS On two attractions, **Kali River Rapids** in Animal Kingdom and **Splash Mountain** in the Magic Kingdom, you are certain to get wet and possibly soaked. If it's really hot and you don't care, then fine. But if it's cool or you're just not up for a soaking, bring a large plastic trash bag to the park. By cutting holes in the top and on the sides, you can fashion a sack poncho that will keep your clothes from getting wet. On the raft ride, you will also get your feet wet. If you're not up for walking around in squishy, soaked shoes, bring a second, smaller plastic bag to wear over your feet while riding.

LILIANE Often little ones fall asleep in their strollers (hallelujah!). Bring a large lightweight cloth to drape over the stroller to cover your child from the sun. A few clothespins will keep it in place.

SUPPLIES FOR INFANTS AND TODDLERS

BASED ON RECOMMENDATIONS from hundreds of *Unofficial Guide* readers, here's what we suggest you carry with you when touring with infants and toddlers:

- A disposable diaper for every hour you plan to be away from your hotel room
- A plastic (or vinyl) diaper wrap with Velcro closures
- A cloth diaper or kitchen towel to put over your shoulder for burping
- Two receiving blankets: one to wrap the baby and one to lay the baby on or to drape over you when you nurse; bring a few clothespins, and you can use a blanket as a makeshift canopy to shelter baby from the sun by attaching it to the roof of the stroller.
- Ointment for diaper rash
- Moistened towelettes such as Wet Ones
- Prepared formula in bottles if you aren't breastfeeding
- A washable bib, baby spoon, and baby food if your infant is eating solid foods

- For toddlers, a small toy for comfort and to keep them occupied during attractions

Baby Care Centers at the theme parks will sell you just about anything that you forget or run out of. As with all things Disney, prices will be higher than elsewhere, but at least you won't need to detour to a drugstore in the middle of your touring day.

TIPS FOR EXPECTANT MOTHERS

LET'S FACE IT: a visit to Walt Disney World is not the ideal vacation for an expectant mom, but we also know that quite a lot of them visit the World every year. The most important advice for expectant moms is to take it easy. If you travel by car or plane, make sure you prepare your schedule in such a manner that you have plenty of rest. Don't stay on your feet all day; stick to a healthy, balanced diet, but most of all don't skip meals; and drink plenty of fluids. Keep the dining options flexible; morning sickness or sudden aversions or preferences to food can be dealt with easily if you don't make reservations and go for whatever you feel like eating. Always carry some snacks and bottled water with you. A plastic bag folded in your pocket in case you feel unwell takes no space but gives peace of mind. You should also discuss your upcoming Walt Disney World visit with your physician. He or she will certainly have valuable tips. From a Branchburg, New Jersey, woman:

> Moms should be really mindful of the temperature. Stay hydrated, and have realistic expectations for how much you'll be able to do. We averaged 5–7 miles of walking per day, and this may have been a bit too much for me. A midday nap or swim break was required.

Comfortable clothes are a must, and so are well-worn-in supporting shoes. You may consider getting a maternity support belt to keep your back from hurting. If you're using a special pillow at night to support your belly, don't forget to bring it with you. If you don't have enough space for it in your suitcase, consider shipping one ahead in a care box. Of course the hotel will provide you with extra pillows if needed.

While there have been no confirmed cases of the Zika virus in the Orlando area to date, there have been a small number of confirmed cases in other parts of Florida. Disney provides free insect repellent to all guests. Pregnant women, or those expecting to become pregnant, may want to take extra precautions.

Maternity bathing suit: If you don't own one, purchase a maternity bathing suit; you will be glad you did. A relaxing afternoon at the pool or a float down the lazy river in the water parks is wonderful.

At the parks, take frequent breaks; put your legs up! The Baby Care Centers also welcome expectant moms, and you can sit and relax in a pleasant atmosphere. Go back to the hotel for a nap during the day, and plan a day away from the parks. Go splurge and have a massage; your back and feet will be grateful. Sleep is precious, so don't overdo it; a good night of sleep is better than all the fireworks in the sky.

Heed the warnings! Here is a short list of rides that are absolutely not suitable for expectant moms: **Alien Swirling Saucers, Avatar Flight of Passage, The Barnstormer, Big Thunder Mountain Railroad, Dinosaur, Expedition Everest, Kali River Rapids, Kilimanjaro Safaris,** *Millennium Falcon:* **Smugglers Run, Mission: Space, Rock 'n' Roller Coaster, Seven Dwarfs Mine Train, Slinky Dog Dash, Space Mountain, Splash Mountain, Star Tours, Star Wars: Rise of the Resistance, Test Track, Tomorrowland Speedway,** and **The Twilight Zone Tower of Terror.** Remember, this is just a short list; use your own best judgment.

A word about the water parks: Obviously, experiencing the offerings of **Crush 'n' Gusher** or **Miss Adventure Falls** at Typhoon Lagoon or barreling down **Summit Plummet** at Blizzard Beach is ill-advised if you're in the family way, but the water parks offer great lazy rivers and pools, as well as shady beaches where you can relax and let the rest of your group enjoy the wild things.

TIPS FOR NURSING MOTHERS

BABY CARE CENTERS are available at all Walt Disney World parks, and nursing mothers will not have difficulty finding a comfortable, clean, and pleasant place to take care of their infants. In addition to breastfeeding rooms equipped with rocking chairs and love seats, the childcare facilities have sinks for washing and a room with toys and videos for your older children. Should you need diapers, baby clothes, children's medicines, and other small necessities, Disney has those items available right there for a fee.

Here are some tips to remember when visiting:

- Getting there by plane: Remember to nurse your child at takeoff and landing. It helps to open the baby's ears and also eliminates discomfort due to pressure changes.
- Nurse your infant at the first sign of hunger. You and the baby will be calmer, and you will attract much less attention if you feed the baby before he or she gets fussy and screams at the top of his or her lungs.
- Wear comfortable clothes. While you can access the Baby Care Centers at any time, there is nothing wrong with nursing your infant in a calm, shady spot anywhere at Walt Disney World or at the pool of your hotel. A dress with buttons in the front and a small baby blanket to put over your shoulder will do the trick. A large T-shirt that allows the baby to nurse "from under" is another option. In case you feel self-conscious, remember that Florida was the first state to protect breastfeeding in public by law in 1993.
- Pick a quiet place to nurse your baby.
- Adequate rest is another must. Schedule several breaks into your day and go back to the hotel for a nap.
- Make sure you plan regular healthy meals. A nursing mom, much like an expectant mother, has increased nutritional needs. In addition to eating a well-balanced diet and drinking plenty of fluids, it's always a good idea to take along some snacks.

- It is hot in Florida, and while it's important for all visitors to drink lots of water, it is crucial for nursing moms, so stay hydrated!
- Schedule a down day into your trip. If you have older children, let Dad take them to the park while you stay behind with the baby. A day of rest works wonders.
- If you plan on a parents' evening out, consider pumping milk for later use or supplementing breast milk with a bottle of formula.
- Nursing is exhausting, and so is touring Walt Disney World. Fatigue can reduce milk flow. Get enough rest and don't stay up past your bedtime. The night of a nursing mom is already short. Leave the park whenever you feel tired, and get enough sleep.
- A bath and a massage calm most fussy babies and are good for mom as well. Bring along some Epsom salts for a relaxing bath, or stop at Basin at Disney Springs and splurge on bath bombs.

TRIAL RUN

IF YOU GIVE THOUGHTFUL CONSIDERATION to all areas of mental, physical, organizational, and logistical preparation discussed in this chapter, what remains is to familiarize yourself with Walt Disney World itself and, of course, to conduct your field test. Yep, that's right; we want you to take the whole platoon on the road for a day to see if you are combat ready. No joke; this is important. You'll learn who poops out first, who is prone to developing blisters, who has to pee every 11 seconds, and, given the proper forum, how compatible your family is in terms of what you like to see and do.

For the most informative trial run, choose a local venue that requires lots of walking, dealing with crowds, and making decisions on how to spend your time. Regional theme parks and state fairs are your best bets, followed by large zoos and museums. Devote the whole day. Kick off the morning with an early start, just like you will at Walt Disney World, paying attention to who's organized and ready to go and who's dragging his or her butt and holding up the group. If you have to drive an hour or two to get to your test venue, no big deal. You'll have to do some commuting at Disney World too. Spend the whole day, eat a couple meals, and stay late.

Don't bias the sample (that is, mess with the outcome) by telling everyone you're practicing for Walt Disney World. Everyone behaves differently when they know they're being tested or evaluated. Your objective is not to run a perfect drill but to find out as much as you can about how the individuals in your family, as well as the family as a group, respond to and deal with everything they experience during the day. Pay attention to who moves quickly and who is slow; to who is adventuresome and who is reticent; to who keeps going and who needs frequent rest breaks; to who sets the agenda and who is content to follow; to who is easily agitated and who stays cool; to who tends to dawdle or wander off; to who is curious and who is bored; to who is demanding and who is accepting. You get the idea.

Evaluate the findings of the test run the next day. Don't be discouraged if your test day wasn't perfect; few (if any) are. Distinguish between problems that are remediable and problems that are intrinsic to your family's emotional or physical makeup (no amount of hiking, for example, will toughen up some people's feet).

Establish a plan for addressing remediable problems (further conditioning, setting limits before you go, trying harder to achieve family consensus, and so on) and develop strategies for minimizing or working around problems that are a fact of life (waking sleepyheads 15 minutes early, placing moleskin on likely blister sites before setting out, packing familiar food for the toddler who balks at restaurant fare). If you are an attentive observer, a fair diagnostician, and a creative problem solver, you'll be able to work out a significant percentage of the issues you're likely to encounter at Walt Disney World before you ever leave home.

WALT DISNEY WORLD *for* GUESTS *with* SPECIAL NEEDS

FIRST, CHECK OUT SERVICES and facilities at disneyworld.disney .go.com/guest-services/guests-with-disabilities, as well as the frequently asked questions page. For specific requests, such as those for special accommodations at hotels or on the Disney transportation system, call ☎ 407-939-7807. When booking your room, let the reservation agent know of any special needs you have.

Much of the Disney transportation system is disabled-accessible. All Disney lots have close-in parking for disabled visitors. All monorails and most rides, shows, restrooms, and restaurants accommodate wheelchairs. Even if an attraction doesn't accommodate wheelchairs or electric convenience vehicles (ECVs), nonambulatory guests may usually ride if they can transfer from a wheelchair to the ride's vehicle. Disney staff, however, aren't permitted to assist with transfers; guests must be able to board the ride unassisted or have a member of their party assist them. Members of the nonambulatory guest's party will be permitted to ride with him or her. Only **Peter Pan's Flight,** the **Swiss Family Treehouse,** the **Tomorrowland Transit Authority PeopleMover,** and **Tom Sawyer Island** (all at the Magic Kingdom) require that guests be ambulatory. Make sure to ask for boarding instructions as soon as you arrive at an attraction. See the tables on the next page; if an attraction is not listed, guests may remain in the ECV or wheelchair to experience it.

Guest Relations at the parks provide free assistive-technology devices to sight- and hearing-impaired guests. Braille guidebooks are available at Guest Relations at the parks, and Braille menus are available at some theme park restaurants. Disney provides sign-language

GUESTS MUST TRANSFER FROM AN ECV TO A WHEELCHAIR

THE MAGIC KINGDOM

- BUZZ LIGHTYEAR'S SPACE RANGER SPIN • *ENCHANTED TALES WITH BELLE*
- IT'S A SMALL WORLD • THE MAGIC CARPETS OF ALADDIN
- THE MANY ADVENTURES OF WINNIE THE POOH • PRINCE CHARMING REGAL CARROUSEL
- UNDER THE SEA: JOURNEY OF THE LITTLE MERMAID
- WALT DISNEY WORLD RAILROAD

EPCOT

- GRAN FIESTA TOUR STARRING THE THREE CABALLEROS
- LIVING WITH THE LAND • THE SEAS WITH NEMO & FRIENDS

DISNEY'S ANIMAL KINGDOM

- AFFECTION SECTION • KILIMANJARO SAFARIS • TRICERATOP SPIN

DISNEY'S HOLLYWOOD STUDIOS

- TOY STORY MANIA!

GUESTS MUST TRANSFER TO A RIDE VEHICLE

THE MAGIC KINGDOM

- ASTRO ORBITER • THE BARNSTORMER • BIG THUNDER MOUNTAIN RAILROAD
- DUMBO THE FLYING ELEPHANT • THE HAUNTED MANSION • MAD TEA PARTY
- PIRATES OF THE CARIBBEAN • SEVEN DWARFS MINE TRAIN • SPACE MOUNTAIN
- SPLASH MOUNTAIN • TOMORROWLAND SPEEDWAY

EPCOT

- FROZEN EVER AFTER • MISSION: SPACE • REMY'S RATATOUILLE ADVENTURE *(opens 2020)*
- SOARIN' • SPACESHIP EARTH • TEST TRACK

DISNEY'S ANIMAL KINGDOM

- AVATAR FLIGHT OF PASSAGE • DINOSAUR • EXPEDITION EVEREST
- KALI RIVER RAPIDS • NA'VI RIVER JOURNEY • PRIMEVAL WHIRL

DISNEY'S HOLLYWOOD STUDIOS

- ALIEN SWIRLING SAUCERS • *MILLENNIUM FALCON:* SMUGGLERS RUN
- ROCK 'N' ROLLER COASTER • SLINKY DOG DASH
- STAR TOURS—THE ADVENTURES CONTINUE
- STAR WARS: RISE OF THE RESISTANCE • THE TWILIGHT ZONE TOWER OF TERROR

interpretations of live shows at the theme parks on certain days of the week. Get confirmation of the interpreted-performance schedule a minimum of 1 week in advance by calling Disney World information at ☎ 407-824-4321 (voice) or 407-827-5141 (TTY). You'll be contacted before your visit with a show schedule that lists the names, dates, and times of the interpreted performances.

The schedule is updated weekly. You can obtain the schedule by emailing WDPRsignlanguageservices@disney.com, or if you're already in Orlando, at any Guest Relations location.

With a minimum of 14 days advance notice, sign-language interpretation can also be requested for some special events and dinner shows, such as the *Hoop-Dee-Doo Musical Revue, Spirit of Aloha,* or the Keys to the Kingdom Tour.

Service animals are welcome in all Disney resorts and in the parks. The relief areas for the service animals are marked on hotel and theme park maps. Service animals are even allowed on some rides. Read more at disneyworld.disney.go.com/guest-services/service-animals.

Disney's "Guide for Guests with Cognitive Disabilities" is available for download at tinyurl.com/WDWCogGuide. If you have a family member with a developmental disability, we recommend visiting autismattheparks.com, which was awarded the 2015 Sunshine Blog Award for Best Cause Blog. Maureen Deal, creator of autismattheparks.com, an informational guide for those who have family members with autism or other developmental disabilities, regularly shares with us her tips for navigating Orlando's theme parks and resorts with your autistic child. Read her latest tips at tinyurl.com/autismthemeparks. A word of caution from a dad from Massachusetts:

> *I have an 18-year-old with autism. Your recommendation to arrive at the park at rope drop is very useful, but a word to the wise: autistic children who have auditory issues—such as difficulty with loud noises, singing, clapping, and so on—should avoid the rope drop. I suggest hanging back until just after the rope is dropped. The time you lose in line is well worth keeping your special needs child from entering the park loaded with anxiety.*

Disability Access Service

Disney's Disability Access Service (DAS) is designed to accommodate guests who can't wait in regular standby lines. You must obtain a DAS card at the Guest Relations window of the first theme park you visit. The same card works in every subsequent park you visit. Once your DAS card is issued, you can use it to receive a return time for an attraction based on the current wait times. As soon as you finish one attraction, you can get a return time for another.

Guests whose disability requires only a wheelchair or mobility vehicle do not need a DAS. If you or your family member has any condition that qualifies for DAS, such as sensory issues, let the cast member at Guest Relations know so you can receive the right level of assistance.

The DAS is good for parties of up to six people. For parties of more than six, see Guest Relations. The DAS is good for the duration of your vacation OR for 14 days (60 days for annual pass holders), whichever is shortest. Bring the MagicBands or park cards of everyone in your group to Guest Relations. All of your group's MagicBands/cards will be linked to the DAS.

You can also use FastPass+ while you're using the DAS. In fact, cast members suggest that you do so. It may take some extra planning on the front end, but using FastPass+ helps your DAS access. Disney's My Disney Experience mobile app will show your FastPass+ and DAS reservations too. Visit tinyurl.com/DASfactsheet to find out what is needed for DAS prior to leaving home. You can also email disability.services@disneyparks.com or call ☎ 407-560-2547 for more information.

REMEMBERING *Your* TRIP

1. Purchase a notebook for each child and spend some time each evening recording the events of the day. If your children have trouble getting motivated or don't know what to write about, start a discussion; otherwise, let them write or draw whatever they want to remember from the day's events.

SABRINA I always collect extra park maps to remember my trip. They're also useful for scrapbooks.

2. Collect mementos along the way and create a treasure box in a small tin or cigar box. Months or years later, it's fun to look at postcards, pins, or park cards to jump-start a memory.

3. Add inexpensive postcards to your photographs to create an album; then write a few words on each page to accompany the images.

4. Give each child a disposable camera to record his or her version of the trip. One 5-year-old snapped photos that never showed anyone above the waist—his view of the world—and they were priceless.

5. Many families take cameras or make videos with their smartphones and tablets, though we recommend using one sparingly—parents end up viewing the trip through the lens rather than being in the moment. If you must, take your device of choice along, but record only a few moments of major sights (too much is boring anyway). And let the kids record and narrate. On the topic of narration, speak loudly so as to be heard over the not-insignificant background noise of the parks. Make use of lockers at all of the parks when the equipment becomes a burden or when you're going to experience an attraction that might damage it or get it wet. Unless you have a waterproof camera or smart device, leave it behind on Splash Mountain, Kali River Rapids, and any other ride where water is involved.

   Selfie sticks are not allowed at any Walt Disney World theme park.

6. Polaroid cameras are back in fashion, and the instant pictures will become the stars of your scrapbook.

7. At the Magic Kingdom, collect any button that applies to your visit (such as First Visit, Birthday, Just Married, Engaged, and so on); each is available for free at City Hall/Guest Relations.

8. At the Main Street Fire Station, you can get a free pack of the Sorcerers of the Magic Kingdom cards for each member of the family. Get the cards even if you don't play the game—they're great keepsakes. You can obtain one new pack every day you visit the Magic Kingdom.

Finally, when it comes to taking photos and collecting mementos, don't let the tail wag the dog. You're not going to Disney World to build the biggest scrapbook in history. Or as this Houston mom put it:

Tell your readers to get a grip on the photography thing. We were so busy shooting pictures that we kind of lost the thread.

HOW TO HAVE FUN BEFORE AND AFTER YOUR VISIT—OR, THINGS BOB WOULD NEVER DO

PREPARING FOR YOUR Walt Disney World vacation is important, but it's equally important to have a good time. Doing so before you leave is yet another way to get the whole family involved.

The weekend before your departure, plan a party for all who are going to Walt Disney World. Pick a Disney movie the entire family will enjoy and plan a meal in front of the TV. A chocolate cake or cookies shaped like the famous mouse head will be a guaranteed success and add to the fun.

BOB Liliane throws a party at the least provocation—Groundhog Day, National Tulip Day, Bless the Reptiles Day, you name it. But scheduling a wingding the weekend before you go to Disney World is to me like holding an Easter egg hunt in a cattle stampede—just a little too much going on to add one more thing.

This is the perfect time to go over the must-see list and reiterate the dos and don'ts.

LILIANE Don't forget to send Bob an invitation.

A similar event can be planned upon your return, when it's time to share the pictures and maybe even the movie you made during your visit to Disney World.

Great Websites

ARTS AND CRAFTS AND PARTY TIPS: family.disney.com

SOME SERIOUS COOKING: magicalkingdoms.com/wdw/recipes

TRY LILIANE'S RECIPE FOR THE MASTER'S CUPCAKE, or the Grey Stuff, as Lumière calls it in *The Beauty and the Beast*. You, too, can make these delicious cupcakes, served at Be Our Guest inside Fantasyland at the Magic Kingdom: themouseforless.com/blog_world/2015/08/grey-stuff -masters-cupcake-recipe.

PART SIX

READY, SET, TOUR!

TOURING RECOMMENDATIONS

HOW MUCH TIME IS REQUIRED TO SEE EACH PARK?

THE MAGIC KINGDOM AND EPCOT offer such a large number of attractions and special live-entertainment options that it's impossible to see everything in a single day, with or without a midday break. For a reasonably thorough tour of each, allocate a minimum of 1.5 days and preferably 2 days. The Animal Kingdom can be seen in a day, though planning on a day and a half allows for a more relaxed visit. If you're a *Star Wars* fan, be prepared to spend at least 2 days at Disney's Hollywood Studios (DHS).

WHICH PARK TO SEE FIRST?

THIS QUESTION IS LESS OBVIOUS than it appears, especially if your party includes children or teenagers. Children who see the Magic Kingdom first expect the same type of entertainment at the other parks. At Epcot, they're often disappointed by the educational orientation (as are many adults). And children may not find Animal Kingdom as exciting as the Magic Kingdom or DHS—real animals, after all, can't be programmed to entertain on cue.

First-time visitors should see Epcot first; you'll be able to enjoy it without having been preconditioned to think of Disney entertainment as solely fantasy or adventure. See Animal Kingdom second. Like Epcot, it's educational, but its live animals provide a change of pace.

Next, see DHS, which helps you transition from the educational Epcot and Animal Kingdom to the fanciful Magic Kingdom. Also, because DHS has fewer substantial attractions, you won't walk as much.

We recommend saving the Magic Kingdom for last, though we do recognize that, for many readers, the Magic Kingdom *is* Disney World. If you can't postpone the Magic Kingdom without a major revolt, at least see Epcot first. Adult orientation notwithstanding, there's lots that children age 7 and up will love, younger children not so much. Be sure to participate in Agent P's World Showcase Adventure and Kidcot, described in Part Eight. They'll be the highlight of your child's day. If seeing Mickey is your kid's top priority, be advised that you can see him in each of the major theme parks. Any cast member can tell you where to find him.

OPERATING HOURS

THE DISNEY WORLD WEBSITE publishes preliminary park hours 180 days in advance, but **schedule adjustments can happen at any time, including the day of your visit.** Check disneyworld.com or call ☎ 407-824-4321 for the exact hours before you arrive. Off-season, parks may be open as few as 9 hours (9 a.m.–6 p.m.). At busy times (particularly holidays), they may operate 8 a.m.–2 a.m.

When Disney launches new attractions or lands, that drives up demand and contributes to unbearably long lines such as those seen at Pandora at Animal Kingdom, as well as at Star Wars: Galaxy's Edge and Toy Story Land at DHS. To absorb the crowds, Disney sometimes runs morning Extra Magic Hours (see page 53) for resort guests every day at a park, instead of one or two days a week. The problem is that Disney doesn't get the message out very well, resulting in guests arriving at the previously posted opening time only to find the park already jam-packed. To be safe, call the number in the previous paragraph if you're going to Animal Kingdom or DHS and you want to be there at or before opening.

OFFICIAL OPENING VERSUS REAL OPENING

WHEN YOU CALL, you're given "official" hours. Sometimes parks open earlier. If the official hours are 9 a.m.–9 p.m., for example, Hollywood Boulevard at DHS might open at 8:30 a.m., and the remainder of the park at 9 a.m.

The Magic Kingdom is a special case: Main Street, U.S.A., opens a full hour before the park's official opening time on days without morning Extra Magic Hours. If the listed opening time is 9 a.m., then most of Main Street and the Central Plaza will be open for photos, shopping, and getting in line for rides by 8 a.m. This significantly alters the Magic Kingdom's early-morning traffic patterns by dumping up to 500 people at Seven Dwarfs Mine Train the instant the park opens. Get a FastPass+ or arrive 75–90 minutes before opening to ride.

Disney surveys local hotel reservations, estimates how many visitors to expect on a given day, and opens the theme parks early to avoid bottlenecks at parking facilities and ticket windows, as well as to absorb crowds as they arrive.

Attractions shut down at approximately the official closing time. Main Street in the Magic Kingdom remains open 30 minutes to an hour after the rest of the park has closed, though as mentioned earlier, high-demand rides such as those in Star Wars: Galaxy's Edge and

Avatar Flight of Passage in Pandora will stay open to serve those still waiting in line at closing.

THE RULES

SUCCESSFUL TOURING OF THE MAGIC KINGDOM, Epcot, Animal Kingdom, or DHS hinges on five rules:

1. Determine in Advance What You Really Want to See

What rides and attractions appeal most to you? Which additional rides and attractions would you like to experience if you have some time left? What are you willing to forgo?

To help you set your touring priorities, we describe each theme park and its attractions later in this book. In each description, we include the authors' evaluation of the attraction and the opinions of Walt Disney World guests expressed as star ratings. Five stars is the best possible rating.

Finally, because attractions range from midway-type rides to high-tech extravaganzas, we've developed a hierarchy of categories to pinpoint an attraction's magnitude:

SUPER-HEADLINERS The best attractions the theme park has to offer. Mind-boggling in size, scope, and imagination, they represent the cutting edge of modern attraction technology and design.

HEADLINERS Full-blown, multimillion-dollar, full-scale themed adventures and theater presentations. Modern in technology and design and employing a complete range of special effects.

MAJOR ATTRACTIONS Themed adventures on a more modest scale but incorporating state-of-the-art technologies. Or, larger-scale attractions of older design.

MINOR ATTRACTIONS Midway-type rides, small dark rides (cars on a track, zigzagging through the dark), small theater presentations, transportation rides, and elaborate walk-through attractions.

DIVERSIONS Exhibits, both passive and interactive. Include playgrounds, video arcades, and street theater.

Not every attraction fits neatly into these descriptions, but it's a handy way to compare any two. Remember that bigger and more elaborate doesn't always mean better. Peter Pan's Flight, a minor attraction in the Magic Kingdom, continues to be one of the park's most beloved rides. Likewise, for many young children, no attraction, regardless of size, surpasses Dumbo.

2. Arrive Early! Arrive Early! Arrive Early!

This is the single most important key to efficient touring and avoiding long lines. First thing in the morning, there are no lines for attractions and fewer people. The same four rides you experience in 1 hour in the early morning can take as long as 3 hours after 10:30 a.m. Eat breakfast before you arrive at the park; don't waste prime touring time sitting in a restaurant.

The earlier a park opens, the greater your advantage. This is because most vacationers won't rise early and get to a park before it opens. Fewer people are willing to make an 8 a.m. opening than a 9 a.m. opening. If you visit during midsummer, arrive at the turnstile 30–40 minutes before opening. During holiday periods, arrive 45–60 minutes early. By arriving, we mean to be at the turnstiles at the recommended time. Consider that you'll have to clear security before advancing to the turnstiles.

LILIANE You'll be able to see and do much more if you arrive early.

If getting the kids up earlier than usual makes for rough sailing, don't despair: you'll have a great time no matter when you get to the park. Many families with young children have found that it's better to accept the relative inefficiencies of arriving at the park a bit late than to jar the children out of their routine. We include a number of touring plans for sleepyheads in this guide.

3. Avoid Bottlenecks

Crowd concentrations and/or faulty crowd management cause bottlenecks. Avoiding bottlenecks involves being able to predict where, when, and why they occur. Concentrations of hungry people create bottlenecks at restaurants during lunch and dinner. Concentrations of people moving toward the exit at closing time create bottlenecks in gift shops en route to the gate. Concentrations of visitors at new and popular rides and at rides slow to load and unload create bottlenecks and long lines. To help you get a grip on which attractions cause bottlenecks, we've developed a Bottleneck Scale with a range of 1–10. If an attraction ranks high on the Bottleneck Scale, try to experience it during the first 2 hours the park is open. The scale is included in each attraction profile in Parts Seven through Eleven.

The best way to avoid bottlenecks, however, is to use one of our field-tested touring plans available in clip-out form, complete with a map, on pages 478–504. The plans will save you as much as 4.5 hours of standing in line in a single day.

4. Go Back to Your Hotel for a Rest in the Middle of the Day

You may think we're beating a dead horse with this midday nap thing, but if you plug away all day at the theme parks, you'll understand how the dead horse feels. No joke; resign yourself to going back to the hotel in the middle of the day for swimming, reading, and a snooze.

5. Let Off Steam

Time at a Disney theme park is extremely regimented for younger children. Often held close for fear of losing them, they are ushered from line to line and attraction to attraction throughout the day. After a couple of hours of being on such a short leash, it's not surprising that they're in need of some physical freedom and an opportunity to discharge that pent-up energy. If you don't return to your hotel for a break, consider one of the creative play areas in the parks. At the Magic Kingdom, the best place for kids to let off steam is Tom Sawyer Island. At the Animal Kingdom, The Boneyard offers plenty of opportunity for exploration.

LILIANE If you can't calm them—dunk them. Whenever my son was too wound up to nap or go to bed at night, I took him to the pool—water works wonders.

Less contained but wonderful on a hot summer day are the splash zones at Epcot, the Magic Kingdom, and Disney Springs. Just remember to bring a change of clothes and keep the footwear dry. Touring the park in wet sneakers is a recipe for blisters. And please parents, stay off your smartphones and keep an eye on your kids, as all play areas are fairly large, and it's pretty easy to misplace a child while he or she is playing.

YOUR DAILY ITINERARY

PLAN EACH DAY in three blocks:

1. Early morning theme park touring
2. Midday break
3. Late-afternoon and evening theme park touring

BOB We strongly recommend deferring parades, stage shows, and other productions until the afternoon or evening.

Choose the attractions that interest you most and check their bottleneck ratings along with what time of day we recommend you visit. If your children are 8 years old or younger, review the attraction's fright-potential rating. Use one of our touring plans or work out a step-by-step plan of your own and write it down. Experience attractions with a high bottleneck rating as early as possible, transitioning to attractions with ratings of 6–8 around midmorning. Plan on departing the park for your midday break by 11:30 a.m. or so.

For your late-afternoon and evening touring block, you don't necessarily have to return to the same theme park. If you purchased the Park Hopper option, you may opt to spend the afternoon/evening block somewhere different. In any event, as you start your afternoon/evening block, see attractions with low bottleneck ratings until about 5 p.m. After 5 p.m., any attraction with a rating of 1–7 is fair game. If you stay into the evening, try attractions with ratings of 8–10 during the hour just before closing.

In addition to attractions, each theme park offers a broad range of live entertainment. In the morning, concentrate on the attractions. For the record, we regard live shows that offer five or more daily performances (except street entertainment) as attractions. Thus, *Indiana Jones Epic Stunt Spectacular!* at Disney's Hollywood Studios is an attraction, as is *Festival of the Lion King* at the Animal Kingdom.

The evening fireworks at Epcot or the parades at the Magic Kingdom, on the other hand, are live-entertainment events. A schedule of live performances is listed in the *Times Guide* available at the entrance of each park. When planning your day, also be aware that major live events draw large numbers of guests from the attraction lines. Thus, a good time to see an especially popular attraction is during a parade or other similar event.

TOURING PLANS

OUR TOURING PLANS are step-by-step guides for seeing as much as possible with a minimum of standing in line. They're designed to help you avoid crowds and bottlenecks on days of moderate-to-heavy attendance. On days of lighter attendance (see "When to Go to Walt Disney World," page 41), the plans will still save time, but they won't be as critical to successful touring. *Unofficial Guide* touring plans, it seems, have side effects. As two readers attest, the plans can fan the embers of love and help you impress your friends. First from a 30-something mother of two from Oconomowoc, Wisconsin:

LILIANE Don't get obsessed with the touring plans. It's your vacation, after all. You can amend or even scrap the plans if you want.

> *My husband was a bit doubtful about using a touring plan, but on our first day at Magic Kingdom, when we had done all of the Fantasyland attractions and ridden Splash Mountain twice before lunch, he looked at me with amazement and said, "I've never been so attracted to you."*

And from a young Gardner, Massachusetts, reader:

> *I went with my school for Magic Music Days. I've been to Disney World before several times, and my parents have always used the guide. I looked crazy to my friends, with my book marked and well-worn and a stack of clip-out touring plans in my hand. The group that traveled around with me were amazed, commenting that it seemed like we were in front of a huge crowd. As soon as we left a ride we had walked on with no wait minutes before, there would be a line! Thank you for helping me impress my friends!*

What You Can Realistically Expect from the Touring Plans

The best way to see as much as possible with the least amount of waiting is to arrive early. Several of our touring plans require that you be on hand when the park opens. Because this is often difficult and sometimes impossible for families with young children or nocturnal teens, we've developed additional touring plans for families who get a late start. You won't see as much as with the early-morning plans, but you'll see significantly more than visitors without a plan.

Variables That Will Affect the Success of the Touring Plans

The touring plans' success will be affected by how quickly you move from ride to ride; when and how many breaks you take; when, where, and how you eat meals; and your ability (or lack thereof) to find your way around. Smaller groups almost always move faster than larger groups, and parties of adults generally cover more ground than families with young kids. Switching off (see page 248), also known as the Baby Swap or child swapping, among other things, inhibits families with little ones from moving expeditiously among attractions.

Many of the plans already include time for meeting the most popular characters at their dedicated venues. However, the spontaneous appearance of a Disney character strolling the park can stop a touring plan in its tracks. If your kids collect character autographs, anticipate these interruptions by including character greetings when creating your online touring plans, or else negotiate some understanding with your children about when you'll collect autographs. Note that queues for autographs are sometimes as long as the queues for major attractions. The only time-efficient ways to collect autographs are to use FastPass+ where available or to line up at the character-greeting areas first thing in the morning. Early morning is also the best time to experience popular attractions, so you may have some tough choices to make.

LILIANE Character meals are another way to collect autographs and might be something you could promise your avid collector in exchange for a full day of touring when the signature hunt is off.

While we realize that following the touring plans isn't always easy, we nevertheless recommend continuous, expeditious touring until around noon.

A multigenerational family from Aurora, Ohio, wonders how to know if you're on track or not, writing:

> It seems like the touring plans were very time-dependent, yet there were no specific times attached to the plan outside of the early morning. On more than one day, I often had to guess as to whether we were on track. Having small children and a grandparent in our group, we couldn't move at a fast pace.

There is no objective measurement for being on track—each family's or touring group's experience will differ to some degree. Nevertheless, the sequence of attractions in the touring plans will allow you to enjoy the greatest number of attractions in the least possible amount of time. Two quickly moving adults will probably take in more attractions in a specific time period than will a large group made up of children, parents, and grandparents. However, each will maximize their touring time and experience as many attractions as possible.

What To Do if You Lose the Thread

If unforeseen events interrupt a plan:

1. If you're following a touring plan in our **Lines** app (touringplans.com/lines), just press the optimize button when you're ready to start touring again. Lines will figure out the best possible plan for the remainder of your day.

2. If you're following a printed touring plan, skip a step on the plan for every 20 minutes' delay. For example, if you lose your phone and spend an hour hunting for it, skip three steps and pick up from there.

3. Forget the plan and organize the remainder of the day using the standby wait times listed in Lines.

What to Expect When You Arrive at the Parks

Because most touring plans are based on being present as soon as the theme park opens, you need to know about opening procedures. Disney transportation to the parks begins 1–2 hours before official opening. The parking lots open at around the same time.

Each park has an entrance plaza outside the turnstiles. Usually, you're held there until 30 minutes before the official opening time, when you're admitted. What happens next depends on the park you're visiting, the season, and the day's crowds.

1. **Standard Opening Procedures** On days when morning Extra Magic Hours are not in effect at the **Magic Kingdom,** you'll be admitted past the turnstiles up to an hour before park opening, but you'll be confined to Main Street, U.S.A. and the central hub until official opening time. Ropes and a human wall of Disney cast members keep you there until opening, when the wall speed-walks you to the headliner attractions (to prevent anyone from running or getting trampled). The effects of this procedure are instant, hour-long waits at Seven Dwarfs Mine Train as soon as the park opens, and more-moderate waits at other headliners.

   On busier days at **Animal Kingdom,** guests without Avatar Flight of Passage FastPasses will start lining up outside the park entrance about 90 minutes before official opening. Guests will usually be admitted past the turnstiles about 30-60 minutes prior to official opening. Once admitted, guests visiting Asia, Africa, or DinoLand are usually walked through Discovery Island and held until park opening at the bridges that connect those lands to Discovery Island.

   The vast majority of guests, however, are headed to Pandora. To reduce crowd pressure, Disney will move guests in stages from Discovery Island to Pandora's attractions: the crowd might first be held on Discovery Island, for example. Once that crowd is large enough, guests will be walked across the bridge to Pandora and stopped just before the land's entrance. Shortly before Pandora's attractions open, the crowds will be split into lines for Avatar Flight of Passage and Na'vi River Journey. The Flight of Passage line will often be long enough to extend from Pandora to the walkway to Africa. If you arrive at Pandora after park opening, look for cast members holding signs that say something like "This is the end of the line for Avatar Flight of Passage."

   Epcot allows guests past the main entrance turnstiles 15-30 minutes before official opening. Most of the time, guests are held in Future World Plaza until about 10 minutes before official opening, at which time rides start running and guests are released to enjoy them. Frozen Ever After opens at official park opening and is a good first stop if you can't get a FastPass+. If you enter the park through the International Gateway, you will be directed clockwise; you will have to walk all the way to Canada and through Mexico toward Norway, even if you have a FastPass+ for the ride. Liliane recently experienced this and tried to avoid the detour by telling the cast member she was going to Les Halles Boulangerie–Patisserie in France, which opens at 9 a.m. However, she was stopped by a cast member in France when trying to make her way to Norway counterclockwise. The next time she tried this, she had no problem leaving France for Norway via Morocco. Try at your own risk, and let us know how you fare!

At **Disney's Hollywood Studios,** after Galaxy's Edge opened: You've seen news clips of shoppers lining up at 6 p.m. the night before 4 a.m. doorbuster sales on Black Friday? Imagine that with light sabers, and that's what the opening of Galaxy's Edge is at the Studios. The only way to experience the rides without 3- to 6-hour waits is to arrive early. We anticipate guests will start lining up at the park entrance as soon as Disney's security team allows. If that's 4 a.m., people will get in line at 4 a.m. We expect the park's operating hours to begin between 6 and 8 a.m. and extend to 11 p.m. or midnight on a regular basis. If you plan to arrive after the park's official opening, it's possible that either Galaxy's Edge or the entire park will be filled to capacity, with no further guests admitted. Have alternate park plans in mind. At press time, Disney hadn't yet said what other special procedures it will put in place for these crowds, but we're pretty sure it will need them.

2. **High-Attendance Days** When large crowds are expected, you'll usually be admitted through the turnstiles up to 30 minutes before official opening at Epcot, the Studios, and Animal Kingdom, and at least an hour at the Magic Kingdom. Much of the park may be operating, and Disney may permit you to head to your first attraction immediately upon entering.

In the first scenario above, you gain a big advantage if you're already past the turnstiles when the park opens. While everyone else is stuck in line waiting for the people ahead to figure out how the biometric scans work, the lucky few already in the park will be in line for their first attraction. You'll probably be done and on your way to your second before many of them are even in the park, and the time savings accrue throughout the rest of the day.

HOW TO FIND THE TOURING PLAN THAT'S BEST FOR YOU

THE DIFFERENT TOURING PLANS FOR EACH PARK are described in the chapter pertaining to that park. The descriptions will tell you for whom (for example, teens, parents with preschoolers, grandparents, and so on) or for what situation (such as sleeping late or enjoying the park at night) the plans are designed. The actual touring plans are located on pages 478–504. Each plan includes a numbered map of the park in question to help you find your way around. Clip out the plan of your choice and take it with you to the park.

Our best touring plans are those provided in this guide. However, customized plans are available at touringplans.com; there you can create specific plans based on your family setup, your favorite attractions, restaurants, and more.

Will the Plans Continue to Work Once the Secret Is Out?

Yes! First, most of the plans require that a patron be there when a park opens. Many Disney World patrons simply won't get up early while on vacation. Second, less than 2% of any day's attendance has been exposed to the plans—too few to affect results. Last, most groups tailor the plans, skipping rides or shows according to taste.

How Frequently Are the Touring Plans Revised?

We revise them every year, and updates are always available at touring plans.com. Most complaints we receive come from readers using out-of-date editions of *The Unofficial Guide*. Even if you're up-to-date, though, be prepared for surprises. Opening procedures and showtimes may change, for example, and you can't predict when an attraction might break down.

"Bouncing Around"

Disney generally tries to place its popular rides on opposite sides of the park. In the Magic Kingdom, for example, the most popular attractions are positioned as far apart as possible—in the north, east, and west corners of the park—so that guests are more evenly distributed throughout the day.

It's often possible to save a lot of time in line by walking across the park to catch one of these rides when crowds are low. Some readers object to this crisscrossing. A woman from Decatur, Georgia, told us she "got dizzy from all the bouncing around." Believe us, we empathize.

In general, our touring plans recommend crossing the park only if you'll save more than 1 minute in line for every 1 minute of extra walking. We sometimes recommend crossing the park to see a newly opened ride too; in these cases, a special trip to visit the attraction early avoids much longer waits later. Also, live shows, especially at the Studios, sometimes have performance schedules so at odds with each other (and the rest of the park's schedule) that orderly touring is impossible.

If you want to experience headliner attractions in 1 day without long waits, you can see those first (requires crisscrossing the park), use FastPass+ (if available), or hope to squeeze in visits during parades and the last hour the park is open (may not work).

Touring Plans and the Obsessive-Compulsive Reader

We suggest sticking to the plans religiously, especially in the mornings, if you're visiting during busy times. The consequence of touring spontaneity in peak season is hours of standing in line. When using the plans, however, relax and always be prepared for surprises and setbacks.

If you find your type-A brain doing cartwheels, reflect on the advice of a woman from Trappe, Pennsylvania:

> *I had planned for this trip for 2 years and researched it using guide-books, websites, and information received from WDW. On night three of our trip, I took an unscheduled trip to the emergency room. When the doctor asked what the problem was, I responded, "I don't know, but I can't stop shaking, and I can't stay here very long because I have to get up in a couple hours to go to Disney's Hollywood Studios." Diagnosis: an anxiety attack caused by my excessive itinerary.*

However, a vet from Annandale, Virginia, warns:

I'm retired Navy, and planning a Disney visit today is almost like planning an amphibious landing for the invasion! I pity any free spirit who blithely shows up at a Disney park for the first time without any advance planning and expects to flit from ride to ride without a care in the world. Disney World will eat you alive if you're not careful!

Touring Plan Rejection

Some folks don't respond well to the regimentation of a touring plan. If you encounter this problem with someone in your party, roll with the punches, as this Maryland couple did:

The rest of the group was not receptive to the use of the touring plans. Rather than argue, I left the touring plans behind as we ventured off for the parks. You can guess the outcome. We recorded our trip and watched the movies when we returned home. About every 5 minutes or so, there's a shot of us all gathered around a park map trying to decide what to do next.

A reader from Royal Oak, Michigan, ran into trouble by not getting her family on board ahead of time:

If one member of the family is doing most of the research and planning (like I did), communicate what the book/touring plans suggest. I failed to do this and it led to some, shall we say, tense moments between my husband and me on our first day. However, once he realized how much time we were saving, he understood why I was so bent on following the plans.

Finally, note that our mobile app, **Lines,** can be used to find attractions with low wait times, even if you're not using a touring plan.

Touring Plans for Low-Attendance Days

We receive a number of letters each year similar to the following one from Lebanon, New Jersey:

The guide always assumed there would be large crowds. We had no lines. An alternate tour for low-traffic days would be helpful.

There are, thankfully, still days on which crowds are low enough that a full-day touring plan isn't needed. However, some attractions in each park bottleneck even if attendance is low:

- **MAGIC KINGDOM** Space Mountain, Splash Mountain, The Many Adventures of Winnie the Pooh, *Enchanted Tales with Belle,* Peter Pan's Flight, and Seven Dwarfs Mine Train
- **EPCOT** Frozen Ever After, Meet Anna and Elsa at Royal Sommerhus, Test Track, and Soarin'
- **ANIMAL KINGDOM** Avatar Flight of Passage, Na'vi River Journey, Kilimanjaro Safaris, Expedition Everest, and Dinosaur

- **DISNEY'S HOLLYWOOD STUDIOS** Alien Swirling Saucers, *Millennium Falcon:* Smugglers Run, Rock 'n' Roller Coaster, Slinky Dog Dash, Star Wars: Rise of the Resistance, The Twilight Zone Tower of Terror, and Toy Story Mania!

For this reason, we recommend that you follow a touring plan at least through the first five or six steps. If you're pretty much walking onto every attraction, scrap the remainder of the plan. Alternatively, you can see the aforementioned attractions immediately after the park is open, or use FastPass+.

Extra Magic Hours and the Touring Plans

If you're a Disney resort guest and use your morning Extra Magic Hours privileges, complete your early-entry touring before the general public is admitted and position yourself to follow the touring plan. When the public is admitted, the park will suddenly swarm. A Wilmington, Delaware, mother advises:

> *The early-entry times went like clockwork. We were finishing up at Toy Story Mania! when Disney's Hollywood Studios opened to the public, and we had to wait in line quite a while for Voyage of the Little Mermaid, which sort of screwed up everything thereafter. Early-opening attractions should be finished up well before regular opening time so you can be at the plan's first stop as early as possible.*

In the Magic Kingdom, early-entry attractions currently operate in Fantasyland and Tomorrowland. At Epcot, they're in the Future World section and Norway Pavilion. At Animal Kingdom, they're in DinoLand U.S.A., Asia, Discovery Island, Africa, and Pandora. At Disney's Hollywood Studios, they're dispersed. Practically speaking, see any attractions on the plan that are open for early entry, crossing them off as you do. If you finish all early-entry attractions and have time left before the general public is admitted, sample early-entry attractions not included in the plan. Stop touring about 10 minutes before the public is admitted, and position yourself for the first attraction on the plan that wasn't open for early entry. During early entry in the Magic Kingdom, for example, you can almost always experience Seven Dwarfs Mine Train and Under the Sea: Journey of the Little Mermaid in Fantasyland, plus Space Mountain in Tomorrowland. As official opening nears, go to the boundary between Fantasyland and Liberty Square and be ready to blitz Splash and Big Thunder Mountains according to the touring plan when the rest of the park opens.

Evening Extra Magic Hours, when a designated park remains open for Disney resort guests 2 hours beyond normal closing time, have less effect on the touring plans than early entry in the morning. Parks are almost never scheduled for both early entry and evening Extra Magic Hours on the same day. Thus a park offering evening Extra Magic Hours will enjoy a fairly normal morning and early afternoon. It's not until late afternoon, when park hoppers coming from the other theme parks descend, that the late-closing park will become especially crowded. By that time, you'll be well toward the end of your touring plan.

FASTPASS+

FASTPASS+ IS DISNEY'S free ride-reservation system. Somewhat like making a reservation at a restaurant, FastPass+ allows you to reserve a ride on an attraction at a Disney theme park at a specific day and time. Like restaurant reservations, you're encouraged to book FastPass+ reservations far in advance: up to 60 days out if you're staying at a hotel on Disney property (including the Swan, Dolphin, Four Seasons, Shades of Green, Hilton Orlando Bonnet Creek, Waldorf Astoria Orlando, and Disney Springs Resort Area hotels, at least through 2020) and 30 days in advance if you're not.

You must use a computer, mobile device, or in-park terminal to make and modify FastPass+ reservations (see the next page), and you must use your MagicBand or park card to redeem the reservation.

FastPass+ can help you see more with less waiting. But FastPass+ comes with rules that restrict how it can be used, so understanding how to use it is important when using our touring plans, especially if you want to experience lots of attractions or you're unable to arrive at park opening. See "FastPass+ Rules" on page 242.

FastPass+ does *not* eliminate the need to arrive early at a theme park. Because each park offers a limited number of FastPass+ attractions, and a limited number of reservations for those attractions each day, you still have to make an early start if you want to avoid long lines at non-FastPass+ attractions.

FastPass+ reduces waits by distributing guests at the designated attractions throughout the day. It provides an incentive—a shorter

wait—for guests willing to postpone experiencing a given attraction until later in the day. The system also, in effect, imposes a penalty—standby status—on guests who don't use it. However, spreading out guest arrivals sometimes decreases waits for standby guests as well.

Making a FastPass+ Reservation

Anyone with an upcoming stay at a Walt Disney World hotel can make FastPass+ reservations up to 60 days in advance at mydisneyexperience .com and through the My Disney Experience (MDE) app; annual pass holders staying off-property may reserve up to 30 days in advance, as may day guests with a valid ticket.

Some resort guests may purchase three extra FastPass+ selections per day for $50 per person. The program is only available to guests staying a minimum of 3 nights in certain rooms, including club-level rooms at Animal Kingdom Lodge, Beach Club Resort, BoardWalk Inn, Contemporary Resort, Grand Floridian Resort, Polynesian Village Resort, Wilderness Lodge, and Yacht Club Resort, as well as presidential, governor, and parlor suites and premium alcove rooms at the Swan and Dolphin, the bungalows of Polynesian Village, and the cabins of Copper Creek. Guests who purchase these FastPasses have a booking window up to 90 days in advance for the three additional FastPass+ selections and can book them at multiple top-tier attractions at different parks if they have valid Park Hopper tickets. They also receive one preferred viewing location for a nighttime spectacular per day. The other three FastPasses (which all on-property guests receive) can be booked 60 days out as usual, but no earlier. The additional FastPasses cannot be booked through MDE. A Disney Signature Services cast member will make the FastPass+ selections at the time of booking. This paid FastPass+ option must be purchased in advance and is not offered to guests upon check-in.

If you buy your admission the day you arrive at the park or you want to change your previous FastPass+ selections once you're inside, you can do so using the mobile app or in-park kiosks. See page 241 for instructions on how to do this.

Once you've used all three of your advance FastPass+ reservations, you can make an additional reservation from your phone (make sure you download the app) or a FastPass+ kiosk within the park. Also, the day-of FastPass+ reservations you make don't have to be in the park where you started. This is a big plus for those who have Park Hopper tickets.

To make advance FastPass+ reservations, you'll first need to register for an MDE account. If you have difficulty with the app or site, call ☎ 407-939-4357 for assistance. While we provide navigational instructions here, Disney's web designers move things around all the time, so you may have to hunt around to find some features.

BEFORE YOU BEGIN Set aside at least 30–40 minutes to complete this process. Make sure you have the following items on hand:

- A valid admission ticket or confirmation number for everyone in your group
- Your hotel-reservation number, if you're staying on-site
- A schedule of the parks you'll be visiting each day, including arrival and departure times and the times of any midday breaks
- The dates, times, and confirmation numbers of any dining or recreation reservations you've already made

GETTING STARTED Now go to disneyworld.disney.go.com/plan and click "Create Account" in the upper right corner. You'll be asked for your email address, along with your name, home address, and birth date. (Disney uses your home address to send your MagicBands and, if applicable, hotel reservation information.) You'll also be asked to choose security questions and answers—write these down and store them in a safe place, or save them as a text file. If you forget your login information, Disney will ask you these questions to verify your identity.

DISNEY HOTEL INFORMATION Next, MDE asks whether you'll be staying at a Disney hotel. If you are, enter your reservation number. This associates your MDE account with your hotel stay in Disney's computer systems. If you've booked a travel package that includes theme park admission, Disney computers will automatically link the admission to your MDE account, allowing you to skip the "Linking Tickets" step. If you've booked a Disney hotel through a third-party site like Expedia or Hotels .com, that site should send you a Disney reservation number to use here.

REGISTER FRIENDS AND FAMILY In the upper-right corner of the home page, hover over "My Disney Experience," and click the "My Family & Friends" link; then enter the names and ages of everyone traveling with you. You can do this later too, but you'll need this information when you make your FastPass+ and dining reservations.

LINKING TICKETS You will need to have purchased theme park admission for each member of your group, and linked them to each member's MDE profile, before making some reservations.

If you haven't purchased your admission, do so now. Disney's website doesn't have the cheapest prices for theme park tickets of 3 or more days. See page 62 for where to find better deals. If you have a voucher that needs to be converted to a ticket at the parks, you can still register it by calling Disney tech support at ☎ 407-939-4357.

If you've already purchased tickets but have not linked them, in the upper-right corner of the home page, click "My Disney Experience" to access a welcome page. Hover over "Park Tickets," and click on "Link Tickets." On each ticket is printed a unique ID code, usually a string of 12–20 numbers, located in one corner on the back; on MagicBands, look for a 12-digit number printed inside the band. Enter the ID code for each ticket you have.

MAKING FASTPASS+ RESERVATIONS You can make FastPass+ reservations for as many days as there are on your ticket 30–60 days in advance (see page 238). If you decide later to extend your stay, you'll be able to make reservations for additional days.

In the upper-right corner of the home page, hover over "My Disney Experience," and click "FastPass+." Next, select "Add FastPass+." On the next screen, indicate which members of your group will be with you. On the screen after that, choose the park and the date on which you're visiting. You can make advance FastPass+ reservations at just one park per day, and you can only make three reservations in advance. Once you've used all three passes (or after they have expired), you may book day-of FastPasses (one at a time) at the same park or, if you have Park Hopper tickets, at another park via the MDE app or a FastPass+ kiosk, placed in strategic locations around the four theme parks. If you got a FastPass+ for evening fireworks, you won't be able to get another FastPass+ until that pass is used or the time window has elapsed.

The website will show you which attractions have FastPass+ reservations available and three possible return times. The default view shows morning FastPass+ availability, but you can select afternoon, evening, or specific times to display.

If you're unsure of the attractions or times of day you should use FastPass+, see the touring plans on pages 478–500. Select the attractions and return times that most closely fit your plans for the day. After confirming your selections, you can check for alternative return-time windows for each attraction. If an attraction isn't selectable, either all of its available FastPass+ reservations are gone or the attraction is closed at the time shown. Those attractions are listed at the bottom of the page as not available.

You'll need to repeat these steps for every day you want to use FastPass+ in the theme parks.

If at any time the initial set of FastPass+ return times you picked conflicts with your plans, you can always check to see whether alternate times are available that better fit your schedule. The good news is that you can change each attraction's return times separately. Plus, if none of the return times for a particular attraction work for you, you can pick another attraction.

We strongly recommend installing the MDE app on your phone to avoid going to a FastPass+ kiosk for changes or additional passes.

MAKING DINING RESERVATIONS See page 145 for instructions.

Once you've made your initial set of FastPass+ and dining reservations, you'll be able to view and edit them (along with your hotel reservation) in the "My Plans" section of MDE.

Buying Tickets and Making FastPass+ Reservations on Arrival

If (1) you buy your admission the day you arrive at the parks or (2) you have to delay making your FastPass+ selections until you're inside, you can use your My Disney Experience app or one of the kiosks throughout the parks to make reservations; we've listed the specific locations in each theme park's chapter. Each set of terminals—look for the F P + K I O S K signs—is staffed cast members who can walk you through the reservation process.

We strongly recommend that you download the app and get acquainted with FastPass+ reservations via your phone. Cast members will gladly help you along the way, but you will still need your MDE user name and password to get the job done.

RETURNING TO RIDE Each FastPass+ reservation lasts for an hour, and Disney officially enforces the ride return time. Thus, if you make a FastPass+ reservation to ride Space Mountain at 7:30 p.m., you have until 8:30 p.m. to either use it or change it to something else. Your FastPass+ will be canceled if you don't show up on time; in practice, however, we've found that you can usually be up to 15 minutes late to use your reservation.

When you return to Space Mountain at the designated time, you'll be directed to a FASTPASS+ RETURN line. Before you enter the line, you'll need to validate your reservation by touching your MagicBand or park card to a reader at the FastPass+ Return entrance. Then you'll proceed with minimal waiting to the attraction's preshow or boarding area.

If technical problems cause an attraction to be closed during your return time, Disney will automatically adjust your FastPass+ reservation in one of three ways:

1. If it's early in the day, Disney will offer you the chance to return to the attraction at any point in the day after it reopens.

2. Alternatively, Disney may let you choose any FastPass+ attraction in the same park, on the same day.

3. If it's late in the day, Disney will automatically give you another selection good for any FastPass+ attraction at any park the following day.

Note that you will receive an email advising you of the technical problem at the attraction of your choice and reminding you of the options you have.

At the FastPass+ attractions listed below, the time gap between getting your pass and returning to ride can range from 3 to 7 hours. To ensure that you have enough time to ride on the day of your visit, either book FastPass+ in advance for these attractions or reserve them in the parks as early in the day as possible.

GET FASTPASS+ *before 11 a.m.* FOR THE FOLLOWING:
MAGIC KINGDOM All character meet and greets, *Enchanted Tales with Belle,* Peter Pan's Flight, Seven Dwarfs Mine Train, Space Mountain, Splash Mountain
EPCOT Frozen Ever After, Mission: Space (Orange), Soarin', Test Track
ANIMAL KINGDOM Avatar Flight of Passage, Expedition Everest, *Festival of the Lion King,* Kilimanjaro Safaris, Meet Favorite Disney Pals at Adventurers Outpost, Na'vi River Journey
DHS Rock 'n' Roller Coaster, Slinky Dog Dash, Star Tours, Toy Story Mania!, The Twilight Zone Tower of Terror, as well as *Millennium Falcon:* Smugglers Run and Star Wars: Rise of the Resistance (if offered)

FastPass+ Rules

Disney has put rules in place to prevent guests from obtaining certain combinations of FastPass+ reservations before they get to the parks:

RULE #1: You can obtain only one advance FastPass+ reservation per attraction, per day, but you can get more once you're in the park and you've used your first set of three. You can't make multiple advance FastPass+ reservations for, say, Toy Story Mania!—you must select three different attractions. But once you've entered Hollywood Studios for the day and your first three reservations have been used or have expired, you can obtain more for Toy Story Mania! if they're available.

It's generally a bad idea to make advance FastPass+ reservations for any of the evening shows or fireworks because you won't be able to get any more reservations while you're in the park. We suggest checking around 4 p.m. to see if any reservations are available. If they are and you're done with the headliner attractions, go ahead and grab a FastPass+.

If your heart is set on experiencing Animal Kingdom's nighttime show *Rivers of Light: We Are One,* you will likely have to use a Fast-Pass+, as the show is very popular and FastPass+ is almost never available the day of. On days the park is open until 11 p.m. and two shows are offered, choose the first show. If you decide to use your three Fast-Passes+ for other attractions, such as the rides in Pandora: The World of Avatar, try seeing the second showing of *Rivers of Light* on standby, as it will probably be less busy.

RULE #2: FastPass+ reservation times can't overlap—Disney's computer system doesn't allow it. If you have a FastPass+ reservation for 2–3 p.m., you can't make another reservation later than 2 p.m. and earlier than 3 p.m. in the same park.

RULE #3: FASTPASS+ TIERS Disney also prohibits guests from using FastPass+ on all of a park's headliner attractions. The practice, known informally as FastPass+ tiers, is currently in effect at Epcot, Disney's Animal Kingdom, and Disney's Hollywood Studios. At Epcot, by way of example, the FastPass+ attractions are divided into the following two tiers:

TIER A (*Choose 1*)	
• Fireworks Show	• Soarin'
• Frozen Ever After	• Test Track
TIER B (*Choose 2*)	
• Disney & Pixar Short Film Festival	• The Seas with Nemo & Friends
• Journey into Imagination with Figment	• Spaceship Earth
• Living with the Land	• *Turtle Talk with Crush*
• Mission: Space (Green or Orange)	

FastPass+ lets you choose only one attraction from Tier A and two attractions from Tier B. Note that Tier A comprises the attractions with the longest lines: this ensures that most guests get to choose Frozen Ever After, Soarin', or Test Track. Also, note that few of the attractions in Tier B actually require FastPass+ for most of the year. In practice, it's difficult to score a FastPass+ at the park for the Tier A attractions you didn't select in advance. The only reliable strategy for avoiding long waits is to be on hand at park opening and experience these attractions before the park gets crowded.

The tiers don't apply beyond your first three advance FastPass+ reservations—any reservations you make beyond the first three when you're in the parks are totally up to you.

Note: Disney's Hollywood Studios currently has severe tier restrictions in place in conjunction with the 2019 opening of Star Wars: Galaxy's Edge. All FastPass+ rides have moved to Tier A, with shows and theater presentations in Tier B. Disney is likely taking these steps because there isn't enough capacity at the park's existing rides to give larger crowds two ride FastPasses each. We believe this will change, though, once Mickey & Minnie's Runaway Railway opens in 2020—its high capacity should enable more ride FastPasses to be distributed. Also of note, neither Galaxy's Edge ride will open with FastPass+, to keep standby wait times down.

RULE #4: BOOKING WINDOW If you have reservations for a resort in Walt Disney World, you can begin making your FastPass+ reservations 60 days before your arrival. You'll be able to make FastPass+ reservations for as many days as your Disney tickets have theme park admission. Thus, if you have a 7-day theme park ticket, you'll be able to make FastPass+ reservations for all 7 days of your trip on the 60th day before you arrive.

How FastPass+ Affects Your Waits in Line

FastPass+ has a noticeable effect on standby lines. Standby wait times are down significantly at the following attractions:

- Rock 'n' Roller Coaster
- Toy Story Mania!
- Expedition Everest
- Test Track

Wait times are *up* at these attractions:

- Pirates of the Caribbean
- Dinosaur
- The Haunted Mansion
- Spaceship Earth
- The Magic Carpets of Aladdin
- Primeval Whirl
- Journey Into Imagination with Figment

LILIANE Lines at Pirates of the Caribbean and Spaceship Earth? Give me a break!

BOB Assume that using the FastPass+ line will take 15%–25% as long as the posted standby time—about 9-15 minutes for an attraction with a 60-minute posted wait.

WAITS WITH FASTPASS+ You'll still wait to actually board the ride, even if you're using FastPass+. The time you'll wait can vary considerably, from almost nothing to 40 minutes or more.

How FastPass+ Affects Your Touring Plans

We've spent a lot of time observing just how wrong things can go at a FastPass+ return point. The most common issue we see is a family arriving too early or too late for their reservation. That's understandable

LILIANE I strongly recommend taking a screenshot of your three FastPass+ reservations, so you have the times handy on your phone. Another option is to carry a printout with you.

because MagicBands don't display reservation times, and the times are cumbersome to find on My Disney Experience.

The next most frequent problem we see is from families, particularly those whose native language isn't English, who simply don't get how FastPass+ works. For example, many families seem to think that just wearing the MagicBand allows them access to the FastPass+ line, without their having to make a reservation.

When a MagicBand doesn't work at a FastPass+ return point, a cast member can usually resolve the problem fairly quickly. When the problem is more complex, the line stops while the issue is sorted.

Remember that after your initial three FastPass+ reservations have been used, you are able to make new reservations one at a time. You can make those additional FastPass+ reservations directly from the MDE app, eliminating the need to go to a FastPass+ kiosk. You can even make a reservation at a different park if you have a Park Hopper ticket.

What to Do If You Can't Get an Advance FastPass+ at a Popular Ride

The touring plans in this guide, which all incorporate FastPass+, are our most efficient, provided you're willing to arrive at the park 35–60 minutes before opening.

However, the entire supply of FastPasses for popular rides like Avatar Flight of Passage can be snapped up a few seconds after they're available. Getting one of those—especially one at the exact time you want—is like winning the lottery: so many people are trying to do the same thing that your odds of succeeding are essentially zero. There are two ways to deal with this: Get the next-best FastPasses you can, or wait for day-of FastPasses.

 BOB Disney holds back a certain amount of each ride's FastPass+ daily capacity as a hedge against ride breakdowns. If the park's rides operate smoothly, this extra FastPass+ capacity is released throughout the day for in-park guests to use.

GET WHAT YOU CAN Our software can adjust any touring plan to use whatever FastPass+ reservations you have. For example, if you can't get a FastPass+ for Avatar Flight of Passage, try for Kilimanjaro Safaris next. Then tell the software what attractions and times you ended up with; the software will adjust your plan accordingly.

DAY-OF FASTPASS+ While Disney typically sets aside around 80% of a ride's capacity for FastPass+ reservations 60 days before your visit, it doesn't make all 80% available at once. The rest are released on the day of your visit.

When you're in the park, you can tell Lines to re-optimize your plan based on your day-of FastPass+ times.

THE FUTURE OF FASTPASS+ As this edition of the *Guide* was going to press, we were hearing rumors that Disney may change the FastPass+ system to include more paid options.

Readers React to FastPass+

FastPass+ generates more comments than anything we've seen in years. A mother from Kansas likes the ability to schedule rides in advance:

It was great to schedule our FastPasses ahead of time and know when and where we were going to be. If a ride was closed during our scheduled time, we got an email, and we were able to go back at any time the rest of the day or switch the attraction or time.

A Columbia, Maryland, woman, however, laments that ride reservations are yet another chore on her vacation to-do list:

Between the need for scheduling meals 180 days in advance and rides 60 days out, Disney World has become a vacation for those who enjoy planning every hour of their day.

From a Ross-on-Rye, United Kingdom, grandfather:

This was our first trip with our grandchildren, and I found the amount of planning required to get appropriate FastPasses for our multigenerational group intimidating.

A woman from Shoreview, Minnesota, offered this:

FastPass+ was a nightmare. I don't think we used all of our passes on any of the days, and 90% of the FP+ we made at 60 days were changed at least once.

From a Springfield, Oregon, senior:

If you can't get an attraction or don't get the time you want, try again the week or two before you leave, and even the day of your visit. People change their minds—I know I did—and FastPasses become available even for the most sought-after rides.

From a Biddeford, Maine, reader:

We enjoyed our off-property experience. However, because we weren't in the Disney bubble, we only had a 30-day window for Fast-Passes. By that time, the biggies, like Avatar Flight of Passage, Toy Story Mania!, Seven Dwarfs Mine Train, etc., were impossible to get.

A common complaint is that FastPass+ is targeted to tech-savvy younger guests, as this 60-something from Bemidji, Minnesota, notes:

Many seniors, and a surprising number of others, aren't into technology. There are a LOT of us, young and old, who don't have gadgets or don't want to use them on vacation. It seems that those without smartphones, etc., are at a disadvantage.

As discussed earlier, you can make changes to your FastPass+ reservations, or set up new reservations, at FastPass+ kiosks in the park or via the MDE app. An "up East" family of four reported their experience:

Though Disney says you can get an additional FastPass+ after you've used your selections, I wouldn't count on it—the most popular attractions are usually out of FastPass+ times early in the day.

HEIGHT REQUIREMENTS

A NUMBER OF ATTRACTIONS REQUIRE CHILDREN to meet minimum height and age requirements; see the table below. If you have children too short or too young to ride, you have several options, including switching off (see page 248). Though the alternatives may resolve some practical and logistical issues, be forewarned that your smaller children might be resentful of their older (or taller) siblings who qualify to ride. A mom from Virginia bumped into just such a situation, writing:

You mention height requirements for rides but not the intense sibling jealousy this can generate. Frontierland was a real problem in that respect. Our very petite 5-year-old, to her outrage, was stuck hanging around while our 8-year-old went on Splash Mountain and Big Thunder Mountain with Grandma and Granddad, and the nearby alternatives weren't helpful (too long a line for rafts to Tom Sawyer Island, etc.). If we had thought ahead, we would have left the younger kid with one of the grown-ups for another roller coaster or two and then met up later at a designated point.

The reader makes a valid point, though in practical terms splitting the group and meeting up later can be more complicated than she might imagine. If you choose to split up, ask the Disney greeter at the entrance to the attraction(s) with height requirements how long the wait is. Tack on 5 minutes for riding onto the anticipated wait, and then add 5 or so minutes to exit and reach the meeting point for an

ATTRACTION AND RIDE RESTRICTIONS

THE MAGIC KINGDOM

- **THE BARNSTORMER** 35" minimum height
- **BIG THUNDER MOUNTAIN RAILROAD** 40" minimum height
- **SEVEN DWARFS MINE TRAIN** 38" minimum height
- **SPACE MOUNTAIN** 44" minimum height   • **SPLASH MOUNTAIN** 40" minimum height
- **TOMORROWLAND SPEEDWAY** 32" to ride, 54" to drive unassisted

EPCOT

- **MISSION: SPACE** 40" minimum height   • **SOARIN'** 40" minimum height
- **TEST TRACK** 40" minimum height

DISNEY'S ANIMAL KINGDOM

- **AVATAR FLIGHT OF PASSAGE** 44" minimum height
- **DINOSAUR** 40" minimum height   • **EXPEDITION EVEREST** 44" minimum height
- **KALI RIVER RAPIDS** 38" minimum height   • **PRIMEVAL WHIRL** 48" minimum height

DISNEY'S HOLLYWOOD STUDIOS

- **ALIEN SWIRLING SAUCERS** 32" minimum height
- *MILLENNIUM FALCON:* SMUGGLERS RUN 38" minimum height
- **ROCK 'N' ROLLER COASTER** 48" minimum height
- **SLINKY DOG DASH** 38" minimum height
- **STAR TOURS—THE ADVENTURES CONTINUE** 40" minimum height
- **STAR WARS: RISE OF THE RESISTANCE** 40" minimum height
- **THE TWILIGHT ZONE TOWER OF TERROR** 40" minimum height

approximate sense of how long the younger kids (and their supervising adult) will have to do other stuff. Our guess is that even with a long line for the rafts, the reader would have had more than sufficient time to take her daughter to Tom Sawyer Island while the sib rode Splash and Big Thunder with the grandparents. For sure she had time to tour the Swiss Family Treehouse in adjacent Adventureland.

WAITING-LINE STRATEGIES FOR ADULTS WITH YOUNG CHILDREN

CHILDREN HOLD UP BETTER through the day if you minimize the time they spend in lines. Arriving early and using our touring plans greatly reduces waiting. Here are other ways to reduce stress for kids:

1. SWITCHING OFF Several attractions have minimum height and/or age requirements. Some couples with children too small or too young forgo these attractions, while others take turns riding. Missing some of Disney's best rides is an unnecessary sacrifice, and waiting in line twice for the same ride is a tremendous waste of time.

ATTRACTIONS WHERE SWITCHING OFF IS USED	
THE MAGIC KINGDOM	**DISNEY'S ANIMAL KINGDOM**
• THE BARNSTORMER • BIG THUNDER MOUNTAIN RAILROAD • SEVEN DWARFS MINE TRAIN • SPACE MOUNTAIN • SPLASH MOUNTAIN • TOMORROWLAND SPEEDWAY	• AVATAR FLIGHT OF PASSAGE • DINOSAUR • EXPEDITION EVEREST • KALI RIVER RAPIDS • PRIMEVAL WHIRL
EPCOT	**DISNEY'S HOLLYWOOD STUDIOS**
• FROZEN EVER AFTER • MISSION: SPACE • SOARIN' • TEST TRACK	• ALIEN SWIRLING SAUCERS • *MILLENNIUM FALCON:* SMUGGLERS RUN • ROCK 'N' ROLLER COASTER • SLINKY DOG DASH • STAR TOURS—THE ADVENTURES CONTINUE • STAR WARS: RISE OF THE RESISTANCE • THE TWILIGHT ZONE TOWER OF TERROR

Instead, take advantage of switching off, also known as The Baby Swap or The Rider Swap (or The Baby/Rider Switch). To switch off, there must be at least two adults. Adults and children wait in line together. When you reach a cast member, say you want to switch off. The cast member will divide the group into those riding first and those riding second—that is, the nonriding child and up to three supervising adults. The first group will enter the ride. The cast member will scan the MagicBands of the adults riding second, who then wait with the nonriding child in a designated spot near the ride entrance.

When the first group returns, those adults take over watching the nonriding child while the other adults return to the FastPass+ line. The cast member will scan the second group's Magic Bands again, after which the group enters the ride's FastPass line. The entire group reunites after the second group finishes their ride.

Rider Switch passes—which are digital entitlements that are scanned into your MagicBand—must be used within 90 minutes of the same day that they're issued. You can only hold one Rider Switch pass at a time, but it will not interfere with any other FastPasses. There is no cost to use the switching-off option.

2. LINE GAMES Wise parents anticipate restlessness in line and plan activities to reduce the stress and boredom. In the morning, have waiting children discuss what they want to see and do during the day. Later, watch for and count Disney characters or play simple guessing games such as 20 Questions. Lines move continuously, so games requiring pen and paper are impractical. The holding area of a theater attraction, however, is a different story. Here, tic-tac-toe, hangman, drawing, and coloring make the time fly by. As an alternative, we've provided a trivia game for each park at the end of each park chapter.

3. PHONE FUN They're a great tool for staying entertained while waiting in a queue. If your kids have their own phones, they'll find something to entertain themselves. If your kids don't have their own phones, load some age-appropriate games on yours. Multiperson games are difficult while moving through an attraction queue, but there are a lot of single-person games above and beyond Angry Birds and Candy Crush Saga. Even though it's one person per each available phone, social features allow you to compare scores or play head-to-head with members of your party or even Facebook friends. Some apps are free of charge; make sure to check before downloading. For a good list of games see tinyurl.com/bestgamesapps or learn4good.com/games/mobile_phone _games.htm. Last but not least, bring lots of battery power!

4. LAST-MINUTE COLD FEET If your young child gets cold feet just before boarding a ride where there's no age or height requirement, you usually can arrange a switch-off with the loading attendant. (This happens frequently in Pirates of the Caribbean's dungeon waiting area.)

No law says you have to ride. If you reach the boarding area and someone is unhappy, tell an attendant you've changed your mind and you'll be shown the way out.

▌ CHARACTER ANALYSIS

THE LARGE, FRIENDLY COSTUMED versions of Mickey, Minnie, Donald, Goofy, and others—known as Disney characters—provide a link between Disney animated films and the theme parks. To people emotionally invested, the characters in Disney films are as real as next-door neighbors, never mind that they're just cartoons. In recent years, theme park personifications of the characters have also become real to us. It's not just a person in a mouse costume we see; it's Mickey himself. Similarly, meeting Goofy or Snow White is an encounter with a celebrity, a memory to be treasured.

BOB Check your *Times Guide* to find out any character's whereabouts in the parks.

While Disney animated-film characters number in the hundreds, only about 250 have been brought to life in costume. Of these, fewer than a fifth mix with guests; the others perform in shows or parades.

WDW CHARACTER-GREETING VENUES

MAGIC KINGDOM

MICKEY AND HIS POSSE

- **Daisy, Donald, Goofy, Minnie, Pluto** Pete's Silly Sideshow
- **Mickey** Town Square Theater (FastPass+)

DISNEY ROYALTY *(Princesses, Princes, Suitors, and Such)*

- **Aladdin, Jasmine** Adventureland • **Anna, Elsa** On float during the Festival of Fantasy Parade and in *Mickey's Royal Friendship Faire* stage show • **Ariel** Ariel's Grotto (FastPass+) • **Belle** *Enchanted Tales with Belle* (FastPass+) • **Cinderella, Elena of Avalor, Rapunzel, and Tiana** Princess Fairytale Hall (FastPass+)
- **Gaston** Fountain outside Gaston's Tavern • **Merida** Fairytale Garden
- **Snow White** Next to City Hall
- **The Tremaines and Fairy Godmother** In Fantasyland near Cinderella's Castle

FAIRIES

- **Tinker Bell** Town Square Theater (FastPass+)

MISCELLANEOUS

- **Alice** (*Alice in Wonderland*) Mad Tea Party
- **Buzz Lightyear** (*Toy Story*) Tomorrowland
- **Captain Jack Sparrow** (*Pirates of the Caribbean*) Adventureland
- **Mary Poppins** Liberty Square
- **Peter Pan** Fantasyland next to Peter Pan's Flight
- **Stitch** (*Lilo & Stitch*) Tomorrowland
- **Winnie the Pooh, Tigger** Fantasyland by The Many Adventures of Winnie the Pooh

EPCOT

MICKEY AND HIS POSSE

- **Daisy** *The American Adventure* • **Donald** Mexico • **Minnie*** World Showcase Gazebo • **Mickey, Goofy*** Innoventions West (Mickey will move to the Imagination! Pavilion; opening date unknown) • **Pluto*** Legacy Plaza West

DISNEY ROYALTY

- **Anna, Elsa** Norway • **Aurora** France gazebo • **Belle** France
- **Jasmine** Morocco • **Mulan** China • **Snow White** Germany

MISCELLANEOUS

- **Alice, Mary Poppins,** and (on rare occasions) **Bert** United Kingdom
- **Ralph, Vanellope** (*Wreck-It Ralph*) ImageWorks
- **Winnie the Pooh** United Kingdom

DISNEY'S ANIMAL KINGDOM

MICKEY AND HIS POSSE

- **Daisy** DinoLand U.S.A., Lower Cretaceous Trail
- **Donald** DinoLand U.S.A., Celebration Welcome Center
- **Goofy, Pluto** DinoLand U.S.A., gas station near Primeval Whirl
- **Mickey, Minnie** Adventurers Outpost on Discovery Island (FastPass+)

DISNEY ROYALTY

- **Pocahontas** Discovery Island at Character Landing

MISCELLANEOUS

- **Chip 'n' Dale** DinoLand U.S.A., Upper Cretaceous Trail
- **Flik** (*A Bug's Life*) Discovery Island across from Creature Comforts
- **Kevin** (*Up*) Discovery Island and near *UP! A Great Bird Adventure Show*
- **Launchpad McQuack** DinoLand U.S.A., Aerial Adventure Base
- **Russell** (*Up*) Discovery Island (**Dug** may appear randomly.)
- **Scrooge McDuck** DinoLand U.S.A., near Restaurantosaurus

* If you are a Chase Disney Visa cardholder, a special meet and greet, complete with free digital downloads from your PhotoPass account, is held in a small air-conditioned area outside the Imagination Pavilion. You will meet some combination of Minnie, Mickey, Pluto, and Goofy.

WDW CHARACTER-GREETING VENUES (continued)

DISNEY'S HOLLYWOOD STUDIOS
MICKEY AND HIS POSSE
- **Chip 'n' Dale** Grand Avenue
- **Daisy, Donald** Near park entrance
- **Goofy** Grand Avenue across from BaseLine Tap House
- **Minnie, Sorcerer Mickey** Red Carpet Dreams on Commissary Lane
- **Pluto** Animation Courtyard

DISNEY CHANNEL STARS
- **Doc McStuffins and Friends** Animation Courtyard near *Disney Junior Dance Party!*
- **Fancy Nancy** Animation Courtyard near *Disney Junior Dance Party!*
- **Vampirina** Animation Courtyard

MISCELLANEOUS
- **Buzz, Jessie, Woody, Green Army Men** (*Toy Story*) Toy Story Land
- **Cruz Ramirez** (*Cars*) Lightning McQueen's Racing Academy
- **Mike and Sulley** (*Monsters, Inc.*) Walt Disney Presents
- **Olaf** (*Frozen*) Celebrity Spotlight in Echo Lake
- **Chewbacca, Kylo Ren, BB-8** (*Star Wars*) Star Wars Launch Bay
- **Chewbacca, Kylo Ren, BB-8, Stormtroopers, Rey** (*Star Wars*) In Galaxy's Edge

BLIZZARD BEACH
- **Goofy** Appears seasonally, usually from spring break to Labor Day at park entrance

TYPHOON LAGOON
- **Lilo, Stitch** (*Lilo & Stitch*) Singapore Sal's near the park entrance. They meet in the spring and summer months on a rotational basis.

Characters are found in all major theme parks and at Disney Deluxe resorts that host character meals. They also often visit the Disney water parks and occasionally appear at Disney Springs.

See page 201 for tips on preparing your young children to meet the Disney characters for the first time.

CHARACTER WATCHING

FAMILIES PURSUE CHARACTERS relentlessly, armed with autograph books and cameras. Some characters are only rarely seen, so character watching has become character collecting. (To cash in on character collecting, Disney sells autograph books throughout the World.) Mickey, Minnie, and Goofy seem to be everywhere. But some characters, such as the Queen of Hearts and Friar Tuck, seldom come out, and quite a few appear only in parades or stage shows. Other characters appear only in a location consistent with their starring role. Buzz Lightyear (Tomorrowland) and Alice in Wonderland, Winnie the Pooh, and Peter Pan (Fantasyland) appear close to their eponymous attractions.

LILIANE The only way to meet The Beast at the Magic Kingdom is after dinner at Be Our Guest.

A Brooklyn, New York, dad complains that character collecting has gotten out of hand:

When we took our youngest child, he had already seen his siblings' collection and was determined to outdo them. Because the characters are available practically all day long at different locations, according to a printed schedule, which our son was old enough to read, we spent more time standing in line for autographs than we did for the most popular rides!

A family from Birmingham, Alabama, found some benefit in their children's pursuit of characters:

After my daughters got Pocahontas to sign your guidebook (we had no blank paper), we quickly bought an autograph book and gave in. It was actually the highlight of their trip, and my son even got into the act by helping get places in line for his sisters. They LOVED looking for characters. It was an amazing, totally unexpected part of our visit.

FROZEN FEVER

THERE IS NO DOUBT that the *Frozen* gals are here to stay. A movie sequel debuts in late 2019, and Cindy learned to reckon with the power of a northeaster, vacated the castle during the holiday season, and learned to "let it go." Here are our recommendations on how to have the most *Frozen* fun while visiting Walt Disney World.

Magic Kingdom

The Festival of Fantasy Parade is a must, and you can see Anna and Elsa on their float without standing in line. Anna and Elsa are also part of *Mickey's Royal Friendship Faire,* the castle forecourt stage show.

Epcot

Frozen Ever After is, of course, an absolute must. The ride's popularity draws long lines all day. Frozen Ever After is a Tier A FastPass+, but Meet Anna and Elsa at Royal Sommerhus doesn't offer FastPass+.

Disney's Hollywood Studios

For the First Time in Forever: A Frozen Sing-Along Celebration at the Hyperion Theater is a fun and interactive show where Anna, Elsa, Kristoff, and the royal historians of Arendelle tell the story of their kingdom. Olaf, the quirky snowman, takes up residence inside the Celebrity Spotlight at Echo Lake.

When All Els(a)e Fails

You won't find anything *Frozen* related at the Animal Kingdom. But there is always Disney Springs, where you can give your princess a total Anna or Elsa makeover at Bibbidi Bobbidi Boutique. If this, too, fails, there is only one thing left to do: let it go!

CHARACTER DINING: WHAT TO EXPECT

BECAUSE OF THE INCREDIBLE POPULARITY of character dining, reservations can be hard to come by if you wait until a couple of months before your vacation to book your choices. What's more, you must provide Disney with a credit card number. Your card will be charged $10 per person if you don't show or you cancel your reservation less than 24 hours in advance; you may, however, reschedule with no penalty. See "Getting Advance Reservations at Popular Restaurants" (page 145) for the full story.

LILIANE Even with Advance Reservations, expect to wait 10–20 minutes to be seated.

At very popular character meals like the breakfast at Cinderella's Royal Table, you're required to make a for-real reservation and guarantee it with a for-real deposit.

Character meals are bustling affairs held in hotels' or theme parks' largest full-service restaurants. Character breakfasts offer a fixed menu served individually, family-style, or on a buffet. The typical breakfast includes scrambled eggs; bacon, sausage, and ham; hash browns; waffles or French toast; biscuits, rolls, or pastries; and fruit. Family-style meals, such as at Akershus, are served in large skillets or platters at your table. Seconds (or thirds) are free.

Character-dinner buffets, such as those at 1900 Park Fare at the Grand Floridian and Chef Mickey's at the Contemporary Resort, separate the kids' fare from the grown-ups', though everyone is free to eat from both lines. Typically, the children's buffet includes hamburgers, hot dogs, pizza, fish sticks, chicken nuggets, macaroni and cheese, and peanut-butter-and-jelly sandwiches. Selections at the adult buffet usually include prime rib or other carved meat, baked or broiled seafood, pasta, chicken, an ethnic dish or two, vegetables, potatoes, and salad.

At all meals, characters circulate around the room while you eat. During your meal, each of the three to five characters present will visit your table, arriving one at a time to cuddle the kids (and sometimes the adults), pose for photos, and sign autographs. Keep autograph books (with pens) handy and cameras or phones at the ready. For the best photos, adults should sit across the table from their children. Seat the children where characters can easily reach them. If a table is against a wall, for example, adults should sit with their backs to the wall and children on the aisle.

FELICITY Chef Mickey's is my favorite place to eat. I always have ice cream with lots of toppings and give Mickey and the gang a big hug. The napkin twirling is much fun.

FELICITY The stepsisters at 1900 Park Fare are so much fun. We made ugly faces instead of posing for photos, and it was hilarious. I liked the food, and cast members were helpful when I had a problem with my autograph book.

Servers generally don't rush you to leave after you've eaten—you can stay as long as you wish to enjoy the characters. Remember, however, that lots of eager kids and adults are waiting not so patiently to be admitted.

When to Go

Attending a character breakfast usually prevents you from arriving at the theme parks in time for opening. Because early morning is best for touring and you don't want to burn daylight lingering over breakfast, we suggest the following:

continued on page 255

CHARACTER-MEAL HIT PARADE

1. CINDERELLA'S ROYAL TABLE MAGIC KINGDOM

MEALS SERVED Breakfast, lunch, and dinner **SETTING** ★★★★
CHARACTERS Cinderella, Ariel, Aurora, Jasmine, Snow White, Fairy Godmother
TYPE OF SERVICE Fixed menu **FOOD VARIETY & QUALITY** ★★★
NOISE LEVEL Quiet **CHARACTER–GUEST RATIO** 1:26

2. AKERSHUS ROYAL BANQUET HALL EPCOT

MEALS SERVED Breakfast, lunch, and dinner **SETTING** ★★★★
CHARACTERS 4–6 characters chosen from Ariel, Belle, Snow White, Aurora,
Mary Poppins (occasionally), and Cinderella
TYPE OF SERVICE Family-style and menu (all you can eat)
FOOD VARIETY & QUALITY ★★★½
NOISE LEVEL Quiet **CHARACTER–GUEST RATIO** 1:54

3. CHEF MICKEY'S CONTEMPORARY RESORT

MEALS SERVED Breakfast, brunch, and dinner **SETTING** ★★★
CHARACTERS Mickey, Minnie, Donald, Goofy, Pluto
TYPE OF SERVICE Buffet
FOOD VARIETY & QUALITY Breakfast and brunch ★★★ Dinner ★★★½
NOISE LEVEL Very loud **CHARACTER–GUEST RATIO** 1:56

4. 1900 PARK FARE GRAND FLORIDIAN RESORT

MEALS SERVED Breakfast and dinner **SETTING** ★★★
CHARACTERS *Breakfast:* Mary Poppins, Alice, Mad Hatter, Pooh, Tigger
Dinner: Cinderella, Prince Charming, Lady Tremaine, the two stepsisters
TYPE OF SERVICE Buffet **FOOD VARIETY & QUALITY** Breakfast ★★★ Dinner ★★★½
NOISE LEVEL Moderate **CHARACTER–GUEST RATIO** Breakfast 1:54 Dinner 1:44

5. TUSKER HOUSE RESTAURANT ANIMAL KINGDOM

MEALS SERVED Breakfast, lunch, and dinner **SETTING** ★★★
CHARACTERS Donald, Daisy, Mickey, Goofy
TYPE OF SERVICE Buffet **FOOD VARIETY & QUALITY** ★★★
NOISE LEVEL Very loud **CHARACTER–GUEST RATIO** 1:112

6. THE CRYSTAL PALACE MAGIC KINGDOM

MEALS SERVED Breakfast, lunch, and dinner **SETTING** ★★★
CHARACTERS Pooh, Eeyore, Piglet, Tigger **TYPE OF SERVICE** Buffet
FOOD VARIETY & QUALITY Breakfast ★★½ **LUNCH AND DINNER** ★★★
NOISE LEVEL Very loud
CHARACTER–GUEST RATIO Breakfast 1:67 Lunch and dinner 1:89

7. ARTIST POINT WILDERNESS LODGE

MEAL SERVED Dinner **SETTING** ★★★★
CHARACTERS Snow White, Dopey, Grumpy, Evil Queen
TYPE OF SERVICE Fixed menu with several choices
FOOD VARIETY & QUALITY ★★★½
NOISE LEVEL Moderate **CHARACTER–GUEST RATIO** 1:35

8. TRATTORIA AL FORNO BOARDWALK

MEAL SERVED Breakfast **SETTING** ★★★½
CHARACTERS Rapunzel, Flynn Rider, Ariel, Prince Eric
TYPE OF SERVICE Fixed menu with several choices
FOOD VARIETY & QUALITY ★★★½
NOISE LEVEL Quiet **CHARACTER–GUEST RATIO** 1:50

CHARACTER-MEAL HIT PARADE *(continued)*

9. HOLLYWOOD & VINE   DISNEY'S HOLLYWOOD STUDIOS

MEALS SERVED Breakfast, lunch, and dinner   **SETTING** ★★½
CHARACTERS *Breakfast:* Goofy, Sofia the First, Doc McStuffins, Vampirina; *Lunch and dinner:* Minnie's Seasonal Dining: Minnie Mouse, Mickey Mouse, Donald Duck, Daisy Duck, and Goofy with seasonal table activities and music
TYPE OF SERVICE Buffet   **FOOD VARIETY & QUALITY** ★★★
NOISE LEVEL Moderate   **CHARACTER–GUEST RATIO** 1:71

10. CAPE MAY CAFE   BEACH CLUB RESORT

MEAL SERVED Breakfast   **SETTING** ★★★
CHARACTERS Goofy, Donald, Minnie, Daisy
TYPE OF SERVICE Buffet   **FOOD VARIETY & QUALITY** ★★½
NOISE LEVEL Moderate   **CHARACTER–GUEST RATIO** 1:67

11. 'OHANA   POLYNESIAN VILLAGE RESORT

MEAL SERVED Breakfast   **SETTING** ★★
CHARACTERS Lilo and Stitch, Mickey, Pluto
TYPE OF SERVICE Family-style   **FOOD VARIETY & QUALITY** ★★½
NOISE LEVEL Loud   **CHARACTER–GUEST RATIO** 1:57

12. GARDEN GRILL RESTAURANT   EPCOT

MEAL SERVED Breakfast, lunch, and dinner   **SETTING** ★★★★
CHARACTERS Mickey, Pluto, Chip 'n' Dale
TYPE OF SERVICE Family-style   **FOOD VARIETY & QUALITY** ★★★½
NOISE LEVEL Very quiet   **CHARACTER–GUEST RATIO** 1:46

13. GARDEN GROVE   SWAN

MEALS SERVED Breakfast (Sat. and Sun.), dinner (nightly)   **SETTING** ★★½
CHARACTERS Chip 'n' Dale, Goofy, Pluto
TYPE OF SERVICE Buffet   **FOOD VARIETY & QUALITY** ★★½
NOISE LEVEL Moderate   **CHARACTER–GUEST RATIO** 1:198, frequently much better

continued from page 253

1. Schedule your in-park character breakfast for the first seating if the park opens at 9 a.m. or later. You'll be admitted to the park before other guests (admission is still required) through a special line at the turnstiles. Arrive early to be among the first parties seated.

2. Go to a character dinner or lunch instead of breakfast. It will be a nice break.

3. Schedule the last seating for breakfast. Have a light snack such as cereal or bagels before you head to the parks for opening, hit the most popular attractions until 10:15 a.m. or so, and then head to brunch. The buffet should keep you fueled until dinner, especially if you eat another light snack in the afternoon.

4. Go on your arrival or departure day. The day you arrive and check in is usually good for a character dinner. Settle at your hotel, swim, and then dine with the characters. This strategy has the added benefit of exposing your children to the characters before chance encounters at the parks. Some children, moreover, won't settle down to enjoy the parks until they have seen Mickey. Departure day is also good for a character meal. Schedule a character breakfast on your checkout day before you head for the airport or begin your drive home.

5. Go on a rest day. If you plan to stay 5 or more days, you'll probably take a day or half-day from touring to rest or do something else.

How to Choose a Character Meal

Many readers ask for advice about character meals. This question from a Waterloo, Iowa, mom is typical:

Are all character breakfasts pretty much the same, or are some better than others? How should I go about choosing one?

LILIANE If you've secured Advance Reservations for a character meal, I say roll out the costume chest. Dress up your little one—from princess to pirate, anything goes.

In fact, some are better, sometimes much better. When we evaluate character meals, we look for these things:

1. **THE CHARACTERS** The meals offer a diverse assortment of characters. Select a meal that features your kids' favorites. Check out our Character-Meal Hit Parade table (see pages 254–255) to see which characters are assigned to each meal. Most restaurants stick with the same characters. Even so, check the lineup when you call to make Advance Reservations.

2. **ATTENTION FROM THE CHARACTERS** At all character meals, characters circulate among guests, hugging children, posing for pictures, and signing autographs. How much time a character spends with you and your children depends primarily on the ratio of characters to guests. The more characters and fewer guests, the better. Because many character meals never fill to capacity, the character-to-guest ratios found in our Character-Meal Hit Parade table have been adjusted to reflect an average attendance. Even so, there's quite a range. The best ratio is at Cinderella's Royal Table, where there's approximately 1 character to every 26 guests. However, Cindy does not actually join the diners (but the other characters at the Royal Table do); rather, she sees her guests for a quick chat and photo opportunity upon arrival.

   The worst ratio is theoretically at the Swan hotel's Garden Grove, where there could be as few as 1 character for every 198 guests. We say *theoretically*, however, because in practice there are far fewer guests at the Garden Grove than at character meals in Disney-owned resorts, and often more characters.

3. **THE SETTING** Some character meals are in exotic settings. Our table rates each meal's setting with the familiar scale of zero (worst) to five (best) stars. Two restaurants, Cinderella's Royal Table in the Magic Kingdom and Garden Grill Restaurant in The Land Pavilion at Epcot, deserve special mention. Cinderella's Royal Table is on the first and second floors of Cinderella Castle in Fantasyland, offering guests a look inside the castle. The Garden Grill is a revolving restaurant overlooking several scenes from the Living with the Land boat ride. Also at Epcot, the popular princess character meals are held in the castlelike Akershus Royal Banquet Hall. Though Chef Mickey's at the Contemporary Resort is rather sterile in appearance, it affords a great view of the monorail running through the hotel. Themes and settings of the remaining character-meal venues, while apparent to adults, will be lost on most children.

4. **THE FOOD** Though some food served at character meals is quite good, most is average (palatable but nothing to get excited about). In variety, consistency, and quality, restaurants generally do a better job with breakfast than with lunch or dinner (if served). Some restaurants offer a buffet, while others opt for one-skillet family-style service, in which all hot items are served from the same pot or skillet. To help you sort it out, we rate the food at each character meal in our table using the five-star scale.

5. **THE PROGRAM** Some larger restaurants stage modest performances where the characters dance, lead a parade around the room, or lead songs and cheers. For some guests, these activities give the meal a celebratory air; for others, they turn what was already mayhem into absolute chaos. Either way, the antics consume time the characters could spend with families at their table.

6. **NOISE** If you want to eat in peace, character meals are a bad choice. That said, some are much noisier than others. Our table gives you an idea of what to expect.

7. **WHICH MEAL** Though breakfasts seem to be most popular, character lunches and dinners are usually more practical because they don't interfere with early-morning touring. During hot weather, a character lunch can be heavenly.

8. **COST** Dinners cost more than lunches, and lunches cost more than breakfasts. Prices for meals vary considerably from the least expensive to the most expensive restaurant. Breakfasts run $60–$65 for adults and $35–$40 for kids ages 3–9. For character lunches or dinners, expect to pay $71–$82 for adults and $38–$48 for kids. Tax and gratuity are included. Little ones age 2 years and younger eat free. The meals at the high end of the price range are at Cinderella's Royal Table in the Magic Kingdom and Akershus Royal Banquet Hall at Epcot.

9. **ADVANCE RESERVATIONS** You can make Advance Reservations for character meals 180 days before you wish to dine (Disney resort guests can reserve 180 days out for the entire length of their trip, up to 10 days). Advance Reservations for most character meals are easy to obtain even if you call only a couple of weeks before you leave home. Meals at Cinderella's Royal Table, Be Our Guest, and Story Book Dining at Artist Point are another story. For these three, you'll need our strategy (see Part Four), as well as help from Congress and the Pope.

10. **"FRIENDS"** For some venues, Disney has stopped specifying characters scheduled for a particular meal. Instead, a specific character "and friends"— for example, "Pooh and friends," meaning Eeyore, Piglet, and Tigger, or some combination thereof, or "Mickey and friends" with some assortment chosen among Minnie, Goofy, Pluto, Donald, Daisy, Chip, and Dale—are listed.

11. **THE BUM'S RUSH** Most character meals are leisurely affairs, and you can usually stay as long as you want. An exception is Cinderella's Royal Table in the Magic Kingdom. Because Cindy's is in such high demand, the restaurant does everything short of prechewing your food to move you through, as this European mother of a 5-year-old can attest:

> We dined a lot, including three character meals and a few Signature restaurants, and every meal was awesome except for lunch with Cinderella in the castle. While I'd often read it wouldn't be a rushed affair, it was exactly that. We had barely sat down when the appetizers were thrown on our table, the princesses each spent just a few seconds with our daughter—almost no interaction—and the side dishes were cold. We were out of there within 40 minutes and felt very stressed. Considering the price for the meal, I cannot recommend it.

12. **BOYS** To answer a common reader question, most character meals featuring Disney princesses include some element to appeal to the young roughnecks. A Texas mom shares her experience:

We ate at Cinderella's Royal Table for lunch, and my sons were made to feel very welcome. They loved the swords they received and have enjoyed "fighting off the dragons" with them.

Getting an Advance Reservation at Cinderella's Royal Table

Once upon a time, breakfast was the only character meal at Cinderella Castle in the Magic Kingdom. Reservations for every table were gone within minutes of becoming available each morning. Disney responded to this popularity by adding character lunches and dinners—and jacking up the price to $65–$82 per adult. As a result, it's now much easier to get into Cinderella's Royal Table for some meals during your stay. Also, the opening of the wildly popular Be Our Guest Restaurant in Fantasyland has taken a lot of pressure off Cindy's. The new kid on the block is Story Book Dining at Artist Point with Snow White (Wilderness Lodge). Book as soon as your 180-day window opens. If you're visiting during peak periods or you have to have a reservation at a specific, popular time, see our Advance Reservation tips starting on page 145.

DISNEY'S ROYAL ALTERNATIVES If you're unwilling to fund Cinderella's shoe habit or you simply weren't able to get an Advance Reservation before young Ariel graduates from college, rest assured there are other venues that will feed you in the company of princesses.

Akershus Royal Banquet Hall, in the Norway Pavilion of Epcot's World Showcase, serves family-style breakfast, lunch, and dinner. Ariel, Cinderella, Snow White, and Belle are regulars. Entrées are a combination of traditional buffet fare and the occasional Scandinavian dish.

LILIANE The character meals at Akershus are my all-time favorite. There are plenty of princesses, and I love the food.

Dinner at the Grand Floridian's **1900 Park Fare** features the whole crew from *Cinderella,* including Lady Tremaine and the stepsisters (breakfast is a supercalifragilisticexpialidocious affair with Mary Poppins and friends, which currently includes Alice in Wonderland, the Mad Hatter, Winnie the Pooh, and Tigger). At $40–$56 per adult and $25–$31 for children age 9 and under (prices are seasonal and include tax but not tip), this is a far more economical option for diners wishing to get their princess on, and the stepsisters are an absolute hoot. This meal is also a little more boy-friendly if you're entertaining a mixed crowd. Finally, remember that your princess may be feeding off your own excitement over eating in the castle—she might be just as happy with a plastic crown purchased in the gift shop and a burger from Cosmic Ray's. We recommend visiting 1900 Park Fare on a day when you're not visiting the parks.

If you were unable to get a FastPass+ for the Frozen Ever After ride and your little Anna and Elsa really want to experience the ride without a minimum hour wait in line, consider breakfast at Akershus Royal Banquet Hall. Pick a day when the park opens at 9 a.m. with no early morning hours. Next, book the first breakfast seating available, probably 8 a.m. Enjoy the breakfast, and by 8:45 a.m. make your way outside to the ride, right next to the restaurant, and be the first in line to ride without a FastPass+ reservation.

Story Book Dining at **Artist Point** with Snow White is a new character dinner at Wilderness Lodge. The prix fixe dinner comes with shared appetizers and desserts, and guests choose their own entrée. Prime rib, roasted chicken, and braised veal shank are among the choices. One of the desserts comes in a smoking box called The Hunter's Gift to the Queen. While you can't keep the box, you may enjoy the maple popcorn and chocolate ganache hearts inside. During the meal, Snow White, Dopey, and Grumpy entertain guests with sing-alongs and a mini parade around the restaurant to the tune of "Whistle While You Work." All three also visit each table for pictures and autographs. At the end of the meal, guests can meet the Evil Queen in front of a themed backdrop.

Meeting the fairest of them all is pricey (adults $60, children ages 3–9 $35), but the fun setting comes with above-average food and includes not-often-seen characters.

OTHER CHARACTER EVENTS

A CAMPFIRE AND SING-ALONG are held nightly (times vary with the season) near the Meadow Trading Post at **Fort Wilderness Resort & Campground.** Chip 'n' Dale lead the songs, and a Disney film is shown. The free program is open to Disney resort guests (☎ 407-824-2900).

WHEN KIDS GET LOST

IF ONE OF YOUR CHILDREN gets separated from you, don't panic. All things considered, Walt Disney World is about the safest place to get lost we can think of. Disney cast members are trained to watch for seemingly lost kids, and because children become detached from parents so frequently in the theme parks, cast members know exactly what to do.

If you lose a child in the Magic Kingdom, report it to a Disney employee, and then check at the Baby Care Center and at City Hall, where lost-children logs are kept. At Epcot, report the loss, then check at the Baby Care Center. At Animal Kingdom, go to the Baby Care Center in Discovery Island. At Disney's Hollywood Studios, report the loss at Guest Relations, at the entrance end of Hollywood Boulevard. Paging isn't used, but in an emergency, an all-points bulletin will be issued throughout the park(s) via internal communications. If a Disney cast member encounters a lost child, he or she will take the child immediately to the park's Baby Care Center.

BOB We suggest that children younger than age 8 be color-coded by dressing them in vacation uniforms with distinctively colored T-shirts or equally eye-catching apparel.

As comforting as this knowledge is, however, it's nevertheless scary when a child turns up missing. Fortunately, circumstances surrounding a child becoming lost are fairly predictable and, for the most part, are also preventable.

Iron on or sew a label into each child's shirt that states his or her name, your name, the name of your hotel, and, if you have one, your cell phone number. Accomplish the same thing by writing the information on a strip of masking tape or by attaching a MagicBand to the child's clothing (resist the urge to put it on like a dog collar).

Other than just blending in, children tend to become separated from their parents under remarkably similar circumstances:

1. PREOCCUPIED SOLO PARENT In this situation, the party's only adult is preoccupied with something like buying refreshments, taking pictures, or using the restroom. Junior is there one second and gone the next.

2. THE HIDDEN EXIT Sometimes parents wait on the sidelines while two or more young children experience a ride together. Parents expect the kids to exit in one place and, lo and behold, the youngsters pop out somewhere else. Exits from some attractions are distant from the entrances. Make sure you know exactly where your children will emerge before letting them ride by themselves. If in doubt, ask a cast member.

3. AFTER THE SHOW At the end of many shows and rides, a Disney staffer will announce, "Check for personal belongings and take small children by the hand." When dozens, if not hundreds, of people leave an attraction simultaneously, it's surprisingly easy for parents to lose contact with their children unless they have them directly in tow.

4. RESTROOM PROBLEMS Mom tells 6-year-old Tommy, "I'll be sitting on this bench when you come out of the restroom." Three possibilities: One, Tommy exits through a different door and becomes disoriented (Mom may not know there's another door). Two, Mom decides she also will use the restroom, and Tommy emerges to find her gone. Three, Mom pokes around in a shop while keeping an eye on the bench but misses Tommy when he comes out.

If you can't find a companion- or family-accessible restroom, make sure there's only one exit. The restroom on a passageway between Frontierland and Adventureland in the Magic Kingdom is the all-time worst for disorienting visitors. Children and adults alike have walked in from the Adventureland side and walked out on the Frontierland side (and vice versa). Adults realize quickly that something is wrong. Children, however, sometimes fail to recognize the problem. Designate a distinctive meeting spot and give clear instructions: "I'll meet you by this flagpole. If you get out first, stay right here." Have your child repeat the directions back to you.

5. PARADES There are many parades and shows at which the audience stands. Children tend to jockey for a better view. By moving a little this way and that, the child quickly puts distance between you before either of you notices.

6. MASS MOVEMENTS Be on guard when huge crowds disperse after fireworks or a parade, or at park closing. With 20,000–40,000 people at once in an area, it's very easy to get separated from a child or others in your party. Use extra caution after the evening fireworks or any other day-capping event. Families should have specific plans for where to meet if they get separated.

7. CHARACTER GREETINGS Children sometimes become lost at character encounters. Usually, there's a lot of activity around a character, with both adults and children touching it or posing for pictures. Most commonly, Mom and Dad stay in the crowd while Junior approaches the character.

BOB Our advice for parents with preschoolers is to stay with the kids when they meet characters, stepping back only to take a quick picture.

In the excitement and with the character moving around, Junior heads in the wrong direction to look for Mom and Dad. In the words of a Salt Lake City mom: "Milo was shaking hands with Dopey one minute, then some confusion happened and Milo was gone."

8. GETTING LOST AT ANIMAL KINGDOM It's especially easy to lose a child in Animal Kingdom, particularly at the Oasis entryway, on the Maharajah Jungle Trek, and on the Gorilla Falls Exploration Trail. Mom and Dad will stop to observe an animal. Junior stays close for a minute or so and then, losing patience, wanders to the exhibit's other side or to a different exhibit.

9. LOST . . . IN THE ZONE More often than you'd think, kids don't realize they're lost. They are so distracted that they sometimes wander around for quite a while before they notice their whole family has disappeared. Fortunately, Disney cast members are trained to look out for kids who have zoned out and will either help them find their family or deposit them at the Baby Care Center.

LILIANE'S TIPS FOR KEEPING TRACK OF YOUR BROOD

ON A GOOD DAY, it's possible for Liliane to lose a cantaloupe in her purse. Thus challenged, she works overtime developing ways to hang on to her possessions. Here's what she has to say:

I've seen parents write their cell phone numbers on a child's leg with a felt-tip marker . . . effective but crude. Before you resort to that, or perhaps a cattle brand, consider some of the tips I've dreamed up. My friends, some much ditzier than I, have used them with great success.

- On your very first day in the parks, teach your kids how to recognize a Disney cast member by pointing out the Disney name tags they wear. Instruct your children to find someone with such a name tag if they get separated from you.

- Same-colored shirts for the whole family will help you gather your troops in an easy and fun way. Opt for just a uniform color or go the extra mile and have the shirts printed with a logo such as "The Brown Family's Assault on the Mouse." You might also include the date or the year of your visit.

- Clothing labels are great. If you don't sew, buy labels that you can iron on the garment. If you own a cell phone, be sure to include the number on the label. If you don't own a cell phone, put in the phone number of the hotel where you'll be staying. Another option is a custom-made temporary tattoo with all the pertinent info. They're cheap, last 2 weeks, don't wash off, and solve the problem of having to sew or iron a label on every garment. (They can be purchased online at safetytat.com or tattooswithapurpose.com.)

- In pet stores you can have name tags printed for a very reasonable price. These are great to add to necklaces and bracelets or attach to your child's shoelace or belt loop.

- When you check in to the hotel, take a hotel business card for each member in your party, especially those old enough to carry wallets and purses.

- Agree on a meeting place before you see a parade, fireworks, or nighttime spectacles such as Epcot's fireworks show, *Rivers of Light,* and *Fantasmic!* Make sure the meeting place is in the park (as opposed to the car or outside the front gate).

- If you have a digital camera or phone camera, take a picture of your kids every morning. If they get lost, the picture will show what they look like and what they're wearing.

- If all the members of your party have cell phones, it's easy to locate each other. Be aware, however, that the ambient noise in the parks is so loud that you probably won't hear your phone ring. Your best bet is to carry your phone in a front pants pocket and to program the phone to vibrate. Even better, send text messages. If any of your younger kids carry cell phones, secure the phones with a strap. Please make sure your cell phone still has power at the end of the day. Carry an extra battery or use mealtimes to recharge all phones.

- Save key tags and luggage tags for use on items you bring to the parks, including your stroller, diaper bag, and backpack or hip pack.

- Don't underestimate the power of the permanent marker, such as a Sharpie. They are great for labeling pretty much anything. Mini-Sharpies are sold as clip-ons and are handy for collecting character autographs. The Sharpie also serves well for writing down the location of your car in the parking lot.

- Finally, a word about keeping track of your MagicBands: they're difficult, but not impossible, to lose. Most adults will be fine, but slender children without much articulation between the forearm and wrist need to wear the band more tightly. If you're worried about the band slipping off, ask for a park card instead (see page 64). Alternatively, have your child wear the MagicBand on a chain, much like a necklace. For very young children, I strongly recommend that an adult holds on to the MagicBand—no need to put yourself through all that stress.

STROLLERS

LILIANE Rental strollers are too large for all infants and many toddlers. If you plan to rent a stroller for your infant or toddler, bring pillows, cushions, or rolled towels to buttress him in.

STROLLERS ARE AVAILABLE for rent at all four theme parks and Disney Springs (single stroller, $15 per day with no deposit, $13 per day for multiday rentals; double stroller, $31 per day with no deposit, $27 per day for multiday rentals; stroller rentals at Disney Springs require a $100 credit card deposit). Strollers are

welcome at Blizzard Beach and Typhoon Lagoon, but no rentals are available.

With multiday rentals, you can skip the rental line entirely after your first visit—just head to the stroller-handout area, show your receipt, and you'll be wheeling out in no time. If you rent a stroller at the Magic Kingdom and you decide to go to Epcot, Animal Kingdom, or Disney's Hollywood Studios, turn in your Magic Kingdom stroller and present your receipt at the next park. You'll be issued another stroller at no additional charge.

You can rent a stroller in advance; this allows you to bypass the payment line and go straight to the pickup line. Disney resort guests can pay ahead at their resort's gift shop, so hang on to your receipts!

Several Orlando companies undercut Disney's prices, provide more comfortable strollers, and deliver them to your hotel. Most of the larger companies offer the same stroller models (the Baby Jogger City Mini Single, for example), so the primary differences between the companies are price and service.

Regarding service, Disney currently allows just a handful of stroller companies to drop off and pick up at a Disney hotel without your having to be physically present to meet the delivery person, thus freeing you to run around the parks instead of waiting around at your hotel. The first three companies reviewed below are part of the **Disney Preferred Stroller Provider** program, a fact they mention prominently on their websites. Before renting from another company, check to see if it's on the featured list too.

We had mom and touringplans.com writer Angela Dahlgren rent strollers from different companies, use them in the parks, and then return them. Her evaluations cover the overall experience, from the ease with which the stroller was rented to the delivery of the stroller, its condition on arrival, usability in the parks, and the return process.

Kingdom Strollers (☎ 407-271-5301; kingdomstrollers.com) topped Angela's list, getting top marks for website ease of use, stroller selection, condition, and overall service. The stroller was also much easier to use than Disney's standard stroller, had more storage, and had an easier-to-use braking system. A rental of 1–3 nights costs $45, and 4–7 nights is $65. That makes the break-even point for choosing Kingdom Strollers over Disney somewhere around 5 days.

Angela also recommends **Orlando Stroller Rentals, LLC** (☎ 800-281-0884; orlandostrollerrentals.com), which has similar prices, plus an excellent website that allows you to easily compare the features of different strollers.

Disney recommends **Magic Strollers** (☎ 866-866-6177; magicstrollers.com), and it offers the same services. Prices are $35 for a single (with a 2-night minimum), plus $7 per day, or $45 for a double, plus $8 a day.

In 2019 Disney introduced new rules regarding the maximum allowable dimensions for strollers, banning oversized strollers and stroller wagons from its parks. The new regulation requires strollers to be less than 31 inches (79 centimeters) wide and 52 inches (132 centimeters) long. **Fantasy Strollers** (fantasystrollers.com) announced that its new strollers, themed after Cinderella's pumpkin carriage or a spaceship, will comply with the new directives and be permitted inside the parks.

Another important matter is protection against the sun. Liliane always used a stroller with an adjustable canopy and also had lightweight pieces of cloth handy to protect her child from the sun. You can use anything for that purpose; a receiving blanket works well. Liliane used clothespins and safety pins to attach the pieces to the canopy. Don't overdo it, though. While it's important to protect your child from the sun, make sure there is enough air circulating—temperatures climb quickly in enclosed spaces.

Strollers are a must for infants and toddlers, but we've observed many sharp parents renting strollers for somewhat older children (up to age 5 or so). The stroller keeps parents from having to carry kids when they sag and provides a convenient place to carry water and snacks.

A family from Tulsa, Oklahoma, recommends springing for a double stroller:

We rent a double for baggage room or in case the older child gets tired of walking.

If you go to your hotel for a break and intend to return to the park, leave your rental stroller by an attraction near the park entrance, marking it with something personal, such as a bandanna. When you return, your stroller will be waiting.

A Charleston, West Virginia, mom recommends a backup plan:

Strollers are not allowed in lines for rides, so if you have a small child (ours was 4) who needs to be held, you might end up holding him a long time. If I had it to do over, I'd bring along some kind of child carrier for when he was out of the stroller.

Bringing your own stroller is permitted. However, only collapsible strollers are allowed on monorails, parking lot trams, and buses. Your stroller is unlikely to be stolen, but mark it with your name. If you're bringing your own stroller to save money, you're flying, and you're checking the stroller as luggage, see if the airline's luggage fees outweigh the cost of renting or buying in Orlando.

BOB Don't try to lock your stroller to a fence, post, or anything else at WDW. You'll get in big trouble.

Having her own stroller was indispensable to a Mechanicsville, Virginia, mother of two toddlers:

> How I was going to manage to get the kids from the parking lot to the park was a big worry for me before I made the trip. I didn't read anywhere that it was possible to walk to the entrance of the parks instead of taking the tram, so I wasn't sure I could do it.
>
> I found that for me personally, since I have two kids aged 1 and 2, it was easier to walk to the entrance of the park from the parking lot with the kids in my own stroller than to take the kids out of the stroller, fold the stroller (while trying to control the two kids and associated gear), load the stroller and the kids onto the tram, etc. No matter where I was parked, I could always just walk to the entrance.

An Oklahoma mom, however, reports a bad experience with bringing her own stroller:

> The first time we took our kids, we had a large stroller (big mistake). It is so much easier to rent one in the park. The large (personally owned) strollers are nearly impossible to get on the buses and are a hassle at the airport. I remember feeling dread when a bus pulled up that was even semifull of people. People look at you like you have a cage full of live chickens when you drag a heavy stroller onto the bus.

Liliane recommends that you bring your own stroller or rent a stroller for the entire duration of your stay. It is so much easier to get around with your child in a stroller, especially at the end of the day when you leave the park and have to return to your hotel via the parking lot or bus station. Once you are back at the hotel, you may also have quite a walk to your room.

STROLLER WARS Sometimes strollers disappear while you're enjoying a ride or show. Disney staff often rearrange strollers parked outside an attraction. This may be done to tidy up or to clear a walkway. Don't assume that your stroller is stolen because it isn't where you left it. It may be neatly arranged a few feet away—or perhaps more than a few feet away.

Sometimes, however, strollers are taken by mistake or ripped off by people not wanting to spend time replacing one that's missing. Don't be alarmed if yours disappears. You won't have to buy it, and you'll be issued a new one.

You'd be surprised at how many people are injured by strollers pushed by parents who are aggressive or in a hurry. Given the number of strollers, pedestrians, and tight spaces, mishaps are inevitable on both sides. A simple apology and a smile are usually the best remediation.

A mom from New Hampshire reports:

> If you're at park opening going toward a headliner attraction with a stroller, think of the stroller as a tractor-trailer during rush hour traffic—everyone cuts in front of you, and they get mad if you run into them. ABANDON the stroller and proceed on foot!

A mom from Arkansas reports:

When we exited Spaceship Earth, we were so turned around the first time we parked our stroller that it took us quite a while to find it. Find a central location to a few of the rides you want to explore, and park your stroller strategically. You will save time and steps that way.

While waiting at rope drop to head to the Frozen Ever After ride at Epcot, Bob and Liliane were horrified to see an expectant mom being run over by a stroller. Please look out for your fellow guests. The ride will still be there and is not worth the injuries nor the remorse.

PART SEVEN

The MAGIC KINGDOM

OPENED IN 1971, THE MAGIC KINGDOM was the first of Walt Disney World's four theme parks to be built. Many of the attractions found here are originals from that park opening, and a few—including **Cinderella Castle, Pirates of the Caribbean,** and **Splash Mountain**—have helped define the basic elements of theme park attractions the world over. Indeed, the Magic Kingdom is undoubtedly what most people think of when they think of Walt Disney World.

But the Magic Kingdom is also welcoming the future, as a roller coaster–style attraction, similar to Tron Lightcycle Power Run at Disney's Shanghai park, is currently being built in Tomorrowland next to Space Mountain. Construction required an adjustment to the track of the Tomorrowland Speedway, which reopened in May, and a temporary shutdown of Walt Disney World Railroad, which will be closed throughout 2019, with no reopening date announced as we went to print. The *Tron* attraction is slated to open in 2021, in time for Walt Disney World's 50th anniversary.

Stroller, wheelchair, and **ECV/ESV rentals** are to the right of the train station, and **lockers** are on the station's ground floor. The lockers operate with a digital keypad system; they accept cash but can only give a maximum of $15 change, so don't try to pay with a $100! On your left as you enter Main Street is **City Hall,** the center for information, Guest Relations, lost and found, guided tours, and entertainment schedules. **ATMs** are underneath the Main Street railroad station, near the Transportation and Ticket Center (TTC), near City Hall, near the Frontierland Shootin' Arcade, near Pinocchio Village Haus in Fantasyland, and inside the Tomorrowland Arcade. Down Main Street and left around the Central Plaza (toward Adventureland) are the **Baby Care Center** and **First Aid.** Across from Disney's Port Orleans Resorts, **Best Friends Pet Care** provides a comfortable home away from home for Fido, Fluffy, and all their pet pals.

continued on page 270

The Magic Kingdom

FP+ Attraction Offers FastPass+

Use FP+ FastPass+ Recommended

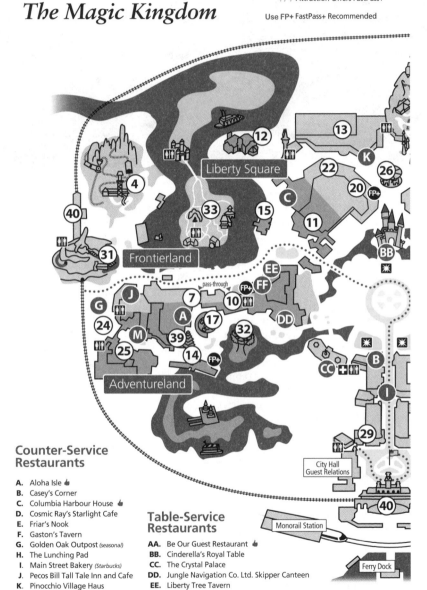

Liberty Square

Frontierland

pass-through

Adventureland

City Hall
Guest Relations

Monorail Station

Ferry Dock

Counter-Service Restaurants

A. Aloha Isle
B. Casey's Corner
C. Columbia Harbour House
D. Cosmic Ray's Starlight Cafe
E. Friar's Nook
F. Gaston's Tavern
G. Golden Oak Outpost *(seasonal)*
H. The Lunching Pad
I. Main Street Bakery *(Starbucks)*
J. Pecos Bill Tall Tale Inn and Cafe
K. Pinocchio Village Haus
L. Tomorrowland Terrace Restaurant *(seasonal)*
M. Tortuga Tavern *(seasonal)*

Table-Service Restaurants

AA. Be Our Guest Restaurant
BB. Cinderella's Royal Table
CC. The Crystal Palace
DD. Jungle Navigation Co. Ltd. Skipper Canteen
EE. Liberty Tree Tavern
FF. The Diamond Horseshoe *(seasonal)*
GG. The Plaza Restaurant
HH. Tony's Town Square Restaurant

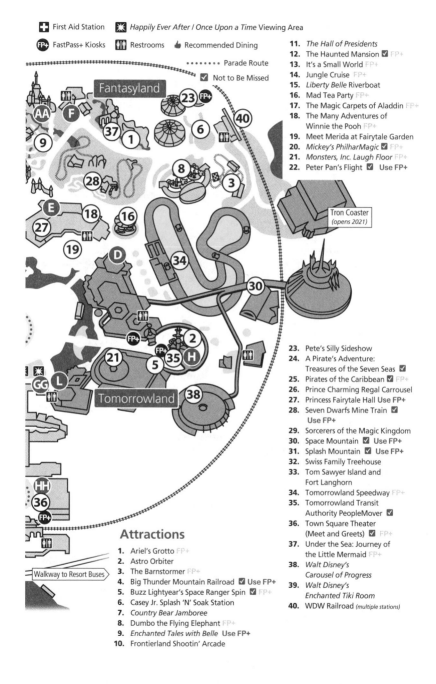

First Aid Station

FP+ FastPass+ Kiosks

🚻 Restrooms

👆 Recommended Dining

✶ *Happily Ever After / Once Upon a Time* Viewing Area

••••••• Parade Route

☑ Not to Be Missed

Fantasyland

Tron Coaster
(opens 2021)

Tomorrowland

Walkway to Resort Buses

11. *The Hall of Presidents*
12. The Haunted Mansion ☑ FP+
13. It's a Small World FP+
14. Jungle Cruise FP+
15. *Liberty Belle* Riverboat
16. Mad Tea Party FP+
17. The Magic Carpets of Aladdin FP+
18. The Many Adventures of
     Winnie the Pooh FP+
19. Meet Merida at Fairytale Garden
20. *Mickey's PhilharMagic* ☑ FP+
21. *Monsters, Inc. Laugh Floor* FP+
22. Peter Pan's Flight ☑ Use FP+

23. Pete's Silly Sideshow
24. A Pirate's Adventure:
     Treasures of the Seven Seas ☑
25. Pirates of the Caribbean ☑ FP+
26. Prince Charming Regal Carrousel
27. Princess Fairytale Hall Use FP+
28. Seven Dwarfs Mine Train ☑
     Use FP+
29. Sorcerers of the Magic Kingdom
30. Space Mountain ☑ Use FP+
31. Splash Mountain ☑ Use FP+
32. Swiss Family Treehouse
33. Tom Sawyer Island and
     Fort Langhorn
34. Tomorrowland Speedway FP+
35. Tomorrowland Transit
     Authority PeopleMover ☑
36. Town Square Theater
     (Meet and Greets) ☑ FP+
37. Under the Sea: Journey of
     the Little Mermaid FP+
38. *Walt Disney's*
     Carousel of Progress
39. *Walt Disney's*
     Enchanted Tiki Room
40. WDW Railroad *(multiple stations)*

Attractions

1. Ariel's Grotto FP+
2. Astro Orbiter
3. The Barnstormer FP+
4. Big Thunder Mountain Railroad ☑ Use FP+
5. Buzz Lightyear's Space Ranger Spin ☑ FP+
6. Casey Jr. Splash 'N' Soak Station
7. *Country Bear Jamboree*
8. Dumbo the Flying Elephant FP+
9. *Enchanted Tales with Belle* Use FP+
10. Frontierland Shootin' Arcade

continued from page 267

Get a **park map** as you enter the park underneath the Main Street Railroad Station or at City Hall. The map lists all attractions, shops, and eateries; provides helpful information about first aid, baby care, and assistance for the disabled; and gives tips for good photos. Additionally, it tells where to find Disney characters.

The guide map is supplemented by a daily entertainment schedule known as the *Times Guide,* which provides info on Disney character appearances, shows and performances, parades, and street entertainment. It also identifies attractions closed for refurbishment and which quick-service locations offer mobile ordering.

Main Street, U.S.A., ends at the **Central Plaza,** from which branch the entrances to the other five sections of the Magic Kingdom: **Adventureland, Frontierland, Liberty Square, Fantasyland,** and **Tomorrowland.**

In this and the following four chapters, we rate the individual attractions at each of the four major Disney theme parks and the two Universal theme parks. The **authors' rating,** which uses the same scale as the appeal by age ratings, is from the perspective of an adult. The authors, for example, might rate a ride such as Dumbo much lower than the age group for which the ride is intended, in this case, children. The authors' star rating is located next to the attraction's name. **Appeal by Age ratings** are expressed on a scale of zero to five stars— the more stars, the better the attraction. The **bottleneck rating** ranges 1–10; the higher the rating, the more congested the attraction. In general, try to experience attractions with a high bottleneck rating early in the morning (that is, 8–10:30 a.m.) before the park gets crowded, or late in the day when the crowd has diminished.

LILIANE You can save a lot of time by getting a car service to drop you off at the Contemporary Resort and walk to the Magic Kingdom. On busy days (WDW Marathon weekend, holidays) it's a lifesaver. Repeat when you leave at night. Put the $25 parking fee toward convenience— you'll be glad you did!

OPENING PROCEDURES Main Street, U.S.A. may open a full hour before the park's official opening time for photos, shopping, and getting in line for rides. The downside—and this is significant—is that the extra hour creates large crowds in the central hub to get in line for popular rides such as Seven Dwarfs Mine Train. Similar, smaller lines form on the walkways to Tomorrowland for Space Mountain, and in Adventureland and Frontierland for Splash Mountain and Big Thunder Mountain Railroad. Upon opening, a mini show takes place on the Castle Forecourt Stage.

FASTPASS+ AT THE MAGIC KINGDOM

WHILE THE MAGIC KINGDOM offers FastPass+ for about two dozen attractions (see the table on the next page), our touring plan software identifies just 10 as frequently needing FastPass+: **Peter Pan's Flight, Seven Dwarfs Mine Train, Big Thunder Mountain Railroad, Splash Mountain, Princess Fairytale Hall with Rapunzel and Tiana, Pirates of the Caribbean, Jungle Cruise, Space Mountain, The Haunted Mansion,** and **Buzz Lightyear's Space Ranger Spin.**

MAGIC KINGDOM FASTPASS+ ATTRACTIONS	
ADVENTURELAND	**FANTASYLAND** (continued)
• Jungle Cruise	• Under the Sea: Journey of the Little
• The Magic Carpets of Aladdin	Mermaid
• Pirates of the Caribbean	**FRONTIERLAND**
FANTASYLAND	• Big Thunder Mountain Railroad
• Ariel's Grotto	• Splash Mountain
• The Barnstormer	**LIBERTY SQUARE**
• Dumbo the Flying Elephant	• The Haunted Mansion
• *Enchanted Tales with Belle*	**MAIN STREET, U.S.A.**
• It's a Small World	• Town Square Theater Meet and Greets
• Mad Tea Party	(separate FastPass needed to meet
• The Many Adventures of Winnie the Pooh	Mickey and Minnie or Tinker Bell)
• *Mickey's PhilharMagic*	**TOMORROWLAND**
• Peter Pan's Flight	• Buzz Lightyear's Space Ranger Spin
• Princess Fairytale Hall (separate	• *Monsters, Inc. Laugh Floor*
FastPass needed to meet each pair of	• Space Mountain
princesses)	• Tomorrowland Speedway
• Seven Dwarfs Mine Train	

Peter Pan is listed first because it's nobody's choice as the first attraction to visit. And no matter where you go first, you'll probably visit at least one other attraction nearby next. That means you're not getting to Peter Pan within the first 30 minutes the park is open. Second, Peter Pan appears on virtually every Magic Kingdom touring plan. Third, though it's not a headliner, Peter Pan develops long lines throughout the day. The ride's hourly capacity is around 1,100 guests—a little more than half of Buzz Lightyear's and far less than half of Pirates of the Caribbean's.

Seven Dwarfs Mine Train, in the second spot, is usually the first FastPass+ that our software recommends, often with a start time between 9 and 10 a.m. If you're doing a comprehensive tour of the Magic Kingdom that allows you to visit Space Mountain and Buzz Lightyear as soon as the park opens, then you can ride Seven Dwarfs Mine Train with little wait. It also puts you in a good position to ride a couple of secondary Fantasyland attractions before a 10 a.m. FastPass+ reservation for Peter Pan—and that helps cut down on how much walking you have to do in the park.

Big Thunder and Splash Mountain are on the list too. While they don't normally get a huge influx of guests immediately at park opening, lines of 20–40 minutes can develop around midmorning at Splash Mountain and Big Thunder Mountain as crowds make their way from Tomorrowland and Fantasyland.

Meeting Rapunzel and Tiana at Princess Fairytale Hall (and, in general, any princess meet and greet) makes the top five because lines don't build as fast there as at other attractions.

Our software usually recommends Pirates of the Caribbean and the Jungle Cruise as day-of FastPasses that you'd get in the early afternoon inside the Magic Kingdom, not one of the three you'd get in advance. These aren't in the top tier of popular attractions in the park, and they have enough capacity to move a lot of people per hour and thus have moderate waits. In addition, it's possible to get "instant" FastPasses for Pirates of the Caribbean by playing two games of A Pirate's Adventure (see page 276).

Space Mountain made the list because of Seven Dwarfs Mine Train. The low height requirement of Seven Dwarfs makes it a more family-friendly attraction than Space Mountain, which also makes FastPass+ reservations much harder to get for Seven Dwarfs than for Space Mountain. When FastPass+ isn't available for Seven Dwarfs, our touring plans usually suggest riding very early or very late, making a FastPass+ for Space Mountain the best possible alternative.

FastPass+ kiosk locations in the Magic Kingdom are as follows:

- In the walkway between Adventureland and Liberty Square, near The Diamond Horseshoe and Swiss Family Treehouse
- At the entrance to Jungle Cruise in Adventureland
- Outside *Mickey's PhilharMagic* in Fantasyland
- In the tent next to Pete's Silly Sideshow in Fantasyland
- Near the Tomorrowland bridge
- At Buzz Lightyear's Space Ranger Spin in Tomorrowland

Same-Day FastPass+ Availability

The preceding advice tells you which attractions to focus on when making your *advance* FastPass+ reservations before you get to the park. You can make more FastPass+ reservations in the park once your advance reservations have been used or have expired. The table on the opposite page shows which attractions are likely to have day-of FastPasses available, and the approximate times at which they'll run out.

You'll notice that many attractions have more day-of FastPass+ availability on days with moderate crowds than with low crowds. Disney can change the capacity of some rides by adding vehicles. It can also change how much of a ride's hourly capacity is dedicated to FastPass+ and increases this number on days of higher attendance. For example, on days of low crowds, Peter Pan's Flight might dedicate 75% of its hourly capacity to FastPass+ riders, 85% on days of moderate crowds.

Finally, the Magic Kingdom holds back a certain amount of each ride's FastPass daily capacity as a hedge against ride breakdowns. If the park's rides operate smoothly, this extra FastPass capacity is released throughout the day for in-park guests to use.

▌█ MAIN STREET, U.S.A.

YOU'LL BEGIN AND END YOUR VISIT ON MAIN STREET, which may open 30 minutes–1 hour before and closes 30 minutes–1 hour after the rest of the park. It's easy to get sidetracked when entering Main

MAGIC KINGDOM
When Same-Day FP+ Runs Out, by Crowd Level

ATTRACTION	LOW CROWDS*	MODERATE CROWDS*	HIGH CROWDS*
• Ariel's Grotto	NA	NA	NA
• The Barnstormer	2 p.m.	4 p.m.	3 p.m.
• Big Thunder Mountain	NA	NA	NA
• Buzz Lightyear's Space Ranger Spin	2 p.m.	3 p.m.	2 p.m.
• Dumbo the Flying Elephant	3 p.m.	6 p.m.	2 p.m.
• Enchanted Tales with Belle	NA	NA	NA
• The Haunted Mansion	noon	1 p.m.	11 a.m.
• It's a Small World	3 p.m.	6 p.m.	6 p.m.
• Jungle Cruise	1 p.m.	2 p.m.	noon
• Mad Tea Party	3 p.m.	5 p.m.	6 p.m.
• Monsters, Inc. Laugh Floor	3 p.m.	3 p.m.	3 p.m.
• The Magic Carpets of Aladdin	2 p.m.	4 p.m.	4 p.m.
• The Many Adventures of Winnie the Pooh	3 p.m.	5 p.m.	6 p.m.
• Mickey's PhilharMagic	3 p.m.	3 p.m.	3 p.m.
• Peter Pan's Flight	NA	NA	NA
• Pirates of the Caribbean	3 p.m.	3 p.m.	1 p.m.
• Princess Fairytale Hall: Cinderella and Friends	NA	NA	NA
• Princess Fairytale Hall: Rapunzel and Tiana	9 a.m.	9 a.m.	NA
• Seven Dwarfs Mine Train	NA	NA	NA
• Space Mountain	NA	11 a.m.	NA
• Splash Mountain	NA	noon	10 a.m.
• Tomorrowland Speedway	1 p.m.	2 p.m.	1 p.m.
• Town Square Theater: Mickey Mouse Meet and Greet	NA	NA	NA
• Town Square Theater: Tinker Bell Meet and Greet	NA	NA	NA
• Under the Sea: Journey of the Little Mermaid	3 p.m.	5 p.m.	5 p.m.

* **LOW CROWDS** (Levels 1–3 on TouringPlans.com Crowd Calendar)

* **MODERATE CROWDS** (Levels 4–7 on TouringPlans.com Crowd Calendar)

* **HIGH CROWDS** (Levels 8–10 on TouringPlans.com Crowd Calendar)

NA = no availability

Street, U.S.A.: this Disneyfied turn-of-the-19th-century small-town street is lovely, with exceptional attention to detail. But remember, time is of the essence, and the rest of the park is waiting to be discovered. The same goes for the one and only **Cinderella Castle.** Stick with your touring plan and return to the castle and Main Street after you've experienced the must-dos on your list.

Sorcerers of the Magic Kingdom ★★★

APPEAL BY AGE PRESCHOOL ★★★ GRADE SCHOOL ★★★★½ TEENS ★★★★
YOUNG ADULTS ★★★★ OVER 30 ★★★½ SENIORS ★★★½

What it is Free interactive game in which players must defeat villains spread around different lands. **Scope and scale** Minor attraction. **Fright potential** Not frightening in any respect. **Bottleneck rating** 7. **When to go** Anytime. **Comments** Expect waits to play at each station. **Duration of experience** About 2 minutes per step, 4 or 5 steps per game. **Probable waiting time per step** 5–10 minutes.

Sorcerers of the Magic Kingdom combines aspects of role-playing games such as Dungeons and Dragons with Disney characters and theme park attractions in a free, trading card–based game. The wizard Merlin sends you on adventures in different parts of the Magic Kingdom to fight evildoers intent on taking over the park. Each land hosts a different adventure, with different villains in each. Pick up the cards, plus a map showing where in the park you can play the game, at the Fire Station on Main Street, U.S.A. You'll need your MagicBand or park card to pick up your first set of cards and start the game.

When you pick up your cards, you'll view an instructional video; then you'll be sent to another location to start your first adventure. Each location in the park is associated with a unique symbol such as an eye or a feather. Look for these symbols on the map to find the best route to your starting point.

Each adventure consists of four or five stops in a particular land. At each stop, another story will play on a computer screen, outlining what your villain is trying to do. Merlin will ask you to cast a spell to stop the villain. To do so, hold one or more of your cards up to the video display. Cameras in the display read your card, deploy the spell, and show you the results.

The audio at each step holds clues to which cards you should use against advanced villains. For example, if a villain says something like, "Don't toy with me!," then you should look for cards with characters that are toys, such as the *Toy Story* characters.

The game has three levels: easy, medium, and hard. In the easy version, appropriate for small children, holding up any one of your character cards is enough to defeat any villain. In more-advanced levels of the game, you need to display two or more character cards in specific combinations to defeat a particular villain; here, different card combinations produce different spells, and only some spells work on certain characters.

The game has about 70 unique cards; you can obtain 5 new ones per day. Don't worry if you play more than once and end up with duplicate cards—a small trading market exists within the park.

> Every time you visit the Magic Kingdom, get your free set of Sorcerers of the Magic Kingdom cards. Even if you don't play, they're a great keepsake.

Sabrina

Town Square Theater Meet and Greets: Mickey Mouse and Tinker Bell *(FastPass+)* ★★★★

APPEAL BY AGE   PRESCHOOL ★★★★½   GRADE SCHOOL ★★★★½   TEENS ★★★★½ YOUNG ADULTS ★★★★½   OVER 30 ★★★★½   SENIORS ★★★★½

What it is Character greeting venue. **Scope and scale** Minor attraction. **Fright potential** Not frightening in any respect. **Bottleneck rating** 7. **When to go** Before 10 a.m. or after 4 p.m., or use FastPass+. **Comments** Mickey and Tinker Bell have 2 separate queues, requiring 2 separate waits in line. It all started with this mouse; not to be missed. **Duration of experience** 2 minutes per character. **Average wait in line per 100 people ahead of you** 45 minutes. **Queue speed** Slow.

Meet Mickey and Tinker Bell throughout the day at the Town Square Theater, to your right as you enter the park. Lines usually drop during the afternoon parade.

Walt Disney World Railroad*   ★★★

Closed due to construction of a Tron-themed roller coaster in Tomorrowland. At press time, no reopening date had been announced.

Thumbs Up for the Whole Family

What it is Scenic railroad ride around perimeter of the Magic Kingdom; provides transportation to Frontierland and Fantasyland. **Scope and scale** Minor attraction. **Fright potential** Not frightening in any respect. **Bottleneck rating** 6. **When to go** Anytime; closed during parades. **Comments** Main Street is usually the least congested station. Plenty to see. **Duration of ride** About 20 minutes for a complete circuit. **Average wait in line per 100 people ahead of you** 8 minutes; assumes 2 or more trains operating. **Loading speed** Moderate.

Later in the day, when you need a break, this full-circuit ride will give you and your feet 20 minutes of rest. Only folded strollers are permitted on the train, so you can't board with your rented Disney stroller. You can, however, obtain a replacement at your destination. Be advised that the railroad shuts down immediately preceding and during parades. If you're in Frontierland and headed out of the park, it's a nice way to end your visit.

While the railroad is closed, one of four narrow-gauge trains, built between 1916 and 1928, is housed at the Main Street station. Guests can enjoy an up close look at the vintage train and take advantage of special photo ops.

ADVENTURELAND

THE FIRST LAND to the left of Main Street, Adventureland combines an African-safari theme with a tropical-island atmosphere.

Jungle Cruise *(FastPass+)*   ★★★½

What it is Outdoor safari-themed boat ride adventure. **Scope and scale** Major attraction. **Fright potential** Moderately intense, some macabre sights; a good test attraction for little ones. **Bottleneck rating** 10. **When to go** Before 10:30 a.m., the last 2 hours the park is open, or use FastPass+. **Comment** An enduring Disney masterpiece. **Duration of ride** 8-9 minutes. **Average wait in line per 100 people ahead of you** 3½ minutes; assumes 10 boats operating. **Loading speed** Moderate.

During the holiday season the Jungle Cruise turns into the Jingle Cruise. Jingle Bells, Jingle Cruise—do you get it?

Isabelle

You have to put things into perspective to truly enjoy this ride and realize that it was once a super-headliner at the Magic Kingdom—it's fun and relaxing but far from high-tech. Before you make a same-day FastPass+ reservation, check the estimated wait time for the standby queue. We think the ride is better at night.

I didn't really like this ride. The animals weren't real, but it was scary in the dark cave, and the big spider was absolutely terrifying.

Felicity

The Magic Carpets of Aladdin *(FastPass+)* ★★½

APPEAL BY AGE PRESCHOOL ★★★½ GRADE SCHOOL ★★★★ TEENS ★★★½ YOUNG ADULTS ★★★½ OVER 30 ★★★½ SENIORS ★★★½

Thumbs Up for the Whole Family

What it is Elaborate midway ride. **Scope and scale** Minor attraction. **Fright potential** Much like Dumbo; a favorite of most younger children. **Bottleneck rating** 10. **When to go** Before 11 a.m. or after 7 p.m.; FastPass+ rarely necessary. **Comment** An eye-appealing children's ride. **Duration of ride** 1½ minutes. **Average wait in line per 100 people ahead of you** 16 minutes. **Loading speed** Slow.

Keep your guard up when you're near the Magic Carpets of Aladdin. The golden camel spits randomly. I was struck in the ear and also got a glob of water in my eye. Don't say I didn't warn you.

A. J.

Like Dumbo, Aladdin is a must for parents with preschoolers. Try to get your kids on in the first 30 minutes the park is open or just before park closing. Beware of the spitting camel positioned to spray jets of water on riders. The front-seat control moves your "carpet" up and down, while the backseat control pitches it forward or backward. Sweet, but oh-so-slow loading. Jasmine and Aladdin are on hand for meeting and greeting in the nearby Agrabah Bazaar.

Movie Tip

This ride is inspired by the 1992 Disney movie Aladdin.
Did you know that Robin Williams was the voice of the Genie?

A Pirate's Adventure: Treasures of the Seven Seas ★★★½

APPEAL BY AGE PRESCHOOL ★★★★ GRADE SCHOOL ★★★★ TEENS ★★★★ YOUNG ADULTS ★★★★ OVER 30 ★★★★ SENIORS ★★★★

What it is Interactive game. **Scope and scale** Diversion. **Fright potential** Some exhibits, such as skulls and sudden sounds, may frighten small children. **Bottleneck rating** 4. **When to go** Open noon–6 p.m. **Comment** Simple, fast, and fun. **Duration of experience** About 25 minutes to play entire game. **Probable waiting time per step** 5 minutes or less.

Similar to Agent P's World Showcase Adventure at Epcot, A Pirate's Adventure features interactive areas with physical props and narrations that lead guests through a quest to find lost treasure, all within Adventureland.

Guests begin their journey at The Crow's Nest near Golden Oak Outpost—this is the central hub for adventurers helping to locate missing treasure. Groups of up to six people are given a talisman (an RFID card) that will help them on their journey. The talisman activates a video screen that assigns your group to one of five different missions. Your group is then given a map and sent off to find your first location.

Once at the location, one member of the party touches the talisman to the symbol at the station, and the animation begins. Each adventure has four or five stops throughout Adventureland, and each stop contains 30–45 seconds of activity. No strategy or action is required: Watch what unfolds, get your next destination, and head off. For each mission completed, you'll receive a Treasure Finder collectible card; an additional card is received upon completing all five pirate raids. If you're not yet convinced to play, watch the faces of the kids playing when they do something that triggers smoke, noise, or other effects. The game can be played daily, noon–6 p.m.

A Pirate's Adventure serves as a good introduction to other interactive games, such as Sorcerers of the Magic Kingdom (see page 273). While we think everyone should try A Pirate's Adventure, it isn't a must if time is tight.

If your group completes two missions of A Pirate's Adventure, you will get a free FastPass+ to Pirates of the Caribbean. If you don't have a FastPass+ for Pirates and the wait is 30 minutes or more, we think it's worth playing two games to get the FastPass+. Ask a cast member if the bonus is still offered before playing.

Pirates of the Caribbean *(FastPass+)* ★★★★

**APPEAL BY AGE PRESCHOOL ★★★½ GRADE SCHOOL ★★★★ TEENS ★★★★
YOUNG ADULTS ★★★★½ OVER 30 ★★★★½ SENIORS ★★★★½**

What it is Indoor pirate-themed adventure boat ride. **Scope and scale** Headliner. **Fright potential** Slightly intimidating queuing area; intense boat ride with gruesome (though humorously presented) sights and a short, unexpected slide down a flume. **Bottleneck rating** 7. **When to go** Before 11 a.m., after 7 p.m., or use FastPass+. **Comment** Disney Audio-Animatronics at their best; not to be missed. **Duration of ride** About 7½ minutes. **Average wait in line per 100 people ahead of you** 3 minutes; assumes 1 line for FastPass+ and 1 for standby. **Loading speed** Fast.

Dark Loud Scary

This indoor ride cruises through sets depicting a pirate raid on a Caribbean port. It's been a favorite for decades, but with the release of *Pirates of the Caribbean: The Curse of the Black Pearl* (2003), *Pirates of the Caribbean: Dead Man's Chest* (2006), *Pirates of the Caribbean: At World's End* (2007), *Pirates of the Caribbean: On Stranger Tides* (2011), and *Pirates of the Caribbean: Dead Men Tell No Tales* (2017), its popularity has soared to new heights. Playing two games of A Pirate's Adventure may earn your group instant FastPasses+ for this ride. Find details in the previous profile.

The ride starts off scary because it's very dark and there are skeletons and loud voices. But it's great fun to try to spot Jack Sparrow. It was very silly of him to hide behind a lady's dress. I loved the boat ride and the music.

Felicity

See the movies before you go to Walt Disney World. They're a blast.

Swiss Family Treehouse ★★★

**APPEAL BY AGE PRESCHOOL ★★★½ GRADE SCHOOL ★★★½ TEENS ★★★
YOUNG ADULTS ★★★ OVER 30 ★★★½ SENIORS ★★★½**

What it is Outdoor walk-through tree house. **Scope and scale** Minor attraction. **Fright potential** Kids who are afraid of heights might want to skip it; otherwise, not frightening. **Bottleneck rating** 6. **When to go** Anytime. **Comments** Requires climbing a lot of stairs. A visual delight. **Duration of tour** 10–15 minutes. **Average wait in line per 100 people ahead of you** 7 minutes.

Thumbs Up for the Whole Family

This king of all tree houses is perfect for the 10-and-under crowd. Though a minor attraction, it's a great place to expend pent-up energy. Parents might be inclined to sit across the walkway and watch their aspiring Tarzans, but in truth the tree house is fun for adults too.

Swiss Family Robinson is a 1960 film adaptation of the Johann David Wyss novel and was the inspiration for the Swiss Family Treehouse.

Walt Disney's Enchanted Tiki Room ★★★

APPEAL BY AGE **PRESCHOOL** ★★★★ **GRADE SCHOOL** ★★★½ **TEENS** ★★★
YOUNG ADULTS ★★★½ **OVER 30** ★★★½ **SENIORS** ★★★★

What it is Audio-Animatronic Pacific Island musical-theater show. **Scope and scale** Minor attraction. **Fright potential** Young children might be frightened by the thunder-and-lightning storm, plus the theater is at times plunged into utter darkness. **Bottleneck rating** 4. **When to go** Before 11 a.m. or after 3:30 p.m. **Comment** Very, very . . . unusual. **Duration of show** 15½ minutes. **Preshow** Talking birds. **Probable waiting time** 15 minutes.

The tiki birds are a great favorite of the 8-and-under age set. The outright absurdity of the whole concept saves the show for older patrons—if you can look beyond the cheese, it's actually hilarious. The air-conditioned theater is a great place to cool off and rest your feet.

We always seem to end up here because it's raining, but it's actually good fun. The singing birds are really clever, and the songs get stuck in your head.

Felicity

FRONTIERLAND

THIS LAND ADJOINS ADVENTURELAND as you move clockwise around the Magic Kingdom. Frontierland's focus is on the Old West, with stockade-type structures and pioneer trappings.

Big Thunder Mountain Railroad *(FastPass+)* ★★★★

APPEAL BY AGE **PRESCHOOL** ★★★½ **GRADE SCHOOL** ★★★★½ **TEENS** ★★★★½
YOUNG ADULTS ★★★★½ **OVER 30** ★★★★½ **SENIORS** ★★★★

What it is Western mining–themed roller coaster. **Scope and scale** Headliner. **Fright potential** Visually intimidating from outside, with moderately intense visual effects; roller coaster. **Bottleneck rating** 9. **When to go** Before 10 a.m., in the hour before closing, or use FastPass+. **Comments** Must be 40″ tall to ride; children younger than age 7 must ride with an adult. Switching-off option (see page 248). Great effects; not to be missed. **Duration of ride** Almost 3½ minutes. **Average wait in line per 100 people ahead of you** 2½ minutes; assumes 5 trains operating. **Loading speed** Moderate–fast.

Zooming on a runaway train around a mountain and through a deserted mining town is Disney at its best (if only one could concentrate on the scenery). The ride is rough, and if you don't like roller coasters, this one is going to remind you why. The air-conditioned queue features first-rate examples of Disney creativity; a realistic mining town, geysers, swinging possums, petulant buzzards, and the like will keep kids busy while waiting in line. Ride after dark if you can. Seats in the back offer a better experience.

Country Bear Jamboree ★★★½

APPEAL BY AGE **PRESCHOOL** ★★★★ **GRADE SCHOOL** ★★★½ **TEENS** ★★★
YOUNG ADULTS ★★★½ **OVER 30** ★★★½ **SENIORS** ★★★★

What it is Audio-Animatronic country hoedown. **Scope and scale** Minor attraction. **Fright potential** Not frightening in any respect. **Bottleneck rating** 6. **When to go** Anytime. **Comment** Old and worn but pure Disney. **Duration of show** 11 minutes. **Probable waiting time** 11–22 minutes on a busy day between noon and 5:30 p.m.

A charming cast of Audio-Animatronic bears sings and stomps in a Western-style hoedown. *Country Bear Jamboree* has run for so long that the geriatric bears are a step away from assisted living. Reader comments tend to echo the need for something new. From a Sandy Hook, Connecticut, mom:

> *I know they consider it a classic, and kids always seem to love it, but could they PLEASE update it after half a century?*

Frontierland Shootin' Arcade ★½

**APPEAL BY AGE   PRESCHOOL ★★★½   GRADE SCHOOL ★★★★   TEENS ★★★½
YOUNG ADULTS ★★★½   OVER 30 ★★★½   SENIORS ★★★½**

What it is Electronic shooting gallery. **Scope and scale** Diversion. **Fright potential** Frightening to children scared of guns. **Bottleneck rating** 1. **When to go** Anytime. **Comments** Costs $1 per play. Fun for kids but not a must.

Would-be gunslingers get around 35 shots per $1 play. Each shot is followed by a short delay before the next shot can be taken—this prevents small children from accidentally using all the shots in 5 seconds. It's barely noticeable for adults. Bring lots of quarters.

Splash Mountain *(FastPass+)*   ★★★★★

**APPEAL BY AGE   PRESCHOOL ★★★★†   GRADE SCHOOL ★★★★½   TEENS ★★★★★
YOUNG ADULTS ★★★★★   OVER 30 ★★★★½   SENIORS ★★★★½**

†Many preschoolers are too short to ride, and others freak out when they see it from the waiting line. Among preschoolers who actually ride, most love it.

What it is Indoor/outdoor water-flume adventure ride. **Scope and scale** Super-headliner. **Fright potential** Visually intimidating from outside, with moderately intense visual effects. The ride, culminating in a 52-foot plunge down a steep chute, is somewhat hair-raising for all ages. **Bottleneck rating** 10. **When to go** As soon as the park opens, during afternoon or evening parades, just before closing, or use FastPass+. **Comments** Must be 40" tall to ride; children younger than age 7 must ride with an adult. Switching-off option (see page 248). A wet winner; not to be missed. **Duration of ride** About 10 minutes. **Average wait in line per 100 people ahead of you** 3½ minutes; assumes ride is operating at full capacity. **Loading speed** Moderate.

The first time I rode Splash Mountain, I spent the entire time worrying about every drop to come until the big one. Don't make the same mistake. Yes, there are multiple drops, but you'll know when the big one is coming. So in the meantime, enjoy the ride.

A. J.

Lose Things   Wet   Scary

Zip-a-dee-doo-dah, having fun yet? My, oh, my, will you get wet! This 0.5-mile ride through swamps, caves, and backwoods bayous is wonderful. Based on the 1946 Disney film *Song of the South,* the log flume ride takes you through Uncle Remus's tales of Br'er Rabbit. Three small drops lead up to the big one—a five-story plunge at 40 miles per hour!

Bring a change of clothes, or wear a bathing suit or a poncho, because you might get very wet.

Sabrina

Movie Tip

Unavailable in the United States, Song of the South *will become public domain in 2039, and Disney might rerelease the movie before it loses the rights to it. If you're interested in the history of this controversial movie, visit songofthesouth.net.*

I liked going through Br'er Bear's village, but the big drop made me feel very woozy. We also got really wet.

Felicity

Tom Sawyer Island and Fort Langhorn ★★★

APPEAL BY AGE	PRESCHOOL ★★★★	GRADE SCHOOL ★★★★	TEENS ★★★½
YOUNG ADULTS ★★★½	OVER 30 ★★★½	SENIORS ★★★½	

Thumbs Up for the Whole Family

What it is Outdoor walk-through exhibit and rustic playground. **Scope and scale** Minor attraction. **Fright potential** Not frightening in any respect, other than dark tunnels that can be avoided. **Bottleneck rating** 4. **When to go** Midmorning–late afternoon. **Comments** Closes at dusk. The place for rambunctious kids.

This is a great place for kids age 5 and up to unwind. The wildest and most uncooperative youngster will relax after exploring caves and climbing around in an old fort. It's also a great place for a picnic, but there is no food, so bring your own. Access is by raft with a (usually short) wait both coming and going. Plan to give your kids at least 20 minutes on the island—left to their own devices, they would likely stay all day.

> I love Tom Sawyer Island. It's the perfect place to take a break or have a picnic; plus, it's a great place for nursing moms to find a quiet spot. Be aware, though, that raft transportation to the island stops at sunset.
>
> Liliane

▌█ LIBERTY SQUARE

THIS LAND RE-CREATES AMERICA at the time of the American Revolution. The architecture is Federal or Colonial. The **Liberty Tree,** a live oak more than 150 years old, lends dignity and grace to the setting.

The Hall of Presidents ★★★

APPEAL BY AGE	PRESCHOOL ★★½	GRADE SCHOOL ★★★	TEENS ★★★½
YOUNG ADULTS ★★★½	OVER 30 ★★★★	SENIORS ★★★★½	

What it is Audio-Animatronic historical theater presentation. **Scope and scale** Minor attraction. **Fright potential** Not frightening in any respect. **Bottleneck rating** 4. **When to go** Anytime. **Comment** Impressive and moving. **Duration of show** Almost 23 minutes. **Probable waiting time** About 15 minutes. It would be exceptionally unusual not to be admitted to the next show.

Thumbs Up for the Whole Family

The Hall of Presidents combines a wide-screen theater presentation of the highlights and milestones in the United States' political history with a short stage show, including life-size animatronic replicas of every US president, plus speeches delivered by Presidents George Washington and Donald Trump. *The Hall of Presidents* is definitely a must-see for adults, but kids are likely to fidget or fall asleep.

Liliane

> Did you know that famous Western actor Royal Dano is the voice of President Lincoln? Dano was also the voice of Lincoln for Disneyland's *Great Moments with Mr. Lincoln* program, first presented at the 1964–65 World's Fair in New York City.

The Haunted Mansion *(FastPass+)* ★★★★½

APPEAL BY AGE	PRESCHOOL ★★★	GRADE SCHOOL ★★★★	TEENS ★★★½
YOUNG ADULTS ★★★★½	OVER 30 ★★★★½	SENIORS ★★★★½	

What it is Haunted-house dark ride. **Scope and scale** Major attraction. **Fright potential** The name raises anxiety, as do the sounds and sights of the waiting area. An intense attraction with humorously presented macabre sights, the ride itself is gentle. **Bottle-neck rating** 8. **When to go** Before 11 a.m. or the last 2 hours the park is open; use Fast-Pass+ when touring 2 days or more, or get it as your first day-of FastPass. **Comment** Some of Disney World's best special effects; not to be missed. **Duration of ride** 7-minute ride plus a 1½-minute preshow. **Average wait in line per 100 people ahead of you** 2½ minutes; assumes both "stretch rooms" operating. **Loading speed** Fast.

Dark   Scary

Don't let the apparent spookiness of the old-fashioned Haunted Mansion put you off. This is one of the best attractions in the Magic Kingdom. It's not scary, except in the sweetest of ways, but it will remind you of the days before ghost stories gave way to slasher flicks. The Haunted Mansion takes less than 10 minutes to ride, preshow included, but you may have to do it more than once—it's jam-packed with visual puns, special effects, hidden Mickeys, and really lovely Victorian-spooky sets. The Haunted Mansion also has a photo opportunity. As your Doom Buggy journeys through the haunted chambers, watch out for ghosts and smile for the camera.

Liberty Belle Riverboat ★★½

APPEAL BY AGE   PRESCHOOL ★★★   GRADE SCHOOL ★★★½   TEENS ★★★
YOUNG ADULTS ★★★½   OVER 30 ★★★½   SENIORS ★★★★

What it is Outdoor scenic boat ride. **Scope and scale** Minor attraction. **Fright potential** Not frightening in any respect. **Bottleneck rating** 4. **When to go** Anytime. **Comment** Slow, relaxing, and scenic. **Duration of ride** About 16 minutes. **Average wait to board** 10–14 minutes.

Thumbs Up for the Whole Family

This fully narrated 16-minute trip is relaxing and offers great photo ops. It's also a good choice at night, when the boat and the attractions along the waterfront are lighted. Did you know that the *Liberty Belle* runs on a track hidden just below the water?

▌▐ FANTASYLAND

THE HEART OF THE MAGIC KINGDOM, Fantasyland is a truly enchanting place spread gracefully like a miniature alpine village beneath the steepled towers of Cinderella Castle.

Fantasyland is divided into three distinct sections. Directly behind Cinderella Castle and set on a snowcapped mountain is Beast's Castle, part of a *Beauty and the Beast*-themed area. Most of this section holds dining and shopping. Outside Beast's Castle is Belle's Village. Nestled inside lush and beautifully decorated grounds, with gardens, meadows, and waterfalls, is Maurice's cottage, home of *Enchanted Tales with Belle*.

The far-right corner of Fantasyland, including Dumbo, The Barnstormer kiddie coaster, and the Fantasyland Train Station, is called **Storybook Circus** as an homage to the *Dumbo* films. These are low-capacity amusement park rides appropriate for younger children. Also located here is Pete's Silly Sideshow, a character greeting venue.

LILIANE The only way to visit Beast's Castle is by eating at Be Our Guest. Reservations are fully booked months in advance.

The middle of Fantasyland holds the headliners, including Under the Sea: Journey of the Little Mermaid and Seven Dwarfs Mine Train. The **original part of Fantasyland,** behind Cinderella Castle, contains classic attractions, such as Peter Pan's Flight and The Many Adventures of Winnie the Pooh. It also hosts the popular Princess Fairytale Hall meet and greet.

Finally, when nature calls, don't miss the *Tangled*-themed restrooms and outdoor seating, near Peter Pan's Flight and It's a Small World. The electric phone charger outlets are hidden in the faux tree trunks. And no, you can't visit Rapunzel's Tower. Sometimes a restroom is just that, a restroom.

Ariel's Grotto *(FastPass+)* ★★★

APPEAL BY AGE   PRESCHOOL ★★★★½   GRADE SCHOOL ★★★★½   TEENS ★★★★
YOUNG ADULTS ★★★★   OVER 30 ★★★★   SENIORS ★★★★

What it is Character greeting venue. **Scope and scale** Minor attraction. **Fright potential** Not frightening in any respect. **Bottleneck rating** 8. **When to go** Before 10:30 a.m. or the last 2 hours the park is open, or use FastPass+. **Duration of experience** Maybe 30–90 seconds. **Average wait in line per 100 people ahead of you** 45 minutes. **Queue speed** Slow.

Ariel's home base is next to Under the Sea: Journey of the Little Mermaid. In the base of the seaside cliffs under Prince Eric's Castle, Ariel (in mermaid form) greets guests from a seashell throne. The queue (not air-conditioned) isn't as detailed as other character greeting venues in the park.

Meeting Ariel was superspecial; I was dressed as a mermaid too. Ariel was so nice to me. She is so pretty.

Felicity

The Barnstormer *(FastPass+)* ★★

APPEAL BY AGE   PRESCHOOL ★★★★   GRADE SCHOOL ★★★★   TEENS ★★★
YOUNG ADULTS ★★★   OVER 30 ★★★   SENIORS ★★★

What it is Small roller coaster. **Scope and scale** Minor attraction. **Fright potential** Frightens some preschoolers. **Bottleneck rating** 9. **When to go** Before 11 a.m., during parades, or the last 2 hours the park is open; not a good use of FastPass+. **Comments** Must be 35″ tall to ride. Switching-off option (see page 248). Great for little ones but not worth the wait for adults. **Duration of ride** About 53 seconds. **Average wait in line per 100 people ahead of you** 7 minutes. **Loading speed** Slow.

Rough

Scary

Remember that the height requirement for this ride is 35 inches. If you want to see how your child handles riding coasters, The Barnstormer is the perfect testing ground. (Seven Dwarfs Mine Train would be the next to try.)

Liliane

Yours truly screamed big-time from start to end (thankfully it only lasted a minute), and no way would I let the apple of my eye ride alone unless he or she were 6 years or older.

Liliane is a gentle and sensitive soul. Most kids experience rides wilder than The Barnstormer on their tricycles. When I heard Liliane wailing like a banshee on this dinky coaster, I thought her appendix must have ruptured.

Bob

Casey Jr. Splash 'N' Soak Station   ★★★

APPEAL BY AGE   PRESCHOOL ★★★★½   GRADE SCHOOL ★★★★   TEENS ★★★
YOUNG ADULTS ★★★½   OVER 30 ★★★★   SENIORS ★★★★

What it is Opportunity to get wet. **Scope and scale** Diversion. **Fright potential** Not frightening in any respect. **Bottleneck rating** 0. **When to go** When it's hot. **Comment** Great way to cool off.

Wet

Casey Jr., the circus train from *Dumbo,* hosts an absolutely drenching experience outside the Fantasyland Train Station in the Storybook Circus area. Expect a cadre of captive circus beasts to spray water on you in this elaborate water-play area. It's a marvel to watch. Be sure to bring a change of clothes and a big towel.

Dumbo the Flying Elephant *(FastPass+)*   ★★★½

APPEAL BY AGE   PRESCHOOL ★★★★½   GRADE SCHOOL ★★★★   TEENS ★★★
YOUNG ADULTS ★★★   OVER 30 ★★★½   SENIORS ★★★★

What it is Disneyfied midway ride. **Scope and scale** Minor attraction. **Fright potential** Very tame; a favorite of most young children. **Bottleneck rating** 10. **When to go** Before 11 a.m. or after 6 p.m.; not a good use of FastPass+. **Comment** Disney's signature ride for children. **Duration of ride** 1½ minutes. **Average wait in line per 100 people ahead of you** 5 minutes. **Loading speed** Slow.

Thumbs Up for the Whole Family

Making sure your kids get their fill of this tame, happy children's ride is what mother love is all about. The 90-second ride is hardly worth waiting in line, unless, of course, you're under 7 years old. Dumbo has a play area with interactive elements. If you have a wait, you'll be given a pager that will buzz when it's your turn to ride.

Movie Tip

If you haven't seen Dumbo *(first released in 1941 and winner of an Academy Award for original music score), you have an elephant-size gap in your Disney education. Watch the movie, fun for all ages, when you get home. In 2019 Disney released the live-action adaptation of* Dumbo. *The film is directed by Tim Burton, who has worked on many memorable films, including* Alice in Wonderland *(2010),* Edward Scissorhands, Alice Through the Looking Glass, The Nightmare Before Christmas, *and* Charlie and the Chocolate Factory *(2005), just to name a few.*

Enchanted Tales with Belle (FastPass+)   ★★★★

APPEAL BY AGE   PRESCHOOL ★★★★½   GRADE SCHOOL ★★★★   TEENS ★★★
YOUNG ADULTS ★★★½   OVER 30 ★★★★   SENIORS ★★★★

What it is Interactive character show. **Scope and scale** Minor attraction. **Fright potential** Not frightening in any respect. **Bottleneck rating** 10. **When to go** As soon as the park opens, during the last 2 hours before closing, or use FastPass+. **Comment** The prettiest meet and greet in the park. **Duration of presentation** About 20 minutes. **Probable waiting time** 30 minutes.

A multiscene *Beauty and the Beast* experience takes guests into Maurice's workshop, through a magic mirror, and into Beast's library, where the audience shares a story with Belle.

Felicity

This is so much fun, especially if you get chosen to play one of the characters. I did, and even my parents got a part. It's a great way to meet Belle and have your photo taken with her.

You enter the attraction by walking through Maurice's cottage, where you see mementos tracing Belle's childhood, including her favorite books, and lines drawn on one wall showing how fast Belle grew every year.

Then you go into Maurice's workshop at the back of the cottage. An assortment of Maurice's odd wood gadgets covers every inch of the floor, walls, and ceiling. Take a moment to peruse the gadgets, and then focus your attention on the mirror on the wall to the left of the entry door.

Soon enough, the room gets dark and the mirror begins to sparkle. With magic and some really good carpentry skills, the mirror turns into a full-size doorway, through which guests enter into a wardrobe room. Once you reach the wardrobe room, the attraction's premise is explained: You're supposed to reenact the story of *Beauty and the Beast* for Belle on her birthday, and guests are chosen to act out key parts in the play.

After the parts are cast, everyone walks into the castle's library and takes a seat. Cast members explain how the play will take place and introduce Belle, who gives a short speech about how thrilled she is for everyone to be there. The play is acted out within a few minutes, and the actors get a photo op with Belle and receive a small bookmark as a memento.

Enchanted Tales with Belle is surely the prettiest and most elaborate meet and greet in Disney World. For the relative few who get to act in the play, it's also a chance to interact with Belle in a way that isn't possible in other character encounters.

It's a Small World (*FastPass+*) ★★★½

APPEAL BY AGE   PRESCHOOL ★★★★½   GRADE SCHOOL ★★★★   TEENS ★★★
YOUNG ADULTS ★★★½   OVER 30 ★★★½   SENIORS ★★★★

What it is World brotherhood–themed indoor boat ride. **Scope and scale** Major attraction. **Fright potential** Not frightening in any respect. **Bottleneck rating** 7. **When to go** Before 11 a.m., during parades, or after 7 p.m.; FastPass+ is unnecessary. **Comment** Exponentially "cute." **Duration of ride** About 11 minutes. **Average wait in line per 100 people ahead of you** 3½ minutes; assumes busy conditions with 30 or more boats operating. **Loading speed** Fast.

Small boats carry visitors on a tour around the world, with singing and dancing dolls showcasing the dress and culture of each nation. At the end of the ride, look for the panel bidding you (and your MagicBand) a personal goodbye. Of course, there's no escaping the brain-numbing tune. Just when you think you've repressed it, the song will resurface without warning to torture you some more.

> It's such a happy ride, and it was so cool to see our names at the end.
>
> **Felicity**

Mad Tea Party (*FastPass+*) ★★

APPEAL BY AGE   PRESCHOOL ★★★★½   GRADE SCHOOL ★★★★½   TEENS ★★★★
YOUNG ADULTS ★★★★   OVER 30 ★★★½   SENIORS ★★★

What it is Midway-type spinning ride. **Scope and scale** Minor attraction. **Fright potential** Low, but this type of ride can induce motion sickness in all ages. **Bottleneck rating** 9. **When to go** Before 11 a.m. or after 5 p.m.; not a good choice for FastPass+. **Comments** You can make the teacups spin faster by turning the wheel in the center of the cup. Fun but not worth the wait. **Duration of ride** 1½ minutes. **Average wait in line per 100 people ahead of you** 7½ minutes. **Loading speed** Slow.

Queasy

Teenagers love to lure unsuspecting adults into the spinning teacups and then turn the wheel in the middle (making the cup spin faster) until the grown-ups are plastered against the sides and on the verge of throwing up. Unless you aspire to be a living physics experiment, don't even *consider* getting on this one with anyone younger than 21. This ride is notoriously slow-loading. Ride the morning of your second day if your schedule is more relaxed. Characters from *Alice in Wonderland,* including Alice herself, meet intermittently in front of the ride.

Movie Tip

Did you know that the voice of Alice, British voice actress and schoolteacher Kathryn Beaumont, is also the voice of Wendy in Peter Pan?

The Many Adventures of Winnie the Pooh (FastPass+) ★★★½

APPEAL BY AGE   PRESCHOOL ★★★★½   GRADE SCHOOL ★★★★   TEENS ★★★½
YOUNG ADULTS ★★★½   OVER 30 ★★★½   SENIORS ★★★★

Thumbs Up for the Whole Family

What it is Indoor track ride. **Scope and scale** Minor attraction. **Fright potential** Frightens a few preschoolers. **Bottleneck rating** 8. **When to go** Before 10 a.m., the last hour the park is open, or use FastPass+. **Comment** Cute as the Pooh bear himself. **Duration of ride** About 4 minutes. **Average wait in line per 100 people ahead of you** 4 minutes. **Loading speed** Moderate.

This attraction is sunny, upbeat, and charming without being saccharine. You ride a "hunny pot" through the pages of a huge picture book into the Hundred Acre Wood, where you encounter Pooh, Piglet, Eeyore, Owl, Rabbit, Tigger, Kanga, and Roo as they contend with a blustery day. Pooh is a perfect test to assess how your very young children will react to indoor (dark) rides. It's also a good choice for FastPass+ if you have small children and you're touring over 2 or more days. Near the ride, Winnie the Pooh and Tigger meet little fans throughout the day.

Movie Tip

Did you know Paul Winchell won a Grammy for his voicing of Tigger? He also voiced a Chinese cat in The Aristocats *and Boomer the woodpecker in* The Fox and the Hound; *plus, he provided the voice of the evil Gargamel in the animated TV series* The Smurfs.

Meet Merida at Fairytale Garden ★★★½

APPEAL BY AGE   PRESCHOOL ★★★★½   GRADE SCHOOL ★★★★   TEENS ★★★½
YOUNG ADULTS ★★★½   OVER 30 ★★★½   SENIORS ★★★★

What it is Storytelling session and character meet and greet. **Scope and scale** Diversion. **Fright potential** Not frightening in any respect. **Bottleneck rating** 7. **When to go** See *Times Guide* for schedule. **Comment** Lovely lass, lovely locale. **Duration of experience** About 10 minutes. **Probable waiting time** 30 minutes.

Merida, the flame-haired Scottish princess from *Brave,* greets guests in Fairytale Garden, next to Cinderella Castle on the Tomorrowland side, between the castle and Cosmic Ray's Starlight Cafe. Princess meet and greets tend to be popular, so expect lines.

Mickey's PhilharMagic (FastPass+) ★★★★

APPEAL BY AGE   PRESCHOOL ★★★★   GRADE SCHOOL ★★★★   TEENS ★★★★
YOUNG ADULTS ★★★★   OVER 30 ★★★★   SENIORS ★★★★½

What it is 3-D movie. **Scope and scale** Major attraction. **Fright potential** Scares some preschoolers. **Bottleneck rating** 6. **When to go** Anytime; never a good use of Fast-Pass+. **Comment** Not to be missed; a zany masterpiece. **Duration of show** About 12 minutes. **Probable waiting time** 10–15 minutes.

Mickey's PhilharMagic combines three fabulous ideas: Mickey and Donald mix and meet with latter-day Disney stars such as Aladdin, Jasmine, Ariel, the Beast's pantry servants (such as Lumière and Mrs. Potts), and Simba; it uses a form of computer-enhanced 3-D video technology that is truly impressive; and the whole shebang is projected on a 150-foot-wide, 180-degree screen. *Mickey's PhilharMagic* even employs some of those famous Disney scent effects and turns the old sorcerer's apprentice trick back on Mickey. However, we think the attraction would benefit from a digital quality upgrade. Adding a few new musical numbers and experiences wouldn't hurt either.

Where other Disney 3-D movies are loud, in-your-face affairs, this one is softer and cuddlier. Things pop out of the screen, but they're really not scary. It's the rare child who is frightened—but there are always exceptions, as was the case with the 3-year-old child of this North Carolina mom:

> *Our family found* PhilharMagic *way too violent (minutes on end of Donald getting the crap kicked out of him by musical instruments). I had to haul my screaming child out of the theater and submit to a therapeutic carousel ride afterward.*

Happily, an Oregon mom has an easy way to nip the willies in the bud:

> *My advice to parents is simply to have their kids not wear the 3-D glasses. We took my daughter's off right away, and then she began giggling and having a good time watching the movie.*

Peter Pan's Flight *(FastPass+)* ★★★★

**APPEAL BY AGE PRESCHOOL ★★★★½   GRADE SCHOOL ★★★★   TEENS ★★★½
YOUNG ADULTS ★★★★   OVER 30 ★★★★   SENIORS ★★★★**

Thumbs Up for the Whole Family

What it is Indoor track ride. **Scope and scale** Minor attraction. **Fright potential** Not frightening in any respect. **Bottleneck rating** 8. **When to go** First or last 30 minutes the park is open, or use Fast-Pass+. **Comment** Happy, mellow, and well done. **Duration of ride** A little more than 3 minutes. **Average wait in line per 100 people ahead of you** 5½ minutes. **Loading speed** Moderate–slow.

Peter Pan's Flight is superbly designed and absolutely delightful, with a happy theme uniting some favorite Disney characters, beautiful effects, and charming music. This dark (indoor) ride takes you on a relaxing trip in a "flying pirate ship" over old London and thence to Never Land, where Peter saves Wendy from walking the plank and Captain Hook rehearses for *Dancing with the Stars* on the snout of the ubiquitous crocodile. There's nothing here that will jump out at you or frighten young children. An interactive queuing area alleviates the pain of waiting in line as guests go through the Darlings' house before boarding their ride to Never Land.

Because Peter Pan's Flight is very popular, count on long lines all day. You can meet the boy who never grew up, and at times Wendy, next to the ride.

There are many little details to discover when riding Peter Pan's Flight. Be on the lookout for Ariel in the mermaid lagoon.

Isabelle

It was brilliant! I felt like flying, and I got to see Tink.

Felicity

Disney's animated film version of Peter Pan *is, of course, the inspiration for this wonderful ride. While the original is easy to find, the sequel,* Return to Never Land, *is not. Try to get a copy at a library or find a used one at amazon.com and reunite with Peter, Wendy, Tinker Bell, Mr. Smee, the Lost Boys, and Captain Hook. But most of all: never grow up.*

Pete's Silly Sideshow ★★★½

**APPEAL BY AGE PRESCHOOL ★★★★★ GRADE SCHOOL ★★★★★ TEENS ★★★★
YOUNG ADULTS ★★★★ OVER 30 ★★★★ SENIORS ★★★★**

What it is Character greeting venue. **Scope and scale** Minor attraction. **Fright potential** Not frightening in any respect. **Bottleneck rating** 8. **When to go** Before 11 a.m. or in the last 2 hours the park is open. **Comment** Well themed, with unique character costumes. **Duration of experience** 3 minutes per character. **Average wait in line per 100 people ahead of you** 25 minutes. **Queue speed** Slow.

Pete's Silly Sideshow is a circus-themed character greeting area in the Storybook Circus part of Fantasyland. The characters' costumes are distinct from the ones normally used around the parks. Characters include Goofy as The Great Goofini, Donald Duck as The Astounding Donaldo, Daisy Duck as Madame Daisy Fortuna, and Minnie Mouse as Minnie Magnifique. On non–Extra Magic Hour days, Pete's opens 45 minutes later than the rest of the park and usually closes at the same time as the first fireworks show. The queue is indoors and air-conditioned. Note that there is one queue for the male characters (Goofy and Donald) and a second queue for the female characters (Minnie and Daisy). You can meet two characters at once but must line up twice to meet all four.

Prince Charming Regal Carrousel ★★★

**APPEAL BY AGE PRESCHOOL ★★★★½ GRADE SCHOOL ★★★★ TEENS ★★★½
YOUNG ADULTS ★★★½ OVER 30 ★★★½ SENIORS ★★★½**

What it is Merry-go-round. **Scope and scale** Minor attraction. **Fright potential** Not frightening in any respect. **Bottleneck rating** 7. **When to go** Anytime. **Comments** Adults enjoy the beauty and nostalgia of this ride. A beautiful children's ride. **Duration of ride** About 2 minutes. **Average wait in line per 100 people ahead of you** 5 minutes. **Loading speed** Slow.

You'll have a long wait, but the beauty of the carousel (formerly known as Cinderella's Golden Carrousel) captures everyone. The carousel, built in 1917, was discovered in New Jersey, where it was once part of an amusement park. It is beautifully maintained and especially magical at night when all the lights are on. Check out your children's delighted expressions as the painted ponies go up and down.

A shy 9-year-old girl from Rockaway, New Jersey, thinks our rating of the carousel should be higher:

> *I want to complain. I went on the Prince Charming Regal Carrousel four times, and I loved it! Raise those stars right now!*

It was so enjoyable riding up and down on a lovely horse. I felt like a princess.

Felicity

Princess Fairytale Hall *(FastPass+)* ★★★

**APPEAL BY AGE PRESCHOOL ★★★★★ GRADE SCHOOL ★★★★½ TEENS ★★★★
YOUNG ADULTS ★★★★ OVER 30 ★★★★ SENIORS ★★★★**

What it is Character-greeting venue. **Scope and scale** Minor attraction. **Fright potential** Not frightening in any respect. **Bottleneck rating** 9. **When to go** Before 10:30 a.m. or after 4 p.m. **Duration of experience** 7–10 minutes. **Average wait in line per 100 people ahead of you** 35 minutes. **Queue speed** Slow.

Princess Fairytale Hall is royalty central in the Magic Kingdom. Inside are two greeting venues, with each holding a small reception area for two royals. Thus, there are four royals meeting and greeting at any time, and you can see two of them at once. Signs outside the entrance tell you which line leads to which royal pair and how long the wait will be. Rapunzel usually leads one side with Tiana, and Cinderella is typically joined by Elena of Avalor, Disney's first Latina princess, on the other side.

About 5–10 guests are admitted to each greeting area, where there's plenty of time for small talk, a photo, and a hug from each princess.

Seven Dwarfs Mine Train *(FastPass+)*   ★★★★

APPEAL BY AGE PRESCHOOL ★★★★   GRADE SCHOOL ★★★★½ TEENS ★★★★½ YOUNG ADULTS ★★★½   OVER 30 ★★★★½   SENIORS ★★★★½

Thumbs Up for the Whole Family

What it is A musical roller-coaster journey into the diamond mine of the Seven Dwarfs. **Scope and scale** Headliner. **Fright potential** Marginally wild ride, dark scenes, and special effects may frighten children age 7 and younger. **Bottleneck rating** 10. **When to go** As soon as the park opens, or use FastPass+. **Comments** The swinging effect is more noticeable the farther back you're seated in the train; must be 38″ tall to ride. Switching-off option (see page 248). Not to be missed. **Duration of ride** About 4 minutes. **Average wait in line per 100 people ahead of you** 4 minutes. **Loading speed** Fast.

Scary

Seven Dwarfs Mine Train is geared to older grade-school kids who have been on amusement park rides before. There are no loops, inversions, or rolls in the track and no massive hills or steep drops; the Mine Train's trick is that the ride vehicle's seats swing side to side as you go through turns. And—what a coincidence!—Disney has designed a curvy track with steep turns. An elaborate indoor section shows the dwarfs' underground operation. The exterior design includes waterfalls, forests, and landscaping.

While it's a charming ride in a lovely setting, Liliane isn't smitten. See her review of this and other Fantasyland attractions at tinyurl.com/newfantasylandreview.

This mom from Utah concurs with Liliane:

> Seven Dwarfs Mine Train is the most overrated ride EVER. My kids (ages 6 and 7) were completely bored standing in line and unimpressed with the ride. If you have kids over 40″ tall, skip it and save your time and FastPass+ for Space Mountain and Big Thunder Mountain Railroad.

It's difficult to get FastPass+ reservations for Mine Train, so if they're available for any time of day, grab them. If not, make advance FastPass+ reservations for around 9:30 a.m. at Big Thunder Mountain Railroad and around 3:30 p.m. at Space Mountain. On the day of your visit, ride Seven Dwarfs Mine Train as soon as the park opens, then Splash Mountain. If you have two mornings, do Seven Dwarfs Mine Train, Splash Mountain, and Big Thunder Mountain on one day and Space Mountain the next.

The Seven Dwarfs Mine Train was a total and utter disappointment. No sharp turns, no drops, and not much speed. Don't waste your time if you like thrills. It's a good test coaster for small children though.

A. J.

To get any momentum going downhill, try to sit
in the back of the Seven Dwarfs Mine Train.

Brendan

Under the Sea: Journey of the Little Mermaid
(FastPass+) ★★★½

APPEAL BY AGE   PRESCHOOL ★★★½   **GRADE SCHOOL** ★★★★   **TEENS** ★★★½
YOUNG ADULTS ★★★★   **OVER 30** ★★★★   **SENIORS** ★★★★

What it is Dark ride retelling the film's story. **Scope and scale** Major attraction. **Fright
potential** Evil Ursula and dark effects frighten kids under age 7. **Bottleneck rating** 8.
When to go Before 10:30 a.m. or the last 2 hours the park is open; rarely a good
choice for FastPass+. **Comment** Cute, but most effects are too simple for an attraction
this big. **Duration of ride** About 5½ minutes. **Average wait in line per 100 people
ahead of you** 3 minutes. **Loading speed** Fast.

I was disappointed! The ride feels very much like a clone of
The Seas with Nemo & Friends at Epcot. The queuing area
is whimsical, but who wants to be stuck in a queuing area?

Liliane

Under The Sea takes riders through almost a dozen scenes retelling the story
of *The Little Mermaid* film, with Audio-Animatronics, video effects, and a
vibrant 3-D set the size of a small theater. Guests board a clamshell-shaped
ride vehicle running along a continuously moving track (similar to The
Haunted Mansion's). Once you're on board, the ride descends "under water,"
past Ariel's grotto, and to King Triton's undersea kingdom. The most detailed
animatronic is Ursula the octopus, and she's a beauty. Other scenes hit the
film's highlights, including Ariel meeting Prince Eric, her deal with Ursula to
become human, and, of course, the happy couple at the end.

Try to ride early in the morning or late at night.

TOMORROWLAND

AT VARIOUS POINTS IN ITS HISTORY, Tomorrowland's attractions presented life's possibilities in adventures ranging from the
modern-day to the distant future. The problem that stymied Disney
repeatedly was that the future came faster and looked different than
what they'd envisioned.

Today, Tomorrowland's theme makes the least sense of any area
in any Disney park. Its current attractions are based on gas-powered
race cars, rocket travel (two rides), a look back at 20th-century technology, an attraction with aliens, and a comedy show with monsters.
It's not so much a vision of the future as it is a collection of attractions
that don't fit anywhere else in the park.

Construction has started on a new roller coaster themed to Disney's *Tron* movie, expected to open in 2021. Most of the ride will
be behind the Tomorrowland Speedway and outside the current park
boundary. Construction impacts to the land's attractions are minimal.

Astro Orbiter   ★★

APPEAL BY AGE   PRESCHOOL ★★★★   **GRADE SCHOOL** ★★★★   **TEENS** ★★★½
YOUNG ADULTS ★★★   **OVER 30** ★★★   **SENIORS** ★★★

What it is Buck Rogers–style rockets revolving around a central axis. **Scope and scale** Minor attraction. **Fright potential** Visually intimidating waiting area for a relatively tame ride. **Bottleneck rating** 10. **When to go** Before 11 a.m. or the last hour the park is open. **Comments** This attraction is not as innocuous as it appears. Not worth the wait. **Duration of ride** 1½ minutes. **Average wait in line per 100 people ahead of you** 13½ minutes. **Loading speed** Slow.

Parents, beware! If you're prone to motion sickness, this ride a) spins round and round; b) is faster than Dumbo; and c) for added "fun," a joystick lets you raise and lower the rocket throughout your 1½-minute journey. We like to ride the Astro Orbiter at night. The combination of lighting and the view is spectacular.

Buzz Lightyear's Space Ranger Spin *(FastPass+)* ★★★★
APPEAL BY AGE PRESCHOOL ★★★★½ GRADE SCHOOL ★★★★½ TEENS ★★★★
YOUNG ADULTS ★★★★ OVER 30 ★★★★ SENIORS ★★★★

What it is Combination space travel–themed indoor ride and shooting gallery. **Scope and scale** Minor attraction. **Fright potential** Dark ride with cartoonlike aliens may frighten some preschoolers. **Bottleneck rating** 8. **When to go** First or last hour the park is open, or use FastPass+. **Comments** A real winner! Not to be missed. **Duration of ride** About 4½ minutes. **Average wait in line per 100 people ahead of you** 3 minutes. **Loading speed** Fast.

Once you get the hang of it, you'll come back for more, to infinity and beyond!

> *The ride is based on the space-commando character Buzz Lightyear from the 1995 Disney-Pixar feature* Toy Story. *Did you know that Tom Hanks and Tim Allen are the voices of Woody and Buzz?*

Monsters, Inc. Laugh Floor (FastPass+) ★★★½
APPEAL BY AGE PRESCHOOL ★★★★ GRADE SCHOOL ★★★★½ TEENS ★★★★
YOUNG ADULTS ★★★★ OVER 30 ★★★★ SENIORS ★★★★½

What it is Interactive animated comedy routines. **Scope and scale** Major attraction. **Fright potential** Not much is frightening, but they are monsters, after all. **Bottleneck rating** 8. **When to go** Before 11 a.m. or after 4 p.m. **Comments** Audience members may be asked to participate in skits. Good concept; jokes are hit-or-miss. **Duration of show** About 15 minutes including preshow. **Probable waiting time** 25 minutes.

> *The show is based on the 2001 Pixar film* Monsters, Inc., *starring Billy Crystal (voice) in the role of Mike Wazowski. It won an Oscar for best song.*

We learned in Disney-Pixar's *Monsters, Inc.* that children's screams could be converted into electricity, which was used to power a town inhabited by monsters. During the film, the monsters discovered that children's laughter was an even better source of energy. In this attraction, the monsters have set up a comedy club to capture as many laughs as possible. Mike Wazowski, the one-eyed character from the film, emcees the club's three comedy acts. Each consists of an animated monster (most not seen in the film) trying out various bad puns, knock-knock jokes, and comedy routines. Using the same cutting-edge technology as Epcot's *Turtle Talk with Crush,* behind-the-scenes Disney employees voice the characters and often interact with audience members during the skits. As with any comedy set, some performers are funny and some are not, but Disney has shown a willingness to experiment with new routines and jokes. A Sioux Falls, South Dakota, mom is a big fan:

Laugh Floor was great. It's amazing how the characters interact with the audi- ence. I got picked on twice without trying. Plus, kids can text jokes to Roz.

Space Mountain *(FastPass+)* ★★★★

†*Some preschoolers love Space Mountain; others are frightened by it.*

What it is Roller coaster in the dark. **Scope and scale** Super-headliner. **Fright potential** Very intense roller coaster in the dark; the Magic Kingdom's wildest ride and a scary roller coaster by any standard. **Bottleneck rating** 10. **When to go** When the park opens or use FastPass+. **Comments** Great fun and action; much wilder than Big Thunder Mountain Railroad. Must be 44″ tall to ride; children younger than age 7 must be accompanied by an adult. Switching-off option (see page 248). An unusual roller coaster with excellent special effects; not to be missed. **Duration of ride** Almost 3 minutes. **Average wait in line per 100 people ahead of you** 3 minutes; assumes two tracks, one dedicated to FastPass+ riders, dispatching at 21-second intervals. **Loading speed** Moderate–fast.

Dark Rough Queasy Scary

Space Mountain is one of Walt Disney World's zippiest (and darkest) rides, lasting a little less than 3 minutes and including numerous abrupt turns and plummets. However, the top speed is only about 28 miles per hour, a leisurely pace by 21st-century standards.

Space Mountain involves sudden blackouts. Those who suffer from claustrophobia (Liliane), who tend to panic in the dark (Liliane), or who have vision problems with extremes of light and darkness (Liliane) should avoid this attraction, as should those with neck or back problems or vertigo. Plunged into darkness and bouncing around like a marble in a spittoon, many warmly recall Space Mountain as the longest 3 minutes of their lives. Your kids will love it. There are no long drops or swooping hills as there are on a traditional roller coaster—only quick, unexpected turns and small drops.

Periodic refurbishments have added new lighting and effects and an improved sound system and soundtrack. Look for special effects during Halloween. If you don't catch Space Mountain first in the morning, use FastPass+ or try again during the 30 minutes before closing.

I dream of riding Space Mountain at the pace of Spaceship Earth in Epcot. At last, I would be able to enjoy the twinkling lights.

Liliane

Tomorrowland Speedway *(FastPass+)* ★★

What it is Drive-'em-yourself minicars. **Scope and scale** Major children's attraction. **Fright potential** Noise of the waiting area frightens some young kids; otherwise, not frightening. **Bottleneck rating** 9. **When to go** Before 10 a.m. or in the last 2 hours the park is open. **Comments** Must be 54″ tall to drive unassisted; must be 32″ tall to ride with parent. Switching-off option (see page 248). Boring for adults; great for preschoolers. **Duration of ride** About 4¼ minutes. **Average wait in line per 100 people ahead of you** 4½ minutes; assumes 285-car turnover every 20 minutes. **Loading speed** Slow.

The sleek cars and racetrack noise will get your younger kids hopped up to ride this extremely prosaic attraction. The younger (or shorter) set will have to ride with an adult. After getting into the car, shift your child over behind the steering wheel. From your position, you will still be able to control the foot pedals. Children will feel like they're really driving, and because the car travels on a self-guiding track, there's no way they can make a mistake while steering. The loading and unloading speeds are excruciatingly slow, and the attraction offers hardly any protection from the sun.

Tomorrowland Transit Authority PeopleMover ★★★½

**APPEAL BY AGE   PRESCHOOL ★★★★   GRADE SCHOOL ★★★★   TEENS ★★★★
YOUNG ADULTS ★★★★½   OVER 30 ★★★★½   SENIORS ★★★★½**

Thumbs Up for the Whole Family

What it is Scenic tour of Tomorrowland. **Scope and scale** Minor attraction. **Fright potential** Not frightening in any respect. **Bottleneck rating** 3. **When to go** During hot, crowded times of day (11:30 a.m.–4:30 p.m.). **Comments** A good way to check out the lines at Space Mountain and the Speedway. Scenic and relaxing. **Duration of ride** 10 minutes. **Average wait in line per 100 people ahead of you** 1½ minutes; assumes 39 trains operating. **Loading speed** Fast.

The ride is ideal for taking a break. It's also a great way to see Tomorrowland all aglow at night. The route gives a sneak preview of Buzz Lightyear's Space Ranger Spin, and you can check on those screams emanating from Space Mountain. Most of the time cast members will let you ride several times in a row without having to get off. This, according to many moms, makes the ride a great option for nursing.

Walt Disney's Carousel of Progress ★★★

**APPEAL BY AGE   PRESCHOOL ★★★½   GRADE SCHOOL ★★★½   TEENS ★★★½
YOUNG ADULTS ★★★★   OVER 30 ★★★★   SENIORS ★★★★½**

What it is Audio-Animatronic theater production. **Scope and scale** Major attraction. **Fright potential** Not frightening in any respect. **Bottleneck rating** 4. **When to go** Anytime. **Comment** Nostalgic, warm, and happy. **Duration of show** 21 minutes. **Preshow** Documentary on the attraction's long history. **Probable waiting time** Less than 10 minutes.

Walt Disney's Carousel of Progress offers a nostalgic look at how technology and electricity have changed the lives of an animatronic family over several generations from circa 1900 to 1990. The family is easy to identify with, and a cheerful, sentimental tune bridges the generations. Adults will be amused at

---

FAVORITE EATS IN THE MAGIC KINGDOM

LAND | SERVICE LOCATION | FOOD SELECTIONS

MAIN STREET Main Street Bakery | Sandwiches and salads; pretty much anything that Starbucks has

ADVENTURELAND Tortuga Tavern (*seasonal*) | Chipotle barbecue short ribs

FANTASYLAND Friar's Nook | Hot dogs and tots
Pinocchio Village Haus | Pepperoni flatbread

FRONTIERLAND Pecos Bill Tall Tale Inn & Cafe | Tacos three ways and a fajita platter

LIBERTY SQUARE Columbia Harbour House | Lobster roll and New England clam chowder | **Sleepy Hollow** | Funnel cake

TOMORROWLAND Cosmic Ray's Starlight Cafe | Barbecue pulled pork platter; kosher choices | **The Lunching Pad** | Hot dogs, barbecue pulled pork sandwich, and frozen soda

the references to laser discs and car phones as examples of modern technology; kids will be confused.

Though dated, *Carousel of Progress* was almost entirely conceived and guided by Walt Disney himself, rare among Magic Kingdom attractions. It's the only Magic Kingdom attraction to display Walt's optimistic vision of a better future through technology and industry. If you're interested in the man behind the mouse, this show is a must-see.

Carousel handles big crowds effectively and is a good choice during busier times of day. Because of its age, this attraction seems to have more minor operational glitches than most attractions, so you may be subjected to the same dialog and songs several times.

LIVE ENTERTAINMENT *and* PARADES *in the* MAGIC KINGDOM

IT'S IMPOSSIBLE TO TAKE IN all the many live-entertainment offerings at the Magic Kingdom in a single day. To experience both the attractions and the live entertainment, we recommend you allocate at least 2 days to this park. In addition to parades, stage shows, and fireworks, check the daily entertainment schedule (via the My Disney Experience app or the *Times Guide*) or ask a cast member about concerts in Fantasyland, the Flag Retreat at Town Square, and the appearances of the various bands, singers, and street performers who roam the park daily. WDW live-entertainment guru Steve Soares usually posts the Magic Kingdom's performance schedule about a week in advance at wdwent.com.

The **Dapper Dans** sing soulful Americana a cappella; be sure to see them as they put on a show for whomever is wandering the street. The **Casey's Corner pianist** plays tunes from a bygone era next to the eatery of the same name. He even takes requests! The legendary **Main Street Philharmonic** performs tunes from classic Disney films, mixed with ragtime and swing, at several locations in the park. The funny characters of **Citizens of Main Street, U.S.A.** can be spotted along Main Street throughout the day. The **Royal Majesty Makers** give little princes and princesses "lessons" in horse riding, swordsmanship, and more in Fantasyland. Check the *Times Guide* for showtimes.

LILIANE The afternoon parade is a must-see—great music, outstanding costumes, and more than 100 live performers. The 26-foot-tall Maleficent dragon is awe-inspiring. Disney really went big with this one.

Parades at the Magic Kingdom are full-fledged spectaculars with dozens of Disney characters and amazing special effects. Remember that parades disrupt traffic, making it nearly impossible to move around the park when one is going on. Parades also draw thousands of guests away from the attractions, making parade time the perfect moment to catch your favorite attraction with a shorter line. Finally, be advised that the Walt Disney World Railroad shuts down during parades.

The best place to view a parade is the upper platform of the **Walt Disney Railroad station,** but you'll have to stake out your position 30–45 minutes before the event. Try also, especially on rainy days, the **covered walkway between Liberty Tree Tavern and The Diamond Horseshoe,** on the border of Liberty Square and Frontierland.

Following is a short list of daily events with special appeal for families with children:

AFTERNOON PARADE Usually staged at 3 p.m., this parade features floats and marching Disney characters. **Festival of Fantasy** (★★★★) has an original score and floats paying tribute to *The Little Mermaid, Brave,* and *Frozen,* among other Disney films. Many of the floats' pieces spin and swing to extremes not normally found in Disney parades: the *Tangled* platform has characters swinging wood hammers from one side of the street to the other. The most talked-about float is Maleficent (the villain from *Sleeping Beauty*) in dragon form—she spits actual fire at a couple of points along the route. Evening parades only take place during Mickey's Not-So-Scary Halloween Party and Mickey's Very Merry Christmas Party.

LUCY Watching the Festival of Fantasy Parade is a must, but if you've already seen it, you can use that time to get on rides, as they are less crowded during that time

BAY LAKE AND SEVEN SEAS LAGOON ELECTRICAL WATER PAGEANT ★★★★ Performed at nightfall at about 9 p.m. most of the year on Seven Seas Lagoon and Bay Lake, this pageant is the perfect culmination of a wonderful day. You have to leave the Magic Kingdom to see the show—take the monorail to the Polynesian Village Resort, get the kids a snack and yourself a drink, and walk to the end of the pier to watch. Pure magic, less the crowds. The pageant floats past the Polynesian at 9 p.m., Grand Floridian at 9:15 p.m., Wilderness Lodge at 9:30 p.m., Fort Wilderness Resort & Campground around 9:45 p.m., the Contemporary at 10:10 p.m., and outside the entrance to the Magic Kingdom at 10:35 p.m.

CASTLE FORECOURT STAGE ★★★½ *Mickey's Royal Friendship Faire* brings to life beloved Disney stories, both classic and contemporary. Tiana, Naveen, and Louis from *The Princess and the Frog* have traveled from New Orleans to be with their friends; Rapunzel and Flynn Rider from *Tangled* are the special guests of Daisy Duck; while Olaf, Anna, and Elsa from *Frozen* bring some icy magic to the party.

LILIANE Where is the mistress of the house? I am all for change, but there should have been a role for Cinderella in the show. This is, after all, her castle!

CHARACTER SHOWS AND APPEARANCES A number of characters are usually on hand to greet guests when the park opens. Because they snarl pedestrian traffic and stop most kids dead in their tracks, this is sort of a mixed blessing. Check your daily *Times Guide* for character greeting locations and times, or see our table on pages 250–251.

FIREWORKS SHOWS The 18-minute *Happily Ever After* presentation (★★★★★) combines memorable vignettes from popular animated films with a stellar fireworks display. The amazing show projected on the castle is best viewed right in front of it. If you only want to see the fireworks and intend to remain in the park, our two favorite spots are in Fantasyland, between Seven Dwarfs Mine Train and *Enchanted Tales with Belle*, or on the bridge between the Central Plaza and Tomorrowland. Anywhere along Main Street is also a good viewing location, especially if you plan to leave the park immediately afterward.

At the **Fireworks Dessert Party,** you can view *Happily Ever After* from the Tomorrowland Terrace area; it costs $84 per adult and $50 per child, tax included. The viewing area is available starting 1 hour before the show, and the event includes a dessert buffet and nonalcoholic beverages. Reservations can be made 180 days in advance online or by calling ☎ 407-WDW-DINE (939-3463). If you make a reservation more than 2 weeks in advance, you'll be given a default reservation time of 6 p.m. for the dessert party and told to call back within 2 weeks of your trip for the actual time.

LUCY Watching the fireworks is simply the best. Make sure you get a good spot before they start.

On the **Ferrytale Fireworks: A Sparkling Dessert Cruise,** guests board one of the ferries at the Transportation and Ticket Center for desserts, souvenir glow glasses, and a view of the fireworks. Unlike the dessert party at the Tomorrowland Terrace, this event includes alcoholic beverages for adults. Unlike the pontoon cruise, this is not a private event for just your party. Pricing is $99 for adults and $69 for children, plus tax. To reserve, call ☎ 407-939-7529 or online through Disney Dining.

For a different view, you can watch the fireworks from Seven Seas Lagoon aboard a chartered pontoon boat on a **Specialty Fireworks Cruise.** The charter costs $320 for up to 8 people and $372 for 10 (tax included). Chips, soda, and water are provided; sandwiches and more-substantial food items may be arranged through reservations. Your Disney captain will take you for a little cruise and then position the boat in a perfect place to watch the fireworks. Life jackets are provided, but wearing them is at your discretion. To reserve a charter, call ☎ 407-WDW-PLAY (939-7529) at exactly 7 a.m. Eastern about 180 days before the day you want to cruise.

LILIANE If all you want is a serene spot to watch the fireworks or the Bay Lake and Seven Seas Lagoon Electrical Water Pageant, you don't need to spend big bucks. The gardens of the Grand Floridian are perfect for the fireworks, and the beach of the Polynesian Village Resort does the trick for the pageant.

At the **After Fireworks Dessert Party,** guests watch the nighttime spectacular from a reserved viewing space in the Plaza Garden, followed by an exclusive dessert party at Tomorrowland Terrace after the show's finale. The menu includes savory snacks such as spinach dip and house-made mini egg rolls, as well as the popular Ooey Gooey Toffee Cake from Liberty Tree Tavern. In addition to special holiday fireworks, guests taking part in the After Fireworks Party on July 3–4 or select nights of Mickey's Not-So-Scary Halloween Party and Mickey's Very Merry Christmas Party can enjoy holiday-themed treats. Admission to the party is $69 for adults and $41 for children plus tax.

On July 3 and 4, the Magic Kingdom celebrates our nation's birthday in red, white, and blue with *Disney's Celebrate America! A Fourth of July Concert in the Sky* at 9:15 p.m. The New Year is welcomed on December 30 and 31 with special *Fantasy in the Sky Fireworks.* Check the *Times Guide* for showtimes.

FLAG RETREAT At 5 p.m. daily at Town Square (railroad-station end of Main Street). Sometimes performed with great fanfare and college marching bands, sometimes with a smaller Disney band.

LET THE MAGIC BEGIN A 5-minute show on the Castle Forecourt starts each day at the Magic Kingdom. It's a diversion at best and not worth you diverting from your touring plans.

MAGIC KINGDOM BANDS Banjo, Dixieland, steel-drum, and marching bands play daily throughout the park.

MOVE IT! SHAKE IT! MOUSEKEDANCE IT! STREET PARTY (★★★) Starting at the railroad end of Main Street, U.S.A., and working toward the Central Plaza, this small parade incorporates about a dozen floats, Disney characters (including Nick Wilde and Judy Hopps from *Zootopia)*, and entertainers. An original tune called "It's a Good Time!" serves as the theme song, and there's a good amount of interaction between the entertainers and the crowd.

THE MUPPETS PRESENT . . . GREAT MOMENTS IN AMERICAN HISTORY Check out this hilarious interactive experience that takes place at Liberty Square, in the upper windows of a building next to *The Hall of Presidents.* Kermit the Frog, Miss Piggy, Fozzie Bear, The Great Gonzo, and James Jefferson (the town crier of Liberty Square) bring to life American history, the Muppet way! The tales include the midnight ride of Paul Revere and the Declaration of Independence. Check the *Times Guide* for showtimes. The building hosting the Muppet mayhem is also home to the second Guest Relations location.

ONCE UPON A TIME (★★★★½) In this show, Mrs. Potts from *Beauty and the Beast* shares bedtime stories with Chip, taking guests on a magical trip through the most adventurous scenes from favorite Disney films like *Cinderella, Peter Pan, The Many Adventures of Winnie the Pooh,* and *Alice in Wonderland.* Videos and special effects are set to music and projected on Cinderella Castle. Disney regularly updates the show's content to keep it fresh. While the show's soundtrack is invariably excessively sentimental, the visuals more than make up for it. We rate this as not to be missed.

For the winter holidays, *Once Upon a Time* gets a *Frozen*-inspired retheming. The castle's projections include Anna, Elsa, Olaf, and other stars from that blockbuster, plus the usual classic Disney characters.

TINKER BELL'S FLIGHT Watch Tinker Bell (a real cast member, not a special effect) fly high above Cinderella Castle during the *Happily Ever After* fireworks show.

TOMORROWLAND STAGE Located behind the Astro Orbiter, the stage occasionally hosts DJ-led dance parties. They are fun at Halloween and

Christmas but totally skippable. Little tykes will like shaking their sillies out though.

EXIT STRATEGIES

BOB Digital displays at the Magic Kingdom exit show the wait to board the monorails and ferry. Take the one with the shorter line.

ARMIES OF GUESTS leave the Magic Kingdom after evening fireworks. The Disney transportation system gets overwhelmed, causing long waits in boarding areas.

If you're parked at the Transportation and Ticket Center (TTC) and are intent on beating the crowd, leave the park before the fireworks begin. If you're staying at a hotel serviced by the ferry, try to catch the ferry that will be crossing Seven Seas Lagoon while the fireworks are in progress. The best vantage point is on the top deck to the right of the pilothouse as you face the Magic Kingdom. If you don't want to board the boat that's loading, stop at the gate and let people pass you. You'll be the first to board the next boat.

If you don't have a stroller, catch the Walt Disney World Railroad (if running) in Frontierland and ride to the park exit at Main Street.

If you're on the Tomorrowland side of the park, a passageway runs between The Plaza Restaurant and Tomorrowland Terrace, behind the east side of Main Street, to Tony's Town Square Restaurant near the park exit. If you're on the Adventureland side of the park, another path runs from First Aid to the Main Street Fire Station near the park exit. However, these passageways aren't always open.

If the path is closed, cut through Tomorrowland Terrace. Before you reach Main Street, bear left into the side door of the corner shop. Main Street shops have interior doors allowing you to pass from one shop to the next without having to get on Main Street. Work your way from shop to shop until you reach Town Square. At Town Square, bear left and move to the train station and the park exit.

Strollers, wheelchairs, and ECVs make navigating the crowds difficult. If you have one of these, or you're staying at a Disney hotel not served by the monorail and must depend on Disney transportation, watch the fireworks, and enjoy a few attractions. Let the throngs of people exit the park and then leave.

MAGIC KINGDOM HARD-TICKET EVENTS

DISNEY EARLY MORNING MAGIC Early Morning Magic is a special extra-cost event offered on certain Tuesdays and Sundays in select months. For $84 per adult and $73 per child (with tax), guests get a breakfast buffet at Cosmic Ray's Starlight Cafe and unlimited access to seven Fantasyland attractions (Mad Tea Party, Princess Fairytale Hall, It's a Small World, Peter Pan's Flight, The Many Adventures of Winnie the Pooh, Under the Sea: Journey of the Little Mermaid, and Seven Dwarfs Mine Train) starting about 75 minutes before regular park opening. Regular park admission is required in addition to the above-mentioned fee, making this event rather pricey.

Consider this upcharge only if you have small children and limited time to see the Magic Kingdom. On EMM days the official park opening is 9 a.m. You will have to be at the park entrance by 7:15 a.m. (check in starts at 7:30 a.m.) at the latest to take full advantage of early access to the rides. If you have small children, keep in mind that you will have to get your family out of the hotel room by about 6 a.m., and by noon, everyone will be ready for a long nap!

Don't waste time on breakfast prior to official park opening, as the buffet at Cosmic Ray's Starlight Café is served until 10 a.m.

DISNEY AFTER HOURS This 3-hour event begins after the Magic Kingdom's regular closing. A ticket purchased in advance costs $113 per adult or child, and $137 per adult or child on the day of the event. Hours are 10 p.m.–1 a.m. For that price you get short lines for the park's best rides and character greetings. Also included are all the ice cream, popcorn, and soda you can consume (from select vendors). This event is only worthwhile if your kids are able to stay up late at night. Even teenagers may balk at doing anything before noon the next morning. The big advantage of this special event is that Disney After Hours' guests can enter the park at 7 p.m. Regular park admission is *not* required.

DISNEY VILLAINS AFTER HOURS During select months, this event offers guests unique, wicked experiences for 3 hours after the park closes to daytime guests. More than 20 popular Magic Kingdom attractions are open with low wait times. A villains show takes place in front of Cinderella's Castle, and the fire-breathing Maleficent's dragon makes its way through the park several times during the evening for guests to enjoy photo ops. Unlimited ice cream novelties, popcorn, and bottled beverages—available at carts stationed throughout the parks—are included in the cost of admission. A ticket purchased in advance costs $148 per adult or child, and $153 per adult or child on the day of the event. Disney Villains ticket holders may enter the park at 7 p.m. The event takes place 10 p.m.–1 a.m.

MICKEY'S HALLOWEEN AND CHRISTMAS PARTIES The Magic Kingdom hosts special after-hours, holiday-themed events August–December, celebrating Halloween and Christmas. These events require separate admission (see pages 47 and 49, respectively, for details) and can sell out.

MAGIC KINGDOM TOURING PLANS

OUR STEP-BY-STEP TOURING PLANS are field-tested, independently verified itineraries that will keep you moving counter to the crowd flow and allow you to see as much as possible in a single day with minimum time wasted in line.

Some plans offer a midday break of at least 3 hours back at your hotel. It's debatable whether the kids will need the nap more than you, but you'll thank us later, we promise.

If you have just 1 day to spend in the Magic Kingdom, our 1-day plans allow you to see the best attractions for kids while avoiding crowds and long waits in line. If you're looking for a more relaxed, less structured tour of the park, try the 1.5-, 2-day, or Sleepyhead plan. These alternatives have less backtracking. The Sleepyhead plan assumes that you'll get to the park around 11 a.m., so it's great for mornings when you don't feel like getting out of bed early.

BOB Don't worry that other people will be following the plans and render them useless. Fewer than 2 in every 100 people in the park have been exposed to this info.

In the Magic Kingdom, the 19 attractions rated highest by kids age 12 and under are character greetings, parades, or fireworks. The Mad Tea Party is the ride kids rate highest. The same is true when teens are included: 20 of the top 25 attractions aren't rides at all. Our touring plans for kids, therefore, include more character greetings, along with the parades and fireworks we've always recommended.

We generally recommend eating lunch outside the Magic Kingdom, but if you can get an Advance Reservation for **Be Our Guest Restaurant,** go for it—it serves the best food in the Magic Kingdom. Our other favorites in the park are the **Columbia Harbour House** in Liberty Square, **Pecos Bill Tall Tale Inn and Cafe** in Frontierland, and **Cosmic Ray's Starlight Cafe** in Tomorrowland.

LILIANE Switching off allows adults to enjoy the more adventuresome attractions while keeping the group together.

The different touring plans are described below. The descriptions will tell you for whom (for example, tweens, parents with preschoolers, grandparents, and so on) or for what situation (such as sleeping late) the plans are designed. The actual touring plans are located on pages 478–486. Each plan includes a numbered map of the park to help you find your way around.

Each plan lists the attractions most likely to need FastPass+ and the approximate return times for which you should try to make reservations. Visit touringplans.com if any attractions, FastPasses, or times need changing, either while planning or in the parks.

HAPPY FAMILY 1-DAY TOURING PLAN This 1-day touring plan includes something for everyone in the family: small children, tweens (ages 8–12), teenagers, parents, and seniors. The plan keeps everyone together for most of the day, including dinner. A midday break is integrated into the parents' plans; teens can visit the park's thrill rides at this time, using day-of FastPasses to minimize their waits in line.

2-DAY TOURING PLAN FOR PARENTS WITH SMALL CHILDREN This 2-day touring plan is designed specifically to eliminate extra walking and backtracking. It's a comprehensive touring plan of the Magic Kingdom and includes nearly every child-friendly attraction in the park. The plan features long midday breaks for lunch and naps outside the park.

2-DAY SLEEPYHEAD TOURING PLAN FOR PARENTS WITH SMALL CHILDREN Another version of the 2-day touring plan described above, this plan allows families with young children to sleep in, arrive at the park in the late morning, and still see the very best attractions in the Magic Kingdom over 2 days.

PARENTS' TOURING PLAN—1 AFTERNOON AND 1 FULL DAY This day-and-a-half plan works perfectly if you're arriving in Orlando late in the morning of your first vacation day and can't wait to start touring. It also works great for families who want to sleep in one morning after spending a full day in the Magic Kingdom the day before.

The plan employs FastPass+ and takes advantage of lower evening crowds to visit other popular attractions. It should work well during the more crowded times of the year.

1-DAY TOURING PLAN FOR TWEENS AND THEIR PARENTS This 1-day plan for parents with children ages 8–12 sets aside ample time for lunch and dinner and includes about 2 hours of free time in the late afternoon to explore other parts of the park. If time permits, consider meeting Ariel at her grotto or more princesses at Fairytale Hall, both in Fantasyland.

1-DAY TOURING PLAN FOR GRANDPARENTS WITH SMALL CHILDREN This plan has a slightly slower walking speed needed to get between attractions. The result should be more fun with less effort. At Pete's Silly Sideshow, you'll have the opportunity to choose which characters to meet, based on your grandchildren's preferences.

PRELIMINARY INSTRUCTIONS FOR ALL MAGIC KINGDOM TOURING PLANS

ON DAYS OF MODERATE-TO-HEAVY ATTENDANCE, follow your chosen touring plan exactly, deviating only:

1. When you aren't interested in an attraction it lists. Simply skip it and proceed to the next step.

2. When you encounter a very long line at an attraction the touring plan calls for. Crowds ebb and flow at the park, and an unusually long line may have gathered at an attraction to which you're directed. It's possible that this is a temporary situation caused by several hundred people arriving en masse from a recently concluded performance of a nearby show. If this is the case, skip it and go to the next step, returning later to retry.

BEFORE YOU GO

1. Call ☎ 407-824-4321 or check disneyworld.com for operating hours.

2. Purchase admission and make FastPass+ reservations before you arrive.

3. Familiarize yourself with park-opening procedures (described on pages 233 and 270) and reread the touring plan you've chosen.

MAGIC KINGDOM TRIVIA QUIZ

1. In 2021 Tomorrowland is debuting a new ride. On what movie series is that ride based?
   a. *Star Wars*
   b. *Avengers*
   c. *Tron*
   d. *Avatar*

2. Which princess does *not* meet guests at the Magic Kingdom?
   a. Belle
   b. Ariel
   c. Rapunzel
   d. Elsa

3. Whom does Princess Tiana marry in *The Princess and the Frog*?
   a. Prince Eric
   b. Prince Naveen
   c. Prince Charming
   d. Prince Philip

4. What body of water does the *Liberty Belle* Riverboat travel?
   a. The Sassagoula River
   b. Seven Seas Lagoon
   c. The Rivers of America
   d. Echo Lake

5. Which character does *not* meet guests at Pete's Silly Sideshow?
   a. Mickey
   b. Minnie
   c. Donald
   d. Daisy

6. What was the Prince Charming Regal Carrousel formerly called?
   a. Merida's Wild Ride
   c. Cinderella's Golden Carrousel
   b. Ariel's Carrousel Under the Sea
   d. Prince Eric's Royal Carrousel

7. Who plays Madame Leota in the *Haunted Mansion* movie?
   a. Jennifer Tilly
   b. Demi Moore
   c. Raquel Alessi
   d. Eva Mendes

8. What is inside Beast's Castle?
   a. A store
   b. A ride
   c. A restaurant
   d. A show

9. Which attraction is inspired by the movie *Song of the South*?
   a. It's a Small World
   b. Splash Mountain
   c. *Walt Disney's Enchanted Tiki Room*
   d. *Country Bear Jamboree*

10. What is the name of the attraction that opened in 2014 at Fantasyland?
    a. Pete's Silly Sideshow
    b. Ariel's Grotto
    c. Seven Dwarfs Mine Train
    d. Casey Jr. Splash 'N' Soak Station

Answers can be found on page 450.

PART EIGHT

EPCOT

EDUCATION, INSPIRATION, AND CORPORATE IMAGERY are the focus at Epcot, the most adult of the Walt Disney World theme parks. What it gains in taking a futuristic, visionary, and technological look at the world, it loses, just a bit, in warmth, happiness, and charm. Some people find the attempts at education to be superficial; others want more entertainment and less education. Most visitors, however, are in between, finding plenty of amusement *and* information.

Epcot's themed areas are distinctly different. **Future World** is in flux. Its older attractions examine where mankind has come from and where it's going, while newer attractions are themed to Disney's make-believe universe of characters. The next phase of Future World construction is likely to include an expansion of World Showcase's almost year-round food festivals into this part of the park. **World Showcase,** which features landmarks, cuisine, and culture from almost a dozen nations, is meant to be a sort of permanent world's fair.

After years of neglect, much-needed updates and new experiences are coming to Epcot. Two new headliner attractions—a family-friendly ride in France based on the Pixar film *Ratatouille* (**Remy's Ratatouille Adventure**) and an indoor roller coaster themed to the *Guardians of the Galaxy* movie series—are scheduled to open by 2020 and 2021, respectively, in time for the 50th anniversary of Walt Disney World. These will be the first completely new attractions in Epcot in almost 15 years.

In the meantime, 2019 saw the opening of an Experience Center at the Odyssey Events Pavilion. Here guests can learn about all the transformations and additions coming to the park. In case you were wondering, the Leave A Legacy photos will be moved to a new location right outside the park's entrance.

But there's more. At the end of summer 2019 Disney retired *Illumi-Nations: Reflections of Earth*. An **all-new nighttime fireworks show** will be coming to the park in 2020. No date has been announced, but in the meantime, guests may enjoy the limited-run fireworks show *Epcot Forever*. See page 326 for more about the nighttime shows.

In Japan the table-service restaurant **Takumi-Tei** opened in summer 2019 as a Signature Dining experience. A **space-themed table-service restaurant** (operated by the Patina Group, which also runs Tutto Italia and Via Napoli at Epcot and Morimoto Asia at Disney Springs), code-named Space 220, is set to open in Future World in late 2019 and will be located between Mission: Space and Test Track. Near Remy's Ratatouille Adventure, Disney is building a *crêperie*—featuring the cuisine of celebrity chef Jérôme Bocuse and offering both table-service and quick-service—that will open by 2021.

At the France Pavilion, a new *Beauty and the Beast* **sing-along** will play in rotation with *Impressions de France*. The *O Canada!* attraction will be getting a new Circle-Vision 360° film, as will the movie at the China Pavilion. A new film, *Awesome Planet,* is coming to the Harvest Theater inside the Land Pavilion; the theater was formerly the home of the film *Circle of Life: An Environmental Fable*. The films are rumored to debut in early 2020.

The park's Festival Center will also receive a complete transformation. The yet-to-be-named pavilion will represent a futuristic city devoted to immersive and interactive experiences.

Bear in mind that the announced rides, restaurants, and experiences will open in stages. We expect all projects to wrap by 2022 in celebration of Epcot's 40th anniversary.

While all these improvements are great news for a park in dire need of new rides and attractions, the next two years will be a challenge, as much of Future World and the park's main entrance will be a construction zone.

As we went to press, Epcot had started its major overhaul of the park's entrance. Expect this part of the commute, including the security screening, to be cumbersome and time-consuming. Keep these delays in mind when planning your visit. If you can, use the International Gateway entrance, which will put you closer to Remy's Ratatouille Adventure (once open).

Epcot is more than twice as large as the Magic Kingdom, so unless 1 day is all you have, plan on spending 2 days at Epcot to savor all it has to offer. Unlike the Magic Kingdom, Epcot may not seem to be a natural for kids at face value, but rest assured that families can have as much fun here as at any of the other theme parks. However, if you're visiting Walt Disney World for 4 days or fewer in 2019 and you have small children, you may find more things to do in 2 days at the Magic Kingdom and 1 each at the Animal Kingdom and Disney's Hollywood Studios.

Now for the practical stuff: Future World always opens first; that's where you start your day. While most of its attractions stay open until the entire park closes, a few close around 7 p.m. most of the year. If you're lodging at a Disney hotel, consider visiting when the park offers morning or evening Extra Magic Hours.

continued on page 306

Epcot

Attractions

1. Agent P's World Showcase Adventure
2. *The American Adventure* ☑
3. *Awesome Planet* (opens 2020)
4. Club Cool ★
5. Disney & Pixar Short Film Festival FP+
6. Epcot Character Spot FP+ ★
7. Fireworks Show ☑ FP+
8. Frozen Ever After FP+
9. Gran Fiesta Tour Starring the Three Caballeros
10. *Impressions de France*
11. Innoventions East
12. Journey into Imagination with Figment FP+
13. Living with the Land ☑ FP+
14. Meet Anna and Elsa at Royal Sommerhus
15. Mission: Space ☑ Use FP+
16. *O Canada!*
17. *Reflections of China*
18. Remy's Ratatouille Adventure (opens 2020)
19. SeaBase
20. The Seas with Nemo & Friends Use FP+
21. Soarin' ☑ Use FP+
22. Spaceship Earth ☑ FP+
23. Test Track ☑ Use FP+
24. *Turtle Talk with Crush* ☑ FP+

★ At press time, several locations were temporarily closing and moving to new unknown locations.

FP+ Attraction Offers FastPass+   ✚ First Aid Station   💥 Fireworks Top Viewing Spot

Use FP+ FastPass+ Recommended   FP+ FastPass+ Kiosks   🚻 Restrooms   🍴 Recommended Dining

↗ "I Can't Believe It's Disney" Fountains   ☑ Not to Be Missed

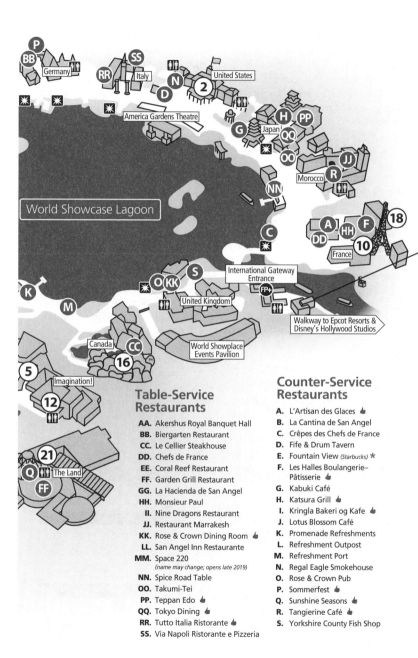

Table-Service Restaurants

AA. Akershus Royal Banquet Hall
BB. Biergarten Restaurant
CC. Le Cellier Steakhouse
DD. Chefs de France
EE. Coral Reef Restaurant
FF. Garden Grill Restaurant
GG. La Hacienda de San Angel
HH. Monsieur Paul
II. Nine Dragons Restaurant
JJ. Restaurant Marrakesh
KK. Rose & Crown Dining Room 🍴
LL. San Angel Inn Restaurante
MM. Space 220
    (name may change; opens late 2019)
NN. Spice Road Table
OO. Takumi-Tei
PP. Teppan Edo 🍴
QQ. Tokyo Dining 🍴
RR. Tutto Italia Ristorante 🍴
SS. Via Napoli Ristorante e Pizzeria

Counter-Service Restaurants

A. L'Artisan des Glaces 🍴
B. La Cantina de San Angel
C. Crêpes des Chefs de France
D. Fife & Drum Tavern
E. Fountain View *(Starbucks)* ★
F. Les Halles Boulangerie–
    Pâtisserie 🍴
G. Kabuki Café
H. Katsura Grill 🍴
I. Kringla Bakeri og Kafe 🍴
J. Lotus Blossom Café
K. Promenade Refreshments
L. Refreshment Outpost
M. Refreshment Port
N. Regal Eagle Smokehouse
O. Rose & Crown Pub
P. Sommerfest 🍴
Q. Sunshine Seasons 🍴
R. Tangierine Café 🍴
S. Yorkshire County Fish Shop

continued from page 303

World Showcase typically opens 2 hours later than Future World (generally 11 a.m.); the exceptions are Norway's Frozen Ever After and Meet Anna and Elsa at Royal Sommerhus, which open with Future World and close with World Showcase. (We expect Remy's Ratatouille Adventure to open with these too.) The perfect breakfast venue, Les Halles Boulangerie–Patisserie in the France Pavilion, is also ready to serve at the earlier time! Guests who enter through the International Gateway are also admitted as soon as Future World opens.

Once you arrive, pick up a park map and the ***Times Guide*** daily entertainment schedule, which lists all the attractions open during both regular hours and Extra Magic Hours. If you intend to stay for Extra Magic Hours in the evening, each member of your party will need to have his or her MagicBand.

Stroller, wheelchair, and **ECV/ESV rentals** are available inside the main entrance to the left, toward the rear of the Entrance Plaza, and at the International Gateway entrance. For **storage lockers,** turn right at Spaceship Earth; there are also lockers at the International Gateway. The **Baby Care Center** is on the World Showcase side of the Odyssey Center complex, to the rear of Test Track. At the same location are the **First Aid Center** and **Lost Persons. Guest Relations** is to the left of Spaceship Earth. **Lost and found** is located at the main entrance at the gift shop and at Guest Relations. **ATMs** are available outside the main entrance, on the Future World bridge, and in World Showcase at the Germany Pavilion. Across from Disney's Port Orleans Resorts, **Best Friends Pet Care** provides a comfortable home away from home for Fido, Fluffy, and all their pet pals.

LUCY Epcot is a great place to meet characters. My favorites are Ralph and Vanellope, Belle, Snow White, and Anna and Elsa.

FASTPASS+ ATTRACTIONS AT EPCOT

EPCOT OFFERS FASTPASS+ at the following attractions:

TIER A *(Choose 1)*	
• Fireworks show	• Soarin'
• Frozen Ever After	• Test Track
TIER B *(Choose 2)*	
• Disney & Pixar Short Film Festival	• The Seas with Nemo & Friends
• Journey into Imagination with Figment	• Spaceship Earth
• Living with the Land	• *Turtle Talk with Crush*
• Mission: Space (Green or Orange)	
COMING SOON	
• We think Remy's Ratatouille Adventure (opens 2020) will debut in Tier A.	

Because the tiers limit the number and combinations of FastPass+ attractions you can experience, much of our Epcot touring strategy is dictated by the attractions in Tier A, which include **Frozen**

Ever After, Soarin', and **Test Track,** and will likely include **Remy's Ratatouille Adventure** when it opens in 2020. Because you're visiting with young kids, we suggest obtaining a midmorning FastPass+ reservation for either Frozen Ever After or Remy's Ratatouille Adventure. When you arrive at Epcot, visit the other Tier A attractions first thing in the morning. For the sake of crowd control, we think Disney will allow access to Remy's Ratatouille Adventure at park opening. If your kids can ride Test Track and don't mind using the single-rider line, do so.

Meet Anna and Elsa at Royal Sommerhus does not offer FastPass+, but if meeting the *Frozen* gals is a must for your little princess, get there as soon as the rope drops. The Norway Pavilion at World Showcase opens at the same time as Future World; note that guests who had breakfast at Akershus Royal Banquet Hall will already be in front of you. The rest of World Showcase opens as usual 2 hours later. Get a FastPass+ for **Frozen Ever After** any time after 1 p.m., so it doesn't cut into your morning chance to meet Anna and Elsa, or any other touring you *might* be able to fit into your morning.

The **evening fireworks** are a must-see, and FastPass+ gets you into a special viewing area for the show, but you still have to arrive a good 30–40 minutes in advance to get a good spot. What's more, there are so many other good viewing spots around World Showcase Lagoon that it's difficult to recommend FastPass+ for the fireworks.

Our most frequent FastPass+ recommendation is for **Spaceship Earth** in Future World, usually around lunch. Because wait times can reach 30–40 minutes, it's one of the best choices in Tier B.

Our touring plan software gives **Mission: Space (Orange)** the second-highest number of FastPass+ recommendations. Waits here can easily exceed an hour or more, but its spot in Tier B means you can get a FastPass+ reservation for it without affecting your ability to get FastPass+ reservations at Tier A headliners.

The Seas with Nemo & Friends is recommended frequently in our plans for parents with small children, as is **Journey into Imagination with Figment.**

FastPass+ isn't necessary for **Disney & Pixar Short Film Festival,** the nonspinning **Mission: Space (Green),** and *Turtle Talk with Crush.*

Look for Epcot FastPass+ kiosks in the following locations:

- At the International Gateway entrance to the park
- At Future World West
- At the Innoventions breezeway (Future World East)

Same-Day FastPass+ Availability

The preceding advice tells you which attractions to focus on when making your FastPass+ reservations *before* you get to the park. In the park, you can make additional FastPass+ reservations once your advance reservations have been used or have expired. The table on the next page shows which attractions are likely to have day-of FastPasses available, and the approximate times at which they'll run out.

Disney often holds back some FastPass+ availability as a hedge against unexpected ride breakdowns. If everything is running well at Soarin' and Test Track, Disney usually releases these day-of FastPasses at 11:30 a.m., 1:30 p.m., and 3:30 p.m.

	EPCOT When Same-Day FP+ Runs Out, by Crowd Level		
ATTRACTION	**LOW CROWDS***	**MODERATE CROWDS***	**HIGH CROWDS***
• Disney & Pixar Short Film Festival	4 p.m.	3 p.m.	3 p.m.
• Frozen Ever After	NA	NA	NA
• Journey into Imagination with Figment	3 p.m.	3 p.m.	1 p.m.
• Living with the Land	3 p.m.	2 p.m.	2 p.m.
• Mission: Space (Orange)	NA	NA	NA
• The Seas with Nemo & Friends	5 p.m.	5 p.m.	5 p.m.
• Soarin'	4 p.m.	1 p.m.	NA
• Spaceship Earth	5 p.m.	3 p.m.	11 p.m.
• Test Track	Noon	NA	NA
• *Turtle Talk with Crush*	5 p.m.	4 p.m.	2 p.m.

* **LOW CROWDS** (Levels 1–3 on TouringPlans.com Crowd Calendar)

* **MODERATE CROWDS** (Levels 4–7 on TouringPlans.com Crowd Calendar)

* **HIGH CROWDS** (Levels 8–10 on TouringPlans.com Crowd Calendar)

NA = no availability. *(Remy's Ratatouille Adventure wasn't open at press time.)*

FUTURE WORLD

IMMENSE, GLEAMING FUTURISTIC STRUCTURES define the first themed area just beyond Epcot's main entrance. Broad thoroughfares are punctuated with billowing fountains, all reflected in shiny space-age facades. Front and center is **Spaceship Earth,** flanked by **Innoventions East and West.** Pavilions to the east are dedicated to mankind's technological achievements; those to the west celebrate human imagination and the natural world. Some attractions, restaurants, and shops may be closed or relocated during the remodeling of Future World.

In time for Walt Disney World's 50th anniversary in 2021, a *Guardians of the Galaxy* thrill ride will open in what used to be *Universe of Energy: Ellen's Energy Adventure,* which closed in August 2017. The new attraction won't be a version of the Guardians of the Galaxy—Mission: Breakout! ride at Disney California Adventure in Anaheim but rather an entirely new experience; Disney says it will be one of the world's longest enclosed roller coasters. While no other details were given, the Guardians ride will have an Epcot story. The spin here is that, as a young boy, Peter Quill, also known as Star-Lord, actually visited Epcot. See page 302 for more about what's coming to Epcot by 2022 (Epcot's 40th anniversary).

CLUB COOL

This Coca-Cola–sponsored exhibit provides free unlimited samples of soft drinks from around the world. Kids love to fill their own tasting cups and move from one sampling station to the next. In Peru, bubble gum–flavored Inca Kola is in; in Zimbabwe, a raspberry cream soda called Sparberry is popular. Club Cool lives up to its name—it's air-conditioned. As part of Epcot's renovation, Club Cool is currently closed and will receive a remodel and a new location. No reopening date or new location had been announced at press time.

Epcot Character Spot *(temporarily closed)* ★★★

APPEAL BY AGE PRESCHOOL ★★★★★ GRADE SCHOOL ★★★★½ TEENS ★★★★ YOUNG ADULTS ★★★★ OVER 30 ★★★★ SENIORS ★★★★

What it is Character greeting venue. **Scope and scale** Diversion. **Fright potential** Not frightening in any respect. **Bottleneck rating** 7. **When to go** Before 11 a.m., or use FastPass+. **Comment** Indoors and air-conditioned. **Duration of experience** 8 minutes. **Probable waiting time** 20–40 minutes.

In Future World West, Epcot Character Spot offers the chance to meet Disney characters indoors, in air-conditioned comfort. Please note that while the characters are all in the same location, they meet in separate areas with separate queues.

At press time, Epcot Character Spot was closed due to extensive renovation at Epcot, with no reopening date announced. In the meantime, Minnie will meet guests at the World Showcase Gazebo, and Daisy will make appearances at *The American Adventure.* Mickey and Goofy are temporarily greeting guests at Innoventions West, and Mickey will get a new permanent home at the Imagination! Pavilion. Joy from Pixar's *Inside Out* and Goofy will also find new permanent homes eventually.

Innoventions West ★

APPEAL BY AGE PRESCHOOL ★★★ GRADE SCHOOL ★★★ TEENS ★★★ YOUNG ADULTS ★★½ OVER 30 ★★½ SENIORS ★★½

What it is Static and hands-on exhibits relating to products and technologies of the near future. **Scope and scale** Diversion. **Fright potential** Not frightening in any respect. **Bottleneck rating** 8. **When to go** On your second day at Epcot or after seeing all major attractions. **Comments** Most exhibits demand time and participation to be rewarding; not much is gained here by a quick walk-through. We're hoping for a spectacular refurbishment.

All of Innoventions East and nearly all of Innoventions West is currently closed, and we expect virtually all of it to be demolished or repurposed by 2021. In the meantime, only one show is worth your visit if time permits.

SpectacuLAB, a funny and interactive show, uses actual scientists to demonstrate various scientific principles. (Because the venue is out of the way and easy to miss, your chances of getting on stage are pretty good.) The 20-minute show is performed four or five times a day, usually 10:30 a.m.–4:30 p.m.; check the daily *Times Guide* for showtimes.

Spend time at Innoventions on your second day at Epcot. If you have only 1 day, visit late if you have the time and endurance.

Mission: Space *(FastPass+)* ★★★★

APPEAL BY AGE PRESCHOOL ★★★½ GRADE SCHOOL ★★★★ TEENS ★★★★½ YOUNG ADULTS ★★★★½ OVER 30 ★★★★ SENIORS ★★★★

What it is Space flight simulation ride. **Scope and scale** Super-headliner. **Fright potential** Intense thrill ride may frighten guests of any age. Switching-off option (see page 248). **Bottleneck rating** 9. **When to go** First or last hour the park is open, or use FastPass+. **Comments** Not recommended for pregnant women or anyone who is prone to motion sickness; must be 40" tall to ride; a gentler nonspinning version (green) is also available. Impressive. **Duration of ride** About 5 minutes plus preshow. **Average wait in line per 100 people ahead of you** 4 minutes. **Loading speed** Moderate–fast.

  In this attraction, you join three other guests in a four-person crew to fly a space mission. Each guest plays a role (commander, pilot, navigator, or engineer) and is required to perform certain functions during the flight. Mission: Space has an Orange Mission to Mars, where guests experience g-forces. A less intense Green Mission takes guests on an orbital adventure around our planet, with visuals similar to Soarin'.

Rough   Queasy

 Follow the Orange brick road; it's much more fun. The ride is too intense for little ones and people prone to motion sickness, but grade-schoolers, teens, and brave moms and dads will love it!

Liliane

The host during your expedition is Gary Sinise, known for his roles in the space flicks Apollo 13 *and* Mission to Mars.

Movie Tip

THE "MOM, I CAN'T BELIEVE IT'S DISNEY!" FOUNTAINS

On a broiling Florida day, when you think you might suddenly combust, fling yourself into one of these two fountains and dance, skip, sing, jump, splash, stick your toes down the spouts, or catch the water in your mouth! Toddlers and preschoolers, along with hippies, especially love the fountain. Pack a pair of dry shorts and turn the kids loose, but make sure they don't go into the fountain with sneakers—wet shoes are a recipe for blisters.

Spaceship Earth *(FastPass+)* ★★★★

APPEAL BY AGE PRESCHOOL ★★★½ GRADE SCHOOL ★★★★ TEENS ★★★★ YOUNG ADULTS ★★★★ OVER 30 ★★★★ SENIORS ★★★★½

Thumbs Up for the Whole Family

What it is Educational dark ride through past, present, and future. **Scope and scale** Headliner. **Fright potential** Dark and imposing presentation intimidates a few preschoolers. **Bottleneck rating** 7. **When to go** Before 10 a.m., after 4 p.m., or use FastPass+. **Comments** If lines are long when you arrive, try again after 4 p.m. One of Epcot's best; not to be missed. **Duration of ride** About 16 minutes. **Average wait in line per 100 people ahead of you** 3 minutes. **Loading speed** Fast.

This ride spirals through the 18-story interior of Epcot's premier landmark, taking guests through Audio-Animatronic scenes depicting mankind's development in communications, from cave painting to the internet. It's actually more fun than it sounds and is carried off with a lot of humor. Spaceship Earth draws crowds like a magnet first thing in the morning because it's so close to the park entrance. We hear that Spaceship Earth may close for a lengthy refurbishment in 2020.

TEST TRACK PAVILION

SPONSORED BY CHEVROLET, this pavilion consists of the Test Track attraction and Inside Track, a collection of transportation-themed exhibits and multimedia presentations. The pavilion is the last one on the left before World Showcase.

Test Track *(FastPass+)* ★★★★

**APPEAL BY AGE PRESCHOOL ★★★★ GRADE SCHOOL ★★★★½ TEENS ★★★★★
YOUNG ADULTS ★★★★½   OVER 30 ★★★★½   SENIORS ★★★★½**

What it is Automobile test-track simulator ride. **Scope and scale** Super-headliner. **Fright potential** Intense thrill ride may frighten guests of any age. Switching-off option (see page 248). **Bottleneck rating** 10. **When to go** First 30 minutes the park is open, just before closing, or use FastPass+. **Comments** Must be 40″ tall to ride. Not to be missed. **Duration of ride** About 4 minutes. **Average wait in line per 100 people ahead of you** 4½ minutes. **Loading speed** Moderate–fast.

Test Track takes you through the process of designing a new vehicle and then "testing" your car in a high-speed drive through and around the pavilion. After hearing about auto design, you enter the Chevrolet Design Center to create your own concept car. Using a large touch screen interface (like a giant iPad), groups of up to three guests drag their fingers to design their car's body, engine, wheels, trim, and color. Next, you board a six-seat ride vehicle, attached to a track on the ground, for an actual drive through Chevrolet's test track. The vehicle's tests include braking maneuvers, cornering, and acceleration, culminating in a spin around the outside of the pavilion at speeds of up to 65 miles per hour.

Test Track is a favorite attraction of teens. If nobody in your family wants to join you on the ride and you don't have FastPass+ reservations, join the single-rider line, which moves much faster (but skips the auto design preshow). Test Track breaks down more often than any other ride in Walt Disney World, experiencing an outage roughly 4 in every 10 days of operation. The attraction is often offline even at park opening. Check with a cast member to determine whether the ride is operating before you make the trek to this corner of Future World.

I was super nervous going on Test Track. Seeing the design room and the big posh cars calmed my nerves, but the ride was too dark, too fast, too high, and way too twisty! Way too scary for me to go on again.

Felicity

Test Track breaks down a lot, especially when it rains, and my family and I found ourselves not being able to ride it at all. If you can, plan on visiting it on a sunny day.

A. J.

IMAGINATION! PAVILION

THIS MULTIATTRACTION PAVILION is situated on the southwest side of Innoventions West and down the walk from The Land. Outside are an "upside-down" waterfall and "jumping" water, a fountain that hops over the heads of unsuspecting passersby.

Disney & Pixar Short Film Festival *(FastPass+)* ★★

APPEAL BY AGE	PRESCHOOL ★★★★½	GRADE SCHOOL ★★★★½	TEENS ★★★★
YOUNG ADULTS ★★★★	OVER 30 ★★★★½	SENIORS ★★★★½	

What it is Movie trailers for upcoming Disney-Pixar movies. **Scope and scale** Diversion. **Fright potential** Not frightening in any respect. **Bottleneck rating** 0. **When to go** When it's raining and you need shelter. **Duration of movie** 20 minutes. **Probable waiting time** About 13 minutes.

The air-conditioned space shows Disney and Pixar animated 4-D short movies, 10–15 minutes long. The short films are fun and enjoyable even for young viewers but are in no way a headliner. Enjoy the attraction on a second day at Epcot, during inclement weather, or when it's hot and your feet need a break. These are the same movie previews that you can see online for free, on Apple TV, or before actual movies in actual theaters.

Don't waste a FastPass+ for this experience, as lines are never long.

Liliane

Journey into Imagination with Figment *(FastPass+)* ★★½

APPEAL BY AGE	PRESCHOOL ★★★★	GRADE SCHOOL ★★★★	TEENS ★★★
YOUNG ADULTS ★★★	OVER 30 ★★★	SENIORS ★★★½	

What it is Dark fantasy-adventure ride. **Scope and scale** Major-attraction wannabe. **Fright potential** Frightens a few preschoolers. **Bottleneck rating** 6. **When to go** Anytime—FastPass+ is unnecessary. **Comment** *Meh*. **Duration of ride** About 6 minutes. **Average wait in line per 100 people ahead of you** 2 minutes. **Loading speed** Fast.

"One little spark of inspiration is at the heart of all creation," croons the ever-popular Figment, as he takes you on a tour of the Imagination Institute with the help of your five senses. Young children will love the little purple dragon, but grown-ups and teens will be only mildly amused (and probably bored).

This ride was special. I have never been on a ride that features a dragon. Figment is too funny. I loved all the interactive stuff at the end.

At the end of Journey into Imagination with Figment, make sure to play the fun games. There is also a cool gift shop.

Isabelle

Felicity

THE LAND PAVILION

THIS HUGE PAVILION contains two attractions and two restaurants. When the pavilion was originally built, its emphasis was on farming, but now it focuses on environmental concerns. Dry as that sounds, kids really enjoy The Land's attractions. Note that The Land gets super-crowded during mealtimes.

Awesome Planet *(opens early 2020)*

What it is A film about Earth and its environment. **Scope and scale** Minor attraction. **Fright potential** Not frightening in any respect. **Bottleneck rating** 5. **When to go** Anytime.

Awesome Planet is a movie that highlights Earth's geography, animals, and people. Created by Industrial Light & Magic, a company founded by George Lucas of *Star Wars* fame, the movie will be shown at the Harvest Theater. The theater once housed the *Circle of Life: An Environmental Fable* film, which closed in 2018 after a 22-year run.

Living with the Land *(FastPass+)* ★★★★

APPEAL BY AGE **PRESCHOOL** ★★★½ **GRADE SCHOOL** ★★★½ **TEENS** ★★★½
YOUNG ADULTS ★★★★ **OVER 30** ★★★★ **SENIORS** ★★★★½

What it is Indoor boat-ride adventure through the past, present, and future of US farming and agriculture. **Scope and scale** Major attraction. **Fright potential** Not frightening in any respect but loud. **Bottleneck rating** 9. **When to go** Before 11 a.m., after 1 p.m., or use FastPass+. **Comments** Go early and save other Land attractions (except for Soarin') for later in the day. The ride is on the pavilion's

Thumbs Up for the Whole Family

lower level. Informative without being dull; not to be missed. **Duration of ride** About 14 minutes. **Average wait in line per 100 people ahead of you** 3 minutes; assumes 15 boats operating. **Loading speed** Moderate.

This boat ride through four experimental growing areas is inspiring and educational. Kids like seeing the giant fruits and vegetables. Teens will be fascinated by the imaginative ways to grow crops—without soil, hanging in the air, and even on a space station. A lot of the produce grown here is served to guests in the restaurants at Epcot.

Soarin' *(FastPass+)* ★★★★½

APPEAL BY AGE **PRESCHOOL** ★★★★ **GRADE SCHOOL** ★★★★½ **TEENS** ★★★★½
YOUNG ADULTS ★★★★½ **OVER 30** ★★★★½ **SENIORS** ★★★★★

What it is Flight simulator ride. **Scope and scale** Super-headliner. **Fright potential** Frightens almost no one who meets the minimum height requirements, except those with a fear of heights. **Bottleneck rating** 10. **When to go** First 30 minutes the park is open, or use FastPass+. **Comments** Entrance on the lower level of The Land Pavilion. May induce motion sickness; must be 40″ tall to ride; switching-off option (see page 248). Exciting and mellow at the same time; not to be missed. **Duration of ride** 5 minutes. **Average wait in line per 100 people ahead of you** 4 minutes; assumes 3 concourses operating. **Loading speed** Moderate.

Queasy

This attraction is the closest you'll come to hang gliding without trying the real thing. Once you're "airborne," IMAX-quality aerial images of the world are projected all around you, and the flight simulator moves in sync with the movie. In 2016 a new version of the film debuted, taking guests on an epic journey that spans six continents and shows some of the greatest wonders of the world, such as the Great Wall of China and the Sydney Opera House. A third ride theater and a 4-D projection system were added to the attraction, increasing the ride's capacity by 50%. The images are well chosen and drop-dead beautiful. Special effects include wind, sound, and even smell. The ride itself is thrilling but perfectly smooth. Any child (or adult) who meets the 40-inch minimum height requirement will love Soarin'. Expect all FastPass+ reservations to be gone by 1 p.m. on days of moderate attendance; on days with high crowds, there may not be any day-of reservations available. Landmarks such as the Eiffel Tower look distorted from seats on the far ends. For an ideal viewing experience, we recommend politely asking a cast member to be seated in row B1.

I loved Soarin', especially since this was the first time I went on the ride with my eyes open! It was exquisite and very realistic. Make sure you put all your belongings under your seat, so you don't have to worry about dropping anything during the flight.
Felicity

A. J.

Soarin' is my favorite ride at Epcot. I didn't expect it to be so good. You literally feel like you're soaring.

THE SEAS WITH NEMO & FRIENDS PAVILION

FEATURING CHARACTERS from Disney-Pixar's *Finding Nemo* and *Finding Dory*, this area encompasses one of America's top marine aquariums, a ride that tunnels through the aquarium, an interactive animated film, and a number of first-class educational walk-through exhibits. Altogether it's a stunning package, not to be missed. With The Seas with Nemo & Friends and *Turtle Talk with Crush*, The Seas is one of Epcot's more popular venues.

SeaBase ★★★½

APPEAL BY AGE PRESCHOOL ★★★★½ GRADE SCHOOL ★★★★½ TEENS ★★★★ YOUNG ADULTS ★★★★ OVER 30 ★★★★ SENIORS ★★★★

Thumbs Up for the Whole Family

What it is A huge saltwater aquarium, plus exhibits on oceanography, ocean ecology, and sea life. **Scope and scale** Major attraction. **Fright potential** Not frightening in any respect. **Bottleneck rating** 7. **When to go** Before 11:30 a.m. or after 5 p.m., or especially after 9 p.m. during evening Extra Magic Hours. **Comments** Watch for tank feeding times 3–3:30 p.m. An excellent marine exhibit.

Take a *Finding Nemo*–themed ride (see next profile) to SeaBase Alpha to start your discovery of The Seas' main tank and exhibits, which feature fish, mammals, and crustaceans in a simulation of an ocean ecosystem. Visitors can observe the activity through windows below the surface (including inside the Coral Reef Restaurant). Children will be enchanted to discover the substantial fish population and the many exhibits offered. While we think the exhibits need updating and reimagining, the tank alone makes this pavilion not to be missed. Save the exhibits for later, after experiencing the ride and *Turtle Talk*.

The Seas with Nemo & Friends *(FastPass+)* ★★★

APPEAL BY AGE PRESCHOOL ★★★★½ GRADE SCHOOL ★★★★ TEENS ★★★½ YOUNG ADULTS ★★★½ OVER 30 ★★★½ SENIORS ★★★½

What it is Ride through a tunnel in The Seas' main tank. **Scope and scale** Major attraction. **Fright potential** Not frightening in any respect. **Bottleneck rating** 7. **When to go** Before 10:30 a.m., after 3 p.m., or use FastPass+. **Comment** Educational *and* fun. **Duration of ride** 4 minutes. **Average wait in line per 100 people ahead of you** 3½ minutes. **Loading speed** Fast.

Upon entering The Seas, you proceed to the loading area, where you'll be made comfortable in a "clamobile" for your journey through the aquarium. The technology used makes it seem as if the animated characters are swimming with the live fish. Meet characters from *Finding Nemo,* such as Mr. Ray, and help Dory, Bruce, Marlin, Squirt, and Crush find Nemo. This cool ride attracts lots of the lovable clown fish's fans, so ride early.

See Finding Nemo *before your visit if you haven't already. You won't soon forget this superb family movie, which won the 2004 Oscar for best animated feature. In 2016* Finding Dory, *a sequel to* Finding Nemo, *brought back Ellen DeGeneres as the voice of the adorably forgetful blue tang.*

Movie Tip

Turtle Talk with Crush (FastPass+) ★★★★

APPEAL BY AGE   PRESCHOOL ★★★★½   GRADE SCHOOL ★★★★½   TEENS ★★★½   YOUNG ADULTS ★★★★   OVER 30 ★★★★   SENIORS ★★★★

What it is An interactive animated film. **Scope and scale** Minor attraction. **Fright potential** Not frightening in any respect. **Bottleneck rating** 9. **When to go** Before 11 a.m., after 3 p.m., or use FastPass+. **Comment** A real spirit lifter; not to be missed. **Duration of show** 15 minutes. **Probable waiting time** 10–20 minutes.

This interactive theater show starring the 150-year-old surfer-dude turtle from *Finding Nemo* starts like a typical theme park movie but quickly turns into an interactive encounter, as Crush begins conversing with audience members. With the release of *Finding Dory,* Dory the blue tang, Destiny the whale shark, Bailey the beluga whale, and Hank the seven-legged octopus joined Crush in his "Human Tank," providing lots of *awesome,* fun interactions for little dudes. It's unusual to wait more than one or two shows to get in. If you find long lines in the morning, try back after 3 p.m., when more of the crowd has moved on to World Showcase, or use FastPass+.

▌ WORLD SHOWCASE

EPCOT'S OTHER THEMED AREA, World Showcase is an ongoing world's fair encircling a picturesque 40-acre lagoon. The cuisine, culture, history, and architecture of almost a dozen countries are permanently displayed in individual pavilions spaced along a 1.2-mile promenade. The pavilions replicate familiar landmarks and depict representative street scenes from the host countries.

World Showcase will also receive some TLC in the coming years. The main new attraction will be Remy's Ratatouille Adventure in France, but new movies for the China and Canada Pavilions are also in the works, and a sing-along show at the France Pavilion is slated to run in rotation with *Impressions de France.*

If you have a sweet tooth like me, you can play a sweet game by trying a treat or candy from each of the 11 countries in World Showcase.

Lucy

Agent P's World Showcase Adventure ★★★★

APPEAL BY AGE   PRESCHOOL ★★★½   GRADE SCHOOL ★★★★½   TEENS ★★★★   YOUNG ADULTS ★★★½   OVER 30 ★★★½   SENIORS ★★★

What it is Interactive scavenger hunt in select World Showcase pavilions. **Scope and scale** Minor attraction. **Fright potential** Not frightening in any respect. **Bottleneck rating** 1. **When to go** Anytime. **Comment** Fun activity, especially for return visitors. It's best

Thumbs Up for the Whole Family

experienced if your group has at least two pairs. **Duration of experience** Allow 30 minutes per adventure. **Probable waiting time** None.

In their eponymous Disney Channel show, Phineas and Ferb have a pet platypus named Perry. In the presence of humans, Perry doesn't do a whole lot. When the kids aren't looking, though, Perry takes on the role of Agent P—a fedora-wearing, James Bond–esque secret agent who battles the evil Dr. Doofenshmirtz to prevent world domination.

In Agent P's World Showcase Adventure, you become a secret agent who helps Perry in his fight. You sign up online at agentpwsa.com using your smartphone and Epcot's Wi-Fi; then you're dispatched on a mission to your choice of six World Showcase pavilions.

Guests who have the My Disney Experience app open may receive a message from Major Monogram, recruiting them to help stop Dr. Doofenshmirtz. The messages are sent from three different locations (the Future World bridge, International Gateway, and Mexico bridge). If you're interested in saving the world from evil, all you have to do is tap a button on the app, and you will be taken to the game's website.

Once you arrive at a pavilion (each one hosts a different 30- to 45-minute adventure), you will receive various clues on your phone to help you solve a set of simple puzzles necessary for defeating Doofenshmirtz's plan. As you discover each clue, you'll find special effects, such as talking statues and flaming lanterns, that physically animate some of the story you're following. Your game is saved for only 1 day, so if you don't finish by the time the park closes, you will need to restart it upon your return.

Note that the show is no longer produced; therefore, older kids and teens (and their parents) will likely be more familiar with the characters than preschoolers.

KIDCOT FUN STOPS AND PASSPORT KITS

This program is designed to make Epcot more interesting for younger visitors. At each pavilion in World Showcase, cast members discuss their native country with the children and give them stickers and cards. The traveler cards have fun facts about the country on one side and a picture for coloring on the other. Kids also receive a zip-top bag that looks like a suitcase in which to carry their cards. Look for the brightly colored Kidcot signs.

Shops in Epcot also sell Passport Kits for about $13. Each kit contains a blank "passport" and stamps for every World Showcase country. As kids visit each country, they tear out the appropriate stamp and stick it in the passport. Disney has built a lot of profit into this little product, but guests—namely parents—don't seem to mind the cost. Liliane feels that the free Kidcot activities are just as much fun.

An adult version of collecting traveler cards, known as Drinking Around the World, has been the base of many complaints we received in the past year. Complaints have also come from guests visiting the Animal Kingdom. While Bob loves his wine and Liliane her margaritas, we sincerely hope that Disney will curb the bad behavior that ruins the experience of all guests, not just those visiting with young ones. As a dad from New Hampshire wrote:

Though Disney might not be actively pushing alcohol consumption, they were very obviously not policing it either. If it gets any worse than it was this year, I can see where families might start taking their vacations elsewhere—there was nothing fun or relaxing about it. Folks were either way too drunk or having to do battle to protect their families from those who were.

NOW, MOVING CLOCKWISE around the World Showcase promenade, here are the nations represented and their attractions:

MEXICO PAVILION

SPANISH 101	
HELLO: Hola	**Pronunciation:** *Oh-la*
GOODBYE: Adios	**Pronunciation:** *Ah-dee-ohs*
THANK YOU: Gracias	**Pronunciation:** *Grah-see-ahs*
MICKEY MOUSE: El Ratón Miguelito	**Pronunciation:** *El Rah-tone Mee-gell-lee-toe*

A PRE-COLUMBIAN PYRAMID dominates the architecture of this exhibit. Inside you'll find authentic and valuable artifacts, a village scene complete with restaurant, and the **Gran Fiesta Tour** boat ride. The meet and greet for **Donald Duck** is outside on the right side of the pavilion. Several times a day, **Mariachi Cobre,** with the help of *folklórico* dancers, recounts in a child-friendly approach the story of *Coco* and the importance of family, life, and death. Guests are invited to join the celebration, and Miguel Rivera himself appears in the form of a handcrafted puppet. It's not to be missed! Check the *Times Guide* and try to see the first performance of the day. The *Coco*-inspired show doesn't replace the regular Mariachi Cobre show, as they continue delighting Epcot guests with performances of traditional mariachi music—as they've done since 1982.

Gran Fiesta Tour Starring the Three Caballeros ★★½

APPEAL BY AGE PRESCHOOL ★★★★ GRADE SCHOOL ★★★★ TEENS ★★★½
YOUNG ADULTS ★★★½ OVER 30 ★★★½ SENIORS ★★★½

What it is Indoor boat ride. **Scope and scale** Minor attraction. **Fright potential** Not frightening in any respect. **Bottleneck rating** 5. **When to go** Before noon or after 5 p.m. **Comment** Light and relaxing. **Duration of ride** About 7 minutes (plus 1½-minute wait to disembark). **Average wait in line per 100 people ahead of you** 4½ minutes; assumes 16 boats in operation. **Loading speed** Moderate.

Thumbs Up for the Whole Family

Gran Fiesta Tour's story line features Donald Duck, José Carioca (a parrot), and Panchito (a Mexican charro rooster) from the 1944 Disney film *The Three Caballeros;* the story has our heroes racing to Mexico City for a gala reunion performance. Guests are treated to detailed scenes done in eye-catching colors.

I would love to see the Gran Fiesta Tour ride get a *Coco* overlay. It would be a fitting use of the boat ride on El Rio del Tiempo. Who's with me?

Liliane

NORWAY PAVILION

NORWEGIAN 101	
HELLO: God dag	**Pronunciation:** *Good dagh*
GOODBYE: Ha det	**Pronunciation:** *Hah deh*
THANK YOU: Takk	**Pronunciation:** *Tahk*
MICKEY MOUSE: Mikke Mus	**Pronunciation:** *Mikeh Moose*

SURROUNDING A COURTYARD is an assortment of traditional Scandinavian buildings, including a replica of the late 13th-century **Akershus Castle,** now home to princess-hosted character meals. The major attraction is the boat ride **Frozen Ever After.** Make sure to visit the replica of a Norwegian stave church. The church currently displays *Gods of the Vikings*, an exhibit showcasing the Norse gods and goddesses that Scandinavian Vikings celebrated in their day. Learn about the original Thor, Odin, Freya, and Loki through authentic Viking artifacts, but be on the lookout for Disney's comical versions of Thor and Loki who roam the land.

It's hard to say no to the mouthwatering pastries at Kringla Bakeri Og Kafe in Norway. This is one of my favorite stops at the end of the day to pick up my next day's breakfast.

Liliane

Frozen Ever After *(FastPass+)* ★★★★

**APPEAL BY AGE   PRESCHOOL ★★★★½   GRADE SCHOOL ★★★★½   TEENS ★★★★
YOUNG ADULTS ★★★★   OVER 30 ★★★★   SENIORS ★★★★**

What it is Indoor boat ride. **Scope and scale** Major attraction. **Fright potential** Dark; ends with a plunge down a 20-foot flume. **Bottleneck rating** 10. **When to go** Before noon, after 7 p.m., or use FastPass+. **Comment** Switching-off option (see page 248). **Duration of ride** 4½ minutes. **Average wait in line per 100 people ahead of you** 6½ minutes; assumes 12 or 13 boats operating. **Loading speed** Fast.

Dark

Frozen Ever After is a boat ride through Arendelle, the fictional kingdom from the movie *Frozen.* The ride's queue features the Wandering Oaken's Trading Post. Waiting in line you'll hear Oaken call, "Yoo-hoo!" while steam pours from his sauna's windows.

Next you board the boats formerly used in the Maelstrom ride, and following the same path, you are off to Arendelle to celebrate the Winter in Summer Festival, where Elsa uses her magical powers to make it snow during the hottest part of the year.

The ride features Anna, Elsa, Olaf, Kristoff, Sven, and Marshmallow (the snowman Elsa created with the adorable Snowgies from the *Frozen Fever* short) singing songs from the movie.

Halfway through the ride, the boat moves backward for a few seconds; this is followed by a short downhill and a small splash that most kids take in stride.

Because Frozen Ever After is in the same FastPass+ tier as Soarin' and Test Track, you'll have to choose between a long hike to World Showcase and back in the morning, or long lines at one of those three attractions.

Unlike most of World Showcase, Frozen Ever After opens as soon as Epcot does. Along with Soarin' and Test Track, it's one of the three attractions that most guests head to first. However, Frozen Ever After experiences more breakdowns than most Walt Disney World attractions. If you're planning to experience the ride first thing in the morning, ask a cast member if it's running before you hike all the way to Norway.

Along with popularity and frequent breakdowns, Frozen Ever After can only handle around 900 riders per hour, making it one of the biggest bottlenecks in Epcot. The opening of Remy's Ratatouille Adventure in 2020 should take much of the park-opening crowd away from Frozen.

> Frozen Ever After is the BEST ride at Epcot. I loved everything—
> the ice palace, Elsa singing, and the amazing Olaf.

Felicity

Meet Anna and Elsa at Royal Sommerhus ★★★★

APPEAL BY AGE **PRESCHOOL** ★★★★★ **GRADE SCHOOL** ★★★★½ **TEENS** ★★★★
YOUNG ADULTS ★★★★ **OVER 30** ★★★★ **SENIORS** ★★★★

What it is Meet and greet with the *Frozen* royalty. **Scope and scale** Minor attraction. **Fright potential** Not frightening in any respect. **Bottleneck rating** 10. **When to go** Before noon or after 7 p.m. **Duration of experience** 4 minutes. **Average wait in line per 100 people ahead of you** 15–25 minutes. **Queue speed** Slow.

Norway's Royal Sommerhus is a character meet and greet set inside Anna and Elsa's summerhouse. The house is nicely decorated with tokens of the *Frozen* gals' childhood and attempts to give the look and feel of Norwegian architecture and crafts. Inside the house, a tapestry pays tribute to the three-headed troll from the now-extinct Maelstrom attraction. This meet and greet has multiple rooms, with Anna and Elsa operating simultaneously, so waits are usually manageable to see these princesses.

> The best meet and greet I ever had. Anna and Elsa are my heroes!

Felicity

CHINA PAVILION

CHINESE (Mandarin) 101	
HELLO: Ni hao	**Pronunciation:** *Knee how*
GOODBYE: Zai jian	**Pronunciation:** *Zy jehn*
THANK YOU: Xiè xie	**Pronunciation:** *Chi-eh chi-eh*
MICKEY MOUSE: Mi Lao Shu	**Pronunciation:** *Me Lah-oh Su*

THERE IS NO RIDE AT THE CHINA PAVILION, but the majestic half-size replica of the **Temple of Heaven** in Beijing will surely make it into your photo album. See *Reflections of China,* an impressive film about the people and natural beauty of China. Don't dismiss this beautiful pavilion. Kids love meeting **Mulan,** who holds court outside most of the time or inside the Temple of Heaven during inclement weather, and the entire family will appreciate the performance of the **Jeweled Dragon Acrobats.** Check the *Times Guide* for showtimes.

Reflections of China ★★★½

APPEAL BY AGE **PRESCHOOL** ★★½ **GRADE SCHOOL** ★★★ **TEENS** ★★★½
YOUNG ADULTS ★★★½ **OVER 30** ★★★★ **SENIORS** ★★★★

What it is Film about the Chinese people and country. **Scope and scale** Major attraction. **Fright potential** Not frightening in any respect. **Bottleneck rating** 4. **When to**

go Anytime. **Comments** Audience stands throughout performance. Beautifully produced film. **Duration of show** About 14 minutes. **Probable waiting time** 10 minutes.

Warm and appealing, *Reflections of China* is a brilliant (albeit politically sanitized) introduction to the people and natural beauty of China. Disney is currently shooting a brand-new movie; a release date has not been announced.

GERMANY PAVILION

GERMAN 101	
HELLO: Hallo	**Pronunciation:** *Hall-o*
GOODBYE: Auf wiedersehen	**Pronunciation:** *Owf veeh-der-zain*
THANK YOU: Danke	**Pronunciation:** *Dan-keh*
MICKEY MOUSE: Micky Maus	**Pronunciation:** *Me-key Mouse*

THE MAIN FOCUS in the Germany Pavilion, which has no rides, is **Biergarten,** a full-service (reservations recommended) restaurant serving German food and beer. Yodeling and oompah band music are regularly performed during mealtimes. Be sure to check out the large, elaborate model railroad just beyond the restrooms as you walk from Germany toward Italy. **Snow White** signs autographs at the well just as you reach the Germany Pavilion.

> The Germany Pavilion is the perfect place to introduce your kids to a great snack: Gummibärchen (gummy bears), my favorite candy.
>
> Liliane

ITALY PAVILION

ITALIAN 101	
HELLO: Buon giorno	**Pronunciation:** *Bon jor-no*
GOODBYE: Ciao (informal)	**Pronunciation:** *Chow*
THANK YOU: Grazie	**Pronunciation:** *Grah-zee-eh*
MICKEY MOUSE: Topolino	**Pronunciation:** *To-po-lee-no*

THE ENTRANCE TO ITALY is marked by an 83-foot-tall **campanile (bell tower)** intended to mirror the one in St. Mark's Square in Venice. Left of the campanile is a replica of the 14th-century **Doge's Palace.**

Streets and courtyards in the Italy Pavilion are among the most realistic in the World Showcase. You really do feel as if you're in Italy. Because there's no film or ride, you can tour anytime. **Sergio,** an Italian mime and juggler, performs five days a week.

UNITED STATES PAVILION

THIS IMPOSING BRICK STRUCTURE—home to a very moving and patriotic, albeit sanitized, retrospective of US history—is reminiscent of Colonial Philadelphia. The American Heritage Gallery hosts an exhibit called *Creating Tradition: Innovation and Change in American Indian Art,* made possible through the collaboration of the Museum of Indian Arts & Culture in Santa Fe, New Mexico, and the Smithsonian's National Museum of the American Indian in Washington, D.C. Among the featured artists with works on display are fashion designer Loren Aragon (Acoma Pueblo), noted doll maker Glenda McKay (Ingalik Athabascan), and Juanita Growing Thunder Fogarty (Assiniboine Sioux) from the Growing Thunder family of Montana.

Don't miss the performances of Voices of Liberty, an a cappella choir that performs regularly either in the rotunda of the United States Pavilion or across the plaza in the America Gardens Theatre, Epcot's premier venue for concerts and stage shows.

Liliane

The American Adventure ★★★★

APPEAL BY AGE   PRESCHOOL ★★½   GRADE SCHOOL ★★★½   TEENS ★★★½
YOUNG ADULTS ★★★★   OVER 30 ★★★★   SENIORS ★★★★½

What it is Patriotic mixed-media and Audio-Animatronic theater presentation on US history. **Scope and scale** Headliner. **Fright potential** Not frightening in any respect. **Bottleneck rating** 6. **When to go** Anytime. **Comment** Disney's best historic/patriotic attraction. **Duration of presentation** About 29 minutes. **Preshow** Voices of Liberty a cappella choir. **Probable waiting time** 25 minutes.

Thumbs Up for the Whole Family

The 29-minute multimedia show is narrated by animatronic Mark Twain and Ben Franklin. The show reminds you of a contest: tell us everything you love about America in 30 minutes or less. Only four female figures are among the 12 personified ideals around the theater, one of them representing the rather ambiguous "tomorrow" by virtue of holding a baby. The North American continent seemingly did not exist before the landing of the *Mayflower.*

JAPAN PAVILION

JAPANESE 101	
HELLO: Konnichiwa	**Pronunciation:** *Ko-nee-chee-wah*
GOODBYE: Sayonara	**Pronunciation:** *Sigh-yo-nah-ra*
THANK YOU: Arigato	**Pronunciation:** *Ah-ree-gah-to*
MICKEY MOUSE: Mikki Mausu	**Pronunciation:** *Mikkee Mou-su*

Did you know you can get great Pokémon merchandise at the Japan Pavilion?!

THE FIVE-STORY, BLUE-ROOFED PAGODA, inspired by an 8th-century shrine in Nara, sets this pavilion apart. A hill garden behind it encompasses waterfalls, rocks, flowers, lanterns, paths, and rustic bridges. There are no attractions, unless you count the huge Japanese retail venue. Not to be missed, though, are the **Matsuriza Taiko drummers.** The drums can often be heard throughout the World Showcase, but you need to be up close to see the graceful way they're played.

Brendan

MOROCCO PAVILION

ARABIC 101	
HELLO: Salaam alekoum	**Pronunciation:** *Sah-lahm ah-leh-koom*
GOODBYE: Ma'salama	**Pronunciation:** *Mah sah-lah-mah*
THANK YOU: Shoukran	**Pronunciation:** *Shoe-krah-n*
MICKEY MOUSE: Mujallad Miki	**Pronunciation:** *Muh-jahl-lahd Me-key*

THE BUSTLING MARKET, winding streets, a lofty minaret, and stuccoed archways re-create the romance and intrigue of Marrakesh and Casablanca. Attention to detail makes Morocco one of the most exciting World Showcase pavilions. The Morocco Pavilion is also home to **Jasmine** and **Aladdin. Spice Road Table** serves up tasty tapas-style Mediterranean dishes and excellent views of the nighttime fireworks—along with high prices. At the full-service **Restaurant Marrakesh,** guests can dine while enjoying traditional music and belly dancing. For a quick lunch, try **Tangierine Café,** one of Epcot's highest-rated restaurants. A Moroccan rock band occasionally plays from a small stage at the front of the pavilion.

FRANCE PAVILION

FRENCH 101	
HELLO: Bonjour	**Pronunciation:** *Bon-jure*
GOODBYE: Au revoir	**Pronunciation:** *Oh reh-vwa*
THANK YOU: Merci	**Pronunciation:** *Maer-si*
MICKEY MOUSE: Mickey	**Pronunciation:** *Mee-keh*

BIENVENUE TO PARIS, the Eiffel Tower, and more. There's not much for kids here, but you won't have any trouble luring them into **Les Halles Boulangerie–Patisserie** for scrumptious French pastries or **L'Artisan des Glaces** for yummy ice cream. **Givenchy,** the famed French fashion and beauty house, has a shop at the pavilion and is the only retail location in the United States that offers the full line of Givenchy makeup and skin-care products, as well as a large selection of fragrances. **Remy's Ratatouille Adventure,** a 3-D dark ride based on the 2007 Disney-Pixar animated film *Ratatouille,* is coming to the France Pavilion. The ride, which resembles the one currently delighting guests at Disneyland Paris, is being built in an area past the Eiffel Tower. An opening date for the new ride had not been announced prior to going to print.

Don't miss **Serveur Amusant,** an acrobatic comedy team performing several times a day at the pavilion. If you're looking for **Belle,** search no more—she meets fans at the pavilion throughout the day. **Aurora** meets at the gazebo here. Character appearances are intermittent, so check your *Times Guide.*

> Try some of the many handmade ice creams or sorbets at L'Artisan des Glaces. So many flavors to choose from! !
>
> Isabelle

Impressions de France ★★★½

APPEAL BY AGE	PRESCHOOL ★★★	GRADE SCHOOL ★★★½	TEENS ★★★½
YOUNG ADULTS ★★★★	OVER 30 ★★★★	SENIORS ★★★★½	

What it is Film essay on the French people and country. **Scope and scale** Major attraction. **Fright potential** Not frightening in any respect. **Bottleneck rating** 7. **When to go** Anytime. **Comment** Exceedingly beautiful film. **Duration of presentation** About 18 minutes. **Probable waiting time** 15 minutes.

France, here we come! This truly lovely 18-minute movie will make you want to pack your suitcase. An added bonus is that the showing is *très civilisé,* as you get to sit down and rest your weary feet.

The movie is outdated, and we wouldn't be surprised to see another film commissioned soon. A *Beauty and the Beast* sing-along show will soon play in rotation with *Impressions de France.* A starting date was not available when we went to print.

Remy's Ratatouille Adventure *(opens 2020)*

What it is Indoor dark ride. **Scope and scale** Major attraction. **Fright potential** Dark ride; may frighten young children. **Bottleneck rating** 9. **When to go** As soon as the park opens, or use FastPass+ or the single-rider line. **Duration of ride** 4½ minutes. **Average wait in line per 100 people ahead of you** About 3 minutes; assumes hourly capacity of around 2,200 riders. **Loading speed** Moderate.

The ride should be very similar to the original Ratatouille: L'Aventure Totalement Toquée de Rémy ride at Disneyland Paris. In that version, you're shrunk down to the size of a rat and whisked through Paris for a quick retelling of the *Ratatouille* film. As one of Remy's rat friends, you watch him ascend from a rodent with a dream, to one of Paris's celebrated chefs.

The storytelling combines three-dimensional films shown on room-size screens with large, detailed, ride-through sets, including water and heat effects. A couple of frenetic scenes, including one in which Remy is chased with a cleaver, may frighten small children.

This is the first all-new major attraction in Epcot in more than a decade, and the first in World Showcase since 1988. It's also family-friendly, with good theming and a well-liked lead character. We expect lines to form as soon as the park opens.

DISNEY DISH WITH JIM HILL

HAMMING IT UP When Remy's Ratatouille Adventure makes its debut in 2020, get ready to see oversize props on a scale that you've never encountered before. One is a 20-foot-tall ham hanging inside the fridge at Gusteau's. This prop—which weighs **1.2 tons**—is so massive that the Reedy Creek Fire Department (which serves WDW) decided it needed its own automatic sprinkler system installed inside.

We expect the ride to offer FastPass+ and a single-rider line, as it does in Disneyland Paris, and we expect it to be in FastPass+ Tier A. Regardless of its FastPass+ tier, it will likely be very difficult to obtain FastPasses. Try to get one for the first hour the park is open, midafternoon, or after dinner. A midafternoon reservation will work well with a counterclockwise tour of World Showcase; an evening reservation calls for a clockwise tour. Reservations from midmorning to early afternoon will likely require you to walk from Future World to the far reaches of World Showcase and back.

If FastPasses aren't available, your best bet for riding without long waits is to arrive at the International Gateway at least 45 minutes before the park opens. (If you're driving, the easiest approach is to valet park at one of the Epcot resorts; Beach Club and BoardWalk are the closest, and valet parking currently costs $33 per day plus gratuity.) That will give you a 10-minute head start on folks walking from the park's front entrance. You might also consider using a ride-share service to drop you off at these hotels.

As soon as the park opens, ride Remy. If you have small children, head next for Frozen Ever After in Norway, a walk of about 0.5 mile either way around World Showcase.

UNITED KINGDOM PAVILION

A BLEND OF ARCHITECTURE attempts to capture Britain's city, town, and rural atmospheres. One street alone has a thatched-roof cottage, a four-story timber-and-plaster building, a pre-Georgian plaster building, a formal Palladian exterior of dressed stone, and a city square with a Hyde Park bandstand (whew!). There are no attractions, but don't miss **The British Revolution.** The band performs the greatest UK hits, from The Beatles to the music of Led Zeppelin and The Who. The **Rose & Crown Pub Musicians** perform daily at the Rose & Crown Pub. **Alice in Wonderland** and **Mary Poppins** greet their fans outside the little English cottage.

If your child loves Mary Poppins, your best chance to meet her is here.

Liliane

CANADA PAVILION

THE CULTURAL, NATURAL, AND ARCHITECTURAL diversity of Canada are reflected in this large, impressive pavilion. Older kids will be interested in the 30-foot-tall totem poles that embellish a Canadian Indian village.

O Canada! ★★★½

APPEAL BY AGE	PRESCHOOL ★★★	GRADE SCHOOL ★★★½	TEENS ★★★½
YOUNG ADULTS ★★★½	OVER 30 ★★★★	SENIORS ★★★★	

What it is Film essay on the Canadian people and their country. **Scope and scale** Major attraction. **Fright potential** Not frightening in any respect. **Bottleneck rating** 5. **When to go** Anytime. **Comments** Audience stands. Makes you want to catch the first plane to Canada! **Duration of show** About 14 minutes. **Probable waiting time** 9 minutes.

O Canada! showcases Canada's natural beauty and population diversity and demonstrates the immense pride that Canadians have in their country. A film starring Martin Short features clips of Canada's stunning landscape, from Prince Edward Island to Vancouver. Visitors leave the theater through **Victoria Gardens,** inspired by the famed Butchart Gardens of British Columbia. A brand-new movie is currently in production, but a release date has not been announced.

This large-capacity attraction (guests must stand) gets moderate late-morning attendance, as Canada is the first pavilion encountered as one travels counterclockwise around World Showcase Lagoon.

LIVE ENTERTAINMENT *at* EPCOT

IN FUTURE WORLD

KIDS WILL LOVE THE CREW of drumming janitors (**The JAMMitors**), as well as **Sergio** the mime and juggler, at home at the Italy Pavilion. The biggest hit, however, is **Mariachi Cobre Presents . . . The**

FAVORITE EATS IN EPCOT

| PAVILION | SERVICE LOCATION | FOOD SELECTIONS |

THE SEAS Coral Reef Restaurant* | Food with a view—fish menu. The aquarium will keep the kids happy for quite some time.

THE LAND Sunshine Seasons | Healthy choices—our all-time favorite

MEXICO La Cantina de San Angel | Kid's plate with empanada, tortilla chips, and drink

NORWAY Kringla Bakeri Og Kafe | Salmon-and-egg bagel and pastries

CHINA Lotus Blossom Café | Vegetable stir-fry, Mongolian beef noodles, and egg rolls

GERMANY Sommerfest | Bratwurst or frankfurter with sauerkraut and apple strudel

ITALY Tutto Italia* | Good pasta and kids' menu | **Via Napoli** | Best pizza in WDW

UNITED STATES Regal Eagle Smokehouse | If you're craving smoked barbecue

JAPAN Katsura Grill | Beef and chicken teriyaki

MOROCCO Tangierine Café | Shawarma, hummus, couscous, and kids' meals; outdoor seating

FRANCE Crêpes des Chefs de France | Crepes and espresso

Les Halles Boulangerie–Patisserie | Croissants, chocolate mousse, and yummy sandwiches on baguettes | **L'Artisan des Glaces** | The place to go for ice cream

UNITED KINGDOM Yorkshire County Fish Shop | Fish-and-chips and Victoria sponge cake for dessert

*Table service only—Advance Reservations highly recommended

Story of Coco, a musical celebration presented several times a day at the Mexico Pavilion.

AROUND WORLD SHOWCASE

STREET PERFORMANCES in and around World Showcase are what set live entertainment at Epcot apart from the other Disney theme parks. A mariachi group can be found in Mexico; street actors in France; the **Voices of Liberty** in the United States; traditional drummers in Japan; and British rock music in the United Kingdom. Check your *Times Guide* for performance times. Some restaurants get in on the act too: you can enjoy raucous Oktoberfest entertainment at Germany's **Biergarten** and see belly dancing at Morocco's **Restaurant Marrakesh.**

The street entertainment at Epcot frequently undergoes changes, and limited-time musical acts come and go throughout World Showcase. While we don't mind change, our major complaint is that the frequency of the performances has been substantially reduced.

Liliane

WDW live-entertainment guru Steve Soares usually posts the Epcot performance schedule about a week in advance at wdwent.com.

AMERICA GARDENS THEATRE

THIS AMPHITHEATER ON THE LAGOON across from the United States Pavilion features pop (and oldies pop) musical acts throughout much of the year, as well as Epcot's popular **Candlelight Processional** for the Christmas holidays. Showtimes are listed on a board outside the exits and in the daily *Times Guide.*

Epcot Forever (FastPass+)

What it is Nighttime fireworks show at World Showcase Lagoon. **Scope and scale** Super-headliner. **Fright potential** Not frightening in any respect. **Bottleneck rating** 7 when leaving. **When to go** Stake out a viewing position 60–100 minutes before the show (45–90 minutes during less-busy periods); FastPass+ not recommended except as noted below. Showtime is listed in the *Times Guide*. **Comments** Audience stands. **Duration of show** About 18 minutes.

The limited-time *Epcot Forever* show opened in October 2019, immediately after the permanent closing of *IllumiNations: Reflections of Earth*. The interim show is a tribute to the history of Epcot and includes fireworks, laser lights, music celebrating the past of Epcot, and eight personal watercrafts towing special effects–enabled kites.

> *IllumiNations* was a good fireworks show. I am sad that it's gone.
>
> Sabrina

A Celebration of Disney Music (opens 2020) (FastPass+)

What it is Nighttime fireworks show at World Showcase Lagoon. **Scope and scale** Super-headliner. **Fright potential** Not frightening in any respect. **Bottleneck rating** 7 when leaving. **When to go** Stake out a viewing position 60–100 minutes before the show (45–90 minutes during less-busy periods); FastPass+ not recommended except as noted below. Showtime is listed in the *Times Guide*. **Comments** Audience stands. **Duration of show** About 18 minutes.

> I really don't want to be in the shoes of those creating the new permanent show. *IllumiNations* has a powerful soundtrack, and it will take a huge effort to top it. I am hoping against all odds to be pleasantly surprised.
>
> Liliane

The new permanent nighttime spectacular, possibly called *A Celebration of Disney Music,* will debut sometime in 2020. It is rumored that the new show will feature music and/or clips of Disney movies related to the 11 countries of World Showcase. Think *Frozen* for Norway, *Ratatouille* for France, *Coco* for Mexico, *Mary Poppins* for the United Kingdom, and so on. We wouldn't be surprised if the new show includes drones, such as the ones used during the 2016 holiday show at Disney Springs.

The best places to view the fireworks show are from the lakeside veranda of **La Cantina de San Angel** (or from **La Hacienda de San Angel**) at the Mexico Pavilion, **Spice Road Table** in Morocco, or the **Rose & Crown Pub** at the United Kingdom Pavilion. The drawback is—you guessed it—that you will have to claim this spot at least 90 minutes beforehand. When choosing a spot on the verandas, select a table alongside the lake. The verandas are huge, and not all tables are created equal.

FastPass+ gets you into a special viewing area for the show—in **Showcase Plaza,** on the south shore of World Showcase Lagoon, directly north of Future World—but you still have to arrive a good half hour or so in advance to get a good spot. What's more, there are so many other good viewing spots around the lagoon that the fireworks really aren't a good use of FastPass+—the consequence is an hour-long wait at Soarin', Test Track, or Frozen Ever After. The one exception is if you're visiting World Showcase for an evening.

For other great viewing spots, check out the map on pages 304–305. Note that the boat dock opposite Germany may be exposed to a lot of smoke from the fireworks because of Epcot's prevailing winds.

Nighttime fireworks are the climax of every day at Epcot, so keep in mind that once the show is over, you'll be leaving the park and so will almost everybody else. For suggested exit strategies, see below.

For a really good view of the show, you can charter a pontoon boat for $320 for up to 8 people and $372 for 10 (tax included). Your captain will take you for a little cruise and then position the boat in a perfect place to watch the show. For more information, call ☎ 407-WDW-PLAY (939-7529).

Special dessert parties that include a reserved viewing area for the nightly fireworks are offered throughout the year. Call ☎ 407-939-3463 for information and reservations.

EXIT STRATEGIES

MORE GROUPS GET SEPARATED and more children lost after the evening fireworks than at any other time. Make sure that you've preselected a meeting point in the Epcot entrance area, such as the flower beds just behind Spaceship Earth. Warn your group not to leave through the exit turnstiles until everyone is reunited.

- If you're staying at the Swan, Dolphin, Yacht & Beach Club Resorts, or BoardWalk Inn & Villas, watch the fireworks from somewhere between Italy and the United Kingdom, and exit the park through the International Gateway. You can walk or take a boat back to your hotel. The Skyliner aerial gondola system, just beyond the International Gateway exit, will take you to Disney's Hollywood Studios, Caribbean Beach, the Riviera, Pop Century, or Art of Animation.

- If you have a car in the Epcot lot, find a viewing spot at the Future World end of World Showcase Lagoon (Showcase Plaza) and leave immediately after the fireworks. The problem is not the traffic—it's making your way to, and finding, your car. Make sure that you write down or take a picture of where you're parked—this is not the time to rely on your memory. If you're parked near the entrance, skip the tram and walk. If you walk, watch your children closely and hang on to them for all you're worth.

■┃ EPCOT TOURING PLANS

OUR STEP-BY-STEP TOURING PLANS are field-tested, independently verified itineraries that will keep you moving counter to the crowd flow and allow you to see as much as possible in a single day with minimum time wasted in line.

Touring Epcot is much more strenuous and demanding than touring the other theme parks. Epcot requires about twice as much walking and has no effective in-park transportation. Our plans will help you avoid crowds and bottlenecks on days of moderate-to-heavy attendance, but they can't shorten the distance you have to walk. (Wear comfortable shoes.) On days of lighter attendance, when crowd conditions aren't a critical factor, the plans will help you organize your tour.

We love Epcot, and we really wanted our small children to enjoy it too. The key for us was to brief our children on what they were likely to see in each attraction and tie it back to something they could relate to. During the tour of the greenhouse in Living with the Land, for example, we made a game of finding foods they like. (They have cocoa beans—chocolate—so we think that covers almost everyone.) While riding Test Track, we asked the kids to figure out which parent's driving was most like the ride's. The Future World attractions can be a lot more palatable to young children if they're engaged and prepared going in.

The different touring plans are described below. The descriptions will tell you for whom or for what situation the plans are designed. The actual touring plans are located on pages 487–491. Each plan includes a numbered map of the park to help you find your way around.

Each plan lists the attractions most likely to need FastPass+ and the approximate return times for which you should try to make reservations. Visit touringplans.com if any attractions, FastPasses, or times need changing, either while planning or in the parks.

Last but not least, getting through security at Epcot's main entrance is much more time-consuming than at the other parks. Take this delay into consideration when using one of our Epcot touring plans.

1-DAY TOURING PLAN FOR PARENTS WITH SMALL CHILDREN This plan is designed for parents of children ages 3–8 who wish to see the very best age-appropriate attractions in Epcot. Every attraction has a rating of at least three-and-a-half stars (out of five) from preschool and grade-school children surveyed by *The Unofficial Guide*. Special advice is provided for touring the park with small children. The plan keeps walking and backtracking to a minimum.

1-DAY SLEEPYHEAD TOURING PLAN FOR PARENTS WITH SMALL CHILDREN A relaxed plan that allows families with small children to sleep late and still see the highlights of Epcot. The plan begins around 11 a.m., sets aside ample time for lunch, and includes the very best child-friendly attractions in the park.

PARENTS' TOURING PLAN—1 AFTERNOON AND 1 FULL DAY This touring plan is for families who want to tour Epcot comprehensively over 2 days. Day one uses early-morning touring opportunities. Day two begins in the afternoon and continues until closing. The afternoon plan also works great if you're arriving to Orlando in the morning and want to tour a park after you've checked in.

1-DAY TOURING PLAN FOR TWEENS AND THEIR PARENTS A 1-day touring plan for parents with children ages 8–12. It includes attractions rated three-and-a-half stars and higher by this age group, and it sets aside ample time for lunch and dinner.

BEFORE YOU GO

1. Call ☎ 407-824-4321 or check disneyworld.com for operating hours.

2. Make reservations at the Epcot full-service restaurant(s) of your choice 180 days before your visit.

3. Make FastPass+ reservations 60 or 30 days in advance.

EPCOT TRIVIA QUIZ

1. Who is no longer performing at World Showcase?

    a. Mariachi Cobre   **c.** Off Kilter

    b. The British Revolution   **d.** Voices of Liberty

2. What is the fastest attraction at Epcot?

    a. Soarin'   **c.** Mission: Space

    b. Test Track   **d.** Spaceship Earth

3. Which Disney princess is *not* found at Epcot?

    a. Belle   **c.** Merida

    b. Mulan   **d.** Snow White

4. Which character's meet and greet do you encounter at the Mexico Pavilion?

    a. Donald Duck   **c.** Mickey

    b. Goofy   **d.** Pluto

5. Which country do you find between France and Canada?

    a. Germany   **c.** Morocco

    b. United Kingdom   **d.** Japan

6. Where can you find the Frozen Ever After ride?

    a. Canada   **c.** Norway

    b. China   **d.** Italy

7. Which team do you join if you want to experience the spinning version of Mission: Space?

    a. The Red team   **c.** The Orange team

    b. The Green team   **d.** The Blue team

8. What drink is available free of charge at Club Cool?

    a. Mello Yello   **c.** Orangina

    b. Beverly   **d.** Mountain Dew

9. What kind of ride is Living with the Land?

    a. A simulation ride   **c.** A water-flume ride

    b. A boat ride   **d.** A roller coaster

10. What event does *not* take place at Epcot?

    a. Candlelight Processional   **c.** International Flower & Garden Festival

    b. International Food & Wine Festival   **d.** Mickey's Very Merry Christmas Party

Answers can be found on page 450.

PART NINE

DISNEY'S ANIMAL KINGDOM

WITH ITS LUSH FLORA, winding streams, meandering paths, and exotic setting, Disney's Animal Kingdom is a stunningly beautiful theme park. Add a population of more than 1,700 animals, replicas of Africa's and Asia's most intriguing architecture, and a diverse array of attractions, and you have the most distinctive of all Disney World theme parks.

The park is arranged somewhat like the Magic Kingdom. The lush, tropical **Oasis** serves as Main Street, funneling visitors to **Discovery Island,** the park's retail and dining center. From Discovery Island, guests can access the respective theme areas: **Africa, Asia, Rafiki's Planet Watch, DinoLand U.S.A.,** and **Pandora,** which brings the flora and fauna of James Cameron's *Avatar* to the park.

On Discovery Island, on your left just before you cross the bridge to Africa, are the **Baby Care Center** and **First Aid.** To your right near the turnstiles, you'll find an **ATM.** As you pass through the turnstiles, **wheelchair** and **stroller rentals** (at Garden Gate Gifts) are to your right. **Guest Relations**—the park headquarters for information, hand-out park maps, entertainment schedules, missing persons, and lost and found—is to the left. **Lockers** are just inside the main entrance to the left. Across from Disney's Port Orleans Resorts, **Best Friends Pet Care** provides a comfortable home away from home for Fido, Fluffy, and all their pet pals.

During slower or colder times of year, Disney may delay the daily opening of the park's secondary attractions: Kali River Rapids and Maharajah Jungle Trek in Asia, as well as the Boneyard playground and Dinosaur in DinoLand U.S.A. The Wildlife Express Train and Conservation Station may have a delayed opening as well.

These procedures may change, so check the *Times Guide* for the schedule when you arrive. The rest of the attractions come online at official park opening time.

Animal Kingdom currently holds two morning Extra Magic Hours sessions per week. Even with the extended hours, expect the attractions listed above to close around 30–60 minutes before sunset during late fall and winter; Kilimanjaro Safaris in Africa may also close earlier than the rest of the park. Thus, as days get shorter with the change of seasons, the attractions close earlier in the day.

The park's nighttime spectacular, *Rivers of Light: We Are One,* takes place on the Discovery River, between Discovery Island and Expedition Everest, and features live music, floating lanterns, water screens, and swirling animal imagery in amphitheater-style viewing areas facing the Discovery River. (See the profile on page 349.)

You can also experience a nighttime version of Kilimanjaro Safaris. Live entertainment (**Burudika** and **Bollywood Beats**) brings music and lively performances to Discovery Island and Harambe Village in Africa. And the theme park's symbol, the **Tree of Life,** is brought to life by magical fireflies (read: twinkling lights) when the sun sets.

FASTPASS+ ATTRACTIONS AT DISNEY'S ANIMAL KINGDOM

FASTPASS+ IS OFFERED at the following attractions:

TIER A (*Choose 1*)	
• Avatar Flight of Passage	• Na'vi River Journey
TIER B (*Choose 2*)	
• The Animation Experience	• Kali River Rapids
• Dinosaur	• Kilimanjaro Safaris
• Expedition Everest	• Meet Favorite Disney Pals at Adventurers Outpost
• *Festival of the Lion King*	• Primeval Whirl
• *Finding Nemo—The Musical*	• *Rivers of Light: We Are One*
• *It's Tough to Be a Bug!*	• *Up! A Great Bird Adventure*

Kilimanjaro Safaris is the attraction that most frequently uses FastPass+ in our Animal Kingdom touring plans because it appeals to everyone, from small children to seniors. Another advantage of using FastPass+ for Kilimanjaro is that you can choose whether to experience the standard daytime safari or try the nighttime version.

We recommend FastPass+ for the Pandora attractions—**Avatar Flight of Passage** and **Na'vi River Journey**—more than any other Animal Kingdom attraction except Kilimanjaro Safaris. Both rides are in the same FastPass+ tier, so you have to choose one for your advance FastPass+. If you plan to ride Flight of Passage, we think that choice will save you the most time in line, assuming you can get it. Otherwise, get a FastPass+ for Na'vi River Journey.

Beyond those attractions, your choices for a best FastPass+ attraction depend on the ages of your family. The **Adventurers Outpost** character meet and greet shows up on our touring plans for parents with small children. Using FastPass+ at the outpost will generally save more time in line than using it at any other child-friendly attraction in our plans. **Expedition Everest,** as a popular thrill ride, appears next on

continued on page 334

Disney's Animal Kingdom

Africa

Discovery Island

Pandora: The
World of Avatar

The Oasis

Bag Checks

FP+ FastPass+ Kiosks

🚻 Restrooms

✚ First Aid Station

FP+ Attraction Offers FastPass+

Use FP+ FastPass+ Recommended

👍 Recommended Dining

☑ Not to Be Missed

Attractions

1. The Animation Experience FP+
2. Avatar Flight of Passage ☑ Use FP+
3. The Boneyard
4. Conservation Station and Affection Section
5. Dinosaur ☑ Use FP+
6. Expedition Everest ☑ Use FP+
7. *Festival of the Lion King* ☑ FP+
8. Gorilla Falls Exploration Trail
9. Kali River Rapids Use FP+
10. Kilimanjaro Safaris ☑ Use FP+

11. Maharajah Jungle Trek
12. Meet Favorite Disney Pals at Adventurers Outpost Use FP+
13. Na'vi River Journey ☑ Use FP+
14. Primeval Whirl FP+
15. *Rivers of Light: We Are One* FP+
16. Theater in the Wild/ *Finding Nemo—The Musical* ☑ FP+
17. Tree of Life/ *It's Tough to Be a Bug!* FP+
18. TriceraTop Spin
19. *Up! A Great Bird Adventure*
20. Wilderness Explorers ☑
21. Wildlife Express Train

Rafiki's Planet Watch

Asia

DinoLand U.S.A.

Table-Service Restaurants

AA. Rainforest Cafe
BB. Tiffins
CC. Tusker House Restaurant 🍴
DD. Yak & Yeti Restaurant 🍴

Counter-Service Restaurants

A. Creature Comforts *(Starbucks)* 🍴
B. Flame Tree Barbecue 🍴
C. Harambe Market 🍴
D. Kusafiri Coffee Shop & Bakery 🍴
E. Pizzafari
F. Restaurantosaurus
G. Satu'li Canteen 🍴
H. Thirsty River Bar & Trek Snacks
I. Yak & Yeti Local Food Cafes 🍴

continued from page 331

our list of best FastPass+ attractions at Animal Kingdom for tweens and whole-family touring plans.

Rivers of Light, **Kali River Rapids,** and **Dinosaur** are reasonable FastPass+ recommendations in some scenarios, such as days with late arrivals. The park's other FastPass-enabled attractions are good choices only in rare circumstances.

FastPass+ kiosk locations in Animal Kingdom are as follows:

- Near Kali River Rapids entrance in Asia
- Across the walkway near Island Mercantile on Discovery Island
- Near Tusker House in Africa

Same-Day FastPass+ Availability

The preceding advice tells you which attractions to focus on when making your *advance* FastPass+ reservations before you get to the park. In the park, you can make more FastPass+ reservations once your advance reservations have been used or have expired. The table below shows which attractions are likely to have day-of FastPasses available, and the approximate times at which they'll run out.

Disney usually holds back some day-of FastPasses for Avatar Flight of Passage as insurance against ride breakdowns. If the ride is running smoothly, Disney often releases these FastPasses at 11 a.m., 1 p.m., and 3 p.m.

ANIMAL KINGDOM When Same-Day FP+ Runs Out, by Crowd Level			
ATTRACTION	**LOW CROWDS***	**MODERATE CROWDS***	**HIGH CROWDS***
• Adventurers Outpost	11 a.m.	NA	NA
• The Animation Experience	NA	NA	NA
• Avatar Flight of Passage	NA	NA	NA
• Dinosaur	4 p.m.	5 p.m.	1 p.m.
• Expedition Everest	4 p.m.	2 p.m.	NA
• *Festival of the Lion King*	3 p.m.	1 p.m.	11 a.m.
• *Finding Nemo—The Musical*	2 p.m.	2 p.m.	1 p.m.
• *It's Tough to Be a Bug!*	5 p.m.	5 p.m.	5 p.m.
• Kali River Rapids	4 p.m.	3 p.m.	Noon
• Kilimanjaro Safaris *(daytime version)*	3 p.m.	NA	NA
• Na'vi River Journey	NA	NA	NA
• Primeval Whirl	5 p.m.	5 p.m.	3 p.m.
• *Rivers of Light: We Are One*	5 p.m.	5 p.m.	6 p.m.
• *Up! A Great Bird Adventure*	2 p.m.	Noon	11 a.m.

* **LOW CROWDS** (Levels 1–3 on TouringPlans.com Crowd Calendar)
* **MODERATE CROWDS** (Levels 4–7 on TouringPlans.com Crowd Calendar)
* **HIGH CROWDS** (Levels 8–10 on TouringPlans.com Crowd Calendar)
  NA = no availability or too new to analyze (The Animation Experience)

The OASIS

THOUGH THE FUNCTIONAL PURPOSE OF THE OASIS is to funnel guests to the center of the park, it also sets the stage and gets you into the right mood to enjoy Animal Kingdom. There's no one broad thoroughfare but rather multiple paths; each delivers you to Discovery Island at the center of the park, but the path you choose and what you see along the way are up to you. The natural-habitat zoological exhibits are primarily designed for the comfort and well-being of the animals. A sign will identify the animal(s) in each exhibit, but there's no guarantee that the animals will be immediately visible. Because most habitats are large and provide ample terrain for the occupants to hide, you must concentrate, looking for small movements in the vegetation. The Oasis is a place to linger and appreciate—if you're a blitzer in the morning, definitely set aside some time here on your way out of the park. The Oasis usually closes 30–60 minutes after the rest of the park.

DISCOVERY ISLAND

THIS ISLAND OF TROPICAL GREENERY and whimsical equatorial African architecture connects to the other lands by bridges. Discovery Island is the hub from which guests can access the park's various themed areas; it's also the park's central shopping and services headquarters. For the best selection of Disney merchandise, try **Island Mercantile.** Counterservice food and snacks are available, as is the **Tiffins** sit-down restaurant. In addition to several wildlife exhibits, Discovery Island's **Tree of Life** hosts the film *It's Tough to Be a Bug!* The indoor **Adventurers Outpost** character meet and greet is just before the bridge to Asia.

Walking trails winding behind the Tree of Life offer several animal-viewing opportunities, from otters and kangaroos to lemurs, storks, and porcupines. Besides the animals, you'll find verdant landscaping, waterfalls, and quiet spots to sit and reflect on your relationship with nature.

During the evening hours, the Tree of Life awakens with thousands of lights, as a sound and light show is projected onto its branches. **Flik,** your favorite ant from *A Bug's Life,* meets near the entrance to *It's Tough to Be a Bug!* Discovery Island is also home to **Pocahontas,** as well as **Russell** and **Dug** from *Up!* The latest addition from the *Up!* gang is **Kevin.** This free-roaming bird loves surprising guests anywhere between the Anandapur Theater in Asia and Discovery Island. Kevin is huge, measuring 10 feet tall from the plumage adorning her head to her feet! Chip 'n' Dale, Daisy Duck, Donald Duck, Goofy, Launchpad McQuack, and Scrooge McDuck can all be found at DinoLand U.S.A. Check the *Times Guide* for character meeting times.

Meet Favorite Disney Pals at Adventurers Outpost
(FastPass+) ★★★½

APPEAL BY AGE **PRESCHOOL** ★★★★★ **GRADE SCHOOL** ★★★★½ **TEENS** ★★★★
YOUNG ADULTS ★★★★ **OVER 30** ★★★★ **SENIORS** ★★★★

What it is Character greeting venue. **Scope and scale** Minor attraction. **Fright potential** Not frightening in any respect. **Bottleneck rating** 7. **When to go** First thing in the morning, after 5 p.m., or use FastPass+. **Comment** Nicely themed. **Duration of experience** About 2 minutes. **Probable waiting time** About 20 minutes. **Queue speed** Moderate.

An indoor, air-conditioned character greeting location for Mickey and Minnie, Adventurers Outpost is decorated with photos, memorabilia, and souvenirs from the Mouses' world travels. Two greeting rooms house two identical sets of characters, so lines move fairly quickly. Good use of Fast-Pass+ if you have kids too small to ride Expedition Everest or Dinosaur.

> You can meet quite a few characters in the park, but my favorite place to meet lots of them is during breakfast at Tusker House. Lucy

Tree of Life / *It's Tough to Be a Bug!* (FastPass+) ★★★★

APPEAL BY AGE **PRESCHOOL** ★★★ **GRADE SCHOOL** ★★★★ **TEENS** ★★★½
YOUNG ADULTS ★★★★ **OVER 30** ★★★★ **SENIORS** ★★★★

What it is 3-D theater show. **Scope and scale** Major attraction. **Fright potential** Very intense and loud, with special effects that startle viewers of all ages and potentially terrify young children. **Bottleneck rating** 9. **When to go** Before noon or after 4 p.m. **Comments** The theater is inside the tree. Zany and frenetic. **Duration of show** Approximately 8 minutes. **Probable waiting time** Less than 20 minutes.

Dark Loud Scary

Before entering the show, take a close look at the Tree of Life, the remarkable home of this 3-D movie. The primary icon and focal point of Animal Kingdom, the tree features a trunk with high-relief carvings depicting 325 animals.

It's Tough to Be a Bug! is cleverly conceived but very intense. For starters, the show is about bugs, and bugs always rank high on the ick-factor scale. That, coupled with some startling special effects and a very loud soundtrack, make *It's Tough to Be a Bug!* a potential horror show for the age-7-and-under crowd, but you can prepare your kids by watching *A Bug's Life* before you leave home—many of the characters are the same.

> The closing lines of the show tipped me off when it was announced that "honorary bugs [read: audience members] remain seated while all the lice, bedbugs, maggots, and cockroaches exit first." In other words, if you don't like bugs crawling on you, even simulated ones, keep your feet off the floor. Liliane

Wilderness Explorers ★★★★

APPEAL BY AGE **PRESCHOOL** ★★★★ **GRADE SCHOOL** ★★★★½ **TEENS** ★★★½
YOUNG ADULTS ★★★½ **OVER 30** ★★★★ **SENIORS** ★★★½

What it is Park-wide scavenger hunt and puzzle-solving adventure game. **Scope and scale** Diversion. **Fright potential** Not frightening in any respect. **Bottleneck rating** 6. **When to go** Sign up first thing in the morning and complete activities throughout the day. **Comments** Collecting all 32 badges takes 3–5 hours, which can be done over several days. One of the best attractions in any Disney park; not to be missed.

Wilderness Explorers is a scavenger hunt based on Russell's Boy Scout-esque troop from the movie *Up!* Players earn "badges"—stickers given out by cast members—for completing predefined activities throughout the park. For example, to earn the Gorilla Badge, you walk the Gorilla Falls Exploration Trail to observe how the primates behave, and then mimic that behavior back to a cast member to show what you've seen. Register for the game near the bridge from The Oasis to Discovery Island. You'll be given an instruction book and a map showing the park location for each badge to be earned. It's tons of fun for kids and adults; we play it every time we're in the park. Activities are spread throughout the park, including Pandora and some areas to which many guests never venture. You have to ride specific attractions to earn certain badges, so using FastPass+ for those will save time.

I love Wilderness Explorers! The interaction between the field guides (cast members) and the young explorers is absolutely fabulous. Make sure to meet Russell and Dug from *Up!* near the entrance to *It's Tough to be a Bug!* It's a great opportunity to get your Wilderness Explorers handbook autographed. Wilderness must be explored!

Liliane

PANDORA:
The World of Avatar

INSPIRED BY JAMES CAMERON'S MOVIE *Avatar,* this land is comprised of lush flora, winding streams, and meandering paths—an exotic destination that will keep you busy from sunrise to sunset, and beyond!

LILIANE The inhabitants of Pandora communicate in the Na'vi language, a constructed language such as Sindarin and Quenya, J. R. R. Tolkien's elvish tongues. I love languages, and even though I'm still learning, here are the basics: "Please" is *rutxe,* "thank you" is *irayo,* and "hello" is *kaltxì.*

The Valley of Mo'ara is the port of entry to Pandora. Beautiful during the day, the valley is even more mesmerizing at night, as a mixture of real and man-made plants creates a host of special effects.

The ultimate discovery, however, is the view of the floating mountains of Pandora. Waterfalls seem to float in midair, and a combination of sparkling creeks and canopied paths creates a soothing atmosphere.

Within the valley, guests are invited to play instruments at the Na'vi-built drum circle. Several times a day, a high-energy show combines tribal drum beating and chanting in the Na'vi language. Toward the end, guests are invited to participate.

LILIANE I am not charmed. What ever happened to the Na'vi? I want blue people!

In April 2018 the Pandora Utility Suit interactive character made its debut in the land. Unlike its military AMP Suit version, which is still on display in front of Pongu Pongu, the pilot of this suit interacts with guests, conveying to them what he learned while studying life on Pandora.

There is much to see, and you will certainly want to return at nightfall, when the exotic, bioluminescent-like plants of Pandora come to life.

If exploring Pandora makes you hungry, the international-inspired **Satu'li Canteen** is the perfect place to sit down and enjoy a meal. The beverage and snack stand **Pongu Pongu** serves Pandora-inspired specialty drinks.

BRENDAN To enjoy Pandora more, you may want to watch *Avatar* before your visit.

At **Windtraders,** the obligatory gift shop, you can find T-shirts, plush toys, and other collectibles. The big hit, however, is the mechanical pet banshee on a leash. The banshee is connected to a small hand unit, allowing you to control your pet by making his head move and his wings flap.

Pandora is a beautifully executed addition to Animal Kingdom, and you don't have to see the movie *Avatar* to enjoy the land and its rides.

Lines for the rides will be long for the foreseeable future. Attractions aside, simply walking around the immersive themed area is worth your while.

Avatar Flight of Passage *(FastPass+)* ★★★★½

APPEAL BY AGE   PRESCHOOL ★★★   GRADE SCHOOL ★★★★★   TEENS ★★★★★
YOUNG ADULTS ★★★★★   OVER 30 ★★★★★   SENIORS ★★★★★

What it is Flight simulator. **Scope and scale** Super-headliner. **Fright potential** Frightens almost no one who meets the minimum height requirements. **Bottleneck rating** 10. **When to go** As soon as the park opens, or use FastPass+. **Comments** May induce motion sickness; snug restraint system may cause some claustrophobic guests to exit before riding; ride is not suitable for larger riders; must be 44″ tall to ride; switching-off option (see page 248). Not to be missed. **Duration of ride** About 6 minutes. **Average wait in line per 100 people ahead of you** About 5 minutes. **Loading speed** Moderate.

Queasy

The queue and preshow of this ride take you through caves covered with petroglyphs and paintings, nocturnal jungle scenes, and the Alpha Centauri Expedition (ACE) research center. The laboratory displays experiments and studies about the planet's wildlife. Nothing, however, is as mesmerizing as the sight of the sleeping Na'vi avatar floating inside a huge water-filled tube. The avatar moves only so slightly, never awakening, yet it's difficult to take your eyes away from him.

At the end of the queue, guests are taken, 16 at a time, into a room where they are "decontaminated" in preparation for their flight and watch a video. In the next room, guests are handed 3-D glasses and mount what look like 16 bicycles; restraints are deployed along your calves and lower back, ensuring that you don't fall off during your flight.

The Flight of Passage line is boring, and so is the video you watch, especially if you haven't seen the movie. The ride is scary-fun. *Fun* because you get to see Pandora, and *scary* when you go through caves, really high up in the sky, and under water. Next time I will ride it with my eyes open longer. Felicity

Now connected with your banshee, the room goes dark, and with a flash of light similar to going into hyperspace on Star Tours, guests are off on a simulated flight. As you fly over Pandora's plains, soar through its mountains, and skim its sea, you can hear and feel the banshee breathing beneath you.

The banshee vibrates like it's breathing. It's so cool.

Sabrina

The ride is just a tad wilder than Epcot's Soarin', and most guests will tolerate the movements and special effects. Unlike Soarin' you will not have other guests' feet dangling overhead, but you can still see other riders next to you. Depending on where you are seated, you will see all of the riders when you divert your attention from the screen. The flight over Pandora is absolutely amazing and the visuals stunning, so keep your eyes on that screen and enjoy what is the most exciting simulated ride we have ever experienced.

Flight of Passage is super intense and so much fun.

Brendan

Two caveats worth mentioning: The bikes do not accommodate riders of all body shapes; they are not suitable for larger riders. A tall Oklahoman experienced this issue:

> *I am 6'6", and I was too tall to ride. Two others from my pod were also too tall/large.*

The snug restraint system, coupled with the confined space of the room, may cause some claustrophobic guests to exit before riding.

Last but not least, while the ride's queue is absolutely stunning, you don't want to be stuck in it—the queue can absorb 3–4 hours of waiting guests inside the attraction itself. At times cast members direct the queue all the way along the path toward Africa and back before you reach the actual queue of the attraction. This loop alone is at least an additional 60–90 minutes. If the wait is not long, go standby after you've experienced the ride with a FastPass+.

Flight of Passage remains one of the most popular rides in Disney World, and it can be difficult to figure out how to ride without devoting half a day to standing in line. Compounding the problem is that almost all FastPasses are snapped up by Disney resort guests months in advance, and the passes are nearly impossible to score on the day of your visit. So suck it up, day guests, and join the queue.

The other primary complicating factor is how variable the park's opening procedure is. A reader from Napa, California, shares this typical experience:

> *We did rope drop at Animal Kingdom during spring break on a day with park opening at 7 a.m. for resort guests. By 6:30 a.m., the line to get in was out in the parking lot. It's also kind of stressful with everyone bumping into each other trying to get to Flight of Passage.*

Several reasons contribute to the erratic park-opening procedures, but it's primarily a matter of safety and traffic control. To forestall a huge mob collecting at the park entrance with an ensuing (and possibly dangerous) stampede to Pandora, Disney elects to absorb the crowd as it arrives and usher guests safely into a queue. But Animal Kingdom's walkways are the narrowest in all the Disney theme parks, which creates choke points. This makes getting guests out of the rushing current and into a calm eddy even more critical.

The tide of arrivals is stunning every morning but overwhelming on days with morning Extra Magic Hours, when buses disgorge teeming hordes of resort guests at the park entrance. A woman from Longueuil, Quebec, who encountered this phenomenon offers this advice:

> *NEVER go to Flight of Passage on a day with morning Extra Magic Hours— we waited 5 hours! (But my God, this ride is beautiful!) My advice is to see Rivers of Light at 8 p.m., sit near the stairs, and then rush to Flight of Passage. If there is no show, just go to the ride in the last 30 minutes before the park closes—they let you in even if the wait time goes beyond the park closure. We waited only 1 hour.*

If your intent is to be among the first in the park:

1. Check online or call the night before your visit to confirm official park-opening time.

2. Go on a non–Extra Magic Hour day, and arrive 90 minutes before official opening (2 hours early on holidays).

3. Don't depend on Disney transportation. Use a cab or ride-sharing service rather than your own car, so you don't get stuck waiting to pay for parking.

4. Have your admission in hand, thus avoiding the ticket booth.

5. Look for a turnstile that seems to be processing people smoothly. (We got hung up for 15 minutes because of an erratic finger scanner.)

6. There are restrooms to the left of the entrance. Use them if you need to—Disney has a process for letting you run to the loo and rejoin your party, but it involves everyone waiting to reunite at the FastPass merge point.

7. Walk briskly to Pandora. Once there (or at some point before), a cast member will place you in the queue for Flight of Passage.

Na'vi River Journey *(FastPass+)* ★★★★

APPEAL BY AGE PRESCHOOL ★★★★   GRADE SCHOOL ★★★★   TEENS ★★★★½
YOUNG ADULTS ★★★★   OVER 30 ★★★★   SENIORS ★★★★

What it is Indoor boat ride. **Scope and scale** Headliner. **Fright potential** Dark ride but not frightening. **Bottleneck rating** 10. **When to go** Before 9:30 a.m., the last 2 hours before closing, or use FastPass+. **Duration of ride** 5 minutes. **Average wait in line per 100 people ahead of you** About 5 minutes. **Loading speed** Moderate.

A less exciting but absolutely charming experience awaits you at the family-friendly Na'vi River Journey boat ride. Travel through the nighttime jungle on a sacred river, discover the creatures of the rain forest, and meet the Na'vi shaman of songs. She is the most sophisticated animatronic we have ever seen, and it's impossible not to fall under her spell.

There is no height restriction for the ride; while it is a dark ride, it's not scary at all. We think of the ride as It's a Small World on steroids.

The queue of the ride, while filled with beautiful details, is not built to handle huge crowds. Ride before 9:30 a.m. or during the last 2 hours before closing if the lines are not long. Because Na'vi River Journey and Avatar Flight of Passage are both Tier A attractions, we recommend you use your FastPass+ for Flight of Passage.

Liliane

Eywa ngahu, a popular greeting in the Na'vi language, means "May Eywa be with you." It sure feels as if Eywa is with you on this ride, as Eywa keeps the ecosystem of Pandora in perfect equilibrium.

Movie Tip

The first Avatar *movie was released in 2009 and is still the world's top-grossing film at the global box office, with earnings of $2.8 billion. Mark your calendars for the next four sequels of* Avatar, *scheduled to be released December 17, 2021; December 22, 2023; December 19, 2025; and December 17, 2027.*

The Na'vi River Journey is a beautiful ride, but it really is just another boat ride. Don't stand in line for it too long.

Isabelle

The Na'vi River Journey makes you feel like you're visiting a different world. It's quite dark, but that's OK because it's all lit up with lights from another planet. The music and the realistic shaman at the end are amazing.

Felicity

AFRICA

GUESTS ENTER THE LARGEST of the Animal Kingdom's lands through **Harambe,** Disney's idealized and immensely sanitized version of a modern rural African town, with shops, a sit-down buffet, limited counter service, and snack stands. Harambe serves as the gateway to the African veld habitat, Animal Kingdom's largest zoological exhibit. Access the veld via **Kilimanjaro Safaris.** Harambe is also the departure point for the train to **Rafiki's Planet Watch** and **Conservation Station** (the park's veterinary headquarters), as well as the home of *Festival of the Lion King,* a long-running live theatrical show. A walkway by *Lion King* connects Africa to Pandora.

Festival of the Lion King (FastPass+) ★★★★

**APPEAL BY AGE PRESCHOOL ★★★★½ GRADE SCHOOL ★★★★½ TEENS ★★★★½
YOUNG ADULTS ★★★★½   OVER 30 ★★★★½   SENIORS ★★★★★**

What it is Theater-in-the-round stage show. **Scope and scale** Major attraction. **Fright potential** A bit loud but otherwise not frightening. **Bottleneck rating** 9. **When to go** Before 11 a.m., after 4 p.m., or use FastPass+; check the handout park map or *Times Guide* for showtimes. **Comment** Upbeat and spectacular; not to be missed. **Duration of show** 30 minutes. **Probable waiting time** 20-35 minutes.

Fantastic pageantry, dazzling costumes, a mini–Broadway show, and air-conditioning too. *Festival of the Lion King* at the Animal Kingdom was the precursor to the Broadway production of *The Lion King.*

Try to score front-row seats. Kids are invited to play musical instruments and join the performance. (Your chances are best if you're celebrating a special day.) Ask a cast member if a cast meet and greet will occur after the performance; often there is one.

Liliane

The show is based on the animated feature The Lion King, *a must-see movie. Did you know that James Earl Jones, the voice behind Mufasa (father of Simba), was also the voice behind Darth Vader in several of the* Star Wars *movies?*

Movie Tip

I love the movie and the show. I was picked to shake maracas and walk around with the performers—that was very cool.

Felicity

One of my favorite shows at the Animal Kingdom is the *Festival of the Lion King.* It gets a 10 out of 10 and is not to be missed.

Lucy

Gorilla Falls Exploration Trail ★★★★

**APPEAL BY AGE PRESCHOOL ★★★★   GRADE SCHOOL ★★★★   TEENS ★★★★
YOUNG ADULTS ★★★★   OVER 30 ★★★★   SENIORS ★★★★**

What it is Walk-through zoological exhibit. **Scope and scale** Major attraction. **Fright potential** Not frightening in any respect. **Bottleneck rating** 9. **When to go** Before or after Kilimanjaro Safaris. Also check the *Times Guide* for early off-season closures. **Comment** Closes at sunset. **Duration of tour** About 20-25 minutes.

The Gorilla Falls Exploration Trail is lush, beautiful, and filled with people much of the time—particularly unpleasant if you have to wiggle your way through with a stroller. Walk the trail before 10 a.m. or after 4:30 p.m., or get a FastPass+ for Kilimanjaro Safaris 60-90 minutes after the park opens. That's long enough for an uncrowded, leisurely tour of the trail and a quick snack before you go on safari.

Kilimanjaro Safaris *(FastPass+)* ★★★★★

**APPEAL BY AGE   PRESCHOOL ★★★★½   GRADE SCHOOL ★★★★½   TEENS ★★★★½
YOUNG ADULTS ★★★★½   OVER 30 ★★★★½   SENIORS ★★★★★**

What it is Truck ride through a simulated African wildlife reservation. **Scope and scale** Super-headliner. **Fright potential** A "collapsing" bridge and the proximity of real animals make a few young children anxious. **Bottleneck rating** 10. **When to go** As soon as the park opens, in the 2 hours before closing, or use FastPass+. **Comment** Truly exceptional. **Duration of ride** About 20 minutes. **Average wait in line per 100 people ahead of you** 4 minutes; assumes full-capacity operation with 18-second dispatch interval. **Loading speed** Fast.

Off you go in an open safari vehicle through a simulated African savanna, looking for hippos, zebras, giraffes, lions, and rhinos. Many readers have asked us whether fewer animals are visible from Kilimanjaro Safaris around lunchtime than at park opening, out of concern that the animals might be less active in the midday heat. To help answer that question, we sent a team of researchers to ride continuously during 1 week in the summer and had them count the number and type of animals visible at different times of day. Our results indicate that you'll probably see the same number of animals regardless of when you visit. This finding is almost certainly due to Disney's deliberate placement of water, food, and shade near the safari vehicles. Kilimanjaro Safaris also operates nighttime safaris. The path through the African savanna is adjusted during these sunset tours, and the trucks make longer stops, allowing guests more time to spot animals. The start time for the nighttime tours depends on what time the sun sets. Some amazing technology ensures that the magical sunset lasts about 4–5 hours every night. To give the animals the rest they need, different animals are in the savanna at night.

I absolutely love Kilimanjaro Safaris, day and night. Remember, flash photography is NOT allowed during the nighttime safari.

I liked seeing the animals up close. It was very funny to see an elephant doing a poo and a wee.

Liliane

Winding through the safari is **Disney's Wild Africa Trek,** a behind-the-scenes walking tour of the Animal Kingdom that takes you into several of Kilimanjaro Safaris' animal enclosures.

Felicity

Bob

If you want to see lots of animals on Kilimanjaro Safaris, it's best to go early in the morning. I think the animals are more awake and active because they're being fed.

Lucy

RAFIKI'S PLANET WATCH

THIS AREA ISN'T REALLY a land. Disney uses the name as an umbrella for Conservation Station, the petting zoo, and the environmental exhibits accessible from Harambe via the Wildlife Express Train. After a nearly yearlong closing for refurbishment, Rafiki's Planet Watch reopened in late summer 2019. The educational area features a few new enhancements, experiences based on Disney's animated feature *The*

Lion King, and **The Animation Experience.** Check the *Times Guide* before you trek out there; the area opens later than the rest of the park.

The Animation Experience *(FastPass+)*

What it is Character-drawing class. **Scope and scale** Minor attraction. **Fright potential** Not frightening in any respect. **Bottleneck rating** 3. **When to go** Check the *Times Guide*. **Duration of experience** About 25 minutes. **Probable waiting time** None.

Thumbs Up for the Whole Family

The latest addition to the area is The Animation Experience, where guests are taught to draw some of Disney's most famous animal characters in a 25-minute class. If you want to discover how Disney animators bring your favorite characters to life, use FastPass+.

Conservation Station and Affection Section   ★★★

APPEAL BY AGE   PRESCHOOL ★★★½   GRADE SCHOOL ★★★★   TEENS ★★★½
YOUNG ADULTS ★★★½   OVER 30 ★★★½   SENIORS ★★★½

What it is Behind-the-scenes walk-through educational exhibit and petting zoo. **Scope and scale** Minor attraction. **Fright potential** Not frightening in any respect. **Bottleneck rating** 6. **When to go** Check the *Times Guide* for hours.

This is the Animal Kingdom's veterinary and conservation headquarters. Guests can meet wildlife experts, observe some of the ongoing projects, and learn about the park operations. A rehabilitation area for injured animals, a nursery for recently born (or hatched) critters, and a petting zoo are included.

What you see will largely depend on what's going on when you arrive. Some readers think there isn't enough happening to warrant waiting in line twice (coming and going) for the train, but others have had better luck, as a university biologist from Springfield, Missouri, attests:

> *If you get to Conservation Station between 10 a.m. and noon, you can see the vet techs actually doing some routine procedures as they maintain the health of the animals. Our aspiring 7-year-old vet LOVED visiting with the technician. She spent 20 minutes asking her all kinds of questions.*

Conservation Station is interesting, but you have to invest a little effort, and it helps to be inquisitive. Because it's so removed from the rest of the park, you'll never bump into Conservation Station unless you take the train round-trip from Harambe.

Wildlife Express Train   ★★

APPEAL BY AGE   PRESCHOOL ★★★★   GRADE SCHOOL ★★★½   TEENS ★★★½
YOUNG ADULTS ★★★½   OVER 30 ★★★½   SENIORS ★★★★

What it is Scenic railroad ride to Rafiki's Planet Watch and its attractions. **Scope and scale** Minor attraction. **Fright potential** Not frightening in any respect. **Bottleneck rating** 7. **When to go** Anytime. **Comments** Opens 30 minutes after the rest of the park and stops running 4:30 p.m. or earlier. Ho-hum. **Duration of ride** About 5–7

Thumbs Up for the Whole Family

minutes one-way. **Average wait in line per 100 people ahead of you** 9 minutes. **Loading speed** Moderate.

Take the train only if you have small kids who would really enjoy the Affection Section petting zoo at Rafiki's Planet Watch. If you have a future veterinarian in your family, it's also worth checking out the behind-the-scenes exhibits at Conservation Station. All ages will enjoy The Animation Experience.

ASIA

CROSSING THE BRIDGE FROM DISCOVERY ISLAND, you enter this land through the village of **Anandapur,** a veritable collage of Asian themes inspired by the architecture and ruins of India, Thailand, Indonesia, and Nepal. Anandapur provides access to an animal exhibit and to Asia's two feature attractions, the **Kali River Rapids** whitewater raft ride and **Expedition Everest.** Also in Asia is *Up! A Great Bird Adventure,* an educational production about birds, and *Rivers of Light: We Are One,* a nighttime show held on the Discovery River (see page 349).

Expedition Everest *(FastPass+)* ★★★★½

APPEAL BY AGE   PRESCHOOL ★★★   GRADE SCHOOL ★★★★½   TEENS ★★★★★
YOUNG ADULTS ★★★★★   OVER 30 ★★★★★   SENIORS ★★★★½

What it is High-speed outdoor roller coaster through Nepalese mountain village. **Scope and scale** Super-headliner. **Fright potential** Frightens guests of all ages. **Bottleneck rating** 8. **When to go** Before 9:30 a.m., after 3 p.m., or use FastPass+. **Comments** Must be 44" to ride; switching-off option (see page 248). A single-rider line is available. Not to be missed. **Duration of ride** 4 minutes. **Average wait in line per 100 people ahead of you** 4 minutes; assumes 2 tracks operating. **Loading speed** Moderate–fast.

As you enjoy one of the most spectacular panoramas in Walt Disney World, you wish this expedition would never end. But you get over that in a hurry as the train starts whirring through the guts of Disney's largest man-made mountain. After a high-speed encounter with a large, smelly (and often AWOL) yeti and a dead stop at the base camp of Mount Everest, the 50-mile-per-hour chase continues backward. The ride is very smooth and rich both in visuals and special effects. The backward segment is one of the most creative and exciting 20 seconds in roller coaster annals.

I didn't like this ride, not one bit. It made me feel really sick.

Be on the lookout for the yeti toward the end of Expedition Everest.

Felicity

Isabelle

Kali River Rapids *(FastPass+)* ★★★½

APPEAL BY AGE   PRESCHOOL ★★★★   GRADE SCHOOL ★★★★½   TEENS ★★★★½
YOUNG ADULTS ★★★★   OVER 30 ★★★★   SENIORS ★★★★

What it is Whitewater raft ride. **Scope and scale** Headliner. **Fright potential** Potentially frightening and certainly wet for guests of all ages. **Bottleneck rating** 9. **When to go** First or last hour the park is open, or use FastPass+. **Comments** Must be 38" tall to ride; you're guaranteed to get wet; opens 30 minutes after the rest of the park and may close early on off-peak or cold days. Switching-off option (see page 248). Short but scenic. **Duration of ride** About 5 minutes. **Average wait in line per 100 people ahead of you** 5 minutes. **Loading speed** Moderate.

This tame raft ride lets you take in the outstanding scenery as you drift through a dense rain forest, past waterfalls and temple ruins. There are neither big drops nor terrifying rapids;

nevertheless, Disney still manages to drench you. Nonriding park guests, especially those who don't meet the height requirement, will take great pleasure squirting water at the rafters from above.

If you ride early in the morning or on a cool day, use raingear and make sure your shoes stay dry. Touring in wet clothes is no fun, and walking all day in soaked sneakers is a recipe for blisters.

Liliane

A. J.

Kali River Rapids can get you anywhere from sprinkled with water to soaking wet. Make sure your possessions are protected. A wet wallet and a soaked cell phone are no fun.

Oh my goodness, this ride is trouble. I rode it with my dad, and we got drenched. The line is fun, like a nature walk. Watch out for people squirting you with water! If you don't want to walk around in dripping wet clothes, wear a poncho.

Felicity

Maharajah Jungle Trek ★★★★

**APPEAL BY AGE   PRESCHOOL ★★★★   GRADE SCHOOL ★★★★   TEENS ★★★★
YOUNG ADULTS ★★★★   OVER 30 ★★★★   SENIORS ★★★★½**

What it is Walk-through zoological exhibit. **Scope and scale** Headliner. **Fright potential** Some children may balk at the bat exhibit. **Bottleneck rating** 5. **When to go** Anytime. **Comments** May open later and close earlier than the rest of park. A standard-setter for natural habitat design. **Duration of tour** About 20–30 minutes.

The Jungle Trek is less congested than the Gorilla Falls Exploration Trail and is a good choice for midday touring. Tigers, water buffalo, and birds are waiting to be discovered along a path winding through the fabulous ruins of the maharajah's palace.

Up! A Great Bird Adventure (FastPass+) ★★★★

**APPEAL BY AGE   PRESCHOOL ★★★½   GRADE SCHOOL ★★★★   TEENS ★★★
YOUNG ADULTS ★★★½   OVER 30 ★★★   SENIORS ★★★½**

What it is Stadium show about birds. **Scope and scale** Major attraction. **Fright potential** Swooping birds startle some younger children. **Bottleneck rating** 6. **When to go** Performance times are listed in the handout park map or *Times Guide*. **Comment** Unique. **Duration of show** 30 minutes. **Probable waiting time** 10–15 minutes.

Thumbs Up for the Whole Family

In this bird show, Russell and Dug from the hit film *Up!* discover bird species from around the world. The show, which debuted in spring 2018 in celebration of the 20th anniversary of the Animal Kingdom, replaces *Flights of Wonder*. Diwali, the Hindu festival of lights, is incorporated into the show during the holidays.

DISNEY DISH WITH JIM HILL

A NEW IDEA TAKES FLIGHT Disney has tried a new script and new characters to boost flagging attendance at the *Up!* exotic-bird show, but to no avail. Now the Imagineers are considering retheming the show around Blu and Jewel, the romantically involved Spix's macaws voiced by Jesse Eisenberg and Anne Hathaway in Blue Sky Studios' *Rio* movies, which Disney now owns.

DINOLAND U.S.A.

THIS MOST TYPICALLY DISNEY of Animal Kingdom's lands is a cross between an anthropological dig and a quirky roadside attraction. Accessible via the bridge from Discovery Island, DinoLand U.S.A. is home to a children's play area, a nature trail, and **Dinosaur,** one of Animal Kingdom's three thrill rides. *Finding Nemo—The Musical* is shown at Theater in the Wild. **Donald, Daisy, Goofy, Chip 'n' Dale, Launchpad McQuack,** and **Scrooge McDuck** all make appearances here; see page 348.

The Boneyard ★★★

APPEAL BY AGE   PRESCHOOL ★★★★★   GRADE SCHOOL ★★★★½   TEENS ★★★
YOUNG ADULTS ★★½   OVER 30 ★★★   SENIORS ★★½

What it is Elaborate playground. **Scope and scale** Diversion. **Fright potential** Not frightening in any respect. **Bottleneck rating** 5. **When to go** Anytime. **Comments** Opens 30 minutes after the rest of the park. Stimulating fun for children.

Time to play! This elaborate playground for kids age 12 and younger is a great place for them to let off steam and get dirty (or at least sandy). The playground equipment consists of skeletal replicas of *Triceratops, Tyrannosaurus rex, Brachiosaurus,* and the like. In addition, there are climbing mazes, plus sandpits where little ones can scrounge for bones and fossils.

The Boneyard can get very hot in the scorching Florida sun, so make sure your kids are properly hydrated and protected against sunburn. The playground is huge, and parents might lose sight of a small child. Fortunately, however, there's only one entrance and exit. Your little ones are going to love The Boneyard, so resign yourself to staying awhile.

Dinosaur *(FastPass+)* ★★★★

**APPEAL BY AGE   PRESCHOOL ★★½   GRADE SCHOOL ★★★★   TEENS ★★★★
YOUNG ADULTS ★★★★   OVER 30 ★★★★   SENIORS ★★★★**

What it is Motion-simulator dark ride. **Scope and scale** Headliner. **Fright potential** High-tech thrill ride rattles riders of all ages. **Bottleneck rating** 5. **When to go** Before 10:30 a.m., after 4:30 p.m., or use FastPass+. **Comments** Must be 40″ tall to ride; switching-off option (see page 248). Not to be missed. **Duration of ride** 3½ minutes. **Average wait in line per 100 people ahead of you** 3 minutes; assumes full-capacity operation with 18-second dispatch interval. **Loading speed** Fast.

Dark   Rough   Scary

Here you board a time capsule to return to the Jurassic age in an effort to bring back a live dinosaur before a meteor hits Earth and wipes them out. The bad guy in this epic is the little-known *Carnotaurus,* an evil-eyed, long-in-the-tooth, *Tyrannosaurus rex*-type fellow. A combination track ride and motion simulator, Dinosaur is not for the fainthearted—you get tossed and pitched around in the dark, with pesky dinosaurs jumping out at you. Dinosaur has left many an adult weak-kneed. Most kids under age 9 find it terrifying. Lines should be relatively light through midmorning, and more FastPasses should be available for day-of use.

*Dinosaur is one of my favorite rides at Animal Kingdom,
but it might scare the poop out of little kids.
Make sure you warn them before going on the ride.*

A. J.

Primeval Whirl (*FastPass+*) ★★★

APPEAL BY AGE   PRESCHOOL ★★★½   GRADE SCHOOL ★★★★   TEENS ★★★★
YOUNG ADULTS ★★★½   OVER 30 ★★★½   SENIORS ★★★½

What it is Small roller coaster. **Scope and scale** Minor attraction. **Fright potential** Scarier than it looks. **Bottleneck rating** 9. **When to go** During the first hour the park is open, in the hour before park closing, or use FastPass+. **Comments** Must be 48″ tall to ride; switching-off option (see page 248). Wild Mouse on steroids. **Duration of ride** Almost 2½ minutes. **Average wait in line per 100 people ahead of you** 4½ minutes. **Loading speed** Slow.

Scary   Rough   Queasy

This tricky little coaster has short drops, curves, and tight loops—not to mention the coaster cars spin. The problem is that, unlike with those evil teacups, you can't control the spinning. Complete spins are fun, but watch out for the screeching-stop half-spins.

Theater in the Wild / *Finding Nemo—The Musical* (*FastPass+*) ★★★★

APPEAL BY AGE   PRESCHOOL ★★★★½   GRADE SCHOOL ★★★★½   TEENS ★★★★
YOUNG ADULTS ★★★★   OVER 30 ★★★★½   SENIORS ★★★★½

What it is Open-air venue for live stage shows. **Scope and scale** Major attraction. **Fright potential** Generally not frightening—but see below. **Bottleneck rating** 6. **When to go** Performance times are listed in the handout park map or *Times Guide*. **Comment** Not to be missed. **Duration of show** 30 minutes. **Probable waiting time** 30 minutes.

Thumbs Up for the Whole Family

Based on the Disney-Pixar animated feature, *Finding Nemo—The Musical* is an elaborate stage show headlining puppets, dancers, acrobats, and special effects. It is arguably the most elaborate live show in any Disney World park. A few scenes, such as one in which Nemo's mom is eaten (!), may be too intense for some very small children. Some of the mid-show musical numbers slow the pace, so the main concern for parents is whether the kids can sit still for an entire show. With that in mind, we advise parents to catch a pre-lunchtime performance—around 11:30 a.m.

To get a seat, show up 20–25 minutes in advance for morning and late-afternoon shows and 30–35 minutes in advance for shows scheduled noon–4:30 p.m. Access to the theater is via a relatively narrow pedestrian path; if you arrive as the previous show is letting out, you'll feel like a salmon swimming upstream.

When the line is very long, don't assume that you'll get into the next show just by queuing up. Ask a cast member whether you're likely to get into the next show.

Liliane

TriceraTop Spin ★★

APPEAL BY AGE   PRESCHOOL ★★★★½   GRADE SCHOOL ★★★★   TEENS ★★★
YOUNG ADULTS ★★★   OVER 30 ★★★   SENIORS ★★★

What it is Hub-and-spoke midway ride. **Scope and scale** Minor attraction. **Fright potential** May frighten preschoolers. **Bottleneck rating** 9. **When to go** Before noon or after 3 p.m. **Comment** Dumbo's prehistoric forebear. **Duration of ride** 1½ minutes. **Average wait in line per 100 people ahead of you** 10 minutes. **Loading speed** Slow.

Instead of Dumbo, you get Dino spinning around a central axis. It's fun for little ones, but this slow-loader is infamous for inefficiency and long waits.

LIVE ENTERTAINMENT
at ANIMAL KINGDOM

WDW LIVE-ENTERTAINMENT GURU Steve Soares usually posts the Animal Kingdom performance schedule about a week in advance at wdwent.com.

ANIMAL ENCOUNTERS Throughout the day, Disney staff conduct impromptu short lectures on specific animals at the park. Look for a cast member in safari garb holding a bird, reptile, or small mammal.

GOODWILL AMBASSADORS A number of Asian and African cast members are on hand throughout the park. Gracious and knowledgeable, they're delighted to discuss their native countries and the wildlife in them. Look for them in Harambe and along the Gorilla Falls Exploration Trail in Africa, and in Anandapur and along the Maharajah Jungle Trek in Asia. They can also be found near the main entrance and at The Oasis.

DONALD'S DINO-BASH Donald Duck takes over DinoLand U.S.A. to celebrate his recent discovery that ducks are descendants of dinosaurs. Characters usually appear intermittently starting at 10 a.m. as follows: Chip 'n' Dale, across from TriceraTop Spin until 4:30 p.m.; Daisy, Donald, and Goofy until 5:30 p.m. at Chester and Hester's Dino-Rama; and Launchpad McQuack and Scrooge McDuck at The Boneyard until 4 p.m. See our review at theunofficialguides.com/2018/06/21/dino-bash.

HOLIDAY EVENTS New holiday decorations in the form of animal-inspired luminaries are coming to Discovery Island, and during the day, life-size puppets of winter animals such as reindeers, foxes, polar bears, and penguins will interact with guests. The Tree of Life *Awakening* will get an overlay of a series of wintry tales, while over at DinoLand U.S.A. Chip 'n' Dale host a **Holiday Hoopla Dance Party.** In Asia, *Up! A Great Bird Adventure* will pay tribute to Diwali, the Indian festival of lights.

FAVORITE EATS AT ANIMAL KINGDOM

LAND | SERVICE LOCATION | FOOD SELECTIONS

DISCOVERY ISLAND　Flame Tree Barbecue | Ribs and chicken with baked beans
Pizzafari | Pizza, Romaine salad with chicken, garlic knots, and shrimp flatbread

AFRICA　Tamu Tamu Eats & Refreshments | Dole Whips and sundaes
Tusker House Restaurant | Rotisserie chicken, curried rice, and salmon. Tusker House has a character breakfast, lunch, and dinner featuring Donald, Daisy, Goofy, and Mickey. *Buffet*

ASIA　Yak & Yeti Restaurant | Korean beef and coconut shrimp | *Table service only*

DINOLAND U.S.A.　Restaurantosaurus | Black bean burger; grilled chicken BLT; kid's cheeseburger or chicken nuggets served in a sand pail, complete with a shovel

OUTSIDE ENTRANCE　Rainforest Cafe | Beef lava nachos; rib, steak, and shrimp trio. Breakfast, lunch, and dinner in a tropical rain forest setting with a huge saltwater aquarium, gorillas going wild once in a while, and simulated thunderstorms. The place to take the kids if you want to sit down! They'll love you for it. | *Table service only*

Africa's village of Harambe will offer new holiday presentations, and diners at Tusker House will be treated to much holiday cheer by Mickey and friends.

Ex-pats living on Pandora will display kitschy holiday decor, mixing vintage Earth pieces with handcrafted items made from materials native to Pandora.

Animal Kingdom's Yuletide fun starts November 8.

STREET PERFORMERS Far and away the most intriguing is the performer you can't see—at least not at first. A perfect fusion between fantasy and reality, **DiVine** (★★★★) is an artist best described as half vine and half creeping plant. She blends perfectly with the foliage at Animal Kingdom and is noticeable only when she moves—which can be quite startling if you're not aware of her presence. DiVine is most often found at The Oasis; if you don't encounter her, ask a cast member when and where she can be found. Video of her is available at **YouTube** (go to youtube.com and search for "DiVine Disney's Animal Kingdom").

But DiVine isn't the only performer at Animal Kingdom worth seeing. Make sure you take a moment to enjoy **Viva Gaia Street Band** at Discovery Island, as well as the **Tam Tam Drummers** of Harambe and the **Burudika** band in Africa. High-energy entertainment includes the new **Bollywood Beats** show in Asia and a dance party held on the Discovery Island stage.

TREE OF LIFE *AWAKENINGS* This nighttime show is shown several times per night at the Tree of Life. It combines digital video projections with music; special projection effects make it appear that some animals carved into the tree trunk have come alive. Each show lasts about 3 minutes and features an original musical score. It's a must-see.

WINGED ENCOUNTERS—THE KINGDOM TAKES FLIGHT This outdoor show features macaws and their handlers in front of the Tree of Life. Guests can talk to the animals' trainers and see the birds fly around the middle of the park. Check the *Times Guide* for showtimes.

Rivers of Light: We Are One (FastPass+) ★★★★★

APPEAL BY AGE PRESCHOOL ★★★★	GRADE SCHOOL ★★★★	TEENS ★★★½
YOUNG ADULTS ★★★★ OVER 30 ★★★★	SENIORS ★★★★	

What it is Nighttime sound-and-light show. **Scope and scale** Major attraction. **Fright potential** Loud. May frighten young children, but most like it. **Bottleneck rating** 10. **When to go** Check *Times Guide* for showtimes; use FastPass+. **Comment** Not to be missed. **Duration of show** 15 minutes. **When to arrive** 60 minutes before showtime if standby.

The sound-and-light show takes place along the lagoon formed by the Discovery River. The show centers on four lotus-flower lanterns floating on the lagoon. They are joined by two boats carrying shamans, who conjure the forces of fire and water to reveal the majesty of the natural world, mostly as video projections on a huge water screen at the back of the lagoon. Unfortunately, the wind patterns on the lagoon sometimes blur many of the videos projected onto the water screens. The highlight is the appearance of four immense, color-changing floats in the shape of a tiger, a turtle, an elephant, and an owl.

The latest changes to the show are mostly new water screen video projections of popular Disney characters and songs, resulting in a revised show called *Rivers of Light: We Are One.*

The bridge between Expedition Everest and DinoLand is a good viewing option. But remember, you won't be the only one, so arrive early to claim your spot! You can also position yourself along the walkway between the Yak & Yeti Restaurant and Expedition Everest. We do not recommend the spot in the waterside seating area of Flame Tree Barbecue, as the water screens and projections come from there, and you won't be able to see much of the show from this location.

If seeing *Rivers of Light* is a must, use one of your advance FastPasses or get the dining package. Half of the show's 5,000 seats are reserved for Fast-Pass+. The other half are for standby guests and those with dining packages. There are also limited, partially obstructed viewing areas around the river. Arrive about 45 minutes in advance to get a standby seat.

Finally, the area's prevailing winds are from the south and east, so mist from the show's fountains should head away from the seating areas. If the weather forecast calls for winds from the north or west, especially during colder months, bring ponchos or blankets just in case.

Rivers of Light is definitely worth your time. I believe that, to really take in all the sights and sounds, you ought to see it twice.

Liliane

Rivers of Light Dining Packages

Breakfast at **Tusker House** starts at $40 for adults and $25 for children ages 3–9. Lunch and dinner prices start at $52 for adults and $32 for children ages 3–9. Lunch and dinner packages at **Tiffins** start at $68 for adults and $26 for children ages 3–9. This is a worthwhile alternative if day-of FastPasses aren't available and you were already planning to eat at one of them.

At the ***Rivers of Light* Dessert Party** ($79 for adults, $47 for children, tax included), guests can add a sweet ending to their day with an array of Animal Kingdom–themed desserts, snacks, and specialty drinks (alcoholic and non) before enjoying VIP viewing of *Rivers of Light.* Check-in is 1 hour prior to the main show at the Asia viewing area across from Expedition Everest. The experience is available on select nights.

If you are a lucky FastPass+ holder, or if you purchased a dining package, you should still arrive at least 30 minutes prior to the show to claim your seat. There are several entrances: one in Asia near Expedition Everest (FastPass+ seating), one across from the *Finding Nemo* theater entrance (dining package seating area), and one a little farther toward DinoLand U.S.A. (standby seating area).

While it's possible to leave the theater (cast members will give you a lanyard to wear, allowing you to return), we recommend you stay put. Bring a snack and a drink, and relax before the show. The theater has no restrooms, so take care of business prior to entering.

ANIMAL KINGDOM HARD-TICKET EVENTS

ANIMAL KINGDOM AFTER HOURS This special extra-cost event provides guests with 3 hours of unlimited access to Expedition Everest, Dinosaur,

It's Tough to Be a Bug!, TriceraTop Spin, Avatar Flight of Passage, and Na'vi River Journey, as well as several character meet and greets. The Tree of Life *Awakenings* also takes place, as well as *Rivers of Light.* A ticket purchased in advance costs $113 per adult or child, and $137 per adult or child on the day of the event. Also included are all the ice cream, popcorn, and soda you can consume (from select vendors). This event is only worthwhile if your kids are able to stay up late at night. Even teenagers may balk at doing anything before noon the next morning. On Mondays, the event is held 10 p.m.–1 a.m.; on all other days, it's held 9 p.m.–midnight. The big advantage of this special event is that Disney After Hours' guests can enter the park at 7 p.m. Regular park admission is *not* required.

ANIMAL KINGDOM TOURING PLANS

OUR STEP-BY-STEP TOURING PLANS are field-tested, independently verified itineraries that will keep you moving counter to the crowd flow. The plans will also allow you to see as much as possible in a single day with minimum time wasted in line. Because Animal Kingdom has fewer attractions than the other parks, you can take them in during a single day, even when traveling with young children.

The different touring plans are described below. The descriptions will tell you for whom (for example, tweens, parents with preschoolers, and so on) or for what situation (such as sleeping late) the plans are designed. The actual touring plans are located on pages 492–495. Each plan includes a numbered map of the park to help you find your way around.

Each plan lists the attractions most likely to need FastPass+ and the approximate return times for which you should try to make reservations. Visit touringplans.com if any attractions, FastPasses, or times need changing, either while planning or in the parks.

1-DAY TOURING PLAN FOR PARENTS WITH SMALL CHILDREN This plan is designed for parents of children ages 3–8 who wish to see the very best age-appropriate attractions in the Animal Kingdom. Every attraction has a rating of at least three-and-a-half stars (out of five) from preschool and grade-school children surveyed by *The Unofficial Guide.* Special advice is provided for touring the park with small children, including restaurant recommendations. The plan keeps walking and backtracking to a minimum.

1-DAY SLEEPYHEAD TOURING PLAN FOR PARENTS WITH SMALL CHILDREN A relaxed plan that allows families with small children to sleep late and still see the highlights of the Animal Kingdom. The plan begins around 11 a.m., sets aside ample time for lunch, and includes the very best child-friendly attractions in the park.

1-DAY TOURING PLAN FOR TWEENS AND THEIR PARENTS A 1-day plan for parents with kids ages 8–12, it includes every attraction rated three stars and higher by this age group and sets aside ample time for lunch.

1-DAY HAPPY FAMILY TOURING PLAN A plan for families of all ages, it includes time-saving tips for teens and adults visiting the Animal Kingdom's thrill rides, as well as age-appropriate attractions for parents with small children. The entire family stays together as much as possible (including lunch), but this plan allows groups with different interests to explore their favorite attractions without having everyone wait around.

BEFORE YOU GO

1. Call ☎ 407-824-4321 or check disneyworld.com for operating hours.

2. Buy your admission and make FastPass+ reservations before you arrive.

DISNEY'S ANIMAL KINGDOM TRIVIA QUIZ

1. Which attraction is inside the iconic Tree of Life?

    a. Pocahontas and Her Forest Friends   **b.** *It's Tough to Be a Bug!*
    c. Wilderness Explorers   **d.** *Up! A Great Bird Adventure*

2. What parade ran for 14 years at Animal Kingdom?

    a. Festival of Fantasy Parade   **c.** Mickey's Jammin' Jungle Parade
    b. Festival of the Lion King Parade   **d.** Mickey's Soundsational Parade

3. In which land do you find Kali River Rapids?

    a. Africa   **c.** Thailand
    b. India   **d.** Asia

4. What show plays at Theater in the Wild?

    a. *Indiana Jones Epic Stunt Spectacular!*
    b. *Voyage of the Little Mermaid*
    c. *Finding Nemo—The Musical*
    d. *Beauty and the Beast—Live on Stage*

5. Which restaurant can be accessed without paying entrance to Animal Kingdom?

    a. Tusker House   **c.** Flame Tree Barbecue
    b. Rainforest Cafe   **d.** Yak & Yeti

6. The newest land in Animal Kingdom is based on which movie?

    a. *The Jungle Book*   **c.** *Tarzan*
    b. *Avatar*   **d.** *A Bug's Life*

7. Which one of the following attractions can only be experienced in a vehicle?

    a. Gorilla Falls Exploration Trail   **c.** Kilimanjaro Safaris
    b. Wilderness Explorers   **d.** Maharajah Jungle Trek

8. What is the closest water park to Animal Kingdom?

    a. Volcano Bay   **c.** Blizzard Beach
    b. Typhoon Lagoon   **d.** Aquatica

9. What is Animal Kingdom's interactive adventure game?

    a. Kids' Discovery Club
    c. *Finding Nemo*

    b. Wilderness Explorers
    d. Expedition Everest

10. What was the first animal to be born in Animal Kingdom?

    a. A black rhino
    c. A Masai giraffe

    b. A Micronesian kingfisher chick
    d. A kudu (a large African antelope)

Answers can be found on page 450.

PART TEN

DISNEY'S HOLLYWOOD STUDIOS

ABOUT HALF OF DISNEY'S HOLLYWOOD STUDIOS (DHS) is set up as a theme park; the other half is off-limits to guests. The *Studios* in "Disney's Hollywood Studios" is of little significance today: movie and TV production ceased here long ago, and nothing remains that offers a peek behind the scenes. Though modest in size, the Studios' open-access areas are confusingly arranged (a product of the park's hurried expansion in the early 1990s).

As at the Magic Kingdom, you enter the park and pass down a main street, only this time it's the **Hollywood Boulevard** of the 1920s and 1930s. The boulevard leads to the magnificent replica of the **Grauman's Chinese Theatre,** home of **Mickey and Minnie's Runaway Railway** ride (opening 2020).

The 11-acre **Toy Story Land** opened in the summer of 2018; see page 371 for a full description. If visiting the new attractions is a priority, make sure to get there at park opening or use FastPass+.

In August 2019 the eagerly awaited 14-acre **Star Wars: Galaxy's Edge** opened. The land is themed to a small town on the planet of Batuu, a remote outpost on the galaxy's edge. The *Star Wars*–inspired land is a collection of squat, sand-colored buildings set amid rock outcrops and surrounded by a green forest. In addition to the two main rides, the land has several shops and eateries. However, the land opened with only the *Millennium Falcon:* **Smugglers Run** operating. **Star Wars: Rise of the Resistance** is scheduled to open later in 2019.

Guest Relations, on your left as you enter, serves as the park headquarters and information center. Go there for a schedule of live performances, lost persons, general information, first aid, or in an emergency. If you haven't picked up a map of the Studios, get one here. To the right of the entrance are **locker, stroller,** and **wheelchair rentals,** as well as package pickup and **lost and found.**

The **Baby Care Center** is located at Guest Relations, and **Oscar's** sells baby food and other necessities. Camera supplies for those precious moments can be purchased at **The Darkroom,** on the right side of Holly-wood Boulevard just past Oscar's. The closest **ATMs** are just inside the park, to the right of the turnstiles, and beside Echo Lake. Across from Disney's Port Orleans Resorts, **Best Friends Pet Care** provides a com-fortable home away from home for Fido, Fluffy, and all their pet pals.

OPENING PROCEDURES AT DHS

WE DON'T THINK THE STUDIOS has enough ride or restaurant capacity to handle the anticipated demand of Galaxy's Edge. Disney will handle some of that by opening the park at 6 a.m. (you read that right) for at least the first two months of operation, and probably on holidays as well. Disney has also placed new, substantial FastPass+ restrictions on its other rides. Going forward Disney will continue to reevaluate the crowds and therefore the opening procedures.

We anticipate it will be something similar to how Disney managed crowds for the Pandora attractions at Animal Kingdom, at a much larger scale. Then, guests lined up as early as 6 a.m. to be near the front of the line for Avatar Flight of Passage, when the park opened at 9 a.m.

Galaxy's Edge will open for morning Extra Magic Hours (EMHs) at 6 a.m., daily through October 2019 at least. These EMHs will run through 9 a.m. If you want to be at the front of that line, we expect on-site guests will begin lining up at 4 a.m. or earlier. Disney is likely to run a similar schedule during holidays and other times of peak attendance, such as when Rise of the Resistance opens.

Cast members will direct guests headed to Galaxy's Edge into a special holding area to prevent that crowd from blocking other guests' walking paths to the rest of the park. We expect this holding area to be near the Grand Avenue section of the park. Guests waiting to enter other areas of the park may be held on Hollywood or Sunset Boule-vard until the park opens.

These daily, extended morning EMHs put off-site guests at a tre-mendous disadvantage for experiencing the Galaxy's Edge rides. By the time off-site guests are admitted into the park, the lines for Gal-axy's Edge's attractions should be many hours long. For more details, see page 366.

FASTPASS+ ATTRACTIONS AT DHS

THE STUDIOS IMPLEMENTS tiering (see page 358) to restrict the number of FastPass+ reservations you can have at its headliners:

Disney says that *Millennium Falcon:* **Smugglers Run** and **Star Wars: Rise of the Resistance** won't offer FastPass+ at the outset; assuming they will eventually, FastPasses for Rise of the Resistance will be the most valuable. We also expect Disney to use timed entry at Galaxy's Edge: you'll be given a window during which you can enter the land and enjoy its offerings—but once you leave, reentry won't be possible.

continued on page 358

Disney's Hollywood Studios

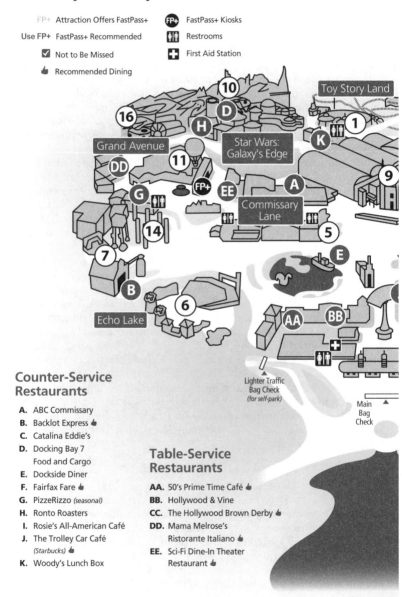

FP+ Attraction Offers FastPass+

Use FP+ FastPass+ Recommended

☑ Not to Be Missed

👍 Recommended Dining

FP+ FastPass+ Kiosks

👫 Restrooms

➕ First Aid Station

Toy Story Land

Grand Avenue

Star Wars: Galaxy's Edge

Commissary Lane

Echo Lake

Lighter Traffic
Bag Check
(for self-park)

Main
Bag
Check

Counter-Service Restaurants

A. ABC Commissary
B. Backlot Express 👍
C. Catalina Eddie's
D. Docking Bay 7 Food and Cargo
E. Dockside Diner
F. Fairfax Fare 👍
G. PizzeRizzo *(seasonal)*
H. Ronto Roasters
I. Rosie's All-American Café
J. The Trolley Car Café *(Starbucks)* 👍
K. Woody's Lunch Box

Table-Service Restaurants

AA. 50's Prime Time Café 👍
BB. Hollywood & Vine
CC. The Hollywood Brown Derby 👍
DD. Mama Melrose's Ristorante Italiano 👍
EE. Sci-Fi Dine-In Theater Restaurant 👍

Attractions

1. Alien Swirling Saucers FP+
2. *Beauty and the Beast—Live on Stage/ Theater of the Stars* FP+
3. *Disney Junior Dance Party!* FP+
4. *Fantasmic!* ☑ Use FP+
5. *For the First Time in Forever: A Frozen Sing-Along Celebration* FP+
6. *Indiana Jones Epic Stunt Spectacular!* FP+
7. *Jedi Training: Trials of the Temple*

8. *Lightning McQueen's Racing Academy*
9. Mickey & Minnie's Runaway Railway *(opens 2020)* ☑ Use FP+
10. *Millennium Falcon:* Smugglers Run
11. *Muppet-Vision 3-D* ☑ FP+
12. Rock 'n' Roller Coaster Starring Aerosmith ☑ Use FP+
13. Slinky Dog Dash ☑ Use FP+
14. Star Tours—The Adventures Continue ☑ Use FP+
15. Star Wars Launch Bay
16. Star Wars: Rise of the Resistance
17. Toy Story Mania! ☑ Use FP+
18. The Twilight Zone Tower of Terror ☑ Use FP+
19. *Voyage of the Little Mermaid* FP+
20. *Walt Disney Presents*

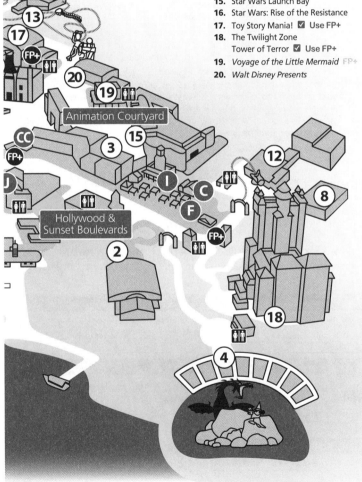

continued from page 355

Anticipating large crowds, Disney has also effectively limited your advance FastPass+ choices at the Studios to one ride and up to two shows (see the table below). Limiting advance selections to a single ride per person allows more people to use FastPass+ for that ride.

For now, four FastPass+ strategies have emerged for the Studios—use these in combination with the recommendations immediately following for non–Galaxy's Edge attractions:

1. See Galaxy's Edge as soon as the park opens, having already made advance FastPass+ reservations for other rides and shows to begin around the time you expect to be done. This option makes the most sense if you want to experience as much of Galaxy's Edge as possible.

2. To see as much of the park as you can as soon as it opens, make early-morning FastPass+ reservations for other rides and shows; then enter Galaxy's Edge in the afternoon and plan to stay until the park closes.

3. Split your tour of Galaxy's Edge between morning and evening and tour the rest of the park in between, again using advance FastPass+ reservations. This should allow you to experience at least one Galaxy's Edge ride with relatively short waits while also experiencing other rides, shows, and live entertainment. This option works only if Disney isn't restricting entry into Galaxy's Edge to one time per person, per day.

4. Tour the Studios over 2 days, splitting them between Galaxy's Edge and the rest of the park to maximize your FastPass+ use.

Our touring plan software seems to think the second option is best, especially if timed entry is in effect—that will effectively limit crowds (and thus lines) at Galaxy's Edge and push everyone else to the Studios' other rides. Seeing those other rides first will minimize the total time you spend in line throughout the day.

Aside from the Galaxy's Edge attractions, **Mickey & Minnie's Runaway Railway** is likely to be one of the highest-capacity rides Disney

TIER A *(Choose 1)*	
• Alien Swirling Saucers	• Toy Story Mania!
• Rock 'n' Roller Coaster	• The Twilight Zone Tower of Terror
• Slinky Dog Dash	
TIER B *(Choose 2)*	
• *Beauty and the Beast—Live on Stage*	• *Muppet-Vision 3-D*
• *Disney Junior Dance Party!*	• *Voyage of the Little Mermaid*
• *For the First Time in Forever: A Frozen Sing-Along Celebration*	
• *Indiana Jones Epic Stunt Spectacular!*	
COMING SOON	
• We think Mickey & Minnie's Runaway Railway (opens 2020) will debut in Tier A.	

has opened in years—that will definitely help keep wait times manageable and reduce the need for FastPass+. And if you're not planning to ride the Galaxy's Edge attractions, Runaway Railway should be a good choice for FastPass+.

Parents with small children should try to obtain advance Fast-Passes for one of the Toy Story Land attractions: **Alien Swirling Saucers, Slinky Dog Dash,** or **Toy Story Mania!** We don't know yet whether Runaway Railway will end up in the same FastPass+ tier as these three—in any case, they make a good alternative or second choice (if available). Teens and adults, along with older kids who are willing and able to experience thrill rides, will benefit most from using FastPass+ at **Rock 'n' Roller Coaster** or **The Twilight Zone Tower of Terror** until the Galaxy's Edge attractions get FastPass+.

Finally, our touring plan software rarely recommends using Fast-Pass+ for shows at the Studios. Because there will inevitably be huge crowds for Galaxy's Edge, and because the Studios has relatively little ride capacity, we expect Disney to run a full schedule of shows and live performances on most days, making it easier to get into them. That said, if your child's happiness depends on sitting up front for *For the First Time in Forever: A Frozen Sing-Along Celebration,* then by all means make that live show one of your FastPass+ choices.

All things considered, a good overall FastPass+ strategy may be to make exactly one early-morning reservation for any ride as described above, and nothing else. Once you've used that reservation, you'll be able to obtain same-day FastPasses for any rides that have them.

FastPass+ kiosk locations at the Studios are as follows:

- At the wait-times board on the corner of Hollywood and Sunset Boulevards
- Near Toy Story Mania! inside Toy Story Land
- Outside The Twilight Zone Tower of Terror, to the left of the entrance, on Sunset Boulevard
- Near *Muppet-Vision 3-D* on Grand Avenue

Same-Day FastPass+ Availability

The preceding advice tells you which attractions to focus on when making your *advance* FastPass+ reservations before you get to the park. Once you're in the park, you can make additional FastPass+ reservations after your advance reservations have been used or have expired. The table on the next page shows which attractions are likely to have day-of Fast-Passes available, and the approximate times at which they'll run out.

Disney often holds back some FastPass+ availability as a hedge against unexpected ride breakdowns. If everything is running well, Disney usually releases these day-of FastPasses around 9:30 a.m., noon, 2:30 p.m., and 5 p.m.

DISNEY'S HOLLYWOOD STUDIOS
When Same-Day FP+ Runs Out, by Crowd Level

ATTRACTION	LOW CROWDS*	MODERATE CROWDS*	HIGH CROWDS*
• Alien Swirling Saucers	NA	NA	NA
• *Beauty and the Beast—Live on Stage*	3 p.m.	3 p.m.	1 p.m.
• *Disney Junior Dance Party!*	3 p.m.	Noon	Noon
• *Fantasmic!* (no FastPass+ at press time)	6 p.m.	6 p.m.	6 p.m.
• *For the First Time in Forever: A Frozen Sing-Along Celebration*	4 p.m.	4 p.m.	2 p.m.
• *Indiana Jones Epic Stunt Spectacular!*	4 p.m.	4 p.m.	4 p.m.
• *Muppet-Vision 3-D*	5 p.m.	5 p.m.	5 p.m.
• Rock 'n' Roller Coaster	NA	NA	NA
• Slinky Dog Dash	NA	NA	NA
• Star Tours (no FastPass+ at press time)	5 p.m.	3 p.m.	NA
• Toy Story Mania!	3 p.m.	NA	NA
• The Twilight Zone Tower of Terror	3 p.m.	NA	NA
• *Voyage of the Little Mermaid*	5 p.m.	4 p.m.	2 p.m.

* **LOW CROWDS** (Levels 1–3 on TouringPlans.com Crowd Calendar)
* **MODERATE CROWDS** (Levels 4–7 on TouringPlans.com Crowd Calendar)
* **HIGH CROWDS** (Levels 8–10 on TouringPlans.com Crowd Calendar)
NA = no availability. *(Mickey & Minnie's Runaway Railway,* Millennium Falcon: Smugglers Run, and Star Wars: Rise of the Resistance weren't open at press time. Fantasmic! and Star Tours were dropped from FastPass+ at press time, but this may be subject to change.)*

HOLLYWOOD *and* SUNSET BOULEVARDS

WITH ITS ART DECO AND MODERN architecture, Hollywood Boulevard is reminiscent of Tinseltown's yesteryears. Most of the Studios' service facilities are located here, interspersed with eateries and shops. The famous **Hollywood Brown Derby** restaurant is also located here. The boulevard leads straight to the iconic replica of the Grauman's Chinese Theatre, the home of **Mickey & Minnie's Runaway Railway** when it opens in the spring of 2020.

The first right off Hollywood Boulevard brings you onto the palm-lined Sunset Boulevard, evoking the glamour of the 1940s. It's home to **The Twilight Zone Tower of Terror, Rock 'n' Roll Coaster Starring Aerosmith,** the *Beauty and the Beast—Live on Stage* show, and the incredible, not-to-be-missed *Fantasmic!* There are plenty of shopping opportunities and small eateries on Sunset Boulevard.

Roving Hollywood characters perform on both boulevards.

Beauty and the Beast—Live on Stage/ Theater of the Stars ★★★★

APPEAL BY AGE   PRESCHOOL ★★★★½ GRADE SCHOOL ★★★★ TEENS ★★★★
YOUNG ADULTS ★★★★   OVER 30 ★★★★½   SENIORS ★★★★½

What it is Live musical, featuring Disney characters; performed in an open-air theater. **Scope and scale** Major attraction. **Fright potential** Not frightening in any respect. **Bottleneck rating** 5. **When to go** Performances are listed in the daily *Times Guide*. Evenings are cooler. **Comment** Excellent. **Duration of show** 25 minutes. **Probable waiting time** 20–30 minutes.

Join Cogsworth, Lumière, Chip, and Mrs. Potts as they help Belle to break the spell. This musical stage show of Disney's *Beauty and the Beast* will charm everybody. The show is popular, so show up 30 minutes early to get a seat.

Liliane

The decor, the costumes, the actors, the music: everything is in perfect harmony. Little girls fond of Belle will want that ball gown, and young boys will be eager to teach that mean Gaston a lesson.

Shows are a great way to take a break. My favorite shows are *Voyage of the Little Mermaid, Beauty and the Beast,* and *Fantasmic!*

Lucy

Lightning McQueen's Racing Academy ★★½

What it is Theater show and meet and greet. **Scope and scale** Minor attraction. **Fright potential** Not frightening but loud. **Bottleneck rating** 8. **When to go** Check the *Times Guide* for showtimes. **Comments** Audience sits on benches. A must for families with preschoolers. **Duration of show** 10 minutes. **Probable waiting time** 30 minutes.

This *Cars*-themed show, which opened in early 2019, is held inside Sunset Showcase Theater, adjacent to Rock 'n' Roller Coaster. The all-new show stars Lightning McQueen, a full-sized audio animatronic, interacting in a humorous way with Cruz Ramirez and Tow Mater, who appear on a wraparound screen. After the show, guests get a chance to snap a photo with trainer-turned-racer Cruz Ramirez just outside the academy. Ka-Chow!

DISNEY DISH WITH JIM HILL

COVER YOUR MOUSE EARS Ever notice how once you hear the theme song to It's a Small World, you can't get it out of your head? Well, you may want to invest in a set of earplugs before climbing aboard Mickey & Minnie's Runaway Railway. The word coming out of Imagineering is that the theme song for this new attraction is so catchy that you'll be humming it for the rest of your vacation . . . whether you want to or not.

Mickey & Minnie's Runaway Railway (FastPass+) (opens 2020)

What it is Indoor dark ride through the new Mickey Mouse cartoon universe. **Scope and scale** Major attraction. **Fright potential** The darkness may frighten some preschoolers.

Disney hasn't said much about Runaway Railway other than it will be a family-friendly, 3-D-ish experience. We're pretty sure it involves an out-of-control railroad car (we're smart like that),

Thumbs Up for the Whole Family

video projection mapping, lots of zigzagging inside the theater, and plenty of sight gags. This will likely be the Studios' sleeper hit of the decade, in which case you should expect long lines throughout the day.

Rock 'n' Roller Coaster Starring Aerosmith
(FastPass+) ★★★★

APPEAL BY AGE   PRESCHOOL ★★   GRADE SCHOOL ★★★★½   TEENS ★★★★★
YOUNG ADULTS ★★★★★   OVER 30 ★★★★½   SENIORS ★★★★

What it is Rock music–themed roller coaster. **Scope and scale** Headliner. **Fright potential** Extremely intense for all ages; the ride is one of Disney's wildest. **Bottleneck rating** 10. **When to go** First 30 minutes the park is open, or use FastPass+. **Comments** Must be 48″ tall to ride; children younger than age 7 must ride with an adult. Switching-off option (see page 248). Not to be missed. **Duration of ride** Almost 1½ minutes. **Average wait in line per 100 people ahead of you** 2½ minutes; assumes all trains operating. **Loading speed** Moderate–fast.

Aerosmith once did a tour called Route of All Evil, and this notorious ride at the Studios makes good on their fans' expectations. Expect loops, corkscrews, and drops that make Space Mountain seem like the Jungle Cruise. You are launched from 0 to 57 miles per hour in less than 3 seconds, and by the time you enter the first loop, you'll be pulling five g's—two more than astronauts experience at liftoff on a space shuttle. If Space Mountain or Big Thunder Mountain Railroad pushes your limits, stay away from Rock 'n' Roller Coaster.

If you can't ride first thing in the morning, waits should be manageable during *Fantasmic!* Alternatively, consider using the single-rider line or FastPass+.

Aerosmith describes this ride best in one of their songs: "Livin' on the Edge."

My parents told me I would like the Rock 'n' Roller Coaster, and I was excited when the limo pulled up, but as soon as we shot off, I felt really sick. I kept my eyes closed the whole time and just wished it was over soon. I hated being in the dark and going upside down. I don't want to do this ride again.

The Twilight Zone Tower of Terror *(FastPass+)* ★★★★★

APPEAL BY AGE   PRESCHOOL ★★½   GRADE SCHOOL ★★★★   TEENS ★★★★★
YOUNG ADULTS ★★★★★   OVER 30 ★★★★½   SENIORS ★★★★½

What it is Sci-fi–themed indoor thrill ride. **Scope and scale** Super-headliner. **Fright potential** Visually intimidating to young children; contains intense, realistic special effects. The plummeting elevator at the ride's end frightens many adults. Switching-off option (see page 248). **Bottleneck rating** 10. **When to go** First or last 30 minutes the park is open, or use FastPass+. **Comments** Must be 40″ tall to ride. Not to be missed. **Duration of ride** About 4 minutes plus preshow. **Average wait in line per 100 people ahead of you** 4 minutes; assumes all elevators operating. **Loading speed** Moderate.

And suddenly the cable went *snap*. If riding a capricious elevator in a haunted hotel sounds like fun to you, this is your ride. Erratic yet thrilling, the Tower of Terror is an experience to savor. The Tower has great potential for terrifying young children and rattling more mature visitors. Random ride-and-drop sequences keep you guessing about when, how far, and how many times the elevator drops.

We suggest using teenagers in your party as experimental probes. If they report back that they really, really liked the Tower of Terror, run quickly in the opposite direction.

If you're up to it, experience the ride first thing in the morning or use Fast-Pass+. Tower Hotel Gifts at the exit of the ride offers a photo experience. For $19.95 plus tax, you can purchase an 8-by-10-inch lenticular print that transforms you into your spirited form.

My favorite part of the Tower of Terror is when you go down and you get pulled off your seat.

Tower of Terror is too scary. I had to leave the line via the chicken exit.

Sabrina

Little kids will feel like they're flying out of their seat when riding Tower of Terror and may be frightened by this.

Felicity

Isabelle

ECHO LAKE

TOWERING OVER ECHO LAKE is Gertie the dinosaur, a tribute to one of the first popular animated characters in the history of film. Echo Lake has several quick-service eateries and two sit-down restaurants, including the **50's Prime Time Café,** where servers treat you like family (including scolding you if you put your elbows on the table), and **Hollywood & Vine,** home of the Disney Junior Play and Dine character breakfast and Minnie's Seasonal Dining at dinner. Echo Lake showcases one attraction, **Star Tours,** and three shows, *Jedi Training: Trials of the Temple, Indiana Jones Epic Stunt Spectacular!,* and the musical *For the First Time in Forever,* based on *Frozen.*

For the First Time in Forever: A Frozen Sing-Along Celebration (FastPass+) ★★★★

APPEAL BY AGE   PRESCHOOL ★★★★½   GRADE SCHOOL ★★★★½   TEENS ★★★★
YOUNG ADULTS ★★★★   OVER 30 ★★★★½   SENIORS ★★★★½

What it is Sing-along based on the popular 2013 film *Frozen.* **Scope and scale** Major attraction for *Frozen* fans; minor attraction for everyone else. **Fright potential** Not frightening in any respect. **Bottleneck rating** 8. **When to go** Check the *Times Guide.* **Comments** If you have *Frozen* fans in your family, save your sanity and get FastPass+. A must for families with preschoolers and grade-school kids. **Duration of show** 25 minutes. **Probable waiting time** 30 minutes if you don't have FastPass+.

Scenes from the movie, projected on a drive-in movie–size screen in the background, provide continuity and familiarize those who haven't seen the film with the characters and story line. Live performers, including two "royal historians" and several characters from *Frozen,* lay down some stand-up comedy shtick to facilitate the narrative and add some corny and occasionally punchy humor. Most of the story is related at a leisurely pace, but the ending is presented in a nanosecond, leaving much of the audience stupefied. Of course, the finale features another rousing round of "Let It Go." Even if you're not a fan, you'll enjoy the show's spirit, as well as that of a theater full of enraptured children—it's contagious. Using FastPass+ grants you access to a preferred-seating section closer to the stage, while standby guests are seated in whatever seats are left.

> Everything in the theater was so sparkly, and I loved singing along with all the other children. I was so surprised and excited when the real Elsa appeared at the end of the show.
>
> **Felicity**

Indiana Jones Epic Stunt Spectacular! ★★★½

APPEAL BY AGE　PRESCHOOL ★★★½　GRADE SCHOOL ★★★★½　TEENS ★★★★ YOUNG ADULTS ★★★★　OVER 30 ★★★★　SENIORS ★★★★½

What it is Movie-stunt demonstration and action show. **Scope and scale** Headliner. **Fright potential** An intense show with powerful special effects, including explosions. Presented in an educational context that young children generally handle well. **Bottleneck rating** 8. **When to go** First two shows or last show. Performance times posted on a sign at the entrance to the theater and in *Times Guide*. **Comment** Done on a grand scale. **Duration of show** 30 minutes. **Preshow** Selection of extras from audience. **Probable waiting time** None.

Thumbs Up for the Whole Family

Professional stuntmen and -women demonstrate dangerous stunts with a behind-the-scenes look at how they're done. Most kids handle the show well. The indoor theater is one of Disney's largest and most comfortable, with excellent sight lines from every seat. Crowd management when entering the theater is a little confusing, but once you're inside it sorts itself out. To be chosen as an extra, arrive early, sit down front, and display unmitigated enthusiasm. Unfortunately, "victims" must be 18 years old and up.

> An amazing show with fiery explosions and nonstop action. Did you know that the folks at Disney have a vault filled with sound effects ranging from gunshots to magical twinkles? When a show is created, they pick and choose from this treasure chest and upload the sounds into their state-of-the-art computerized mixing table.
>
> **Liliane**

> Huh? What's a magical twinkle sound like? But now that I think about it, I sure remember the noise my innards made after eating about a dozen magical twinkles.
>
> **Bob**

> Those were Twinkies, Mr. Tiki-Birdbrain!
>
> **Liliane**

Jedi Training: Trials of the Temple ★★★½

APPEAL BY AGE　PRESCHOOL ★★★★½　GRADE SCHOOL ★★★★½　TEENS ★★★½ YOUNG ADULTS ★★★½　OVER 30 ★★★★　SENIORS ★★★★

What it is Outdoor stage show. **Scope and scale** Minor attraction. **Fright potential** It does involve battle with Darth Vader, but the good guys always win; children typically love it. **Bottleneck rating** 8. **When to go** First two shows of the day. **Comment** A treat for young Star Wars lovers. **Duration of show** About 20 minutes. **When to arrive** 15 minutes before showtime.

Jedi Training: Trials of the Temple is to the left of the Star Tours building entrance, opposite Backlot Express. Young Skywalkers-in-training are taught the ways of the Force and do battle against the likes of Darth Vader, Kylo Ren, and the

Seventh Sister Inquisitor (from the *Star Wars Rebels* cartoon). If all this sounds too intense, it's not—Stormtroopers provide comic relief, and just as in the movies, the Jedi always wins. Space is limited, and kids ages 4–12 must register to be in the show. To sign up, visit the Indiana Jones Adventure Outpost shop (near 50's Prime Time Café) early in the day to reserve a spot for your youngling.

> If fighting the Dark Lord is important to your child, I recommend arriving 30 minutes prior to park opening. Once the rope drops, head directly to the registration area. The young Padawan must be with you to register.

Liliane

Star Tours—The Adventures Continue ★★★½

APPEAL BY AGE PRESCHOOL ★★★★   GRADE SCHOOL ★★★★½ TEENS ★★★★½ YOUNG ADULTS ★★★★½   OVER 30 ★★★★½   SENIORS ★★★★½

What it is Indoor space flight–simulation ride. **Scope and scale** Headliner. **Fright potential** Extremely intense visually for all ages; too intense for children under age 8. **Bottleneck rating** 8. **When to go** Before 10 a.m., during lunch, or after 5 p.m. **Comments** Expectant mothers and anyone prone to motion sickness are advised against riding. Must be 40″ tall to ride. Switching-off option (see page 248). **Duration of ride** About 7 minutes. **Average wait in line per 100 people ahead of you** 5 minutes; assumes all simulators operating. **Loading speed** Moderate–fast.

Rough   Queasy   Scary

Based on the *Star Wars* movie series, the ride is a 3-D motion simulator with more than 50 combinations of opening and ending scenes. Hold on tight as you experience dips, turns, twists, and light speed, only to exit hyperspace above Coruscant; on Naboo, Tatooine, or Endor; or inside the dreaded Death Star. You could ride Star Tours all day without seeing the same film segment twice. Despite having the same theme as the Galaxy's Edge rides, Star Tours is located in Echo Lake.

> Oh, no! We're caught in a tractor beam!

Liliane

■ GRAND AVENUE

THE FORMER STREETS OF AMERICA, which incorporate what was once Muppet Courtyard, now portray present-day downtown Los Angeles and serve as a pedestrian thoroughfare to Galaxy's Edge. Here you'll find *Muppet-Vision 3-D,* **PizzeRizzo, Mama Melrose's Ristorante Italiano,** and **BaseLine Tap House,** a pub specializing in beer and wines from California.

Muppet-Vision 3-D ★★★★

APPEAL BY AGE PRESCHOOL ★★★★   GRADE SCHOOL ★★★★   TEENS ★★★½ YOUNG ADULTS ★★★★ OVER 30 ★★★★ SENIORS ★★★★

What it is 3-D movie starring the Muppets. **Scope and scale** Major attraction. **Fright potential** Intense and loud but not frightening. **Bottleneck rating** 8. **When to go** Anytime. **Comment** Uproarious; not to be missed. **Duration of show** 17 minutes. **Preshow** Muppets on television. **Probable waiting time** 12 minutes.

Kermit, Miss Piggy, and the rest of the gang will lift your spirits as they unleash their hilarious mayhem. Because adults tend to associate Muppet characters with the children's show *Sesame Street,* many bypass this attraction. Big mistake. *Muppet-Vision 3-D* operates on several planes, and there's as much here for oldsters as for youngsters. The presentation is intense and sometimes loud, but most preschoolers handle it well. If your child is a little scared, encourage him to watch without the 3-D glasses at first. A New Brunswick, Canada, reader thinks the Muppets are heaven-sent:

> *Muppet-Vision 3-D is a godsend: 1) It NEVER has a line (even on our visit on New Year's Day). 2) Everyone ages 1–100 gives the show high marks. 3) Between the preshow and the movie, it's half an hour seated comfortably in an air-conditioned theater. 4) Between the live actors and animatronics, it's so much more than just another silly 3-D movie. 5) IT'S THE MUPPETS! Who doesn't love these hysterical creatures and their 3-D shenanigans?*

Waits generally peak around lunchtime, and it's unusual to find a wait of more than 20 minutes. Because it's near one of the main pathways to Galaxy's Edge, *Muppet-Vision* may get more traffic. Watch for throngs waiting to enter or coming from Galaxy's Edge—if you do encounter a long line, try again later.

This show is extremely silly. I loved seeing all the things coming out of the screen and flying right at me.

Felicity

STAR WARS: *Galaxy's Edge*

STAR WARS: GALAXY'S EDGE is an outpost in the village of Black Spire, on the planet of Batuu. Formerly a busy trading port and way-point before the invention of light speed–capable transportation, it's now a dusty backwater filled with bounty hunters, smugglers, and those who make a living by not being recognized. As if that wasn't enough, members of the Resistance and First Order live in and around Black Spire in an uneasy coexistence.

Galaxy's Edge has two access points, via Grand Avenue and Toy Story Land. Entering through Grand Avenue puts you in the middle of the Resistance's encampment, while the entrance at Toy Story Land is controlled by the First Order. However, for crowd-control reasons, we expect that the Toy Story Land entrance will be used as an exit only for the foreseeable future.

In the Resistance section of the park, guests complete a critical mission on the ***Millennium Falcon:* Smugglers Run.** How you do on the mission has high stakes: perform with skill, and you may earn extra galactic credits, while bringing the ship back banged up could put you on the list of bounty hunter Harkos, and you may face a problem if you show up at the local cantina.

On the First Order side of the land, **Star Wars: Rise of the Resistance** makes guests feel like they're inside a hangar bay in the middle of a fight between the First Order and the Resistance. The ride will have a large amount of animatronics and scenes with almost life-size AT-ATs.

SHOPPING Between the two sections, a merchant's alley is home to shops and merchant stalls. One stall is overseen by a **Toydarian,** a creature fans first encountered on Tatooine in *Star Wars: The Phantom Menace;* it's the home of playthings and dolls. **Dok-Ondar's Den of Antiquities** sells ancient artifacts, also known as memorabilia from the movies and prebuilt legacy lightsabers. **Creature Stall** has unique companions, such as cackling Kowakian monkey-lizards, for you to take home. The biggest hits, however, are **The Droid Depot,** where guests can build their own droid, and **Savi's Workshop,** where guests design their own one-of-a-kind lightsaber. With Savi's Workshop's limited capacity, Disney will most likely implement a reservation system for it, which may include guaranteed entry into Galaxy's Edge. But be warned that a credit card will be required to make a reservation, and you will be charged a $200 cancellation fee if you are a no-show. Costumes and Galaxy's Edge–related clothes are available at **Black Spire Outfitters.** Hats, pins, badges, and souvenirs are sold at **Resistance Supply,** for those who are with the force, and at **First Order Cargo,** for those who have crossed to the dark side.

The Droid Depot and Savi's Workshop fill up quickly, and if your heart is set on building a droid or lightsaber, stop there first, as long lines form, especially for Savi's Workshop, which can only accommodate 14 builders per session (20 minutes per session). The cost of a droid unit is $99.99 plus tax; the price includes a carrying box and instructions. Accessories for your unit are available for an additional charge. Building

LILIANE The Milk Stand's blue and green milk are an acquired taste, to say the least. I strongly recommend that you purchase one drink for all to taste before ordering one for each member of your party.

your own lightsaber (which includes a carrying box) will cost you $199.99 plus tax. Additional customization items can be purchased at Dok-Ondar's Den of Antiquities.

DINING The main eatery inside the land is **Docking Bay 7 Food and Cargo,** a quick-service restaurant. According to Disney lore, it's the home of chef Strono "Cookie" Tuggs, the former chef at Maz Kanata's castle on Takodana from *The Force Awakens.* The restaurant, housed in a working hangar bay, serves beef pot roast, roasted chicken or fish, and vegetarian dishes. At **Oga's Cantina,** the galaxy's most infamous watering hole, join smugglers, rogue traders, and bounty hunters for Bespin Fizz, Bloody Rancor, Dagobah Slug Slinger, Jedi Mind Trick, and T-16 Skyhopper, just to name a few. Oga's Cantina is a super-headliner, so long lines form as soon as visitors arrive, and Disney is likely to implement a virtual queue here too. In that case you will be able to make a reservation for the cantina, but a no-show fee of $10 per person will be charged to your credit card if you decide not to go or use the reservation solely to obtain guaranteed entry into Galaxy's Edge. **Ronto Roasters** serves meats roasted over an old pod racer's engine (wraps filled with spiced grilled sausage and roasted pork). At **The Milk Stand** try the famous blue or green milk. A popcorn stand dubbed **Kat Saka's Kettle** sells a sweet and salty popcorn snack with a hint of spice.

INTERACTIVITY IN GALAXY'S EDGE Within the land, guests encounter familiar characters from the movies, including Chewbacca, members of the First Order, and—among many others—Captain Rex, the RX-series droid pilot of Star Tours fame, who takes on a new role in the land as a DJ at Oga's Cantina.

On Batuu, cast members interact in character at all times with visitors. Stormtroopers and Kylo Ren roam the land on the lookout for guests suspected to help the Resistance. Rey and Chewbacca also engage with visitors. It's a treat to watch Chewie trying to fix ships of the Resistance's fleet.

Make sure to download the **Play Disney Parks** app before you get to the park. Once inside Galaxy's Edge, the app turns into a "datapad" and allows you to interact with the land's many control panels and droids. It's up to you to pledge your alliance to the Resistance or the First Order. Beware that if you play the game, there will be consequences. If you survive an encounter with Kylo Ren, you'll be hailed as a hero and get extra points from the Resistance, but bang up the *Millennium Falcon,* and you'll see your score go down.

OPENING PROCEDURES Star Wars: Galaxy's Edge is one of the most detailed and immersive lands ever created. And even though the land opened with only the *Millennium Falcon:* Smugglers Run operating, the new land will be very popular for a long time.

Opening procedure and access to the land might change according to popularity, but for now, we believe Disney will walk the first wave of guests to enter the park each morning straight into Galaxy's Edge. However, once the area approaches its maximum capacity, which is determined by how many riders the attractions inside can process, direct entry to the land is shut off. At this point, guests must use their smartphones and go to the Walt Disney World app (or kiosks located around the park) to secure a spot in a free, virtual queue. While Disney may choose to let guests ride the *Millennium Falcon* only once, we believe that there won't be a limit on how long you can stay inside Galaxy's Edge.

Handing out wristbands could be part of the management plan. How Disney handles the crowds will affect wait times at all rides. If it's a free-for-all and people have to wait in line to get into Galaxy's Edge, wait times could go down at other attractions.

Even if Disney eventually adds FastPass+ to the rides, there will be so much competition for them that the odds will be like winning the Powerball.

At times, the Studios could reach capacity and simply stop admitting guests. As we went to press, no opening date for the second headliner ride, Star Wars: Rise of the Resistance, had been announced. With the opening of Star Wars: Galaxy's Edge, the Studios became the second busiest park in Walt Disney World. To enjoy all there is to see and do, consider setting aside more than 1 day for the Studios.

If money is not an issue, staying at the BoardWalk, Yacht Club, Beach Club, Swan, or Dolphin will put you in walking to Disney's Hollywood Studios. Staying at one of these is likely a better option than taking a boat to the park. Resorts along the Skyliner route may or may not have an advantage in reaching Star Wars: Galaxy's Edge, as the gondolas' efficiency remains to be seen.

Additionally, staying at a Disney property will put you at an advantage, as you will have access to the land for Extra—and get this—Extra, Extra Magic Hours. The latter will open the park as early as 6 a.m. Keep in mind that you won't be the only one taking advantage of these hours, and you may have to leave the comfort of your bed as early as 4 a.m.

All this being said, we also think the park simply does not have enough rides and restaurants to handle so many people. May the Force be with you!

Opening an incomplete land is an unusual step and raises questions about what the reaction will be to a land that *Star Wars* fans have been eagerly awaiting. If fans nevertheless flock to the new land, how will Disney handle the crowds? We expect some kind of free reservation system that will not require guests to stay on property.

Down the road, Disney will probably offer Early Morning Magic and After Hours opportunities to get into Galaxy's Edge before the park opens or after it closes. This special access will of course come with a price but might be the only way to experience Galaxy's Edge without huge crowds.

Movie Tip *In 1977 George Lucas put the galaxy on a map, and fans eagerly followed him to a galaxy far, far away. Now, 40 years and 9 movies later, Star Wars has found a home at Disney's Hollywood Studios. With more movies and a Star Wars–themed hotel scheduled over the next 2 years, there is no doubt that the Force is very strong indeed.*

THE HOTEL Last but not least, Disney is building a *Star Wars*–themed resort on the south side of DHS, just east of World Drive. The hotel will be connected seamlessly to Star Wars: Galaxy's Edge. The new resort will offer a *Westworld*-like experience, in which guests are given new identities and tasks once they arrive at the hotel. The resort, which resembles a starship and offers views of space instead of the park and surrounding landscape, will combine luxury with complete immersion into an authentic *Star Wars* story. (No opening date was announced at press time.)

At the resort, guests become active citizens of the galaxy and can dress up in the proper attire. The good news is that it's going to be out of this world; the bad news is that we expect it to require a minimum stay of 2–3 nights at a rate of $500 and up, per night, per person. The daily rate may or may not include entry to DHS.

LILIANE I have started sewing costumes and can't wait to board the ship.

STAR WARS: GALAXY'S EDGE UPDATES

We expect Disney to adapt and change its opening hours, access, and FastPass+ procedures. Check out updated information, for free, as it becomes available at theunofficialguides.com/2019/07/03/a-guide -to-star-wars-galaxys-edge-at-disneys-hollywood-studios.

Millennium Falcon: **Smugglers Run** ★★★★★

What it is Advanced flight simulator. **Scope and scale** Super-headliner. **Fright potential** Intense visuals may frighten children under 8. **Bottleneck rating** 10. **When to go** As soon as the park opens, in the last hour of the day, use the single-rider line, or use FastPass+ if it becomes available. **Comments** Must be 38" tall to ride; switching-off option (see page 248). Not to be missed. **Duration of ride** 4½ minutes. **Average wait in line per 100 people ahead of you** 3½ minutes. **Loading speed** Moderate–fast.

Queasy

Riding in the cockpit of the fabled *Millennium Falcon* fulfills the dreams of many *Star Wars* fans, including coauthor Liliane. Hondo Ohnaka, a well-known businessman (also known as a smuggler), has cut a deal with Chewbacca to use the *Falcon*, and he's recruiting a flight crew to help him deliver hard-to-find items to his clientele. This is where you come in. As you wait in the ride's queue, you are handed boarding cards, which break riders into groups of six: two pilots, two engineers, and two gunners. Before getting into the cockpit, riders are led into the lounge of the *Millennium Falcon,* complete with the famous Dejarik (holochess) table. Once the boarding call comes, riders are let into the exceptionally detailed cockpit of the ship. With the jobs assigned, it's time to jump into hyperspace.

The motion simulator ride is similar to Star Tours, except that you and the rest of the crew are given partial control of the *Millennium Falcon,* and what happens next depends on the actions of the six people controlling the ship. Furthermore, your actions in the cockpit have consequences and will follow you throughout your stay at Galaxy's Edge. Be prepared to do your best, because who wants to be known throughout the galaxy as the one who wrecked the *Millennium Falcon?*

There are more than 100 buttons, switches, and levers in the cockpit, and each one does something when activated; watch for indicator rings to illuminate around certain controls, clueing you into the correct moment to punch them. Your randomly selected mission (there are reportedly three) may see you running guns to the Resistance or escaping the maw of an interstellar Leviathan. Two stationary simulators allow disabled guests to experience the attraction without interrupting operations for other guests.

> After experiencing the entire *Millennium Falcon* queue once, see if the single-rider line is operating. The experience is not much diminished.

Star Wars: Rise of the Resistance *(opens late 2019)*

Liliane

What it is Unique multifaceted dark ride. **Scope and scale** Super-headliner. **Fright potential** Intense ride; may frighten children under 8. **Bottleneck rating** 10. **When to go** As soon as the park opens, in the last hour of the day, or use FastPass+ if it becomes available. **Comments** Must be 40" tall to ride; switching-off option (see page 248). Not to be missed. **Duration of ride** About 25 minutes with all preshows; about 5 minutes for ride. **Average wait in line per 100 people ahead of you** 4 minutes. **Loading speed** Moderate–fast.

Dark

Queasy

Loud

Scary

A mobile Resistance gun turret tucked into a scrubland forest marks the entrance of the most epic indoor dark ride in Disney theme park history. Rise of the Resistance is an innovative attempt to integrate at least four different ride experiences—including trackless vehicles, a motion simulator, walk-through environments, and even an elevator drop—into Disney's longest attraction ever.

The adventure begins as you explore the Resistance military outpost, which has been laser-carved out of ancient stone. An animatronic BB-8 rolls in, accompanied by a hologram of Rey (Daisy Ridley), who recruits you to strike a blow against the First Order. Fifty guests at a time exit the briefing room to board a standing-room-only shuttle craft piloted by Nien Nunb from *Return of the Jedi.* You can feel the rumble as the ship breaks orbit and you see Poe Dameron (Oscar Isaac) accompanying you in his X-Wing, until a Star Destroyer snags you in its tractor beam and sucks you into its belly.

When the doors to your shuttle craft reopen, you've been convincingly transported into an enormous hangar, complete with 50 Stormtroopers, TIE Fighters, and a 100-foot-wide bay window looking into outer space. Cast members clad as First Order officers brusquely herd captive guests into holding rooms to await their interrogation by helmet-headed baddie Kylo Ren (Adam Driver).

Before long, you make a break for it in an eight-passenger (two [four-seat] rows) troop transport with an animatronic astromech droid as your driver; the car is capable of traveling without a fixed track. The ride blends dozens of robotic characters and enormous sets with video projections to create some of the most overwhelming environments ever seen in an indoor ride. One sequence sends you in between the legs of two towering AT-ATs while dodging laser fire from legions of Stormtroopers, while another puts you face-to-face with the Solo-slaying Ren. In the epic finale (spoiler alert), you'll survive an escape pod's dramatic crash back to Batuu, a heart-stopping multistory plunge enhanced by digital projections.

Once open, Rise of the Resistance will become the second-most popular ride in the park, right behind *Millennium Falcon:* Smugglers Run. If it's operating when you visit, make it your first destination of the day or your very last. And while the drop at the end isn't quite as intense as The Twilight Zone Tower of Terror, we recommend that you don't underestimate its ability to loosen your lunch.

TOY STORY LAND

THE 11-ACRE TOY STORY LAND officially opened June 30, 2018. The idea behind it is that you've been shrunk to the size of a toy and placed in Andy's backyard, where you get to play with other toys he's set up.

The new land has three rides (**Alien Swirling Saucers** and **Slinky Dog Dash,** plus the preexisting **Toy Story Mania!**) and a quick-service restaurant named **Woody's Lunch Box,** serving American fare and soda floats (see page 171).

A. J. The potato barrels at Woody's Lunch Box were good. I also liked the grilled cheese, though it could've been cooked a little longer.

SABRINA Toy Story Land is so much fun, and Slinky Dog Dash is awesome! The ride takes you through Andy's room, and you get to see all his toys.

Two stands offer plenty of Toy Story merchandise, including headbands inspired by aliens, Slinky Dog toys, fashion accessories, and T-shirts. **Roundup Rodeo BBQ,** themed around a play area that Andy has set up in his backyard, is a much-needed table-service restaurant coming to Toy Story Land. An opening date has not been announced.

Woody, Buzz, and **Jessie** greet guests throughout the land. **Sarge** and the **Green Army Men Drum Corps** proudly march through the land several times daily. They play "Sarge Says" and are on the lookout for willing cadets for their interactive boot camp. Are you ready to become an official recruit in Andy's Backyard?

 BRENDAN Toy Story Land is so detailed. I love the giant characters.

Toy Story Land is one of two entrances to Star Wars: Galaxy's Edge, the other being Grand Avenue. We would be surprised if Disney allows morning entry to Galaxy's Edge in this very busy area, at least during the land's initial opening, as the combination of large excited crowds, small children, and strollers may raise too many safety and logistical concerns.

In 1995 Pixar debuted Toy Story, *a movie where all toys are secretly alive (unbeknownst to humans). This feature-length film was followed by two more successful installments, with the next adventures of Woody and his gang scheduled to be released June 21, 2019. Now Woody and his friends also have a land to welcome honorary toys. Go ahead and join them, to infinity and beyond!*

Alien Swirling Saucers *(FastPass+)* ★★★

APPEAL BY AGE   PRESCHOOL ★★★★½   GRADE SCHOOL ★★★★   TEENS ★★★½ YOUNG ADULTS ★★★½   OVER 30 ★★★½   SENIORS ★★★

What it is Spinning car ride. **Scope and scale** Minor attraction. **Fright potential** May induce motion sickness in riders of all ages. **Bottleneck rating** 10. **When to go** The first or last hour the park is open. **Comment** Must be 32" tall to ride. Switching-off option (see page 248). **Duration of ride** 3 minutes. **Average wait in line per 100 people ahead of you** 10 minutes. **Loading speed** Slow.

Alien Swirling Saucers is themed around *Toy Story*'s vending machine aliens and their obsession with The Claw. The ride features an electronic space music soundtrack with eight songs that may sound familiar. Use FastPass+ only if this ride is critical to your child's happiness; if not, consider skipping Saucers if the wait exceeds 20 minutes.

Alien Swirling Saucers is wilder than it looks. You really get tossed around. **Brendan**

 I instantly loved Alien Swirling Saucers. It's quite wobbly and you dash all over the place. The music is loud but fun.

Alien Swirling Saucers is not worth the wait. It is slow moving and dull. One of its only highlights is the techno music. **Felicity**

Slinky Dog Dash *(FastPass+)* ★★★★

A.J.

APPEAL BY AGE   PRESCHOOL ★★★★½   GRADE SCHOOL ★★★★★   TEENS ★★★★½ YOUNG ADULTS ★★★★½   OVER 30 ★★★★½   SENIORS ★★★★½

What it is Outdoor roller coaster. **Scope and scale** Major attraction. **Fright potential** May frighten some preschoolers. **Bottleneck rating** 10. **When to go** As soon as the park opens, right before the park closes, or use FastPass+. **Comment** Must be 38" tall to ride. Switching-off option (see page 248). **Duration of ride** 2 minutes. **Average wait in line per 100 people ahead of you** 4 minutes. **Loading speed** Moderate.

Slinky Dog Dash is a long, outdoor roller coaster designed to look like Andy built it out of Tinker Toys. The coaster's trains are themed (naturally) to *Toy Story*'s Slinky Dog. The ride is more intense than the Magic Kingdom's Barnstormer and Seven Dwarfs Mine Train—lots of hills but no loops or high-speed curves—but not as forceful as Big Thunder Mountain Railroad. It's likely to be inundated as soon as the park opens, and stay that way all day.

I rode Slinky Dog Dash twice. It's intense!

All three Toy Story Land rides are in the same FastPass+ tier, meaning that you'll be able to make an advance FastPass+ reservation for only one of the three. Get a FastPass+ for whichever one you can, as early in the day as possible. When the park opens, head immediately for one of the other Toy Story Land attractions based on your preferences and ride.

Brendan

Slinky Dog Dash is my favorite ride at the Studios. You won't want to miss it, and it's a good ride to do at night. The lines are a little shorter than during the day, and the park looks amazing, as everything is lit up with neon lights.

A. J.

Toy Story Mania! *(FastPass+)* ★★★★½

APPEAL BY AGE   PRESCHOOL ★★★★½   GRADE SCHOOL ★★★★★   TEENS ★★★★★ YOUNG ADULTS ★★★★★   OVER 30 ★★★★★   SENIORS ★★★★½

What it is 3-D ride through indoor shooting gallery. **Scope and scale** Headliner. **Fright potential** Dark ride may frighten some preschoolers. **Bottleneck rating** 8. **When to go** As soon as the park opens, during mealtimes (around noon and 6 p.m.) and *Fantasmic!*, or use FastPass+. **Duration of ride** About 6½ minutes. **Average wait in line per 100 people ahead of you** 4½ minutes. **Loading Speed** Fast.

In 2018 Disney moved the entrance to the ride from the former Pixar Place to incorporate the attraction inside the new Toy Story Land. The ride is an interactive shooting gallery, much like Buzz Lightyear's Space Ranger Spin at the Magic Kingdom, but in Toy Story Mania! your vehicle passes through a totally virtual midway, with booths offering such games as ring toss and ball throw. The pull-string cannon on your ride vehicle takes advantage of computer-generated imagery to toss rings, shoot balls, and even throw eggs and pies. Each game booth is manned by a *Toy Story* character who is right beside you in 3-D glory, cheering you on. You also experience vehicle motion, wind, and water spray.

The ride begins with a training round to familiarize you with the nature of the games and then continues through a number of games in which you compete against your riding mate for a higher score. The technology has the ability to self-adjust the level of difficulty, and there are plenty of easy targets for small children to reach. *Tip:* Let the pull-string retract all the way back into the cannon before pulling it again.

Toy Story Mania!, Slinky Dog Dash, and Alien Swirling Saucers are hot tickets. Use FastPass+ or ride as soon as the park opens.

This ride was absolutely awesome. I wanted to ride it again and again.

Felicity

ANIMATION COURTYARD

THIS AREA IS TO THE RIGHT of the Chinese Theatre and contains **Disney Junior Dance Party!,** the popular *Voyage of the Little Mermaid* show, **Walt Disney Presents,** and **Star Wars Launch Bay.**

If you love Disney Junior characters, bring your autograph book. You can meet them in Animation Courtyard.

Lucy

Disney Junior Dance Party! ★★★★

APPEAL BY AGE **PRESCHOOL ★★★★½** **GRADE SCHOOL ★★★★** **TEENS ★**
YOUNG ADULTS ★★½ **OVER 30 ★★★** **SENIORS ★★★**

What it is Live show for preschool children. **Scope and scale** Minor attraction. **Fright potential** Not frightening in any respect. **Bottleneck rating** 8. **When to go** Check the *Times Guide* for showtimes. **Comments** Audience sits on the floor. A must for families with preschoolers. **Duration of show** 25 minutes. **Probable waiting time** 30 minutes.

Disney Junior Dance Party! is a high-energy live show inspired by some of the most popular Disney Junior shows on television, including *Mickey and the Roadster Racers, Doc McStuffins, The Lion Guard,* and *Vampirina.*

The show, hosted by Finn Fiesta and a DJ named Deejay, involves live appearances from many favorite characters and fun music from Disney Junior. Even for adults without children, it's a treat to watch the tykes rev up. For preschoolers, *Disney Junior* will be the highlight of their day, as a Thomasville, North Carolina, mom attests:

> The show was fantastic! My 3-year-old loved it. The children danced, sang, and had a great time.

The Florida mother of a 4-year-old agrees:

> My daughter absolutely LOVED the show! I saw it advertised on the Disney Junior channel and didn't think it looked all that great, but in person it was really fun. If you have preschoolers, this is a MUST!

Disney Junior is the fourth iteration of the stage show since 2007. The show is staged in a huge building to the right of Star Wars Launch Bay. Show up at least 25 minutes before showtime. Once inside, pick a spot on the floor and take a breather until the performance begins. Outside, little ones can meet the stars of Disney Junior, including Doc McStuffins.

Star Wars Launch Bay ★★★

APPEAL BY AGE **PRESCHOOL ★★★★½** **GRADE SCHOOL ★★★★½** **TEENS ★★★★½**
YOUNG ADULTS ★★★★½ **OVER 30 ★★★★½** **SENIORS ★★★★½**

What it is Displays of a few *Star Wars* movie models and props, a movie trailer, and character greetings. **Scope and scale** Minor attraction. **Fright potential** Small children may be scared when meeting Chewbacca because he's huge and Kylo Ren is intimidating, but everyone loves interacting with BB-8. **Bottleneck rating** 6. **When to go** Anytime. **Comments** The movie trailer summarizes the *Star Wars* films released so far and includes plot spoilers. **Probable waiting time** 20–30 minutes each for the movie trailer and character greetings. **Queue speed** Slow.

Located in the back of Animation Courtyard, Star Wars Launch Bay is home to a walk-through exhibit, three meet and greet areas, a theater showing movies (featuring interviews with some of the creators of the new *Star Wars* films), a small mock-up of the Mos Eisley cantina, and the Launch Bay Cargo shop.

If you're a die-hard *Star Wars* fan, you'll want to see it all and you won't mind the huge amount of time it will take. But if meeting Chewie, BB-8, and Kylo Ren are your priorities, get there at park opening and head right away to the meet and greets.

Each character has a separate queuing area, and lines move slowly. Once you exit one, head right away to the next meet and greet.

Voyage of the Little Mermaid ★★★½

What it is Musical stage show featuring characters from the Disney movie *The Little Mermaid*. **Scope and scale** Major attraction for preschoolers and grade-schoolers. **Fright potential** Ursula the sea witch may frighten preschoolers. **Bottleneck rating** 10. **When to go** Anytime. **Comment** Romantic, lovable, and humorous in the best Disney tradition. **Duration of show** 17 minutes. **Preshow** Taped ramblings about the decor in the preshow holding area. **Probable waiting time** Not more than 30 minutes.

This most tender and romantic stage show is a winner, appealing to every age. Once inside the theater, the audience is transported into the wonderful underwater world of Ariel and her friends. Very young children might be frightened by Ursula the sea witch, a 12-foot-tall puppet.

Because the show is well done and located at a busy pedestrian intersection, *Voyage of the Little Mermaid* plays to capacity crowds all day. When the theater doors open, pick a row of seats, and let 6–10 people enter the row ahead of you. The strategy is twofold: to get a good seat and be near the exit.

Walt Disney Presents ★★★

What it is Disney-memorabilia collection plus a short film about Walt Disney. **Scope and scale** Minor attraction. **Fright potential** Not frightening in any respect. **Bottleneck rating** 2. **When to go** Anytime. **Comment** Excellent! **Duration of presentation** 25 minutes. **Probable waiting time** For film, 10 minutes.

As everything else related to film and TV production at the Studios has closed, we anticipate that *Walt Disney Presents,* formerly known as *Walt Disney: One Man's Dream,* will shut its doors in the near future. In the meantime, it is still a tribute to Walt Disney, consisting of an exhibit area showcasing Disney memorabilia and a film documenting Disney's life, which is often replaced with trailers for upcoming Disney or Pixar movies.

My son, a cinematographer, used to take me to this attraction during every visit, and today, when visiting, he still sees the show to, as he says, "pay tribute to the man who started it all." I am sad to see this attraction dwindling, and I hope Disney will consider an even better tribute to Walt Disney in the near future.

Liliane

LIVE ENTERTAINMENT *at* DISNEY'S HOLLYWOOD STUDIOS

THE STUDIOS LIVE ENTERTAINMENT, which is generally as good or better than comparable acts found at the other Disney theme parks, includes theater shows; musical acts; street performers; *Star Wars: A Galactic Spectacular* fireworks; *Star Wars: A Galaxy Far, Far Away* stage show in front of the Chinese Theatre; and *Fantasmic!*, a nighttime water, fireworks, and laser show that draws rave reviews. Read on for details.

FAVORITE EATS AT DISNEY'S HOLLYWOOD STUDIOS

LAND | SERVICE LOCATION | FOOD SELECTIONS

COMMISSARY LANE ABC Commissary | Cheeseburgers, chicken and ribs combo; better options for dinner, such as chimichurri steak, Mediterranean salad with chicken or salmon, and a great Southwest burger

ECHO LAKE Backlot Express | Great burgers & fixin's
Sci-Fi Dine-In Theater | It's not about the food (dismal) but about eating in a vintage convertible car watching old sci-fi movie previews. Teens love it! Great place to cool off. *Table service only*

GRAND AVENUE PizzeRizzo | Pizza and meatball sub

SUNSET BOULEVARD Fairfax Fare | Fairfax salad with barbecue pork, bacon, and corn-tomato salsa; fajita combo; pulled-pork sandwich

TOY STORY LAND Woody's Lunch Box | *Toy Story*–themed specialties, fruit tarts, and soda floats

DISNEY CHARACTERS *Toy Story*'s Buzz, Woody, Jessie, and Green Army Men meet in Toy Story Land, while Minnie and Mickey Mouse can be found on Commissary Lane in an indoor venue dubbed Mickey and Minnie Starring in Red Carpet Dreams. Chip 'n' Dale meet right outside this venue. The star of Echo Lake is Olaf, the quirky snowman from *Frozen*. Disney Junior stars appear next to *Disney Junior Dance Party!* Check the *Times Guide* for times and locations of character appearances.

LILIANE Disney's Hollywood Studios is the only Disney World park without an interactive game. I vote for a *Star Wars*–themed game with trading cards and all.

HOLIDAY EVENTS During the Christmas season, the **Jingle Bell, Jingle BAM!** nighttime show is projected on the Grauman's Chinese Theatre, and Santa takes up residency at the Once

FELICITY I had never met a snowman before. Olaf danced with me and gave me a big, warm hug. Olaf doesn't know how to write, so he can't give you an autograph, but he loves to take pictures with you.

Upon a Time shop on Sunset Boulevard. Once Santa leaves to deliver toys around the world, Santa Goofy takes his place the rest of the year. Check your *Times Guide* for details. On Sunset Boulevard, **Sunset Seasons Greetings**—a sound-and-light show projected on The Twilight Zone Tower of Terror—is performed about every 20 minutes nightly. Like on Main Street, U.S.A., the show comes with lots of magical snow.

Even Echo Lake gets a holiday overhaul, and Gertie, the giant dinosaur, wears a Santa hat! For a complete review of the Yuletide happenings at the Studios, see theunofficialguides.com/2018/11/22disneys-hollywood-studios.

STAR WARS: A GALACTIC SPECTACULAR This 15-minute *Star Wars*–themed fireworks extravaganza is choreographed to John Williams's epic music from *Star Wars: The Force Awakens*. Even if you're not a fan of the galactic saga, the nightly fireworks are an absolute must-see. The best viewing points are along Hollywood Boulevard or on the left side of Center Stage Courtyard, facing the Chinese Theatre.

STAR WARS: A GALAXY FAR, FAR AWAY This live-action stage show is held several times daily on Center Stage and features everybody's favorite Wookiee, Chewbacca, as well as heroes and villains from across the galaxy. No word yet if the show will be incorporated into the new Star Wars: Galaxy's Edge.

STREET ENTERTAINMENT ★★★½ Appearing mainly on Hollywood and Sunset Boulevards, the Citizens of Hollywood, also known as Streetmosphere, portray old-time Tinseltown characters. The performers are not shy about asking you to join in their skits, and you may be asked anything from explaining why you came to "Hollywood" to reciting a couple of lines in one of the directors' new films.

THE WONDERFUL WORLD OF ANIMATION The new laser light and projection show takes viewers on a tour of 90 years of Disney animation. The 12-minute show features animated Pixar and Disney releases and is projected on the Grauman's Chinese Theatre. The show does not replace *Star Wars: A Galactic Spectacular,* which also takes place on the theater's facade. Depending on park hours, guests will be able to see both of the aforementioned shows.

Check your *Times Guide* for any performance schedule changes, as Disney adds or removes performances according to park occupancy.

Fantasmic! ★★★★½

**APPEAL BY AGE   PRESCHOOL ★★★★   GRADE SCHOOL ★★★★½   TEENS ★★★★½
YOUNG ADULTS ★★★★½   OVER 30 ★★★★½   SENIORS ★★★★½**

What it is Mixed-media nighttime spectacular. **Scope and scale** Super-headliner. **Fright potential** Loud and intense with fireworks and some scary villains, but most young children like it. **Bottleneck rating** 9. **When to go** Check *Times Guide* for schedule; if two shows are offered, the second is less crowded. **Comment** Not to be missed. **Duration of show** 25 minutes. **Probable waiting time** 50–90 minutes for a seat; 35–40 minutes for standing room.

  Fantasmic! is a must-see for the whole family. Starring Mickey Mouse in his role as the sorcerer's apprentice from *Fantasia,* the production uses lasers, images projected on a shroud of mist, dazzling fireworks, lighting effects, and powerful music. *Fantasmic!* has the potential to frighten young children. Prepare your children for the show, and make sure that they know that, in addition to all the favorite Disney characters, the Maleficent dragon and the evil Jafar will make appearances. To give you an idea, picture the evil Jafar turning into a cobra 100 feet long and 16 feet high. Rest assured, however, that during the final parade, your kids will cheer on Cinderella and Prince Charming, Belle, Snow White, Ariel and Prince Eric, Jasmine and Aladdin, Donald Duck, Minnie, and Mickey. You can alleviate the fright factor somewhat by sitting back a bit. Also, if you are seated in the first 12 rows, you will get sprayed with water at times.

The theater is huge, but so is the popularity of the show. If there are two performances, the second show will almost always be less crowded. If you attend the first (or only) scheduled performance, show up at least 1 hour in advance. If you opt for the second show, arrive at least 40 minutes early. Plan to use that time for a picnic. If you forget to bring munchies, not to worry; there are food concessions in the theater.

Unless you buy a *Fantasmic!* dining package, you will not have reserved seats, so arrive early for best choice. Try to sit in the middle three or four sections, a bit off-center. No refunds are given if *Fantasmic!* is canceled due to weather or other circumstances.

The number one show in my opinion is *Fantasmic!* You can't miss it.

Brendan

Fantasmic! Dining Packages

Three restaurants offer a ticket voucher for the members of your dining party to enter *Fantasmic!* via a special entrance and sit in a reserved section of seats. The package consists of a buffet at **Hollywood & Vine,** or a fixed-price dinner at **Mama Melrose's Ristorante Italiano** or **The Hollywood Brown Derby** (full-service restaurants). Call ☎ 407-WDW-DINE (939-3463) up to 180 days in advance to request the *Fantasmic!* package. This is a real reservation and must be guaranteed by a credit card at the time of booking. There's a 48-hour cancellation policy.

Prices fluctuate according to season, so call to find out the exact dinner charge for a particular date. If there are two scheduled performances in 1 night, the lunch package will only grant you reserved seating for the first performance.

Allow at least 2 hours to eat. You will receive the ticket vouchers at the restaurant. After dinner, report to the *Fantasmic!* sign on Hollywood Boulevard next to Oscar's (just inside the front entrance to the park) no later than 35 minutes prior to showtime. A cast member will escort you to the reserved section. If *Fantasmic!* is canceled for any reason, such as weather or technical problems, you will not receive a refund. However, you can go to Guest Relations to receive a voucher for a performance within the next 5 days. This only works if you're still in town and if you're willing to pay another admission to the Studios. If you're still around and you have a Park Hopper, go for it!

LILIANE If there are two *Fantasmic!* performances during the time of your visit, you really have no reason to spend extra money on the dining package. Just grab some food, enter the theater at least 40 minutes prior to the show, and relax!

EXIT STRATEGIES

EXITING THE STUDIOS at the end of the day following *Fantasmic!* is not nearly as difficult as leaving after the Epcot fireworks. We recommend that you take it easy and make your way out of the park after the first wave of guests has departed. Pick a spot inside the park and give instructions that nobody is to go through the turnstiles before the group is reunited. Most important, latch on to your kids.

HOLLYWOOD STUDIOS HARD-TICKET EVENTS

EARLY MORNING MAGIC   For $84 per adult and $73 per child (with tax), guests get a breakfast buffet and unlimited access to Toy Story Land starting about 75 minutes before regular park opening. Offered on certain Mondays and Wednesdays in select months, the attractions for Early Morning Magic (EMM) include Toy Story Mania!, Slinky Dog Dash, and Alien Swirling Saucers. Regular park admission is also required. On EMM days the official park opening is 9 a.m. You will have to be at the park entrance by 7:15 a.m. (check in starts at 7:30 a.m.) at the latest to take full advantage of this early access to Toy Story Land. If you have small children, keep in mind that you will have to get your family out of the hotel room by about 6 a.m. Breakfast is available at a quick-service dining location outside of Toy Story Land until 10 a.m. Please note that based on capacity, Disney may make other reservation times available, with breakfast preceding the park experience.

HOLLYWOOD STUDIOS AFTER HOURS   A ticket purchased in advance costs $113 per adult or child, and $137 per adult or child on the day of the event. Guests have 3 hours of unlimited access to Toy Story Mania!, Slinky Dog Dash, Rock 'n' Roller Coaster Starring Aerosmith, Twilight Zone Tower of Terror, Star Tours—The Adventures Continue, several character meet and greets, and Star Wars Launch Bay. Hours are 9:30 p.m.–12:30 a.m. Also included are all the ice cream, popcorn, and soda you can consume (from select vendors). This event is only worthwhile if your kids are able to stay up late at night. Even teenagers may balk at doing anything before noon the next morning. The big advantage of this special event is that Disney After Hours' guests can enter the part at 7 p.m. No word yet on if this event will continue when Galaxy's Edge is open or whether Galaxy's Edge attractions will be included; if it is, expect a price hike. Disney may also offer a Star Wars: Galaxy's Edge package only. Regular park admission is *not* required.

DISNEY'S HOLLYWOOD STUDIOS TOURING PLANS

OUR STEP-BY-STEP TOURING PLANS are field-tested, independently verified itineraries that will keep you moving counter to the crowd flow and allow you to see as much as possible in a single day with a minimum of time wasted in line. You can take in all the attractions at DHS in 1 day, even when traveling with young children. If you aren't interested in an attraction on the touring plan, simply skip it and proceed to the next step. Likewise, if you encounter a very long line at an attraction, skip it. Use of FastPass+ is factored into the touring plans.

The different touring plans are described below. The descriptions will tell you for whom (for example, tweens, parents with preschoolers, and so on) or for what situation (such as sleeping late) the plans are designed. The actual touring plans are on pages 496–500 and include a numbered map of the park to help you find your way around.

1-DAY *STAR WARS* TOURING PLAN A 1-day itinerary for families who love *Star Wars*, this plan includes rides, shopping, and general exploration of Star Wars: Galaxy's Edge. Be sure to try the interactive games in the Play Disney Parks app as you wait in the attraction queues and wander around the land. On busy days Disney may restrict access to Galaxy's Edge and only give guests a limited amount of time (usually 4 hours). If that's the case, you may need to forego some steps of the plan because there won't be enough time to experience everything. If you're limited on time, consider skipping Savi's Workshop and the Droid Depot. They're very cool but also extremely popular and very expensive, and waiting for them will take valuable time you could be using to explore all the beautiful details of the land. The plan also includes *Star Wars* attractions outside the land, including Star Wars Launch Bay, Star Tours–The Adventures Continue, and *Jedi Training: Trials of the Temple.*

1-DAY TOURING PLAN FOR PARENTS WITH SMALL CHILDREN This plan is for parents of children ages 3–8 who wish to see the very best age-appropriate attractions and shows in Hollywood Studios. Every attraction has a rating of at least three-and-a-half stars (out of five) from preschool and grade-school children surveyed by *The Unofficial Guide.* The plan includes a midday break outside the park, so families can rest and regroup. The plan keeps walking and backtracking to a minimum.

1-DAY SLEEPYHEAD TOURING PLAN FOR PARENTS WITH SMALL CHILDREN A relaxed plan that allows families with small children to sleep late and still see the highlights of DHS. The plan begins around 11 a.m., sets aside ample time for lunch and dinner, and includes the very best child-friendly attractions and shows in the park. Special advice is provided for touring the park with small kids.

1-DAY TOURING PLAN FOR TWEENS AND THEIR PARENTS A 1-day plan for parents with children ages 8–12, it includes every attraction rated three-and-a-half stars and higher by this age group and sets aside ample time for lunch and dinner.

1-DAY HAPPY FAMILY TOURING PLAN A 1-day itinerary for multigenerational families, this plan allows teens and older children to experience the Studios' thrill rides while parents and small children visit more age-appropriate attractions. The family stays together most of the day, including lunch and dinner, and each attraction in the plan is rated three-and-a-half stars or higher.

BEFORE YOU GO

1. Call ☎ 407-824-4321 or check disneyworld.com for operating hours.

2. Buy your admission and make FastPass+ reservations before you arrive.

3. Make lunch and dinner Advance Reservations or reserve the *Fantasmic!* dinner package (if desired) before you arrive by calling ☎ 407-WDW-DINE.

4. The schedule of live entertainment changes from week to week and even from day to day. Review the daily *Times Guide* handout, available free throughout Disney's Hollywood Studios.

DISNEY'S HOLLYWOOD STUDIOS TRIVIA QUIZ

1. Rex is Andy's dinosaur. What is the name of Bonnie's dinosaur in *Toy Story*?

   a. Baby Bob   **c.** Barney
   b. Riff   **d.** Trixie

2. Which famous rock band stars in Rock 'n' Roller Coaster?

   a. The Rolling Stones   **c.** The Who
   b. Aerosmith   **d.** Queen

3. The Tower of Terror is based on which TV series?

   a. *The Tower of Terror*   **c.** *The Twilight Hotel*
   b. *Hotel California*   **d.** *The Twilight Zone*

4. What is the name of the lake at Disney's Hollywood Studios?

   a. Echo Lake   **c.** Studio Lake
   b. Bay Lake   **d.** Lake Buena Vista

5. What was the original name of Disney's Hollywood Studios?

   a. Pixar Studios   **c.** DreamWorks
   b. Paramount Studios   **d.** Disney-MGM Studios

6. Where does *Beauty and the Beast—Live on Stage* take place?

   a. Theater of the Stars   **c.** Castle Forecourt Stage
   b. American Gardens Theatre   **d.** Hollywood Hills Amphitheater

7. What is the name of the roller coaster at Toy Story Land?

   a. Alien Swirling Saucers   c. Woody's Lunch Box
   b. Slinky Dog Dash   **d.** Andy's Toy Box

8. What restaurant is not located in Disney's Hollywood Studios?

   a. Hollywood & Vine   **c.** Mama Melrose's Ristorante
   b. Cosmic Ray's Starlight Cafe   **d.** Hollywood Brown Derby

9. What is the name of the nighttime spectacular held at Disney's Hollywood Studios?

   a. *Happily Ever After*   **c.** *IllumiNations: Reflections of Earth*
   b. *Cinematic Spectacular*   **d.** *Fantasmic!*

10. What is the current name of the former Pizza Planet?

   a. PizzeRizzo   **c.** The Flying Zucchini Brothers
   b. The Great Gonzo's Pandemonium   **d.** The Swedish Chef
      Pizza Parlor

Answers can be found on page 450.

PART ELEVEN

UNIVERSAL ORLANDO

UNIVERSAL ORLANDO

UNIVERSAL ORLANDO is a complete destination resort, with two theme parks; a water park; soon to be eight hotels; and **CityWalk,** a shopping, dining, and entertainment complex. A system of roads and two multistory parking facilities are connected by moving sidewalks to City-Walk, which also serves as a gateway to **Universal Studios Florida (USF)** and **Universal's Islands of Adventure (IOA)** theme parks.

And Universal isn't done. Over the last few years, it has acquired hundreds of acres of land along Destination Parkway to Sand Lake Road, more land than Universal Orlando currently sits on. And in the summer of 2018, Universal confirmed it was considering a fourth park. Possible names for the new park include Epic Universe and Fantastic Worlds. Bob and Liliane think this is awesome! While Bob wants Nintendo rides to finally have a home, Liliane is dreaming of a *Lord of the Rings*–themed land. Who knows? We could possibly get both and much more!

Universal has developed into a major, world-class, multifaceted resort destination—one we can no longer adequately cover in the few dozen pages allocated here. For in-depth coverage of the Universal parks, consider *The Unofficial Guide to Universal Orlando,* by Seth Kubersky with Bob Sehlinger and Len Testa. This guide is the most comprehensive on Universal Orlando in print, with more than 400 pages devoted to the subject. Though we'll continue to cover Universal Orlando in this book, we strongly recommend the Universal guide for all of the tips, insights, elaborations, and attention to detail that we can't accommodate in these pages.

Both Universal theme parks are accessed via CityWalk. Crossing CityWalk from the parking garages, you can bear right to USF or left to IOA.

LODGING AT UNIVERSAL ORLANDO

BY MAY 2020 UNIVERSAL will have eight resort hotels. The 750-room **Portofino Bay Hotel** is a gorgeous property set on an artificial bay and themed like an Italian coastal town. The 650-room **Hard Rock Hotel** is an ultracool "Hotel California" replica, and the 1,000-room, Polynesian-themed **Royal Pacific Resort** is sumptuously decorated and richly appointed. These three resorts are on the pricey side, but their guests get free unlimited Universal Express Passes for the length of their stay.

LILIANE If your kids are *Despicable Me* fans, check out the 18 two-room, Minion-themed Kids' Suites at Portofino Bay.

The retro-style **Cabana Bay Beach Resort,** Universal's largest hotel, has 2,200 moderate- and value-priced rooms, plus amenities (bowling alley, lazy river) not seen at comparable Disney resorts. **Sapphire Falls Resort** has a Caribbean theme and is priced between the Royal Pacific and the Cabana Bay Beach Resorts. The 16-story **Aventura Hotel,** a moderately priced 600-room hotel, also features 13 kids' suites, a food hall showcasing five distinct cuisine options, plus a rooftop bar and grill. Located adjacent to Sapphire Falls Resort and across from Cabana Bay Beach Resort, Aventura Hotel is within walking distance of USF, IOA, and Volcano Bay water park. Cabana Bay, Sapphire Falls, and Aventura do *not* offer complimentary Universal Express Passes to any of the three parks.

Universal's **Endless Summer Resort** will have two hotel towers: **Surfside Inn and Suites** opened August 2019, and **Dockside Inn and Suites** will follow suit by May 2020. See pages 115–122 for more on Universal's hotels.

Aventura, Cabana Bay, and Surfside Inn and Suites connect to the rest of the resort via shuttle buses and walking paths; the other four hotels also offer water taxi service. All hotel guests get early admission into The Wizarding World of Harry Potter in one or both theme parks (depending on the season) and Volcano Bay 1 hour before the general public.

LILIANE Universal's hotels offer wake-up calls from the Blue Man Group, the Cat in the Hat, Transformers, Olive Oyl, Betty Boop, Spider-Man, and the Grinch.

ADMISSION OPTIONS

UNIVERSAL OFFERS 1-, 2-, 3-, 4-, and 5-day passes for one or two theme parks; adding Volcano Bay to a multiday ticket costs $55–$75 plus tax, depending on length, and upgrading from one-park-per-day to Park-to-Park access costs $55–$70. Universal charges up to $20 less for 1-day tickets valid only during "Value" or "Regular" seasons; multiday tickets are valid any time but expire 14 days after their first use. Universal also sells a range of two- and three-park annual passes, which include sizable discounts on hotels, food, and merchandise. Passes can be obtained in advance at ☎ 800-711-0080 or universal orlando.com. Prices on page 386 are what you'll pay at the gate and include sales tax.

continued on page 386

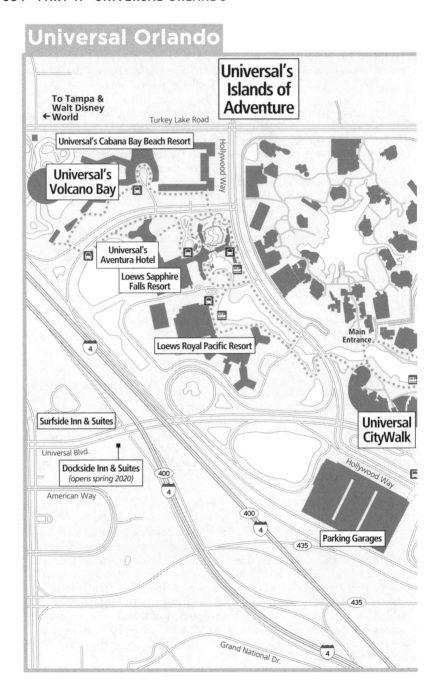

Universal Orlando

To Tampa &
Walt Disney
← World

Turkey Lake Road

Universal's
Islands of
Adventure

Universal's Cabana Bay Beach Resort

Hollywood Way

Universal's
Volcano Bay

Universal's
Aventura Hotel

Loews Sapphire
Falls Resort

Loews Royal Pacific Resort

Main
Entrance

4

Surfside Inn & Suites

Universal Blvd.

Universal
CityWalk

Dockside Inn & Suites
(opens spring 2020)

400

4

American Way

Hollywood Way

400

4

435

Parking Garages

435

Grand National Dr.

4

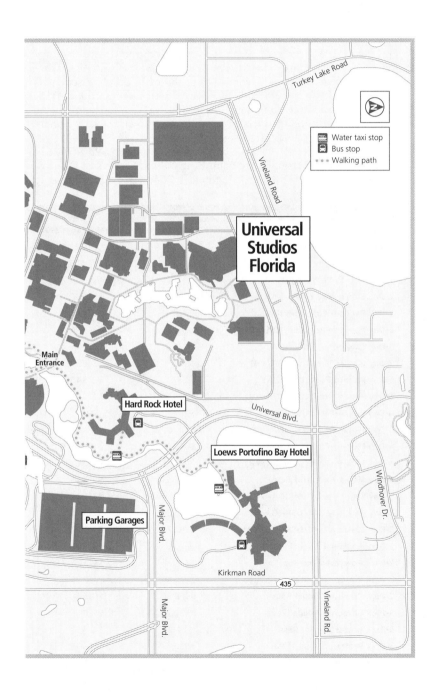

continued from page 383

Be sure to check Universal Orlando's website for seasonal deals and specials. You can save as much as $20 off the gate prices by buying your tickets online. The **Official Ticket Center** (OTC), a ticket discounter (officialticketcenter.com), offers the most deeply discounted Universal tickets we're aware of. Tickets purchased through OTC include tax and free shipping. In addition, OTC often matches or beats the short-term deals Universal offers on its own website, such as a "buy 3 days, get 2 days free" special.

The main Universal Orlando information number is ☎ 407-363-8000, or visit universalorlando.com. Reach Guest Services at ☎ 407-224-4233. The number for lost and found is ☎ 407-224-4233, option 2.

UNIVERSAL ORLANDO ADMISSIONS		
TICKET TYPE	**ADULTS**	**CHILDREN (Ages 3-9)**
1-Day Single-Park (USF/IOA)	$122.48-$143.78	$117.15-$138.45
1-Day Volcano Bay	$85.20-$90.53	$79.88-$85.20
1-Day Park-to-Park (USF/IOA)	$181.05-$202.35	$175.73-$197.03
2-Day Single-Park (USF/IOA)	$260.91	$250.26
2-Day Park-to-Park (USF/IOA)	$324.81	$314.16
2-Day Park-to-Park (USF/IOA/VB)	$383.39	$372.74
3-Day Single-Park (USF/IOA)	$282.21	$271.56
3-Day Single-Park (USF/IOA/VB)	$340.79	$330.14
3-Day Park-to-Park (USF/IOA)	$346.11	$335.46
3-Day Park-to-Park (USF/IOA/VB)	$404.69	$394.04
4-Day Single-Park (USF/IOA)	$292.86	$282.21
4-Day Single-Park (USF/IOA/VB)	$362.09	$351.44
4-Day Park-to-Park (USF/IOA)	$362.09	$351.44
4-Day Park-to-Park (USF/IOA/VB)	$431.31	$420.66
5-Day Single-Park (USF/IOA)	$303.51	$292.86
5-Day Single-Park (USF/IOA/VB)	$383.39	$372.74
5-Day Park-to-Park (USF/IOA)	$378.06	$367.41
5-Day Park-to-Park (USF/IOA/VB)	$457.94	$447.29
2-Park Seasonal Annual Pass	$324.81	$324.81
2-Park Power Annual Pass	$378.06	$378.06
2-Park Preferred Annual Pass	$420.66	$420.66
2-Park Premier Annual Pass	$596.36	$596.36
3-Park Seasonal Annual Pass	$430.25	$430.25
3-Park Power Annual Pass	$494.15	$494.15
3-Park Preferred Annual Pass	$536.75	$536.75
3-Park Premier Annual Pass	$781.70	$781.70

UNIVERSAL EXPRESS

THIS SYSTEM ALLOWS ANY GUEST to "skip the line" and experience an attraction via a special queue with little or no waiting. While Disney's FastPass+ system requires scheduling your ride reservation hours or days ahead of time, Universal Express involves no advance planning; simply visit any eligible operating attraction whenever you choose, no return time windows required. In addition, unlike FastPass+, Universal Express is not free for everyone.

Unlimited Universal Express at the two theme parks is a complimentary perk for guests at Portofino Bay, Hard Rock Hotel, and Royal Pacific; hotel guests may use the Express lines all day long simply by flashing the pass they get at check-in. This perk far surpasses any benefit accorded to guests of Disney resorts and is especially valuable during peak season.

Day guests or ineligible hotel guests can purchase Universal Express for the theme parks for an extra $74.54–$149.09 (for a single park) or $95.84–$170.39 (for both parks) including tax (depending on the season), which provides line-jumping privileges at each Universal Express attraction. You can purchase Universal Express for either single (one ride only on each participating attraction) or unlimited use. The number of Express Passes is limited each day, and they can sell out, so increase your chances of securing passes by buying and printing them at home off Universal's website. You'll need to know when you plan on using it, though, because prices vary depending on the date.

More than 90% of attractions are covered by Universal Express, a much higher percentage than those covered by FastPass+ at Disney World. The exceptions are **Hagrid's Magical Creatures Motorbike Adventure** and **Pteranodon Flyers** at IOA and **Kang & Kodos' Twirl 'n' Hurl** at USF.

You can also buy Universal Express at the theme parks' ticket windows, just outside the front gates, but it's faster to do so inside the parks. Express Passes can be purchased in most park gift shops, as well as from freestanding kiosks that seem to proliferate around the parks like mushrooms during peak seasons.

IS UNIVERSAL EXPRESS WORTH IT? The answer depends on the season you visit, hours of park operation, and crowd levels. If you want to sleep in and arrive at a park after opening, Express is an effective, albeit expensive, way to avoid long lines at the headliner attractions, especially during holidays and busy times.

If, however, you arrive 30 minutes before park opening and you use our Universal Orlando touring plans (see pages 501–504), you should experience the lowest possible waits at both USF and IOA. We encourage you to try the touring plans first, but if waits for rides become intolerable, you can always buy Express in the parks. If you do use Express, bring a lanyard (or buy one from Universal) to wear the pass around your neck, lest you lose it.

UNIVERSAL DINING PROGRAMS

CHARACTER DINING A *Despicable Me* character breakfast is held every Saturday at the Tahitian Room at Royal Pacific Resort. The cost for meeting Gru, Margo, Edith, Agnes, and the Minions is $34.99 for adults and $20.99 for kids ages 3–9. Prices do not include tax and gratuities. For information and reservations, call ☎ 407-503-3463.

At IOA's Café 4 you can dine with Captain America, Spider-Man, Wolverine, Cyclops, Storm, and Rogue. The dinner costs $49.99 for adults ($24.99 kids ages 3–9) and is held Thursday–Sunday at 5 p.m.

During the holiday season, the Grinch brings his special blend of mischief as he joins diners at IOA for breakfast on select days. The Grinch & Friends character breakfast costs $37.27 for adults and $22.36 for kids. Call ☎ 407-224-FOOD (3663) to schedule a character meal in the park.

COCA-COLA FREESTYLE SOUVENIR CUP This perk entitles you to a souvenir sipper cup with 1 day of unlimited fountain soft drinks at all participating Coca-Cola Freestyle locations at both USF and IOA. The cost is $15.99 plus tax for all ages, or $6 with a Universal Dining Plan. The price includes the first day of refills; it can be reactivated for $8.99 plus tax per additional day.

UNIVERSAL DINING PLAN This plan is available exclusively to guests who book a hotel package with Universal. The plan includes one counter-service meal (entrée and nonalcoholic beverage), one table-service meal (entrée, dessert, and nonalcoholic beverage), and one snack and one additional beverage (from a cart or counter-service location) each day. Select CityWalk locations and most in-park dining locations participate. Gratuity is not included, and no substitutions may be made. Eligible restaurants and menu items are indicated by a Universal Dining Plan logo. Price per day is $63.89 for adults, $24.48 for kids. To book your vacation package with the Universal Dining Plan, visit universalorlando.com.

Available to all guests, the **Quick Service Dining Plan** provides one counter-service meal with drink, another soft drink, and one snack. The cost is $25.55 for adults and $17.03 for kids age 9 and younger, plus tax. It's valid at most counter-service eateries in all three parks (including Three Broomsticks in Hogsmeade, the Leaky Cauldron in Diagon Alley, and Fast Food Boulevard in Springfield) and a smattering at Universal CityWalk, but not at the hotels. The plan can be purchased from kiosks or restaurant cashiers.

UNIVERSAL, KIDS, AND SCARY STUFF

THOUGH THERE'S PLENTY FOR YOUNGER CHILDREN to enjoy at the Universal parks, most major attractions can potentially make kids under age 8 wig out. At IOA, watch out for **The Amazing Adventures of Spider-Man, Doctor Doom's Fearfall, Hagrid's Magical Creatures Motorbike Adventure, Harry Potter and the Forbidden Journey, The Incredible Hulk Coaster, Jurassic Park River Adventure,** and *Poseidon's Fury.* Skull

Island: Reign of Kong is visually and psychologically intense; it may be too much for little ones. **Popeye & Bluto's Bilge-Rat Barges** is wet and wild, but most younger children handle it well. **Dudley Do-Right's Ripsaw Falls** is a toss-up, to be considered only if your kids like water-flume rides. Nothing else should pose a problem.

At USF, forget **Hollywood Rip Ride Rockit, Men in Black Alien Attack, Revenge of the Mummy, The Simpsons Ride,** and **Transformers: The Ride 3-D.** The first part of **E.T. Adventure** is a little intense for a few preschoolers, but the end is all happiness and harmony. There are some scary visual effects on both the **Hogwarts Express** train that runs between the two parks and **Harry Potter and the Escape from Gringotts** dark ride–roller coaster, but both are billed as family rides. Interestingly, very few families report problems with *Universal Orlando's Horror Make-Up Show.* Anything we haven't listed is pretty tame.

CHILD SWAP Switching off at Universal is similar to Disney's version but superior in several respects. The entire family goes through the whole line together before being split into riding and nonriding groups near the loading platform. The nonriding parent and child(ren) wait in a designated room, usually with some sort of entertainment (for example, Harry Potter and the Forbidden Journey at IOA shows the first 20 minutes of *Harry Potter and the Sorcerer's Stone* on a loop), a place to sit down, and sometimes restrooms with changing tables. At any theme park, the best tip we can give is to ask the greeter in front of the attraction what you're supposed to do.

BLUE MAN GROUP

THE SHARP AQUOS THEATRE, near CityWalk, is home to the Blue Man Group. The theater can be accessed from inside or outside USF.

The three blue men are just that—blue—and bald and mute. Wearing black clothing and skullcaps slathered with bright-blue grease paint, they deliver a 1-hour, 45-minute fast-paced show that uses music (mostly percussion) and multimedia effects to make light of contemporary art and life in the information age. We recommend getting seats at least 15 rows back from the stage.

Tickets start at $63.90 for adults and $31.95 for children ages 3–9 and can be purchased online or at the Universal box office; tickets purchased at the box office cost $10 more.

UNIVERSAL CITYWALK

HERE YOU'LL FIND GREAT RESTAURANTS, clubs, shops, outdoor entertainment, a concert hall (Hard Rock Live), and a movie theater. City-Walk has a number of combination restaurants and clubs. Open to families with kids until 9 p.m., many of the venues offer live entertainment.

Toothsome Chocolate Emporium & Savory Feast Kitchen is a full-service restaurant, bar, and confectionery that is well worth your visit. The 19th-century–inspired steampunk chocolate factory is funky, and while all things chocolate are fabulous, the rest of the menu is also a winner. **Voodoo Doughnut** serves one-of-a-kind doughnuts.

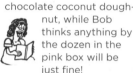

LILIANE I dream of a chocolate coconut doughnut, while Bob thinks anything by the dozen in the pink box will be just fine!

For mom and dad's night out, great entertainment is available at **CityWalk's Rising Star,** a karaoke joint where singers are backed by a live band; **Bob Marley—A Tribute to Freedom,** which has reggae; **Pat O'Brien's** dueling-pianos club; **Fat Tuesday,** specializing in New Orleans–style daiquiris; **Bigfire,** which cooks food over a wood fire at the center of the eatery; a **Hard Rock Cafe** and **Hard Rock Live** concert venue; **Jimmy Buffett's Margaritaville;** the **Red Coconut Club,** a two-story upscale cocktail lounge with live music and dancing; and a dance club called **the groove,** with high-tech lighting and visual effects. If you want to go clubbing, $12.77 admits you to all of the clubs. For details, call Universal CityWalk information at ☎ 407-224-2691.

How To Make It Work

CityWalk is open daily, 11 a.m.–2 a.m., and parking is available in the same garages that serve the theme parks at the rate of $25 a day for cars and $30 for RVs, trailers, and other large rigs. Regular parking is free after 6 p.m. If you stay at one of the Universal resorts, it's a short walk, but water taxi and bus transportation are also available. For added fun, try one of the pedicabs that will take you from CityWalk to your resort for a modest tip. Call ☎ 407-224-FOOD (3663) for dinner reservations. Visit universalorlando.com and select "At CityWalk" under "Events" for special events.

UNIVERSAL'S
ISLANDS *of* ADVENTURE

WHEN ISLANDS OF ADVENTURE (IOA) OPENED IN 1999, it provided Universal with enough critical mass to actually compete with Disney. Doubly interesting is that the second Universal park is a direct competitor to Disney's Magic Kingdom, the most-visited theme park in the world. IOA has kid-friendly rides and cartoon characters (like Fantasyland), thrill rides in a sci-fi city (like Tomorrowland), and a jungle river with robot creatures (like Adventureland). Its layout—a central entry corridor leading to a ring of connected lands—even mimics the classic Disney model, with one major exception: instead of a hub and castle in the center, Universal built a large lagoon, whose estuaries separate the park's thematically diverse "islands" (which are actually peninsulas).

In 2007 Universal's management made one bold bet: securing the rights to build a *Harry Potter*–themed area within IOA. Harry P. is possibly the only fictional character extant capable of trumping Mickey Mouse, and Universal went all-out, under J. K. Rowling's watchful and exacting eye, to create a setting and attractions designed to be the envy of the industry. The Wizarding World of Harry Potter–Hogsmeade opened at IOA in 2010 and was an immediate hit. And there is no sign of letting up: in summer 2019 IOA opened Hagrid's Magical Creatures Motorbike Adventure, and a new *Jurassic Park*–themed roller coaster is under construction.

Disney and Universal officially downplay their fierce competition, pointing out that any new theme park or attraction makes Central Florida a more marketable destination. Behind closed doors, however, the two companies share a Pepsi-versus-Coke rivalry that keeps both working hard to gain a competitive edge. The good news is that all this translates into bigger and better attractions for you to enjoy.

IOA is arranged much like Epcot's World Showcase (in a large circle surrounding a lake), but its themed areas are self-contained "lands" reminiscent of the Magic Kingdom. You first encounter the Moroccan-style **Port of Entry**, where you'll find **Guest Services, lockers, stroller and wheelchair rentals,** an **ATM, lost and found,** and shopping. From Port of Entry, moving clockwise around the lagoon, you access **Marvel Super Hero Island, Toon Lagoon, Skull Island, Jurassic Park, The Wizarding World of Harry Potter–Hogsmeade, The Lost Continent,** and **Seuss Landing.**

BEWARE OF THE WET AND WILD

THOUGH WE'VE DESCRIBED IOA as a direct competitor to the Magic Kingdom, there is one major qualification you should be aware of: whereas most Magic Kingdom attractions are designed to be enjoyed by guests of any age, attractions at IOA are largely created for an under-40 population. The thrill rides at Universal are serious with a capital *S*, making Space Mountain and Big Thunder Mountain Railroad look about as tough as Dumbo. In fact, 9 out of the 14 top attractions at IOA are thrill rides, and of these, 3 not only scare the bejabbers out of you but also drench you with water. Some of the water rides have People Dryers near the exit (they cost $5!), though they don't get you 100% dry.

BOB Roller coasters at Islands of Adventure are the real deal—not for the timid or for little ones.

LILIANE Consider yourself warned: several attractions at Islands of Adventure will drench you to the bone.

LILIANE Check out my post on how to get completely drenched at IOA: theunofficial guides.com/2019/04 /15/islands-of -adventure.

For families, there are three interactive playgrounds as well as six rides that young children will enjoy. Of the thrill rides, only the two in Toon Lagoon (described later) are marginally appropriate for little kids, and even on these rides, your child needs to be fairly hardy.

Universal's Islands of Adventure

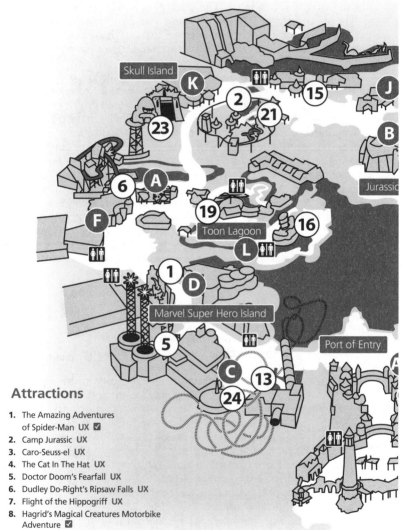

Attractions

1. The Amazing Adventures of Spider-Man UX ☑
2. Camp Jurassic UX
3. Caro-Seuss-el UX
4. The Cat In The Hat UX
5. Doctor Doom's Fearfall UX
6. Dudley Do-Right's Ripsaw Falls UX
7. Flight of the Hippogriff UX
8. Hagrid's Magical Creatures Motorbike Adventure ☑
9. Harry Potter and the Forbidden Journey UX ☑
10. The High in the Sky Seuss Trolley Train Ride! UX
11. Hogwarts Express: Hogsmeade Station UX ☑
12. If I Ran The Zoo
13. The Incredible Hulk Coaster UX ☑
14. Jurassic Park Discovery Center
15. Jurassic Park River Adventure UX ☑
16. Me Ship, *The Olive*
17. Ollivanders
18. One Fish, Two Fish, Red Fish, Blue Fish UX
19. Popeye & Bluto's Bilge-Rat Barges UX ☑
20. *Poseidon's Fury* UX

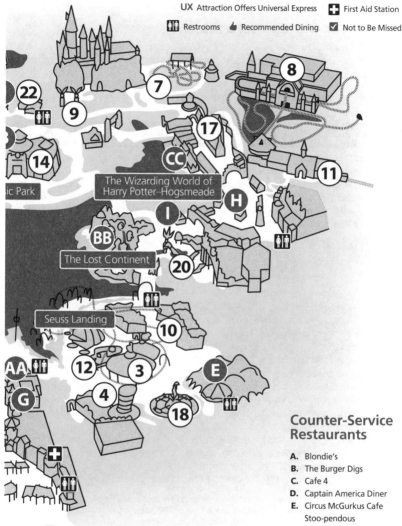

UX Attraction Offers Universal Express ✚ First Aid Station

👫 Restrooms 👍 Recommended Dining ☑ Not to Be Missed

The Wizarding World of Harry Potter–Hogsmeade

The Lost Continent

Seuss Landing

...ic Park

Counter-Service Restaurants

A. Blondie's
B. The Burger Digs
C. Cafe 4
D. Captain America Diner
E. Circus McGurkus Cafe Stoo-pendous
F. Comic Strip Cafe
G. Croissant Moon Bakery
H. Doc Sugrue's Kebab House
I. Fire-Eater's Grill
J. Pizza Predattoria
K. Thunder Falls Terrace 👍
L. Wimpy's *(seasonal)*

Table-Service Restaurants

AA. Confisco Grille
BB. Mythos Restaurant 👍
CC. Three Broomsticks (counter service) 👍

21. Pteranodon Flyers
22. Raptor Encounter
23. Skull Island: Reign of Kong UX ☑
24. Storm Force Accelatron UX

ISLANDS *of* ADVENTURE ATTRACTIONS

MARVEL SUPER HERO ISLAND

THIS ISLAND, WITH ITS FUTURISTIC and retro-future design and comic-book signage, offers shopping and attractions based on Marvel Comics characters.

The Amazing Adventures of Spider-Man
(Universal Express) ★★★★★

APPEAL BY AGE   PRESCHOOL ★½   GRADE SCHOOL ★★★★½   TEENS ★★★★½
YOUNG ADULTS ★★★★½   OVER 30 ★★★★½   SENIORS ★★★★

What it is Indoor adventure simulator ride based on Spider-Man. **Scope and scale** Super-headliner. **Fright potential** Intense; kids tall enough to ride usually take it in stride. **Bottleneck rating** 9. **When to go** The first 40 minutes the park is open. **Comments** Must be 40″ tall to ride. One of the best attractions anywhere. **Duration of ride** 4½ minutes. **Average wait in line per 100 people ahead of you** 4 minutes. **Loading speed** Fast.

Dark   Rough   Scary   Queasy

Soar above buildings without ever leaving the ground! The Amazing Adventures of Spider-Man—covering 1½ acres and combining moving ride vehicles, high-definition 3-D film, and live action—is frenetic, fluid, and astounding. The visuals are rich, and the ride is wild but not jerky. It will leave you in awe.

The story line is that you're a reporter for the *Daily Bugle* newspaper (where Peter Parker, also known as Spider-Man, works as a mild-mannered photographer), when it's discovered that evildoers have stolen—we promise we're not making this up—the Statue of Liberty. You're drafted on the spot by your cantankerous editor to go get the story. After speeding around and being thrust into a battle between good and evil, you experience a 400-foot "sensory drop" from a skyscraper roof all the way to the pavement. Spidey is less frantic than the similar Transformers ride at Universal Studios Florida and features more dialogue and humor.

If you were on hand for early entry, ride after experiencing The Wizarding World, Skull Island: Reign of Kong, and The Incredible Hulk Coaster. If you skip The Wizarding World, ride after the Hulk. The single-rider line can greatly cut your wait, as long as the line doesn't reach the stroller parking area.

I hated the long queue, and I didn't really like that all the bad guys came so close to me. The spinning made me feel sick. I did like being squirted with water though.

Felicity

Doctor Doom's Fearfall *(Universal Express)* ★★★

APPEAL BY AGE   PRESCHOOL ★★   GRADE SCHOOL ★★★★   TEENS ★★★½
YOUNG ADULTS ★★★★½   OVER 30 ★★★½   SENIORS ★★★

What it is Vertical ascent and free fall. **Scope and scale** Headliner. **Fright potential** Frightening for all ages. **Bottleneck rating** 10. **When to go** The first 40 minutes the park is open. **Comments** Must be 52″ tall to ride. More bark than bite. **Duration of ride**

40 seconds. **Average wait in line per 100 people ahead of you** 18 minutes. **Loading speed** Slow.

Here you're strapped into a seat with your feet dangling, blasted 200 feet up in the air, and then allowed to partially free-fall back down. The scariest part of the ride by far is the apprehension that builds as you sit, strapped in, waiting for the ride to launch; blasting up and falling down are actually pleasant. We've seen glaciers that move faster than the line to Doctor Doom. If you want to ride without investing half a day, be one of the first in the park to ride. Doctor Doom also has a singles line, accessed through the arcade, that's nearly always open.

The Incredible Hulk Coaster
(Universal Express) ★★★★½

APPEAL BY AGE	PRESCHOOL ★	GRADE SCHOOL ★★★½	TEENS ★★★★★
YOUNG ADULTS ★★★★★	OVER 30 ★★★★½	SENIORS ★★★½	

What it is Roller coaster. **Scope and scale** Super-headliner. **Fright potential** Frightening for all ages. **Bottleneck rating** 10. **When to go** The first 40 minutes the park is open. **Comments** Must be 54" tall to ride. Items too large to be secured in a pocket must be placed in lockers near the ride. A coaster-lover's coaster. **Duration of ride** 2¼ minutes. **Average wait in line per 100 people ahead of you** 9 minutes. **Loading speed** Moderate.

The Hulk is a great roller coaster, one of the best in Florida, providing a ride comparable to Montu (Busch Gardens). Bolliger & Mabillard, the original builder of the ride, finished a major refurbishment in 2016, completely replacing all tracks and coaster trains. The queue was revamped with a sleek new look, and the replacement trains feature flashing lights and a synchronized soundtrack composed by Fall Out Boy's Patrick Stump. Unfortunately, the reconstructed ride remains rougher than we'd hoped, though it's still a far cry from the side-to-side shaking of Hollywood Rip Ride Rockit at Universal Studios Florida. Our advice is to skip The Wizarding World attractions in the early morning and ride Hulk first thing. Alternatively, if you insist on going to Hogsmeade at rope drop (or you are eligible for Early Park Admission), ride Hulk immediately after the Harry Potter attractions and Skull Island. A single-rider line is usually available.

You-know-who made me ride it, and for the duration of the ride, I lost my very polite European ways.

Unfortunately, Liliane lost her very polite European ways at about 140 decibels. My ears hurt for days.

Storm Force Accelatron (Universal Express) ★★½

APPEAL BY AGE	PRESCHOOL ★★★★	GRADE SCHOOL ★★★★	TEENS ★★★★
YOUNG ADULTS ★★★½	OVER 30 ★★★	SENIORS ★★★	

What it is Spinning ride. **Scope and scale** Minor attraction. **Fright potential** Nauseating but not frightening. **Bottleneck rating** 9. **When to go** Anytime. **Comment** Teacups in the dark. **Duration of ride** 1½ minutes. **Average wait in line per 100 people ahead of you** 21 minutes. **Loading speed** Slow.

Storm Force is a spiffed-up version of Disney's nausea-inducing Mad Tea Party. Ride early or late to avoid long lines. Skip it if you're prone to motion sickness.

TOON LAGOON

THIS LAND TRANSLATES cartoon art into real buildings and settings. Whimsical and gaily colored, with rounded and exaggerated lines, Toon Lagoon is Universal's answer to Storybook Circus in the Magic Kingdom—only you have about a 60% chance of getting soaked at Universal's version. **Comic Strip Lane** is the main street of Toon Lagoon. Here you can visit the domains of Beetle Bailey, Hägar the Horrible, Krazy Kat, the Family Circus, and Blondie and Dagwood, among others of whom your kids have never heard. Shops and eateries tie in to the cartoon strip theme. This is a great place for photo ops with cartoon characters.

Dudley Do-Right's Ripsaw Falls *(Universal Express)* ★★★½

APPEAL BY AGE   PRESCHOOL ★½   GRADE SCHOOL ★★★★½   TEENS ★★★★½
YOUNG ADULTS ★★★★½   OVER 30 ★★★★   SENIORS ★★★★

What it is Flume ride. **Scope and scale** Major attraction. **Fright potential** The big drop frightens guests of all ages. **Bottleneck rating** 8. **When to go** Before 11 a.m. **Comments** Must be 44″ tall to ride. Lockers available for a fee. A minimalist Splash Mountain. **Duration of ride** 5 minutes. **Average wait in line per 100 people ahead of you** 9 minutes. **Loading speed** Moderate.

Inspired by the Rocky and Bullwinkle cartoons, this ride features Canadian Mountie Dudley Do-Right as he attempts to save his girlfriend, Nell Fenwick, from the evil Snidely Whiplash. Story line aside, it's a flume ride, with the inevitable big drop at the end. Universal claims that this is the first flume ride to "send riders plummeting 15 feet below the surface of the water." In reality, though, you're just plummeting into a tunnel. The flume is as good as Splash Mountain's at the Magic Kingdom, and the final drop is a whopper, but the theming and the visuals aren't even in the same league.

The big drop doesn't get you that wet, but beware of the minor drop—that one will get you soaked!

Brendan

This ride will get you wet, but on average not as wet as you might expect (it looks worse than it is). If you want to stay dry, however, bring a poncho or at least a big garbage bag with holes cut out for your head and arms. While younger children are often intimidated by the big drop, those who ride generally enjoy themselves. Ride first thing in the morning after experiencing the Marvel Super Hero rides and Skull Island.

Small children will be intimidated by the big drop. Try Popeye & Bluto's Bilge-Rat Barges first.

Liliane

Right, Liliane. Popeye & Bluto's Bilge-Rat Barges is perfect for small children . . . as long as they have wet suits and life jackets.

Bob

Me Ship, *The Olive* ★ ★ ★

APPEAL BY AGE   PRESCHOOL ★ ★ ★ ★ ★   GRADE SCHOOL ★ ★ ★   TEENS ★ ★
YOUNG ADULTS ★ ★   OVER 30 ★ ★ ½   SENIORS ★ ★

What it is Interactive playground. **Scope and scale** Minor attraction. **Fright potential** Not frightening in any respect. **Bottleneck rating** 4. **When to go** Anytime. **Comment** Colorful and appealing for kids.

The Olive is Popeye's three-story boat come to life as an interactive playground. Younger kids can scramble around in Swee'Pea's Playpen, while older sibs shoot water cannons at riders trying to survive the adjacent Bilge-Rat Barges. If you're into the big rides, save this for later in the day.

Popeye & Bluto's Bilge-Rat Barges (*Universal Express*) ★ ★ ★ ★

APPEAL BY AGE   PRESCHOOL ★ ★ ★   GRADE SCHOOL ★ ★ ★ ★ ½   TEENS ★ ★ ★ ★ ½
YOUNG ADULTS ★ ★ ★ ★ ★   OVER 30 ★ ★ ★ ★ ½   SENIORS ★ ★ ★ ★

What it is Whitewater-raft ride. **Scope and scale** Major attraction. **Fright potential** Ride is wild and wet but not frightening. **Bottleneck rating** 8. **When to go** Before 10:30 a.m. **Comments** Must be 42″ tall to ride. Lockers available for a fee. Bring your own soap. **Duration of ride** 4½ minutes. **Average wait in line per 100 people ahead of you** 7 minutes. **Loading speed** Moderate.

   This whitewater-raft ride for the whole family is engineered to ensure that everyone gets drenched; the ride even provides water cannons for highly intelligent nonparticipants ashore to fire at those aboard. The rapids are rougher and more interesting, and the ride longer, than Animal Kingdom's Kali River Rapids. If you didn't drown on Dudley Do-Right, here's a second chance.

Remember that you *will* get wet. That's OK on a hot summer day, unless it's first thing in the morning. Now is the time to use the raingear or plastic bags to protect yourselves. Most important, keep your footwear dry to avoid blisters later.

Liliane

SKULL ISLAND

LOCATED BETWEEN DUDLEY DO-RIGHT'S RIPSAW FALLS and Thunder Falls Terrace, Skull Island: Reign of Kong is both an attraction and an entire "island" unto itself.

Skull Island: Reign of Kong (*Universal Express*)   ★ ★ ★ ★ ½

APPEAL BY AGE   PRESCHOOL —   GRADE SCHOOL ★ ★ ★ ½   TEENS ★ ★ ★ ★ ½
YOUNG ADULTS ★ ★ ★ ½   OVER 30 ★ ★ ★ ★   SENIORS ★ ★ ★ ★ ★

What it is Indoor/outdoor truck safari with 3-D effects. **Scope and scale** Superheadliner. **Fright potential** Extremely intense; if you or your little one has a fear of darkness, insects, or man-eating monsters, you may want to forgo the monkey. **Bottleneck rating** 10. **When to go** Immediately after park opening or just before closing. **Comments** Must be 34″ tall to ride. The King has returned; not to be missed. **Duration of ride** About 6 minutes. **Average wait in line per 100 people ahead of you** 3 minutes. **Loading speed** Fast.

   The ride is an original adventure set in the 1930s, casting guests as jungle explorers with the 8th Wonder Expedition

Company. The queue experience is phenomenal, featuring an ancient temple inhabited by both lifelike animatronic figures and live haunted house–style actors who startle unwitting guests.

Bob and Liliane agree on the scare factor for little tykes here, as both recently managed to run smack into a wall due to the nearly complete darkness in the queue. Thankfully, the live actors seemed to have been on a break that morning!

Your transportation is an oversize 72-seat open-sided "expedition vehicle" that superficially resembles the trucks at Animal Kingdom's Kilimanjaro Safaris. It's helmed by one of five different animatronic tour guides, each with a unique personality and backstory. Your ride begins with a short loop outside through the jungle (which may be bypassed in inclement weather), ending at the massive torch-framed doors in the center of Skull Island's imposing stony facade. You pass through a maze of caves, where you're swiftly assaulted by icky prehistoric bats, bugs, and beasties, brought to gruesome life through a mix of detailed physical effects and razor-sharp 3-D screens. You're then thrust into the center of a raging battle between vicious *V. rex* dinosaurs and the big ape himself, in a climactic sequence similar (though not identical) to the *King Kong 360* 3-D attraction on Universal Studios Hollywood's tram tour. Finally, just when you think it's all over, you'll have one last face-to-face encounter with the "eighth wonder of the world," only this time in the fur-covered flesh.

JURASSIC PARK

FOR ANYONE WHO'S BEEN ASLEEP FOR 25 YEARS, *Jurassic Park* is a Steven Spielberg film franchise about a fictitious theme park with real dinosaurs. Jurassic Park at IOA is a real theme park (or at least a section of one) with fictitious dinosaurs. A *Jurassic Park*– or *Jurassic World*–themed roller coaster is under construction, but there's no word yet on a name, opening date, or even specs and the manufacturer for the coaster.

Camp Jurassic ★★★½

APPEAL BY AGE PRESCHOOL ★★★★★ GRADE SCHOOL ★★★★★ TEENS ★★★½ YOUNG ADULTS ★★★★½ OVER 30 ★★★½ SENIORS ★★★

What it is Interactive play area. **Scope and scale** Minor attraction. **Fright potential** Not frightening in any respect. **Bottleneck rating** 3. **When to go** Anytime. **Comment** Creative playground; confusing layout.

One of the best theme park playgrounds you'll find anywhere. A sort of dinosaur-themed Tom Sawyer Island (minus the rafts), it allows kids to explore lava pits, caves, mines, and a rain forest.

Jurassic Park Discovery Center ★★½

APPEAL BY AGE PRESCHOOL ★★★ GRADE SCHOOL ★★★½ TEENS ★★ YOUNG ADULTS ★★★½ OVER 30 ★★★ SENIORS ★★★½

What it is Interactive natural-history exhibit. **Scope and scale** Minor attraction. **Fright potential** Not frightening in any respect. **Bottleneck rating** 3. **When to go** Usually opens later than the rest of the park and may close earlier as well; typical hours are 10 a.m.–5 p.m.

This interactive educational exhibit mixes fiction from the movie *Jurassic Park,* such as using fossil DNA to bring dinosaurs back to life, with various skeletal remains and other paleontological displays. Cycle back after experiencing all the rides or on a second day. Most folks can digest this exhibit in 10–15 minutes.

On a hot summer day, it's a great place to cool off. The best exhibit lets guests watch an animatronic raptor being hatched. Young children will delight in the hatching and are afforded an opportunity to name the baby dino. You never know quite when one will emerge, but ask an attendant if you should stick around.

Liliane

Jurassic Park River Adventure *(Universal Express)* ★★★★

APPEAL BY AGE   PRESCHOOL ★★½   GRADE SCHOOL ★★★★   TEENS ★★★★½
YOUNG ADULTS ★★★★½   OVER 30 ★★★★   SENIORS ★★★½

What it is Indoor/outdoor adventure river-raft ride based on the *Jurassic Park* movies. **Scope and scale** Super-headliner. **Fright potential** Visuals and big drop frighten guests of all ages. **Bottleneck rating** 9. **When to go** Before 11 a.m. **Comments** Must be 42″ tall to ride. Lockers available for a fee. **Duration of ride** 6½ minutes. **Average wait in line per 100 people ahead of you** 5 minutes. **Loading speed** Fast.

Wet   Scary

Guests board boats for a water tour of Jurassic Park. Everything is tranquil as the tour begins, and then the tour boat is accidentally diverted into Jurassic Park's maintenance facilities. Here, the boat and its riders are menaced by an assortment of hungry meat-eaters. At the climactic moment, the boat and its passengers escape by plummeting over an 85-foot drop. You can stay relatively dry if you're sitting in an interior seat. Young children must endure a double whammy on this ride: first, they are stalked by giant, salivating (sometimes spitting) reptiles, and then they're sent catapulting over the falls. Unless your children are fairly hardy, wait a year or two before you spring the River Adventure on them.

Don't go on Jurassic Park River Adventure if you don't want to get wet. You've been warned.

Brendan

Pteranodon Flyers ★★

APPEAL BY AGE   PRESCHOOL ★★★★½   GRADE SCHOOL ★★★★½   TEENS ★★★★★
YOUNG ADULTS ★★★½   OVER 30 ★★★½   SENIORS ★★★★

What it is Slow as Christmas. **Scope and scale** Minor attraction. **Fright potential** Not frightening in any respect. **Bottleneck rating** 10. **When to go** When there's no line. **Comments** Adults and older children must be accompanied by a child 36″–52″ tall. All sizzle, no steak. **Duration of ride** 1¼ minutes. **Average wait in line per 100 people ahead of you** 28 minutes. **Loading speed** More sluggish than a hog in quicksand.

This ride swings you along a track that passes over a small part of Jurassic Park. We recommend you skip this one. Why? Because the next ice age will probably end before you reach the front of the line! And your reward for all that waiting? A 1-minute-and-15-second ride.

If your kids are set on riding, look for kiosks outside Camp Jurassic's entrance that dispense timed-return tickets for the Flyers. It will still be a long wait before they're able to ride, but at least you can play elsewhere while waiting.

Raptor Encounter ★★★½

What it is Photo op with lifelike dinosaur. **Scope and scale** Minor attraction. **Fright potential** The velociraptor makes loud, growling noises and sudden, snapping movements that startle even some adults. **Bottleneck rating** 8. **When to go** Check with attraction employees for appearance times. **Comment** Sure to scare the spit out of small kids. **Duration of encounter** About a minute. **Average wait in line per 100 people ahead of you** 30 minutes.

Scary

Several times each hour, the blue siren lights around the predator paddock signal the arrival of the park's semi-tame velociraptor. A game warden briefs one family at a time regarding proper safety procedures (convey calm assurance, move in slowly, and try not to smell like meat) before they step up for a photo. Don't peer too closely over the edge of the raptor enclosure; you'll spot the cleverly camouflaged legs of the puppeteer inside and spoil the illusion.

Selfies are encouraged—just don't be surprised if the dino snaps when you say, "Smile!" Don't try to touch the raptor, or you may come home minus a hand. Surreptitiously feeding your offspring to the dinosaurs is also discouraged by management.

In 2018 Blue, designed after the female velociraptor from 2015's *Jurassic World* and 2018's *Jurassic World: Fallen Kingdom*, joined Raptor Encounter.

Appearances begin around 10 a.m. and run periodically until 6:45 p.m., with brief breaks about every 20 minutes to rotate raptors. Ask a team member stationed outside the paddock approximately how long your wait will be before queuing. Due to construction of the *Jurassic Park*–themed roller coaster, the location of the Raptor Encounter has been moved temporarily to the right of Pizza Predatoria, next to the restrooms. The new location will likely be on the opposite side of Pizza Predatoria.

THE WIZARDING WORLD OF HARRY POTTER–HOGSMEADE

IN 2007 UNIVERSAL INKED A DEAL WITH WARNER BROTHERS Entertainment to create a fully immersive *Harry Potter*–themed environment based on the best-selling children's books by J. K. Rowling and the companion blockbuster movies from Warner Brothers. The project was personally blessed by Rowling, who demanded painstaking accuracy.

Passing beneath a stone archway, you enter the village of **Hogsmeade.** Depicted in winter, the village setting is rendered in exquisite detail: stone cottages and shops have steeply pitched slate roofs; bowed multipaned windows; gables; and tall, crooked chimneys. In keeping with the stores depicted in the *Potter* films, the shopping venues in The Wizarding World of Harry Potter–Hogsmeade are small and intimate—so intimate, in fact, that they feel congested when they're serving only 12–20 shoppers.

ISABELLE Listen for Moaning Myrtle, the female ghost who appears in many of the *Harry Potter* movies, in the ladies' restroom.

Isabelle

With so many avid Potter fans, lines for the shops develop most days by 9:30 or 10 a.m. The lines for the shops are frequently longer than the wait for the rides.

WIZARDING WORLD–HOGSMEADE ATTRACTIONS

Flight of the Hippogriff *(Universal Express)* ★★★

**APPEAL BY AGE PRESCHOOL ★★★★   GRADE SCHOOL ★★★★½ TEENS ★★★½
YOUNG ADULTS ★★★½ OVER 30 ★★★½ SENIORS ★★★½**

What it is Children's roller coaster. **Scope and scale** Minor attraction. **Fright potential** Frightens a small percentage of preschool riders. **Bottleneck rating** 5. **When to go** First 90 minutes the park is open. **Comments** Must be 36" tall to ride. A good beginner coaster. **Duration of ride** 1 minute. **Average wait in line per 100 people ahead of you** 14 minutes. **Loading speed** Slow.

Below and to the right of Hogwarts Castle next to Hagrid's Hut, the Hippogriff is short and sweet but not worth much of a wait. Have your kids ride soon after the park opens. Even if you don't ride, it's worth a stroll down to see the castle from the cliff bottom and to check out Hagrid's Hut (above the path for the regular line) and an adorable animatronic of Buckbeak.

This coaster was just right for me. The queue was long and hot, but the ride was so great that I think it was worth the wait.

Felicity

Hagrid's Magical Creatures Motorbike Adventure ★★★★½

What it is Indoor–outdoor roller coaster. **Scope and scale** Super-headliner. **Fright potential** Intense wild ride with special effects. **Bottleneck rating** 10+. **When to go** First 30 minutes the park is open or just before closing. **Comments** Expect long waits in line; must be 48" tall to ride. Switching-off option (see page 248). Items too large to be secured in a pocket must be placed in lockers near the ride. Muggles will wish that the ride never ends. Not to be missed. **Duration of ride** About 3 minutes. **Average wait in line per 100 people ahead of you** About 4 minutes. **Loading speed** Moderate.

Dark Queasy Scary

Riding either on Hagrid's motorcycle or in a sidecar, guests are taken through indoor and outdoor show scenes. Be prepared to meet centaurs, Cornish pixies, and the iconic Fluffy (the three-headed dog), as well as a never-before-seen-in-the-movies beast. Although guests surge through multiple launches and go as fast as 50 miles per hour, including backward, we think this is still a family-friendly roller coaster. The sidecar sits lower but closer to the effects, so every rider gets a good view.

I am still looking for the Triwizard Tournament's Golden Eggs and the Triwizard Cup.

Liliane

If you feel Universal's attractions are too dependent on video screens and simulated movement, Hagrid is here to answer your prayers with richly detailed scenery, spectacular practical effects, and accelerated airtime that's exhilarating, but not *too* extreme for tweens and parents to enjoy together. Hagrid's has a near-flawless combination of theme and thrills, easily making it the best "story coaster" in Orlando, and a strong contender for the best ride at Universal Orlando.

The coaster replaced the Dragon Challenge roller coasters in June 2019. Ride as early as possible or shortly before park closing. A Virtual Line is offered when the queue grows long; use Universal's smartphone app to secure a return time upon entering the park. Hagrid's ride does not currently offer Universal Express access, but it may in the future. A single-rider queue is available. Larger guests (over 40″ waists) should test the sample seats before lining up; request the motorbike seat to enjoy a little more breathing room than the cramped sidecar.

Harry Potter and the Forbidden Journey
(Universal Express) ★★★★★

What it is Motion simulator dark ride. **Scope and scale** Super-headliner. **Fright potential** Intense special effects and wild ride. **Bottleneck rating** 10. **When to go** Immediately after park opening or in the last hours before closing. **Comments** Must be 48″ tall to ride. Switching-off option (see page 248). Items too large to be secured in a pocket must be placed in lockers near the ride. Marvelous for Muggles; not to be missed. **Duration of ride** 4¼ minutes. **Average wait in line per 100 people ahead of you** 4 minutes. **Loading speed** Fast.

Dark

Rough

Queasy

Scary

This ride provides the only opportunity at Universal Orlando to come in contact with Harry, Ron, Hermione, and Dumbledore as portrayed by the original actors. From Hogsmeade you reach the attraction through the imposing Winged Boar gates and progress along a winding path. Entering the castle on a lower level, you walk through a sort of dungeon festooned with various icons and prop replicas from the *Potter* flicks, including the Mirror of Erised from *Harry Potter and the Sorcerer's Stone*. You later emerge back outside and into the Hogwarts greenhouses. Blessedly, there are water fountains but, alas, no restrooms—take care of that before getting in line for the attraction.

Eventually, you reenter the castle, moving along its fabulously themed halls and passageways. One chamber showcases a multistory gallery of portraits, including those of the four founders of Hogwarts. The founders argue about Quidditch and Dumbledore's controversial decision to host an open house at Hogwarts for Muggles (garden-variety mortals). Don't rush through the gallery—the conversation is essential to understanding the rest of the attraction.

Next, you arrive at Dumbledore's office, where the chief wizard appears on a balcony and welcomes you to Hogwarts. After his welcoming remarks, Dumbledore dispatches you to the Defence Against the Dark Arts classroom to hear a presentation on the history of Hogwarts.

As you gather to await the lecture, Harry, Ron, and Hermione pop out from beneath an invisibility cloak. They suggest you ditch the lecture in favor of joining them for a proper tour of Hogwarts, including a Quidditch match. After receiving preride instructions, it's time to board.

The ride vehicle is mounted to a Kuka robotic arm that can be programmed to replicate all the sensations of flying, including broad swoops, steep dives, sharp turns, sudden stops, and fast acceleration. The ride vehicle moves you through a series of alternating sets and domes, where scenes are projected all around you. You'll soar over Hogwarts Castle, narrowly evade an attacking dragon, spar with the Whomping Willow, get tossed into a Quidditch match, and fight off Dementors inside the Chamber of Secrets.

Bob

The only restrooms in The Wizarding World at IOA, labeled public conveniences, are in the middle of Hogsmeade. Remember where they are—especially if you're prone to motion sickness.

We recommend that you don't ride on an empty stomach. If you start getting queasy, fix your gaze on your feet and try to exclude as much from your peripheral vision as possible.

Liliane

Even if your child meets the height requirement, consider carefully whether Forbidden Journey is an experience he or she can handle. Because the seats on the benches are compartmentalized, kids can't see or touch Mom or Dad if they get scared.

Upon entering Forbidden Journey's interior queue, all riders with bags or loose items must secure them in a free locker. If you don't need a locker, enter through Filch's gift shop and cut through the lockers to save as much as 30 minutes in line.

Because the ride experience is individual (you can't see the other riders, including members of your party), the single-rider line is a great option. It will get you on the ride in only 10–25 minutes. If you use the single-rider line, however, you'll miss much of the interior of the castle.

I hated every moment of this ride. Walking through Hogwarts Castle was scary, and the dark, spinning ride made me really feel sick. I screamed and cried because of all the spiders, and I never want to go on this ride again.

Felicity

Hogwarts Express *(Universal Express)* ★★★★½

APPEAL BY AGE PRESCHOOL ★★★½ **GRADE SCHOOL** ★★★★½ **TEENS** ★★★★½
YOUNG ADULTS ★★★★★ **OVER 30** ★★★★½ **SENIORS** ★★★★★

What it is Transportation attraction. **Scope and scale** Super-headliner. **Fright potential** Potter villains and spirit creatures menace the train. **Bottleneck rating** 10+. **When to go** Immediately after park opening. **Comments** Expect lengthy waits in line; Park-to-Park ticket required to ride. Not to be missed. **Duration of ride** 4 minutes. **Average wait in line per 100 people ahead of you** 7 minutes. **Loading speed** Moderate.

See page 423 for a full description. Because the Hogsmeade Station doesn't include the cool Platform 9¾ effect found at the King's Cross end, expect waits for the one-way trip to be shorter here. If you wish to experience the train going from IOA to USF, do so before midafternoon, when lines can build. On peak days, guests wishing to take a same-day return trip may be relegated to a slower reride queue.

Ollivanders ★★★★

APPEAL BY AGE   PRESCHOOL ★★½ **GRADE SCHOOL** ★★★★½ **TEENS** ★★★½
YOUNG ADULTS ★★★★ **OVER 30** ★★★★ **SENIORS** ★★★½

What it is Combination wizarding demonstration and shopping op. **Scope and scale** Major attraction. **Fright potential** Special effects may startle 6-and-unders. **Bottleneck rating** 10. **When to go** First thing in the morning or after 7:30 p.m. **Comments** Audience stands. Enchanting. **Duration of presentation** 6 minutes. **Average waiting time in line per 100 people ahead of you** 36 minutes.

Ollivanders, located in Diagon Alley in the books and films, somehow sprouted a branch location in Hogsmeade at IOA. Potter scholars pointed out this misplacement, but the wand shop stayed and is one of the most popular features of The Wizarding World. It's also a horrendous bottleneck, with long lines where guests roast in an unshaded queue. Once inside, a Wandkeeper sizes you up and presents a wand, inviting you to try it out; your attempted spells produce unintended, unwanted, and highly amusing consequences. Ultimately, a wand chooses you, with all the attendant special effects. It's great fun, but the tiny shop can accommodate only about 24 guests at a time. Usually just one person in each group gets to be chosen by a wand, and then the whole group is dispatched to the Owl Post and Dervish and Banges to make purchases. Wand prices range from $48.99 for a no-frills model to $55.38 for an interactive gizmo that triggers special effects hidden inside shop windows throughout Hogsmeade. The average wait time during summer and other busy periods is 45–85 minutes between 9:30 a.m. and 7:30 p.m. If you're just looking to buy a wand without the interactive experience, a cart is usually set up near the *Frog Choir* stage, typically with little to no wait.

If your young 'un is selected to test-drive a wand, be forewarned that you'll have to buy it if you want to take it home.

Wizarding World Entertainment

Nearly every retail space sports some sort of animatronic or special effects surprise. At **Dervish and Banges,** the fearsome *Monster Book of Monsters* rattles and snarls at you as Nimbus 2001 brooms strain at their tethers overhead. At the **Hog's Head** pub, the titular porcine part, mounted behind the bar, similarly thrashes and growls. (The pub also serves The Wizarding World's signature nonalcoholic brew, Butterbeer. Outdoor vendors also sell it, but the wait at Hog's Head is generally 10 minutes or less, versus half an hour or more in the lines outside. Also, the outdoor vendors charge a few cents more and don't honor annual pass discounts.)

Roughly across the street from the pub, you'll find shaded benches at the **Owlery,** where animatronic owls (complete with lifelike poop) ruffle and hoot from the rafters. Next to the Owlery is the **Owl Post,** where you can have mail stamped with a Hogsmeade postmark before dropping it off for delivery (an Orlando postmark will also be applied by the real USPS). You can't enter through the Owl Post's front door on busy days, when it serves exclusively as an exit. Because it's so difficult to get into the Owl Post, IOA sometimes stations a team member outside to stamp your postcards with the Wizarding World postmark.

Street entertainment at the Forbidden Journey end of Hogsmeade includes the ***Frog Choir*** (★★★), composed of four singers, two of whom are holding large amphibian puppets sitting on pillows; and the ***Triwizard Spirit Rally*** (★★★), showcasing dancing and martial arts. Performances run about 6–15 minutes.

Don't miss the *Harry Potter*–themed Christmas event held at both Wizarding Worlds November 16, 2019–January 5, 2020. Expect holiday decor and food adapted from the *Harry Potter* novels, as well as an amazing, not-to-be-missed sound-and-light show projected on Hogwarts Castle.

THE LOST CONTINENT

THIS AREA IS AN EXOTIC MIX of Silk Road bazaar and ancient ruins, with Greco-Moroccan accents. (And you thought your decorator was nuts.) This is the land of mythical gods, fabled beasts, and expensive souvenirs. In 2018 the crew of *The Eighth Voyage of Sindbad* took their final bow. Right now The Lost Continent is reduced to *Poseidon's Fury,* a theater attraction, and some food and souvenir stalls. However, kids will love the Mystic Fountain. It speaks, sings, squirts unsuspecting onlookers with water, and is downright mischievous.

Poseidon's Fury *(Universal Express)* ★★★½

APPEAL BY AGE	PRESCHOOL ★	GRADE SCHOOL ★★½	TEENS ★★★
YOUNG ADULTS ★★★★	OVER 30 ★★★½	SENIORS ★★★★½	

What it is High-tech theater attraction. **Scope and scale** Headliner. **Fright potential** Intense visuals and special effects frighten some preschoolers. **Bottleneck rating** 7. **When to go** After experiencing all the rides. **Comment** Audience stands. **Duration of show** 17 minutes, including preshow. **Probable waiting time** 25 minutes.

The Greek god Poseidon tussles with an evil wizardish guy using fire, water, lasers, smoke machines, and angry lemurs. (*Note:* Lemurs aren't actually part of the show—just seeing if you're paying attention.) The plot unfolds in installments as you pass from room to room and finally into the main theater. There's some great technology at work here. Frequent explosions and noise may frighten younger children, so exercise caution with preschoolers. We recommend catching *Poseidon* after experiencing your fill of the rides.

SEUSS LANDING

IN THIS 10-ACRE THEMED AREA based on Dr. Seuss's famous children's books, all of the buildings and attractions replicate a whimsical, brightly colored cartoon style with exaggerated features and rounded lines. There are four rides at Seuss Landing; an interactive play area, **If I Ran the Zoo,** populated by Seuss creatures; and **Oh, the Stories You'll Hear!,** a live musical show (see page 407).

If you have only young children in your party, Seuss Landing is the place to spend lots of happy time. A great stop in Seuss Landing is Dr. Seuss's All the Books You Can Read bookstore. Last but not least, if your kids can't get enough of Dr. Seuss, check out seussville.com.

Liliane

Caro-Seuss-el *(Universal Express)* ★★★

APPEAL BY AGE	PRESCHOOL ★★★★★	GRADE SCHOOL ★★★★	TEENS ★★
YOUNG ADULTS ★★★★	OVER 30 ★★★½	SENIORS ★★★★	

What it is Merry-go-round. **Scope and scale** Minor attraction. **Fright potential** Not frightening in any respect. **Bottleneck rating** 8. **When to go** Anytime. **Comment** Wonderfully unique. **Duration of ride** 2 minutes. **Average wait in line per 100 people ahead of you** 9 minutes. **Loading speed** Slow.

Totally outrageous, the Caro-Seuss-el is a full-scale, 56-mount merry-go-round made up exclusively of Dr. Seuss characters. Waits are usually not too long, even in the middle of the day.

The Cat in the Hat *(Universal Express)* ★★★½

APPEAL BY AGE PRESCHOOL ★★★★★ GRADE SCHOOL ★★★★ TEENS ★★★
YOUNG ADULTS ★★★½ OVER 30 ★★★ SENIORS ★★★★

What it is Indoor adventure ride. **Scope and scale** Major attraction. **Fright potential** Not frightening in any respect. **Bottleneck rating** 8. **When to go** Before 11:30 a.m. or after 4:30 p.m. **Comments** Must be 36″ tall to ride. Dr. Seuss would be proud. **Duration of ride** 3½ minutes. **Average wait in line per 100 people ahead of you** 5 minutes. **Loading speed** Moderate.

A must for preschoolers, guests ride on "couches" through 18 different sets inhabited by animatronic Seuss characters, including The Cat in the Hat, Thing 1, Thing 2, and the beleaguered goldfish who tries to maintain order in the midst of bedlam. Well done overall, with nothing that should frighten younger children. This is fun for all ages. Try to ride early or late in the day after families with young children have started to depart.

> This was my favorite ride at Islands of Adventure.
> The ride made me feel like I was going into the book.
>
> **Felicity**

The High in the Sky Seuss Trolley Train Ride! *(Universal Express)* ★★★½

APPEAL BY AGE PRESCHOOL ★★★★★ GRADE SCHOOL ★★★★ TEENS ★★★
YOUNG ADULTS ★★★ OVER 30 ★★★½ SENIORS ★★★★½

What it is Elevated train. **Scope and scale** Major attraction. **Fright potential** Not frightening in any respect. **Bottleneck rating** 8. **When to go** Before 11:30 a.m. or just before closing. **Comments** Relaxed tour of Seuss Landing; must be 40″ tall to ride. **Duration of ride** 3½ minutes. **Average wait in line per 100 people ahead of you** 9 minutes. **Loading speed** Molasses.

Trains putter along elevated tracks, while a voice reads one of four Dr. Seuss stories over the train's speakers. As each train makes its way through Seuss Landing, it passes a series of animatronic characters in scenes that are part of the story being told. Little tunnels and a few mild turns make this a charming ride. The trains are small, fitting about 20 people, and the loading speed is glacial. Save the train for the end of the day or ride first thing in the morning.

If I Ran the Zoo *(Universal Express)* ★★½

APPEAL BY AGE PRESCHOOL ★★★★★ GRADE SCHOOL ★★★½ TEENS ★★★★
YOUNG ADULTS — OVER 30 — SENIORS —

What it is Interactive playground. **Scope and scale** Minor attraction. **Fright potential** Not frightening in any respect. **Bottleneck rating** 2. **When to go** Anytime. **Comments** Whimsical and funny; great for preschoolers.

A playground with 19 different interactive elements, this area is great silly-dilly fun for little tykes. How silly? The sign at the entrance of this crazy zoo should give you a clue: "Keep track of adults. They get lost all the time." And yes, you should know by now that there is no way the kids will stay dry.

One Fish, Two Fish, Red Fish, Blue Fish
(Universal Express) ★★★

APPEAL BY AGE	PRESCHOOL ★★★★	GRADE SCHOOL ★★★★½	TEENS ★★★½
YOUNG ADULTS ★★½	OVER 30 ★★★	SENIORS ★★★	

What it is Wet version of Dumbo the Flying Elephant. **Scope and scale** Minor attraction. **Fright potential** Not frightening in any respect. **Bottleneck rating** 8. **When to go** Before 10 a.m. **Comment** Who says you can't teach an old ride new tricks? **Duration of ride** 2 minutes. **Average wait in line per 100 people ahead of you** 9 minutes. **Loading speed** Slow.

Wet

Imagine Dumbo with Seuss-style fish instead of elephants and you have half the story—the other half involves yet another opportunity to drown. Guests steer their fish up or down 15 feet in the air while traveling in circles. At the same time, they try to avoid streams of water projected from "squirt posts."

Felicity

The queue was horrendously long, but I didn't care because the ride was super awesome. You can control the fish to avoid the water squirts, but we still got soaked.

I followed Dr. Seuss's advice: If you never did, you should. These things are fun. These things are good. And all wet there I stood! My favorite ride in Seuss Landing!

Liliane

LIVE ENTERTAINMENT *at* ISLANDS *of* ADVENTURE

ISLANDS OF ADVENTURE is home to a music and light show projected on Hogwarts Castle, and the characters from Dr. Seuss's beloved books come to life several times each day in a not-to-be-missed show.

OH! THE STORIES YOU'LL HEAR! (★★★) Featuring many of Dr. Seuss's most beloved characters (including The Lorax, The Grinch, Thing 1 and Thing 2, Sam I Am, and the Cat in the Hat), *Oh! The Stories You'll Hear!* is a fun singing and dancing show staged in an outdoor area between One Fish, Two Fish, Red Fish, Blue Fish and The Cat in the Hat ride. After each show, the characters separate for individual meet and greets and autographs. Shows run daily, usually starting by 10:30 a.m. and continuing every hour until about 4:30 p.m. on a schedule published in the park map. During inclement weather, the show takes place within the Circus McGurkus Cafe Stoo-pendous restaurant nearby.

THE NIGHTTIME LIGHTS AT HOGWARTS CASTLE (★★★½) On select nights, Hogwarts Castle, the home of the Harry Potter and the Forbidden Journey ride, transforms into a dazzling digital projection show. Video-mapping effects are synchronized to the music of John Williams in an absolute must-see. There are no fireworks, but the music and spectacular lighting effects make the performances simply magical. The show repeats every 15–20 minutes after sunset. Check the park map for showtimes.

A new show, the ***Dark Arts at Hogwarts Castle,*** will take place on select nights in late 2019. The more intense show includes Death

Eaters, Dementors, mountain trolls, Inferi, Aragog the Acromantula, and He Who Must Not be Named, complete with a new score by the legendary John Williams. A Patronus spell, executed by drones, saves Hogwarts Castle. We expect Universal to rotate the shows throughout the year.

Christmas at Universal Orlando starts mid-November and lasts through the first week of January. Seasonal decorations adorn the attractions, holiday songs are broadcast from speakers in the streets, and each park has a headliner holiday event.

Expect holiday decor and food adapted from the *Harry Potter* novels, plus a nighttime show inspired by the books that is displayed on Hogwarts Castle. During the day the famous Frog Choir charms onlookers with tunes such as "The Most Magical Yule Ball of All" and "I Cast a Spell on Father Christmas." Check out Liliane's report about Grinchmas and other Yuletide events at Universal Orlando at theunofficialguides.com/2018/11/01/universal-orlando-3.

Universal transforms Seuss Landing into the whimsical world of Grinchmas. Be sure to explore every nook and cranny of this wintry wonderland, as it's filled with special touches that Dr. Seuss fans are sure to adore.

You won't want to miss the ***Grinchmas Who-liday Spectacular Show,*** a live show retelling Dr. Seuss's classic holiday tale, starring The Grinch with music recorded by Mannheim Steamroller. The half-hour musical is performed six to eight times daily through January 1 at the soundstage behind Circus McGurkus Cafe Stoo-pendous.

Throughout the day, Whos from Whoville stroll through Seuss Landing, and The Grinch himself holds court inside the All the Books You Can Read store. The Grinch who stole Christmas takes time to interact before each photograph, which is a lot of fun but results in a long, slow-moving line. If meeting the Grinch is a priority, make this your first stop in the morning. Check the park map for showtimes and character meet and greets.

On select days in November and December feast with the Grinch and enjoy meeting Thing 1 and Thing 2 during **The Grinch & Friends Character Breakfast.** See page 388 for more details.

ISLANDS *of* ADVENTURE TOURING PLANS

WHEN IT COMES TO TOURING IOA efficiently, you have two basic choices, and as you might expect, there are trade-offs. If you're intent on experiencing The Wizarding World first thing, be at the turnstiles at least 30 minutes before the park opens. Once you're admitted, hurry to Hogsmeade and ride **Hagrid's Magical Creatures Motorbike Adventure,**

FAVORITE EATS AT UNIVERSAL'S ISLANDS OF ADVENTURE

LAND	SERVICE LOCATION	FOOD SELECTIONS
PORT OF ENTRY	**Croissant Moon Bakery**	Croissants and sandwiches
TOON LAGOON	**Blondie's**	Hot dogs
JURASSIC PARK	**Pizza Predattoria**	Pizza
Thunder Falls Terrace	Chicken, ribs, and smoked turkey legs	
THE WIZARDING WORLD OF HARRY POTTER–HOGSMEADE		
Three Broomsticks	Shepherd's pie and fish-and-chips	
LOST CONTINENT	**Fire Eater's Grill**	Gyro
Mythos Restaurant	Risotto and Mediterranean flatbread	*Table service only*
SEUSS LANDING	**Circus McGurkus Cafe Stoo-pendous**	Fried chicken and mashed potatoes with gravy

followed by **Forbidden Journey** and then **Flight of the Hippogriff.** Next head to other must-see attractions before the park gets crowded. The catch? Ride difficulties could have you stuck in a long line while crowds—and more lines—spread to other areas of IOA.

Unless you have Early Park Admission at IOA, we recommend skipping Potterville first thing and enjoying other attractions in the meantime, starting at **Marvel Super Hero Island** and then heading for **Skull Island.** The Wizarding World usually clears out in the afternoon and is often empty in the last hour, even on busy days, meaning you can ride Forbidden Journey with a minimal wait if you step in the queue shortly before closing time.

The touring plans are described below. The actual touring plans are located on pages 501 and 503–504. Each plan includes a numbered map of the park to help you find your way around.

1-DAY TOURING PLAN FOR FAMILIES This touring plan is for guests without Park-to-Park tickets and is appropriate for groups of all sizes and ages. It includes thrill rides that may induce motion sickness or get you wet. If the plan calls for you to experience an attraction that doesn't interest you, simply skip it and go to the next step. Be aware that the plan calls for some backtracking.

Because there are so many attractions with the potential to frighten young children, be prepared to skip a few things and to practice switching off (works generally the same way as at Disney World; see page 248). For the most part, attractions designed especially for young children, such as playgrounds, can be enjoyed anytime. Work them into the plan at your convenience.

Be aware that in this park, there are an inordinate number of attractions that will get you wet. If you want to experience them, come armed with ponchos, large plastic garbage bags, or some other protective covering. Failure to follow this prescription will make for a squishy, sodden day.

THE BEST OF UNIVERSAL ORLANDO IN 1 DAY See page 428 for a description of this plan.

UNIVERSAL STUDIOS FLORIDA

OPENED IN JUNE 1990, UNIVERSAL STUDIOS FLORIDA (USF) was, at the time, almost four times the size of Disney's Hollywood Studios, and much more of the facility was accessible to visitors. USF is spacious, beautifully landscaped, meticulously clean, and delightfully varied in its entertainment. Rides are exciting and innovative and, like many Disney attractions, focus on familiar and/or beloved movie characters or situations.

USF is laid out in a *P* configuration, with the rounded part of the *P* sticking out disproportionately from the stem. Beyond the main entrance, a wide boulevard stretches past several shows and rides to the park's New York area. Branching off this pedestrian thoroughfare to the right are four streets that access other areas of the park and intersect a promenade circling a large lake. The area of USF open to visitors is a bit smaller than Epcot.

BOB Get to the park turnstiles with your admission already purchased about 30–45 minutes before official opening time. Arrive 45–60 minutes before official opening time if you need to buy admission. **Be aware that you can't do a comprehensive tour of both Universal parks in a single day.**

The park is divided into eight areas: **Hollywood, Production Central, New York, San Francisco, The Wizarding World of Harry Potter–Diagon Alley, World Expo, Springfield: Home of The Simpsons,** and **Woody Woodpecker's KidZone.** In most of USF, where one area begins and another ends is blurry, but no matter. Guests orient themselves by the major rides, sets, and landmarks and refer, for instance, to "New York," "the waterfront," "over by E.T.," or "by Mel's Diner." Because most USF attractions aren't thematically integrated into the areas of the park in which they reside, we present them alphabetically rather than by area.

The park offers all standard services and amenities, including stroller and wheelchair rental, lockers, diaper-changing and infant-nursing facilities, car assistance, and foreign-language assistance. Most of the park is accessible to disabled guests, and TDDs are available for the hearing-impaired. Almost all services are just inside the main entrance.

UNIVERSAL STUDIOS FLORIDA ATTRACTIONS

Animal Actors on Location! (Universal Express) ★★★½

APPEAL BY AGE	PRESCHOOL ★★★★	GRADE SCHOOL ★★★★½	TEENS ★★★★
YOUNG ADULTS ★★★½	OVER 30 ★★★★		SENIORS ★★★★

What it is Animal tricks and comedy show. **Scope and scale** Major attraction. **Fright potential** Not frightening in any respect. **Bottleneck rating** 4. **When to go** After you've experienced all rides. **Comment** Cute li'l critters. **Duration of show** 20 minutes. **Probable waiting time** 25 minutes.

This show integrates video segments with live sketches, jokes, and animal tricks performed on stage. Live animals, some of which are veterans of television and movies (and many of which were rescued from shelters), take part, and kids are invited to participate. Sit in the center of the stadium about halfway up for the best chance to be selected. Check the daily entertainment schedule for showtimes.

Successful touring of Universal Studios with young children is absolutely possible, and *Animal Actors on Location!* is a must-see!

Liliane

Curious George Goes to Town   ★★★

What it is Interactive playground. **Scope and scale** Minor attraction. **Fright potential** Not frightening in any respect. **Bottleneck rating** 1. **When to go** Anytime. **Comments** You will get soaked. **Probable waiting time** None.

Wet

Preschoolers won't want to leave this interactive water-play area, themed to the hometown of Curious George, the lovable monkey from the children's book series. In addition to spigots, pipes, and spray guns, two giant roof-mounted buckets periodically dump *a 1,000 gallons* of water on unsuspecting visitors below. When you hear the sound of a bell, run—it means that one of the buckets is about to tip over. Be sure to bring a change of clothes, as it will be almost impossible to stay dry. Kids who want to stay dry can mess around in the foam-ball playground equipped with chutes, tubes, and ball blasters. The creatively designed playground is perfect for letting off steam and cooling off on a hot summer day.

Have the kids wear a swimsuit under their clothes so they can enjoy the water features. Simpler still, let the 4-and-unders frolic in their underwear (bring an extra pair).

Liliane

A Day in the Park with Barney (Universal Express) ★★★

What it is Live character stage show. **Scope and scale** Major children's attraction. **Fright potential** Toddlers may balk at Barney's size. **Bottleneck rating** 4. **When to go** Anytime. **Comment** Great hit with preschoolers. **Duration of show** 20 minutes, plus 5-minute preshow and character greeting. **Probable waiting time** 15 minutes.

Barney, the cuddly purple dinosaur of public-television fame, leads a sing-along with the help of the audience and sidekicks Baby Bop and B.J. A short preshow gets the kids lathered up before they enter Barney's Park (the theater). Interesting theatrical effects include wind, falling leaves, clouds and stars in the simulated sky, and snow. After the show, Barney poses for photos with parents and children inside the theater or in the indoor playground at the theater exit.

I love you, you love me . . . this show should be a top priority if you have little ones who like Barney.

Liliane

I loved this show. All the characters were so friendly, and we all sang together. It was great to meet and spend time with Barney when the show was done.

Felicity

continued on page 414

Universal Studios Florida

Attractions

1. *Animal Actors on Location!* UX
2. Curious George Goes to Town
3. *A Day in the Park with Barney* UX
4. Despicable Me Minion Mayhem UX
5. E.T. Adventure UX
6. Fast & Furious: Supercharged UX VL
7. *Fear Factor Live (seasonal)* UX
8. Fievel's Playland
9. Harry Potter and the Escape from Gringotts UX ☑
10. Hogwarts Express: King's Cross Station UX ☑
11. Hollywood Rip Ride Rockit UX
12. Kang & Kodos' Twirl 'n' Hurl UX
13. Men in Black Alien Attack UX ☑
14. Ollivanders
15. Race Through New York Starring Jimmy Fallon UX VL ☑
16. Revenge of the Mummy UX ☑
17. *Shrek 4-D* UX
18. The Simpsons Ride UX ☑
19. Transformers: The Ride–3-D UX ☑
20. *Universal Orlando's Horror Make-Up Show* UX ☑

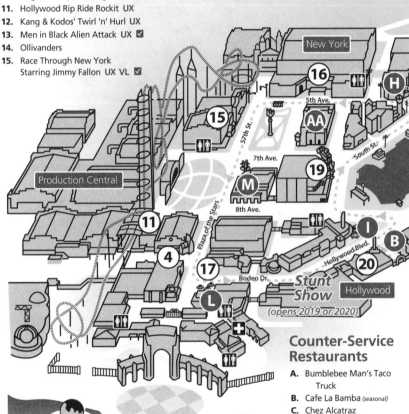

Counter-Service Restaurants

A. Bumblebee Man's Taco Truck
B. Cafe La Bamba *(seasonal)*
C. Chez Alcatraz
D. Duff Brewery
E. Fast Food Boulevard 👍

21. *Universal Orlando's Cinematic Celebration (seasonal)*

22. Woody Woodpacker's Nuthouse Coaster UX

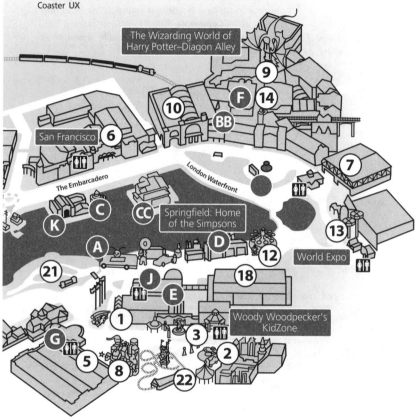

The Wizarding World of Harry Potter–Diagon Alley

9

F **14**

10

BB

San Francisco **6**

7

The Embarcadero

London Waterfront

K

C

CC

Springfield: Home of the Simpsons

13

A

D

12

World Expo

21

J

18

E

1

3

Woody Woodpecker's KidZone

2

G

5

8

22

Table-Service Restaurants

F. Florean Fortescue's Ice-Cream Parlour 👍

G. KidZone Pizza Company *(seasonal)*

H. Louie's Italian Restaurant

I. Mel's Drive-In

J. Moe's Tavern

K. Richter's Burger Co.

L. Today Cafe

M. Universal Studios' Classic Monsters Cafe

AA. Finnegan's Bar & Grill

BB. Leaky Cauldron (counter service) 👍

CC. Lombard's Seafood Grille

UX Attraction Offers Universal Express   **VL** Virtual Line   ✚ First Aid Station   🚻 Restrooms

👍 Recommended Dining   ☑ Not to Be Missed   ⋯ Parade Route

continued from page 411

Despicable Me Minion Mayhem
(Universal Express) ★★★★

APPEAL BY AGE **PRESCHOOL** ★★ **GRADE SCHOOL** ★★★★½ **TEENS** ★★★★
YOUNG ADULTS ★★★★½ **OVER 30** ★★★★ **SENIORS** ★★★

What it is Motion simulator 3-D ride. **Scope and scale** Major attraction. **Fright potential** Ride is wild and jerky but not frightening. **Bottleneck rating** 10. **When to go** First hour after park opening or after 5 p.m. **Comments** Expect long waits in line. Great fun. **Duration of ride** 5 minutes. **Average wait in line per 100 people ahead of you** 7 minutes; assumes all simulators in use. **Loading speed** Moderate.

Rough Queasy

Despicable Me Minion Mayhem involves high-tech motion simulators moving and reacting in sync with a cartoon projected on an IMAX-like screen. The story combines elements from the animated movie *Despicable Me,* starring Gru, the archvillain, along with his adopted daughters and his diminutive yellow Minions. During the queue and preshow, you visit Gru's house and are then ushered into his lab, where you're turned into a Minion. Guests disembark the ride into a disco party with a Minion meet and greet before exiting through the obligatory gift shop.

If you're on hand at park opening and you ride Despicable Me first, you'll have a short wait; however, you'll set yourself up for a long wait at nearby Hollywood Rip Ride Rockit. If the coaster is a priority for you, ride it first and then return to Despicable Me immediately afterward. If, by that time, the wait is intolerable, try again in the late afternoon. Stationary seating is available for those prone to motion sickness and for children less than 40 inches tall.

This is an amazing ride, but the queue is long and boring.

Felicity

E.T. Adventure *(Universal Express)* ★★★½

APPEAL BY AGE **PRESCHOOL** ★★★★ **GRADE SCHOOL** ★★★★ **TEENS** ★★★
YOUNG ADULTS ★★★ **OVER 30** ★★★½ **SENIORS** ★★★★

Thumbs Up for the Whole Family

What it is Indoor adventure ride based on the movie *E.T.* **Scope and scale** Major attraction. **Fright potential** Too intense for some preschoolers. **Bottleneck rating** 8. **When to go** During the first 90 minutes the park is open. **Comments** Must be 34" tall to ride. A happy reunion. **Duration of ride** 4½ minutes. **Average wait in line per 100 people ahead of you** 5 minutes. **Loading speed** Moderate.

Guests aboard a bicycle-like conveyance escape with E.T. from earthly law enforcement officials and then journey to his home planet. The attraction is similar to Peter Pan's Flight at the Magic Kingdom but is longer and has more elaborate special effects. Make sure you give the attendant your name—we recommend you just state your name; don't try to spell it—and relish the end of the ride when E.T. personalizes his goodbye message. Lines build quickly after 10 a.m., and waits can be an hour on busy days. Ride in the morning or late afternoon.

Make sure to give the cast member your name when you enter the ride, so you can hear E.T. telling you goodbye at the end of the ride.

Very cute. Liliane wants to phone home . . .

Isabelle

Movie Tip

E.T. Adventure is based on Steven Spielberg's film E.T.: The Extra-Terrestrial—*a great family movie that won four Oscars in 1982.*

Liliane

Fast & Furious: Supercharged (Universal Express) ★★★

APPEAL BY AGE PRESCHOOL ★ GRADE SCHOOL ★★★ TEENS ★★★
YOUNG ADULTS ★★★ OVER 30 ★★ SENIORS ★★★

What it is Car chase 3-D motion simulator. **Scope and scale** Headliner. **Fright potential** Simulated street-racing action with loud noises may frighten young children. **Bottleneck rating** 4. **When to go** After experiencing the other headliners. **Comment** Must be 40″ tall to ride. **Duration of ride** 5 minutes. **Average wait in line per 100 people ahead of you** 3 minutes. **Loading speed** Fast.

Guests enter the attraction through the distressed facade of San Francisco's historic Oriental Warehouse, which was erected on the site of the park's former *Beetlejuice* stage show. The Supercharged experience starts in the elaborate queue, an industrial warehouse where you can check out some of the high-performance automobiles seen in the films.

In two preshows, live performers interact with prerecorded clips of Mia (Jordana Brewster) and Tej (Chris "Ludacris" Bridges) to establish the backstory for anyone who hasn't yet seen all—or any—of the eight (and counting) *Furious* films.

After boarding specially designed tramlike party buses, you're taken to an underground club, where a postrace rave party is in full swing until the feds crash the party, searching for a crucial crime witness hiding among the guests. Series stars Dominic "Dom" Toretto (Vin Diesel), Luke Hobbs (Dwayne Johnson), Letty Ortiz (Michelle Rodriguez), and Roman Pearce (Tyrese Gibson) appear in holographic form to rescue you from Owen Shaw (Luke Evans), the bad guy from *Fast & Furious 6*. In the attraction's climax, a 360-degree projection tunnel with hydraulic platforms, 400-foot-long screens, and 4K projectors makes it appear as if your ride vehicle is in the midst of a high-stakes car chase, speeding at 100-plus miles per hour through a West Coast urban jungle. The best views are from the center seats in the first bus; stay to the left when the queue splits before the loading dock.

Supercharged periodically offers a free Virtual Line system, which lets you select your ride time using the Universal Orlando mobile app as soon as you enter the park; you can also grab a paper ticket from the ride's kiosks immediately after hitting Despicable Me. You will only save time if the standby wait is more than 30 minutes. Standard standby, Universal Express, and single-rider lines are also available.

Fear Factor Live (Universal Express; seasonal) ★★½

APPEAL BY AGE PRESCHOOL ★ GRADE SCHOOL ★★★★ TEENS ★★
YOUNG ADULTS ★★★ OVER 30 ★★★★ SENIORS ★★

What it is Live version of the gross-out-stunt TV show. **Scope and scale** Headliner. **Fright potential** The stuff of nightmares. **Bottleneck rating** 6. **When to go** Three to five shows daily; crowds are smallest at the first and second-to-last shows. **Comment** *Ewwww*. **Duration of show** 30 minutes. **Probable waiting time** 25 minutes.

Fear Factor Live is a stage version of the stomach-turning reality show that ran on NBC 2001–2006 and again 2011–2012. Six volunteers compete for one prize (a package that contains Universal goodies ranging from park tickets to T-shirts) by doing dumb and yucky things, such as swimming with eels and eating bugs. The show is really payback for adults; adolescents will enjoy watching Mom squirm during the icky parts. For children age 8 and under, *Fear Factor Live* is nightmare material. Whether you participate or simply watch, this show will keep your innards in an uproar.

Fievel's Playland ★★★

What it is Children's play area with waterslide. **Scope and scale** Minor attraction. **Fright potential** Not frightening in any respect. **Bottleneck rating** 1. **When to go** Anytime. **Comment** A much-needed attraction for preschoolers. **Probable waiting time** 20–30 minutes for the waterslide; otherwise, no waiting. **Loading speed** Slow for the waterslide.

> Fievel's Playland is another must for a successful visit to Universal Studios with small children. The playground is themed after the 1991 Steven Spielberg–produced movie *Fievel Goes West*. Young children love to identify with the tales of Fievel Mousekewitz.
>
> Liliane

This is a great playground that features ordinary household items reproduced on a giant scale, seen as a mouse would experience them. Preschoolers and grade-schoolers can climb nets, walk through a huge boot, splash in a sardine-can fountain, seesaw on huge spoons, and climb onto a cow skull. Most of the playground is reserved for preschoolers, but a combination waterslide and raft ride is open to all ages. There's almost no waiting in line here, and you can stay as long as you want. Younger children love the oversize items, and there's enough to keep teens and adults busy while little ones cut loose. The waterslide–raft ride is extremely slow-loading and carries only 300 riders per hour. With an average wait of 20–30 minutes, we don't think the 16-second ride is worth the trouble, and, yes, you *will* get soaked.

Hollywood Rip Ride Rockit *(Universal Express)* ★★★★

What it is Super-high-tech roller coaster. **Scope and scale** Headliner. **Fright potential** Frightening for all ages. **Bottleneck rating** 9. **When to go** Immediately after park opening. **Comments** Expect long waits in line; must be 51″ tall to ride. Items too large to be secured in a pocket must be placed in lockers near the ride. Woo-hoo! (and ouch!). **Duration of ride** 2½ minutes. **Average wait in line per 100 people ahead of you** 3–5 minutes. **Loading speed** Moderate.

Hollywood Rip Ride Rockit has some features that we've never seen before. Let's start with the basics: Rip Ride Rockit is a sit-down X-Car coaster that runs on a 3,800-foot steel track, with a maximum height of 167 feet and a top speed of 65 miles per hour. X-Car vehicles are more maneuverable than most other kinds and use less restrictive restraints, making for an exhilarating ride.

You ascend—vertically—at 11 feet per second to crest the 17-story-tall first hill, the second-highest point reached by any roller coaster in Orlando (Mako at SeaWorld is higher). The drop is almost vertical, too, and launches you into Double Take, a loop inversion in which you begin on the inside of the loop, twist to the outside at the top (so you're upright), and then twist back inside the loop for the descent. Double Take stands 136 feet tall, and its loop is 103 feet in diameter at its widest point. You next hurl (not that hurl—it comes later) into a stretch of track shaped like a musical treble clef. As on Double Take, the track configuration on Treble Clef is a first. A man from Belgium, Wisconsin, warns:

I've ridden many roller coasters, including some over 400 feet tall and with speeds in excess of 120 mph, yet I've never ridden one as painful and as rough as Rip Ride Rockit. With the beating my head and neck took, I'll never ride it again.

The ride starts in the Production Central area; weaves into the New York area near Race Through New York, popping out over the heads of guests in the square below; and then storms out and over the lagoon separating Universal Studios from CityWalk. Each row is outfitted with color-changing LEDs and high-end audio and video technology. Like the Rock 'n' Roller Coaster at Disney's Hollywood Studios, this coaster features a musical soundtrack. With Rip Ride Rockit, however, you can choose the genre of music you want to hear as you ride: classic rock, country, disco, pop, or rap.

After the ride, Universal flogs a digital-video "rip" of your ride, complete with the soundtrack you chose, that you can upload to YouTube, Facebook, and the like. Your only chance to ride without a long wait is to be one of the first to enter the park when it opens.

The incentive for me to try out this thingy has not been invented. Therefore, Bob, stop asking me to ride the monster. The answer is NO.

Liliane, I'm still half-deaf from the last roller coaster I rode with you.

Kang & Kodos' Twirl 'n' Hurl   ★★★

**APPEAL BY AGE   PRESCHOOL ★★★★   GRADE SCHOOL ★★★★½   TEENS ★★★
YOUNG ADULTS ★★★½   OVER 30 ★★★   SENIORS ★★★**

What it is Spinner ride. **Scope and scale** Minor attraction. **Fright potential** Like Dumbo, only louder. **Bottleneck rating** 8. **When to go** After The Simpsons Ride. **Comments** Rarely has a long wait. The world's wittiest spinner. **Duration of ride** 1½ minutes. **Average wait in line per 100 people ahead of you** 21 minutes. **Loading speed** Slow.

The Twirl 'n' Hurl is primarily eye candy for the Springfield section of the park (where the Simpsons live). Think of it as Dumbo with Bart's sense of humor: Kang and Kodos are tentacled aliens who hold pictures of Simpson characters; make the characters speak and spin by steering your craft to the proper altitude. All the while Kang (loudly) exhorts you to destroy Springfield and makes insulting comments about humans. Preschoolers enjoy the ride, while older kids crack up over the snarky narration.

Men in Black Alien Attack *(Universal Express)*   ★★★★½

**APPEAL BY AGE   PRESCHOOL ★★   GRADE SCHOOL ★★★★   TEENS ★★★★
YOUNG ADULTS ★★★★   OVER 30 ★★★★   SENIORS ★★★½**

What it is Interactive dark thrill ride. **Scope and scale** Super-headliner. **Fright potential** Dark and intense; frightens many children age 10 and under. **Bottleneck rating** 9. **When to go** During the first 2 hours the park is open, or anytime using the single-rider line. **Comments** Must be 42" tall to ride. Switching-off option (see page 248). Items too large to be secured in a pocket must be placed in lockers near the ride. Buzz Lightyear's Space Ranger Spin on steroids; not to be missed. **Duration of ride** 2½ minutes. **Average wait in line per 100 people ahead of you** 5 minutes. **Loading speed** Moderate-fast.

Based on the movie of the same name, the story line has you volunteering as a Men in Black (MIB) trainee. After an introduction warning that aliens "live among us" and articulating MIB's mission to round them up, Zed expands on the finer points of alien spotting and familiarizes you with your training vehicle and your weapon, an alien zapper. Following this, you load up and are dispatched on an innocuous training mission that immediately deteriorates into a situation where only you are in a position to prevent aliens from taking over the universe.

Now, if you saw the movie, you understand that the aliens are mostly giant exotic bugs and cockroaches and that zapping the aliens makes them explode into myriad gooey body parts. Thus, the meat of the ride (no pun intended) consists of careening around Manhattan and shooting aliens. Each of the 120 or so alien figures has sensors that activate special effects and respond to your zapper. Aim for the eyes and keep shooting until the aliens' eyes turn red. Targets above you score the most points; look for aliens behind second-story windows. Avoid a long wait and ride during the first 2 hours the park is open, or try the single-rider line if you don't mind splitting your group. You can reride by following the signs for the child swap at the top of the exit stairs. For a special treat, ask an attendant for a free immigration tour of the queue.

Race Through New York Starring Jimmy Fallon
(Universal Express) ★★★½

APPEAL BY AGE	PRESCHOOL ★	GRADE SCHOOL ★★★½	TEENS ★★★★½
YOUNG ADULTS ★★★★	OVER 30 ★★★★½	SENIORS ★★★★	

What it is Comedic 3-D simulator ride. **Scope and scale** Headliner. **Fright potential** Comparable to Despicable Me and a little less wild than the Simpsons Ride but not frightening. **Bottleneck rating** 2. **When to go** According to your Virtual Line return time. **Comment** Must be 40" tall to ride. **Duration of ride** 4 minutes. **Average wait in line per 100 people ahead of you** 5 minutes. **Loading speed** Moderate.

The queue-less experience and the preshow areas get a lot of points. All guests, except those with Express Passes, must first be assigned a virtual-line reservation time via Universal's smartphone app or an automated kiosk. Once your appointed time arrives, return to the ride entrance. Upon entering the building, you are transported to a replica of NBC's historic New York City offices at 30 Rockefeller Center.

You will be directed to the first lobby of the NBC offices. An NBC page will hand you a color-coded card. Hold on to it, and take time to enjoy the artifacts in this first area, as *The Tonight Show* pays tribute to former hosts Steve Allen, Jack Paar, Johnny Carson, Jay Leno, and Conan O'Brien in several displays. When the lobby lights change to the color of your card, that is your cue to move to the building's next floor. Here you await your ride in a fancy lounge, with couches and touch screen tables with video games from the show.

The main attractions, however, are the live appearances by the Ragtime Gals barbershop quintet and Hashtag the Panda. Enjoy the musical performances until it's your time to ride, and get your picture taken with Hashtag the Panda.

When the color of the lights changes once more, it's time for you to make your way to Jimmy Fallon's studio. Here, the star of the show will share safety guidelines before you enter a theater with a large screen. Next, after donning 3-D glasses, you'll be racing against Jimmy Fallon. Starting at the studio of *The Tonight Show,* the race takes you through the streets of New York and eventually to the moon. Fans create wind effects, and there are faint pizza smells, in addition to the obligatory water spray.

The ride is silly and fun, and it features many characters from *The Tonight Show.* It helps if you know the show—and appreciate Jimmy's humor—but it isn't a must. We like the ride but worry that Universal is getting too attached to screens and 3-D rides.

Revenge of the Mummy *(Universal Express)* ★★★★½

APPEAL BY AGE   PRESCHOOL ★   GRADE SCHOOL ★ ★ ★   TEENS ★ ★ ★ ★ ½
YOUNG ADULTS ★ ★ ★ ★ ½   OVER 30 ★ ★ ★ ★ ½   SENIORS ★ ★ ★ ★

What it is Combination dark ride and roller coaster. **Scope and scale** Super-headliner. **Fright potential** Scary for all ages. **Bottleneck rating** 8. **When to go** The first hour the park is open or after 6 p.m. **Comments** Must be 48″ tall to ride. Switching-off option (see page 248). Items too large to be secured in a pocket must be placed in lockers near the ride. Killer! **Duration of ride** 4 minutes. **Average wait in line per 100 people ahead of you** 7 minutes. **Loading speed** Moderate.

Dark   Queasy   Scary

Revenge of the Mummy is an indoor dark ride based on the *Mummy* flicks, where guests fight off "deadly curses and vengeful creatures" while flying through Egyptian tombs and other spooky places on a high-tech roller coaster. The special effects—including video effects, animatronics, lighting, and enough fire-spewing gas vents to rotisserie a chicken—are aging but still pretty good. The ride begins slowly, passing through various chambers, including one where flesh-eating scarab beetles descend on you. Suddenly your vehicle stops, then drops backward and rotates. Next thing you know, you're shot at high speed up the first hill of the roller coaster. Though it's a wild ride by anyone's definition, the emphasis remains as much on the visuals, robotics, and special effects as on the ride itself. Note that the queue contains enough scary stuff to frighten small children all on its own. Try to ride during the first hour the park is open. If lines are long, the single-rider line is often more expedient than using Universal Express.

The mummy scared the willies out of me. This one is definitely not for young children.

Liliane

Shrek 4-D (Universal Express) ★★★½

APPEAL BY AGE   PRESCHOOL ★ ★ ★   GRADE SCHOOL ★ ★ ★ ★   TEENS ★ ★ ★ ½
YOUNG ADULTS ★ ★ ★ ½   OVER 30 ★ ★ ★ ½   SENIORS ★ ★ ★ ½

What it is 3-D movie. **Scope and scale** Headliner. **Fright potential** Loud but not frightening. Preshow area is a little macabre. **Bottleneck rating** 7. **When to go** The first hour the park is open or after 4 p.m. **Comment** Warm, fuzzy mayhem. **Duration of show** 20 minutes. **Probable waiting time** 16 minutes.

The preshow presents the villain from the movie, Lord Farquaad, as he appears on various screens to describe his posthumous plan to reclaim his lost bride, Princess Fiona, who married Shrek. The plan is posthumous because Lord Farquaad ostensibly died in the movie, and it's his ghost making the plans, but never mind. Guests then move into the main theater, don their 3-D glasses, and recline in seats equipped with "tactile transducers" and "pneumatic air propulsion and water spray nodules capable of both vertical and horizontal motion." As the 3-D film plays, guests are also subjected to smells relevant to the on-screen action (oh boy).

This attraction is a real winner. It's irreverent, frantic, laugh-out-loud funny, and iconoclastic. Concerning the last, the film takes a good poke at Disney, with Pinocchio, the Three Little Pigs, and Tinker Bell (among others) all sucked into the mayhem. In contrast to Disney's *It's Tough to be a Bug!*, *Shrek 4-D* doesn't generally frighten children under age 7. Stationary seating is available on request.

Take off the 3-D glasses if it is all too scary, and consider earplugs. Did you know that *Shrek* in German means "the scare"?

Liliane

The Simpsons Ride *(Universal Express)* ★★★★

APPEAL BY AGE   PRESCHOOL ★   GRADE SCHOOL ★★★★   TEENS ★★★★
YOUNG ADULTS ★★★½   OVER 30 ★★★   SENIORS ★★½

What it is Mega-simulator ride. **Scope and scale** Super-headliner. **Fright potential** Visuals not scary but very wild ride. **Bottleneck rating** 9. **When to go** First thing after park opening. **Comments** Must be 40″ tall to ride; not recommended for pregnant women or people prone to motion sickness. Switching-off option (see page 248). **Duration of ride** 4⅓ minutes. **Average wait in line per 100 people ahead of you** 5 minutes. **Loading speed** Moderate.

Rough   Queasy

This attraction is a simulator ride similar to Star Tours at Disney's Hollywood Studios and Despicable Me Minion Mayhem at USF, but with a larger screen more like that of Soarin' at Epcot.

The attraction takes a wild and humorous poke at thrill rides, dark rides, and live shows. Two preshows involve *Simpsons* characters speaking sequentially on different video screens in the queue; their comments help define the characters for guests who are unfamiliar with the TV show. The story line has the conniving Sideshow Bob secretly arriving at Krustyland amusement park and plotting his revenge on Krusty the Clown and Bart who, in a past *Simpsons* episode, revealed that Sideshow Bob had committed a crime for which he'd framed Krusty. Sideshow Bob gets even by making things go wrong with the attractions that the Simpsons (and you) are riding.

Like the show on which it's based, The Simpsons Ride definitely has an edge—and more than a few wild hairs. There will be jokes and visuals that you'll get but will fly over your children's heads—and most assuredly vice versa. You can expect large crowds all day. Some parents may find the humor a little too coarse for younger children.

Transformers: The Ride 3-D ★★★★★

APPEAL BY AGE   PRESCHOOL ★   GRADE SCHOOL ★★★★   TEENS ★★★★½
YOUNG ADULTS ★★★★½   OVER 30 ★★★★   SENIORS ★★½

What it is Multisensory 3-D dark ride. **Scope and scale** Super-headliner. **Fright potential** Loud, intense, and violent; prepare 7-and-unders by previewing a movie trailer before you visit. **Bottleneck rating** 10. **When to go** The first 30 minutes the park is open or after 4 p.m. **Comments** Must be 40″ tall to ride; children 40″–48″ must be accompanied by a rider 14 years or older. **Duration of ride** 4½ minutes. **Average wait in line per 100 people ahead of you** 4½ minutes. **Loading speed** Moderate–fast.

Dark   Rough   Loud   Queasy   Scary

Hasbro's Transformers—those toy robots from the 1980s that

you turned and twisted into trucks and planes—have been, er, transformed into director Michael Bay's blockbuster movie franchise and then to a theme park attraction befitting their pop-culture idols. Recruits to this cybertronic war enlist by entering the N.E.S.T. Base (headquarters of the heroic Autobots and their human allies). Inside, in the queue, video monitors catch you up on the backstory. Basically, the Decepticon baddies are after the AllSpark, source of cybernetic sentience. Your job is to safeguard the shard. The vastly annoying top villain, Megatron, and his pals Starscream and Devastator threaten the mission, but don't worry—you have Sideswipe and Bumblebee on the bench to back you up.

Transformers: The Ride 3-D is a ride you can enjoy even if you don't know the story or haven't seen the movies.

Liliane

The plot amounts to little more than a giant game of keep-away, and the uninitiated will likely be unable to tell one meteoric mass of metal from another, but you'll be too dazzled by the debris whizzing by to notice. The ride's mix of detailed set pieces and high-tech video projections brings these colossi to life in one very intense and immersive thrill ride.

This ride draws crowds—your only solace is that The Wizarding World of Harry Potter–Diagon Alley draws even larger throngs. Follow our touring plan to minimize waits. The single-rider line will get you on board faster but will close if it becomes backed up. Finally, it's hard to focus on the fast-moving imagery from the front row; center seats in the second and third rows provide the best perspective.

Transformer characters Optimus Prime, Bumblebee, and Megatron appear regularly near the ride.

Universal Orlando's Horror Make-Up Show
(Universal Express) ★★★★½

APPEAL BY AGE   PRESCHOOL ★½   GRADE SCHOOL ★★★½   TEENS ★★★½
YOUNG ADULTS ★★★★½   OVER 30 ★★★★   SENIORS ★★★★½

What it is Theater presentation on the art of makeup. **Scope and scale** Major attraction. **Fright potential** Gory but not frightening; may upset young children. **Bottleneck rating** 6. **When to go** After you've experienced all rides. **Comment** A gory knee-slapper. **Duration of show** 25 minutes. **Probable waiting time** 20 minutes.

Thumbs Up for the Whole Family

Lively, well-paced look at how makeup artists create film monsters, realistic wounds, severed limbs, and other unmentionables. Exceeding most guests' expectations, the *Horror Make-Up Show* is the sleeper attraction at Universal. Its humor and tongue-in-cheek style transcend the gruesome effects, and most folks (including preschoolers) take the blood and guts in stride. It usually isn't too hard to get into.

Woody Woodpecker's Nuthouse Coaster
(Universal Express) ★★½

APPEAL BY AGE   PRESCHOOL ★★★★½   GRADE SCHOOL ★★★★½   TEENS ★★½
YOUNG ADULTS —   OVER 30 —   SENIORS —

What it is Kid's roller coaster. **Scope and scale** Minor attraction. **Fright potential** Not frightening in any respect. **Bottleneck rating** 5. **When to go** Anytime. **Comment** Must be 36″ tall. **Duration of ride** About a minute. **Average wait in line per 100 people ahead of you** 8 minutes. **Loading speed** *Slooow.*

The child-size roller coaster is small enough for kids, though its moderate speed might unnerve some smaller children. The family-friendly coaster is very similar to Flight of the Hippogriff. The ride has no loops, inversions, nor rolls. Built in 1999, it was Universal Orlando's first roller coaster.

THE WIZARDING WORLD OF HARRY POTTER–DIAGON ALLEY

SECRETED BEHIND A LONDON STREET SCENE that features **Grimmauld Place** and **Wyndham's Theatre, Diagon Alley** is accessed through a secluded entrance in the middle of the facade. As in the books and films, the unmarked portal is concealed within a magical brick wall that's ordinarily reserved for wizards and the like. (Unfortunately, the wall doesn't actually move, due to safety concerns.) The endless queue of Muggles (plain old humans) in shorts and flip-flops will leave little doubt where that entryway is.

LILIANE I want to sneak into the Wizarding World through the Leaky Cauldron pub. OK, I'll take the Hogwarts Express.

When Early Park Admission is offered, USF admits eligible on-site resort guests 1 hour before the general public, with the turnstiles opening up to 90 minutes before the official opening time. Arrive at least 30 minutes before early entry starts; during peak season, we recommend showing up on the very first boat or bus from your hotel. If you're a day guest visiting on an Early Park Admission day, Diagon Alley will already be packed when you arrive. Even when Early Park Admission isn't offered, all guests may enter Diagon Alley from the front gates up to 30 minutes before park opening, and hotel guests in IOA will arrive via Hogwarts Express a little after that, though Harry Potter and the Escape from Gringotts doesn't begin operating until close to official opening time.

WIZARDING WORLD–DIAGON ALLEY ATTRACTIONS

Harry Potter and the Escape from Gringotts
(Universal Express) ★★★★★

**APPEAL BY AGE   PRESCHOOL ★½   GRADE SCHOOL ★★★★   TEENS ★★★★½
YOUNG ADULTS ★★★★★   OVER 30 ★★★★½   SENIORS ★★★★**

What it is Super-high-tech 3-D dark ride with roller coaster elements. **Scope and scale** Super-headliner. **Fright potential** All scary elements are heaped on this one, though the ride itself is less intense than Forbidden Journey at IOA. **Bottleneck rating** 10+. **When to go** Immediately after park opening or just before closing. **Comments** Must be 42″ tall to ride. Items too large to be secured in a pocket must be placed in lockers near the ride. Not to be missed. **Duration of ride** 4½ minutes. **Average wait in line per 100 people ahead of you** 4 minutes. **Loading speed** Moderate–fast.

Harry Potter and the Escape from Gringotts incorporates a substantial part of the overall experience into its elaborate queue, which even nonriders should experience. Owned and operated by goblins, Gringotts is the Federal Reserve of the wizarding economy. You enter through the bank's lobby, where you're critically appraised by glowering animatronic goblins. Your path takes you to a "security checkpoint," where your photo will be taken (to be purchased afterward as an identity lanyard in the gift shop) and past animated newspapers and office windows where the scenario is set up.

> Even people who don't love roller coasters will enjoy
> Harry Potter and the Escape from Gringotts.
> Brendan

Unlike Forbidden Journey, Gringotts doesn't rush you through its queue, but rather allows you to experience two full preshows before approaching the ride vehicles. The first show takes you into the goblin bank, and then you're off for a convincing simulated 9-mile plunge into the earth aboard an "elevator" with a bouncing floor and ceiling projections. All this is before you pick up your 3-D goggles and board your ride.

Once on board, you enter the bank at the exact moment that Harry, Ron, Hermione, and Griphook have arrived to liberate the Hufflepuff Cup Horcrux from Bellatrix Lestrange's vault. Familiar film moments featuring the vaults' guardian dragon play out in the ride's background as Bellatrix and Voldemort appear to menace you with snakes and sinister spells, whereupon the heroic trio pauses its quest to save your hapless posteriors.

As far as physical thrills go, Gringotts falls somewhere between Disney's Seven Dwarfs Mine Train and Space Mountain, with only one short (albeit unique) drop and no upside-down flips.

The ride feels noticeably different depending on the row you're seated in. The front row is closest to the action and has the scariest view of the drop; 3-D effects look better farther back. The sixth row gets the most coaster action, especially from the initial fall, but the screens are slightly distorted. The far right seat in row four is the sweet spot.

> I was so surprised that the queue was just like in the movie.
> I like this a lot. The ride was scary at times.
> Felicity

Hogwarts Express *(Universal Express)* ★★★★½

**APPEAL BY AGE   PRESCHOOL ★★★★   GRADE SCHOOL ★★★★½   TEENS ★★★★
YOUNG ADULTS ★★★★½   OVER 30 ★★★★½   SENIORS ★★★★★**

What it is Transportation attraction. **Scope and scale** Super-headliner. **Fright potential** Potter villains and spirit creatures menace the train. **Bottleneck rating** 10+. **When to go** Immediately after park opening. **Comments** Expect lengthy waits in line; Park-to-Park ticket required to ride. Not to be missed. **Duration of ride** 4 minutes. **Average wait in line per 100 people ahead of you** 7 minutes. **Loading speed** Moderate.

Diagon Alley at USF is connected to Hogsmeade at Islands of Adventure (IOA) by the Hogwarts Express, just as in the novels and films. The counterpart to Hogsmeade Station in IOA is USF's King's Cross Station, a landmark London train depot that has been re-created a few doors down from Diagon Alley's hidden entrance. (It's important to note that King's Cross has a separate entrance and exit from Diagon Alley: you can't go directly between them without crossing through the London Waterfront.)

The passage to Platform 9¾, from which Hogwarts students depart on their way to school, is concealed from Muggles by a seemingly solid brick wall, which you'll witness guests ahead of you dematerializing through. (Spoiler: The Pepper's Ghost effect creates a clever but congestion-prone photo op, but you experience only a dark corridor with whooshing sound effects when crossing over yourself.)

Once on the platform, you'll pass a pile of luggage before being assigned to one of the three train cars' seven compartments. The train itself looks exactly authentic to the *n*th degree, from the billowing steam to the brass fixtures and upholstery in your eight-passenger private cabin. Along your one-way Hogwarts Express journey, you'll see moving images projected beyond the windows of the car rather than the park's backstage areas, with the streets of London and the Scottish countryside rolling past outside your window. You experience a different presentation coming and going, and in addition to pastoral scenery, there are surprise appearances by secondary characters (Fred and George Weasley, Hagrid) and threats en route (bone-chilling Dementors, licorice spiders), augmented by sound effects in the cars.

Passengers will need a valid Park-to-Park ticket; you can upgrade your 1-Park Base Ticket at the station entrance. Disembarking passengers must enter the second park and, if desired, queue again for their return trip.

Park-to-Park ticket holders should make the train their second stop after Escape from Gringotts if going from Diagon Alley to Hogsmeade. Or, if Diagon Alley is your top priority of the day, enter IOA as early as possible and line up at the Hogsmeade Station for the train to London King's Cross. If the posted wait is 15 minutes or less, it's typically quicker to take the train than to walk to the other Wizarding World.

Ollivanders ★★★★

**APPEAL BY AGE PRESCHOOL ★★½ GRADE SCHOOL ★★★★½ TEENS ★★★★
YOUNG ADULTS ★★★★½ OVER 30 ★★★★½ SENIORS ★★★★½**

What it is Combination wizarding demonstration and shopping op. **Scope and scale** Major attraction. **Fright potential** Special effects may startle 6-and-unders. **Bottleneck rating** 10. **When to go** After riding Harry Potter and the Escape from Gringotts. **Comments** Audience stands. Enchanting. **Duration of presentation** 6 minutes. **Average waiting time in line per 100 people ahead of you** 18 minutes.

Ollivanders, located in Diagon Alley in the books and films, somehow sprouted a branch location in Hogsmeade at IOA (see page 403). In The Wizarding World–Diagon Alley, Ollivanders assumes its rightful place, with much larger digs. The shop has three separate choosing chambers, where wands choose a wizard (rather than the other way around), turning it from a popular curiosity into an actual attraction. As for the IOA location, it continues to operate. If your young 'un is selected to test-drive a wand, be forewarned that you'll have to buy it if you want to take it home.

Wearing wizard robes increases your kid's chance of being picked for the wand ceremony.

Liliane

Wizarding World Entertainment

Take a moment to spot Kreacher (the house elf regularly peers from a second-story window above 12 Grimmauld Place) and chat with the Knight Bus conductor and his Caribbean-accented shrunken head. Look down the alley to the rounded facade of **Gringotts Wizarding Bank,** where a 40-foot fire-breathing Ukrainian Ironbelly dragon (as seen in *Harry Potter and the Deathly Hallows: Part 2*) perches atop the dome.

To the right of Escape from Gringotts is **Carkitt Market,** a canopy-covered plaza where short live shows are staged every half hour or so. **Celestina Warbeck and the Banshees** (★★★★) showcases the singing sorceress swinging to jazzy tunes titled and inspired by J. K. Rowling herself, and **Tales of Beedle the Bard** (★★★½) recounts the Three Brothers fable from *Deathly Hallows* with puppets crafted by Michael Curry (*Festival of the Lion King, Finding Nemo—The Musical*).

Intersecting Diagon Alley near the Leaky Cauldron is **Knockturn Alley,** a labyrinth of twisting passageways where the Harry Potter bad guys hang out. A covered walk-through area with a projected sky creating perpetual night, it features spooky special effects in the faux shop windows (don't miss the creeping tattoos and crawling spiders).

The *Harry Potter*–themed Christmas events held at both Wizarding Worlds November 16, 2019–January 5, 2020, are an absolute must. Even Celestina Warbeck and the Banshees have a special yuletide program. Hearing her perform "My Baby Gave Me a Hippogriff for Christmas" is a hoot. Expect holiday decor and food adapted from the *Harry Potter* novels.

LIVE ENTERTAINMENT *at* UNIVERSAL STUDIOS

IN ADDITION TO THE SHOWS profiled earlier, Universal offers a wide range of street entertainment. Costumed comic-book and cartoon characters (Shrek, Donkey, SpongeBob SquarePants, and Scooby-Doo and the gang), along with movie star look-alikes, roam the park for photo ops. Meet characters like Homer, Bart, Marge, Lisa, and Maggie from *The Simpsons,* as well as the penguins of *Madagascar,* throughout the park. Optimus Prime, Bumblebee, and Megatron meet outside Transformers: The Ride 3-D. The "Character Zones" section in the handout park map provides times and places for musical acts and shows.

THE BLUES BROTHERS SHOW (★★★½) Held on the corner of the New York area, across from the lagoon, *The Blues Brothers Show* features

---

FAVORITE EATS AT UNIVERSAL STUDIOS

LAND | SERVICE LOCATION | FOOD SELECTIONS

PRODUCTION CENTRAL Classic Monsters Cafe | Chicken and rib combo, pizza, and brisket sandwich

NEW YORK Finnegan's Bar and Grill | Irish pub with fish-and-chips, frequently features live music | *Table service only* | **Louie's Italian Restaurant** | Pizza

SAN FRANCISCO Richter's Burger Co. | Burgers

THE WIZARDING WORLD OF HARRY POTTER–DIAGON ALLEY Leaky Cauldron | Bangers and mash, fish-and-chips, and cottage pie

SPRINGFIELD Fast Food Boulevard | Several eateries with food inspired by *The Simpsons* TV series. We love the tacos at **Bumblebee Man's Taco Truck.**

WOODY WOODPECKER'S KIDZONE KidZone Pizza Company | Pizza

HOLLYWOOD Mel's Drive-In | Old-fashioned root beer float, BLT, and burgers

Jake and Elwood performing a few of the hit songs from the classic 1980 movie musical, including "Soul Man" and "Sweet Home Chicago." The brothers are joined on stage by Jazz the saxophone player and his girlfriend, Mabel the waitress, who belts an Aretha Franklin cover to start the show. The concert is a great pick-me-up, and the short run time (12 minutes) keeps the energy high.

MARDI GRAS At Universal Studios this celebration lasts 50 nights! From early February through the end of March, the park brings a family-friendly version of the New Orleans celebration to Florida, where guests excitedly collect beads, which are distributed generously. Prior to the parade at the French Quarter Courtyard, guests can enjoy authentic New Orleans bands and amazing food, such as jambalaya, gumbo, and beignets. On select nights you can also enjoy free Mardi Gras concerts. The Little Jester's parade-viewing area, next to the now-closed *Terminator 2: 3-D* attraction, is reserved for families with kids. This section allows parents to exit the park speedily once the parade is over. Check out Liliane's review of the 2019 event at theunofficial guides.com/2019/03/17/mardi-gras-at-universal-orlando.

MACY'S HOLIDAY PARADE Once the legendary Macy's Thanksgiving Day Parade ends in New York City, many of the balloons and floats are sent to USF to become the star of the Universal Studios Christmas celebration. The parade, held daily, early December–January 1, features marching bands and, of course, an appearance by Santa himself. Check the park map for parade times, and find out more details in Liliane's report about the parade and other holiday events at Universal Orlando: theunofficialguides.com/2018/11/01/universal-orlando-3.

UNIVERSAL'S SUPERSTAR PARADE (★★★½) This Disney-like parade features dancers and performers, four large and elaborate floats inspired by cartoons, and a very mixed bag of street-prowling Universal characters. The parade stops twice for a highly choreographed ensemble number. Though impressive in its scope and coordination, the performance is well-nigh impossible to take in from any given viewing spot.

The parade, marked on our map on pages 412–413, begins at the Esoteric Pictures gate in Hollywood between *Universal Orlando's Horror Make-Up Show* and Cafe La Bamba, proceeds along 5th Avenue, heads toward the front of the park, and disappears backstage through the gate where it entered. The best viewing spots are along 5th Avenue, on the front steps of faux buildings in New York.

If you miss part of the parade in the New York area, you can scoot along the waterfront to Mel's Diner and catch it as it comes down Hollywood Boulevard. If, after watching the parade on the New York streets, you plan to leave the park, you can use the same route to access Hollywood Boulevard and the park exit before the parade arrives.

The same floats are trotted out individually at various times of day for mini-shows, such as a street party with photo opportunities in front of Mel's Drive-In, and character meet and greets. Check with cast members for specific times.

Universal Orlando's Cinematic Celebration (seasonal)
★★★★

APPEAL BY AGE   PRESCHOOL ★★½   GRADE SCHOOL ★★½   TEENS ★★
YOUNG ADULTS ★★½   OVER 30 ★★★   SENIORS ★★½

What it is Fireworks, dancing fountains, and movies. **Scope and scale** Major attraction. **Fright potential** Loud and intense with fireworks and some scary villains, but most young children like it. **Bottleneck rating** 9. **When to go** 1 show a day, usually at park closing. **Comment** Good effort. Movie trailers galore. **Duration of show** 19 minutes. **Probable waiting time** None.

The show, which takes place at the lagoon in the middle of the Studios, is the big nighttime event, designed to cap your day at the park. The presentation runs through clips and music from favorite movies, so be prepared to hear and see roaring dinosaurs from *Jurassic World,* feel the adrenaline rush of high-speed cars from *Fast & Furious,* and watch the mischievous antics of the Minions from *Despicable Me.* Little tykes might be intimidated by some of the clips, especially the giant dinosaurs.

Cinematic Celebration is a great way to end your day in the park. Try to claim a good spot 45 minutes ahead of time on peak attendance days, or 5–10 minutes prior to the show during slower seasons. Central Park, a three-tiered seating and viewing area, is located across the lagoon from San Francisco and has a fountain stage containing more than 100 jets, fog effects, and an underwater catwalk.

If you didn't manage to claim a spot in Central Park, try to see the show directly across the lagoon from Richter's Burger Co., where the sidewalk makes a small protrusion overlooking the water, or between Mel's Diner and Transformers.

UNIVERSAL STUDIOS FLORIDA TOURING PLANS

TOURING UNIVERSAL STUDIOS FLORIDA, including one meal and a visit to Diagon Alley, takes about 10–12 hours. Some theater attractions don't schedule performances until 11 a.m. or after. This means that early in the day, all park guests are concentrated among the limited number of attractions in operation.

As a postscript, you won't have to worry about any of this if you use our Universal Studios touring plan. We'll keep you one jump ahead of the crowd and make sure that any given attraction is running by the time you get there. The touring plans are described below. The actual touring plans are located on pages 502–504. Each plan includes a numbered map of the park to help you find your way around.

1-DAY TOURING PLAN This plan is for guests without Park-to-Park tickets and includes every recommended attraction at USF. If a ride or show is listed that you don't want to experience, skip that step and proceed to the next. Move quickly from attraction to attraction, and if possible, hold off on lunch until after experiencing at least six rides.

THE BEST OF UNIVERSAL ORLANDO IN 1 DAY   This touring plan is for guests with 1-Day Park-to-Park tickets who wish to see the highlights of USF and IOA in a single day. The plan uses Hogwarts Express to get from one park to the other and then back again; you can walk back to the first park for the return leg if the line is too long. The plan includes a table-service lunch at Mythos (make reservations online a few days before your visit) and dinner at the Leaky Cauldron; during holidays, you may need to substitute a quick-service snack for one or both meals to fit in all of the plan's attractions.

PART TWELVE

THE BEST
of the REST

The DISNEY WATER PARKS

WALT DISNEY WORLD has two swimming theme parks. **Typhoon Lagoon** is the most diverse Disney splash pad, while **Blizzard Beach** takes the prize for the most slides and most bizarre theme (a ski resort in meltdown). Blizzard Beach has the best slides, but Typhoon Lagoon has a surf pool where you can bodysurf. Both parks have excellent and elaborate themed areas for toddlers and preschoolers.

BOB During summer and holiday periods, Typhoon Lagoon and Blizzard Beach fill to capacity on weekdays and close their gates before 11 a.m.

Admission costs for each park start at $69 per day for adults and $63 per day for children (ages 3–9), plus tax. Seasonal tickets are $5 cheaper and available late September–mid-May. Florida residents may purchase a no-blackout-date annual pass granting them daily access to both water parks; prices for all ages are $139 plus tax. If you buy your Walt Disney World admission before leaving home and you're considering the **Park Hopper Plus** (PHP) add-on (see page 60), you may want to wait until you arrive and have some degree of certainty about the weather during your stay. You can add the PHP option at any Disney resort or Guest Relations window at the theme parks. This is true regardless of whether you purchased your tickets separately or as part of a package. Also note that if you're planning to visit only one theme park per day and you're planning only 1 day to visit a water park, buying separate water-park admission is almost always cheaper than buying the PHP add-on.

H2O Glow Nights, a special ticketed event, is held on select nights at Typhoon Lagoon late May–late August. The event takes place 8–11 p.m., with guests admitted to the park at 6 p.m. Tickets are $59 per person for adults and $54 per person for children ages 3–9, when purchased in advance (prices do not include tax).

• BLIZZARD BEACH •

ATTRACTION	HEIGHT REQUIREMENT	WHAT TO EXPECT
CHAIR LIFT UP MT. GUSHMORE	32″	Great ride even if you go up only for the view. When the park is packed, use the single-rider line.
CROSS COUNTRY CREEK	none	Lazy river circling the park; grab a tube.
DOWNHILL DOUBLE DIPPER	48″	Side-by-side tube-racing slides. At 25 miles per hour, the tube races through water curtains and free falls. It's a lot of fun but rough.
MELT-AWAY BAY	none	Wave pool with gentle, bobbing waves. The pool is great for younger swimmers.
RUNOFF RAPIDS	none	Three corkscrew tube slides to choose from. The center slide is for solo raft rides; the other two slides offer one-, two-, or three-person tubes. The dark, enclosed tube makes the ride feel as if you've been flushed down a toilet.
SKI PATROL TRAINING CAMP	60″ maximum for T-Bar	A place for preteens to train for the big rides
SLUSH GUSHER	48″	A 90-foot double-humped slide. Ladies, cling to those tops—all others hang on for your lives.
SNOW STORMERS	none	Three mat-slide flumes; down you go on your belly
SUMMIT PLUMMET	48″	A 120-foot free fall at 60 mph. This ride is very intense. Make sure your child knows what to expect. Being over 48 inches tall does not guarantee an enjoyable experience. If you think you'd enjoy washing out of a 12th-floor window during a heavy rain, then this slide is for you.
TEAMBOAT SPRINGS	none	1,200-foot whitewater group raft flume; wonderful ride for the whole family
TIKE'S PEAK	48″ and under only	Kid-size version of Blizzard Beach. This is the place for little ones.
TOBOGGAN RACERS	none	Eight-lane race course. You go down the flume on a mat. The ride is less intense than Snow Stormers.

Summit Plummet is a rough ride and can give you a bad skin chafing. It happened to my dad.

Brendan

Disney water parks allow one cooler per family or group, but no glass and no alcoholic beverages. As of 2019 guests are no longer permitted to bring loose or dry ice into the Disney parks. Bring reusable ice packs, or freeze water inside sealed bags or bottles, to keep your food and drinks cold. Both parks charge the following rental prices: towels are $2; lockers are $10 small, $15 large; life jackets are available at no cost. Strollers are welcome but unavailable for rent.

The best way to avoid standing in lines is to visit the water parks when they're not very crowded. We recommend going on a weekend, when most visitors are traveling, or on a Monday. While Disney once offered morning and evening Extra Magic Hours at its water parks, it's been several years since we last saw them on the operating schedule. It's Disney's prerogative to change its mind, however, especially during summer, so check the schedules online a few days before you go.

Just as at the theme parks, the key to a successful visit to the Disney water parks is to get up early, have breakfast, and arrive at the park 30 minutes before opening. Wear your bathing suit under shorts and a T-shirt so you don't have to bother with lockers or dressing rooms. Wear shoes—paths are relatively easy on bare feet, but there's a lot of

• TYPHOON LAGOON •

ATTRACTION	HEIGHT REQUIREMENT	WHAT TO EXPECT
BAY SLIDES	60" and under	A miniature, two-slide version of Storm Slides, specifically designed for small children. Kids splash down into a far corner of the surf pool.
CASTAWAY CREEK	none	Half-mile lazy river in a tropical setting. Wonderful!
CRUSH 'N' GUSHER	48"	Water roller coaster where you can choose from among three slides: Banana Blaster, Coconut Crusher, and Pineapple Plunger, ranging 410–420 feet long. This thriller leaves you wondering what exactly happened—if you make it down in one piece, that is. It's not for the faint of heart. If your kids are new to water-park rides, this is not the place to break them in, even if they're tall enough to ride.
GANG PLANK FALLS	none	Whitewater raft flume in a multiperson tube
HUMUNGA KOWABUNGA	48"	Speed slides that hit 30 mph. A five-story drop in the dark rattles the most courageous rider. Ladies should ride this in a one-piece swimsuit.
KEELHAUL FALLS	none	Fast whitewater ride in a single-person tube
KETCHAKIDDEE CREEK	48" and under only	Toddlers and preschoolers love this area reserved only for them. Say "splish splash" and have lots of fun.
MAYDAY FALLS	none	The name says it all. Wild single-person tube ride. Hang on!
MISS ADVENTURE FALLS	none; must be able to hold on to the raft handles	Family-friendly wild water raft ride. We like the fact that you don't have to walk upstairs or carry tubes to the top of the attraction. It's nice to simply sit in the raft and be transported up the conveyor belt. If the ride operates properly, it will take a bit over a minute from the moment you board the raft until you arrive at the top of the conveyor belt. The 58-second journey down takes you through tunnels with twists, turns, and waterfalls. It takes several rides to discover the decor along the route, but don't expect anything elaborate.
STORM SLIDES	none	Three body slides down and through Mount Mayday
SURF POOL	none; minimum age is 8; adult supervision required	World's largest inland surf facility with waves up to 6 feet high. Monday–Friday, in the early morning before the park opens, or evenings after the park has closed (hours vary), surfing lessons are offered. Cost is $190 including tax for 2½ hours; class size is 25. Call ☎ 407-WDW-SURF (939-7873). The cost includes a light Continental breakfast. Participants must provide their own surfing equipment. Park admission is not required.

ground to cover. If you or your children have tender feet, wear protective footwear that can be worn in and out of the water as you move around the park. Shops in the parks sell sandals and waterproof shoes.

Obviously, you'll need a towel, sunblock, and money. Carry enough money for the day and your Disney resort ID (if you have one), or use your MagicBand to pay for stuff. Though no location is completely safe, we've felt comfortable hiding our money in our cooler—nobody disturbed our stuff, and our cash was easy to reach. If, however, you're carrying a wad or you're simply a worrywart when it comes to money, rent a locker. Another great device is a water-resistant case with a lanyard to hold park tickets, a credit card, some cash, and your hotel key/card. You can buy these cases at the water parks; more-sophisticated versions are available at any good outdoors or sporting-goods shop.

LILIANE Wallets and purses get in the way, so lock them in your car's trunk or leave them at your hotel.

Personal swim gear (fins, masks, rafts, and so on) is not allowed—everything you need is either provided free or available to rent. If you forget your towel, you can rent one (cheap!). If you forgot your swimsuit or lotion, you can buy it on-site; disposable waterproof cameras are available for sale as well, though you can find them cheaper at area drugstores.

Establish your base for the day. Beautiful sunning and lounging spots are plentiful throughout both water parks; arrive early so you can have your pick. The breeze is best along the beaches of the lagoon at Blizzard Beach and the surf pool at Typhoon Lagoon. At Typhoon Lagoon, if children younger than age 6 are in your party, choose a spot to the left of Mount Mayday near the children's swimming area.

LILIANE While I don't feel any better on a water roller coaster than I do on a dry one, I love the water parks. My all-time favorite water ride is Teamboat Springs, the 1,200-foot whitewater raft flume at Blizzard Beach.

Though Typhoon Lagoon and Blizzard Beach are huge parks with many slides, armies of guests overwhelm them almost daily. If your main reason for going is the slides and you hate long lines, try to be among the first guests to enter the park. Go directly to the slides and ride as many times as you can before the park fills. When lines for the slides become intolerable, head for the surf or wave pool or the tube-floating streams. The lazy rivers at both parks are perfect for relaxation. Float through caves, beneath waterfalls, past gardens, and under bridges.

Wheelchairs can be rented at Typhoon Lagoon from Singapore Sal's, and at Blizzard Beach from Beach Haus. The cost is $12 with a $100 refundable deposit. If you keep your receipt, you won't have to pay for a wheelchair for the rest of the day at the theme parks. However, this does not guarantee availability at the theme parks. Electric conveyance vehicles (ECVs) can be rented at the water parks for $50 plus tax with a $100 refundable deposit.

BOB If you have a car, drive instead of taking a Disney bus.

Direct bus transportation to the water parks is available from all Disney resorts.

Both water parks are large and require almost as much walking as the theme parks. Add to this wave surfing, swimming, and climbing to reach the slides, and you'll definitely be pooped by day's end. Consider a low-key activity for the evening. A Waterloo, Ontario, mom found Typhoon Lagoon to be more strenuous than she anticipated:

> I wish I had been prepared for the fact that we'd have to haul the tubes up the stairs of the Crush 'n' Gusher slides. My daughter was not strong enough to carry hers, so I had to lug the tubes up by myself. I was EXHAUSTED by the end of the day, and my arms ached for a couple of days afterward.

It's as easy to lose a child or become separated from your party at one of the water parks as it is at a major theme park. On arrival, pick a very specific place to meet in the event you are separated. If you split up on purpose, establish times for checking in.

Children under age 14 must be accompanied by an adult. The water parks are great fun for the whole family, but if you have very

FAVORITE EATS AT BLIZZARD BEACH AND TYPHOON LAGOON

PARK | SERVICE LOCATION | FOOD SELECTIONS

BLIZZARD BEACH   Avalunch | Hot dogs and fresh fruit cup
Cooling Hut | Popcorn, chicken wrap, and hummus | **Lottawatta Lodge** | Flatbread, burgers, salads, and kids' meals | **Warming Hut** | Chicken wraps, beef empanadas, and barbecue turkey leg

TYPHOON LAGOON   Happy Landings | Ice cream, cookies, and waffle cones. *Garbage Pail:* Ice cream, fudge, nuts, and sprinkles in a pail with shovel
Leaning Palms | Pizza and kids' meals | **Lowtide Lou's** *(seasonal)* | Chicken wraps and tuna sandwiches | **Typhoon Tilly's** | Fish, barbecue pork, and kids' meals; great beer

Refillable mugs: If you or the kids enjoy soda, your best bet is to get a refillable mug, available at both water parks. For the price of the mug ($11.99), you are entitled to free refills throughout the day (only on the day of purchase). Select locations.

young children or if you aren't a thrill-seeking water puppy, the pool of your hotel might serve just as well. The water parks, however, were made to order for teens. Note that during the winter months, Disney closes Blizzard Beach and Typhoon Lagoon for refurbishment, alternating maintenance in such a way that one water park will be open at all times. If it is very wintry, Disney will close both parks.

LILIANE Lost-children stations at the water parks are so out of the way that neither you nor your child will find them without help from a Disney cast member. Explain to your children how to recognize cast members (by their distinctive name tags) and how to ask for help.

Blizzard Beach and Typhoon Lagoon offer premium spaces for rental that can accommodate up to six people. Four premium spaces in each water park include the personalized services of an attendant, private lockers, all-day drink mugs, a cooler with bottled water, lounge furniture, tables, and rental towels. You can also rent a premium beach chair space at both parks. The deal includes two lounge chairs, umbrella, cocktail table, and two towels. Limit is up to four people; if you have more than four people in your party, a second reservation is needed. These rentals are also available on a same-day basis if any locations are left (check at Shade Shack in Blizzard Beach and at High and Dry Rentals in Typhoon Lagoon). Cost for either setup varies by season and must be paid at time of reservation. Reserve the premium or beach chair spaces in advance by calling ☎ 407-WDW-PLAY (939-7529). Cancellations must be made no later than 9 a.m. the day prior to the reservation to avoid a penalty.

BEFORE YOU GO

1. Call ☎ 407-560-3400 (Blizzard Beach) or 407-560-4120 (Typhoon Lagoon) before you go to get the official park opening time.

2. Purchase admission tickets online before you arrive.

3. Decide if you want to picnic or not, and then plan or pack accordingly (see restrictions on page 430). Pets are not allowed at the water parks.

A WORD FROM THE WEATHERMAN

THUNDERSTORMS ARE COMMON IN FLORIDA. On summer afternoons, such storms often occur daily, forcing the water parks to close temporarily while the threatening weather passes. If the storm is severe and prolonged, it can cause a great deal of inconvenience. The park may actually close for the day, launching a legion through the turnstiles to compete for space on the Disney resort buses. If you depend on Disney buses, leave the park earlier, rather than later, when you see a storm moving in. Most important, though, instruct your children to immediately return to home base at the sight of lightning or when they hear the first rumble of thunder.

We recommend you monitor the local weather forecast the day before you go, checking again in the morning before leaving for the water park. Scattered thunderstorms are to be expected and usually cause no more than a temporary inconvenience, but moving storm fronts are to be avoided.

We get a lot of questions about the water parks during cold-weather months. Did you know that Disney actually heats all the water-park pools in the winter? Orlando-area temperatures can vary from the high 30s to the low 80s during December, January, and February. When it's warm, though, these months can serve up a dandy water-park experience, as this Batavia, Ohio, woman recounts:

> *Going to Blizzard Beach in December was the best decision ever! They told us that if the park didn't reach 100 people by noon, they would be closing. . . . There was no wait for anything all day! In June we waited in line for an hour for Summit Plummet. In December it took us only the amount of time to walk up the stairs. We had the enormous wave pool to ourselves. We did everything in the entire park and had lunch in less than 3 hours. The weather was slightly chilly at 71° and overcast with very light rain, but the water is heated, so we were fine.*

SAFETY FIRST

TOO MUCH FUN IN THE SUN isn't a good thing if you get sunburned or become dehydrated. Drink lots of fluids, use sunscreen, and bring a T-shirt and a hat for extra protection. Lifeguards are on duty throughout the parks. At Typhoon Lagoon, a first aid station is located behind Leaning Palms. The Blizzard Beach first aid station is between Lottawatta Lodge and Beach Haus.

UNIVERSAL'S VOLCANO BAY

VOLCANO BAY IS UNIVERSAL'S first highly themed water park, designed to directly compete with Disney's Blizzard Beach and Typhoon Lagoon. At just under 30 acres, it's the same size as Disney's water parks, excluding parking lots. A single-day admission to Volcano

• UNIVERSAL'S VOLCANO BAY •

ATTRACTION | HEIGHT REQUIREMENT* | LOCATION | WHAT TO EXPECT

HONU IKA MOANA | 42" for ika Moana, 48" for Honu or if riding alone on ika Moana | **River Village** | Honu and ika Moana are two separate slides attached to the same tower, where guests board multiperson animal-themed rafts before speeding down into a pool. The Honu (blue whale raft) side sends you vertically up steep walls before sliding back down; it's the scariest group ride in the park. Ika Moana (green sea turtle raft) is a much gentler ride in and out of twisting green tunnels.

MAKU ROUND RAFT RIDE | 42", 48" if riding alone | **Rainforest Village** | The six-person raft plunges riders through wild waters and bowl-like formations before ending up in a pool surrounded by erupting geysers.

KALA AND TAI NUI SERPENTINE BODY SLIDES | 48" | **Rainforest Village** | After falling through a trapdoor, two riders go down slides simultaneously. Their paths cross several times as they go down translucent, intertwining tubes. Insider tip: The green side is faster.

KO'OKIRI BODY PLUNGE | 48" | **Wave Village** | Hop on this 125-foot slide featuring a trapdoor with a 70-degree-angle descent, and let us know how you fare.

KOPIKO WAI WINDING RIVER | children under 48" must wear life vest and have supervising companion | **River Village** | Lazy river takes guests through the tropical landscape and the volcano itself. Inside Mount Krakatau, watch your TapuTapu interact with the mountain's cavern walls.

KRAKATAU AQUA COASTER | 42", 48" if riding alone | **River Village** | Guests board a specially designed canoe that seats up to four. Next you go through the volcano's interior, all the while twisting and turning before plummeting through a waterfall. The ride uses linear-induction motor technology, which launches the canoe uphill before immediately sending it into a downhill plunge.

KRAKATAU VOLCANO | **Krakatau** | Did you know that you can walk through the volcano? Make sure to chat with the god of the dancing fountains and use your TapuTapu to see the cave walls light up. The walk provides a great view over Waturi Beach and gives you an idea of how huge Krakatau is. It's a must-see.

OHYAH AND OHNO DROP SLIDES | 48" | **Rainforest Village** | Very intense slides that end up with a drop into a pool

PUIHI ROUND RAFT RIDE | 42", 48" if riding alone | **Rainforest Village** | The six-person raft launches down into a dark, winding tunnel before shooting up, causing riders to momentarily experience zero gravity prior to going down once more.

PUKA ULI LAGOON | children under 48" must wear life vest | **Rainforest Village** | Children's play area

PUNGA RACERS | 42", 48" if riding alone | **Rainforest Village** | Guests on racing manta ray mats go down across four lanes and through underwater sea caves.

THE REEF | children under 48" must wear life vest | **Wave Village** | Leisure pool with its own waterfall. Relax and watch guests shoot down the Ko'okiri Body Plunge.

RUNAMUKKA REEF AND TOT TIKI REEF | 48" maximum for slides | **River Village** | Volcano Bay's child-play areas. Tot Tiki Reef is perfect for toddlers, while Runamukka Reef is more suitable for older kids.

TANIWHA TUBES | 42", 48" if riding alone | **Rainforest Village** | A single- or double-rider tube ride down twisting waterslides. Along the way tiki statues make sure you don't stay dry. Bear left to the green Tonga slides for more open-air sections.

TEAWA THE FEARLESS RIVER | 42", 48" if riding alone; children under 48" must wear life vest and have supervising companion | High-speed whitewater river. If you're looking for a lazy river, this is not it!

WATURI BEACH | children under 48" must wear life vest | **Wave Village** | The beach features a multidirectional wave pool at the foot of Krakatau Lagoon.

*All guests are required to maintain proper riding position unassisted.

Bay costs $85.20–$90.53 for adults, $79.88–$85.20 for children ages 3–9, including tax. The park opens at 9 or 10 a.m. (with early admission an hour earlier for all on-site hotel guests) and stays open as late as 9 p.m. during the summer.

Volcano Bay is located directly south of Universal's Cabana Bay Beach Resort, accessible via a walking path, and is a short walk from Universal's Royal Pacific, Aventura, and Sapphire Falls hotels. Guests staying at Universal's Endless Summer Resort will have to use the free shuttle bus to reach the water park. If you're driving from off-site, park at Universal's theme park parking structures and take a shuttle bus to Volcano Bay. If you're staying on International Drive, you can take the International Drive trolley (visit iridetrolley.com for schedules and fees). Do not attempt to park at the Cabana Bay, Royal Pacific, Sapphire Falls, or Aventura hotel. All hotels have hefty parking fees to prevent off-site guests parking on their premises.

The park's four areas are based on the story of the fabled Waturi, an ancient tribe from Polynesia. The tribe set out on outrigger canoes to find a new home, believing that Kunuku, a golden-finned fish, would show them the way. The Waturi visited many Polynesian islands without encountering the elusive fish until they caught sight of Kunuku playing in the waves of Volcano Bay, where the Waturi settled. The park is themed to the islands of the South Pacific, with lush palm trees, tiki carvings, and thatched cabanas.

The heart of the park is **Krakatau,** a 200-foot volcano home to the **Krakatau Aqua Coaster. Wave Village** includes two huge pools and a beautiful beach; **River Village** holds activities for little tykes and the winding river experience; and **Rainforest Village** is home to several raft and speed slides, a pool, and a whitewater rafting experience.

Universal uses virtual lines instead of a traditional queuing system. Every visitor is issued a wearable wristband called TapuTapu, which, in addition to claiming your place in the virtual line, can also be used to reserve and open lockers ($12–$16) and make payments throughout the park when linked to a credit card via the Universal Orlando website or app. Guests tap the band against a totem outside a ride, and the device will alert them when it's time to return to experience the attraction. In the meantime, guests can explore other areas of the park. The TapuTapu bands also trigger special effects throughout Volcano Bay, such as controlling streams of water in **Tot Tiki Reef** or shooting water cannons at other guests who are enjoying the **Kopiko Wai Winding River.**

As with standby queues, you can wait in only one virtual line at a time. You can check wait times for the entire park on boards throughout the park, but the wait times are not yet displaying on the Universal Orlando app. Universal Express Pass is available for Volcano Bay starting at $20 per person for one use per ride; it can be purchased online or inside the park on select days.

Volcano Bay has a capacity of about 6,000 people, and the park can hit capacity in peak season. Wait times for the most popular rides can reach up to 3 hours. Be prepared to only enjoy a few rides if you visit during peak season. Arrive at the park entrance about 30 minutes prior to opening, and go for the headliners such as the Aqua Coaster, the two **Honu ika Moana** rides, the **Ko'okiri Body Plunge,** and the **Maku Puihi** raft rides.

Universal has worked out a lot of the kinks of the TapuTapu system, resulting in better management of lines. Adding wait-time boards is a huge improvement, and we hope that more are coming, preferably near all TapuTapu stations.

Early in the day, the virtual wait system works very well, and guests can often ride a few slides immediately and reserve short waits at others. The problems start as the crowds grow. By lunchtime, the virtual waits for many slides are 60 minutes or more.

If possible, try staying at Aventura, Cabana Bay Beach, or Sapphire Falls Resort, which are connected to the park by a walking path, and take advantage of early entry for Universal hotel guests. During the extra hour, most of the slides are kept at "Ride Now," resulting in relatively short lines.

Liliane thinks Volcano Bay is the most beautiful water park she's ever been to. Here is her report: theunofficialguides.com/2018/04/02/volcano-bay.

While luxury cabanas are available for rent, we don't think they're a must; however, we do recommend the private loungers (about $53.24 including tax, and up): two covered, connected chairs, providing shade and a box to keep items you want to keep close and not put in the sand. Please note all premium seating is date-specific.

LILIANE I could spend an entire day at Volcano Bay just enjoying the amazing view of the volcano, the beach, and the lazy river.

Another novelty for Orlando water parks is that Volcano Bay offers a leisure pool. **The Reef** is to the right of the volcano, and most of the pool is meant for swimmers. Swim up to the edge of the pool overlooking **Waturi Beach** and get a glimpse of the brave souls shooting down Ko'okiri Body Plunge.

Four dining venues serve Caribbean and island-inspired foods. For the less adventurous eaters, there are plenty of chicken fingers, burgers, and pizza to be had. The Universal Dining Plan can be used here.

FAVORITE EATS AT VOLCANO BAY

LAND | SERVICE LOCATION | FOOD SELECTIONS

RAINFOREST VILLAGE   Bambu | Quinoa edamame burger topped with roasted shiitake mushroom and sriracha mayo

Dancing Dragons Boat Bar | Volcano Blossom on tap brewed especially for the park by the Orange Blossom Brewery

The Feasting Frog | Tacos served with plantain chips and salsa

RIVER VILLAGE   Whakawaiwai Eats | Hawaiian pizza with caramelized pineapple, diced ham, and pickled jalapeños

WAVE VILLAGE   Kohola Reef Restaurant & Social Club | Slow-smoked glazed chicken, served with mango slaw and fries, and coconut curry chicken, served with rice and sweet plantains; chocolate lava cake and pineapple upside-down cake

Kunuku Boat Bar | Kona Big Wave on draft, imported from Kailua-Kona, Hawaii

A 1-day quick-service meal plan is available for $25.55 per adult and $17.03 for children ages 3–9 (tax included). The plan comes with an entrée, a snack, and one nonalcoholic beverage.

BEFORE YOU GO

1. Call ☎ 407-363-8000, or visit universalorlando.com/volcanobay, the day before you go to find out the official park opening time.

2. Purchase admission tickets online before you arrive.

3. Visit the website to determine which attractions are appropriate for the kids in your party.

4. Familiarize yourself with the TapuTapu system before you visit the park.

AQUATICA *by* SEAWORLD

AQUATICA IS LOCATED across International Drive from the back side of SeaWorld. From Kissimmee, Walt Disney World, and Lake Buena Vista, take I-4 East, exit onto the Central Florida Parkway, and then bear left on International Drive. From Universal Studios, take I-4 West and exit onto FL 528; then exit onto International Drive.

Admission prices at the gate are $71.36. Tickets purchased online are $10 cheaper. If you don't want to wait in line to buy tickets, buy them in advance at aquatica.com, or use the ticket machines to the left of Aquatica's main entrance. An Aquatica/SeaWorld/Busch Gardens/Adventure Island combo ticket starts at $159.74 online for a visit to two of the parks; for $181.04 you can try out three of the parks; and for $234.29, you can visit all four parks an unlimited number of times within 14 days of first use. All prices include tax.

BOB If you don't purchase your admission in advance, take advantage of the automatic admission machines located to the right of the main entrance. The machines are a pain in the rear, asking for your name, age, home zip code, and billing zip code, but if you have a credit card, the machines are a lot faster than standing in line at the ticket windows.

Aquatica is comparable in size to other water theme parks in the area. Landscaped with palms, ferns, and tropical flowers, it's far less themed than Disney's Typhoon Lagoon and Blizzard Beach or Universal's Volcano Bay. You can take in all the attractions in 1 day, but as with all water parks, remember that an entire day of action in the Florida sun will wear out the most active kids, and most grown-ups too.

As at other water parks, there are lockers, towels, wheelchairs, and strollers to rent; gift shops to browse; and places to eat. The three restaurants at Aquatica are **WaterStone Grill,** offering burgers, wraps, and salads; **Banana Beach Cook-Out,** dishing up pizza, pulled pork, and chicken; and **Mango Market,** a diminutive eatery serving loaded fries and chicken tenders. WaterStone Grill and Mango Market serve beer. If food is important to you, you are out of luck. The eateries at Aquatica are dismal at best; unfortunately, the park does not allow you to bring in your own food.

• AQUATICA BY SEAWORLD •

ATTRACTION | HEIGHT REQUIREMENT* | WHAT TO EXPECT

CUTBACK COVE AND BIG SURF SHORES | none | One cove serves up bodysurfing waves, while the other puts out gently bobbing floating waves. A spacious beach arrayed around the coves is the park's primary sunning venue. Shady spots, courtesy of beach umbrellas, ring the perimeter of the area for sun-sensitive guests.

DOLPHIN PLUNGE | 48"; must be able to maintain proper riding position unassisted | Corkscrewing romp through a totally arced tube until you blast through the clear tube at the end. It's nearly impossible to view the dolphins because you're flushed through the clear tube so fast and with so much water splashing in your face that the ride is over before you've seen anything.

IHU'S BREAKAWAY FALL | 48" | Orlando's steepest multidrop tower slide. This is not a mild journey. Brace yourself, and make sure your swimsuit is securely fastened!

KAREKARE CURL | 48"; maximum 2 people, with a combined weight not exceeding 400 pounds; individual riders must not exceed 250 pounds; single riders not allowed | Aquatica's newest ride opened in April 2019. It's only 361 feet long, lasting about 20 seconds. Thrill seekers will love this high-adrenaline ride in a two-person raft that includes a 35-foot drop down an enclosed tube.

KATA'S KOOKABURRA COVE | 48" and under only | Wading pool and slides for the preschool crowd

LOGGERHEAD LANE | must be in a single or double tube | Take a tube and enjoy this lazy river, which at one point passes through the Fish Grotto, a tank populated by hundreds of exotic tropical fish.

OMAKA ROCKA | 48" | A wide diameter, enclosed, one-person tube ride. The name is derived from the wave action inside the tube, which washes you alternately up one side of the tube and then the other.

RAY RUSH | 42" | A multiperson raft ride with enclosed spirals and manta-inspired elements

ROA'S RAPIDS | 51" and under required to wear a life vest | Floating stream with a very swift current but without any rapids. There is only one place to get in and out.

TASSIE'S TWISTERS | must be able to maintain proper riding position while holding on to both handles unassisted | An enclosed slide tube spits you into an open bowl, where you careen around the edge much in the manner of the ball in a roulette wheel.

TAUMATA RACER | 42"; must be able to maintain proper riding position unassisted | A high-speed mat ride down a steep hill

WALHALLA WAVE | 42"; must be able to maintain proper riding position unassisted | Circular raft that can accommodate up to four people and splashes down a six-story enclosed twisting tube

WALKABOUT WATERS | 36"–42" for slides into main pool and over 42" tall for larger slides | 15,000-square-foot children's adventure area. If your children are under the age of 10, this alone may be worth the admission price. It's impossible not to get wet and impossible not to have fun!

WHANAU WAY | must be able to maintain the proper riding position while holding on to both handles unassisted | Tubes carry one or two passengers down one of four slides with a few twists and one corkscrew.

*Guests under 48" are required to wear a life vest.

BEFORE YOU GO

1. Call ☎ 407-545-5550, or visit aquatica.com, the day before you go to find out the official park opening time.
2. Purchase admission tickets online before you arrive.
3. Visit the website to determine which attractions are appropriate for the kids in your party.

SEAWORLD

MANY DOZENS OF READERS have written to extol the virtues of SeaWorld. The following are representative. An English family writes:

The best-organized park is SeaWorld. The park map included a show schedule and told us which areas were temporarily closed. Best of all, there was almost no queuing. Overall, we rated this day so highly that it's the park we would most like to visit again.

A woman in Alberta, Canada, gives her opinion:

We chose SeaWorld as our fifth day at the World. What a pleasant surprise! It was every bit as good (and in some ways better) than WDW itself. Well worth the admission, an excellent entertainment value, educational, well run, and better value for the dollar in food services. Perhaps expand your coverage to give them their due!

OK, here's what you need to know. SeaWorld (☎ 407-545-5550; seaworld.com/orlando) is a world-class marine-life theme park near the intersection of I-4 and the Beachline Expressway. It's about 10 miles east of Disney World. Opening daily at 9 a.m. and closing between 6 and 10 p.m., depending on the season, SeaWorld charges $106.49 at the gate (including tax). If you purchase online at seaworld.com, the same tickets will cost you about $20 less. Several multipark tickets are available as well, including a three-park ticket, which includes admission to three of the following parks: SeaWorld, Aquatica, Busch Gardens, or Adventure Island. Your three visits can be used at the same park, or at a combination of any of the different parks listed. The tickets, valid 1 year from the date of purchase, are priced at $181.04. The second and third visits must be redeemed within 14 days of your first visit. For $193.70 you can enjoy 12 months of unlimited admission to SeaWorld Orlando; $385.40 provides unlimited admission to 11 parks for 12 months, including SeaWorld and Aquatica in Orlando, San Antonio, and San Diego; Busch Gardens in Tampa Bay and Williamsburg, Virginia; and Sesame Place in Langhorne, Pennsylvania. Prices for Florida residents are the same but come with the option to make monthly payments. Check SeaWorld's website for all ticket options. Stroller rental is $15.98 for a single stroller, $26.63 for a double stroller. Wheelchair rental is $16 per day, and electric scooters are $64 per day. Prices include tax.

BOB Be forewarned that you can't take food or drinks into SeaWorld or its swimming park, Aquatica.

SeaWorld offers an all-day dining plan priced at $42.59 for adults and $21.29 for kids ages 3–9. Guests can eat at participating restaurant locations as often as once every hour until closing time. SeaWorld offers several behind-the-scenes tours, such as Dolphin Encounter and Penguins Up-Close. To book a tour, visit seaworld.com/orlando/tours.

Figure 8–9 hours or more to see everything, 6 or so if you stick to the big deals. SeaWorld is about the size of the Magic Kingdom and

• SEAWORLD •

ATTRACTION | STAR RATING | HEIGHT REQUIREMENT | WHAT TO EXPECT

ANTARCTICA: EMPIRE OF THE PENGUIN | ★★★★ | none | Motion-based trackless dark ride; you exit in a real penguin habitat.

DOLPHIN COVE | ★★★★ | none | 2-acre outdoor dolphin habitat

DOLPHIN DAYS | ★★★★ | none | Educational show with dolphins and tropical birds

DOLPHIN NURSERY | ★★ | none | Outdoor pool for expectant dolphins or mothers and calves

INFINITY FALLS | ★★★★ | 42″ | 4-minute rain forest–themed river rapids ride; a vertical lift raises rafts 40 feet then launches them into the river; you will get soaked!

JEWEL OF THE SEA AQUARIUM | ★★½ | none | Aquarium located under Journey to Atlantis. The jellyfish aquarium is amazing.

JOURNEY TO ATLANTIS | ★★½ | 42″; 42″–48″ must be accompanied by a supervising companion at least 14 years old | Combination roller coaster–flume ride

KRAKEN | ★★★★ | 54″ | Roller coaster

MANATEE REHABILITATION AREA | ★★½ | none | Manatee viewing area

MANTA | ★★★★★ | 54″ | Roller coaster

MANTA AQUARIUM | ★★★½ | none | More than 3,000 marine animals; the pop-up aquarium lets kids feel like they're in the aquarium.

MAKO | ★★★★½ | 54″ | In SeaWorld's own words: the tallest, longest, fastest coaster in Orlando

OCEAN DISCOVERY | ★★★★½ | none | An educational killer whale show that occurs on certain days at the earliest Shamu show

ONE OCEAN | ★★★★½ | none | High-tech Shamu and killer whale show

PACIFIC POINT PRESERVE | ★★★ | none | Sea lions and seals viewing area

PELICAN PRESERVE | ★★ | none | Pelican viewing area

PETS AHOY | ★★★½ | none | Show with performing birds, cats, dogs, and a pig

SEA LION HIGH: THE NEW CLASS | ★★★½ | none | Sea lion, walrus, and otter show

SESAME STREET | ★★★★★ | Abby's Flower Tower: 42″; Big Bird's Twirl 'n' Whirl: 36″; Cookie Drop!: 42″; Elmo's Choo Choo Train: 36″; Slimey's Slider: 42″; Super Grover's Box Car Derby: 38″ | Iconic locations from the beloved TV show, six *Sesame Street*–themed attractions, wet and dry play areas, and a daily parade with Big Bird and friends

SHAMU UNDERWATER VIEWING | ★★★ | none | Whale viewing area

SHARK ENCOUNTER | ★★★½ | none | Shark viewing area

SKY TOWER | ★★ | 48″ or accompanied by a supervising companion at least 14 years old (handheld infants OK) | 400-foot tower with a bird's-eye view of Orlando; rarely open

STINGRAY LAGOON | ★★½ | none | Stingray viewing area

TURTLETREK | ★★★ | none | 3-D film about sea turtles; animal habitats

WILD ARCTIC | ★★★ | 42″; 42″–48″ must be accompanied by a supervising companion at least 14 years old | Simulation ride and Arctic-wildlife viewing

requires about the same amount of walking. In terms of size, quality, and creativity, it's unequivocally on par with Disney's major theme parks. Unlike Walt Disney World, SeaWorld primarily features stadium shows or walk-through exhibits. This means that you'll spend about 80% less time waiting in line during 8 hours at SeaWorld than you would for the same-length visit at a Disney park.

FAVORITE EATS AT SEAWORLD		
LAND	SERVICE LOCATION	FOOD SELECTIONS
KEY WEST AT SEAWORLD **Captain Pete's Island Eats**	Hot dogs and chicken tenders		
THE WATERFRONT **Voyager's Smokehouse**	Barbecue ribs and chicken Seafire Grill	Fried chicken sandwiches, wraps, and salads		
SHARK ENCOUNTER **Sharks Underwater Grill**	Fish, pasta, and coconut chicken tenders; floor-to-ceiling glass allows guests to observe some 50 sharks and fish.	*Table service only*		
WILD ARCTIC **Mango Joe's**	Pizza and kids' meals		
FRONT GATE PLAZA **Sweet Sailin' Candy Shop**	Candies and hand-dipped chocolate turtles		

But you'll notice immediately as you check the performance times that the shows are scheduled so that it's almost impossible to see them back-to-back. A Cherry Hill, New Jersey, visitor confirms this rather major problem, complaining:

The shows were timed so we could not catch all the major ones in a 7-hour visit.

Much of the year, you can get a seat for the stadium shows by showing up 10 or so minutes in advance. When the park is crowded, however, you need to be at the stadiums at least 20 minutes in advance (30 minutes in advance for a good seat). All of the stadiums have splash zones, specified areas where you're likely to be drenched with ice-cold salt water by whales, dolphins, and sea lions. Finally, Sea-World has three of the best coasters—**Mako, Manta,** and **Kraken**—in Florida. If you're a coaster lover, be on hand before park opening and ride all three rides as soon as the park opens.

A new **Sesame Street** land opened in 2019, replacing the Shamu's Happy Harbor children's playground. The 6-acre environment, which re-creates iconic locations from the beloved TV show, includes both wet and dry play areas, a kid-size roller coaster, and a daily parade featuring Big Bird and friends.

The **Seven Seas Food Festival** is held every weekend mid-February–early May. The festival offers delightful Asian, Latin, Polynesian, European, and Mediterranean flavors at food kiosks throughout the park. In addition, concerts feature well-known artists such as Lynyrd Skynyrd, Styx, the Village People, Alabama, Daughtry, the Commodores, and Grupo Manía. Prices range from $3.75 to $6.50 per dish with the option to buy a sampling lanyard for $50 (10 items) or $65 (15 items), plus tax. The quality and variety of the food is topped only by the generous serving sizes. Check out Liliane's review of the 2018 festival at theunofficialguides.com/2019/03/25/seven-seas-food-festival-2.

DISCOVERY COVE

ALSO OWNED BY SEAWORLD, this intimate park is a welcome departure from the hustle and bustle of other Orlando parks. Its slower pace could be the overstimulated family's ticket back to mental health.

The main draw at Discovery Cove is the chance to swim with an **Atlantic bottlenose dolphin.** The 50-minute experience (30 minutes in the water) is open to visitors age 6 and up who are comfortable in the water. Trainers lead an orientation and allow participants to ask questions. Next, small groups wade into shallow water to get an introduction to the dolphin in its habitat. The experience culminates with guests swimming into deeper water for closer interaction with the dolphin before being towed back to shore by the mammal.

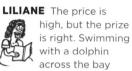

LILIANE The price is high, but the prize is right. Swimming with a dolphin across the bay was one of the most amazing things I've ever done in my life.

LILIANE With a focus on personal guest service and one-on-one animal encounters, Discovery Cove admits only 1,300 guests per day.

Snorkel or swim in the **Grand Reef,** which houses thousands of exotic fish and rays, as well as an underwater shipwreck and hidden grottoes. The **Freshwater Oasis** is a swimming and wading experience, where you can get up close and personal with otters and marmosets. In the **Explorer's Aviary,** you can touch and feed gorgeous tropical birds. The park is threaded by the **Wind-Away River,** in which you can float or swim, and dotted with beaches that serve as pathways to the attractions.

All guests are required to wear flotation vests when swimming, and lifeguards are omnipresent. You'll need your swimsuit, pool shoes, and a cover-up. On rare days when it's too cold to swim in Orlando, guests are provided with free wet suits. Discovery Cove also provides fish-friendly sunscreen samples; guests may not use their own sunscreen.

Discovery Cove is open daily, 9 a.m.–5 p.m.; check-in begins at 7:15 a.m. Admission is limited, so purchase tickets well in advance; call ☎ 877-557-7404 or visit discoverycove.com. Prices vary seasonally from $211.94 to $383.40 per person, including tax (no children's discount). Prices for Florida residents start at $170, tax included, if bought in advance. Admission includes the dolphin swim; self-parking; Continental breakfast; a substantial lunch; snacks and drinks; and use of beach umbrellas, lounge chairs, towels, lockers, and swim and snorkel gear. If you're not interested in the dolphin swim, you can visit Discovery Cove for the day for $158.69–$266.25 per person, including tax, depending on the season. You can add admission to SeaWorld, Aquatica, Busch Gardens, and/or Adventure Island for an additional fee.

For an additional $49–$69 per person, plus tax, depending on the season, you can experience **SeaVenture,** a 25-minute underwater stroll on the bottom of the Grand Reef aquarium. Participants wear diving helmets (large enough to accommodate eyeglasses), and no experience or SCUBA certification is necessary. Minimum age is 10 years. For $109–$169 plus tax, guests can swim freely alongside several species of sharks. And for $59–$69 plus tax, guests can help feed stingrays and tropical fish, as well as take a private, guided swim of The Grand Reef; the experience is offered Thursday–Monday, 7–8:30 a.m.

DISNEY SPRINGS

THIS SPRAWLING DINING, SHOPPING, and entertainment complex is strung along the banks of Lake Buena Vista, on the east side of Walt Disney World. It consists of the **Marketplace, The Landing, Town Center,** and the **West Side.** You can roam, shop, and eat without paying any sort of entrance fee.

If you have a car, use it. There is bus transportation from all the Disney resorts to Disney Springs, and some resorts offer boat transportation. Starting at 4 p.m. guests can commute from all four theme parks directly to Disney Springs. All guests using bus transportation to Disney Springs are dropped off at The Gateway, which is centrally located at Town Center. The Gateway also has 18 loading zones for return trips to Disney resorts. The former Marketplace bus loop supports other transportation needs, including vehicles serving nearby Good Neighbor hotels, Hotel Plaza Boulevard, and Shades of Green. The boats are better than the buses but take about four times as long as driving your car. The boat route, however, is very pretty and a good choice if you're not in a hurry. The last boat back to the resorts leaves Disney Springs at 11:30 p.m. sharp. Note that boats come to a total standstill during thunderstorms. There is plenty of free parking at Disney Springs.

The Lime Garage brings guests directly into Town Center; the Orange Garage is closest to the West Side entertainment venues. The Grapefruit Garage feeds into Marketplace; the garage is located opposite the Lime Garage and across Buena Vista Drive, connected to Disney Springs via a pedestrian bridge. The high-tech parking garages feature overhead lights that indicate whether spaces are available or not. We recommend parking as close as possible to the elevator banks. Disney parking garages close at 3 a.m.

There are six ATMs at Disney Springs. All major credit cards are accepted, and if you're a Disney resort guest, you can have your purchases delivered to your hotel (this only works if you're not checking out the next day). Pickup is usually at the primary gift shop of your resort (no room delivery), but even so, it beats the heck out of lugging stuff around. Pets are not allowed at Disney Springs.

For more information about all the restaurants at Disney Springs, see the section beginning on page 173.

MARKETPLACE

WITH WORLD OF DISNEY and many activities for children, The Marketplace is the most kid-friendly of the shopping and dining areas. The Marketplace has a small carousel and mini–train rides for a nominal fee. Free kid-oriented dance parties take place in the lakeside amphitheater, and a fountain splash area is great for cooling down. The centerpiece of shopping is the 50,000-square-foot **World of Disney,** the largest store in the country selling Disney-trademarked merchandise. Kids will particularly enjoy the **LEGO Store.** You'll know you're there when you see Brickley, the 30-foot sea serpent made out of over a million LEGO blocks that lives in the lake in front of the store. Outside the store is a play area filled with LEGO blocks for children to enjoy.

Once Upon a Toy is a joy. The biggest draws at this 16,000-square-foot store are classic toys with a Disney twist. Here you can find Mr. Potato Head with Mickey ears or a sorcerer's hat and the classic game Clue set in The Haunted Mansion. One of the most exciting shopping options is found at **Marketplace Co-Op,** a retail space that includes Liliane's favorite—the Cherry Tree Lane store—which has the most amazing dresses and accessories of which even Mary Poppins would approve.

Bibbidi Bobbidi Boutique transforms your little girl into a princess, albeit for a price. A Fairy Godmother–in–training (the shop manager) and her helpers offer salon services for princesses age 3 and up. Hairstyle, manicure, and makeup will cost you $64.95 plus tax; the Castle Package (including your choice of a princess costume with accessories a) starts at $200 plus tax and gratuity. Hairstyling for your young Prince Charming is also available, starting at $19.95 plus tax. Photo packages cost extra. The boutique can be reserved up to 180 days in advance.

LILIANE Save money by getting just the hairstyle and makeup at Bibbidi Bobbidi and taking your own pictures.

The Void collaborated with Lucasfilm and ILMx-LAB to create the virtual reality experience Star Wars: Secrets of the Empire. Prices to join the rebellion start at $32.95 plus tax. Reservations can be made online at thevoid.com. For those not taken with *Star Wars,* the company offers an experience themed to *Wreck-It Ralph.* You must be at least 10 years old and 48 inches tall to play.

THE LANDING AND TOWN CENTER

FEATURING WATERFRONT WALKWAYS and merchandise kiosks, **The Landing** lies between the West Side and Marketplace and affords sweeping views of the water and Saratoga Springs Resort.

The Boathouse, which offers upscale waterfront dining, is also the launching pad for the *Venezia,* a 40-foot wooden Italian water taxi. Kids will enjoy the guided **Amphicar** rides, which take guests on a 20-minute tour of the landmarks of Disney Springs, albeit at an exorbitant price.

Art of Shaving offers high-end grooming essentials for the modern dad, and **Sanuk** sells creatively inspired footwear. The latest sports sunglasses can be found at **Oakley,** and **Havaianas** is your place to go for cool flip-flops plus options to design your own.

Liliane's favorites are **Chapel Hats** ("I really had to control myself to keep from buying a fascinator for the next Kentucky Derby") and **The Ganachery.**

Town Center, situated between The Landing and the parking garage, offers plenty of retail shopping, such as **Zara, Ugg, Tommy Bahama,** and **Vera Bradley.**

continued on page 448

Disney Springs

Disney's Saratoga Springs Resort & Spa

Strawberry Parking Lot

Lake Buena Vista

water taxi

water taxi

West Side Dock

water taxi

The Landing Dock

Virgin Atlantic Check-In

West Side

Parking

WEST SIDE Shopping
1. Curl by Sammy Duvall
2. Disney's Candy Cauldron
3. Disney Style
4. Fit2Run
5. Pelé World Soccer
6. Pop Gallery
7. Something Silver
8. Sosa Family Cigars
9. Star Wars Galactic Outpost
10. Sunglass Icon
11. Super Hero Headquarters

Dining
A. City Works Eatery & Pour House
B. Food Trucks at Exposition Park
C. House of Blues Restaurant & Bar/ The Smokehouse
D. Jaleo/Pepe by José Andrés
E. Starbucks

THE LANDING Shopping
12. The Art of Shaving
13. Chapel Hats
14. **Group 1:** Erwin Pearl, The Ganachery, Oakley, Sanuk, Savannah Bee Company
15. Havaianas

Orange Garage

Dining
F. The Boathouse
G. Chef Art Smith's Homecomin'
H. The Edison
I. Enzo's Hideaway
J. Erin McKenna's Bakery NYC
K. Jock Lindsey's Hangar Bar
L. Joffrey's Coffee & Tea Company
M. Maria & Enzo's Ristorante
N. Morimoto Asia/ Morimoto Street Food
O. Paddlefish
P. Paradiso 37
Q. Pizza Ponte
R. Raglan Road/ Cookes of Dublin
S. STK Orlando
T. Terralina Crafted Italian
U. Vivoli il Gelato
V. Wine Bar George

TOWN CENTER Shopping
16. Coca-Cola Store
17. **Group 1:** American Threads, Johnston & Murphy, Lucky Brand, Tommy Bahama, Ugg
18. **Group 2:** Columbia Sportswear, Everything but Water, Free People, Johnny Was, Kate Spade New York, Lilly Pulitzer, Sperry, Sugarboo, Vera Bradley
19. **Group 3:** Coach, MAC, Origins
20. **Group 4:** Lacoste, Luxury of Time, Sephora, Shore, Stance, Superdry
21. **Group 5:** Levi's, Orlando Harley Davidson, TUMI, Volcom
22. **Group 6:** Alex and Ani, Anthropologie, Ever After Jewelry Co., Francesca's, Kiehl's, Kipling, Melissa Shoes, L'Occitane en Provence, Under Armour, UNOde50
23. **Group 7:** Edward Beiner, Na Hoku, Pandora

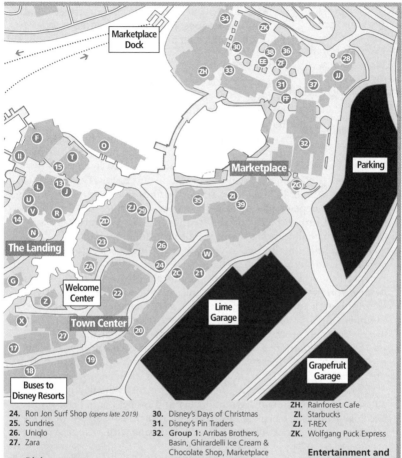

24. Ron Jon Surf Shop *(opens late 2019)*
25. Sundries
26. Uniqlo
27. Zara

Dining
W. Amorette's Patisserie
X. Blaze Pizza, Fast-Fire'd
Y. Chicken Guy
Z. D-Luxe Burger
ZA. Frontera Cocina
ZB. Planet Hollywood Observatory
ZC. The Polite Pig
ZD. Sprinkles
ZE. Wolfgang Puck Bar & Grill

MARKETPLACE Shopping
28. Bibbidi Bobbidi Boutique
29. Build-A-Dino/Dino Store

30. Disney's Days of Christmas
31. Disney's Pin Traders
32. **Group 1:** Arribas Brothers, Basin, Ghirardelli Ice Cream & Chocolate Shop, Marketplace Co-Op, Tren-D
33. **Group 2:** Goofy's Candy Co., Star Wars Trading Post
34. **Group 3:** The Art of Disney, Disney's Wonderful World of Memories
35. LEGO Store
36. Mickey's Pantry
37. Once Upon a Toy
38. The Spice & Tea Exchange
39. World of Disney

Dining
ZF. Earl of Sandwich
ZG. 4 Rivers Cantina Barbacoa Food Truck

ZH. Rainforest Cafe
ZI. Starbucks
ZJ. T-REX
ZK. Wolfgang Puck Express

Entertainment and Attractions
AA. Aerophile
BB. AMC Disney Springs 24 Dine-In Theatres
CC. Cirque du Soleil *(reopening date unknown)*
DD. House of Blues
EE. Marketplace Carousel
FF. Marketplace Train Express
GG. The NBA Experience
HH. Splitsville Luxury Lanes
II. Vintage Amphicar & Italian Water Taxi Tours
JJ. The Void: Step Beyond Reality

continued from page 445

LILIANE You can still get your Sprinkles cupcake even if the store is closed or terribly busy. The cupcake ATM operates daily, 8 a.m.–3 a.m., and a menu tells you what choices are available. $5 cupcake anyone?

Also at Town Center are the gourmet food kiosks **Aristocrepes, Daily Poutine,** and **B.B. Wolf's Sausage Co.,** as well as **Sprinkles.**

WEST SIDE

A NEW CIRQUE DU SOLEIL SHOW will pay homage to Disney's rich history of animation. An opening date for the show has not been announced, but reports indicate a spring 2020 debut.

Splitsville, an upscale bowling, billiards, and dining venue, covers 45,000 square feet on two levels. It has 30 bowling lanes, an outdoor patio with live music, dining options (including two sushi bars), and more. Or try **Aerophile,** where you ascend 400 feet over Disney Springs in a tethered balloon. The weather-dependent ride is 8–10 minutes and runs $20 for adults (age 10 and up) and $15 for children (ages 3–9). Operating 8 a.m.–midnight, the balloon ride is wheelchair accessible.

Fit2Run sells running gear, **Curl by Sammy Duvall** is a surf shop, and **Sunglass Icon** stocks designer shades.

Catch the latest box office hits at the state-of-the-art **AMC Dine-In Disney Springs 24,** showing flicks and serving food in an Art Deco setting. For showtimes and ticket sales, go to amctheatres.com, click "Our Theatres," then "Find a Theatre," and select "AMC Dine-In Disney Springs 24" from the "Orlando/Daytona Beach" list.

The NBA Experience, offering basketball-themed experiences featuring hands-on activities, as well as a restaurant and a retail store, opened in August 2019 in the former location of DisneyQuest.

The place to be for mom and dad's night out is the newly opened **Jaleo** restaurant by award-winning chef and Nobel Peace Prize nominee José Andrés. The restaurant features an extensive menu of tapas reflecting the regional diversity of Spanish cuisine with a modern twist.

OUTDOOR RECREATION

WALT DISNEY WORLD OFFERS a wealth of fun stuff for families besides theme parks, water parks, eating, and shopping. You can fish, canoe, hike, bike, boat, play tennis and golf, ride horses, work out, or take cooking lessons.

Your kids will go nuts for the **Wilderness Lodge Resort,** and so will you. While you're there, have a family-style meal at the kid-friendly **Whispering Canyon Cafe** and rent bikes for a ride on the paved paths of adjacent **Fort Wilderness Resort & Campground.** The outing will be a great change of pace. The only downside is that your kids might not want to go back to their own hotel.

Find more fun at **ESPN Wide World of Sports Complex,** a 220-acre competition and training center. Disney guests are welcome at the sports complex as paying spectators, but none of the facilities are available for guests to use. Prices vary; to book tickets and to learn what events (including Major League Baseball exhibition games) are scheduled during your visit, call ☎ 407-939-1500 or visit espnwwos .com. In 2022 the Special Olympics USA Summer Games will be held at the ESPN Wide World of Sports Complex.

Located 40–60 minutes south of Walt Disney World is the **Disney Wilderness Preserve,** a wetlands-restoration area with hiking trails and an interpretive center, operated by The Nature Conservancy in partnership with Disney. The preserve is open April–October, Monday–Friday, 9 a.m.–4:30 p.m. To confirm its operating hours, call ☎ 407-935-0002 and press 3 for the holiday schedule. Trail access and conditions are occasionally limited due to inclement weather or restoration activities. Check the weather before your visit and call ahead to check trail access. Admission is free, though donations are appreciated. If you're interested, call the preserve directly or visit tinyurl.com/disneywildernesspreserve.

GOLF AND MINIATURE GOLF

IF GOLF IS YOUR THING, call ☎ 407-WDW-GOLF (939-4653) or visit golfwdw.com for information, tee times, and greens fees at **Palm Golf Course, Magnolia Golf Course, Lake Buena Vista Golf Course,** or **Oak Trail Golf Course**.

Fun for the whole family abounds at **Fantasia Gardens Miniature Golf,** across the street from the Walt Disney World Swan, and **Winter Summerland,** right next to Blizzard Beach. Fantasia Gardens is a beautifully landscaped course with fountains, animated statues, topiaries, and flower beds. Winter Summerland offers two 18-hole courses—one has a "blizzard in Florida" theme, while the other sports a tropical-holiday theme, with Christmas ornaments hanging from palm trees.

Fantasia Gardens is quite demanding and not nearly as whimsical as Winter Summerland. Adults and older teens will enjoy the challenge of Fantasia Gardens, but if your group includes children younger than 12, head to Winter Summerland. Winter Summerland can be reached by taking a bus to the Animal Kingdom, where you then transfer to a bus to Blizzard Beach. The course is right next to the entrance to the water park. To access Fantasia Gardens you must take a bus to the Swan and walk to the course from there. Admission to both courses is $14 for adults and $12 for children ages 3–9, plus tax. Hours are daily, 10 a.m.–10 p.m. For more information call ☎ 407-WDW-PLAY (939-7529).

Our favorite minigolf in Orlando is **Hollywood Drive-In Golf,** in Universal CityWalk (☎ 407-802-4848; hollywooddriveingolf.com). One hole has the Creature from the Black Lagoon spitting water over the walkway you need to pass through; another hole has a huge alien ship that you need to walk through and for which you need to press a button so that a door opens, *Star Trek*–style, to let you out. It's a nonstop barrage of clever in-jokes, insanely well-designed holes, and unique lighting elements. There's also an iPhone app for keeping score and misting fans for keeping cool. Open daily, 9 a.m.–2 a.m.; cost (including tax) is $18 for adults, $16 for children ages 3–9.

THEME PARK TRIVIA QUIZ ANSWERS

MAGIC KINGDOM

1. (C)   **2.** (D)   **3.** (B)   **4.** (C)   **5.** (A)   **6.** (C)   **7.** (A)   **8.** (C)   **9.** (B)   **10.** (C)

EPCOT

1. (C)   **2.** (B)   **3.** (C)   **4.** (A)   **5.** (B)   **6.** (C)   **7.** (C)   **8.** (B)   **9.** (B)   **10.** (D)

DISNEY'S ANIMAL KINGDOM

1. (B)   **2.** (C)   **3.** (D)   **4.** (C)   **5.** (B)   **6.** (B)   **7.** (C)   **8.** (C)   **9.** (B)   **10.** (D)

DISNEY'S HOLLYWOOD STUDIOS

1. (D)   **2.** (B)   **3.** (A)   **4.** (A)   **5.** (D)   **6.** (A)   **7.** (B)   **8.** (B)   **9.** (D)   **10.** (A)

INDEX

The Magic Kingdom

MAGIC KINGDOM HAPPY FAMILY 1-DAY TOURING PLAN

1. Arrive at the Magic Kingdom entrance 40 minutes (when morning Extra Magic Hours are in effect) to 70 minutes (on days without morning EMHs) before official opening. Get guide maps and the *Times Guide*. Stroller rentals are under the train station on Main Street, U.S.A.
2. Meet Mickey Mouse at the Town Square Theater on Main Street, U.S.A.
3. Ride Seven Dwarfs Mine Train in Fantasyland.
4. Take a spin on the Mad Tea Party.
5. Ride the Prince Charming Regal Carrousel.
6. Ride Peter Pan's Flight.
7. See *Enchanted Tales with Belle*.
8. Meet a set of princesses at Princess Fairytale Hall.
9. Meet characters at Pete's Silly Sideshow.
10. **PARENTS:** Take about a 4-hour break for lunch and a nap.
11. **TEENS:** Ride Space Mountain in Tomorrowland during the parents' break. Use FastPass+ as much as possible by choosing the earliest available reservation for steps 11–13.
12. **TEENS:** Ride Splash Mountain in Frontierland.
13. **TEENS:** Ride Big Thunder Mountain Railroad.
14. **TEENS:** Play Sorcerers of the Magic Kingdom. Sign up at the fire station on Main Street.
15. **TEENS:** See the afternoon parade from Frontierland.
16. **PARENTS:** Return to the park. If it's warm enough, pack extra clothes and a towel, and let the kids run around in the Casey Jr. Splash 'N' Soak Station in Fantasyland.
17. **PARENTS:** Ride Dumbo the Flying Elephant.
18. Ride The Many Adventures of Winnie the Pooh.
19. See *Mickey's PhilharMagic*.
20. Eat dinner. Good nearby choices are Pecos Bill Tall Tale Inn (20a) in Frontierland and Columbia Harbour House (20b) in Liberty Square.
21. Play two rounds of A Pirate's Adventure: Treasures of the Seven Seas in Adventureland. Sign up near the Golden Oak Outpost.
22. Ride Pirates of the Caribbean.
23. Experience Under the Sea—Journey of the Little Mermaid in Fantasyland.
24. If time permits, meet Ariel at her grotto.
25. See *Monsters, Inc. Laugh Floor* in Tomorrowland.
26. Ride Buzz Lightyear's Space Ranger Spin.
27. If time permits, meet Tinker Bell at Town Square Theater on Main Street.
28. See the *Happily Ever After* fireworks and the *Once Upon a Time* castle projection show.

Suggested start times for your advance FastPass+: Seven Dwarfs Mine Train: 9 a.m.; Peter Pan's Flight: 10 a.m.; Princess Fairytale Hall: 11 a.m. For day-of FastPass+: The Many Adventures of Winnie the Pooh: 4:30 p.m.; Pirates of the Caribbean: 6:30 p.m.

If any of these FastPasses or times aren't available, see tinyurl.com/free-tplans to customize the plan based on the ones you were able to get, at no charge. Also get free real-time updates while you're in the park.

The Magic Kingdom

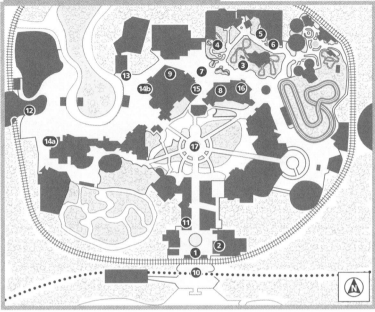

MAGIC KINGDOM 2-DAY TOURING PLAN FOR
PARENTS WITH SMALL CHILDREN: DAY 1

1. Arrive at the Magic Kingdom entrance 40 minutes (when morning Extra Magic Hours are in effect) to 70 minutes (on days without morning EMHs) before official opening. Get guide maps and the *Times Guide*. Stroller rentals are under the train station on Main Street, U.S.A.
2. As soon as the park opens, meet Mickey Mouse at the Town Square Theater on Main Street, U.S.A.
3. Ride the Seven Dwarfs Mine Train in Fantasyland.
4. See *Enchanted Tales with Belle*.
5. Ride Under the Sea—Journey of the Little Mermaid.
6. Meet Ariel at her grotto.
7. Take a spin on the Prince Charming Regal Carrousel.

8. Meet a set of princesses at Princess Fairytale Hall.
9. Take Peter Pan's Flight.
10. Eat lunch and return to your hotel for a midday break of around 4 hours.
11. Return to the park and sign up for Sorcerers of the Magic Kingdom on Main Street. Play a few rounds.
12. Ride Splash Mountain in Frontierland.
13. See The Haunted Mansion in Liberty Square.
14. Eat dinner. Good nearby choices are Pecos Bill Tall Tale Inn (14a) in Frontierland and Columbia Harbour House (14b) in Liberty Square.
15. See *Mickey's PhilharMagic* in Fantasyland.
16. Ride The Many Adventures of Winnie the Pooh.
17. See the *Happily Ever After* fireworks and the *Once Upon a Time* castle projection show.

Suggested start times for your advance FastPass+: Seven Dwarfs Mine Train: 9 a.m.; *Enchanted Tales with Belle*: 10 a.m.; Peter Pan's Flight: 11 a.m. For day-of FastPass+: Splash Mountain: 5 p.m.; The Many Adventures of Winnie the Pooh: 6:45 p.m.

If any of these FastPasses or times aren't available, see tinyurl.com/free-tplans to customize the plan based on the ones you were able to get, at no charge. Also get free real-time updates while you're in the park.

The Magic Kingdom

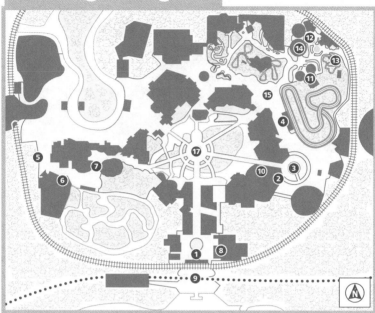

MAGIC KINGDOM 2-DAY TOURING PLAN FOR
PARENTS WITH SMALL CHILDREN: DAY 2

1. Arrive at the Magic Kingdom entrance 40 minutes (when morning Extra Magic Hours are in effect) to 70 minutes (on days without morning EMHs) before official opening. Get guide maps and the *Times Guide*. Stroller rentals are under the train station on Main Street, U.S.A.
2. As soon as the park opens, ride Buzz Lightyear's Space Ranger Spin in Tomorrowland. Ride twice if desired.
3. Take a spin on the Astro Orbiter.
4. Ride the Tomorrowland Speedway.
5. Play two rounds of A Pirate's Adventure: Treasures of the Seven Seas. Sign up near the Golden Oak Outpost.
6. Ride Pirates of the Caribbean.
7. Ride The Magic Carpets of Aladdin.
8. Meet Tinker Bell at the Town Square Theater on Main Street, U.S.A.

9. Leave the park for a midday break. Allow at least 4 hours. If you want to play in the Casey Jr. Splash 'N' Soak Station this afternoon, bring a towel and a change of clothes.
10. Return to the park and see *Monsters, Inc. Laugh Floor* in Tomorrowland.
11. Ride Dumbo the Flying Elephant in Fantasyland.
12. Meet Daring Disney Pals at Pete's Silly Sideshow.
13. Ride The Barnstormer.
14. Try the Casey Jr. Splash 'N' Soak Station.
15. Take a spin on the Mad Tea Party.
16. Eat dinner.
17. See the *Happily Ever After* fireworks and the *Once Upon a Time* castle projection show if you haven't already seen them.

Suggested start times for your advance FastPass+: The Magic Carpets of Aladdin: 10:30 a.m.; Meet Tinker Bell at Town Square Theater: 11:30 a.m.; Dumbo: 4:30 p.m. For day-of FastPass+: The Barnstormer: 5:30 p.m.

If any of these FastPasses or times aren't available, see tinyurl.com/free-tplans to customize the plan based on the ones you were able to get, at no charge. Also get free real-time updates while you're in the park.

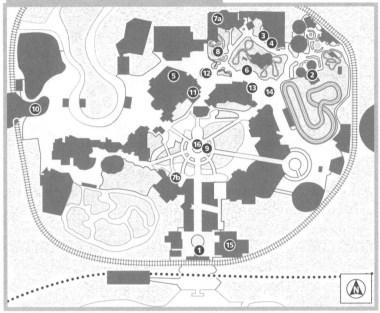

MAGIC KINGDOM 2-DAY SLEEPYHEAD TOURING PLAN FOR PARENTS WITH SMALL CHILDREN: DAY 1

1. Arrive before 11 a.m. Get guide maps and the *Times Guide*. Stroller rentals are under the train station on Main Street, U.S.A.
2. In Fantasyland, ride Dumbo the Flying Elephant.
3. Ride Under the Sea—Journey of the Little Mermaid.
4. Meet Ariel at her grotto if the wait is 20 minutes or less.
5. Ride Peter Pan's Flight.
6. Take the Seven Dwarfs Mine Train.
7. Eat lunch. If you can get reservations at Be Our Guest (7a), it's a great dining choice. If, however, your kids want to meet more characters,

and it's in your budget, then try The Crystal Palace on Main Street, U.S.A. (7b).
8. See *Enchanted Tales with Belle*.
9. See the Festival of Fantasy afternoon parade.
10. Ride Splash Mountain in Frontierland.
11. In Fantasyland, see *Mickey's PhilharMagic*.
12. Ride the Prince Charming Regal Carrousel.
13. See The Many Adventures of Winnie the Pooh.
14. Ride the Mad Tea Party.
15. Meet Mickey Mouse at Town Square Theater on Main Street, U.S.A.
16. See the *Happily Ever After* fireworks and the *Once Upon a Time* castle projection show.

Suggested start times for your advance FastPass+: Peter Pan's Flight: 11 a.m.; Seven Dwarfs Mine Train: 12:15 p.m.; *Enchanted Tales with Belle*: 1:30 p.m. For day-of FastPass+: Splash Mountain: 3 p.m.; The Many Adventures of Winnie the Pooh: 6 p.m.

If any of these FastPasses or times aren't available, see tinyurl.com/free-tplans to customize the plan based on the ones you were able to get, at no charge. Also get free real-time updates while you're in the park.

The Magic Kingdom

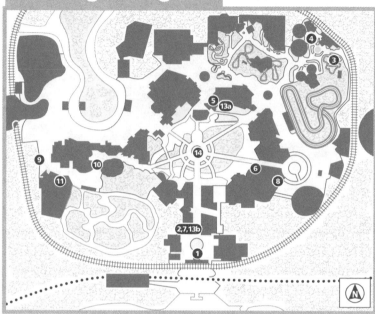

MAGIC KINGDOM 2-DAY SLEEPYHEAD TOURING PLAN
FOR PARENTS WITH SMALL CHILDREN: DAY 2

1. Arrive around 11 a.m. Get guide maps and the *Times Guide*. Stroller rentals are under the train station on Main Street, U.S.A.
2. Sign up for Sorcerers of the Magic Kingdom at the Main Street Fire Station, and play a few rounds.
3. In Fantasyland, ride The Barnstormer.
4. Meet Daring Disney Pals at Pete's Silly Sideshow.
5. Meet Rapunzel and Tiana or Cinderella and Elena at Princess Fairytale Hall.
6. In Tomorrowland, see *Monsters, Inc. Laugh Floor*.
7. Play a few rounds of Sorcerers of the Magic Kingdom.
8. Try Buzz Lightyear's Space Ranger Spin in Tomorrowland.
9. Play two rounds of A Pirate's Adventure: Treasures of the Seven Seas. Sign up near the Golden Oak Outpost.
10. Ride The Magic Carpets of Aladdin.
11. Ride Pirates of the Caribbean.
12. Eat dinner.
13. If time permits, meet more princesses (**13a**) or Disney characters in Fantasyland, or play additional sessions of Sorcerers of the Magic Kingdom (**13b**).
14. If you haven't already done so, see the *Happily Ever After* evening fireworks and the *Once Upon a Time* castle projection show.

Suggested start times for your advance FastPass+: The Barnstormer: 11 a.m.; Princess Fairytale Hall: noon; Buzz Lightyear's Space Ranger Spin: 1 p.m. For day-of FastPass+: The Magic Carpets of Aladdin: 4:30 p.m.
   If any of these FastPasses or times aren't available, see tinyurl.com/free-tplans to customize the plan based on the ones you were able to get, at no charge. Also get free real-time updates while you're in the park.

The Magic Kingdom

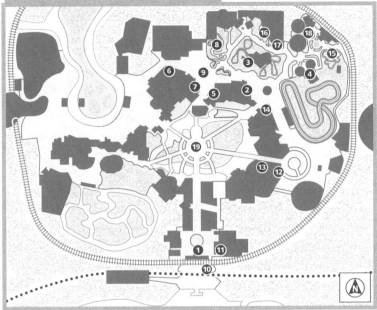

PARENTS' MAGIC KINGDOM PLAN:
1 AFTERNOON AND 1 FULL DAY (FULL DAY)

1. Arrive at the Magic Kingdom entrance 40 minutes (when morning Extra Magic Hours are in effect) to 70 minutes (on days without morning EMHs) before official opening. Get guide maps and the *Times Guide*. Stroller rentals are under the train station on Main Street, U.S.A.
2. In Fantasyland, ride The Many Adventures of Winnie the Pooh.
3. Ride the Seven Dwarfs Mine Train.
4. Experience Dumbo the Flying Elephant.
5. Meet Rapunzel and Tiana or Cinderella and Elena at Princess Fairytale Hall.
6. Ride Peter Pan's Flight.
7. See *Mickey's PhilharMagic*.
8. See *Enchanted Tales with Belle*.
9. Take a spin on the Prince Charming Regal Carrousel.

10. Eat lunch and return to your hotel for a midday break of 3-4 hours.
11. Return to the park and meet Mickey Mouse at Town Square Theater on Main Street, U.S.A.
12. Ride Buzz Lightyear's Space Ranger Spin in Tomorrowland.
13. See *Monsters, Inc. Laugh Floor*.
14. Eat dinner. Cosmic Ray's Starlight Café in Tomorrowland is a good choice.
15. Ride The Barnstormer in Fantasyland.
16. Ride Under the Sea—Journey of the Little Mermaid.
17. Meet Ariel at her grotto.
18. Meet Daring Disney Pals at Pete's Silly Sideshow.
19. See the *Happily Ever After* fireworks and the *Once Upon a Time* castle projection show.

Suggested start times for your advance FastPass+: Seven Dwarfs Mine Train: 9 a.m.; Peter Pan's Flight: 10 a.m. *Enchanted Tales with Belle*: 11:30 a.m. For day-of FastPass+: Buzz Lightyear's Space Ranger Spin: 4 p.m.; Under the Sea—Journey of the Little Mermaid: 6:30 p.m.

If any of these FastPasses or times aren't available, see tinyurl.com/free-tplans to customize the plan based on the ones you were able to get, at no charge. Also get free real-time updates while you're in the park.

The Magic Kingdom

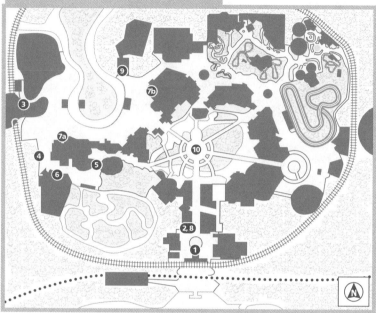

PARENTS' MAGIC KINGDOM PLAN:
1 AFTERNOON AND 1 FULL DAY (AFTERNOON)

1. Arrive at the Magic Kingdom entrance around 11 a.m. Get guide maps and the *Times Guide*. Stroller rentals are under the train station on Main Street.
2. Sign up for the Sorcerers of the Magic Kingdom at the Main Street Fire Station. Tell the cast member that you'll be spending most of your time in Adventureland and Frontierland.
3. Ride Splash Mountain in Frontierland.
4. Play two rounds of A Pirate's Adventure: Treasures of the Seven Seas in Adventureland. Sign up near the Golden Oak Outpost.

5. Ride The Magic Carpets of Aladdin.
6. Ride Pirates of the Caribbean.
7. Eat dinner. Good nearby choices include Pecos Bill Tall Tale Inn and Cafe (7a) in Frontierland and the Columbia Harbour House (7b) in Liberty Square.
8. Play a few rounds of Sorcerers of the Magic Kingdom. Sign up at the Main Street Fire Station.
9. See The Haunted Mansion in Liberty Square.
10. See the *Happily Ever After* fireworks and the *Once Upon a Time* castle projection show.

Suggested start times for your advance FastPass+: Splash Mountain: 4 p.m.; The Magic Carpets of Aladdin: 5:30 p.m.; The Haunted Mansion: 7:30 p.m.

If any of these FastPasses or times aren't available, see tinyurl.com/free-tplans to customize the plan based on the ones you were able to get, at no charge. Also get free real-time updates while you're in the park.

The Magic Kingdom

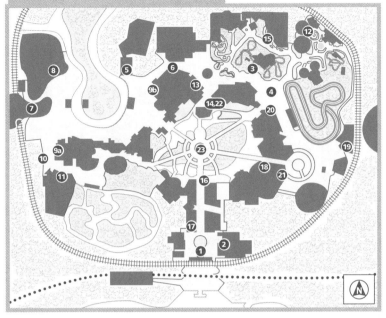

MAGIC KINGDOM 1-DAY TOURING PLAN
FOR TWEENS AND THEIR PARENTS

1. Arrive at the Magic Kingdom entrance 40 minutes (when morning Extra Magic Hours are in effect) to 70 minutes (on days without morning EMHs) before official opening. Get guide maps and the *Times Guide*. Stroller rentals are under the train station on Main Street, U.S.A.
2. Meet Mickey Mouse at the Town Square Theater on Main Street, U.S.A.
3. In Fantasyland, ride the Seven Dwarfs Mine Train.
4. Take a spin on the Mad Tea Party.
5. See The Haunted Mansion in Liberty Square.
6. In Fantasyland, ride Peter Pan's Flight.
7. Ride Splash Mountain in Frontierland.
8. Ride Big Thunder Mountain Railroad.
9. Eat lunch. Good nearby choices are Pecos Bill Tall Tale Inn (9a) in Frontierland and Columbia Harbour House (9b) in Liberty Square.
10. Play two rounds of A Pirate's Adventure: Treasures of the Seven Seas in Adventureland. Sign up near the Golden Oak Outpost.
11. Ride Pirates of the Caribbean.
12. In Fantasyland, meet Daring Disney Pals at Pete's Silly Sideshow.
13. See *Mickey's PhilharMagic*.
14. Meet Rapunzel and Tiana at Princess Fairytale Hall.
15. Ride Under the Sea—Journey of the Little Mermaid.
16. See the afternoon parade on Main Street, U.S.A.
17. Play a few rounds of Sorcerers of the Magic Kingdom.
18. See *Monsters, Inc. Laugh Floor* in Tomorrowland.
19. Ride Space Mountain.
20. Eat dinner. Cosmic Ray's Starlight Café in Tomorrowland has a wide variety from which to choose.
21. Ride Buzz Lightyear's Space Ranger Spin.
22. If time permits, meet Cinderella and Elena at Princess Fairytale Hall.
23. See the *Happily Ever After* fireworks and the *Once Upon a Time* castle projection show.

Suggested start times for your advance FastPass+: Seven Dwarfs Mine Train: 9 a.m.; Peter Pan's Flight: 10 a.m.; Big Thunder Mountain Railroad: 11 a.m. For day-of FastPass+: Space Mountain: 5 p.m.; Buzz Lightyear's Space Ranger Spin: 6:30 p.m.

If any of these FastPasses or times aren't available, see tinyurl.com/free-tplans to customize the plan based on the ones you were able to get, at no charge. Also get free real-time updates while you're in the park.

The Magic Kingdom

MAGIC KINGDOM 1-DAY TOURING PLAN
FOR GRANDPARENTS WITH SMALL CHILDREN

1. Arrive at the Magic Kingdom entrance 40 minutes (when morning Extra Magic Hours are in effect) to 70 minutes (on days without morning EMHs) before official opening. Get guide maps and the *Times Guide*. Stroller rentals are under the train station on Main Street, U.S.A.
2. As soon as the park opens, ride Buzz Lightyear's Space Ranger Spin in Tomorrowland.
3. Ride The Many Adventures of Winnie the Pooh in Fantasyland.
4. Take a spin on the Mad Tea Party.
5. Ride the Seven Dwarfs Mine Train.
6. Try Peter Pan's Flight.
7. See *Enchanted Tales with Belle*.
8. Ride Under the Sea—Journey of the Little Mermaid.
9. Meet Ariel at her grotto if time permits.
10. Leave the park for lunch and a midday break

of around 4 hours.
11. Return to the park and meet Mickey Mouse at Town Square Theater on Main Street, U.S.A.
12. In Tomorrowland, see *Monsters, Inc. Laugh Floor*.
13. Play two rounds of A Pirate's Adventure: Treasures of the Seven Seas. Sign up near the Golden Oak Outpost.
14. Ride Pirates of the Caribbean.
15. Eat dinner. Good nearby choices are Pecos Bill Tall Tale Inn and Cafe (15a) in Frontierland and the Columbia Harbour House (15b) in Liberty Square.
16. Ride the Magic Carpets of Aladdin.
17. Ride Dumbo in Fantasyland.
18. Meet characters at Pete's Silly Sideshow.
19. See the *Happily Ever After* fireworks and the *Once Upon a Time* castle projection show.

Suggested start times for your advance FastPass+: Seven Dwarfs Mine Train: 9 a.m.; Peter Pan's Flight: 10 a.m.; *Enchanted Tales with Belle:* 11 a.m. For day-of FastPass+: Meet Mickey Mouse at Town Square Theater: 4 p.m.; Dumbo: 7:30 p.m.

If any of these FastPasses or times aren't available, see tinyurl.com/free-tplans to customize the plan based on the ones you were able to get, at no charge. Also get free real-time updates while you're in the park.

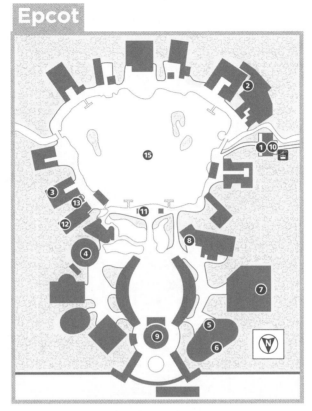

EPCOT 1-DAY TOURING PLAN FOR
PARENTS WITH SMALL CHILDREN

1. Arrive at the International Gateway entrance 40 minutes before opening. Rent strollers. Get guide maps and the *Times Guide.*
2. As soon as the park opens, ride Remy's Ratatouille Adventure in France (if open).
3. Head to Norway, and ride Frozen Ever After. Save the Anna and Elsa character greeting for later.
4. If your kids are tall enough, try Test Track in Future World East.
5. Ride The Seas with Nemo & Friends in Future World West.
6. See *Turtle Talk with Crush* and tour the main tank and exhibits.
7. Take the Living with the Land boat ride at The Land Pavilion.
8. Ride Journey Into Imagination with Figment at the Imagination! Pavilion.
9. Ride Spaceship Earth (if open).
10. Eat lunch and take a midday break back at your hotel.
11. Return to the park and sign up for Agent P's World Showcase Adventure at agentpwsa.com if your children are old enough. Play a game or three around the next few steps in the plan.
12. Begin a clockwise tour of World Showcase with the Mexico Pavilion, and take the Gran Fiesta Tour. Also check the *Times Guide* for live performances, and visit the Kidcot Fun Stops as you tour.
13. Meet Anna and Elsa at Royal Sommerhus in Norway.
14. Eat dinner in World Showcase.
15. See the evening fireworks. Good viewing spots are around Mexico and also between Canada and France.

Suggested start times for your advance FastPass+: Test Track: 11 a.m.; The Seas with Nemo & Friends: noon; Spaceship Earth: 1 p.m. Also check for fireworks FastPasses after you've used your first three.

If any of these FastPasses or times aren't available, see tinyurl.com/free-tplans to customize the plan based on the ones you were able to get, at no charge. Also get free real-time updates while you're in the park.

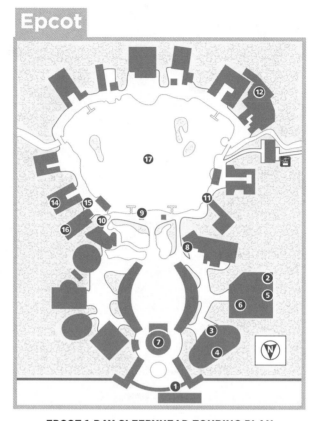

EPCOT 1-DAY SLEEPYHEAD TOURING PLAN
FOR PARENTS WITH SMALL CHILDREN

1. Arrive at the main entrance around 11 a.m. Rent strollers if needed. Get guide maps and the *Times Guide.*
2. Ride Soarin' in The Land Pavilion.
3. See The Seas with Nemo & Friends and tour the main tank and exhibits.
4. Experience *Turtle Talk with Crush.*
5. Take the Living with the Land boat ride at The Land Pavilion.
6. Eat lunch at Sunshine Seasons.
7. Ride Spaceship Earth (if open).
8. Ride Journey Into Imagination with Figment at the Imagination! Pavilion.
9. Sign up for Agent P's World Showcase Adventure at agentpwsa.com if your children are old enough. Plan to play a few games after riding Frozen Ever After.
10. Begin a tour of World Showcase. Check the

Times Guide for live performances, and visit the Kidcot Fun Stops as you tour.
11. If you were able to get FastPasses for Remy's Ratatouille Adventure in France, start in Canada and follow the steps below in the order shown; if you were able to get FastPasses for Frozen Ever After in Norway, start in Mexico and follow the steps in reverse order.
12. Ride Remy's Ratatouille Adventure in France (if open).
13. Eat dinner in World Showcase.
14. Tour Norway, and ride Frozen Ever After.
15. If time permits, meet Anna and Elsa at Royal Sommerhus.
16. Take the Gran Fiesta Tour boat ride in Mexico.
17. See the evening fireworks. Good viewing spots are available around Mexico and also between Canada and France.

Suggested start times for your advance FastPass+: The Seas with Nemo & Friends: noon; Spaceship Earth: 2 p.m.; Remy's Ratatouille Adventure or Frozen Ever After: after 4:30 p.m. Also check for ride or fireworks FastPasses after you've used your first three.

If any of these FastPasses or times aren't available, customize the plan at tinyurl.com/free-tplans based on the FastPasses you were able to get, at no charge. You can also get free real-time updates while you're in the park.

PARENTS' EPCOT TOURING PLAN:
1 AFTERNOON AND 1 FULL DAY (FULL DAY)

1. Arrive at the International Gateway entrance 40 minutes before opening. Rent strollers. Get guide maps and the *Times Guide*.
2. As soon as the park opens, ride Remy's Ratatouille Adventure in France (if open).
3. In Norway, take the Frozen Ever After boat ride. Save the character greeting for later.
4. Head to Future World East and ride Test Track. Consider the single-rider line to save time if you don't have FastPasses.
5. Eat lunch at Sunshine Seasons in The Land Pavilion.
6. Take the Living with the Land boat ride.
7. Sign up for Agent P's World Showcase Adventure at agentpwsa.com if your children

are old enough. Play a few games whenever you're near a pavilion that supports it.
8. Begin a clockwise tour of World Showcase at Mexico, and take the Gran Fiesta Tour boat ride.
9. Tour Norway, and meet Anna and Elsa at Royal Sommerhus.
10. Check the *Times Guide* for performance times of the acts in the next two steps. Work these in around dinner in World Showcase.
11. See China and the acrobatics act.
12. See The Voices of Liberty at the United States Pavilion.
13. See the evening fireworks. Good viewing spots are available between Canada and France.

Suggested start times for your advance FastPass+: Test Track: 10 a.m.; Living with the Land: noon. Also get FastPass+ for the fireworks.

If any of these FastPasses or times aren't available, see tinyurl.com/free-tplans to customize the plan based on the ones you were able to get, at no charge. Also get free real-time updates while you're in the park.

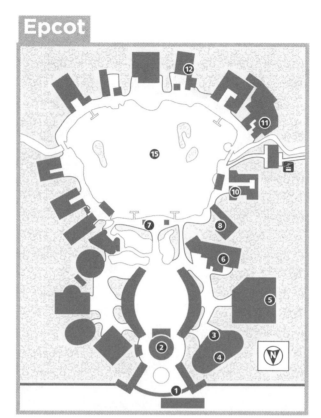

PARENTS' EPCOT TOURING PLAN:
1 AFTERNOON AND 1 FULL DAY (AFTERNOON)

1. Arrive at the main entrance around noon. Rent strollers. Get guide maps and the *Times Guide*.
2. Ride Spaceship Earth at the front of the park (if open).
3. In Future World West, see The Seas with Nemo & Friends and tour the main tank and exhibits.
4. See *Turtle Talk with Crush*.
5. Ride Soarin' at The Land Pavilion.
6. Ride Journey Into Imagination with Figment and play the postride games.
7. If you haven't already done so, sign up for Agent P's World Showcase Adventure at agentpwsa.com if your children are old enough. Play a few rounds once you get to the United Kingdom.
8. Begin a counterclockwise tour of World Showcase at Canada, and see *O Canada!*
9. Check the *Times Guide* for performance times of any live entertainment in World Showcase.
10. Tour the United Kingdom Pavilion, and see British Revolution if it's playing.
11. See Serveur Amusant in France.
12. Tour Japan and the Mitsukoshi department store.
13. Eat dinner in World Showcase.
14. Tour any remaining World Showcase pavilions that interest you.
15. If you haven't already done so, see the fireworks show.

Suggested start times for your advance FastPass+: Spaceship Earth: 11:30 a.m.; Soarin': 12:30 p.m. Also get FastPass+ for the fireworks.

If any of these FastPasses or times aren't available, see tinyurl.com/free-tplans to customize the plan based on the ones you were able to get, at no charge. Also get free real-time updates while you're in the park.

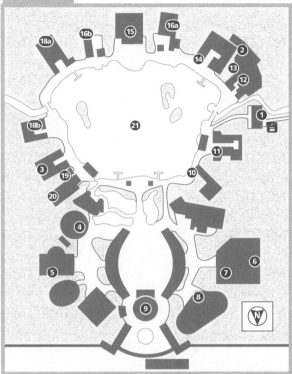

EPCOT 1-DAY TOURING PLAN
FOR TWEENS AND THEIR PARENTS

1. Arrive at the International Gateway entrance 40 minutes before opening. Get guide maps and the *Times Guide*.
2. As soon as the park opens, ride Remy's Ratatouille Adventure in France (if open).
3. In Norway, ride Frozen Ever After. Save the character greeting for later.
4. Head to Future World East and ride Test Track. Consider the single-rider line to save time if you don't have FastPasses.
5. Ride Mission: Space in Future World East.
6. Ride Soarin' in The Land Pavilion.
7. Eat lunch. Sunshine Seasons is the closest, best option.
8. Tour The Seas main tank and exhibits.
9. Ride Spaceship Earth (if open).
10. Begin a counterclockwise tour of World Showcase at Canada.

11. Tour the United Kingdom Pavilion.
12. Tour the France Pavilion. Work in a performance of Serveur Amusant if the schedule permits.
13. See the *Beauty and the Beast* sing-along (or *Impressions de France* film, if that's your thing), if time permits.
14. Tour the Morocco Pavilion.
15. See The Voices of Liberty singing group at the United States Pavilion.
16. Tour the Japan (**16a**) and Italy (**16b**) Pavilions.
17. Eat dinner in World Showcase.
18. Tour Germany (**18a**) and China (**18b**).
19. Tour the Norway Pavilion, and meet Anna and Elsa at Royal Sommerhus.
20. Tour the Mexico Pavilion.
21. See the evening fireworks. Good viewing spots are available between Canada and France.

Suggested start times for your advance FastPass+: Test Track: 10 a.m.; Soarin': 11:30 a.m.; Spaceship Earth: 1:20 p.m. Also check for fireworks FastPasses after you've used your first three.

If any of these FastPasses or times aren't available, see tinyurl.com/free-tplans to customize the plan based on the ones you were able to get, at no charge. Also get free real-time updates while you're in the park.

Disney's Animal Kingdom

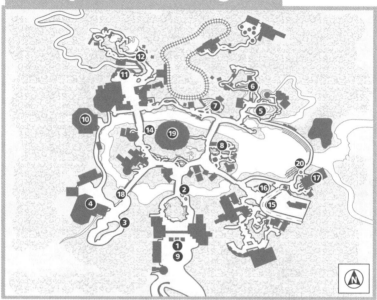

ANIMAL KINGDOM 1-DAY TOURING PLAN FOR PARENTS WITH SMALL CHILDREN

1. Arrive 40 minutes prior to official opening time. Rent strollers, and get guide maps and the *Times Guide*.
2. While waiting for the park to open, sign up for Wilderness Explorers on the bridge between The Oasis and Discovery Island. Play these short, fun games as you follow the tour.
3. As soon as the park opens, take the Na'vi River Journey in Pandora.
4. Experience Avatar Flight of Passage if your kids are tall enough.
5. Ride Kali River Rapids in Asia.
6. Walk the Maharajah Jungle Trek around the next step.
7. See *Up! A Great Bird Adventure*.
8. Meet Mickey and Minnie at Adventurers Outpost on Discovery Island.
9. Eat lunch and return to your hotel for a midday

break of around 4 hours.
10. In Africa, work in a show of *Festival of the Lion King* around the next two steps.
11. Experience the Kilimanjaro Safaris.
12. Walk the Gorilla Falls Exploration Trail.
13. Eat dinner.
14. Tour the Discovery Island Trails. One entrance is just over the bridge from Africa to Discovery Island, on the left. You'll end up near the walkway to DinoLand U.S.A.
15. Try TriceraTop Spin in DinoLand U.S.A.
16. Spend some time in The Boneyard while waiting for the *Nemo* show in the next step.
17. See *Finding Nemo—The Musical*.
18. Tour Pandora after dark.
19. See the Tree of Life *Awakenings* show on Discovery Island.
20. See *Rivers of Light* in Asia.

Suggested start times for your advance FastPass+: Avatar Flight of Passage: 9:30 a.m.; Meet Disney Pals at Adventurers Outpost: 11 a.m.; Kilimanjaro Safaris: 5 p.m. Also check for *Rivers of Light* FastPasses after experiencing Kilimanjaro Safaris.

If any of these FastPasses or times aren't available, see tinyurl.com/free-tplans to customize the plan based on the ones you were able to get, at no charge. Also get free real-time updates while you're in the park.

Disney's Animal Kingdom

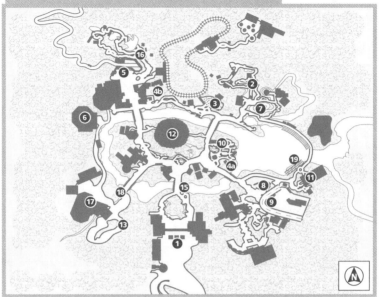

ANIMAL KINGDOM 1-DAY SLEEPYHEAD TOURING PLAN FOR PARENTS WITH SMALL CHILDREN

1. Arrive around 11 a.m. Rent strollers, and get guide maps and the *Times Guide.*
2. Walk the Maharajah Jungle Trek in Asia.
3. See *Up! A Great Bird Adventure.*
4. Eat lunch at either Flame Tree Barbecue (**4a**) on Discovery Island or the Harambe Market (**4b**) in Africa.
5. Experience Kilimanjaro Safaris in Africa.
6. Work in a show of *Festival of the Lion King* around the next two steps.
7. Ride Kali River Rapids in Asia.
8. Play in The Boneyard in DinoLand U.S.A.
9. Try TriceraTop Spin.
10. Meet Mickey and Minnie at the Adventurers Outpost on Discovery Island.
11. See *Finding Nemo—The Musical* in DinoLand U.S.A.
12. See the Tree of Life *Awakenings* show on Discovery Island.
13. Take the Na'vi River Journey in Pandora.
14. Eat dinner.
15. Sign up for the Wilderness Explorers game, on the bridge from The Oasis to Discovery Island. Work in these quick, fun games as you finish the tour.
16. Walk the Gorilla Falls Exploration Trail in Africa.
17. Experience Avatar Flight of Passage in Pandora if your kids are tall enough.
18. Tour the rest of Pandora.
19. See *Rivers of Light* in Asia.

Suggested start times for your advance FastPass+: Kali River Rapids: 3:30 p.m.; Meet Disney Pals at Adventurers Outpost: 4:30 p.m.; Avatar Flight of Passage: after dinner.

If any of these FastPasses or times aren't available, see tinyurl.com/free-tplans to customize the plan based on the ones you were able to get, at no charge. Also get free real-time updates while you're in the park.

Disney's Animal Kingdom

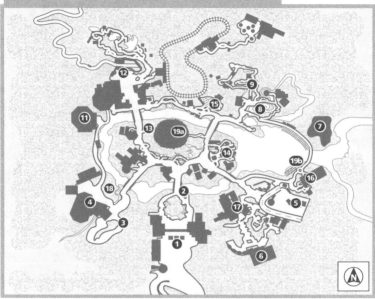

ANIMAL KINGDOM 1-DAY TOURING PLAN
FOR TWEENS AND THEIR PARENTS

1. Arrive 40 minutes prior to official opening time. Rent strollers, and get guide maps and the *Times Guide*.
2. Sign up for the Wilderness Explorers game as you enter the park, on the bridge from The Oasis to Discovery Island. Work in these quick, fun games as you follow the tour.
3. As soon as the park opens, take the Na'vi River Journey in Pandora.
4. Experience Avatar Flight of Passage.
5. Take the Primeval Whirl in DinoLand U.S.A.
6. Ride Dinosaur.
7. Ride Expedition Everest in Asia.
8. Experience Kali River Rapids.
9. Walk the Maharajah Jungle Trek.
10. Eat lunch.
11. Work in a show of *Festival of the Lion King* in Africa around the next two steps.
12. Experience Kilimanjaro Safaris.
13. Tour the Discovery Island Trails. One entrance is just over the bridge from Africa to Discovery Island, on the left. You'll end up on Discovery Island near the bridge to Asia.
14. Meet Mickey and Minnie at the Adventurers Outpost on Discovery Island.
15. See *Up! A Great Bird Adventure* in Asia.
16. See *Finding Nemo—The Musical* in DinoLand U.S.A.
17. Eat dinner. A good choice is Restaurantosaurus.
18. Tour the rest of Pandora.
19. See Tree of Life *Awakenings* (**19a**) on Discovery Island and *Rivers of Light* (**19b**) in Asia.

Suggested start times for your advance FastPass+: Avatar Flight of Passage: 9:30 a.m.; Expedition Everest: 10:30 a.m.; Kilimanjaro Safaris: 12:30 p.m. Also check for FastPasses for Adventurers Outpost and then *Rivers of Light* after experiencing Kilimanjaro Safaris.

If any of these FastPasses or times aren't available, see tinyurl.com/free-tplans to customize the plan based on the ones you were able to get, at no charge. Also get free real-time updates while you're in the park.

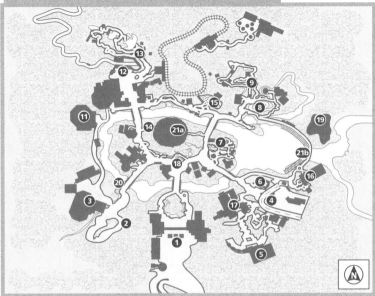

ANIMAL KINGDOM 1-DAY HAPPY FAMILY TOURING PLAN

1. Arrive 40 minutes prior to official opening time. Get guide maps and the *Times Guide*. Stroller rentals are just past the entrance, to the right.
2. In Pandora, take the Na'vi River Journey.
3. Experience Avatar Flight of Passage.
4. **PARENTS:** Ride TriceraTop Spin in DinoLand U.S.A.
5. **TEENS:** Ride Dinosaur.
6. **PARENTS:** Stop off at The Boneyard while the teens finish up at Dinosaur.
7. Meet Mickey and Minnie at the Adventurers Outpost on Discovery Island.
8. Take a ride on Kali River Rapids in Asia. You *will* get wet, so use ponchos or plastic bags to keep dry.
9. Walk the Maharajah Jungle Trek.
10. Eat lunch.
11. Work in a show of *Festival of the Lion King* in

Africa around the next two steps.
12. Experience Kilimanjaro Safaris.
13. Walk the Gorilla Falls Exploration Trail.
14. Tour the Discovery Island Trails. One entrance is just over the bridge from Africa to Discovery Island, on the left. You'll end up on Discovery Island near the bridge to Asia.
15. See *Up! A Great Bird Adventure* in Asia.
16. See *Finding Nemo—The Musical* in DinoLand U.S.A.
17. Eat dinner. A good choice is Restaurantosaurus.
18. **PARENTS:** Tour any remaining animal exhibits at Discovery Island or The Oasis.
19. **TEENS:** Ride Expedition Everest in Asia using the single-rider line.
20. Tour the rest of Pandora.
21. See Tree of Life *Awakenings* (21a) on Discovery Island and *Rivers of Light* in Asia (21b).

Suggested start times for your advance FastPass+: Avatar Flight of Passage: 9:30 a.m.; Meet Disney Pals at Adventurers Outpost: 10:30 a.m.; Kilimanjaro Safaris: 12:30 p.m. Also check for *Rivers of Light* FastPasses after experiencing Kilimanjaro Safaris.

If any of these FastPasses or times aren't available, see tinyurl.com/free-tplans to customize the plan based on the ones you were able to get, at no charge. Also get free real-time updates while you're in the park.

Disney's Hollywood Studios

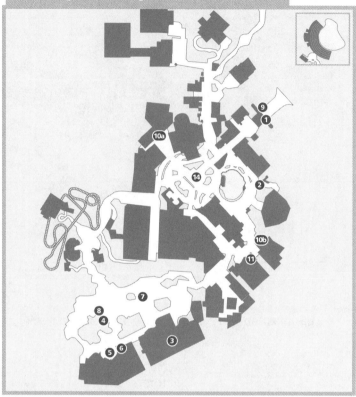

DISNEY'S HOLLYWOOD STUDIOS 1-DAY
EVERYTHING *STAR WARS* TOURING PLAN

1. Avoid visiting DHS if morning Extra Magic Hours are in effect and you're not able or eligible to use them. Arrive at least 60 minutes prior to opening (90–120 minutes during peak times). Grab a park map and *Times Guide*. Rent strollers, if needed, at the gas station on the right side of the park.

2. If your child is interested, sign up for *Jedi Training* at the Indiana Jones Adventure Outpost. Your entire party must be present to register. A late-afternoon time would work best.

3. Enter Galaxy's Edge and ride Rise of the Resistance (if open).

4. Get in line for Savi's Workshop if you want to build a lightsaber (or reserve a spot if possible). It has a substantial nonrefundable cost.

5. Ride *Millennium Falcon: Smuggler's Run*.

6. Eat lunch at Docking Bay 7 Food and Cargo.

7. As you tour the land, be on the lookout for Rey, Chewbacca, and the Stormtroopers.

8. Get in line at the Droid Depot if you want to build a droid. It has a substantial nonrefundable cost.

9. Return to your hotel for lunch and a midday break.

10. Return to the park. Work in the Star Wars Launch Bay (10a) around your *Jedi Training* show (10b).

11. Ride Star Tours-The Adventures Continue in Echo Lake. If your child signed up for *Jedi Training*, work in the ride either just before or after the show.

12. Eat dinner.

13. Visit any other attractions or shows of interest, do some shopping, and explore the park.

14. See *Star Wars: A Galactic Spectacular*.

Get advance FastPasses for Rise of the Resistance or *Millennium Falcon*, if available. Also check for any day-of-ride FastPasses for Star Tours before you leave the park for your break.

If any of these FastPasses or times aren't available, see tinyurl.com/free-tplans to customize the plan based on the ones you were able to get, at no charge. Also get free real-time updates while you're in the park.

Disney's Hollywood Studios

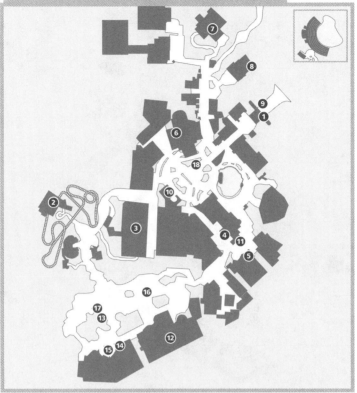

DISNEY'S HOLLYWOOD STUDIOS 1-DAY TOURING PLAN
FOR PARENTS WITH SMALL CHILDREN

1. Avoid visiting DHS if morning Extra Magic Hours are in effect and you're not able or eligible to use them. Arrive at least 60 minutes prior to opening (90–120 minutes during peak times). Ask a cast member if timed-entry reservations are required for Galaxy's Edge; if so, ask what time you should request one for late-afternoon admittance, and do that when the time comes. Grab a park map and *Times Guide*. Rent strollers, if needed, at the gas station on the right side of the park.
2. As soon as the park opens, ride Slinky Dog Dash in Toy Story Land.
3. Ride Toy Story Mania!
4. See Mickey and Minnie Starring in Red Carpet Dreams on Commissary Lane.
5. Ride Star Tours–The Adventures Continue in Echo Lake.
6. See *Disney Junior Dance Party!* in Animation Courtyard.
7. Ride The Twilight Zone Tower of Terror on Sunset Boulevard.
8. See *Beauty and the Beast–Live on Stage*.
9. Return to your hotel for lunch and a midday break of 3–4 hours.
10. Return to the park and ride Mickey and Minnie's Runaway Railway (if open).
11. Meet Olaf at Celebrity Spotlight in Echo Lake.
12. Enter Galaxy's Edge and ride Rise of the Resistance (if open).
13. Get in line for Savi's Workshop if you want to build a lightsaber (or reserve a spot if possible). It has a substantial nonrefundable cost.
14. Eat dinner at Docking Bay 7 Food and Cargo.
15. Ride *Millennium Falcon:* Smuggler's Run.
16. As you tour the land, be on the lookout for Rey, Chewbacca, and the Stormtroopers.
17. Get in line at the Droid Depot if you want to build a droid. It has a substantial nonrefundable cost.
18. Exit Galaxy's Edge to view the fireworks show.

Suggested start times for your advance FastPass+: Toy Story Mania!: 9 a.m.; *Beauty and the Beast:* 11:30 a.m. Also check for any day-of ride FastPasses before you leave the park for your break.

Disney's Hollywood Studios

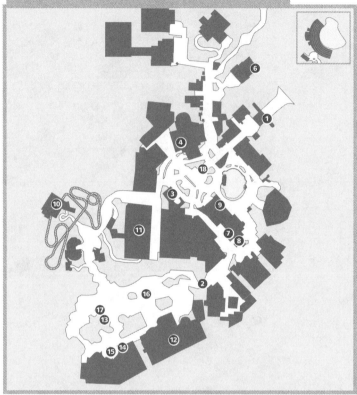

DISNEY'S HOLLYWOOD STUDIOS 1-DAY SLEEPYHEAD TOURING PLAN FOR PARENTS WITH SMALL CHILDREN

1. Avoid visiting DHS if morning Extra Magic Hours are in effect and you're not able or eligible to use them. Arrive at the park entrance around 11 a.m. Grab a park map and *Times Guide*. Rent strollers, if needed, at the gas station on the right side of the park entrance.
2. Ask a cast member if you need a timed-entry reservation to tour Galaxy's Edge. If so, get one now. A late-afternoon return time would be ideal, but take what you can get.
3. Ride Mickey & Minnie's Runaway Railway (if open) at Hollywood Boulevard.
4. Join in the *Disney Junior Dance Party!* in Animation Courtyard.
5. Eat lunch.
6. See *Beauty and the Beast* on Sunset Boulevard. Check the *Times Guide* for showtimes.
7. See Mickey and Minnie Starring in Red Carpet

Dreams on Commissary Lane.
8. Meet Olaf at Celebrity Spotlight in Echo Lake.
9. See *For the First Time in Forever: A Frozen Sing-Along Celebration.*
10. Ride Slinky Dog Dash in Toy Story Land.
11. Ride Toy Story Mania!
12. Enter Galaxy's Edge and ride Rise of the Resistance (if open).
13. Get in line for Savi's Workshop if you want to build a lightsaber (or reserve a spot if possible). It has a substantial nonrefundable cost.
14. Eat dinner at Docking Bay 7 Food and Cargo.
15. Ride *Millennium Falcon:* Smuggler's Run.
16. As you tour the land, be on the lookout for Rey, Chewbacca, and the Stormtroopers.
17. Get in line at the Droid Depot if you want to build a droid. It has a substantial nonrefundable cost.
18. Exit Galaxy's Edge to view the fireworks show.

Suggested start times for your advance FastPass+: Mickey & Minnie's Runaway Railway: 11 a.m.; *Beauty and the Beast:* 12:30 p.m. Check for any day-of ride FastPasses after *Beauty and the Beast.*

If any of these FastPasses or times aren't available, see tinyurl.com/free-tplans to customize the plan based on the ones you were able to get, at no charge. Also get free real-time updates while you're in the park.

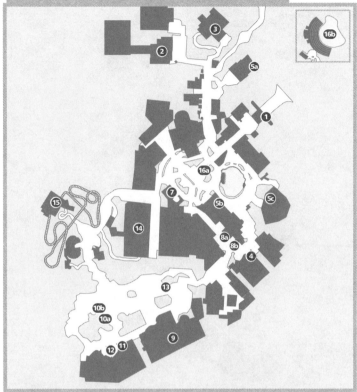

DISNEY'S HOLLYWOOD STUDIOS 1-DAY TOURING PLAN
FOR TWEENS AND THEIR PARENTS

1. Avoid visiting DHS if morning Extra Magic Hours are in effect and you're not able or eligible to use them. Arrive at DHS 90 minutes before opening. Ask a cast member if you need a timed-entry reservation to tour Galaxy's Edge. If so, get one now. A late-afternoon return time would be ideal, but take what you can get.
2. Ride Rock 'n' Roller Coaster on Sunset.
3. Ride The Twilight Zone Tower of Terror.
4. In Echo Lake, ride Star Tours.
5. Work in *Beauty and the Beast* (**5a**) on Sunset, *For the First Time in Forever: A Frozen Sing-Along Celebration* (**5b**) on Hollywood, and the *Indiana Jones Epic Stunt Spectacular!* (**5c**) in Echo Lake around lunch, starting with whichever show's performance is soonest.
6. Eat lunch if you haven't already done so.
7. Ride Mickey & Minnie's Runaway Railway (if open) on Hollywood Boulevard.

8. If time permits, meet Mickey and Minnie at Red Carpet Dreams (**8a**) and Olaf at Celebrity Spotlight (**8b**).
9. Begin touring Galaxy's Edge and ride Rise of the Resistance (if open).
10. Get in line for Savi's Workshop (**10a**) or Droid Depot (**10b**) if you want to build a lightsaber or droid (or reserve a spot if possible). They both have a substantial nonrefundable cost.
11. Eat dinner at Docking Bay 7 Food and Cargo.
12. Ride *Millennium Falcon: Smuggler's Run.*
13. As you tour the land, be on the lookout for Rey, Chewbacca, and the Stormtroopers.
14. Exit Galaxy's Edge through Toy Story Land and ride Toy Story Mania!
15. Ride Slinky Dog Dash.
16. See the *Wonderful World of Animation* or *Star Wars: A Galactic Spectacular* (**16a**), or *Fantasmic!* (**16b**).

Get advance FastPasses for Rise of the Resistance or *Millennium Falcon*, if available, any time after 3 p.m., plus any other show reservations you may be able to get earlier. Get day-of FastPasses for any available rides or shows left to see, such as Slinky Dog Dash or Toy Story Mania!

Disney's Hollywood Studios

DISNEY'S HOLLYWOOD STUDIOS 1-DAY
HAPPY FAMILY TOURING PLAN

1. Avoid visiting DHS if morning Extra Magic Hours are in effect and you're not able or eligible to use them. Arrive at DHS 90 minutes before opening. Ask a cast member if you need a timed-entry reservation for Galaxy's Edge. If so, get one now. A late-afternoon return time is ideal, but take what you can get.
2. Ride Slinky Dog Dash in Toy Story Land.
3. Ride Toy Story Mania!
4. Ride Star Tours—The Adventures Continue in Echo Lake.
5. **TEENS:** Ride The Twilight Zone Tower of Terror on Sunset Boulevard.
6. **PARENTS:** See *Disney Junior Dance Party!* in Animation Courtyard. Check the *Times Guide* for showtimes.
7. Meet Mickey and Minnie Starring in Red Carpet Dreams on Commissary Lane.
8. See *For the First Time in Forever* in Echo Lake.
9. Eat lunch. Try Backlot Express.
10. **PARENTS:** Go back to the hotel for a midday break of 3-4 hours (teens remain in the park).
11. **TEENS:** See *Indiana Jones Epic Stunt Spectacular!* Check the *Times Guide* for times.
12. **TEENS:** Ride Rock 'n' Roller Coaster on Sunset Boulevard. Use the single-rider line if the wait exceeds 25 minutes.
13. Meet back at the park. Ride Mickey & Minnie's Runaway Railway (if open) on Hollywood.
14. Begin touring Galaxy's Edge and ride Rise of the Resistance (if open).
15. Get in line for Savi's Workshop if you want to build a lightsaber (or reserve a spot if possible). It has a substantial nonrefundable cost.
16. Eat dinner at Docking Bay 7 Food and Cargo.
17. If you want to build a droid, visit the Droid Depot. It has a substantial nonrefundable cost.
18. Ride *Millennium Falcon*: Smuggler's Run.
19. As you tour the land, be on the lookout for Rey, Chewbacca, and the Stormtroopers.
20. Exit Galaxy's Edge through Toy Story Land and see the evening fireworks and shows.

Suggested start times for your advance FastPass+: The Twilight Zone Tower of Terror: 10 a.m.; *For the First Time in Forever:* 11 a.m. Also check for day-of ride FastPasses after seeing *For the First Time in Forever.*

Universal's Islands of Adventure

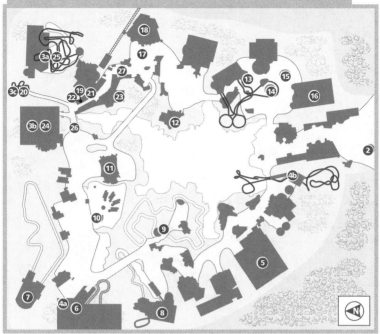

UNIVERSAL'S ISLANDS OF ADVENTURE 1-DAY TOURING PLAN

Assumes: Day guest without Universal Express; 1-Day Base Ticket

1. Buy admission in advance. Call ☎ 407-363-8000 the day before for the official opening time.
2. Arrive at IOA 75–90 minutes before opening if Early Park Admission is offered and you're eligible, or 30–45 minutes before opening for day guests. Get a park map as soon as you enter.
3. Early-entry guests should ride Hagrid's Magical Creatures Motorbike Adventure (**3a**) in The Wizarding World, followed by Harry Potter and the Forbidden Journey (**3b**). Ride Flight of the Hippogriff (**3c**) if you have time.
4. Early-entry guests can exit Hogsmeade into Jurassic Park as early entry ends and ride Skull Island: Reign of Kong (**4a**) as soon as it opens, then continue to Marvel Super Hero Island to ride The Incredible Hulk Coaster (**4b**). Guests without early-entry should start with the Hulk.
5. Ride The Amazing Adventures of Spider-Man.
6. Experience Skull Island if you haven't already.
7. Take the Jurassic Park River Adventure. Put your belongings in a pay locker here and leave them through the next two water rides.
8. Reverse course to ride Dudley Do-Right's Ripsaw Falls in Toon Lagoon.
9. Ride Popeye & Bluto's Bilge-Rat Barges. Retrieve your property from Jurassic Park.
10. Explore Camp Jurassic.
11. If time permits before lunch, check out the exhibits in the Jurassic Park Discovery Center.
12. Eat lunch. A good sit-down choice is Mythos (make reservations at zomato.com).
13. Take The High in the Sky Seuss Trolley Train Ride!
14. Ride the Caro-Seuss-el.
15. Ride One Fish, Two Fish, Red Fish, Blue Fish.
16. Experience The Cat in the Hat.
17. In Lost Continent, chat with the Mystic Fountain.
18. Experience *Poseidon's Fury.*
19. Enter Hogsmeade. See the *Frog Choir* or *Triwizard Spirit Rally* perform on the small stage outside Hogwarts, time permitting.
20. Ride Flight of the Hippogriff if you didn't back in Step 3c.
21. See the wand ceremony at Ollivanders, and buy a wand if you wish.
22. See the other show from Step 19 if you haven't already. Pose for a photo with the Hogwarts Express conductor. Explore Hogsmeade's shops and interactive windows.
23. Have dinner at Three Broomsticks.
24. Ride Harry Potter and the Forbidden Journey during the first Hogwarts Castle nighttime light show of the evening (performed seasonally).
25. Ride Hagrid's Magical Creatures Motorbike Adventure if you didn't back in Step 3a.
26. Watch the last Hogwarts Castle light show before closing, or revisit favorite attractions.

Universal Studios Florida

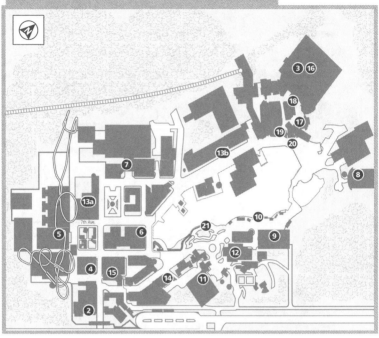

UNIVERSAL STUDIOS FLORIDA 1-DAY TOURING PLAN
Assumes: Day guest without Universal Express; 1-Day Base Ticket

1. Buy admission in advance and call ☎ 407-363-8000 the day before your visit for the official opening time.
2. Arrive at USF 90–120 minutes before opening if Early Park Admission is offered and you're eligible, or 30–45 minutes before opening for day guests. Get a park map and use Universal's app to reserve Virtual Line times for Race Through New York Starring Jimmy Fallon and/or Fast & Furious. Supercharged for early afternoon.
3. Early-entry guests should ride Harry Potter and the Escape from Gringotts if it's operating. If not, enjoy the rest of The Wizarding World–Diagon Alley but don't get in line.
4. Before early entry ends, ride Despicable Me Minion Mayhem. Day guests should wait in the front lot until permitted to ride.
5. Ride Hollywood Rip Ride Rockit.
6. Experience Transformers: The Ride 3-D.
7. Ride Revenge of the Mummy in New York.
8. Ride Men in Black Alien Attack in World Expo.
9. Experience The Simpsons Ride in Springfield.
10. Ride Kang & Kodos' Twirl 'n' Hurl if 50 or fewer people are in line.
11. Ride E.T. Adventure in Woody Woodpecker's KidZone.
12. Work in *Animal Actors on Location!* around

lunch (we recommend Fast Food Boulevard in Springfield), according to the schedule.
13. Ride Race Through New York (13a) and/or Fast & Furious (13b), according to the Virtual Line reservations you made earlier.
14. See *Universal Orlando's Horror Make-Up Show* according to the schedule.
15. See *Shrek 4-D* in Production Central.
16. Enter Diagon Alley and ride the Escape from Gringotts. If it's your first ride, take the standby queue. For rerides, use the single-rider line.
17. See the *Celestina Warbeck* and *Tales of Beedle the Bard* shows.
18. See the wand ceremony at Ollivanders, and buy a wand if you wish.
19. Tour Diagon Alley. Browse the shops, explore Knockturn Alley, and discover the interactive effects. If you're hungry, try the Leaky Cauldron or Florean Fortescue's Ice-Cream Parlour.
20. Chat with the Knight Bus conductor and his shrunken head. Also look for Kreacher in the window of 12 Grimmauld Place, and listen to the receiver in the red phone booth.
21. If it's scheduled, see *Universal Orlando's Cinematic Celebration* from Central Park. Passes may be required to access the viewing area; see the park map or app for details.

Universal Studios Florida

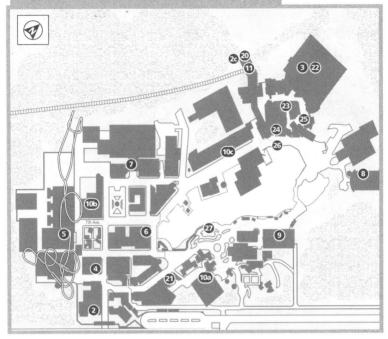

THE BEST OF UNIVERSAL STUDIOS FLORIDA AND ISLANDS OF ADVENTURE IN 1 DAY

Assumes: 1-Day Park-to-Park Ticket

1. Buy your admission in advance; call ☎ 407-363-8000 the day before your visit for the official opening time.
2. Arrive at USF 90–120 minutes before opening if Early Park Admission is offered and you're eligible, or 30–45 minutes before opening for day guests. Line up at the shortest open turnstile, get a park map, and use Universal's app to reserve Virtual Line times for Race Through New York Starring Jimmy Fallon and/or Fast & Furious: Supercharged for midmorning or late afternoon. **Alternative:** If only IOA is open for Early Park Admission and you're eligible, arrive at IOA's turnstiles 75–90 minutes before the official opening time. Ride Harry Potter and the Forbidden Journey (**2a**). Ride Flight of the Hippogriff (**2b**) if you have time. Take the Hogwarts Express train (**2c**) to King's Cross Station before USF officially opens for the day, and continue at the next step.
3. Early-entry guests should ride Harry Potter and the Escape from Gringotts if it's operating. If not, enjoy the rest of Diagon Alley but don't get in line.
4. Before early entry ends, ride Despicable Me Minion Mayhem. Day guests should wait in the front lot until permitted to ride.
5. Ride Hollywood Rip Ride Rockit.
6. Experience Transformers: The Ride 3-D.
7. Ride Revenge of the Mummy in New York.
8. Ride Men in Black Alien Attack in World Expo.
9. Experience The Simpsons Ride in Springfield.
10. If you have small children, ride E.T. Adventure (**10a**) in Woody Woodpecker's KidZone. If not, experience Race Through New York Starring Jimmy Fallon (**10b**) or Fast & Furious: Supercharged (**10c**), according to the Virtual Line reservations you made earlier.
11. Ride Hogwarts Express from King's Cross Station to IOA. Have your park-to-park ticket ready.

(continued on next page)

Universal's Islands of Adventure

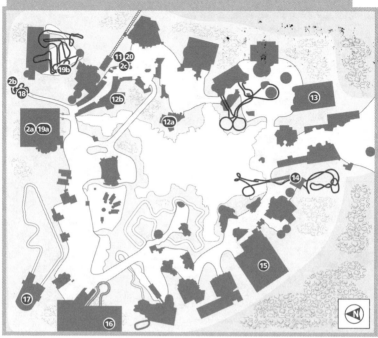

THE BEST OF UNIVERSAL STUDIOS FLORIDA AND ISLANDS OF ADVENTURE IN 1 DAY

(continued from previous page)

12. Eat lunch at Mythos in Lost Continent (**12a**) or Three Broomsticks in Hogsmeade (**12b**).
13. Ride The Cat in the Hat in Seuss Landing.
14. Ride The Incredible Hulk Coaster in Marvel Super Hero Island.
15. Ride The Amazing Adventures of Spider-Man.
16. Continue clockwise through Toon Lagoon, and ride Reign of Kong on Skull Island.
17. Experience Jurassic Park River Adventure.
18. Enter Hogsmeade, and ride Flight of the Hippogriff if the wait isn't too long.
19. Ride Harry Potter and the Forbidden Journey (**19a**), followed by Hagrid's Magical Creatures Motorbike Adventure (**19b**). Use the single-rider lines if waits exceed 30 minutes.
20. Return to USF using the Hogwarts Express from Hogsmeade Station, or walk back to the other park if the posted wait exceeds 20 minutes.

See map on previous page for the following steps.

21. See the next showing of *Universal Orlando's Horror Make-Up Show* upon returning to USF. Also remember your return time for any remaining Virtual Line reservations you made. If you couldn't get a reservation, check at the attractions an hour or two before closing.
22. Enter Diagon Alley and ride Harry Potter and the Escape from Gringotts.
23. See the wand ceremony at Ollivanders, and buy a wand if you wish.
24. Tour Diagon Alley. Browse the shops, explore the dark recesses of Knockturn Alley, and discover the interactive effects. If you're hungry, try the Leaky Cauldron or Florean Fortescue's Ice-Cream Parlour.
25. See the *Celestina Warbeck* and *Tales of Beedle the Bard* shows.
26. Chat with the Knight Bus conductor and his shrunken head. Also look for Kreacher in the window of 12 Grimmauld Place, and listen to the receiver in the red phone booth.
27. If it's scheduled, watch *Universal Orlando's Cinematic Celebration* from Central Park (between Hollywood and Woody Woodpecker's KidZone). Passes may be required to access the viewing area; see the park map or app for details.